# Exeter City

# Mike Blackstone

Published by Rel8 Media
2012

# Exeter City Down The Years

Published by Rel8 Media
Unit 7, Woodend Business Centre, Cowdenbeath, Fife,
KY4 8HG

British Library in Publication Data.
A catalogue record for this volume is available from the British Library.

ISBN 978-0-9555307-9-1

# ABOUT THE AUTHOR

Although Mike Blackstone has lived the greater part of his life in Exmouth, Devon, for the past ten years he has resided 'up north' in a far flung North West corner of Lancashire, in Heysham, Morecambe.

Some 300 miles from his beloved St James' Park, home of Exeter City, he doesn't watch the team play now, but retains the same passion for recording the history of Exeter City as he did when he first set forth inside St James' Park in the 1959-60 season.

An Exeter City statistician and programme collector, Mike started to contribute to the club's match programme in 1969 and became the editor during the 1992-93 season.

Having won a string of awards for the programme, several years in succession, including best match programme in the country on more than one occasion, he stepped aside for the 2011-12 season.

He has contributed to numerous books, magazines, newspapers, and the programmes of many other clubs, and he is also so far the author of five books prior to this one, as listed below.

His enthusiasm for the game, together with his love of reading and writing about it, as well as sampling real ales shows no sign of diminishing.

(see his Beer North West Blog at  http://beerstagger.blogspot.com)

It is hoped that this book will form a useful season by season record of Exeter City Football Club, 1904-2012.

## ALSO BY MIKE BLACKSTONE

* Exeter City: A File of Fascinating Football Facts, ISBN 0-946-65153-1, Obelisk Publications, 1992.
* Plymouth Argyle: A File of Fascinating Football Facts, ISBN 0-946-65165-5, Obelisk Publications, 1993.
* The Brown Sauce Is Off: A North West Non-League Odyssey,
ISBN 0-954-82010-X, Mike Blackstone, 2004.
* Exeter City F.C.: A Grecian Anthology, ISBN 978-0-9548201-1-4,
Mike Blackstone, 2008.
* Exeter City F.C.: A to Z of Players (awaiting publication). 2012.
* A Diary of a Real Ale Drinker (in preparation).
* Exeter City—63/4 Promotion Season—50 Years On (in preparation).

## DEDICATION

To my late father Jim. Together we built up an archive of Exeter City records which have proved to be so useful, again and again, over many years.

To Lynda for her tremendous support and encouragement throughout the writing of this book. How she puts up with my anorak tendencies, one will never know!

## ACKNOWLEDGEMENTS

I would like to thank everyone who has assisted with the writing of this book.

In particular to Georgia Shorrock who kindly allowed me to reproduce the excellent caricatures drawn by her late father, known as 'Stil'. Much of his work originally appeared in the Express and Echo newspaper based in Exeter.

I also thank Exeter City supporter, Brian Ingersent, who loaned the above caricatures to me.

My thanks also to Paul Farley at Exeter City F.C. for his help in locating some old team photographs which were originally displayed at the club.

Finally a big thank you to Andy McGregor of Re8 Media Publishing for his support, suggestions and having faith in the project from day one.

## SOURCES

Other than those already acknowledged elsewhere in the introduction to the book, I have constantly referred to the written history of the Grecians which has appeared in various publications over the years.
Apart from my own comprehensive records of the club, I would like to mention the following publications etc., all of which have been of tremendous value in writing this book:-
Express and Echo newspaper, Exeter.
Western Morning News, Plymouth.
Rothmans Football Yearbooks 1970/1-2002/3.
Sky Sports Football Yearbooks 2003/4-2011/2.
Football League Players' Records 1888-1939 - Michael Joyce, Soccer Data.
The P.F.A. Premier & Football League Players' records 1946-2005 - Barry Hugman, Queen Anne Press.
Football Through The Turnstiles - Brian Tabner, Yore Publications
Exeter City: A Complete Record 1904-1990 - Breedon Books.
A File of Fascinating Football Facts - Mike Blackstone.
Exeter City F.C.: A Grecian Anthology - Mike Blackstone.
Various Exeter City F.C. match programmes and handbooks.

City's league results

| | Home | Away |
|---|---|---|
| 110th Battery Royal Artillery | 2-1 | 3-3 |
| 111th Battery Royal Artillery | 1-0 | 5-1 |
| 112th Battery Royal Artillery | 2-0 | 2-2 |
| Belmont+ | - | 3-1 |
| Dawlish | 2-4 | 3-2 |
| Friernhay | 6-0 | 4-2 |
| Newton Town | 3-1 | 1-0 |
| St Luke's College | 3-1 | 3-0 |

+ Belmont withdrew from the league during the season
and their results were expunged

East Devon Challenge Cup

| Belmont | H | R1 | 4-0 |
|---|---|---|---|
| Exmouth United | H | R2 | 4-1 |
| Newton Town | N* | SF | 1-2 |

* The semi-final was played on the neutral ground of Dawlish.

CITY PLAYING SQUAD 1904-05 (all amateurs)

| Name | Pos | Signed from | App | Gls |
|---|---|---|---|---|
| ??? Andrews | F | St Sidwells United C/S 1904 | 3 | 2 |
| ??? Aplin | FB | St Sidwells United C/S 1904 | 1 | |
| Joseph Ashford | FB | St Sidwells United C/S 1904 | 10 | 1 |
| ??? Bailey | HB | St Sidwells United C/S 1904 | 1 | |
| ??? Campbell | FB | St Sidwells United C/S 1904 | 4 | |
| ??? Coles | W | St Sidwells United C/S 1904 | 3 | 1 |
| ??? Davidson | HB | St Sidwells United C/S 1904 | 13 | 1 |
| 'Ginger' Eveleigh | F | St Sidwells United C/S 1904 | 9 | 1 |
| ??? Fenwick | FB | St Sidwells United C/S 1904 | 4 | |
| ??? Henderson | W | ??? | 1 | |
| ??? Horner | F | ??? | 12 | |
| ??? Keech | F | St Sidwells United C/S 1904 | 2 | |
| ??? Morgan | HB | St Sidwells United C/S 1904 | 14 | |
| ??? Peters | G | ??? | 13 | |
| Reverend Reid | F | Swindon Town C/S 1904 | 11 | 16 |
| ??? Russell | W | St Sidwells United C/S 1904 | 10 | 1 |
| James Sellick | W | St Sidwells United C/S 1904 | 13 | 5 |
| ??? Smeath | F | ??? | 1 | |
| ??? Sturge | G | ??? | 1 | |
| Sidney Thomas | F | St Sidwells United C/S 1904 | 14 | 12 |
| ??? Wallage | HB | St Sidwells United C/S 1904 | 12 | |
| 'Bunker' Wells | HB | St Sidwells United C/S 1904 | 2 | |

* Exeter City Football Club began life in 1904 and entered the East Devon Senior League. They made a successful start becoming champions, although they only played 14 games. They also played a number of friendly fixtures. Home matches were played at St James' Field

* Most of the players had been recruited from the former St Sidwells United club, and details of them are shown, although some of the information available at the time was rather sketchy, such as Christian names etc.

* Football was still regarded as just another sport in the city of Exeter, with Rugby Union being the dominant one in the sporting pages of the local Press.

* Leading goalscorer for Exeter City was the Reverend Reid, who had previously played Southern League football for Swindon Town. He was the curate of St James' Church, Exeter.

* Exeter City's historic first match was against the 110th Battery in a East Devon League fixture, which was played on 10th September 1904. It was reported in the press that ... 'great interest was shown by the soccerites.' ... City won 2-1 before an estimated attendance of 600, with goals from Sidney Thomas and 'Ginger' Eveleigh.

* In order to augment their East Devon League fixture list, City also played a number of friendly matches, the first of which was against Torquay United at home on 24th September 1904. Exeter won 5-0 with Thomas becoming the first player to net a hat-trick for the club. The other goals were scored by Eveleigh and Sellick.

* in the game at the 111th Battery - City winning 5-1 - it was reported that ... 'After having Davidson and Horner badly injured by the same Battery player, there was an excitable demonstration on the part of the spectators who demanded the referee order the defaulting soldier off the field. The referee yielded amid applause.'

* Strictly speaking Exeter City wasn't a new club as such, as it was a continuation of St Sidwells United, who ceased playing at the end of the previous season. However, as the City club didn't exist until 1904, that has always been regarded as the year of formation.

CITY PLAYING SQUAD 1905-06
(All the players were amateurs, although there is some doubt about goalkeeper John
'Jack' Robinson who played professionaly for a number of clubs prior to joining Exeter City)

| Name | Pos | Signed From | App | Gls |
|------|-----|-------------|-----|-----|
| ??? Andrews | F | St Sidwells United C/S 1904 | 11 | 4 |
| ??? Bastin | HB | | 3 | |
| ??? Brooks | HB | | 8 | |
| ??? Clarke | FB | | 2 | |
| ??? Davidson | HB | St Sidwells United C/S 1904 | 12 | |
| ??? Fenwick | FB | St Sidwells United C/S 1904 | 8 | 1 |
| ??? Fitzgerald | HB | | 3 | |
| ??? Hill | FB | | 1 | |
| ??? Horner | F | | 1 | |
| ??? Keech | F | St Sidwells United C/S 1904 | 2 | |
| ??? Kendrick | F | | 1 | |
| ??? Morgan | HB | St Sidwells United C/S 1904 | 10 | |
| ??? Reed | F | | 2 | |
| Reverend Reid | F | Swindon Town C/S 1904 | 12 | 7 |
| ??? Richardson | F | | 1 | |
| John Robinson | G | Plymouth Argyle Dec 1905 | 1 | |
| ??? Russell | W | St Sidwells United C/S 1904 | 12 | |
| ??? Selley | G | | 1 | |
| James Sellick | W | St Sidwells United C/S 1904 | 9 | 2 |
| ??? Sturge | G | | 10 | |
| Sidney Thomas | F | | 10 | 2 |
| E Wells | FB | | 11 | |
| ??? West | W | | 1 | |

OTHER GAMES

With only 12 League games to play, City, like other clubs of the day, filled their fixture list with a series of Friendly games:-

| | | | |
|------|------|------|------|
| 112 Battery RA (H) | 23/9 | 3-1 | |
| United Batteries (H) | 7/10 | 2-2 | |
| Royal Marines (H) | 21/10 | 6-2 | |
| United Batteries (A) | 4/11 | 2-0 | |
| 112 Battery RA (A) | 11/11 | 2-3 | |
| Royal Marines (H) | 25/11 | 2-2 | |
| East Devon Lge (H) | 9/12 | 1-6 | |
| RFA (H) | 23/12 | 2-4 | |
| Plymouth Argyle (H) | 24/12 | 3-2* | |
| Plympton (A) | 26/12 | 1-2 | |
| Holsworthy (A) | 30/12 | 7-3 | |
| Taunton Casuals (A) | 6/1 | 0-1 | |
| Exmouth United (H) | 13/1 | 4-1 | |
| Millbrook Rangers(H) | 27/1 | 0-2 | |
| Holsworthy (H) | 10/2 | 3-1 | |
| St Luke's (A) | 17/2 | 1-4 | |
| United Batteries (H) | 17/3 | 2-2 | |
| Plympton (H) | 16/4 | 2-2 | |
| 111 Battery RA (H) | 18/4 | 2-3 | |
| * Played at County Ground, Exeter | | | |

Many of the opponents were from the Services units stationed in the South West at the time.

* John 'Jack' Robinson, who played one League game for City in 1905/6, was a former England goalkeeper. He won 11 Caps between 1897 and 1901, whilst playing for New Brighton and Southampton. Robinson moved to Plymouth side Green Waves, but returned to Exeter for season 1908/9.

City's league results

| | Home | Away |
|------|------|------|
| Essa | 1-2 | 2-0 |
| Green Waves | 1-2 | 0-1 |
| Millbrook Rangers | 2-0 | 1-4 |
| Plymouth Argyle Res | 1-4 | 0-6 |
| Tavistock | 1-1 | 4-1 |
| Torpoint | 1-3 | 2-3 |

East Devon Challenge Cup

| | | | |
|------|------|------|------|
| Bovey Tracey St John's | H | 10-0 | R1 |
| United Batteries Royal Artillery | A | 1-3 | R2 |

* After one season in the East Devon Senior League, Exeter City switched leagues to join the Plymouth and District League, but found the opposition a lot stronger as they ended the season next to bottom.

* To augment their league fixtures - just 12 of them - a number of friendly games were played throughout the season , including one against Plymouth Argyle on Christmas Day 1905, which was staged at Exeter Rugby Club's County Ground, City winning 3-2.

* Once again the Reverend Reid topped the goalscoring charts in league matches, which included netting a hat-trick in the 4-1 win at Tavistock.

* Figures for attendances at matches were virtually non-existent, although it was reported that 2,000 were present for the visit of Plymouth Argyle reserves on 4th December 1905.

* City recorded their then club record win when they defeated Bovey Tracey St John's 10-0 in the first round of the East Devon Challenge Cup.

CITY PLAYING SQUAD 1906-07
(All the players were amateurs)

| Name | Pos | Signed from | App | Gls |
|------|-----|-------------|-----|-----|
| ??? Andrews | F | St Sidwells United C/S 1904 | 2 | |
| ??? Antliffe | G | | 3 | |
| ??? Aspey | HB | | 9 | 1 |
| ??? Bastin | HB | | 16 | |
| ??? Brown | HB | | 1 | |
| ??? Campbell | HB | | 2 | |
| ??? Chapman | G | | 6 | |
| ??? Coates | FB | | 4 | |
| ??? Davidson | HB | St Sidwells United C/S 1904 | 8 | |
| ??? Ebery | W | | 1 | 1 |
| Edward 'Ginger' Eveleigh | F | | 7 | 1 |
| Richard Fenwick | FB | St Sidwells United C/S 1904 | 21 | 2 |
| ??? Haswell | HB | | 1 | |
| ??? Hawke | F | | 1 | |
| ??? Henry | W | | 1 | |
| ??? Hill | FB | | 5 | |
| ??? Hyde | G | | 1 | |
| ??? Kelly | HB | | 1 | |
| Evelyn Lintott | HB | Woking Dec 1906 | 1 | |
| Benjamin Massey | F | | 13 | 5 |
| ??? Morgan | HB | St Sidwells United C/S 1904 | 2 | 2 |
| ??? Muncey | HB | | 18 | |
| ??? Oliver | HB | | 1 | |
| ??? Pryce | F | | 5 | 3 |
| Reverend Reid | F | Swindon Town C/S 1904 | 18 | 5 |
| ??? Robins | FB | | 1 | |
| ??? Russell | W | St Sidwells United C/S 1904 | 9 | 2 |
| ??? Selley | G | | | |
| James Sellick | W | St Sidwells United C/S 1904 | 23 | 4 |
| H Singlehurst | F | | 3 | 1 |
| ??? Smith | G | | 1 | |
| ??? Sturge | G | | 1 | |
| Sidney Thomas | F | St Sidwells United C/S 1904 | 12 | 2 |
| ??? Tipping | F | | 5 | 6 |
| ??? Tomlinson | F | | 4 | |
| ??? Turner | F | | 8 | 3 |
| ??? Vansinter | F | | 2 | |
| ??? Vibart | G | | 12 | |
| Percival Warner | HB | | 5 | |
| E Wells | FB | | 1 | |
| W 'Bunker' Wells | W | | 23 | |
| ??? Wilson | F | | 3 | 2 |
| ??? Youlden | F | | 3 | 4 |

City's league results

| | Home | Away |
|------|------|------|
| 2nd Devonshire Regiment | 0-1 | 2-4 |
| Devon & Cornwall Light Infantry | 2-0 | 4-3 |
| Essa | 1-1 | 0-1 |
| Green Waves | 0-2 | 0-3 |
| Gunnislake | 1-2 | 2-2 |
| Millbrook Rangers | 2-1 | 3-0 |
| Plymouth Argyle Reserves | 3-5 | 1-3 |
| Rifle Brigade | 3-0 | 1-4 |
| Royal Marines | 1-4 | 1-3 |
| St Michael's | 1-0 | 3-1 |
| Tavistock | 2-1 | 5-2 |
| Torpoint | 3-2 | 1-8 |

Once again a series of Friendly games were arranged to plug gaps in the fixture list:

| RA United (H) | 8/9 | 1-4 |
|---------------|-----|-----|
| 112 Battery RA (A) | 15/9 | 1-3 |
| Barnstaple (A) | 22/9 | 7-0 |
| Taunton Casuals (H) | 29/9 | 5-2 |
| St Luke's College(H) | 1/12 | 0-1 |
| Holsworthy (A) | 15/12 | 2-3 |
| Green Waves (H) | 25/12 | 3-2* |
| North Devon XI (A) | 27/12 | 1-3 |
| Holsworthy (H) | 2/3 | 2-2 |
| 15 Brigade RA (H) | 3/4 | 4-6* |
| Friernhay (H) | 13/4 | 2-0 |

* Games played at County Ground, Exeter

* At the start of the 1906-07 season the local newspaper printed a preview of the season as follows:-
'The Exeter City club officials this year expect an advance all round, and this is already good reason to suppose that the grandstand so often spoken of, is now a thing for the very near future.

'Nearly all last season's players have signed on. In addition to these, numerous new players have come to stop in the district, and no doubt some of them will be seen in the ranks of the first team.

'The club has again entered the Plymouth and District League, in which entries this year are very numerous. The County Ground has again been booked for Christmas Day, and a great attraction will doubtless be provided.

'The playing members have already entered upon a programme of strict training. This programme, it is hoped, will be maintained throughout the whole season and thus to materially improve Exeter City's record in the Plymouth and District League.'

* For the visit of Plymouth Argyle reserves for a Plymouth and District League fixture, such was the interest that Exeter attracted their highest attendance thus far, with an estimated 2,000 spectators inside the ground. Argyle won an eight-goal thriller, by 5-3.

# Exeter City's New Ground Scheme

With Exeter City about to embark on their fourth season, and Interest in the game increasing, the local newspaper printed a preview of the 1907-08 campaign, which concentrated on a possible move to a new ground. The scheme eventually fell through and Exeter City remained at St. James' Park:-

'Association football prospects were never so bright in Exeter at the outset of this another season. Friernhay F.C. start the year as the oldest senior club in the area, while Exeter City have on tap the very important scheme of a new ground at Barnfield. When that scheme is realised soccer will have risen to a position of importance in the City of Exeter, which only the most sanguine could have anticipated five or six years ago.

Nor will its development stop there. The future of the Association code in this district is almost solely in the hands of the premier club, Exeter City, and now that organisation has risen to the possibilities of the future, thanks in not a small degree to the assiduity of the Officials like Mr. Fey and Mr. Thomas, Association will establish a firm and lasting foothold here.

The Barnfield ground, as many people know, will be ready for the opening of another season. The terms upon which the City club will have the lease of it, their plans for laying out of it, on the most modern and up to date lines, its entrances, and capacity are all being gone into.

'Suffice to say now that if the scheme as at present drafted is carried into effect, Barnfield will be an enclosure of which any amateur club would have reason to be proud. And above all, this is where the club will have a tremendous pull. It is ideally situated in almost the very heart of the city.

It behoves every follower of the game, having regard to the ambitious future of this bold venture, that all petty carping and all spirit of jealousy may be sunk in the desire to see Exeter City prosper in all these new schemes. For, after all, as the City club prospers, so will all other soccer organisations in the whole district reap the benefits proportionately.

The Grecians have never entered upon a season when it was more important that they should score playing successes. If they established themselves in public favour by meritous performances during the coming winter, the bigger and more venturesome battle of 1908-09 is half won.

It has been stated that no effort will be spared to encourage the East Devon League reserve team. In the last two or three years the mistake has lain there, for the club has had absolutely no reserves to fall back on, and in the event of a contingency arising, they have had to seek help from local sides.

Things must be different in the future. The backbone of the team remains with the like of W. Wells, Bastin, Fenwick, Warner, Sellick and Singlehurst who are still in the city, and these with some of the promising young bloods which were on show in trial games should provide a useful and serviceable side.

The best advice in summing up, is to encourage the young players of merit, spare no effort to win matches now that the verge of such an ambitious project has been reached, and the City club will be all that it can desire.'

CITY PLAYING SQUAD 1907-08
(All the players were amateurs with the exception of Jack Banks.)

| Name | Pos | Signed From | App | Gls |
|---|---|---|---|---|
| ??? Antliff | G | ??? | 5 | |
| ??? Ashford | FB | ??? | 7 | |
| ??? Aspey | HB | ??? | 4 | |
| ??? Badcock | F | ??? | 8 | 1 |
| Jack Banks | HB | Leyton Dec 1907 | 15 | 2 |
| ??? Bastin | HB | ??? | 2 | |
| ??? Blunden | F | ??? * | 1 | |
| Fred Chenneour | F | ??? | 3 | |
| ??? Clark | W | ??? | 7 | |
| ??? Drew | F | ??? | 9 | 1 |
| Henry Dyer | FB | ??? | 11 | |
| Edward 'Ginger' Eveleigh | F | ??? | 25 | 15 |
| Richard Fenwick | FB | St Sidwells United C/S 1904 | 18 | 1 |
| ??? Goodchild | HB | ??? | 1 | |
| ??? Hyde | G | ??? | 1 | |
| ??? Johnson | F | ??? | 1 | |
| ??? Jones | W | ??? | 1 | |
| ??? Letheran | HB | ??? | 22 | 1 |
| Benjamin Massey | F | ??? | 17 | 10 |
| ??? Mudd | HB | ??? | 20 | 6 |
| ??? Murch | FB | ??? | 1 | |
| ??? Oliver | HB | ??? | 8 | |
| ??? Parsons | FB | ??? | 1 | |
| James Sellick | W | St Sidwells United C/S 1904 | 21 | 3 |
| ??? Sercombe | HB | ??? | 1 | |
| H Singlehurst | F | ??? | 26 | 10 |
| ??? Smith | G | ??? | 1 | |
| ??? Stoneman | W | ??? | 1 | |
| Sidney Thomas | F | St Sidwells United C/S 1904 | 2 | |
| Percival Warner | HB | ??? | 9 | |
| E Wells | FB | ??? | 12 | |
| W 'Bunker' Wells | W | ??? | 25 | |

City's league results

| | HOME | AWAY |
|---|---|---|
| 2nd Devonshire Regiment | 2-1 | 4-1** |
| Essa | 6-1 | 1-0 |
| Green Waves | 0-2* | - |
| Gunnislake | 7-2 | 1-3 |
| Looe | 1-3 | 1-4 |
| Millbrook Rangers | 3-0+ | - |
| Oreston Rovers | 3-2 | 1-3 |
| Plymouth Argyle Reserves | 0-5 | 1-8 |
| Plympton | 2-1 | 0-0 |
| Royal Marines | 2-1 | -31 |
| St Michael's | 1-0 | 1-1 |
| Tavistock | 3-1 | 1-0 |
| Torpoint | 1-3 | 0-6 |
| Woodland Villa | 3-0 | 2-1 |

Friendly Games arranged were as follows:

| | | |
|---|---|---|
| Friernhay (H) | 7/9 | 2-2 |
| Exmouth United (H) | 14/9 | 2-1 |
| 1st Rifle Brigade (H) | 28/9 | 1-3 |
| St Luke's College (H) | 7/12 | 1-0 |
| Yeovil Casuals (H) | 21/12 | 1-0 |
| East Devon (H) | 25/12 | 3-3* |
| Friernhay (H) | 26/12 | 2-1 |
| Exmouth United (H) | 8/2 | 4-1 |
| 15 Brigade RA (H) | 15/2 | 1-3 |

* Played at County Ground, Exeter

* With the game against Green Waves having been postponed twice, the home fixture was played for four points. The away game was therefore not played.

** Both matches against the 2nd Devonshire Regiment were played on Exeter City's ground.

+ The match against Millbrook Rangers was played for four points, a previous game having been abandoned. The away match was therefore not played.

* As the season drew to a close there was much speculation as to whether Exeter City would be applying to join the Southern League. This was confirmed in April 1908 when it was reported:-
'Considerable progress has been made with regard to the professional club scheme. In the haunts where professional players are mostly to be found, advertisements have appeared inviting applications from players for all positions, with the intimation that only good men with good credentials need apply to the Exeter City Football and Athletic Company.

* It was further reported that 'every effort is being made to adapt St James' Park to the requirements, and with making use of every foot of space for banking, staging and stands, this can be achieved.'

# Public Meeting: Professional Team For The Southern League

A public meeting was held on Friday 1st May 1908 to promote Exeter City Football Club as a professional outfit and to apply to join the Southern League. The Express and Echo newspaper report of the meeting was quite comprehensive and it is worth reproducing as follows:-

*The promoters of the Exeter City professional team could not have wished for a better and more enthusiastic public meeting.*

*It was plainly evident that the scheme had caught on and captured the fancy of a large section of the community. The meeting was held at the Royal Public Rooms, Exeter.*
*Captain F.J. Harvey presided and was supported on the platform by the Reverend Philip Williams. Messrs Nat Whittaker (Secretary of the Southern League), W. Knight (secretary of the London League), R.F. Davis (Chairman of Plymouth Argyle), Louis Crabbe (Secretary of Plymouth Argyle), Sydney Cole and J. Jacques (Plymouth Argyle), E. Armfield (Southampton), J. Skeggs (Millwall), Robinson (Sports Traffic Manager, Great Western Railway), J. Bickford (Great Western Railway), J.T. Howcroft (well known referee from Bolton), and possible future directors of Exeter City, namely, M.J. McGahey, J. Parkhouse, N. Kendall, W. Fenwick, A. Alford, T. Oliver, F Collingwood and S. Thomas.*

*The hall was packed some time before the start, the interval being occupied with musical selections by the City Orchestra.*

*The Mayor of Exeter, Alderman G. Gadd. wished the scheme all success and said that a professional team in the city would no doubt popularise soccer throughout the entirety of East Devon.*

*Mr. Armfield said that Southampton were always ready to assist a struggling community who were labouring hard to establish a good Association club. The work was no child's play, and there must be no half heartedness, or the thing was doomed to failure.*

*Mr. Crabbe said that ever since he brought the Argyle reserves to Exeter three years ago for the first time, he was struck by the possibilities of soccer in East Devon. No one could doubt that the first step to success was taken when Banks was engaged as a professional coach. In conclusion he gave as Argyle's message to Exeter - "Plymouth will support you."*

*Mr Skeggs was met with a hearty reception and said that he must confess that once he doubted whether Exeter could support a first class team, for generally he was afraid that Cathedral centres were not good sporting centres, but now he was convinced that Exeter was the exception.*

*Mr. Norman Kendall proposed the following motion:- 'That this representative meeting of the citizens of Exeter pledges its support to the Exeter City Football and Athletic Company Limited in its endeavour to enter the professional Southern League.'*

*The Reverend Philip Williams seconded the resolution and spoke of the growth of soccer in recent years in Exeter. The resolution was carried unanimously.*

*Mr. Kendall proposed a vote of thanks to the officials of the Southern Football League who had given time and trouble to come and speak to them that night. The meeting then broke up amongst much enthusiastic cheering.*

*The City promoters could therefore proceed in the full and complete assurance that the club will secure admission to the First Division of the Southern League, providing that at the meeting of the League they provide proof of the possession of a suitable ground and financial support together with a strong team.*

13

# Exeter City Elected To The Southern League

The following report appeared in the Express and Echo relating to the Annual General Meeting of the Southern League held at the Charterhouse Hotel, London, on 29th May 1908:-

*Mr. Whittaker, the Southern League secretary announced that there were five vacancies and six applicants, namely, Leyton, and New Brompton who retired automatically, Exeter City, Croydon, Southend United and Coventry City.*

*A letter had been received from Hastings to the effect that they had withdrawn their application for entry into the First Division.*

*Representatives of the six applicants were then heard in the following order - New Brompton, Leyton, Southend, Coventry, Croydon and Exeter City.*

*Norman Kendall, who put forward Exeter City's case for acceptance into the League, made a good impression by his report on the team and the ground.*

*He remarked how City had the assistance of the Great Western Railway and if elected would ever be loyal to the Southern League.*

*Thereafter a vote was taken, the result of which was:- Exeter City 33, Leyton 32, New Brompton 31, Southend United 26, Coventry City 25 and Croydon 10.*

*The result of the ballot fully justified Exeter City's optimism as they came top of the poll, although that was rather unexpected.*

*There was scarcely a delegate who did not offer handshakes to the City representatives. Mr. Crabbe of Plymouth Argyle in particular could not disguise his delight.*

*Exeter's rapid rise in the football world was spoken of as wonderful. Mr. McGahey did Exeter a lot of good among the delegates the previous night when they met up in London, and made Exeter City's position very positive and clear.*

*Few questions were asked of Norman Kendall at the meeting, compared to those put to the other clubs, showing that the delegates were quite satisfied with Exeter City.*

## Arthur Chadwick: Appointed Manager

On 1st May 1908, Arthur Chadwick was appointed as Exeter City's first ever manager, but given the title of 'Coach and Advisor.' He would also play as well. He had previously played for Accrington, Burton Swifts, Portsmouth, Southampton and Northampton Town. A Lancastrian, he was expected to use his contacts in that area to bring players to Exeter City.

Chadwick would serve as City's Manager until 1922. He was later Manager at both Reading and Southampton.

He won two full England Caps in 1900, playing against Scotland Wales. At the time he played for Southampton, then in the Southern League.

Chadwick's cousin, Edgar Chadwick, was also a full England international.

14

# 'Well Equipped' For Inaugural Southern League Season.

Prior to Exeter City's big step up into the Southern League, the following preview of their prospects appeared in the local press:-

*'The prospects may be summed up in a few words as follows:- Management, excellent, and players, a fine serviceable lot, well capable of finishing in the first ten in the Southern League table. We allude to the management and in particular to the part which we hope will be played by Arthur Chadwick. He will be essentially the man at the helm, and though nominally only 'Advisor' to the team, we sincerely trust that in the early stages, the directors will rely implicitly upon the guidance of him. To all intents and purposes he is the Manager.*
*Gentleman like Captain F.J. Harvey, Messrs. Norman Kendall, William Fenwick, A. McGahey, T. Oliver and F. Parkhouse, together with the assiduous secretary, Sidney Thomas, may be relied upon to leave no stone unturned to make the undertaking a success, and in Mr. Kendall and Mr. McGahey the club are happy on the possession of two directors of quite unique capabilities in two essentially different directions.*

*They have steered the ship so far with fearless confidence and judgement, but at the same time they realise that in working of a first class club which now lies immediately ahead of them, their experience is by no means such as to warrant their relying entirely on their own initiative.*

*They have a 'man in a hundred' in Arthur Chadwick, and upon him they may depend for pilotage over the many awkward shoals that lie immediately ahead. What he does not know about the game, is hardly worth knowing and we believe that time will prove the appointment of Arthur Chadwick was the wisest of all the management early moves.*

*As everyone realises a lot depends upon the first Southern League game. It would, perhaps, have been better if the City had an easier hurdle to commence operations against, but at the same time local enthusiasts probably know too much about the Southern League strengths to base their estimates entirely upon what City will do at Millwall in the opening game. Few teams ever come away from Millwall with even a point to their credit, and the experience of Plymouth Argyle at Millwall has been anything but encouraging. If therefore, Exeter City get within a goal at the stronghold of the 'Dockers' they will have done remarkably well, and should be sure of a huge welcome when they turn out at St James' Park in the following game against Bristol Rovers.*

*It is a pity that the Athletic sports clash with the opening of St James' Park as a Southern League enclosure, but the crowds which have eagerly gone to the informal practices during the last fortnight convince everyone that the City, despite the counter attractions, will have a splendid send off on 5th September.*

*It would seem that Exeter City's players are well up to Southern League standard and teams like Southend United, New Brompton, Reading, Watford, Coventry City, Leyton, Norwich City and Brentford have nothing to show which would give them the slightest advantage over Exeter.*

*Exeter City are well equipped, and if luck favours them with regard to reasonable immunity from accidents, they are going to win matches, and it certainly will steer them clear of the danger zone.*

*They have at present, as many professionals signed on as Plymouth Argyle, and the club also have a grand set of amateurs in the reserve team should they wish to call upon them for first team duties.'*

The first squad of Exeter City players prior to the start of the Southern League season.
Back row: Arthur Chadwick (Manager), Albert Ambler, Joe Bulcock, James Fletcher, John Crelley, Jack Banks, Levi Copestake, William Wake.
Front row: Tom Drain, Thomas Craig, Samuel Johnson, Robert Watson, Andrew McGuigan, James Bell, Thomas White.
Seated on ground: Herbert Tierney, Frederick Parnell
The team, it will be noted, then played in green shirts with white sleeves and white shorts.

### The Historic First Home Game
An estimated attendance of 8,000 spectators watched Exeter City's first ever Southern League match at St. James' Park on Saturday 5th September 1908.
The visitors were Bristol Rovers and the game ended all square at 3-3, which prompted the following comment in the match report:-
'Exeter City quite satisfied their supporters in their first home match of their career as a professional team, for a win had not been expected. The attack was excellent and little fault could be found with the defence.'

City team: Fletcher, Craig, Bulcock, Ambler, Johnson, Tierney, Parnell, Watson, Drain, Bell, White.

City's league results

| | HOME | AWAY |
|---|---|---|
| Brentford | 1-2 | 2-0 |
| Brighton & H.A. | 1-0 | 2-1 |
| Bristol Rovers | 3-3 | 1-5 |
| Coventry City | 0-3 | 1-0 |
| Crystal Palace | 1-1 | 0-0 |
| Leyton Orient | 3-1 | 2-4 |
| Luton Town | 2-1 | 2-0 |
| Millwall | 2-1 | 2-2 |
| New Brompton | 1-3 | 1-3 |
| Northampton Town | 2-1 | 0-1 |
| Norwich City | 3-2 | 0-2 |
| Plymouth Argyle | 2-1 | 0-4 |
| Portsmouth | 4-1 | 0-2 |
| Queens Park Rangers | 1-0 | 1-1 |
| Reading | 5-1 | 2-1 |
| Southampton | 1-2 | 0-2 |
| Southend United | 2-1 | 0-0 |
| Swindon Town | 1-4 | 1-2 |
| Watford | 1-0 | 1-3 |
| West Ham United | 1-0 | 1-4 |

F.A. Cup

| | | | |
|---|---|---|---|
| Weymouth | H | Q1 | 14-0 |
| Longfleet St Mary | A | Q2 | 1-1 |
| Longfleet St Mary | H | Q2R | 10-1 |
| Whiteheads | H | Q3 | 4-0 |
| Kingswood Rovers | A | Q4 | 2-0 |
| Barnet Alston | A | Q5 | 3-0 |
| Wrexham | A | R1 | 1-1 |
| Wrexham | H | R1R | 2-1 |
| Plymouth Argyle | A | R2 | 0-2 |

CITY MANAGER 1908-09
Arthur Chadwick - Appointed April 1908

| CITY PLAYING SQUAD 1908-09 | | | App | Gls |
|---|---|---|---|---|
| Name | Pos | Signed From | | |
| Albert Ambler | HB | Stockport County C/S 1908 | 35 | |
| Jack Banks | HB | Plymouth Argyle Jan 1908 | 2 | |
| James Bell | F | Barrow C/S 1908 | 39 | 22 |
| Joseph Bulcock | FB | Macclesfield Town C/S 1908 | 23 | |
| Arthur Chadwick | HB | Northampton Town Apr 1908 | 19 | 2 |
| Levi Copestake | W | Bristol City C/S 1908 | 32 | 6 |
| Thomas Craig | FB | Stockport County C/S 1908 | 38 | |
| John Crelley | FB | Everton C/S 1908 | 18 | |
| Thomas Drain | F | Kilmarnock C/S 1908 | 14 | 1 |
| James Fletcher | G | Carlisle United C/S 1908 | 11 | |
| Andy McGuigan | F | Barrow C/S 1908 | 28 | 16 |
| Frederick Parnell | W | Leeds City C/S 1908 | 29 | 3 |
| Willam Plant | W | St Luke's College C/S 1908 | 1 | |
| Jack Robinson | G | Green Waves C/S 1908 | 29 | |
| Herbet Tierney | HB | Bolton Wanderers C/S 1908 | 11 | |
| William Wake | HB | Plymouth Argyle C/S 1908 | 30 | |
| Robert Watson | F | Woolwich Arsenal C/S 1908 | 39 | 6 |
| Thomas White | W | Carlisle United C/S 1908 | 19 | |

SOUTHERN LEAGUE - 1908-09

| | P | W | D | L | F | A | Pts |
|---|---|---|---|---|---|---|---|
| Northampton Town | 40 | 25 | 5 | 10 | 90 | 45 | 55 |
| Swindon Town | 40 | 22 | 5 | 13 | 96 | 55 | 49 |
| Southampton | 40 | 19 | 10 | 11 | 67 | 58 | 48 |
| Portsmouth | 40 | 18 | 10 | 12 | 68 | 60 | 46 |
| Bristol Rovers | 40 | 17 | 9 | 14 | 60 | 63 | 43 |
| EXETER CITY | 40 | 18 | 6 | 16 | 56 | 65 | 42 |
| New Brompton | 40 | 17 | 7 | 16 | 48 | 59 | 41 |
| Reading | 40 | 11 | 18 | 11 | 60 | 57 | 40 |
| Luton Town | 40 | 17 | 6 | 17 | 59 | 60 | 40 |
| Plymouth Argyle | 40 | 15 | 10 | 15 | 46 | 47 | 40 |
| Millwall | 40 | 16 | 6 | 18 | 59 | 61 | 38 |
| Southend United | 40 | 14 | 10 | 16 | 52 | 54 | 38 |
| Claton Orient | 40 | 15 | 8 | 17 | 52 | 55 | 38 |
| Watford | 40 | 14 | 9 | 17 | 51 | 64 | 37 |
| Queens Park Rangers | 40 | 12 | 12 | 16 | 52 | 50 | 36 |
| Crystal Palace | 40 | 12 | 12 | 16 | 62 | 62 | 36 |
| West Ham United | 40 | 16 | 4 | 20 | 56 | 60 | 36 |
| Brighton & H.A. | 40 | 14 | 7 | 19 | 60 | 61 | 35 |
| Norwich City | 40 | 12 | 11 | 17 | 59 | 75 | 35 |
| Coventry City | 40 | 15 | 4 | 21 | 64 | 91 | 34 |
| Brentford | 40 | 13 | 7 | 20 | 59 | 74 | 33 |

* Exeter City entered the 'new world' of professional football when they played in the Southern League in 1908. Formed only four years earlier, the Grecians had previously played in the East Devon League and the Plymouth and District League.

* Player-manager Arthur Chadwick had assembled a virtual new team, the majority of the players having come from the north of England, especially Lancashire, where he had many contacts. Chadwick was a former England international and had played for Accrington, Burton Swifts, Southampton, Portsmouth and Northampton Town. He won two caps for England playing against Scotland and Wales respectively.

* City's first ever home match in the Southern League, against Bristol Rovers, drew an attendance of 8,000 to St James' Park. However, the highest gate of the season at the Park was 11,500 for the visit of Millwall on Christmas Day 1908.

* Exeter were in goalscoring form in the early rounds of the FA Cup. Having beaten Weymouth 14-0 at home in the first qualifying round, they then drew 1-1 at Longfleet St Mary, before winning the replay back in Devon, 10-1.

* City went on to defeat Whiteheads, Kingswood Rovers, Barnet Albion and Wrexham after a replay, before going out of the competition at the second round proper stage, when they lost 2-0 to Plymouth Argyle at Home Park.

* James 'Daisy' Bell was top scorer for City with 22 goals in the Southern League. This included the only hat-trick netted by a City player in a Southern League match that season when Bell scored all three goals that defeated Clapton Orient 3-1 at St James' Park.

* Many of Bell's goals was the result of the tricky wing play of Levi Copestake, who had been signed from Bristol City. Standing just 5' 5" tall, Copestake was the smallest member of the City team.

* The first ever 'Devon derby' at professional level between Exeter City and Plymouth Argyle took place at St James' Park in November 1908, when a crowd of 9,000 saw the Grecians win 2-1, with both their goals being scored by James Bell.

* 20 minutes before kick off in the Exeter versus Plymouth match, the ground was described as thus:- 'The flowerpot stand was three parts full. There were nearly 5,000 in the ground altogether, although few of the Plymouth following had arrived. The grandstand was quickly filling and the enclosure in front of it was packed, but behind the St James' Road goal there was plenty of room.'

* An exciting eight-goal friendly fixture was played at St James' Park on 30th December 1908 when the 2nd Battalion of the Coldstream Guards provided the opposition. City won 5-3, but what made this game even more exciting was the fact that the pitch was covered with four inches of snow! One cannot imagine that modern day footballers would have played!

* Exeter City issued a match programme for the very first time when Wrexham were at St James' Park for an F.A. Cup first round replay on 20th January 1909. City won 2-1.

* The Grecians made their first ever visit to the Crystal Palace ground in Sydenham, South East London, when they drew 0-0 with the Palace in March 1909. The ground had for many years been used to stage the FA Cup Final, but for the visit of Exeter there were only 1,000 spectators present mainly due to the horrendous conditions, which resulted in the pitch being under water in several places.

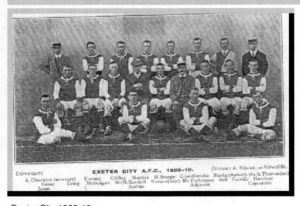

Exeter City 1909-10
Back row: Arthur Chadwick (Player-Manager), Herbert Tierney, John Crelley, Percival Hartley, Harold Sturge, Herbert Crossthwaite, Jack Banks (Trainer), Sydney Thomas (Secretary).
Middle row: Thomas Green, Thomas Craig, Andy McGuigan, Norman Kendall (Director), Robert Watson, Frederick Parkhouse (Director), James Bell, James Garside, Richard Harrison.
Front row, seated on ground: Edwin Jones, Albert Ambler, James Atkinson, Levi Copestake

\* A glance at the fixture list shows just how far City had come in the space of two years. Instead of playing only local teams they were now travelling the length and breadth of southern England— to Essex to play Southend United, into Norfolk to take on Norwich City and as far north as Coventry and Northampton. Nunhead, City's FA Cup opponents hailed from South East London, in the Peckham area.

### City's league results

| | Home | Away |
|---|---|---|
| Brentford | 4-1 | 0-3 |
| Brighton & H.A. | 0-1 | 1-2 |
| Bristol Rovers | 1-1 | 0-1 |
| Clapton Orient | 2-1 | 1-5 |
| Coventry City | 3-0 | 0-6 |
| Croydon Common | 3-1 | 5-2 |
| Crystal Palace | 2-0 | 0-3 |
| Luton Town | 1-2 | 1-3 |
| Millwall | 5-0 | 0-0 |
| New Brompton | 3-2 | 2-3 |
| Northampton Town | 2-3 | 0-0 |
| Norwich City | 2-2 | 0-1 |
| Plymouth Argyle | 2-4 | 0-1 |
| Portsmouth | 5-0 | 1-4 |
| Queen's Park Rangers | 0-0 | 0-2 |
| Reading | 3-1 | 1-0 |
| Southampton | 2-0 | 2-3 |
| Southend United | 3-1 | 0-2 |
| Swindon Town | 0-1 | 1-3 |
| Watford | 1-1 | 3-1 |
| West Ham United | 1-0 | 1-2 |

| F.A. Cup | | | |
|---|---|---|---|
| Nunhead | H | Q4 | 7-1 |
| Stoke | A | Q5 | 0-0 |
| Stoke | H | Q5R | 1-1* |
| Stoke | N | Q52R | 1-2+ |

*Played at County Ground, Exeter
+ Played at Craven Cottage, Fulham

| Southern Charity Cup | | | |
|---|---|---|---|
| Plymouth Argyle | A | R1 | 1-0 |
| Swindon Town | A | R2 | 0-4 |

CITY MANAGER 1909-10
Arthur Chadwick - Appointed April 1908

### CITY PLAYING SQUAD 1909-10

| Name | Pos | Signed From | Apps | Gls |
|---|---|---|---|---|
| Albert Ambler | HB | Stockport County C/S 1908 | 21 | |
| James Atkinson | HB | Brighton & H.A. C/S 1909 | 40 | |
| James Bell | F | Barrow C/S 1908 | 38 | 15 |
| Arthur Chadwick | HB | Northampton Town Apr 1908 | 21 | 4 |
| Levi Copestake | W | Bristol City C/C 1908 | 30 | 4 |
| Thomas Craig | FB | Stockport County C/S 1908 | 13 | |
| John Crelley | FB | Everton C/S 1908 | 30 | |
| Herbert Crossthwaite | G | Fulham C/S 1909 | 41 | |
| Crad Evans | F | Ellacombe Dec 1909 | 3 | 2 |
| James Garside | F | Accrington Stanley May 1907 | 35 | 4 |
| Thomas Green | F | Stockport County C/S 1909 | 31 | 8 |
| Richard Harrison | F | Manchester City C/S 1909 | 8 | 5 |
| Percival Hartley | HB | Chorley St George C/S 1909 | 34 | 4 |
| Edwin Jones | FB | Chorley C/S 1909 | 39 | |
| Andy McGuigan | F | Barrow C/S 1908 | 16 | 4 |
| Harold Sturge | G | Exmouth United C/S 1908 | 1 | 1 |
| Herbert Tierney | NB | Bolton Wanderers C/C 1908 | 21 | 2 |
| Robert Watson | F | Woolwich Arsenal C/S 1908 | 40 | 8 |

### SOUTHERN LEAGUE - 1909-10

| | P | W | D | L | F | A | Pts |
|---|---|---|---|---|---|---|---|
| Brighton & H.A. | 42 | 23 | 13 | 6 | 69 | 28 | 59 |
| Swindon Town | 42 | 22 | 10 | 10 | 92 | 46 | 54 |
| Queens Park Rangers | 42 | 19 | 13 | 10 | 56 | 47 | 51 |
| Northampton Town | 42 | 22 | 4 | 16 | 90 | 44 | 48 |
| Southampton | 42 | 16 | 16 | 10 | 64 | 55 | 48 |
| Portsmouth | 42 | 20 | 7 | 15 | 70 | 63 | 47 |
| Crystal Palace | 42 | 20 | 6 | 16 | 69 | 50 | 46 |
| Coventry City | 42 | 19 | 8 | 15 | 71 | 60 | 46 |
| West Ham United | 42 | 15 | 15 | 12 | 69 | 56 | 45 |
| Clapton Orient | 42 | 16 | 11 | 15 | 60 | 46 | 43 |
| Plymouth Argyle | 42 | 16 | 11 | 15 | 61 | 54 | 43 |
| New Brompton | 42 | 19 | 5 | 18 | 58 | 74 | 43 |
| Bristol Rovers | 42 | 16 | 10 | 16 | 37 | 48 | 42 |
| Brentford | 42 | 16 | 9 | 17 | 50 | 58 | 41 |
| Luton Town | 42 | 15 | 11 | 16 | 72 | 92 | 41 |
| Millwall | 42 | 15 | 7 | 20 | 45 | 59 | 37 |
| Norwich City | 42 | 13 | 9 | 20 | 59 | 78 | 35 |
| Exeter City | 42 | 14 | 6 | 22 | 60 | 69 | 34 |
| Watford | 42 | 10 | 13 | 19 | 51 | 76 | 33 |
| Southend United | 42 | 12 | 9 | 21 | 51 | 90 | 33 |
| Croydon Common | 42 | 13 | 5 | 24 | 52 | 96 | 31 |
| Reading | 42 | 7 | 10 | 25 | 38 | 73 | 24 |

* The second season of professional football at St James' Park proved to be harder than the first one had been, and this was reflected in the final position in the Southern League. James 'Daisy' Bell once again top scored, however, there had been several changes made to the playing staff compared to the previous season.

* Exeter got away to a terrible start to their Southern League season, not recording a win in their opening seven matches. The first win of the season was 4-2 at home to Brentford,

* Prior to the season commencing half of the playing surface was relaid and the drainage system overhauled. However, by October 1909 there were already reports in the local press that the pitch was once again cutting up badly after heavy rain.

* The FA Cup replay against Stoke was staged at the County Ground, home of the Exeter Rugby Club. This was due to the fact that Stoke had protested that City's St James' Park pitch was not long enough and therefore did not meet the F.A.'s minimum size. As a result receipts suffered as City had to pay the Rugby Club a sum of £150 for the hire of the ground.

* During the half time interval in the game at Plymouth Argyle on Christmas Day, the referee gathered the players of both sides together and warned them that he would not tolerate the 'roughness of play' that had gone on in the first half.

* The return meeting between Exeter City and Plymouth Argyle two days later led to a crowd incident prior to kick off. The fences were broken down at the St James' Road end of the ground and some of the City directors, together with the Police, hurried over to prevent the crowd from encroaching onto the field.

* Crad Evans, who made his debut for City against Leyton in December 1909, was picked to appear for the Wales Amateur international team against England in February 1910, a game played on the ground of Huddersfield Town.

* The Grecians travelled to Plymouth Argyle on 9th March 1910 to play in a benefit match for Argyle's international goalkeeper John Sutcliffe. Argyle won 3-1.

* Oxford City visited St James' Park on 20th March 1910, to play a friendly fixture against Exeter City. The Grecians won a seven goal thriller, 4-3, before a crowd of around 2,000.

* City were unbeaten at St James' Park in a Southern League fixture in 1909-10 until the visit of Plymouth Argyle, on 27th December 1909. The Grecians' record on the road though was appalling, with only two victories recorded at Watford and Reading.

* The highest attendance of the season at St James' Park was not surprisingly for the visit of Plymouth Argyle when 14,000 were present. This also proved to be the highest of the entire Southern League campaign, home or away.

* The lowest attendance of the season, just 1,500, was at Watford, where City won 3-1 with goals from Andy McGuigan (2) and Robert Watson.

* City could not have ended the season much worse than they did. In the penultimate game they travelled to Coventry City and lost 6-0. Five days later they were at Clapton Orient where they lost 5-1, with only a goal from James Bell to show for their efforts.

* James Bell scored a hat-trick in the 4-1 home win over Brentford in October 1909, the other goal coming from the penalty spot, converted by player-manager Arthur Chadwick.

* Richard Harrison, a newcomer signed from Manchester City, also netted a hat-trick for the Grecians when he helped the side to a 5-0 thrashing of Portsmouth at St James' Park in November 1909.

Exeter City 1910-11
Back row: Arthur Chadwick (Manager), John Duffy, Spencer Bassett,
William Wells, Walter Whittaker, William Smith, Archibald Hughes, Arthur
Coates, Charles Pratt, Jack Banks (Trainer).
Middle row: Enos Whittaker, Frederick Parnell, Norman Kendall (Director),
Edwin Jones, Tom Oliver (Director), Robert Watson, Frederick Parkhouse
(Director), Thomas Griffiths, Sidney Thomas (Secretary), Francis James,
James Garside.
Seated on ground: James Bell, Nolan Evans, Frederick Prideaux, Arthur
Cooke,

| CITY PLAYING SQUAD 1910-11 | | | | |
|---|---|---|---|---|
| Name | Pos | Signed From | Apps | Gls |
| Spencer Bassett | HB | Woolwich Arsenal C/S 1910 | 32 | |
| James Bell | F | Barrow C/S 1908 | 28 | 14 |
| Arthur Coates | FB | Heywood United C/S 1910 | 23 | |
| Arthur Cooke | W | Sheffield Wednesday C/S 1910 | 4 | |
| John Duffy | W | Bradford City C/S 1910 | 7 | |
| Nolan Evans | FB | St Helens Recreation C/S 1910 | 29 | 1 |
| James Garside | F | Accrington Stanley May 1907 | 32 | 8 |
| Thomas Griffiths | HB | Blackburn Rovers C/S 1910 | 5 | |
| Archibald Hughes | F | Manchester City C/S 1910 | 18 | 7 |
| Francis James | F | Manchester City C/S 1910 | 24 | 6 |
| Edwin Jones | FB | Chorley C/S 1909 | 24 | 2 |
| Thomas Kent | F | St Lukes' College Apr 1911 | 5 | 1 |
| James Maxsted | F | Royal Artillery Nov 1910 | 1 | |
| Frederick Parnell | W | Preston North End C/S 1910 | 33 | 3 |
| Charles Pratt | HB | Everton C/S 1910 | 35 | 1 |
| Frederick Prideaux | HB | Torpoint C/S 1910 | 35 | |
| William Smith | F | South Shields Adelaide C/S 1910 | 12 | 4 |
| Robert Watson | F | Woolwich Arsenal C/S 1908 | 24 | 1 |
| Enos Whittaker | W | Haslingden C/S 1910 | 9 | 1 |
| Walter Whittaker | G | Clapton Orient C/S 1910 | 38 | |
| Own goals | | | | 2 |

## A Most Likely Lot Of Men
There was the usual optimism prior to the start of the
season with one newspaper stating:- *'It appears that
Exeter City have assembled a team from which they can
be expected to achieve success in the coming season.*
*They are the most likely lot of men that Exeter City have
yet had. In fact, most of them, though still young, have
received recognition from clubs of big repute.*
*The majority of clubs in the Southern League will probably
be on par with last season, but Exeter City should almost
certainly be one in the forefront of those who seek
improvement.'*

City's league results

| | Home | Away |
|---|---|---|
| Brentford | 0-0 | 1-3 |
| Brighton & Hove Albion | 2-1 | 2-0 |
| Bristol Rovers | 2-1 | 3-1 |
| Clapton Orient | 3-0 | 0-1 |
| Coventry City | 2-3 | 3-1 |
| Crystal Palace | 3-4 | 0-1 |
| Luton Town | 4-2 | 1-3 |
| Millwall | 1-2 | 1-3 |
| New Brompton | 2-2 | 0-1 |
| Northampton Town | 1-4 | 0-2 |
| Norwich City | 3-1 | 0-0 |
| Plymouth Argyle | 1-3 | 0-0 |
| Portsmouth | 0-2 | 0-0 |
| Queens Park Rangers | 2-2 | 0-1 |
| Southampton | 0-0 | 3-1 |
| Southend United | 1-0 | 2-1 |
| Swindon Town | 2-1 | 1-0 |
| Watford | 2-0 | 2-2 |
| West Ham United | 0-0 | 1-4 |

| F.A. Cup | | | |
|---|---|---|---|
| Reading | A | Q4 | 1-1 |
| Reading | N* | Q4 | 1-1Ab |
| Reading | N* | Q4 | 1-0 |
| Nelson | H+ | R1 | 4-3 |
| Burnley | H$ | R2 | 0-2 |

Ab - Match abandoned 80th minute
* - Played at County Ground, Exeter
+ - Tie switched to Nelson's ground
$ - Tie switched to Burnley's ground

| Southern Charity Cup | | | |
|---|---|---|---|
| Bristol Rovers | A | R1 | 0-1 |

CITY MANAGER 1910-11
Arthur Chadwick - Appointed April 1908

SOUTHERN LEAGUE - 1910-11

| | P | W | D | L | F | A | Pts |
|---|---|---|---|---|---|---|---|
| Swindon Town | 38 | 24 | 5 | 9 | 80 | 31 | 53 |
| Northampton Town | 38 | 18 | 12 | 8 | 54 | 27 | 48 |
| Brighton & H.A. | 38 | 20 | 8 | 10 | 58 | 35 | 48 |
| Crystal Palace | 38 | 17 | 13 | 8 | 55 | 48 | 47 |
| West Ham United | 38 | 17 | 11 | 10 | 63 | 46 | 45 |
| Queens Park Rangers | 38 | 13 | 14 | 11 | 52 | 41 | 40 |
| Clapton Orient | 38 | 16 | 8 | 14 | 57 | 52 | 40 |
| Plymouth Argyle | 38 | 15 | 9 | 14 | 54 | 55 | 39 |
| Luton Town | 38 | 15 | 8 | 15 | 67 | 63 | 38 |
| Norwich City | 38 | 15 | 8 | 15 | 46 | 48 | 38 |
| Coventry City | 38 | 16 | 6 | 16 | 65 | 68 | 38 |
| Brentford | 38 | 14 | 9 | 15 | 41 | 42 | 37 |
| Exeter City | 38 | 14 | 9 | 15 | 51 | 54 | 37 |
| Watford | 38 | 13 | 9 | 16 | 49 | 65 | 35 |
| Millwall | 38 | 11 | 9 | 18 | 42 | 54 | 31 |
| Bristol Rovers | 38 | 10 | 10 | 18 | 42 | 55 | 30 |
| Southampton | 38 | 11 | 8 | 19 | 42 | 67 | 30 |
| New Brompton | 38 | 11 | 8 | 19 | 34 | 65 | 30 |
| Southend United | 38 | 10 | 9 | 19 | 47 | 64 | 29 |
| Portsmouth | 38 | 8 | 11 | 19 | 34 | 53 | 27 |

* Once again there were a number of 'new' players in the City squad for the 1910-11 season, and the team did not make the best of starts, which they never really recovered from. They only won two Southern League matches up until 10th December, drawing another four.

* The highest attendance of the season was 20,000 at Crystal Palace, who defeated the Grecians 1-0. The best crowd figure at St James' Park was 7,500 for the visit of Plymouth Argyle in January 1911.

* It was reported that crowds had dwindled for reserve team matches at St James' Park, with only around 4,000 watching the Plymouth and District League fixtures.

* The City team ran out to the 'sound' of 'Uncle Tom Cobley' at the start of matches at St James' Park. But this was changed later in the season as it had been, quote, "abused." The Devonshire's Regiment march, 'We Lived and Loved Together' being played instead.

* Several railway excursions were run for City supporters to attend the Southern League match at Plymouth Argyle in September 1910, and it was reckoned that 500 fans took advantage of the cheap fares offered.

* Exeter City were ordered to post warning notices around the ground by the Southern League management committee, following an incident after the game at St James' Park against Crystal Palace, which the visitors won 4-3. Mud was hurled at the Palace officials and players while on their way to the railway station by a group of 'rowdy youths.'

* The City directors decided to change the colours of the club to red and white in November 1910. The players had said that the green and white brought them no luck and wanted a change. They petitioned the directors and they agreed. The new red and white striped shirts were worn for the first time in the home match against West Ham United on 12th November, the game ending goalless.

* Once again 'home' FA Cup ties had to be moved away from St James' Park, due to the pitch not being long enough. Exeter Rugby Club's County Ground was used once more, however, the tie against Reading was abandoned due to fog! City had better luck when the game was replayed, but then had to give up ground advantage to both Nelson and Burnley in subsequent rounds, who refused to agree to playing at the County Ground,

* Leading goalscorer James 'Daisy' Bell was transferred to Portsmouth in April 1911, although the fee was reportedly 'not believed to be large one.' His scoring ability had made him a real favourite of the City supporters.

* There was speculation prior to the last away match of the season, that manager Arthur Chadwick had turned down an  offer from the club directors to stay on as manager the following season. This followed on from collections being taken at home matches for a 'Summer Wage Fund' to help the club retain and pay players through that period.

* At the end of April 1911, strong rumours were circulating that Exeter City were in financial difficulty. It had been proposed that no players were to be re-engaged and therefore the Summer wages would be saved until the start of August 1911. Manager Chadwick felt that it was an unfair responsibility to ask him to seek players at such a late stage when the best players would have already been signed by other clubs.

* With the matter of the length of the St James' Park pitch not resolved, it was suggested that negotiations should be entered into with the Exeter Rugby Club in an effort to share their County Ground for all League and Cup fixtures as from the 1911-12 season. St James' Park would be retained by the football club for reserve team football only.

## Better Prospects For The Grecians?

The Exeter City directors felt very optimistic about the 1911-12 season, although manager Arthur Chadwick had only managed to make four new signings to his playing squad during the summer.

The Express and Echo newspaper reported that ...' *although City are not stronger in playing strength, the team will, it is confidently anticipated, do better than the previous season.'*

Their season preview went on ...

'*It is indeed all important that Exeter City do well. The club has been in the limelight with a vengeance this summer. First there was talk of a new ground and the fate of St James' Park as the home of the club hung on the balance. There were pathetic protestations of love for the old home and away over the bridge at the County Ground, St Thomas there were gentle beckonings to another nest at the County Ground.*
*To sum up, the whole playing strength of the Grecians, it would appear that the side is likely to prove a trifle better than last year, and the improvement of course, is in attack.*
*There is no point in making wild prophecies about the League Championship coming to Devon, but it certainly looks as if Exeter City are good enough for the top half of the table this season.'*

*Finally, several prominent football clubs have gone in for adopting pet dogs as mascots. Exeter City are one such club, and the new mascot is a large English sheep dog called 'Laddie' and owned by goalkeeper, Walter Whittaker.'*

### City's league results

|                      | Home | Away |
|----------------------|------|------|
| Brentford            | 1-0  | 1-3  |
| Brighton & H.A.      | 1-3  | 1-2  |
| Bristol Rovers       | 2-1  | 1-2  |
| Clapton Orient       | 1-0  | 0-0  |
| Coventry City        | 0-0  | 1-1  |
| Crystal Palace       | 1-1  | 0-5  |
| Luton Town           | 2-0  | 2-4  |
| Millwall             | 3-1  | 0-5  |
| New Brompton         | 8-1  | 1-4  |
| Northampton Town     | 0-2  | 1-2  |
| Norwich City         | 1-0  | 1-1  |
| Plymouth Argyle      | 0-1  | 1-3  |
| Queens Park Rangers  | 1-1  | 0-0  |
| Reading              | 2-0  | 2-1  |
| Southampton          | 2-2  | 0-3  |
| Stoke                | 1-1  | 3-1  |
| Swindon Town         | 1-4  | 1-0  |
| Watford              | 0-1  | 0-0  |
| West Ham United      | 3-3  | 2-3  |

### F.A. Cup

| Merthyr Town | H  | Q4   | 1-1 |
|--------------|----|------|-----|
| Merthyr Town | A  | Q4R  | 0-0 |
| Merthyr Town | N* | Q4R  | 0-2 |

\* Played at Ashton Gate, Bristol City

### Southern Charity Cup

| Swindon Town    | H | R1  | 2-0 |
|-----------------|---|-----|-----|
| Plymouth Argyle | H | R2  | 0-0 |
| Plymouth Argyle | A | R2R | 1-2 |

CITY MANAGER 1911-12
Arthur Chadwick - Appointed April 1908

### CITY PLAYING SQUAD 1911-12

| Name | Pos | Signed From | Apps | Gls |
|------|-----|-------------|------|-----|
| Spencer Bassett | HB | Woolwich Arsenal C/S 1910 | 38 | 1 |
| William Caddy | FB | Woodland Villa Dec 1911 | 2 | |
| Arthur Chadwick | HB | Southampton Apr 1908 | 1 | |
| John Chapman | G | Bolton Waderers C/S 1911 | 6 | |
| Fred Chenneour | F | Amateur C/S 1910 | 2 | |
| Arthur Coates | FB | Heywood United C/S 1911 | 18 | |
| Frank Coman | F | Nelson C/S 1911 | 28 | 6 |
| William Crute | G | Babbacombe Dec 1911 | 3 | |
| Nolan Evans | FB | St Helens Recreation C/S 1910 | 34 | 1 |
| John Fort | FB | Atherton C/S 1911 | 18 | |
| James Garside | F | Accrington Stanley May 1907 | 24 | 7 |
| Thomas Griffiths | HB | Blackburn Rovers C/S 1910 | 17 | 2 |
| Thomas Kent | F | St Lukes College April 1911 | 8 | 2 |
| Henry Lockett | HB | Nottingham Forest C/S 1911 | 34 | 6 |
| Frederick Parnell | W | Preston North End C/S 1910 | 17 | 2 |
| Charles Pratt | HB | Everton C/S 1910 | 21 | |
| Frederick Prideaux | HB | Torpoint C/S 1910 | 12 | |
| Dick Pym | G | Topsham Dec 1911 | 8 | |
| James Rigby | HB | Accrington Stanley C/S 1911 | 19 | |
| Arthur Rutter | F | Barnsley C/S 1911 | 28 | 10 |
| Albert Tompkinson | F | Glossop Jan 1912 | 1 | 1 |
| Robert Watson | F | Woolwich Arsenal C/S 1908 | 34 | 8 |
| Enos Whittaker | W | Haslingden C/S 1910 | 24 | 2 |
| Walter Whittaker | G | Clapton Orient C/S 1910 | 21 | |

### SOUTHERN LEAGUE - 1911-12

|                      | P  | W  | D  | L  | F  | A  | Pts |
|----------------------|----|----|----|----|----|----|-----|
| Queens Park Rangers  | 38 | 21 | 11 | 6  | 59 | 35 | 53  |
| Plymouth Argyle      | 38 | 23 | 6  | 9  | 63 | 31 | 52  |
| Northampton Town     | 38 | 22 | 7  | 9  | 82 | 41 | 51  |
| Swindon Town         | 38 | 21 | 6  | 11 | 82 | 50 | 48  |
| Brighton & HA        | 38 | 19 | 9  | 10 | 73 | 35 | 47  |
| Coventry City        | 38 | 17 | 8  | 13 | 66 | 54 | 42  |
| Crystal Palace       | 38 | 15 | 10 | 14 | 70 | 46 | 40  |
| Millwall             | 38 | 15 | 10 | 13 | 60 | 57 | 40  |
| Watford              | 38 | 13 | 10 | 15 | 56 | 68 | 36  |
| Stoke                | 38 | 13 | 10 | 15 | 51 | 63 | 36  |
| Reading              | 38 | 11 | 14 | 13 | 43 | 69 | 36  |
| Norwich City         | 38 | 10 | 14 | 14 | 40 | 60 | 34  |
| West Ham United      | 38 | 13 | 7  | 18 | 64 | 69 | 33  |
| Brentford            | 38 | 12 | 9  | 17 | 60 | 65 | 33  |
| Exeter City          | 38 | 11 | 11 | 16 | 48 | 62 | 33  |
| Southampton          | 38 | 10 | 11 | 17 | 46 | 63 | 31  |
| Bristol Rovers       | 38 | 9  | 13 | 16 | 41 | 62 | 31  |
| New Brompton         | 38 | 11 | 9  | 18 | 35 | 72 | 31  |
| Luton Town           | 38 | 9  | 10 | 19 | 49 | 61 | 28  |
| Clapton Orient       | 38 | 7  | 11 | 20 | 27 | 62 | 25  |

* Exeter City managed to get through the close season, but only thanks to the generosity of supporters and well wishers who between them were able to raise £200 towards the Summer wages for players.

* One bit of very good news was that local M.P. Mr. H.E. Duke managed to persuade a landowner at the back of what is now the Big Bank to sell 20 feet of land, so it was possible to lengthen the St James' Park pitch to comply with F.A rules and avoid having cup ties switched to their opponents grounds or be played at the County Ground in Exeter. The newly lengthened pitch was used for the first time for the visit of West Ham United on 14th October 1911.

* Manager Arthur Chadwick made his annual pilgrimage to the North of England during the summer and duly signed four players, Fort from Atherton, Lockett from Nottingham Forest, Cornan from Nelson, and Rutter from Barnsley.

* City had a journey to forget when travelling to Watford for their opening game of the season. Their train to Paddington was late. They took a fleet of taxi's to Euston, where the train was again delayed heading for Watford. As a consequence they arrived just 5 minutes before kick off, the start of game being delayed by a further ten minutes. The game ended goalless.

* Exeter City recorded their record Southern League victory when New Brompton visited St James' Park in September 1911. City won 8-1, which included a hat-trick from Robert Watson.

* The Flowerpot terrace, (later to become the Cowshed and now the Flybe Stand) was extended by 20 yards or so to link up with the Duke Bank terracing. It was used for the first time when Queens Park Rangers were the visitors on 30th September 1911.

* James Garside became the second City player in 1911-12 to score hat-trick in a Southern League fixture, when he helped his side to a 3-1 win at Stoke on 6th November.

* Representatives from Exeter City attended a meeting in London in November 1911 to discuss the possibility of amalgamating the Southern League with the Football League.

* The match referee asked for the kick off time to be brought forward five minutes when he officiated at the Crystal Palace versus Exeter City fixture in December 1911. This, he explained, was so that the game could finish in sufficient light!

* With the St James' Park pitch being a near waterlogged state, it was decided to shorten the pitch and move the goal posts forward, for the game against Brentford on 27th January 1912. The length of the pitch was only two yards longer than it had been before the purchase of the land behind the Duke Bank.

* A friendly match was played against Plymouth Argyle at St James' Park on 20th March 1912, with all the proceeds being used for the Exeter City Summer Wages Fund. City won the game 1-0

* As per usual the Exeter City team travelled home by train after their Good Friday match at Reading. They were joined by the teams and officials from Plymouth Argyle and Luton Town, who had both journeyed from Paddington. Luton stayed the night in Exeter before travelling on to play at the Argyle the following day.

* Exeter City's flag was flown at half mast at St James' Park for the visit of Crystal Palace on 20th April 1912, as a mark of respect for all those who lost their lives with the sinking of the 'Titanic.' A collection was taken for the 'Titanic Fund.'

| CITY PLAYING SQUAD 1912-13 | | | | |
|---|---|---|---|---|
| Name Pos Signed Fr | Pos | Signed From | Apps | Gls |
| Spencer Bassett | HB | Woolwich Arsenal C/S 1910 | 11 | 2 |
| Clifford Brooksbank | F | Blackburn Rovers C/S 1912 | 10 | 3 |
| Thomas Cooper | F | South Liverpool C/S 1912 | 28 | 9 |
| Ellis Crompton | F | Tottenham Hotspur C/S 1912 | 31 | 10 |
| John Fort | FB | Atherton C/S 1911 | 34 | |
| James Garside | F | Accrington Stanley May 1907 | 10 | 1 |
| Martin Golightly | F | Gateshead C/S 1912 | 7 | |
| George Hurst | FB | Walkden Central C/S 1912 | 35 | |
| Benjamin Ives | W | Barrow C/S 1912 | 29 | 8 |
| James Lagan | HB | West Stanley C/S 1912 | 16 | |
| Henry Lockett | HB | Nottingham Forest C/S 1911 | 36 | |
| Ralph Nevin | FB | Gateshead C/S 1912 | 7 | |
| Charles Pratt | HB | Everton C/S 1910 | 14 | |
| Dick Pym | G | Topsham Dec 1911 | 38 | |
| James Rigby | HB | Accrington Stanley C/S 1911 | 38 | 1 |
| Arthur Rutter | F | Barnsley C/S 1911 | 36 | 9 |
| Enos Whittaker | W | Haslingden C/S 1910 | 38 | 4 |
| Own Goals | | | | 1 |

## Football Association Enquiry

Preparations for the 1912-13 season were overshadowed by the Football Association looking into the financial affairs of Exeter City F.C. Needless to say this was reported in some depth in the local newspapers. One such report explained the reasoning behind the concern of the F.A.:-

*'It has been known for some tome past that an F.A. enquiry into certain affairs of Exeter City Football Club was likely to take place. Over two months ago the management were acquainted with the fact that certain complaints had been sent to them by a section of the club directors.*

*The club had to send their accounts books to the F.A. and whilst the matter was 'sub-judice' it did appear, however, that the one of the charges made was that irregular match bonuses were being paid to players.*

*It is also understood that there are other complaints about irregular accounts. If proven it is possible that there will be suspension of officials and those directors associated with the alleged illegal transactions at the time they took place.*

*The worst of the matter is that the said charges emanate from a small section of directors themselves, which is a rare occurrence. The trouble had been brewing for a long time past, starting somewhere about the end of season 1910-11 when there was a difference of opinion as to finding the money for summer wages. Such divisions on a directorate must be fatal to the interests of any club.'*

### City's league results

| | Home | Away |
|---|---|---|
| Brentford | 1-0 | 1-0 |
| Brighton & H.A. | 2-1 | 0-1 |
| Bristol Rovers | 4-0 | 1-1 |
| Coventry City | 3-0 | 1-0 |
| Crystal Palace | 1-1 | 1-0 |
| Gillingham | 2-0 | 4-0 |
| Merthyr Town | 2-4 | 0-2 |
| Millwall | 1-4 | 0-1 |
| Northampton Town | 1-1 | 0-4 |
| Norwich City | 1-0 | 1-1 |
| Plymouth Argyle | 1-0 | 0-3 |
| Portsmouth | 2-1 | 1-2 |
| Queens Park Rangers | 3-1 | 1-2 |
| Reading | 1-0 | 2-2 |
| Southampton | 1-0 | 2-2 |
| Stoke | 1-0 | 2-0 |
| Swindon Town | 1-3 | 2-2 |
| Watford | 1-0 | 0-1 |
| West Ham United | 0-0 | 0-4 |

### F.A. Cup

| | | | |
|---|---|---|---|
| Cardiff City | A | Q4 | 1-5 |

### Southern Charity Cup

| | | | |
|---|---|---|---|
| Plymouth Argyle | A | R1 | 2-0 |
| Swindon Town | H | R2 | 2-0 |
| Queens Park Rangers | A | R3 | 0-2 |

CITY MANAGER 1911-12
Arthur Chadwick - Appointed April 1908

SOUTHERN LEAGUE - 1911-12

| | P | W | D | L | F | A | Pts |
|---|---|---|---|---|---|---|---|
| Plymouth Argyle | 38 | 22 | 6 | 10 | 77 | 36 | 50 |
| Swindon Town | 38 | 20 | 8 | 10 | 66 | 41 | 48 |
| West Ham United | 38 | 18 | 12 | 8 | 66 | 46 | 48 |
| Queens Park Rangers | 38 | 18 | 10 | 10 | 46 | 35 | 46 |
| Crystal Palace | 38 | 17 | 11 | 10 | 55 | 36 | 45 |
| Millwall | 38 | 19 | 7 | 12 | 62 | 43 | 45 |
| Exeter City | 38 | 18 | 8 | 12 | 48 | 44 | 44 |
| Reading | 38 | 17 | 8 | 13 | 59 | 55 | 42 |
| Brighton & H.A. | 38 | 13 | 12 | 13 | 48 | 47 | 38 |
| Northampton Town | 38 | 12 | 12 | 14 | 61 | 48 | 36 |
| Portsmouth | 38 | 14 | 8 | 16 | 41 | 49 | 36 |
| Merthyr Town | 38 | 12 | 12 | 14 | 42 | 60 | 36 |
| Coventry City | 38 | 13 | 8 | 17 | 53 | 59 | 34 |
| Watford | 38 | 12 | 10 | 16 | 43 | 50 | 34 |
| Gillingham | 38 | 12 | 10 | 16 | 36 | 53 | 34 |
| Bristol Rovers | 38 | 12 | 9 | 17 | 55 | 64 | 33 |
| Southampton | 38 | 10 | 11 | 17 | 40 | 72 | 31 |
| Norwich City | 38 | 10 | 9 | 19 | 39 | 50 | 29 |
| Brentford | 38 | 11 | 5 | 22 | 42 | 55 | 27 |
| Stoke | 38 | 10 | 4 | 24 | 39 | 75 | 24 |

* At a special meeting called by the Football Association, and held at the Great Western Hotel, Exeter on 1st June 1912, they considered charges of irregular accounting and match bonuses paid to Exeter City players. Four City directors were censured by the F.A. and the club were fined £20. One director was suspended from acting as such or in any capacity in the Exeter City Football Club.

* Prior to the start of the season the St James' Park playing surface was re-turfed, the grandstand enlarged and new terracing built, increasing the capacity by 1,500.

* An Athletics sports meeting was held at St James' Park on 17th August 1912, followed by a pre-season practice match between the Reds and the Greens, the former winning 3-1.

* Brentford were forced to play with just ten men for the opening 20 minutes of their match at Exeter on 16th November 1912, when one of their players had missed the train from London. He caught a later train and was able to join the game, although by then City had scored the one and only goal of the contest.

* Matches between Exeter City and Plymouth Argyle had already gained something of a reputation and as a result the Southern League appointed a referee who was regarded one of the best in the country for the meeting in January 1913. Referee Mr. Baker, travelled from Nantwich in Cheshire and it was reported that he would "Show us how Devon derbies ought to be conducted."

* The final shot of the above game (a 1-0 win for Exeter) resulted in Argyle keeper Horne tipping the ball over his own bar, which he dislodged. The City ground staff were still replacing the bar when the teams left the field,

* Prior to City's 2-0 win at home to Gillingham on 1st March 1913, the Grecians were fourth in the table and there was much talk about the possibility of the team going on to win the Southern League Championship. By the end of the month, City were top of the table.

* Exeter City reserves reached the final of the Devon Senior Cup, only to lose to their great rivals, Plymouth Argyle (2-1) at Home Park.

* The Grecians transferred left winger Ben Ives to Queens Park Rangers in March 1913, for a fee described as being less than £300, and probably £250. The player said he was happy at Exeter, but would leave if it was to financially benefit the Grecians.

* The highest attendance of the season had been 15,000 who were present for the visit of Exeter City at Millwall. The highest crowd at St James' Park was not surprisingly for the game against Plymouth Argyle, when 12,000 made their way through the turnstiles.

* The lowest crowd of the season at St James' Park was for the final match of the Southern League season, played in pouring rain against Stoke. Only 1,000 were at the Park to see City win 1-0.

* It was reckoned that 750 City supporters had travelled for the F.A. Cup tie at Cardiff. The Exeter City Military Band, under the leadership of George Newman, joined their counterparts from Cardiff on the pitch to entertain the crowd prior to kick off and again at half-time.

* The strangest goal of the season surely had to go to Swindon Town player, Kay, who passed back to his keeper from fully 25-yards out. However, the keeper slipped and fell and could only watch the ball go over his head and trickle into the net to give City a 2-0 lead. Swindon fought back to draw 2-2.

# 1913/14    Southern League                    12th from 20

Back row: S. Greenaway (Trainer), N. Kendall (Director), A. Chadwick (Manager), J. Pengelly (Director), W. Norman (Director), G. Middlewick (Director), S. Thomas (Secretary).
2nd Row: E.Lewis, R.Loram, R.Gerrish, W.Kirby, R.Pym, S.Strettle, A.Evans, F.Munt, J.Manstan (Groundsman).
3rd row: J.Whittaker, J.Fort, J.Rigby, M.McGahey (Chairman), W.Smith, F.Marshall, H.McCann, J.Lee.
Seated on ground: M.Holt, C.Pratt, F.Lovett, J.Lagan, M.Orr, J.Goddard.

City's league results

| | Home | Away |
|---|---|---|
| Brighton & H.A. | 4-1 | 1-2 |
| Bristol Rovers | 1-1 | 1-1 |
| Cardiff City | 0-1 | 1-1 |
| Coventry City | 0-0 | 2-1 |
| Crystal Palace | 1-1 | 0-0 |
| Gillingham | 2-0 | 0-2 |
| Merthyr Town | 3-0 | 0-1 |
| Millwall | 3-1 | 1-3 |
| Northampton Town | 2-0 | 1-2 |
| Norwich City | 0-1 | 1-3 |
| Plymouth Argyle | 0-0 | 0-0 |
| Portsmouth | 1-0 | 2-2 |
| Queens Park Rangers | 0-0 | 3-2 |
| Reading | 0-1 | 2-2 |
| Southampton | 2-0 | 0-2 |
| Southend Uited | 0-0 | 0-1 |
| Swindon Town | 0-2 | 1-1 |
| Watford | 1-1 | 1-0 |
| West Ham United | 1-1 | 1-1 |

F.A. Cup

| | | | |
|---|---|---|---|
| Portsmouth | A | R1 | 4-0 |
| Aston Villa | H | R2 | 1-2 |

Southern Charity Cup

| | | | |
|---|---|---|---|
| Merthyr Town | A | R1 | 1-2 |

CITY MANAGER 1913-14
**Arthur Chadwick - Appointed April 1908**

## CITY PLAYING SQUAD 1913-14

| Name | Pos | Signed From | Apps | Gls |
|---|---|---|---|---|
| Clifford Brooksbank | F | Blackburn Rovers C/S 1912 | 25 | 2 |
| Arthur Evans | F | Manchester City C/S 1913 | 6 | |
| John Fort | FB | Atherton C/S 1911 | 33 | |
| Frederick Goodwin | F | West Ham United Dec 1913 | 14 | 2 |
| Augustus Harding | FB | Chelsea C/S 1913 | 6 | |
| Harold Holt | W | Cardiff City C/S 1913 | 30 | 3 |
| William Kirby | F | Preston North End C/S 1913 | 5 | |
| James Lagan | HB | West Stanley C/S 1912 | 22 | |
| John Lee | W | Clapton Orient C/S 1913 | 6 | 1 |
| Ernest Lewis | F | Amateur Oct 1913 | 3 | |
| William Lovett | F | Rochdale C/S 1913 | 21 | 3 |
| Henry McCann | F | Barnsley C/S 1913 | 35 | 11 |
| Frederick Marshall | D | Hyde United C/S 1913 | 19 | 4 |
| Henry Orr | W | Barnsley C/S 1913 | 2 | |
| Charles Pratt | HB | Everton C/S 1910 | 17 | |
| William Pridham | F | Torquay Town C/S 1913 | 2 | |
| Dick Pym | G | Topsham Dec 1911 | 38 | |
| James Rigby | HB | Accrington Stanley C/S 1911 | 37 | |
| William Smith | HB | Hyde United C/S 1913 | 29 | |
| Samuel Strettle | FB | Chesterfield C/S 1913 | 38 | |
| Enos Whittaker | W | Haslingden C/S 1910 | 30 | 13 |

SOUTHERN LEAGUE - 1913-14

| | P | W | D | L | F | A | Pts |
|---|---|---|---|---|---|---|---|
| Swindon Town | 38 | 21 | 8 | 9 | 81 | 41 | 50 |
| Crystal Palace | 38 | 17 | 16 | 5 | 60 | 32 | 50 |
| Northampton Town | 38 | 14 | 19 | 5 | 50 | 37 | 47 |
| Reading | 38 | 17 | 10 | 11 | 43 | 36 | 44 |
| Plymouth Argyle | 38 | 15 | 13 | 10 | 46 | 42 | 43 |
| West Ham United | 38 | 15 | 12 | 11 | 61 | 60 | 42 |
| Brighton & h.A. | 38 | 15 | 12 | 11 | 43 | 45 | 42 |
| Queens Park Rangers | 38 | 16 | 9 | 13 | 45 | 43 | 41 |
| Portsmouth | 38 | 14 | 12 | 12 | 57 | 48 | 40 |
| Cardiff City | 38 | 13 | 12 | 13 | 46 | 42 | 38 |
| Southampton | 38 | 15 | 7 | 16 | 55 | 54 | 37 |
| Exeter City | 38 | 10 | 16 | 12 | 39 | 38 | 36 |
| Gillingham | 38 | 13 | 9 | 16 | 48 | 49 | 35 |
| Norwich City | 38 | 9 | 17 | 12 | 49 | 51 | 35 |
| Millwall | 38 | 11 | 12 | 15 | 51 | 56 | 34 |
| Southend United | 38 | 10 | 12 | 16 | 41 | 66 | 32 |
| Bristol Rovers | 38 | 10 | 11 | 17 | 46 | 67 | 31 |
| Watford | 38 | 10 | 9 | 19 | 38 | 61 | 28 |
| Coventry City | 38 | 6 | 14 | 18 | 43 | 68 | 26 |

## F.A. Cup Fever

There was great excitement in the city when the Grecians drew Aston Villa at home in the second round of the F.A. Cup, the game being played on Saturday, 31st January 1914.

As soon as the tickets went on sale there was a steady stream of supporters buying them for grandstand seats. Admission was fixed at 5/- for the grandstand; 1/' for the bank terracing; 2/- for the rest of the ground. There were also some 'ring seats' Inside the railing for early ticket buyers, but they were strictly limited.

Villa were taking the tie very seriously as they sent their team to train in Southport from Monday to Thursday prior to the game, before they travelled to Exeter on the Friday.

The attendance for the tie was 9,500 with match receipts totalling £910.

* At the start of the season Exeter City played friendly matches at two newly formed clubs in the County, namely Tiverton and Budleigh Salterton. At the former a crowd of over 700 watched the Grecians win 7-0. After the match both teams were entertained and dined at Harris' Restaurant in the town. City defeated Budleigh 13-0 and again were treated to tea at the Feather's Hotel in the town.

* The Exeter City team travelled by train to Paddington for their game at Watford in October 1913. They were then 'met by a charabanc' to take them to Watford's Cassio Road ground, arriving an hour before kick off. City won 1-0 thanks to a goal from John Lee, the only one he was to score all season.

* The Exeter City Supporters' Club organised a collection at the City versus Northampton Town fixture in October 1913, to raise funds on behalf of the Senghenydd Colliery Disaster Fund. 439 miners were killed following an explosion.

* The Southern League fixture at Portsmouth kicked off earlier than usual to enable the referee to catch his train home to Birmingham after the match. City had travelled the night before by train from Exeter Queen Street and stayed in a Southampton hotel.

* The City team wore an unusual strip for the visit of Southampton to St James' Park on 27th December. With the Saints playing in red and white striped shirts, City changed into a fetching chocolate coloured shirt with yellow sleeves.

* Improvements were made to The Duke Bank terracing in January 1914, which increased the capacity to around 7,000. Extra crush barriers were erected. Terracing was also constructed to the left hand side (Duke Bank) of the grandstand.

* Many of the city centre shop window displays were given over to displaying Exeter City colours etc., prior to the Second Round FA Cup tie against the holders Aston Villa at St James' Park. The night before the game, the Villa and City teams attended a performance at the Exeter Hippodrome.

* Prior to the Villa cup-tie, a goat was bought by local taxi drivers, as a lucky mascot, and paraded through the streets wearing City colours. It was presented to Exeter captain, Jimmy Rigby before kick off. Match receipts totalled £910 - a club record.

* At the end of the season it was announced that Exeter City had reduced their overdraft from £1,600 to £600.

* Officials and players left aboard ship from Southampton docks on 22nd May 1914 to begin a tour of Argentina and Brazil. Exeter City had been chosen to make the trip by the league as being a typical English club.

* They played five matches in Argentina and three in Brazil, including becoming the first ever team to play the full Brazilian national side. the full list of matches and results were as follows:- Argentine North (0-1); Argentine South (3-0); Racing Club, Buenos Aires (2-0); Rosarian League XI (3-1); Combinadoes (5-0); Rio de Janeiro (3-0); Fluminese (5-3), Brazil (0-2).

* The South American trip proved to be eventful, with many stories emanating from it, most of which have appeared elsewhere in other publications. On their voyage home, First World War was declared and the ship's captain was told to watch out for 'German Men of War' in the English Channel. As a result the ship was diverted to dock at Liverpool instead of Southampton.

* 'Fears were entertained for a few days that Exeter City would be without a League team, as nearly the whole of their playing squad were on the sea returning from their South American tour when hostilities broke out,' reported the Express and Echo.

'They consequently ran the risk of capture by the enemy, or being held up at some port or other. But they came safely through, arriving in Exeter on 10th August.'

* The Exeter City directors considered the tour of Argentina and Brazil to be beneficial to all concerned. It not only helped the directors to retain the services of nearly all the players from the previous season, but it also enabled new signing, William Hunter, who went on the tour, to get to know his team mates.

* It was pointed out prior to the start of the season that attendances may show a decline as 'a large number of young men who watch football will have volunteered joining the Armed Services. Two of the City directors, Captain Harvey, was busy with Army work, whilst Norman Kendall was connected with the 4th Devonshire Regiment, and both of them could be required to travel abroad.

* The last game to be played at St James' Park for the duration of the First World War was a Southern League fixture against Reading on Saturday 17th April 1915. A game watched by an attendance of 3,000.

* The Grecians did pay two further matches after that though, the first of which was a friendly against the Army, played at Okehampton, where they won 3-0. They then travelled to Southampton for what was their final away fixture in the Southern League that season, and final game of any sort for a while, as they lost 3-0.

City's league results

|  | Home | Away |
|---|---|---|
| Brighton & H.A. | 1-0 | 1-2 |
| Bristol Rovers | 1-0 | 1-2 |
| Cardiff City | 2-0 | 0-1 |
| Croydon Common | 3-1 | 0-0 |
| Crystal Palace | 1-1 | 0-0 |
| Gillingham | 2-0 | 0-0 |
| Luton Town | 1-2 | 2-0 |
| Millwall | 0-1 | 1-2 |
| Northampton Town | 2-1 | 1-1 |
| Norwich City | 2-0 | 1-3 |
| Plymouth Argyle | 1-1 | 3-1 |
| Portsmouth | 1-1 | 2-1 |
| Queens Park Rangers | 0-1 | 2-0 |
| Reading | 0-1 | 0-1 |
| Southampton | 1-2 | 0-3 |
| Southend United | 7-1 | 2-0 |
| Swindon Town | 0-1 | 0-4 |
| Watford | 4-1 | 1-1 |
| West Ham United | 3-1 | 1-4 |

F.A. Cup
| Aston Villa | A R1 | 0-2 |
|---|---|---|

Southern Charity Cup
| Merthyr Town | H R1 | 2-1 |
|---|---|---|
| Plymouth Argyle | A R2 | 0-1 |

CITY MANAGER 1914-15
Arthur Chadwick - Appointed April 1908

### CITY PLAYING SQUAD 1914-15

| Name | Pos | Signed From | Apps | Gls |
|---|---|---|---|---|
| Stanley Cowie | F | Blackpool C/S 1914 | 1 | |
| Samuel Cox | F | Devon Regiment Mar 1915 | 2 | |
| John Dockray | W | Bury C/S 1914 | 23 | 2 |
| Arthur Evans | F | Manchester City C/S 1913 | 20 | 1 |
| Frederick Goodwin | F | West Ham United Dec 1913 | 26 | 3 |
| William Goodwin | F | Blackburn Rovers C/S 1914 | 36 | 23 |
| Alfred Green | HB | Rotherham Town C/S 1914 | 14 | 7 |
| Augustus Harding | FB | Chelsea C/S 1913 | 1 | |
| Harold Holt | W | Cardiff City C/S 1913 | 38 | 4 |
| William Hunter | F | Clapton Orient C/S 1914 | 5 | 1 |
| James Lagan | HB | West Stanley C/S 1912 | 25 | |
| William Lovett | F | Rochdale C/S 1913 | 32 | 7 |
| Frederick Marshall | D | Hyde United C/S 1913 | 36 | |
| Charles Pratt | HB | Everton C/S 1910 | 11 | |
| Dick Pym | G | Topsham Dec 1911 | 38 | |
| James Rigby | HB | Accrington Stanley C/S 1911 | 35 | 1 |
| William Smith | HB | Hyde United C/S 1913 | 37 | |
| Samuel Strettle | FB | Chesterfield C/S 1913 | 38 | |
| Own Goal | | | | 1 |

### SOUTHERN LEAGUE - 1913-14

|  | P | W | D | L | F | A | Pts |
|---|---|---|---|---|---|---|---|
| Watford | 38 | 22 | 8 | 8 | 68 | 46 | 52 |
| Reading | 38 | 21 | 7 | 10 | 68 | 43 | 49 |
| Cardiff City | 38 | 22 | 4 | 12 | 72 | 38 | 48 |
| West Ham United | 38 | 18 | 9 | 11 | 58 | 47 | 45 |
| Northampton Town | 38 | 16 | 11 | 11 | 56 | 51 | 43 |
| Southampton | 38 | 19 | 5 | 14 | 78 | 74 | 43 |
| Portsmouth | 38 | 16 | 10 | 12 | 54 | 42 | 42 |
| Millwall | 38 | 16 | 10 | 12 | 50 | 52 | 42 |
| Swindon Town | 38 | 15 | 11 | 12 | 77 | 59 | 41 |
| Brighton & H.A. | 38 | 16 | 7 | 15 | 46 | 47 | 39 |
| Exeter City | 38 | 15 | 8 | 15 | 50 | 41 | 38 |
| Queens Park Rangers | 38 | 13 | 12 | 13 | 55 | 56 | 38 |
| Norwich City | 38 | 11 | 14 | 13 | 53 | 56 | 36 |
| Luton Town | 38 | 13 | 8 | 17 | 61 | 73 | 34 |
| Crystal Palace | 38 | 13 | 8 | 17 | 47 | 61 | 34 |
| Bristol Rovers | 38 | 14 | 3 | 21 | 53 | 75 | 31 |
| Plymouth Argyle | 38 | 8 | 14 | 16 | 51 | 61 | 30 |
| Southend United | 38 | 10 | 8 | 20 | 44 | 64 | 28 |
| Croydon Common | 38 | 9 | 9 | 20 | 47 | 63 | 27 |
| Gillingham | 38 | 6 | 8 | 24 | 43 | 82 | 20 |

* Receipts of £25 5s 9d from Exeter City's first pre-season practice match between the Stripes and the Colours was to be presented to the Prince of Wales Patriotic Fund. Pipers of the Highland Light Infantry played musical selections prior to the kick off at St James' Park, and again at the interval.

* It was reported in the local press that many people in Exeter were against the Football Association's decision, in August 1914, to carry on playing despite the outbreak of the First World War, some saying that they were putting football before the Empire.

* Exeter City secretary Sidney Thomas said that many of the players were already contracted on wages of £5 per week  and that they could not be cancelled unless the players agreed to do so, therefore it would be difficult to stop playing. Season ticket sales had, however, slumped from over £200 to barely £20.

* The Grecians placed St James' Park at the disposal of the local military authority and troops were being drilled there every day.  A recruiting Sergeant was attending every home match urging young men to join the forces.

* The match report of City's tedious goalless draw at Crystal Palace stated: 'For the whole of 90 minutes a crowd of over 3,000 spectators were held in bondage until the referee's whistle signalled their deliverance.'

* Alf Green netted a hat-trick in the 7-1 home thrashing of Southend United in November 1914. William Goodwin was the only other City player to score hat-trick in the Southern League during the season when Exeter defeated Croydon Common 3-1.

* The City directors invited a number of wounded soldiers to attend the home match against Millwall in November 1914. They included Sgt. Hyde of the Devon Regiment, a former City player during their amateur days.

* A number of troops stationed in the town attended the Watford versus Exeter City game at Cassio Road on Christmas Day. At half-time they ran onto the pitch and played a game of football among themselves. When the teams appeared for the second half, they returned to their places in the ground.

* For the second season running, Exeter City were paired with Aston Villa in the FA Cup, only this time they had to travel to Villa Park. They lost 2-0 in front of an attendance of 12,000.

* At a special meeting of the Southern League, held in London in April 1915, Exeter City proposed that gate receipts should be pooled. This was met with unanimous support and a percentage of entrance money (not including grandstand receipts) should be paid over to the visiting club. The percentage was still to be decided.

* The season was overshadowed by the First World War and after the final matches were played in the Southern League - City visiting Southampton on 24th of April - it was announced that football would be suspended for the duration.

* The Football Association in conjunction with The Football League and The Southern League declared that all professional football be abandoned until after the War. Situated as they were, in a geographical sense, Exeter City decided they would not play in a regional or part time competition which would be organised for season 1915-16.

* It had been a disastrous season financially for the Grecians, and several other clubs, with attendance's well down, as supporters stayed away from games and indeed signed up for the forces to assist in the War effort.

City's results - all friendly fixtures

|  |  |
|------|--------|
| Mar 1st | Exeter City 0 Crownhill 6 |
| Mar 15th | Exeter City 2 AGLABs (Higher Barracks, Topsham) 0 |
| Mar 22nd | Exeter City 0 Devonport Dockyard 1 |
| Mar 29th | Exeter City 2 Royal Field Artillery 1 |
| Apr 5th | Exeter City 0 Yeovil Aircraft Works 0 |
| Apr 12th | Exeter City 1 Exeter Argyle 1 |
| Apr 18th | Plymouth Argyle 1 Exeter City 2 |
| Apr 19th | Exeter City 10 Royal Field Artillery 2 |
| Apr 21st | Exeter City 2 Plymouth Argyle 1 |
| Apr 26th | Exeter City 2 Devonport Dockyard 1 |

CITY PLAYING SQUAD 1918-19
The following players are known to have appeared for City in friendly fixtures.
Individual details are shown where known.

| Name | Pos | Signed From |
|------|-----|-------------|
| ?? Baxter | F | AGLABS, Higher Barracks, Topsham |
| ?? Brooks | W | Royal Field Artillery |
| ?? Byron | ?? | Former Lancashire League player |
| ?? Cannon | FB | ?? |
| ?? Chappell | FB | Bradninch |
| ?? Chudley | ?? | Formerly Mount Radford School, Exeter |
| ?? Chunney | F | AGLABS, Higher Barracks, Topsham |
| Arthur Coates | HB | Southampton |
| ?? Coppin | W | Formerly with South Shields |
| ?? Cotter | F | Former Lancashire League player |
| William Crawshaw | HB | Army |
| John Dockray | W | Bury C/S 1914 |
| ?? Dunwall | W | ?? |
| ?? Green | HB | Formerly of Barnstaple |
| ?? Herbert | W | ?? |
| Charles Lincoln | W | Formerly of Heavitree |
| ?? Lock | F | ?? |
| Reg Loram | G | |
| ?? Lovell | FB | ?? |
| James Makin | F | Army |
| T Makin | F | ?? |
| ?? Newman F | ?? | |
| ?? Marland | HB | Former Lancashire League player |
| ?? Martin | HB | A Lieutenant in the Services |
| ?? Perry | F | Royal Army Pay Corps |
| ?? Potter | F | Exeter Argyle |
| Charles Pratt | HB | Everton C/S 1910 |
| Dick Pym | G | Topsham Dec 1911 |
| ?? Salter | W | Formerly of Exmouth |
| Samuel Strettle | FB | Chesterfield C/S 1913 |
| ?? Tapp | ?? | Exeter Argyle |

Moves were being made to resume first class football for the 1919-20 season, and as a result a meeting was held by Exeter City Football Club in February 1919 to discuss the possibility of the Grecians getting themselves ready.

A series of friendly fixtures were played, the first of which took place on 1st March, when Plymouth-based side, Crownhill, won 6-0 at St James' Park, before an attendance of 2,000. City fielded only two of their former players, who were with them prior to the First World War, and called upon a number of amateurs to make up the team.

An even bigger attendance, 2,500, were present for the 2-0 home win over AGLABs, and the local newspaper reported:-

*'Exeter City are reaping the reward of their trail of local talent in these practice games. The visitors were drawn from the staffs of the Agricultural Companies, Labour Corps, stationed at the Higher Barracks, Topsham. The queues lining up in St James' Road before the kick off were remindful of the old Southern League days. There can be no doubt in fact that the soccer revival at Exeter is going to be a big thing in the near future., for the enthusiasm displayed today proved that.'*

The major talking point at the time was the possibility that all the Southern League clubs would form a new Third Division of the Football League, as early as the 1920-21 season. Some of the City FC directors felt that this would be a good move for the club, however, they also felt that should they or neighbours Plymouth Argyle win promotion to the Second Division, they would find the financial burden crippling.

City manager Arthur Chadwick returned to the club on 20th February 1919 and at once began the work of preparing for the following season in the Southern League.

* The annual meeting of the Exeter City Football and Athletic Company was held at the Bude Hotel, Exeter on 31st December 1918. It was announced that it was hoped that St James' Park would be in a position to stage competitive matches again by 1st September 1919, for the start and resumption of Southern League fixtures.

* The directors stated that if players could earn £6 a week elsewhere then good luck to them, but they certainly could not do so at Exeter City.

* City Director, Norman Kendall urged that practice matches should be staged at St James' Park at the earliest opportunity so that local talent could be "brought out in their midst."

*Some of the club Directors thought it would be a good thing for the Club if the Southern League were amalgamated with The Football League, however, should the Grecians be promoted to the Second Division in the future, it would improve impossible to sustain the Club financially as costs would be crippling.

* Club Chairman, Mr. McGahey said that Exeter City had earned a place in first class football. He added: "We mean to keep that place. And when the result of the February meeting between the Football League and the Southern League is known, a general meeting of all supporters will be called with a view of getting into shape again and seeing about next season's team."

* Some of the pre-First World War Exeter City players had fared badly during the conflict. Arthur Evans was killed in the first battle of the Somme; Fred Goodwin was reportedly killed, although not confirmed; Billy Smith had a leg amputated; Fred Marshall, badly wounded and retired from playing.

* Two City players were awarded the Military Medal, namely Sammy Strettle and Ernest Lewis.

* Manager Arthur Chadwick returned to Exeter on 20th February 1919 and immediately began work in preparing for the following season.

* The first match to be played at St James' Park at the end of the First World War took place on 1st March 1919, when a crowd of around 2,000 were present to see Exeter City lose 6-0 to Crownhill, Plymouth.

* City played against a team called AGLABs, and their players were drawn from the permanent staffs of the Agricultural Companies, Labour Corps, stationed at the Higher Barracks, Topsham.

* The Devonport Dockyard side that played at Exeter City on 22nd March 1919, included three Plymouth Argyle players. As a result the Argyle manager, Bob Jack, accompanied the team to St James' Park.

* A crowd of 12,000 were present at Home Park for the friendly fixture between Plymouth Argyle and Exeter City on Good Friday, 18th April 1919.

* Admission price for the game at St James' Park between Exeter City and Plymouth Argyle on the Easter Monday, 21st April 1919, was one shilling.

* The match report for the game between Exeter City and Devonport Dockyard played on 26th April 1919, stated:- 'Referees are naturally there for the purpose of controlling the game and to pull players up when they infringe the rules, but it can be overdone., which in this case it was. It cannot be said there was a lack of 'tootling', but unfortunately there was a lack of first class football.'

## Southern League Outlook

The following preview appeared in the local press prior to the start of the 1920-21 season:-

*'The Exeter City players reported for strict training in the second week in August under the direction of Arthur Chadwick, who has the assistance of Charlie Pratt in this connection.*

*The prospects of the City in the Southern League appear to be distinctly rosy, the new men have linked up with those retained from 1915 in the happiest possible fashion, and the whole seems to constitute the right blend.*

*There are some changes in the Southern League this season. To begin with it now contains the maximum of clubs permitted - 22. West Ham United has joined the Football League and Croydon Common has been wound up. The five vacancies thus created have been filled by the re-election of Gillingham, and the promotion from Division Two of Brentford, Merthyr, Swansea and Newport County.*

*St James' Park is once again assuming its former smart appearance and will be ready in good time for the practice matches. The club directors have under consideration the erection of a covered stand for about 5,000 spectators on the popular side.'*

City's league results

| | HOME | AWAY |
|---|---|---|
| Brentford | 0-0 | 1-2 |
| Brighton & H.A. | 4-1 | 0-0 |
| Bristol Rovers | 2-1 | 2-4 |
| Cardiff City | 1-1 | 0-1 |
| Crystal Palace | 2-1 | 0-1 |
| Gillingham | 2-1 | 0-0 |
| Luton Town | 3-2 | 1-3 |
| Merthyr Town | 3-0 | 1-2 |
| Millwall | 3-1 | 0-1 |
| Newport County | 1-2 | 1-4 |
| Northampton Town | 2-4 | 1-3 |
| Norwich City | 2-1 | 0-0 |
| Plymouth Argyle | 0-1 | 1-3 |
| Portsmouth | 2-0 | 0-2 |
| Queens Park Rangers | 0-1 | 0-0 |
| Reading | 2-2 | 1-0 |
| Southampton | 4-1 | 1-1 |
| Southend United | 3-0 | 0-2 |
| Swansea Town | 2-1 | 1-0 |
| Swindon Town | 3-1 | 1-1 |
| Watford | 3-0 | 1-0 |

F.A. Cup

| | | |
|---|---|---|
| Newport County | A R1 | 0-1 |

CITY MANAGER 1919-20
Arthur Chadwick - Appointed April 1908

CITY PLAYING SQUAD 1919-20

| Name | Pos | Signed From | Apps | Gls |
|---|---|---|---|---|
| Joseph Coleburne | FB | Atherton C/S 1919 | 42 | |
| Edwin Connor | W | Fulham C/S 1919 | 14 | 1 |
| William Crawshaw | HB | Royal Artillery C/S 1919 | 15 | |
| John Dockray | W | Bury C/S 1914 | 41 | 3 |
| James Gill | F | Bury Mar 1920 | 3 | |
| William Goodwin | F | Blackburn Rovers C/S 1914 | 37 | 17 |
| Alfred Green | HB | Rotherham Town C/S 1914 | 3 | 1 |
| James Henderson | F | South Shields Dec 1919 | 6 | 3 |
| Sydney Hetherington | F | ?? C/S 1919 | 1 | |
| Charles Lincoln | W | Heavitree United C/S 1919 | 2 | |
| William Lovett | F | Rochdale C/S 1913 | 34 | 5 |
| James Makin | F | Army C/S 1919 | 31 | 14 |
| Henry Medcalf | FB | Bideford Nov 1919 | 5 | |
| John Mitton | HB | Bury C/S 1919 | 42 | |
| Percival Nutland | F | Amateur C/S 1919 | 1 | |
| Percival Oldacre | F | Stoke C/S 1919 | 33 | 8 |
| Stanley Popplewell | HB | Barrow C/S 1919 | 41 | 4 |
| Benjamin Potter | FB | Exeter Argyle C/S 1919 | 2 | |
| Charles Pratt | HB | Everton C/S 1910 | 1 | |
| Dick Pym | G | Topsham Dec 1911 | 42 | |
| George Reader | F | St Luke's College Jan 1920 | 1 | 1 |
| James Rigby | HB | Accrington Stanley C/S 1911 | 28 | |
| Charles Shreeve | W | Army C/S 1919 | 2 | |
| Christopher Southcombe | W | South Molton C/S 1919 | 1 | |
| Samuel Strettle | FB | Chesterfield C/S 1913 | 34 | |

SOUTHERN LEAGUE - 1919-20

| | P | W | D | L | F | A | Pts |
|---|---|---|---|---|---|---|---|
| Portsmouth | 42 | 23 | 12 | 7 | 73 | 27 | 58 |
| Watford | 42 | 26 | 6 | 10 | 69 | 42 | 58 |
| Crystal Palace | 42 | 22 | 12 | 8 | 69 | 43 | 56 |
| Cardiff City | 42 | 18 | 17 | 7 | 70 | 43 | 53 |
| Plymouth Argyle | 42 | 20 | 10 | 12 | 57 | 29 | 50 |
| Queens Park Rangers | 42 | 18 | 10 | 14 | 62 | 50 | 46 |
| Reading | 42 | 16 | 13 | 13 | 51 | 43 | 45 |
| Southampton | 42 | 18 | 8 | 16 | 72 | 63 | 44 |
| Swansea Town | 42 | 16 | 11 | 15 | 53 | 45 | 43 |
| Exeter City | 42 | 17 | 9 | 16 | 57 | 51 | 43 |
| Southend United | 42 | 13 | 17 | 12 | 46 | 48 | 43 |
| Norwich City | 42 | 15 | 11 | 16 | 64 | 57 | 41 |
| Swindon Town | 42 | 17 | 7 | 18 | 65 | 68 | 41 |
| Millwall | 42 | 14 | 12 | 16 | 52 | 55 | 40 |
| Brentford | 42 | 15 | 10 | 17 | 52 | 59 | 40 |
| Brighton & H.A. | 42 | 14 | 8 | 20 | 60 | 72 | 36 |
| Bristol Rovers | 42 | 11 | 13 | 18 | 61 | 78 | 35 |
| Newport County | 42 | 13 | 7 | 22 | 45 | 70 | 33 |
| Northampton Town | 42 | 12 | 9 | 21 | 64 | 103 | 33 |
| Luton Town | 42 | 10 | 10 | 22 | 51 | 76 | 30 |
| Merthyr Town | 42 | 9 | 11 | 22 | 47 | 78 | 29 |
| Gillingham | 42 | 10 | 7 | 25 | 34 | 74 | 27 |

* Exeter City resumed competitive football after the First World War by playing a 'Peace Match' at Plymouth Argyle on 26th July 1919. An attendance of over 6,000 saw the teams draw 1-1, with John Mitton scoring for City.

* The Grecians made a great start to their Southern League season, being undefeated in their opening seven matches.

* Due to a railway strike, Watford were unable to travel to Exeter for their Southern League fixture on 27th September 1919. Instead the Grecians welcomed local amateur side, Friernhay, to St James' Park and won 7-1 before a crowd of 3,000. Watford, incidentally, were later fined £50 by the Southern League for non fulfilment of the fixture.

* The lady members of the Exeter City Supporters' Club handed out red and white rosettes to City fans as they entered the ground for the match against Millwall on 25th October 1919.

* The City first team travelled to play against a North Devon XI at Barnstaple's Rose and Crown Ground in an Exhibition match in November 1919. Exeter won 2-1 with goals from William Goodwin and Charles Pratt.

* A collection was made prior to the home match against Northampton Town, on behalf of former City player Billy Smith, who had a leg amputated after being wounded in the First World War.

* The Exeter City officials and team travelled to away matches by train and there were many reports of their travel arrangements in the local press. For example, for their FA Cup tie at Newport the party had left Exeter St David's at 0850, had lunch at Bristol Temple Meads station, and then went on to Newport to arrive at 12.30.

* Exeter City made their 'first' visit to Selhurst Park, the new home of Crystal Palace in November 1919. However, the Grecians had played there before when the ground was used by Croydon Common FC, that club having gone into liquidation. Unfortunately the game against the Palace was abandoned in the 85th minute due to fog and City had to visit again the following March for the rearranged fixture.

* The Grecians played in claret and amber shirts when the visited Southampton for a Southern League fixture in January 1920. The change was made due to the fact that the Saints played in red and white stripes.

* Goalkeeper Dick Pym and winger John Dockray played for the Southern League representative team against Cambridge University in March 1920. Pym had earlier played for the Southern League against the Welsh League.

* Exeter City played another exhibition match at Seaton Town in April 1920, where they won 6-2 and it was reported:- 'The whole population turned out and the Grecians were given a wonderful reception.'

* The Exeter City Military Band marched from North Street, through the city centre to St James' Park, where they played various musical selections prior to the last Southern League home match of the season against Merthyr Town.

* For the fourth season running, goalkeeper Dick Pym was an ever present in Southern League matches. A total of 156 consecutive appearances.

* The highest attendance of the season at St James' Park was 11,000 for the visit of Bristol Rovers in April 1920. The highest attendance for a City away game in the Southern League was 15,000 at Plymouth Argyle on Christmas Day 1919.

* William Goodwin picked up where he had left off. For in the 1914-15 season he was City's top scorer with 23 Southern League goals, and he led the way again in 1919-20 with 17.

# The Football League Beckons

On 18th May 1920 it was announced that Exeter City could be playing in The Football League as from the start of the next season.

A meeting was held in Sheffield between representatives of the Football League and the Southern League when the following resolution was proposed by Watford F.C. and seconded by Norwich City F.C.:-

'That this meeting of the First Division of the Southern League clubs is of the opinion that the time is opportune for an application to form a Third Division, consisting of a Northern Section and a Southern Section. Further, the clubs comprising of the Southern League First Division be selected to form the Southern Section.'

A vote was taken amongst the Southern League clubs at the meeting, with 19 in favour, one against and one abstention.

Eleven days later at the Annual General Meeting of The Football League it was agreed 'that subject to the consent of the Football Association, that a Third Division of The Football League be formed. That clubs at present forming the First Division of the Southern League comprise the Third Division for the season 1920-21.'

Exeter City's manager, Arthur Chadwick was delighted that he would now be guiding the Grecians in The Football League.

"It is the finest thing that could have happened," he declared.

Chadwick had feared that The Football League would have taken two thirds of the Southern League members in which case City would not have been part of the new Third Division.

Throughout the summer preparations were made on and off the field by Exeter City for the start of their new 'adventure.'

On 18th August 1920 it was announced by the Exeter City Board of Directors that charge for admission to the ground for first team matches would be one shilling and threepence.

The decision was arrived at unanimously after very careful consideration of the club's financial position and heavy commitments for the season.

Chairman , Mr. M.J. McGahey said that a variety of reasons actuated the Directors on the matter.

A large sum of money had been spent on the terracing of the popular bank and the improvement of the ground in general.

A considerable increased number of players had been signed in order for the club to be able to compete both in The Football League and the Third Division of the Western League.

This had resulted in a much increased wage bill, reportedly 150% more than on the previous season. Travelling expenses would also be higher than ever before. The Directors had also decided to fall in line with other clubs and pay the players the bonus of £2 for a win and £1 for a draw in Football League Third Division matches.

It was therefore, in view of the above, that the Directors felt that the increase in admission of threepence was justified and not a "serious burden to the individual spectator."

# Improvements To St James' Park

At a meeting of the Exeter City Supporters' Club held on Thursday 10th June 1920, it was unanimously decided to give the Directors of Exeter City Football Cub a sum of £180, with a request that it be used solely towards defraying the cost of enclosing the pitch at St James' Park with iron railings.

In attendance at the meeting were the City F.C. club Chairman, Mr. M.J. McGahey, and Directors, Mr. J. Pengelly, Mr. N. Kendall and Mr. E. Head. Mr. Pengelly explained that it would be impracticable to proceed with the building of a new stand in readiness for the first season in the Football League, and the Directors had decided to concentrate on making ground improvements instead.

The popular bank was to be stepped with timber and cinders, whilst the enclosure at the St. James' Road end of the ground had been widened by taking a strip of turf from the actual playing area. The pitch would be enclosed by four foot high iron railings. The Directors added that they would not tell the Supporters Club how to spend their £180, but if they would care to invest it in iron railings, it would have an immediate benefit to supporters and help to improve the appearance of St. James' Park.

Mr. Pengelly added that the popular bank would consist of 24 steppings of 15 inches in width, each with 5 inch steps which would give every person a good view of the play. If the club were to have a successful season, then further improvements to the ground would be undertaken in twelve months time. The fencing around the ground would be completed by a supporter free of charge, who wished to remain anonymous.

Mr. McGahey said that the improvements to the ground in the summer months would involve an expenditure of close on £1,000 and would improve the comfort of Exeter City supporters. When the ground improvements are complete, club secretary Sidney Thomas said there would be room for 4,000 spectators at St James' Park.

Mr. Head added that the Directors' job was to keep the players happy and contented. Their idea was to present the very best they could for supporters and do their utmost to keep Exeter City at the very high position that it now occupied. Ideas from outside were always welcome and if practicable, would be acted upon. The Directors were out to achieve success and wanted a team to be proud of, and on some future occasion would not find itself in the Third Division, but the Second.

It was also decided that the reserve team would be playing in the Western League as from the 1920-21 season. It was stated: 'The Western League with its headquarters in Bristol, embraces some very strong teams and is much on a par with the new Southern League.'

Travelling expenses for the reserves would be much higher than playing in the Plymouth and District League, and to meet that added expense, and the bigger wage bill rendered necessary by the signing of more players, the Directors intended to introduce a uniform admission price to all matches.

Ground season tickets were priced at £1 7s 6d; Enclosure £2; Lady's tickets £1 10s; Stand £2 5s; Lady's tickets £2; Centre Stand £3; Lady's tickets £2 10s.

'It is up to the soccer public to support the club and make the new arrangements a success," said a City Director.

Exeter City's first ever Football League squad prior to the start of the 1920-21 season.

**CITY PLAYING SQUAD 1920-21**

| Name | Pos | Signed From | Apps | Gls |
|------|-----|-------------|------|-----|
| Leonard Appleton | W | Blackpool C/S 1920 | 37 | 2 |
| William Betteridge | FB | Boscombe C/S 1920 | 2 | |
| Walter Brayshaw | F | Sheffield United C/S 1920 | 5 | |
| Joseph Coleburne | FB | Atherton C/S 1919 | 30 | |
| James Carrick | HB | Plank Lane C/S 1920 | 41 | 3 |
| William Crawshaw | HB | Royal Artillery C/S 1919 | 28 | |
| John Dockray | W | Bury C/S 1914 | 42 | 2 |
| John Feebery | HB | Bolton Wanderers C/S 1920 | 42 | 2 |
| Alfred Green | HB | Rotherham Town C/S1914 | 31 | |
| Thomas Hesmondhalgh | F | Rochdale C/S 1920 | 1 | |
| Sydney Hetherington | F | ?? C/S 1919 | 8 | 1 |
| Percival Hilton | HB | Everton C/S 1920 | 1 | |
| John Hinton | F | Thorneycrofts Mar 1921 | 4 | 1 |
| William Lakin | FB | Barnsley C/S 1920 | 6 | |
| Thomas McIntyre | W | Services C/S 1920 | 5 | |
| James Makin | F | Army C/S 1919 | 39 | 6 |
| John Mitton | HB | Bury C/S 1919 | 11 | |
| Robert Pollard | FB | Plank Lane C/S 1920 | 7 | |
| Dick Pym | G | Topsham Dec 1911 | 39 | |
| James Rigby | HB | Accrington Stanley C/S 1911 | 7 | |
| Robert Shields | F | Huddersfield Town Dec 1920 | 19 | 4 |
| George Taylor | HB | Skelmersdale United C/S 1920 | 6 | |
| Charles Vowles | F | Army C/S 1920 | 31 | 9 |
| Charles Waller | G | Army C/S 1920 | 3 | |
| William Wright | F | Tranmere Rovers C/S 1920 | 17 | 9 |

* Exeter City started on a 'new' adventure in the 1920-21 season, being members of the newly formed Third Division of The Football League. The Southern League clubs of the previous season joined en-bloc.

* At a meeting of the Exeter City Supporters' Club in June 1920 it was agreed to give the Directors the sum of £180 to be used to enclose the pitch from spectators with iron railings.

City's league results

| | HOME | AWAY |
|------|------|------|
| Brentford | 3-0 | 0-0 |
| Brighton & H.A. | 1-0 | 1-1 |
| Bristol Rovers | 1-0 | 0-5 |
| Crystal Palace | 1-1 | 1-2* |
| Gillingham | 2-1 | 1-2 |
| Grimsby Town | 1-1 | 0-2 |
| Luton Town | 1-0 | 0-3 |
| Merthyr Town | 3-3 | 1-7 |
| Millwall | 4-0 | 0-2 |
| Newport County | 0-1 | 0-2 |
| Northampton Town | 4-0 | 3-3 |
| Norwich City | 1-1 | 0-0 |
| Plymouth Argyle | 1-1 | 0-0 |
| Portsmouth | 0-0 | 1-2 |
| Queens Park Rangers | 0-1 | 1-2 |
| Reading | 1-0 | 0-1 |
| Southampton | 1-0 | 0-3 |
| Southend United | 0-0 | 0-0 |
| Swansea Town | 1-2 | 1-2 |
| Swindon Town | 1-0 | 1-1 |
| Watford | 1-2 | 0-0 |

* Match payed at The Dell, Southampton.
Crystal Palace's ground was closed.

F.A. Cup
Watford                    A  R1      0-3

CITY MANAGER 1919-20
Arthur Chadwick - Appointed April 1908

FOOTBALL LEAGUE - DIVISION THREE

| | P | W | D | L | F | A | Pts |
|------|---|---|---|---|---|---|-----|
| Crystal Palace | 42 | 24 | 11 | 7 | 70 | 34 | 59 |
| Southampton | 42 | 19 | 16 | 7 | 64 | 28 | 54 |
| Queens Park Rangers | 42 | 22 | 9 | 11 | 61 | 32 | 53 |
| Swindon Town | 42 | 21 | 10 | 11 | 73 | 49 | 52 |
| Swansea City | 42 | 18 | 15 | 9 | 56 | 45 | 51 |
| Watford | 42 | 20 | 8 | 14 | 59 | 44 | 48 |
| Millwall | 42 | 18 | 11 | 13 | 42 | 30 | 47 |
| Merthyr Town | 42 | 15 | 15 | 12 | 60 | 49 | 45 |
| Luton Town | 42 | 16 | 12 | 14 | 61 | 56 | 44 |
| Bristol Rovers | 42 | 18 | 7 | 17 | 68 | 57 | 43 |
| Plymouth Argyle | 42 | 11 | 21 | 10 | 35 | 34 | 43 |
| Portsmouth | 42 | 12 | 15 | 25 | 46 | 48 | 39 |
| Grimsby Town | 42 | 15 | 9 | 18 | 49 | 59 | 39 |
| Northampton Town | 42 | 15 | 8 | 19 | 59 | 75 | 38 |
| Newport County | 42 | 14 | 9 | 19 | 43 | 64 | 37 |
| Norwich City | 42 | 10 | 16 | 16 | 44 | 53 | 36 |
| Southend United | 42 | 14 | 8 | 20 | 44 | 61 | 36 |
| Brighton & H.A. | 42 | 14 | 8 | 20 | 42 | 61 | 36 |
| Exeter City | 42 | 10 | 15 | 17 | 39 | 54 | 35 |
| Reading | 42 | 12 | 7 | 23 | 42 | 59 | 31 |
| Brentford | 42 | 9 | 12 | 21 | 42 | 67 | 30 |
| Gillingham | 42 | 8 | 12 | 22 | 34 | 74 | 28 |

* The club made several ground improvements to St James' Park in readiness for the Football League. These included stepping the Big Bank with timber and cinders, whilst the St James' Road end was widened. Expenditure would be approximately £1,000.

* Forward William Goodwin was transferred to Manchester United in June 1920 for a fee of £650 - a then record for Exeter City.

* It was announced that Exeter City had made a profit of £1,084 14s 10d on the previous year. Match receipts had totalled £9,570, whilst wages cost £3,361 and travelling £1,205.

* Exeter City's first ever game in The Football League was played at St James' Park on Saturday 28th August 1920, when they defeated Brentford 3-0 before an attendance of 7,000. The distinction of becoming City's first ever scorer in The Football League fell to William Wright.

* Following Exeter City's match at Brentford on Saturday 4th September, the team stayed in Lowestoft until Wednesday of the following week, then travelling to play at Norwich City, where they were held to a goalless draw.

* The club transfer record was broken for the second time in a few months as John Mitton was transferred to Sunderland for £2,000 in October 1920.

* Crystal Palace had to play their 'home' match against Exeter City at 'The Dell', Southampton on 27th November 1920, as their own Selhurst Park ground had been ordered by The Football League to be closed for 14 days following crowd disturbances. An attendance of 13,000 watched Palace win 2-1.

* In December 1920, the City Supporters Club asked the Directors to consider reducing admission charges which had been increased by the club to one shilling and threepence at the start of the season. Attendances had gone down partly due to unemployment and short term working in the area. However, the Directors turned down the request, but relented in April 1921 for the last few games.

* St James' Park was purchased outright by the Board of Directors in December 1920, plus a small strip of land at the rear of the Duke Bank. The transfer fees received for players had been used to fund the purchase.

* It was estimated that over 1,000 spectators gained free entry to the ground for the match against Plymouth Argyle at St James' Park. They had climbed the fence by the railway bank at the Well Street entrance. The official attendance was 14,664 - a then club record.

* The night before their FA Cup tie at Watford, the City team and officials were guests of the Palace Theatre, Watford, where they watched a performance of 'Aladdin.'

* Goalkeeper Dick Pym missed his first game since March 1912, when he was sidelined through injury for the game against Brighton and Hove Albion in January 1921.

* Lack of goals scored had hindered City throughout the season, and as a result no one player managed to reach double figures. The Grecians only managed to score more than one goal in a League match on six occasions.

* Strong rumours were circulating by the end of the season that talented goalkeeper Dick Pym was being watched by a club, who were going to make an offer during the summer months.

## City Purchase St. James' Park

The purchase of St. James' Park was completed on Friday 24th June 1921. City Chairman Mr. M.J. McGahey said that the major portion of the ground was the property of the Trustees of Lady Anne Clifford's charity.

The residue of the ground, a garden at the back and a house abutting on Old Tiverton Road, was the property of Sir Henry Duke. It would be recalled that Mr. Duke, when he was M.P. for Exeter, purchased the land in order to permit the extension of the old City ground. The club had been paying rental in respect of the land occupied by them ever since.

Total cost of the purchase was £2,500 each to Sir Henry Duke and to the Trustees of Lady Anne Clifford respectively.

Mr. McGahey added that the purchase was very wise because unless they bought, the terms of their lease they were subject to, meant that their could be increases in rent having to be paid. One condition was that if the club gave up possession of St James' Park, the ground had to be restored to its original state.

### City's league results

| | HOME | AWAY |
|---|---|---|
| Aberdare Athletic | 0-1 | 2-0 |
| Brentford | 1-0 | 2-5 |
| Brighton & H.A. | 0-3 | 1-3 |
| Bristol Rovers | 2-2 | 3-1 |
| Charlton Athletic | 1-0 | 0-1 |
| Gillingham | 1-1 | 0-3 |
| Luton Town | 0-1 | 0-4 |
| Merthyr Town | 1-0 | 0-0 |
| Millwall | 1-0 | 0-1 |
| Newport County | 2-2 | 1-1 |
| Northampton Town | 2-0 | 3-2 |
| Norwich City | 2-0 | 0-0 |
| Plymouth Argyle | 0-2 | 0-0 |
| Portsmouth | 1-4 | 0-2 |
| Queens Park Rangers | 0-1 | 1-2 |
| Reading | 1-3 | 0-0 |
| Southampton | 0-0 | 0-2 |
| Southend United | 4-1 | 1-0 |
| Swansea Town | 1-1 | 1-2 |
| Swindon Town | 1-4 | 1-1 |
| Watford | 1-3 | 0-0 |

### F.A. Cup

| | | | |
|---|---|---|---|
| Bristol Rovers | A | Q5 | 0-0 |
| Bristol Rovers | H | Q5R | 0-2 |

**CITY MANAGER 1921-22**
Arthur Chadwick - Appointed April 1908

### CITY PLAYING SQUAD 1921-22

| Name | Pos | Signed from | Apps | Gls |
|---|---|---|---|---|
| Frank Brown | HB | Blackpool C/S 1921 | 6 | |
| Eli Bullock | F | Macclesfield Town C/S 1921 | 27 | 4 |
| James Congdon | F | Millbrook Rangers Jul 1921 | 6 | |
| Ellis Crompton | HB | Bristol Rovers Jun 1921 | 39 | 4 |
| John Dockray | W | Bury C/S 1914 | 39 | 5 |
| Thomas Edge | W | Oldham Athletic C/S 1921 | 3 | |
| Henry Fryer | G | Luton Clarence C/S 1921 | 32 | |
| Richard Gaskell | FB | Ashton National Jun 1921 | 14 | |
| Joseph Graham | HB | Stockport County C/S 1921 | 12 | |
| Alfred Green | HB | Rotherham Town C/S1914 | 12 | |
| Jasper Green | F | Preston North End Jun 1921 | 6 | |
| Percival Hill | F | Luton Town C/S 1921 | 14 | 2 |
| Harold Kirk | F | Plymouth Argyle Mar 1922 | 14 | 9 |
| John McCulloch | F | Dykehead Nov 1921 | 1 | |
| John MacKechnie | FB | Northampton Town Jul 1921 | 18 | |
| James Mitton | HB | Stockport County C/S 1921 | 40 | 1 |
| Frank Newman | W | Burslem Port Vale Jul 1921 | 39 | 1 |
| Robert Pollard | FB | Plank Lane C/S 1920 | 24 | |
| James Rigby | HB | Accrington Stanley C/S 1911 | 34 | |
| Charles Squires | HB | Maerdy Mar 1922 | 2 | |
| Robert Stewart | FB | Oldham Athletic Jun 1921 | 25 | |
| Thomas Townsend | F | Torquay United Feb 1922 | 7 | |
| Charles Vowles | F | Army C/S 1920 | 23 | 11 |
| James Watson | G | Luton Town Aug 1921 | 10 | |
| George Williams | F | Southampton C/S 1921 | 11 | 1 |
| Henry Wilson | HB | Amateur, C/S 1921 | 4 | |

### FOOTBALL LEAGUE - DIVISION THREE SOUTH

| | P | W | D | L | F | A | Pts |
|---|---|---|---|---|---|---|---|
| Southampton | 42 | 23 | 15 | 4 | 68 | 21 | 61 |
| Plymouth Argyle | 42 | 25 | 11 | 6 | 63 | 24 | 61 |
| Portsmouth | 42 | 18 | 17 | 7 | 62 | 39 | 53 |
| Luton Town | 42 | 22 | 8 | 12 | 64 | 35 | 52 |
| Queens Park Rangers | 42 | 18 | 13 | 11 | 53 | 44 | 49 |
| Swindon Town | 42 | 16 | 13 | 13 | 72 | 60 | 45 |
| Watford | 42 | 13 | 18 | 11 | 54 | 48 | 44 |
| Aberdare Athletic | 42 | 17 | 10 | 15 | 57 | 51 | 44 |
| Brentford | 42 | 16 | 11 | 15 | 52 | 43 | 43 |
| Swansea Town | 42 | 13 | 15 | 14 | 50 | 47 | 41 |
| Merthyr Town | 42 | 17 | 6 | 19 | 45 | 56 | 40 |
| Millwall | 42 | 10 | 18 | 14 | 38 | 42 | 38 |
| Reading | 42 | 14 | 10 | 18 | 40 | 47 | 38 |
| Bristol Rovers | 42 | 14 | 10 | 18 | 52 | 67 | 38 |
| Norwich City | 42 | 12 | 13 | 17 | 50 | 62 | 37 |
| Charlton Athletic | 42 | 13 | 11 | 18 | 43 | 56 | 37 |
| Northampton Town | 42 | 13 | 11 | 18 | 47 | 71 | 37 |
| Gillingham | 42 | 14 | 8 | 20 | 47 | 60 | 36 |
| Brighton & H.A. | 42 | 13 | 9 | 20 | 45 | 51 | 35 |
| Newport County | 42 | 11 | 12 | 19 | 44 | 61 | 34 |
| Exeter City | 42 | 11 | 12 | 19 | 38 | 59 | 34 |
| Southend United | 42 | 8 | 11 | 23 | 34 | 74 | 27 |

\* This proved to be a very poor season for Exeter City which ultimately led them to applying for re-election to the Football League. Goalscoring again proved a problem for the team, with less than one per game being netted.

*Long serving goalkeeper Dick Pym was transferred to Bolton Wanderers in June 1921 for a fee of £5,000 - easily a club record at that time.

* It was announced in July 1921 that the club had made a profit of £4,419 on the year's working. Match receipts had totalled £12,420. Transfer of players had brought in £4,421.

* Exeter City became the first club to visit Charlton Athletic's new ground at The Valley when they travelled there on the opening day of the season, 27th August 1921, and lost 1-0 before an attendance of 11,000.

* On the morning of their match at Portsmouth on 17th September 1921, the City players paid a visit to Lord Nelson's flagship, 'H.M.S. Victory.' That afternoon, City lost the game 2-0.

* It was reported that the poor attendance of 4,000 for the Southend United versus Exeter City fixture was due to the fact that a further 1,600 people were attending a fishing competition off Southend Pier, with double that number watching!

* At the request of the referee .... 'Exeter changed their colours to white shirts and blue knickers, Swindon Town undertaking to oblige Exeter next Saturday in the return game at St James' Park.'

* The Grecians made a fruitless journey for their match at Gillingham on 26th November. Having stayed in Chatham overnight, the game was called off due to thick fog.

* City played a home tie in the FA Cup for the first time in seven years, when they lost 0-2 in a fifth qualifying round replay against Bristol Rovers in December 1921.

* Jasper Green sustained a broken leg in the game at Watford on 17th December 1921, after a collision with the home goalkeeper, who suffered concussion. Both players were helped from the field, the game being held up for ten minutes.

* A new entrance to the St James' Park ground from Well Street was used for the first time for the game against Watford on Christmas Eve.

* A record attendance of 16,000 were present at St. James' Park for the visit of Plymouth Argyle on Boxing Day. Argyle won 2-0.

* Winger Tom Edge was selected to play for the Southern League representative team against the Central League at Wolverhampton in March 1922.

* Harold 'Jazzo' Kirk was sent off for deliberately kicking the ball out of the ground after disputing a free-kick decision, when City played at Torquay United in a friendly in March 1922. Kirk refused to leave the field, and after consultation between the players and match officials, he was allowed to play on.

* A rallying call was made by the chairman of the Exeter City Supporters' Club in April 1922, as he warned that the football club had endured a very poor season financially. He said it was up to all well wishers of the Club to rally round and help.

* Only three players managed to score more than once in a game, namely, Charlie Vowles with two against Southend United in a 4-1 home win; John Dockray two against Northampton Town in a 3-2 victory; Harold Kirk netting two (one a penalty) in a 3-1 win at Bristol Rovers.

* Highest attendance of the season at St James' Park was not surprisingly for the visit of Plymouth Argyle, (16,000), and the day after in the return fixture at Home Park, this also produced the highest away crowd that City were to play in front of, 22,000.

\* A highly successful years working was reported at the Annual General Meeting of the Exeter City Supporters' Club in September 1922. Results of the various schemes promoted to increase interest among followers of the Football Club were reported. These included sports meetings, a fete, whist drives and a poultry draw.

During the year the Supporters' Club had provided new iron railings at the foot of the popular bank, an improvement that was greatly appreciated by the Directors and spectators.

Receipts for the years activities totalled £907 0s 2d. Deducting from this was the cost of the new iron railings and the cost of fixing them, a total of £76 12s 7d.

Exeter City FC secretary Sid Thomas dwelt on the need for covered accommodation on the popular side of the ground (The Flowerpot terracing). The club, he said, must have lost £100 or more at a recent game against Watford owing to the inclement weather. If the club could put their supporters under cover, they would not be as dependent on favourable weather.

\* Following the FA Cup 5th Qualifying round exit at home to Southern League, Bath City, the Express and Echo described it as a humiliating defeat against a team which was placed lower than the City reserves. They wrote: 'The Directors must strengthen the team. The situation cannot be left any longer. Exeter City cannot afford to make another re-election plea to the Football League or they will be playing Southern League football themselves next season.'

### City's league results

| | HOME | AWAY |
|---|---|---|
| Aberdare Athletic | 1-0 | 1-3 |
| Brentford | 0-2 | 1-0 |
| Brighton & H.A. | 1-0 | 0-3 |
| Bristol City | 0-0 | 1-1 |
| Bristol Rovers | 0-0 | 3-3 |
| Charlton Athletic | 0-0 | 0-0 |
| Gillingham | 0-1 | 1-2 |
| Luton Town | 1-2 | 0-6 |
| Merthyr Town | 2-1 | 1-3 |
| Millwall | 2-1 | 0-3 |
| Newport County | 4-0 | 2-6 |
| Northampton Town | 1-2 | 0-3 |
| Norwich City | 2-0 | 0-6 |
| Plymouth Argyle | 0-0 | 1-5 |
| Portsmouth | 2-3 | 4-3 |
| Queens Park Rangers | 1-2 | 0-2 |
| Reading | 4-0 | 3-1 |
| Southend United | 2-1 | 0-5 |
| Swansea Town | 1-0 | 1-5 |
| Swindon Town | 2-1 | 1-2 |
| Watford | 1-2 | 0-4 |

### F.A. Cup

| Bournemouth & B.A. | H | Q4 | 0-0 |
|---|---|---|---|
| Bournemouth & B.A. | A | Q4R | 3-1 |
| Bath City | H | Q5 | 1-2 |

### CITY MANAGER 1922-23
Arthur Chadwick - Appointed April 1908
Fred Mavin - Appointed January 1923

### CITY PLAYING SQUAD 1922-23

| Name | Pos | Signed from | Apps | Gls |
|---|---|---|---|---|
| John Ackroyd | FB | Scunthorpe & Lindsey United Jun 1922 | 30 | |
| Edwin Bell | FB | Welton Rovers May 1922 | 1 | |
| Horace Clarke | HB | Chesterfield May 1922 | 16 | |
| Ernest Coopland | HB | Arsenal Feb 1923 | 9 | |
| Harold Crockford | F | Fulham C/S 1922 | 30 | 17 |
| Ellis Crompton | HB | Bristol Rovers Jun 1921 | 36 | |
| John Davis | F | Torquay United Feb 1923 | 17 | 4 |
| William Devlin | F | Newport County Jun 1922 | 12 | 5 |
| John Dockray | W | Bury C/S 1914 | 30 | |
| John Duke | HB | Bristol City Dec 1922 | 1 | |
| Andrew Flynn | FB | Mexborough May 1922 | 13 | |
| Henry Fryer | G | Luton Clarence C/S 1921 | 26 | |
| Harold Kirk | F | Plymouth Argyle Mar 1922 | 29 | 11 |
| Allan Mathieson | F | Luton Town Aug 1922 | 26 | 4 |
| Alfred Matthews | w | Bristol City May 1922 | 39 | 2 |
| James Mitton | HB | Stockport County C/S 1921 | 32 | 1 |
| Frank Newman | W | Burslem Port Vale Jul 1921 | 3 | |
| Sydney Pavey | G | Taunton United Nov 1922 | 16 | |
| Robert Pollard | FB | Plank Lane C/S 1920 | 39 | |
| James Rigby | HB | Accrington Stanley C/S 1911 | 19 | |
| George Shelton | W | Sheffield Wednesday May 1922 | 13 | |
| Leonard Southway | HB | Bristol City May 1922 | 15 | |
| Charles Vowles | F | Army C/S 1920 | 10 | |
| Own Goals | | | | 3 |

### FOOTBALL LEAGUE - DIVISION THREE SOUTH

| | P | W | D | L | F | A | Pts |
|---|---|---|---|---|---|---|---|
| Bristol City | 42 | 24 | 11 | 7 | 66 | 40 | 59 |
| Plymouth Argyle | 42 | 23 | 7 | 12 | 61 | 29 | 53 |
| Swansea Town | 42 | 22 | 9 | 11 | 78 | 45 | 53 |
| Brighton & H.A. | 42 | 20 | 11 | 11 | 52 | 34 | 51 |
| Luton Town | 42 | 21 | 7 | 14 | 68 | 49 | 49 |
| Millwall | 42 | 14 | 18 | 10 | 45 | 40 | 46 |
| Portsmouth | 42 | 19 | 8 | 15 | 58 | 52 | 46 |
| Northampton Town | 42 | 17 | 11 | 14 | 54 | 44 | 45 |
| Swindon Town | 42 | 17 | 11 | 14 | 62 | 56 | 45 |
| Watford | 42 | 17 | 10 | 15 | 57 | 54 | 44 |
| Queens Park Rangers | 42 | 16 | 10 | 16 | 54 | 49 | 42 |
| Charlton Athletic | 42 | 14 | 14 | 14 | 55 | 51 | 42 |
| Bristol Rovers | 42 | 13 | 16 | 13 | 35 | 36 | 42 |
| Brentford | 42 | 13 | 12 | 17 | 41 | 51 | 38 |
| Southend United | 42 | 12 | 13 | 17 | 49 | 54 | 37 |
| Gillingham | 42 | 15 | 7 | 20 | 51 | 59 | 37 |
| Merthyr Town | 42 | 11 | 14 | 17 | 39 | 48 | 36 |
| Norwich City | 42 | 13 | 10 | 19 | 51 | 71 | 36 |
| Reading | 42 | 10 | 14 | 18 | 36 | 55 | 34 |
| Exeter City | 42 | 13 | 7 | 22 | 47 | 84 | 33 |
| Aberdare Athletic | 42 | 9 | 11 | 22 | 42 | 70 | 29 |
| Newport County | 42 | 8 | 11 | 23 | 40 | 70 | 27 |

* On the eve of the season it was reported in the local Press:- 'The club realises fully that many seasons like the last two would spell goodbye to the Football League. Re-elected and revived, Exeter City are out to establish themselves high up in the Southern Division.'

* The players went on a pre-season day out on 16th August 1922, using two charabancs to Sidmouth, and then on to Seaton late afternoon where they played a friendly - Red and Whites against Blue and Whites. In Sidmouth some players had watched the cricket, whilst others watched a Punch and Judy show.

* For their opening game of the season at Aberdare Athletic, the City team travelled by train to Cardiff, then ...' a 26 mile charabanc drive through towns and villages, beautiful still, despite the endless chain if mining towns and villages, railway sidings and slag heaps.'

* It was announced that Exeter City had made a profit on the year ending April 30th of £1,136 6s. Match receipts had totalled £14,991 12s, but wages accounted for £7,712, and travel and expenses, £1,751 7s 6d.

* Exeter City played a benefit match against Bolton Wanderers for two of their players, Jimmy Rigby and John Dockray, in September 1922. Added interest was the fact that former City goalkeeper, Dick Pym was in the visitors' side, and an attendance of over 5,000 saw the Wanderers run out 2-0 winners.

* The Grecians' paid their first ever visit to Watford's new Vicarage Road ground on 30th September 1922, but it proved to be an unhappy day as the Grecians lost 4-0. Watford had previously played at Cassio Road.

* The players held a meeting in early October to discuss the teams poor start to the season, which had seen them win just twice in their opening nine matches. It had an immediate effect as City won 1-0 at Brentford in the next game.

* In October 1922, the Board of Directors decided to cut admission charges for the reserve team's Southern League matches at St James' Park, from one shilling to eightpence.

* With first choice goalkeeper Harry Fryer reporting sick, City full-back Andrew Flynn played in goal for the FA Cup fourth qualifying round tie at home to Boscombe, the game ending goalless. Flynn also played in goal for the replay, which the Grecians won 3-0. He kept his place for the 5th qualifying round at home to Southern League Bath City, but Exeter lost 2-1.

* The game at home to Southend United kicked off 40 minutes late as the visitors had missed their train to Exeter, their arrival at Paddington being delayed by a problem on the London Underground.

* Exeter City's long serving manager Arthur Chadwick resigned in December 1922, after fourteen years in charge of the club. He was later replaced by Fred Mavin.

* Exeter City wore royal blue shirts (loaned to them by their hosts) in the match at Swindon Town in January 1923, the change being made at the request of the referee to help him distinguish between the two teams.

* Harold Kirk scored all four Exeter City goals in the 4-3 win at Portsmouth in March 1923.

* After the final Football League fixture it was reported that their had been acute disappointment with how the season had ended. In the last ten matches of the season, City lost nine and drew one. The report stated:- 'There was a time when it seemed that the City would finish at least halfway up the League ladder. Instead they are escaping the fatal bottom berths by the narrowest of margins.'

## Up For The Cup!

* In order to prepare for their match at Newport County in the FA Cup fourth qualifying round, the Exeter City team travelled the day before by train as far as Bristol where they stayed overnight at the George Hotel near Temple Meads station,. In the evening they attended a show at the Bristol Hippodrome. Also staying at the same hotel were the Nelson FC team, who were to play Bristol City the following day.

* A story appeared in the press concerning the above Newport County versus Exeter City Cup-tie and a black cat. The report read:-

*'The County players had enticed the little creature to their dressing room before the match in the hope that he would bring the good luck associated with such pets. Hardly had the City team arrived on the ground before the kitten forsook the Newport dressing room and commenced miaowing outside the Exeter quarters. Needless to say the little animal was welcomed with open arms and in the Grecians' dressing room. He stayed until the players went out onto the field.'*

* Around 4,000 Exeter City supporters gathered at St David's station to give the team and officials a tremendous reception following their 1-0 win at Bristol Rovers in the FA Cup. The team had difficulty in making their way through the crowd to the waiting club charabanc which took them back to St James' Park.

City's league results

| | HOME | AWAY |
|---|---|---|
| Aberdare Athletic | 1-1 | 0-0 |
| Bournemouth & B.A. | 0-2 | 0-1 |
| Brentford | 1-0 | 0-1 |
| Brighton & H.A. | 0-1 | 0-1 |
| Bristol Rovers | 3-1 | 0-0 |
| Charlton Athletic | 0-0 | 0-1 |
| Gillingham | 2-1 | 1-1 |
| Luton Town | 2-1 | 0-1 |
| Merthyr Town | 1-0 | 0-3 |
| Millwall | 2-0 | 1-3 |
| Newport County | 5-0 | 0-2 |
| Northampton Town | 2-1 | 0-1 |
| Norwich City | 1-2 | 0-4 |
| Plymouth Argyle | 0-4 | 0-4 |
| Portsmouth | 0-0 | 0-4 |
| Queens Park Rangers | 3-0 | 0-2 |
| Reading | 1-2 | 0-1 |
| Southend United | 2-0 | 0-0 |
| Swansea Town | 1-0 | 0-1 |
| Swindon Town | 3-1 | 1-0 |
| Watford | 1-0 | 0-4 |

F.A. Cup

| | | | |
|---|---|---|---|
| Newport County | A | Q4 | 2-0 |
| Bristol Rovers | H | Q5 | 2-2 |
| Bristol Rovers | A | Q5R | 1-0 |
| Sittingbourne | A | Q6 | 2-0 |
| Grimsby Town | H | R1 | 1-0 |
| Watford | H | R2 | 0-0 |
| Watford | A | R2R | 0-1 |

CITY MANAGER 1923-24
Fred Mavin - Appointed January 1923

CITY PLAYING SQUAD 1923-24

| Name | Pos | Signed from | Apps | Gls |
|---|---|---|---|---|
| Harry Bailey | G | Luton Town C/S 1923 | 41 | |
| John Batten | F | Bradford Park Avenue C/S 1923 | 9 | 1 |
| Stanley Charlton | FB | Rochdale May 1923 | 39 | 1 |
| Joseph Coleburne | FB | Swindon Town May 1923 | 39 | 3 |
| William Crawshaw | HB | Accrington Stanley May 1923 | 5 | |
| Ellis Crompton | HB | Bristol Rovers Jun 1921 | 26 | |
| John Davis | F | Torquay United Feb 1923 | 24 | 5 |
| John Dockray | W | Bury C/S 1914 | 30 | 5 |
| James Edmondson | F | Swansea Town Sept 1923 | 6 | 1 |
| Andrew Flynn | FB | Mexborough May 1922 | 7 | 1 |
| Thomas Gallogley | F | Plymouth Argyle C/S 1923 | 21 | 1 |
| Donald Gilchrist | HB | Portsmouth C/S 1923 | 29 | 1 |
| George Hunter | HB | Sunderland May 1923 | 18 | |
| Harold Kirk | F | Plymouth Argyle Mar 1922 | 37 | 8 |
| Wilfred Llevesley | F | Manchester United C/S 1923 | 16 | 3 |
| Frank Lowson | F | Bradford Park Avenue C/S 1923 | 4 | |
| George McIntosh | HB | Workington C/S 1923 | 16 | |
| Alfred Matthews | W | Bristol City May 1922 | 29 | 5 |
| George Murray | F | Reading C/S 1923 | 14 | 1 |
| Sydney Pavey | G | Taunton United Nov 1922 | 1 | |
| Robert Pollard | FB | Plank Lane C/S 1920 | 19 | |
| Albert Potter | FB | Pinhoe C/S 1922 | 7 | |
| George Shelton | W | Sheffield Wednesday May 1922 | 23 | 1 |
| Hugh Whelan | HB | Bradford City C/S 1923 | 2 | |

FOOTBALL LEAGUE - DIVISION THREE SOUTH

| | P | W | D | L | F | A | Pts |
|---|---|---|---|---|---|---|---|
| Portsmouth | 42 | 24 | 11 | 7 | 87 | 30 | 59 |
| Plymouth Argyle | 42 | 23 | 9 | 10 | 70 | 34 | 55 |
| Millwall | 42 | 22 | 10 | 10 | 64 | 38 | 54 |
| Swansea Town | 42 | 22 | 8 | 12 | 60 | 48 | 52 |
| Brighton & H.A. | 42 | 21 | 9 | 12 | 68 | 37 | 51 |
| Swindon Town | 42 | 17 | 13 | 12 | 58 | 44 | 47 |
| Luton Town | 42 | 16 | 14 | 12 | 50 | 44 | 46 |
| Northampton Town | 42 | 17 | 11 | 14 | 64 | 47 | 45 |
| Bristol Rovers | 42 | 15 | 13 | 14 | 52 | 46 | 43 |
| Newport County | 42 | 17 | 9 | 16 | 56 | 64 | 43 |
| Norwich City | 42 | 16 | 8 | 18 | 60 | 59 | 40 |
| Aberdare Athletic | 42 | 12 | 14 | 16 | 45 | 58 | 38 |
| Merthyr Town | 42 | 11 | 16 | 15 | 45 | 65 | 38 |
| Charlton Athletic | 42 | 11 | 15 | 16 | 38 | 45 | 37 |
| Gillingham | 42 | 12 | 13 | 17 | 43 | 58 | 37 |
| Exeter City | 42 | 15 | 7 | 20 | 37 | 52 | 37 |
| Brentford | 42 | 14 | 8 | 20 | 54 | 71 | 36 |
| Reading | 42 | 13 | 9 | 20 | 51 | 57 | 35 |
| Southend United | 42 | 12 | 10 | 20 | 53 | 84 | 34 |
| Watford | 42 | 9 | 15 | 18 | 45 | 54 | 33 |
| Bournemouth & B.A. | 42 | 11 | 11 | 20 | 40 | 65 | 33 |
| Queens Park Rangers | 42 | 11 | 9 | 22 | 37 | 77 | 31 |

* Railings were erected in front of the Big Bank prior to the start of the season, so that all four sides of the ground had now been similarly treated. Improvements were also made to the dressing rooms.

* Despite leaving at 9am by train for their game at Bournemouth in September 1923, City only made it to the ground with ten minutes to spare. There had been a delay on the Somerset and Dorset line and a fleet of taxi's met the team to ferry them to Dean Court.

* At a meeting of the Exeter City Supporters' Club at the end of September 1923, the possibility of putting a roof over the popular bank terracing (later known as the Cowshed) was discussed. The Club's directors had stated that they planned to make the improvements at some stage in the future,

* It was reported that the Club had made a loss of £2,257 4s 6d on the 12 months ending 30th April 1923. Match receipts had totalled £9,917 15s 6d and a profit of £129 was made on the match programme. Wages had cost £7,169 10s, whilst travelling and hotel expenses accounted for £1,191.

* Exeter had high hopes of forward James Edmondson who they signed from Swansea Town in September 1923, as he had a good goal scoring track record. Unfortunately he badly dislocated his shoulder after just six outings and never played again that season.

* Half-back Hugh Whelan, who had signed from Bradford City in the summer of 1923, was released in October of that year due to .... 'the climate did not suit him and he has been unable to touch his best form."

* An F.A. enquiry took place following the referee's report of the Luton Town versus Exeter City match. A player from each side had been sent off and seven City players were injured during the course of the game. City ended the match with eight men, whilst Luton finished with nine! The enquiry took into account that the referee was not in the best of health at the time of the game.

* Exeter's game at Charlton Athletic on 19th January 1924, played at The Mount, Catford, was abandoned four minutes into the second half due to bad light. Exeter were drawing 1-1 at the time,

* The night before the FA Cup first round tie, both the Exeter City and Grimsby Town teams attended a performance at the Exeter Hippodrome, On the day of the match the Grimsby team walked to St James' Park from their Rougemont Hotel headquarters.

* Four City players were involved in a car crash when returning from the game at Norwich City in February 1924. They had been in a taxi, one of three, transporting the team form Liverpool Street station for their train home to Exeter from Paddington. Fortunately none of the four were injured, and they were able to continue their journey in another taxi.

* Half-back Donald Gilchrist had to rush to Portsmouth in April 1924, when he heard that his younger brother, Duncan, had died whilst playing for the Portsmouth reserve team, having collapsed on the pitch.

* Goalscoring was a huge problem for City throughout the season, and they went on a run of 12 league matches where they only scored two goals. Away from home, they never found the net until Andrew Flynn hit the only goal of the game at Swindon Town in February 1924.

* The highest attendance of the season for a league fixture at St James' Park was 13,000 for the visit of Plymouth Argyle on Boxing Day.

## Preview Of The Season

The local newspaper once again included their usual season preview for Exeter City:-

*'There is an air of comradeship at Exeter City headquarters that augers well, and the Directors policy in retaining from last season all the men that really mattered, apart from John Dockray, and securing in addition just a few keen young men of the right sort to fit in as the occasion depends, is the one that commends itself to everybody.*

*The optimistic mood which expression is given in official quarters and in the training room would appear to be particularly justified at the present time. A good fighting side should be available in each of the two main competitions, the Football League and the Southern League, with the chiefs proving a force to be reckoned with in away matches, as well as on their own ground.*

*There should be a lot less in the unfortunate matter of injuries which came in the way of the club last season, and not merely because of the reversion to the old system of League fixtures, but also because the wet summer has kept the playing field just right for football.'*

**City's league results**

| | Home | Away |
|---|---|---|
| Aberdare Athletic | 3-1 | 1-3 |
| Bournemouth & B.A. | 2-1 | 1-1 |
| Brentford | 5-1 | 5-2 |
| Brighton & H.A. | 2-0 | 0-2 |
| Bristol City | 0-2 | 1-0 |
| Bristol Rovers | 1-1 | 1-0 |
| Charlton Athletic | 2-1 | 0-1 |
| Gillingham | 3-3 | 1-1 |
| Luton Town | 0-1 | 1-1 |
| Merthyr Town | 2-1 | 1-0 |
| Millwall | 0-0 | 0-2 |
| Newport County | 4-3 | 1-2 |
| Northampton Town | 0-0 | 1-2 |
| Norwich City | 1-0 | 1-0 |
| Plymouth Argyle | 3-0 | 1-1 |
| Queens Park Rangers | 1-3 | 4-1 |
| Reading | 1-0 | 1-1 |
| Southend United | 0-1 | 0-3 |
| Swansea Town | 2-0 | 1-2 |
| Swindon Town | 1-0 | 0-1 |
| Watford | 4-0 | 0-3 |

**F.A. Cup**

| | | | |
|---|---|---|---|
| Newport County | H | Q5 | 1-1 |
| Newport County | A | Q5R | 3-3 |
| Newport County | N* | Q5R | 1-0 |
| Barnet | H | Q6 | |
| Southampton | A | R1 | 0-5+ |
| Southampton | A | R1 | 1-3 |

\* 2nd replay at Ashton Gate, Bristol City.
\+ Match abandoned due to fog in 77th minute

**CITY MANAGER 1924-25**
Fred Mavin - Appointed January 1923

**CITY PLAYING SQUAD 1924-25**

| Name | Pos | Signed From | App | Gls |
|---|---|---|---|---|
| George Appleyard | F | Barnsley C/S 1924 | 8 | 1 |
| Harry Bailey | G | Luton Town C/S 1923 | 42 | |
| Harold Blackmore | F | Silverton United C/S 1924 | 11 | 6 |
| Stanley Charlton | FB | Rochdale May 1923 | 30 | 1 |
| Joseph Coleburne | FB | Swindon Town May 1923 | 6 | |
| William Compton | W | Bristol City May 1924 | 39 | 11 |
| William Crawshaw | HB | Accrington Stanley May 1923 | 6 | |
| Ellis Crompton | HB | Bristol Rovers Jun 1921 | 37 | 2 |
| John Davis | F | Torquay United Feb 1923 | 27 | 9 |
| Andrew Flynn | FB | Mexborough May 1922 | 13 | |
| Richard Jones | HB | Stockport County C/S 1924 | 10 | |
| Harold Kirk | F | Plymouth Argyle Mar 1922 | 33 | 12 |
| Wilfred Llevesley | F | Manchester United C/S 1923 | 24 | 5 |
| Alfred Matthews | W | Bristol City May 1922 | 42 | 4 |
| George Murray | F | Reading C/S 1923 | 6 | |
| Robert Pollard | FB | Plank Lane C/S 1920 | 41 | |
| Albert Potter | FB | Pinhoe C/S 1922 | 32 | 1 |
| Robert Pullan | HB | Bristol City May 1924 | 37 | 2 |
| George Shelton | W | Sheffield Wednesday May 1922 | 13 | 3 |
| Thomas Smelt | F | Accrington Stanley C/S 1924 | 5 | 1 |
| Own Goals | | | | 1 |

**FOOTBALL LEAGUE - DIVISION THREE SOUTH**

| | P | W | D | L | F | A | Pts |
|---|---|---|---|---|---|---|---|
| Swansea Town | 42 | 23 | 11 | 8 | 68 | 35 | 57 |
| Plymouth Argyle | 42 | 23 | 10 | 9 | 77 | 38 | 56 |
| Bristol City | 42 | 22 | 9 | 11 | 60 | 41 | 53 |
| Swindon Town | 42 | 20 | 11 | 11 | 66 | 38 | 51 |
| Millwall | 42 | 18 | 13 | 11 | 58 | 38 | 49 |
| Newport County | 42 | 20 | 9 | 13 | 62 | 42 | 49 |
| Exeter City | 42 | 19 | 9 | 14 | 59 | 48 | 47 |
| Brighton & H.A. | 42 | 19 | 8 | 15 | 59 | 45 | 46 |
| Northampton Town | 42 | 20 | 6 | 16 | 51 | 44 | 46 |
| Southend United | 42 | 19 | 5 | 18 | 51 | 61 | 43 |
| Watford | 42 | 17 | 9 | 16 | 38 | 47 | 43 |
| Norwich City | 42 | 14 | 13 | 15 | 53 | 51 | 41 |
| Gillingham | 42 | 13 | 14 | 15 | 35 | 44 | 40 |
| Reading | 42 | 14 | 10 | 18 | 37 | 38 | 38 |
| Charlton Athletic | 42 | 13 | 12 | 17 | 46 | 48 | 38 |
| Luton Town | 42 | 10 | 17 | 15 | 49 | 57 | 37 |
| Bristol Rovers | 42 | 12 | 13 | 17 | 42 | 49 | 37 |
| Aberdare Athletic | 42 | 14 | 9 | 19 | 54 | 67 | 37 |
| Queens Park Rangers | 42 | 14 | 8 | 20 | 42 | 63 | 36 |
| Bournemouth & B.A. | 42 | 13 | 8 | 21 | 40 | 58 | 34 |
| Brentford | 42 | 9 | 7 | 26 | 38 | 91 | 25 |
| Merthyr Town | 42 | 8 | 5 | 29 | 35 | 77 | 21 |

* Having won their opening three matches of the season, against Reading, Bristol City and Merthyr Town, Exeter City topped the Division Three South table for the first time ever.

* The City Directors arranged a day out (11th Sept 1924) for the staff and players, and a friendly fixture at Holsworthy (which was duly won 1-0). The report read: 'A party of 40, made the journey to Holsworthy in two well equipped charabancs, supplied by the Central Garage Company, Exeter.'

* In the 20th minute of Exeter City's game at Newport County, the referee had to stop the match and go over to speak to spectators on the popular side of the ground who had been barracking the Exeter players.

* A' Felix the Cat' mascot was presented by some 'Exeter ladies' to City captain, Stan Charlton, before the start of the F.A. Cup tie against Newport County in November 1924. Charlton tied the mascot to one of the posts supporting the net of the Exeter goal. The game ended in a 1-1 draw.

* Harold Blackmore travelled with the City team to Ashton Gate, Bristol City, to watch their FA Cup second replay against Newport County. He was then asked to play at the last minute due to an injury to Harold Kirk. As a result he had to borrow pair of boots from the Bristol City club and duly scored the only goal of the game!

* Exeter's thirteen match unbeaten run almost came to an end in spectacular fashion when they visited Southampton for an F.A. Cup first round tie in January 1925, where they were losing 5-0, only for the match to be abandoned in the 77th minute due the ever thickening fog. The tie was played again four days later and Southampton won 3-1.

* In February 1925 it was reported that the Club needed the sum of £2,000 to put it on an even financial footing and it was suggested that one, or more players may have had to be transferred to raise that sum.

* After playing at Norwich City on 14th March 1925 (City won 1-0), the team travelled to Holland where they played a friendly against Ajax. Harold Kirk netted a hat-trick as the Grecians won 5-1.

* Full-back Stan Charlton was selected to play for the Football Association XI to tour Australia in the Summer of 1925. He missed the last few matches of City's season as the F.A. team set sail for Australia at the end of March.

* Swansea Town attracted their then record attendance of 25,000 to the Vetch Field for the visit of Exeter City in what was the final match of the season. The Swans had to win if they were to gain the Third Division South Championship, and they did, beating the Grecians 2-1.

* The local St Sidwells Traders Association set about the task of raising much need finance for Exeter City Football Club in May 1925, by means of shares, donations etc. The money was needed to pay the summer wages at St James' Park, which the Club would struggle to meet.

* Finance was also needed for the erection of further covered accommodation at St James' Park. It was stated that no other members of The Football League had such scanty shelter to offer spectators on wet days.

* A concert and presentation evening was held at The Exeter Trades and Labour Hall in May 1925. Former City goalkeeper Dick Pym was in attendance to receive a water colour portrait of himself in recognition of the great service he gave to the Grecians prior to his transfer to Bolton Wanderers.

\* Exeter City full-back, Stan Charlton, returned to the club in September 1925, having been away playing for the F.A. XI on their tour of Australia since the previous April. He captained the team in the final game and appeared in 20 of the 26 matches that they played. The local newspaper reported that on his return, Charlton looked as if he had developed physically and was as fine a sportsman and athlete as anyone could wish to see.

\* Reports were not very complimentary about Exeter City's kit when they entertained Norwich City at St. James' Park in October 1925. 'There was a marked contrast in the appearance of the teams,' it was stated. 'Norwich looked very smart in their white shirts with a 'V' back and front in yellow and green, but Exeter's red jerseys were very washed out looking.'

\* Rain was falling heavily when Reading visited St James' Park on 2nd January 1926. Prior to kick off, the referee called the respective captains over to the touchline, due to the waterlogged state of the centre circle. The usual flip of a coin took place to determine which way the teams would kick. By the second half both sets of players were virtually unrecognisable covered from head to toe in mud as the rain continued to fall. City won 3-2.

\* Had Exeter City player Harold 'Jazzo' Kirk not been a footballer, it was said he could have earned a living on stage as an entertainer, for he was an accomplished pianist and singer. He could tell jokes and recite poetry and had recently learned to play the Ukelele and the Banjolele.

## City's league results

| | HOME | AWAY |
|---|---|---|
| Aberdare Athletic | 4-0 | 0-5 |
| Bournemouth & B.A. | 0-1 | 1-2 |
| Brentford | 6-1 | 0-2 |
| Brighton & H.A. | 2-4 | 3-1 |
| Bristol City | 1-1 | 0-1 |
| Bristol Rovers | 3-0 | 1-0 |
| Charlton Athletic | 5-3 | 0-1 |
| Crystal Palace | 0-1 | 2-3 |
| Gillingham | 2-1 | 0-2 |
| Luton Town | 2-2 | 1-1 |
| Merthyr Town | 6-2 | 1-3 |
| Millwall | 3-1 | 0-3 |
| Newport County | 2-1 | 0-3 |
| Northampton Town | 1-0 | 1-2 |
| Norwich City | 0-1 | 1-3 |
| Plymouth Argyle | 4-0 | 2-2 |
| Queens Park Rangers | 3-0 | 0-0 |
| Reading | 3-2 | 2-3 |
| Southend United | 0-1 | 1-3 |
| Swindon Town | 1-2 | 1-2 |
| Watford | 6-1 | 1-3 |

F.A. Cup

| Swansea Town | H R1 | 1-3 |
|---|---|---|

CITY MANAGER 1925-26
Fred Mavin - Appointed January 1923

### CITY PLAYING SQUAD 1925-26

| Name | Pos | Signed from | Apps | Gls |
|---|---|---|---|---|
| John Anderson | F | South Molton | 1 | |
| Harry Bailey | G | Luton Town C/S 1923 | 32 | |
| Harold Blackmore | F | Silverton United C/S 1924 | 27 | 14 |
| David Bolam | F | Lincoln City C/S 1925 | 1 | |
| Walter Casson | F | Pontypridd C/S 1925 | 8 | 3 |
| Stanley Charlton | FB | Rochdale May 1923 | 34 | 5 |
| William Compton | W | Bristol City May 1924 | 42 | 12 |
| Ellis Crompton | HB | Bristol Rovers Jun 1921 | 7 | |
| Andrew Flynn | FB | Mexborough May 1922 | 1 | |
| John Garratt | HB | Torquay United Mar 1926 | 2 | |
| Horace Hawkins | FB | Denaby United C/S 1925 | 4 | |
| Harold Kirk | F | Plymouth Argyle Mar 1922 | 27 | 5 |
| Wilfred Lievesley | F | Manchester United C/S 1923 | 29 | 18 |
| Wilfred Lowton | FB | Heavitree United C/S 1924 | 13 | 1 |
| William McDevitt | HB | Liverpool C/S 1925 | 24 | 2 |
| Alfred Matthews | W | Bristol City May 1924 | 28 | 2 |
| Colin Myers | F | Queens Park Rangers C/S 1925 | 19 | 3 |
| Frank Newman | W | Halifax Town C/S 1925 | 14 | 1 |
| Sydney Pavey | G | Taunton Town Nov 1922 | 10 | |
| Robert Pollard | FB | Plank Lane C/S 1920 | 40 | |
| Albert Potter | FB | Pinhoe C/S 1922 | 33 | 1 |
| Robert Pullan | HB | Bristol City May 1924 | 40 | |
| George Shelton | W | Sheffield Wednesday May 1922 | 26 | 4 |
| Own Goals | | | | 1 |

### FOOTBALL LEAGUE - DIVISION THREE SOUTH

| | P | W | D | L | F | A | Pts |
|---|---|---|---|---|---|---|---|
| Reading | 42 | 23 | 11 | 8 | 77 | 52 | 57 |
| Plymouth Argyle | 42 | 24 | 8 | 10 | 107 | 67 | 56 |
| Millwall | 42 | 21 | 11 | 10 | 73 | 39 | 53 |
| Bristol City | 42 | 21 | 9 | 12 | 72 | 51 | 51 |
| Brighton & H.A. | 42 | 19 | 9 | 14 | 84 | 73 | 47 |
| Swindon Town | 42 | 20 | 6 | 16 | 69 | 64 | 46 |
| Luton Town | 42 | 18 | 7 | 17 | 80 | 75 | 43 |
| Bournemouth B.A. | 42 | 17 | 9 | 16 | 75 | 91 | 43 |
| Aberdare Athletic | 42 | 17 | 8 | 17 | 74 | 66 | 42 |
| Gillingham | 42 | 17 | 8 | 17 | 53 | 69 | 42 |
| Southend United | 42 | 19 | 4 | 19 | 78 | 73 | 42 |
| Northampton Town | 42 | 17 | 7 | 18 | 82 | 80 | 41 |
| Crystal Palace | 42 | 19 | 3 | 20 | 75 | 79 | 41 |
| Merthyr Town | 42 | 14 | 11 | 17 | 69 | 75 | 39 |
| Watford | 42 | 15 | 9 | 18 | 73 | 89 | 39 |
| Norwich City | 42 | 15 | 9 | 18 | 58 | 73 | 39 |
| Newport County | 42 | 14 | 10 | 18 | 64 | 74 | 38 |
| Brentford | 42 | 16 | 6 | 20 | 69 | 94 | 38 |
| Bristol Rovers | 42 | 15 | 6 | 21 | 66 | 69 | 36 |
| Exeter City | 42 | 15 | 5 | 22 | 72 | 70 | 35 |
| Charlton Athletic | 42 | 11 | 13 | 18 | 48 | 68 | 35 |
| Queens Park Rangers | 42 | 6 | 9 | 27 | 37 | 84 | 21 |

* The long awaited improvement to the 'Flowerpot' side of St James' Park, later known as the Cowshed, was completed in time for the start of the season. The Exeter City Supporters' Club funded the erection of cover over the terracing.

* The Mayor of Exeter attended the home game against Bournemouth & Boscombe Athletic. It was reported ....'The arrival of the Mayor of Exeter was the signal for a little ceremony, the crowd standing bare headed while the Exeter City Military Band played the National Anthem. Both teams lined up and the Mayor shook hands with all the players.'

* Gillingham arrived at St James' Park just 15 minutes before kick off for their game on 19th September 1925. The team had experienced delays on the train journey from London. The Grecians won 2-1.

* The main grandstand was totally destroyed by fire on 17th November 1925, and with it all the playing kit. The fire took hold extremely quickly and was first spotted by groundsman Andy Tucker who was returning from his lunch break. He could do little to save anything and had to await the arrival of the fire brigade. The fire totally engulfed the structure with the roof buckling and collapsing. It was reckoned damage totalled £6,000. It was established that the fire had started when some shirts had caught alight whilst they were left out to dry by the coke stove.

* The first game to be played at St James' Park four days after the fire, was a Southern League fixture, when Weymouth were the visitors. Both teams changed at the nearby Red Lion Hotel in Sidwell Street.

*Tents were placed on the site of the destroyed grandstand, for use of the match officials and players during the interval, when Swansea Town visited the Park for a first round FA Cup tie on 28th November 1925. The Swansea team changed at Messrs' Neal's in St James' Road, whilst City used the Red Lion.

* Plans were rapidly drawn up for the replacement of the grandstand and it was hoped that the new structure would be in place for the start of the 1926-27 season. It would have seating for 2,000 spectators. It was still in use for season 2012-13.

* The final position of 20th in the Division Three South league table was extremely disappointing,. especially after such a good season twelve months earlier.

* The 6-1 home win over Brentford in December 1925, was the biggest win for City since the First World War. Harold Blackmore netted a hat-trick.

* One other City player scored a hat-trick, that being Wilf Lievesley, who accomplished the feat on two occasions, in the 5-3 home win over Charlton Athletic, and again in a 4-0 win against Aberdare Athletic at St James' Park

* The highest attendance of the season was 20,000 who were at Home Park to see Plymouth Argyle play Exeter City. Best crowd of the season at St James' Park was 11,000, when Swindon Town were the visitors in April 1926.

* One notable name appeared for the first time, that of Cliff Bastin, who was attending Ladysmith Road School in Exeter. He was chosen for the England Schoolboys team, the start of an illustrious career which saw him play for Exeter City and Arsenal.

* There had been much talk during the season of City full-back Stan Charlton being transferred to Bolton Wanderers, but no firm bid was ever received.

* The Grecians signed eleven new players for the start of the season, to add to the 12 players who had been retained from the previous campaign. It was hoped ... 'that between them, these Grecians will perform so well as to fill the handsome, spacious new grandstand on all first team occasions, not to mention the enclosure and ground generally.

* As well as the construction of the new grandstand at St. James' Park, much work had been undertaken on the pitch. An extensive re-turfing scheme had been completed in the centre of the pitch and in the two goal areas. Hundreds of tons of soil had been removed, and 'good earth substituted for it.' As a result it was hoped that the very heavy, muddy patches which were so conspicuous the previous season were a thing of the past.

* When Plymouth Argyle visited St James' Park for a league fixture on 27th December 1926, it was reported that 'railway excursions had brought big crowds up from Plymouth.' The grandstand was full long before kick off. New seating was brought into use on the railway bank alongside the stand, while new crush barriers at the Big Bank ensured the safety of spectators. The attendance was 19,221, with Argyle winning the match 2-0.

* At the end of the season mention was made of the fact that Exeter City had done better at home than in any previous season since the war. The Grecians had called upon a total of 22 players in their League matches, one less than in the 1925-26 campaign. Only one player appeared in every match, that being captain and left-back Stan Charlton.

### City's league results

| | Home | Away |
|---|---|---|
| Aberdare Athletic | 2-1 | 1-3 |
| Bournemouth & B.A. | 4-0 | 3-4 |
| Brentford | 3-1 | 1-6 |
| Brighton & H.A. | 0-0 | 2-5 |
| Bristol City | 1-1 | 2-3 |
| Bristol Rovers | 1-1 | 1-3 |
| Charlton Athletic | 1-0 | 0-1 |
| Coventry City | 8-1 | 0-0 |
| Crystal Palace | 3-1 | 0-1 |
| Gillingham | 5-1 | 2-3 |
| Luton Town | 1-2 | 2-2 |
| Merthyr Town | 3-0 | 3-3 |
| Millwall | 1-1 | 2-4 |
| Newport County | 2-1 | 0-2 |
| Northampton Town | 3-2 | 2-2 |
| Norwich City | 1-0 | 4-4 |
| Plymouth Argyle | 0-2 | 0-2 |
| Queens Park Rangers | 0-2 | 1-1 |
| Southend United | 2-0 | 2-1 |
| Swindon Town | 3-1 | 2-4 |
| Watford | 2-0 | 0-1 |

### F.A. Cup

| | | | |
|---|---|---|---|
| Aberdare Athletic | H | R1 | 3-0 |
| Northampton Town | H | R2 | 1-0 |
| Accrington Stanley | H | R3 | 0-2 |

**CITY MANAGER 1926-27**

Fred Mavin - Appointed January 1923

### CITY PLAYING SQUAD 1926-27

| Name | Pos | Signed from | Apps | Gls |
|---|---|---|---|---|
| Harry Bailey | G | Luton Town C/S 1923 | 28 | |
| Harold Blackmore | F | Silverton United C/S 1924 | 33 | 25 |
| Stanley Charlton | FB | Rochdale May 1923 | 42 | 3 |
| William Compton | W | Bristol City May 1924 | 37 | 7 |
| Frederick Dent | F | Bristol City C/S 1926 | 14 | 3 |
| John Ditchburn | HB | Sunderland C/S 1926 | 30 | |
| John Garratt | HB | Torquay United Mar 1926 | 8 | |
| Hugh Good | HB | Middlesbrough C/S 1926 | 4 | |
| Wilfred Lievesley | F | Manchester United C/S 1923 | 26 | 12 |
| Wilfred Lowton | FB | Heavitree United C/S 1924 | 19 | 3 |
| William McDevitt | HB | Liverpool C/S 1925 | 28 | 2 |
| Charles Miller | FB | Plymouth Argyle C/S 1926 | 10 | |
| Frank Newman | W | Halifax Town C/S 1925 | 2 | |
| Thomas Parkin | W | Durham City C/S 1926 | 5 | 1 |
| Arthur Phoenix | F | Barnsley C/S 1926 | 16 | 7 |
| Robert Pollard | FB | Plank Lane C/S 1920 | 23 | |
| Alexander Pool | HB | Bristol City C/S 1926 | 27 | 1 |
| Albert Potter | FB | Pinhoe C/S 1922 | 17 | 1 |
| Robert Pullan | HB | Bristol City May 1924 | 26 | |
| George Purcell | F | Swindon Town C/S 1926 | 41 | 7 |
| Oswald Randall | G | Swindon Town C/S 1926 | 14 | |
| James Walker | F | Plymouth Argyle C/S 1926 | 12 | 2 |
| Own Goals | | | | 2 |

### FOOTBALL LEAGUE - DIVISION THREE SOUTH

| | P | W | D | L | F | A | Pts |
|---|---|---|---|---|---|---|---|
| Bristol City | 42 | 27 | 8 | 7 | 104 | 54 | 62 |
| Plymouth Argyle | 42 | 25 | 10 | 7 | 95 | 61 | 60 |
| Millwall | 42 | 23 | 10 | 9 | 89 | 51 | 56 |
| Brighton & H.A. | 42 | 21 | 11 | 10 | 79 | 50 | 53 |
| Swindon Town | 42 | 21 | 9 | 12 | 100 | 85 | 51 |
| Crystal Palace | 42 | 18 | 9 | 15 | 84 | 81 | 45 |
| Bournemouth & B.A. | 42 | 18 | 8 | 16 | 78 | 66 | 44 |
| Luton Town | 42 | 15 | 14 | 13 | 68 | 66 | 44 |
| Newport County | 42 | 19 | 6 | 17 | 57 | 71 | 44 |
| Bristol Rovers | 42 | 16 | 9 | 17 | 78 | 80 | 41 |
| Bristol Rovers | 42 | 16 | 9 | 17 | 78 | 80 | 41 |
| Brentford | 42 | 13 | 14 | 15 | 70 | 61 | 40 |
| Exeter City | 42 | 15 | 10 | 17 | 76 | 73 | 40 |
| Charlton Athletic | 42 | 16 | 8 | 18 | 60 | 61 | 40 |
| Queens Park Rangers | 42 | 15 | 9 | 18 | 65 | 71 | 39 |
| Coventry City | 42 | 15 | 7 | 20 | 71 | 86 | 37 |
| Norwich City | 42 | 12 | 11 | 19 | 59 | 71 | 35 |
| Merthyr Town | 42 | 13 | 9 | 20 | 63 | 80 | 35 |
| Northampton Town | 42 | 15 | 5 | 22 | 59 | 87 | 35 |
| Southend United | 42 | 14 | 6 | 22 | 64 | 77 | 34 |
| Gillingham | 42 | 11 | 10 | 21 | 54 | 72 | 32 |
| Watford | 42 | 12 | 8 | 22 | 57 | 87 | 32 |
| Aberdare Athletic | 42 | 9 | 7 | 26 | 62 | 101 | 25 |

* The new grandstand at St James' Park, with a capacity of 2,000, was described as 'being as smart as any in the South.' The stand included dressing rooms, offices, refreshment kiosks etc. Owing to a strike there was a delay in supply of materials to the builders, however, it was used for the first time for the opening fixture of the 1926-27 season against Merthyr Town.

* Club secretary Sidney Thomas issued a statement prior to the start of the season stating: 'We are looking forward with confidence to the 1926-27 season. It appears from the players available that the Directors will have a difficult task in deciding who will be given immediate places in the first team."

* It was reported that up to 2,000 Exeter City supporters travelled on the Great Western Railway excursions for the game at Bristol City on 16th October 1926. The Grecians lost 3-2.

* Exeter City recorded their then record victory in a Football League match when they demolished visiting Coventry City, 8-1, on 4th December 1926. They led 3-0 at half-time, but ran riot in the second half.

* In the week prior to their FA Cup third round tie against Accrington Stanley at St James' Park, the players stayed and trained in Sidmouth from Wednesday evening to Saturday morning. A Director said: "This is a new departure for the club, but the men have had a very hard task during recent weeks, and in many cases they have had to play when probably not fit to do so."

* The Accrington Stanley team had travelled to stay overnight in Teignmouth to ...'refresh themselves in the sea breezes of the South Devon resort.'

* The state of the pitch at Queens Park Rangers left a lot to be desired when Exeter City visited for match on 24th February. It was described thus: 'The ground was in a deplorable condition. Scarcely a blade of grass could be seen.'

* Harold Blackmore broke the record for the most league goals scored in a season since Exeter City had turned professional in 1908. The record, held by James 'Daisy' Bell in that very first season, stood at 23 goals. Blackmore went on to net 25.

* Blackmore netted twice against Bolton Wanderers in a benefit match for City player, Bob Pollard. Exeter won 3-2. His goals and performance was enough to convince Bolton to sign the player immediately afterwards. Negotiations for his transfer had begun much earlier, but were concluded that evening, with a fee of £2,500 being paid.

* Wilf Livesley scored four times in the 5-1 home win over Gillingham on 2nd April 1927.

* Southampton visited St James' Park on 4th May 1927, to play against Exeter City in a benefit match for former Grecian Ellis Crompton, who had retired at the end of the previous season, The game ended 1-1.

* The Grecians secured more points and scored more goals at St James' Park than in any of their seven preceding seasons. They scored 46 and conceded just 18.

* City netted 76 league goals in total, whereas their previous record was 72, which they reached in the previous campaign.

* The attendance for the visit of Plymouth Argyle to St James' Park on 27th December 1925, was estimated to be 20,000, with at least a further 500 non-paying spectators, including some who climbed the trees!

* Only 600 people were at the Aberdare Athletic versus Exeter City Third Division South fixture on 26th March 1927. This was reportedly due to .... 'the distress underlying the community in the district. The Exeter supporters were the only signs of cheerfulness in a drab and dismal setting at Yns Park.'

Local player Reg Clarke made his debut for Exeter City in 1927-28, the first of 315 league matches that he was to play for the Club, when he moved to Aldershot in the summer of 1937.

CITY PLAYING SQUAD 1927-28

| Name | Pos | Signed from | Apps | Gls |
|------|-----|-------------|------|-----|
| Harold Andrews | F | Torquay United C/S 1927 | 2 | |
| Clifford Bastin | W | School Dec 1927 | 3 | 3 |
| Robert Chambers | HB | Carlisle United C/S 1927 | 1 | |
| Stanley Charlton | FB | Rochdale May 1923 | 18 | |
| Reginald Clarke | HB | Southern Railway, Exeter C/S 1927 | 9 | |
| William Compton | W | Bristol City May 1924 | 33 | 9 |
| Frederick Dent | F | Bristol City C/S 1926 | 34 | 26 |
| John Ditchburn | HB | Sunderland C/S 1926 | 20 | |
| Thomas Edwards | F | Aberdare Athletic Feb 1928 | 3 | |
| Harold Gee | HB | New Brighton C/S 1927 | 29 | 2 |
| Thomas Holland | G | Weymouth C/S 1927 | 29 | |
| Thomas Jenkins | W | Merthyr Town C/S 1927 | 4 | |
| Robert Kirk | W | Bristol City C/S 1927 | 8 | |
| Wilfred Lievesley | F | Manchester United C/S 1923 | 2 | |
| Wilfred Lowton | FB | Heavitree United C/S 1924 | 7 | |
| Patrick McDade | F | Liverpool C/S 1927 | 2 | |
| William McDevitt | HB | Liverpool C/S 1925 | 36 | 3 |
| Samuel Mason | HB | Gillingham C/S 1927 | 20 | 1 |
| Charles Miller | FB | Plymouth Argyle C/S 1926 | 25 | |
| Thomas Parkin | W | Durham City C/S 1926 | 3 | |
| Arthur Phoenix | F | Barnsley C/S 1926 | 28 | 2 |
| Robert Pollard | FB | Plank Lane C/S 1920 | 36 | |
| Alexander Pool | HB | Bristol City C/S 1926 | 23 | 1 |
| George Purcell | F | Swindon Town C/S 1926 | 40 | 13 |
| William Vaughan | F | Burton Town C/S 1927 | 33 | 9 |
| Thomas Wainwright | G | Cardiff City C/S 1927 | 13 | |
| Henry Warren | HB | Blackpool C/S 1927 | 1 | |
| Own Goals | | | | 1 |

## FOOTBALL LEAGUE - DIVISION THREE SOUTH

| | P | W | D | L | F | A | Pts |
|---|---|---|---|---|---|---|-----|
| Millwall | 42 | 30 | 5 | 7 | 127 | 50 | 65 |
| Northampton Town | 42 | 23 | 9 | 10 | 102 | 64 | 55 |
| Plymouth Argyle | 42 | 23 | 7 | 12 | 85 | 54 | 53 |
| Brighton & H.A. | 42 | 19 | 10 | 13 | 81 | 69 | 48 |
| Crystal Palace | 42 | 18 | 12 | 12 | 79 | 72 | 48 |
| Swindon Town | 42 | 19 | 9 | 14 | 90 | 69 | 47 |
| Southend United | 42 | 20 | 6 | 16 | 80 | 64 | 46 |
| Exeter City | 42 | 17 | 12 | 13 | 70 | 60 | 46 |
| Newport County | 42 | 18 | 9 | 15 | 81 | 84 | 45 |
| Queens Park Rangers | 42 | 17 | 9 | 16 | 72 | 71 | 43 |
| Charlton Athletic | 42 | 15 | 13 | 14 | 60 | 70 | 43 |
| Brentford | 42 | 16 | 8 | 18 | 76 | 74 | 40 |
| Luton Town | 42 | 16 | 7 | 19 | 94 | 87 | 39 |
| Bournemouth & B.A. | 42 | 13 | 12 | 17 | 72 | 79 | 38 |
| Watford | 42 | 14 | 10 | 18 | 68 | 78 | 38 |
| Gillingham | 42 | 13 | 11 | 18 | 62 | 81 | 37 |
| Norwich City | 42 | 10 | 16 | 16 | 66 | 70 | 36 |
| Walsall | 42 | 12 | 9 | 21 | 75 | 101 | 33 |
| Bristol Rovers | 42 | 14 | 4 | 24 | 67 | 93 | 32 |
| Coventry City | 42 | 11 | 9 | 22 | 67 | 96 | 31 |
| Merthyr Town | 42 | 9 | 13 | 20 | 53 | 91 | 31 |
| Torquay United | 42 | 8 | 14 | 20 | 53 | 103 | 30 |

City's league results

| | Home | Away |
|---|------|------|
| Bournemouth & B.A. | 4-1 | 0-2 |
| Brentford | 0-1 | 1-1 |
| Brighton & H.A. | 0-3 | 2-0 |
| Bristol Rovers | 4-1 | 2-1 |
| Charlton Athletic | 2-1 | 0-0 |
| Coventry City | 0-1 | 0-0 |
| Crystal Palace | 2-2 | 0-2 |
| Gillingham | 2-2 | 1-1 |
| Luton Town | 3-2 | 1-2 |
| Merthyr Town | 2-0 | 3-0 |
| Millwall | 2-4 | 0-2 |
| Newport County | 5-1 | 0-1 |
| Northampton Town | 1-1 | 0-5 |
| Norwich City | 2-2 | 2-2 |
| Plymouth Argyle | 2-0 | 2-1 |
| Queens Park Rangers | 4-0 | 1-0 |
| Southend United | 3-2 | 2-1 |
| Swindon Town | 0-0 | 0-3 |
| Torquay United | 5-1 | 1-1 |
| Walsall | 3-0 | 1-5 |
| Watford | 3-3 | 2-3 |

| F.A. Cup | | | | |
|----------|---|-----|-----|---|
| Aberdare Athletic | H | R1 | 9-1 | |
| Ilford | H | R2 | 5-3 | |
| Rotherham United | A | R3 | 3-3 | |
| Rotherham United | H | R3R | 3-1 | |
| Blackburn Rovers | H | R4 | 2-2 | |
| Blackburn Rovers | A | R4R | 1-3 | |

| CITY MANAGER 1928-29 |
|----------------------|
| Frank Mavin - Appointed January 1923 |
| David Wilson - Appointed March 1928 |

* Torquay United became members of The Football League for the 1927-28 season, and their first ever opponents were Exeter City on 27th August. A then record attendance of 11,625 for Plainmoor, saw the teams draw 1-1, with William Vaughan equalising for City six minutes from time.

* It was announced that City manager, Fred Mavin, was to leave the club in November 1927. He was to take over as manager of Crystal Palace. He had told the Directors that the offer was too good to turn down.

* It was decided to advertise the vacant manager's position at St James' Park and the Directors received over 100 applications.

* Exeter City outclassed their Southern League opposition, Aberdare Athletic, in the first round of the F.A. Cup, going on to win 9-1. Fred Dent scored four times. City had led 4-1 at half-time.

* The appointed match referee was held up on the train due to snow storms and didn't arrive at the Exeter City versus Plymouth Argyle fixture on Boxing Day until half an hour after kick off. St James' Park had to be cleared of snow prior to kick off and rival spectators enjoyed themselves throwing snow balls at one another.

* Exeter performed the League double over Plymouth Argyle for the first time. The Grecians won 2-0 at St James' Park, and in the return meeting at Home Park the following day, won 2-1.

* Four Exeter City players wore knee pads for protection from the frost bound ground when they lined up against visiting Torquay United. City won 5-0 before an attendance of 9,000.

* 300 City supporters travelled to the third round F.A. Cup tie at Rotherham United reportedly:- 'Resplendent in red and white streamers and equipped with all the usual cup tie paraphernalia, bells, bugles and rattles.'

* The replay against Rotherham was on a Wednesday afternoon, and City chairman Mr. M. J. McGahey appealed via the pages of the local Press for employers to allow their staff to attend the game. The largest employers in the city, Messrs Willey and Co Ltd, closed for the afternoon.

* The attendance of 28,348 for the Blackburn Rovers versus Exeter City F.A. Cup fourth round replay, was the biggest crowd that the Grecians had ever played before.

* Half-back Harold Gee sustained a broken leg in the 2-1 victory at Bristol Rovers in March 1928. The injury was to end his career, and he eventually received £280 compensation.

* Although the game kicked off at 5pm, the referee felt that the light was so bad, that it was unlikely that the Gillingham versus Exeter City fixture would finish. However, by not having a half-time interval, the game did run its course, and ended 1-1.

* In March 1929 it was announced that Exeter City had finally appointed a new manager. David Wilson, a former Scottish international had been appointed to succeed Fred Mavin. Having formerly played for St. Mirren, Bradford City and Oldham Athletic, Wilson had also managed Nelson.

* 16-year-old Cliff Bastin, became the youngest ever player to make his debut for Exeter City when he lined up in the Grecians team for a visit to Coventry City, a game that ended goalless. A few days later he scored twice in 5-1 home win over Newport County.

*At the end of the season it was suggested that the Flowerpot terrace, opposite the main stand, be developed still further and extended around to join up with the Big Bank increasing the capacity of St James' Park. It was hoped that a new entrance to the ground could then be made via Old Tiverton Road.

Exeter City 1928-29
Back row: Reg Clarke, David Wilson (Manager), Wilf Lowton, Thomas Holland, Charlie Miller, William Jones (Trainer), Leslie Dennington
Front row: George Purcell, Billy McDevitt, Arthur Doncaster, Harold Houghton, William Death, Alexander Pool

| City's league results | Home | Away |
|---|---|---|
| Bournemouth & B.A. | 6-3 | 1-3 |
| Brentford | 2-3 | 2-4 |
| Brighton & H.A. | 4-1 | 2-3 |
| Bristol Rovers | 2-2 | 1-1 |
| Charlton Athletic | 2-5 | 1-3 |
| Coventry City | 2-3 | 1-1 |
| Crystal Palace | 1-2 | 0-1 |
| Fulham | 1-4 | 0-0 |
| Gillingham | 4-2 | 3-1 |
| Luton Town | 1-1 | 0-4 |
| Merthyr Town | 5-0 | 1-1 |
| Newport County | 6-1 | 1-1 |
| Northampton Town | 2-0 | 0-4 |
| Norwich City | 3-1 | 0-5 |
| Plymouth Argyle | 1-2 | 0-0 |
| Queens Park Rangers | 1-1 | 0-1 |
| Southend United | 1-2 | 0-1 |
| Swindon Town | 1-1 | 0-2 |
| Torquay United | 1-3 | 3-1 |
| Walsall | 1-1 | 2-7 |
| Watford | 2-2 | 0-3 |

| F.A. Cup | | | |
|---|---|---|---|
| Barking Town | H | R1 | 6-0 |
| Torquay United | A | R2 | 1-0 |
| Leeds United | H | R3 | 2-2 |
| Leeds United | A | R3R | 1-5 |

CITY MANAGER 1928-29
David Wilson - Appointed March 1928
Billy McDevitt - Appointed February 1929

| FOOTBALL LEAGUE - DIVISION THREE SOUTH | P | W | D | L | F | A | Pts |
|---|---|---|---|---|---|---|---|
| Charlton Athletic | 42 | 23 | 8 | 11 | 86 | 60 | 54 |
| Crystal Palace | 42 | 23 | 8 | 11 | 81 | 67 | 54 |
| Northampton Town | 42 | 20 | 12 | 10 | 96 | 57 | 52 |
| Plymouth Argyle | 42 | 20 | 12 | 10 | 83 | 51 | 52 |
| Fulham | 42 | 21 | 10 | 11 | 101 | 71 | 52 |
| Queens Park Rangers | 42 | 19 | 14 | 9 | 82 | 61 | 52 |
| Luton Town | 42 | 19 | 11 | 12 | 89 | 73 | 49 |
| Watford | 42 | 19 | 10 | 13 | 79 | 74 | 48 |
| Bournemouth & B.A. | 42 | 19 | 9 | 14 | 84 | 77 | 47 |
| Swindon Town | 42 | 15 | 13 | 14 | 75 | 72 | 43 |
| Coventry City | 42 | 14 | 14 | 14 | 62 | 57 | 42 |
| Southend United | 42 | 15 | 11 | 16 | 80 | 75 | 41 |
| Brentford | 42 | 14 | 10 | 18 | 56 | 60 | 38 |
| Walsall | 42 | 13 | 12 | 17 | 73 | 79 | 38 |
| Brighton & H.A. | 42 | 16 | 6 | 20 | 58 | 76 | 38 |
| Newport County | 42 | 13 | 9 | 20 | 69 | 86 | 35 |
| Norwich City | 42 | 14 | 6 | 22 | 69 | 81 | 34 |
| Torquay United | 42 | 14 | 6 | 22 | 66 | 84 | 34 |
| Bristol Rovers | 42 | 13 | 7 | 22 | 60 | 79 | 33 |
| Merthyr Town | 42 | 11 | 8 | 23 | 55 | 103 | 30 |
| Exeter City | 42 | 9 | 11 | 22 | 67 | 88 | 29 |
| Gillingham | 42 | 10 | 9 | 23 | 43 | 83 | 29 |

| CITY PLAYING SQUAD 1928-29 | | | | |
|---|---|---|---|---|
| Name | Pos | Signed from | Apps | Gls |
| Clifford Bastin | W | School Dec 1927 | 14 | 3 |
| Edward Cameron | F | Stafford Rangers C/S 1928 | 24 | 9 |
| James Campbell | G | Partick Thistle C/S 1928 | 17 | |
| Alexander Christie | HB | Rochdale C/S 1928 | 4 | |
| Reginald Clarke | HB | Southern Railway, Exeter C/S 1927 | 38 | 3 |
| William Death | W | Sunderland Sep 1928 | 21 | 5 |
| Leslie Dennington | HB | Reading Nov 1928 | 19 | |
| John Ditchburn | HB | Sunderland C/S 1926 | 1 | |
| Arthur Doncaster | F | Bolton Wanderers C/S 1928 | 24 | 7 |
| William Hick | F | Bristol City Race 1929 | 16 | 8 |
| Thomas Holland | G | Weymouth C/S 1927 | 25 | |
| Harold Houghton | F | Everton Jun 1928 | 27 | 8 |
| Robert Kirk | W | Bristol City C/S 1927 | 2 | |
| Wilfred Lowton | FB | Heavitree United C/S 1924 | 36 | 5 |
| William McDevitt | HB | Liverpool C/S 1925 | 21 | 2 |
| Samuel Mason | HB | Gillingham C/S 1927 | 10 | |
| Charles Miller | FB | Plymouth Argyle C/S 1926 | 40 | |
| Arthur Phoenix | F | Barnsley C/S 1926 | 8 | |
| Robert Pollard | FB | Plank Lane C/S 1920 | 17 | |
| Alexander Pool | HB | Bristol City C/S 1926 | 24 | 1 |
| George Purcell | F | Swindon Town C/S 1926 | 42 | 8 |
| Alexander Sheffield | HB | Mansfield Town C/S 1928 | 12 | |
| Stanley Streets | HB | Clapton Orient C/S 1928 | 9 | 2 |
| James Taylor | HB | Droylsden C/S 1928 | 2 | |
| Edward Wade | F | New Brighton C/S 1928 | 9 | 5 |
| Own Goals | | | | 1 |

* Robert Kirk travelled with the Exeter City team for an overnight stay in Birmingham to play at Coventry City the following afternoon. But whilst his team mates attended a theatre performance on the Friday evening, Kirk boarded a train and headed off to his Glasgow home. This left the team a player short and Arthur Doncaster had to travel to Coventry, early on the day of the game, to make up the numbers. Kirk's contract was cancelled the following week.

* Winger William Death was signed by manager David Wilson from Sunderland. The deal was completed late Friday afternoon and the pair of them then boarded an overnight train arriving in Exeter at 9am the following morning. Death made his debut the same afternoon in a 2-0 home win over Northampton Town.

* The annual report for the Exeter City Football Club was issued for September 1928, and it showed a loss on the year's working up to and including 30th April 1928 of £226 0s 8d. Match receipts had risen to £14,239, however, wages had totalled £8,653 19s 6d and travelling cost £765. Hotel expenses accounted for £596.

* Supporters of both teams mixed freely and stood on the Big Bank, singing and playing bugles, when Plymouth Argyle visited St James' Park in October 1928. It was the first time that Argyle had visited Exeter since Plymouth had been bestowed the honour of becoming a 'city.'

* The Barking team left it late to arrive at St James' Park for their F.A. Cup first round tie against Exeter City. They left Paddington by train at 10.30am, arrived in Exeter at 1.25pm. The game kicked off 50 minutes later! Barking lost 6-0.

* When Exeter lost 7-2 at Walsall in December 1928, this was partly due to the fact that goalkeeper Thomas Holland had to leave the field injured., being replaced by outfield player, Wilf Lowton. At the time City were losing 1-0.

* Prior to their FA Cup third round tie at Exeter, the Leeds United officials and players stayed at the Rougemont Hotel in Exeter, attended a show at the Hippodrome, and on the morning of the match walked to the ground. The tie ended 2-2.

* With the team struggling in the league, City manager David Wilson resigned his position on 13th February 1929. It was decided to continue without a replacement for the time being with secretary Sidney Thomas taking on some of the managerial duties.

* The home match against Brighton and Hove Albion, due to be played on 16th February 1929, was called off at 2pm due to persistent heavy snowfalls. Secretary Sid Thomas said that he could not recall a first team fixture being postponed at St James' Park since the club turned professional in 1908.

* On 11th April 1929, the Directors of Exeter City F.C. announced that they had appointed club captain, Billy McDevitt, as player-manager. they said: "McDevitt has a very wide knowledge of the game and of its exponents in all parts of the country, and his knowledge should prove of material benefit to the Club."

* Exeter had to win their final match of the season at Swindon Town to avoid having to apply for re-election to the Football League. However, they slipped to a 2-0 defeat. But their home form had been a contributing factor to a poor season, with only seven victories in the 21 matches played.

* Half-back Sam Mason missed almost all of the season after suffering from a 'serious illness.' He had travelled to play at Gillingham in October 1928, but was taken ill on the Friday night. As a result he had to be taken 'home' to Exeter on the morning of the match to receive medical treatment.

Exeter City 1929-30
Back row: Alex Sheffield, Jimmy Gray, John Alderson, Robert Shanks,
Leslie Dennington
Front row: George Purcell, Harold Houghton, George Cyril Guyan,
Hemingway, Arthur Doncaster, John Ditchburn

**CITY PLAYING SQUAD 1929-30**

| Name Pos | Pos | Signed from | Apps | Gls |
|---|---|---|---|---|
| John Alderson | G | Sheffield United C/S 1929 | 36 | |
| William Armfield | W | Aston Villa C/S 1929 | 7 | 1 |
| Richard Baugh | FB | West Bromwich Albion May 1929 | 9 | |
| Reginald Clarke | HB | Southern Railway, Exeter C/S 1927 | 24 | |
| William Death | W | Sunderland Sep 1928 | 4 | 1 |
| Leslie Dennington | HB | Reading Nov 1928 | 30 | |
| John Ditchburn | HB | Sunderland C/S 1926 | 18 | |
| Arthur Doncaster | F | Bolton Wanderers C/S 1928 | 29 | 6 |
| James Gray | FB | Liverpool Jan 1930 | 20 | |
| John Gurkin | HB | Stalybridge Celtic C/S 1929 | 2 | |
| George Guyan | F | Connah's Quay Nomads Jun 1929 | 28 | 14 |
| Cyril Hemingway | F | Torquay United C/S 1929 | 39 | 19 |
| William Henderson | F | Torquay United C/S 1929 | 5 | |
| Thomas Holland | G | Weymouth C/S 1927 | 5 | |
| Harold Houghton | F | Everton Jun 1928 | 34 | 11 |
| George Howson | FB | Bath City C/S 1929 | 13 | |
| William McDevitt | HB | Liverpool C/S 1925 | 16 | |
| David McMullan | HB | Belfast Celtic May 1929 | 19 | |
| Samuel Mason | HB | Gillingham C/S 1927 | 23 | 1 |
| Charles Miller | FB | Plymouth Argyle C/S 1926 | 6 | |
| George Purcell | F | Swindon Town C/S 1926 | 40 | 12 |
| Robert Shanks | FB | Huddersfield Town C/S 1929 | 36 | 1 |
| Alexander Sheffield | HB | Mansfield Town C/S 1928 | 12 | |
| Alwyn Thomas | F | Torquay United C/S 1929 | 1 | |
| Percy Varco | F | Norwich City Feb 1930 | 6 | |
| Own Goals | | | | 1 |

**City's league results**

| | Home | Away |
|---|---|---|
| Bournemouth & B.A. | 1-2 | 0-3 |
| Brentford | 0-0 | 0-2 |
| Brighton & H.A. | 1-4 | 1-1 |
| Bristol Rovers | 5-2 | 0-1 |
| Clapton Orient | 4-0 | 0-3 |
| Coventry City | 1-1 | 3-3 |
| Crystal Palace | 6-1 | 1-1 |
| Fulham | 2-1 | 2-2 |
| Gillingham | 3-0 | 0-2 |
| Luton Town | 2-2 | 4-0 |
| Merthyr Town | 1-1 | 2-0 |
| Newport County | 0-4 | 1-4 |
| Northampton Town | 6-4 | 2-2 |
| Norwich City | 3-0 | 1-3 |
| Plymouth Argyle | 1-1 | 1-4 |
| Queens Park Rangers | 0-2 | 0-2 |
| Southend United | 0-1 | 3-1 |
| Swindon Town | 5-1 | 0-1 |
| Torquay United | 0-0 | 1-2 |
| Walsall | 0-2 | 2-5 |
| Watford | 1-0 | 1-2 |

**F.A. Cup**

| | | | |
|---|---|---|---|
| Walsall | A | R1 | 0-1 |

**CITY MANAGER 1929-30**
Billy McDevitt - Appointed April 1929

**FOOTBALL LEAGUE - DIVISION THREE SOUTH**

| | P | W | D | L | F | A | Pts |
|---|---|---|---|---|---|---|---|
| Plymouth Argyle | 42 | 30 | 8 | 4 | 98 | 38 | 68 |
| Brentford | 42 | 28 | 5 | 9 | 94 | 44 | 61 |
| Queens Park Rangers | 42 | 21 | 9 | 12 | 80 | 68 | 51 |
| Northampton Town | 42 | 21 | 8 | 13 | 82 | 58 | 50 |
| Brighton & H.A. | 42 | 21 | 8 | 13 | 87 | 63 | 50 |
| Coventry City | 42 | 19 | 9 | 14 | 88 | 73 | 47 |
| Fulham | 42 | 18 | 11 | 13 | 87 | 83 | 47 |
| Norwich City | 42 | 18 | 10 | 14 | 88 | 77 | 46 |
| Crystal Palace | 42 | 17 | 12 | 13 | 81 | 74 | 46 |
| Bournemouth & B.A. | 42 | 15 | 13 | 14 | 72 | 61 | 43 |
| Southend United | 42 | 15 | 13 | 14 | 69 | 59 | 43 |
| Clapton Orient | 42 | 14 | 13 | 15 | 55 | 62 | 41 |
| Luton Town | 42 | 14 | 12 | 16 | 64 | 78 | 40 |
| Swindon Town | 42 | 13 | 12 | 17 | 73 | 83 | 38 |
| Watford | 42 | 15 | 8 | 19 | 60 | 73 | 38 |
| Exeter City | 42 | 12 | 11 | 19 | 67 | 73 | 35 |
| Walsall | 42 | 13 | 8 | 21 | 71 | 78 | 34 |
| Newport County | 42 | 12 | 10 | 20 | 74 | 85 | 34 |
| Torquay United | 42 | 10 | 11 | 21 | 64 | 94 | 31 |
| Bristol Rovers | 42 | 11 | 8 | 23 | 67 | 93 | 30 |
| Gillingham | 42 | 11 | 8 | 23 | 51 | 80 | 30 |
| Merthyr Town | 42 | 6 | 9 | 27 | 60 | 135 | 21 |

* Prior to the season starting, Exeter City transferred their 17-year-old wing-sensation, Cliff Bastin to Arsenal for a fee of £2,000, easily a club record for someone so young. Indeed this was at a time when the English transfer fee record stood at £11,000.

* The City Directors were confident that the team would improve greatly on the previous season, when the club successfully applied for re-election to the Football League.

* As the match referee was about the start the game, he called for Exeter City goalkeeper John Alderson to change his white jersey as it clashed with the visiting Fulham players' shirts. Alderson changed into a crimson one.

* Winger Billy Death sustained a knee injury early in the season against Walsall, which proved to be cartilage trouble. He never played for City again. Injury also struck full-back Billy Armfield, who dislocated his shoulder in the match at Fulham. This required an operation and he too missed a large part of the season.

* What were described as 'disgraceful scenes' took place at the end of the Merthyr Town versus Exeter City fixture. The home supporters were most unhappy with the referee who had denied them a penalty and at the final whistle he was hit by a stone thrown from the crowd. City won 2-0.

* The Great Western Railway ran three excursion trains from Plymouth to Exeter for the City versus Argyle match at St James' Park on 1st March 1930. It was estimated that over 3,000 Argyle supporters were in the crowd of 16,000. Four supporters had climbed onto the roof of the covered terrace, but were asked to get down by the Police. The teams drew 1-1.

* Exeter City played a friendly match at Torquay United in March 1930 to help raise funds to assist the Plainmoor club to repair the grandstand which had been damaged in gale force winds. An attendance of 1,792 produced receipts of £77. The Grecians won the game, 3-0.

* Half-back David McMullan took over in goal for the injured John Alderson after just 20 minutes in the game at Clapton Orient. Alderson had collided with a post as Orient took the lead. The Grecians eventually went down 3-0.

* Former Exeter City goalkeeper and favourite, Dick Pym, travelled from his Bolton home to watch the Grecians defeat Northampton Town 6-4 in April 1930. Pym was on the injury list and jumped at the chance of returning to watch his former club. Cyril Hemingway netted four times for City.

* McMullan again played in goal for Exeter, but this time for the whole 90 minutes, when City lost 4-0 at home to Newport County on 26th April 1930. He had to play between the posts as both regular keepers Tom Holland and John Alderson were injured. McMullan decided not to wear gloves or a cap.

* As well as netting four times in the game against Northampton Town, Cyril Hemingway also recorded a hat-trick as he helped City to a 5-1 home win over Swindon Town earlier in the season. With eight goals in four matches at one stage, not surprisingly Hemingway was City's top scorer for the season.

* The lowest attendance of the season for a Third Division South fixture was 3,000 for the Merthyr Town versus Exeter City game. The lowest at St James' Park was 4,000 for the visits of Bournemouth and Boscombe Athletic and Fulham respectively.

* City had a run of five league matches without scoring towards the start of the season, going almost a month without hitting the back of the net.

## CITY PLAYING SQUAD 1930-31

| Name | Pos | Signed From | Apps | Gls |
|---|---|---|---|---|
| Jack Angus | HB | Scunthorpe & Lindsey C/S 1930 | 15 | |
| William Armfield | W | Aston Villa C/S 1929 | 34 | 9 |
| Stan Barber | HB | Bristol City C/S/ 1930 | 35 | 1 |
| Richard Baugh | FB | West Bromwich Albion May 1929 | 30 | 4 |
| Reg Clarke | HB | Southern Railway, Exeter, C/S 1927 | 31 | 1 |
| Frederick Courtney | W | South Molton C/S 1930 | 2 | |
| Arthur Davies | G | Everton C/S 1930 | 37 | |
| Leslie Dennington | HB | Reading Nov 1928 | 16 | |
| John Ditchburn | HB | Sunderland C/S 1926 | 14 | |
| Arthur Doncaster | W | Bolton Wanderers C/S 1928 | 32 | 10 |
| James Gray | FB | Liverpool Jan 1930 | 12 | |
| James Gumm | W | St James', Exeter, Apr 1931 | 1 | |
| William Halliday | F | Connahs Quay C/S 1930 | 6 | 1 |
| Harold Houghton | F | Everton Jun 1928 | 42 | 23 |
| William Inglis | HB | Reading C/S 1930 | 15 | |
| Frederick Jones | G | Manchester City C/S 1930 | 5 | |
| Robert Lister | W | West Ham United C/S 1930 | 8 | 1 |
| John McCosh | F | Queen of the South C/S 1930 | 1 | |
| Charles Miller | FB | Plymouth Argyle C/S 1926 | 37 | |
| Jacob Parsons | F | Accrington Stanley C/S 1930 | 3 | |
| George Purcell | F | Swindon Town C/S 1926 | 42 | 7 |
| Robert Shanks | FB | Huddersfield Town C/S 1929 | 5 | |
| Percy Varco | F | Norwich City Feb 1930 | 39 | 26 |
| Own Goals | | | | 2 |

## THIRD DIVISION SOUTH - 1930-31

| | P | W | D | L | F | A | Pts |
|---|---|---|---|---|---|---|---|
| Notts County | 42 | 24 | 11 | 7 | 97 | 46 | 59 |
| Crystal Palace | 42 | 22 | 7 | 13 | 107 | 71 | 51 |
| Brentford | 42 | 22 | 6 | 14 | 90 | 64 | 50 |
| Brighton & H.A. | 42 | 17 | 15 | 10 | 68 | 53 | 49 |
| Southend United | 42 | 22 | 5 | 15 | 76 | 60 | 49 |
| Northampton Town | 42 | 18 | 12 | 12 | 77 | 59 | 48 |
| Luton Town | 42 | 19 | 8 | 15 | 76 | 51 | 46 |
| Queens Park Rangers | 42 | 20 | 3 | 19 | 82 | 75 | 43 |
| Fulham | 42 | 18 | 7 | 17 | 77 | 75 | 43 |
| Bournemouth & B.A. | 42 | 15 | 13 | 14 | 72 | 73 | 43 |
| Torquay United | 42 | 17 | 9 | 16 | 80 | 84 | 43 |
| Swindon Town | 42 | 18 | 6 | 18 | 89 | 94 | 42 |
| EXETER CITY | 42 | 17 | 8 | 17 | 84 | 90 | 42 |
| Coventry City | 42 | 16 | 9 | 17 | 75 | 65 | 41 |
| Bristol Rovers | 42 | 16 | 8 | 18 | 75 | 92 | 40 |
| Gillingham | 42 | 14 | 10 | 18 | 61 | 76 | 38 |
| Walsall | 42 | 14 | 9 | 19 | 78 | 95 | 37 |
| Watford | 42 | 14 | 7 | 21 | 72 | 75 | 35 |
| Clapton Orient | 42 | 14 | 7 | 21 | 63 | 91 | 35 |
| Thames | 42 | 13 | 8 | 21 | 54 | 93 | 34 |
| Norwich City | 42 | 10 | 8 | 24 | 47 | 76 | 28 |
| Newport County | 42 | 11 | 6 | 25 | 69 | 111 | 28 |

\* What a strange season 1930-31 proved to be for Exeter City. Disappointment in the Third Division South, where the goals flowed for and against, but a monumental run in the FA Cup that took the Grecians to the quarter-final stage.

### City's league results

| | HOME | AWAY |
|---|---|---|
| Bournemouth & B.A. | 4-1 | 1-3 |
| Brentford | 4-0 | 1-2 |
| Brighton & H.A. | 2-2 | 2-3 |
| Bristol Rovers | 0-3 | 1-1 |
| Clapton Orient | 6-1 | 3-2 |
| Coventry City | 2-3 | 1-3 |
| Crystal Palace | 4-3 | 2-7 |
| Fulham | 3-2 | 2-4 |
| Gillingham | 3-0 | 5-3 |
| Luton Town | 1-1 | 1-3 |
| Newport County | 3-0 | 0-4 |
| Northampton Town | 3-3 | 0-1 |
| Norwich City | 1-0 | 2-1 |
| Notts County | 3-3 | 2-1 |
| Queens Park Rangers | 2-0 | 2-7 |
| Southend United | 1-1 | 1-5 |
| Swindon Town | 3-1 | 1-2 |
| Thames | 4-3 | 0-1 |
| Torquay United | 2-2 | 0-0 |
| Walsall | 2-5 | 1-2 |
| Watford | 2-1 | 1-0 |

### F.A. Cup

| | | | |
|---|---|---|---|
| Northfleet United | A | R1 | 3-0 |
| Coventry City | H | R2 | 1-1 |
| Coventry City | A | R2R | 2-1 |
| Derby County | H | R3 | 3-2 |
| Bury | A | R4 | 2-1 |
| Leeds United | H | R5 | 3-1 |
| Sunderland | A | R6 | 1-1 |
| Sunderland | H | R6R | 2-4 |

### CITY MANAGER 1930-31
Billy McDevitt - Appointed February 1929

* City sustained three heavy defeats in the league, 2-7 at Crystal Palace, and 2-7 at Queens Park Rangers. they also crashed 2-5 at home to Walsall. On the other hand they also stuck four goals past Bournemouth, Brentford, Crystal Palace, Thames, five against Gillingham and six against Clapton Orient!

* City endured one miserable run of away matches in November and December which saw them concede 16 goals in just four matches.

* It was in the FA Cup though that City excelled beyond their wildest dreams as they defeated Northfleet United, Coventry City (after a replay), Derby County, Bury and Leeds United, to face Sunderland at Roker Park in the quarter final. Amazingly they held the Wearsiders to a 1-1 draw.

* The replay back at St James' Park drew a club record attendance of 20,984 and on a very wet afternoon, Sunderland ended the City dream as they won 4-2.

* Cornishman Percy Varco top scored for City with 26 league goals. He had been signed the previous season from Norwich City. Varco was later to retire to Fowey in Cornwall where he became town Mayor.

* With the temperature soaring into the 80s at St James' Park, two spectators at the game against Norwich City in August 1930, were treated for heat stroke during the interval. They had been watching the match from the Big Bank. Buckets of water were provided throughout the ground for spectators to use.

* Highest attendance of the season for a league match at St James' Park was 8,000 for the visit of Torquay United in September 1930.

* East London club, Thames FC, made their first ever visit to St James' Park for a Third Division South fixture on 18th October 1930, Thames wore dark red and blue quartered shirts and white shorts, and were captained by former Plymouth Argyle favourite, Moses Russell.

* The Christmas Day fixtures drew good crowds, but it was mixed fortunes as far as Exeter City were concerned. The first team went down 4-0 at Newport County's Somerton Park ground before an attendance of 6,000. Meanwhile back at the Park, City reserves defeated Newport County reserves 7-0 in the Southern League, a game watched by 1,800.

* On the evening prior to the FA Cup third round meeting between Exeter City and Derby County, both teams attended a pantomime at the Theatre Royal, Exeter. Derby arrived at the ground on the day of the tie with sprays of lucky white heather. It didn't do them any good as they lost 3-2.

* The well known Exeter City Military Band entertained the crowd prior to all the Cup ties at St James' Park, with their most notable rendition being that of 'There's A Good Time Coming' - the title of which was used for a City Fanzine many years later.

* The coach driver who was conveying the Exeter City team to Gigg Lane, Bury for their FA Cup fourth round tie, went past the ground. After being told of his error by the City players, he shouted that he had decided to drive the team direct to Wembley!

* On the afternoon of the FA Cup quarter-final replay against Sunderland at St James' Park, many Exeter businesses closed for the duration of the game to allow their employees to see the match. Other firms made special arrangements so that as many workers as could be spared could attend the Park. Several schools in the city were closed for the afternoon.

CITY PLAYING SQUAD 1931-32

| Name | Pos | Signed from | Apps | Gls |
|------|-----|-------------|------|-----|
| John Angus | HB | Scunthorpe & Lindsey U C/S 1930 | 11 | |
| William Armfield | W | Aston Villa C/S/ 1929 | 31 | 4 |
| Stanley Barber | HB | Bristol City C/S 1930 | 42 | 4 |
| Richard Baugh | FB | West Bromwich Albion C/S 1929 | 14 | 1 |
| Stanley Bright | FB | Cullompton C/S 1929 | 1 | |
| Arthur Childs | HB | Hull City C/S 1931 | 28 | 1 |
| Reg Clarke | HB | Friernhay 1927 | 39 | 2 |
| Fred Courtney | W | South Molton C/S 1930 | 1 | |
| Arthur Davies | G | Everton C/S 1930 | 42 | |
| John Ditchburn | HB | Sunderland C/S 1928 | 2 | |
| Arthur Doncaster | F | Bolton Wanderers C/S 1928 | 41 | 8 |
| James Gray | FB | Liverpool Jan 1930 | 30 | |
| James Gumm | W | St James' C/S 1930 | 1 | |
| William Halliday | F | Connah's Quay C/S 1930 | 5 | |
| Harold Houghton | F | Everton Jun 1928 | 33 | 16 |
| Charles Miller | FB | Plymouth Argyle C/S 1926 | 40 | |
| George Purcell | F | Swindon Town C/S 1928 | 22 | 4 |
| Leslie Roberts | F | Manchester City Feb 1932 | 11 | 4 |
| Charles Robinson | HB | Blackpool C/S 1931 | 2 | |
| Percy Varco | F | Norwich City C/S 1930 | 36 | 16 |
| Fred Whitlow | F | Charlton Athletic C/S 1931 | 23 | 15 |
| William Woodward | F | Spennymoor United C/S 1931 | 7 | 2 |

*   The Express and Echo reported ...'The desirability of promotion for Exeter City has been stressed often and has been put in a nutshell by club secretary, Mr. S.H. Thomas, who pointed out that the slump in league attendances following the FA Cup ties of the previous season was a clear indication of the need for a new match programme of wider interest. He stated "We have got to follow Plymouth Argyle into the Second Division and the sooner the better," It is clear that there would be great enthusiasm if the Grecians fought their way into the Second Division in the same great hearted way in which they defeated some of the giants in the FA Cup last season.'

* When Exeter City visited The Nest, the home ground of Norwich City in November 1931, it was described as ...'a peculiarly shaped ground.'

* Prior to Exeter City's first practice match on 15th August 1931 it was reported .... 'Splendid entertainment was provided by the sports meeting held at the Park, by the Exeter City Athletic Club. 4,000 spectators enjoyed all the events in an excellent and varied programme of foot and cycle contests.'

* Harold Houghton had played for the Football Association XI on their tour of Canada during the summer of 1931.

City's league results

| | Home | Away |
|---|------|------|
| Bournemouth & B.A. | 1-0 | 2-5 |
| Brentford | 4-1 | 2-2 |
| Brighton & H.A. | 3-1 | 1-1 |
| Bristol Rovers | 1-0 | 4-2 |
| Cardiff City | 3-1 | 2-5 |
| Clapton Orient | 4-3 | 2-2 |
| Coventry City | 3-0 | 0-4 |
| Crystal Palace | 0-1 | 0-3 |
| Fulham | 0-3 | 1-3 |
| Gillingham | 4-0 | 1-0 |
| Luton Town | 1-1 | 3-6 |
| Mansfield Town | 3-0 | 1-3 |
| Northampton Town | 0-0 | 1-2 |
| Norwich City | 3-0 | 1-0 |
| Queens Park Rangers | 6-2 | 0-1* |
| Reading | 4-0 | 0-2 |
| Southend United | 3-0 | 1-0 |
| Swindon Town | 1-1 | 1-2 |
| Thames | 4-1 | 0-0 |
| Torquay United | 3-1 | 1-2 |
| Watford | 2-0 | 0-1 |

*Played at White City, London.

F.A. Cup
Grimsby Town          A R1       1-4

CITY MANAGER 1931-32
Billy McDevitt - Appointed April 1929

FOOTBALL LEAGUE - DIVISION THREE SOUTH

| | P | W | D | L | F | A | Pts |
|---|---|---|---|---|---|---|-----|
| Fulham | 42 | 24 | 9 | 9 | 111 | 62 | 57 |
| Reading | 42 | 23 | 9 | 10 | 97 | 67 | 55 |
| Southend United | 42 | 21 | 11 | 10 | 77 | 53 | 53 |
| Crystal Palace | 42 | 20 | 11 | 11 | 74 | 63 | 51 |
| Brentford | 42 | 19 | 10 | 13 | 68 | 52 | 48 |
| Luton Town | 42 | 20 | 7 | 15 | 95 | 70 | 47 |
| Exeter City | 42 | 20 | 7 | 15 | 77 | 62 | 47 |
| Brighton & H.A. | 42 | 17 | 12 | 13 | 73 | 58 | 46 |
| Cardiff City | 42 | 19 | 8 | 15 | 87 | 73 | 46 |
| Norwich City | 42 | 17 | 12 | 13 | 76 | 67 | 46 |
| Watford | 42 | 19 | 8 | 15 | 81 | 79 | 46 |
| Coventry City | 42 | 18 | 8 | 16 | 108 | 97 | 44 |
| Queens Park Rangers | 42 | 15 | 12 | 15 | 79 | 73 | 42 |
| Northampton Town | 42 | 16 | 7 | 19 | 69 | 69 | 39 |
| Bournemouth & B.A. | 42 | 13 | 12 | 17 | 70 | 78 | 38 |
| Clapton Orient | 42 | 12 | 11 | 19 | 77 | 90 | 35 |
| Swindon Town | 42 | 14 | 6 | 22 | 70 | 84 | 34 |
| Bristol Rovers | 42 | 13 | 8 | 21 | 65 | 92 | 34 |
| Torquay United | 42 | 12 | 9 | 21 | 72 | 106 | 33 |
| Mansfield Town | 42 | 11 | 10 | 21 | 75 | 108 | 32 |
| Gillingham | 42 | 10 | 8 | 24 | 40 | 82 | 28 |
| Thames | 42 | 7 | 9 | 26 | 53 | 109 | 23 |

* The match between Exeter City and Brighton & Hove Albion kicked off at 5.30pm, instead of the advertised 5.40pm start. The half-time interval was also dispensed with and teams 'turned straight around' for the second half. This was to avoid the game being abandoned due to bad light. City won 3-1.

* Queen's Park Rangers kicked off a player short when they visited Exeter on 17th October, Lewis, their inside forward, having missed the train from Paddington. He caught a later train and eventually took to the field four minutes after the game had started.

* Former Exeter City winger, Cliff Bastin, won his first full England cap when he played against Wales on 18th November 1931. The match was played at Liverpool's Anfield ground with England winning 3-1.

* Prior to Exeter City's F.A. Cup tie at Grimsby Town, several of the players walked to see the 'famous' Grimsby Fish Market, and one seller told them: "If your team is as good as our fish, then you will win the Cup!" City lost 4-1, so the fish must have been better than the team. However, pre-match, the City players had eaten oysters sent to them by local tradesmen.

* The Grecians visited the White City Stadium in London for the first time when they played against Queens Park Rangers on 27th February 1932. Although it had a capacity of 129,000, only 14,000 were present for the game which Rangers won 1-0.

* For the game at Swindon Town on Easter Saturday, forward Fred Whitlow asked to be 'rested' as he was suffering from a lack of confidence. Percy Varco took his place and scored in the 2-1 defeat.

* Full-back George Purcell was granted a benefit match by Exeter City and Plymouth Argyle provided the opposition at St James' Park on 2nd May 1932. Argyle won 4-2 before an attendance of 3,000.

* After the final match of the season the following appeared in the Express and Echo newspaper:- 'In the mind of the true soccer follower, the game never sleeps. It may doze off for a few minutes now and again, but on the cricket field and lawn tennis courts quite a lot of discussion will take place this summer as to how Exeter City missed promotion in the campaign of 1931-32.'

* In May 1932, Exeter City announced that they hoped to raise £5,000 which would pay to cover the 'popular bank' terracing, and also to help pay the summer wages.

* Two City players netted hat-tricks during the course of the season. Fred Whitlow netted three goals against Queen's Park Rangers in a 6-2 home win, and in the previous game, Percy Varco scored three in 3-1 victory against Cardiff City.

* The highest attendance of the season at St James' Park was 14,000 who were at the Boxing Day game against Southend United. The highest attendance away was 20,000 who were at Reading's Elm Park to see them beat the Grecians 2-0.

* City were beaten on just two occasions at home in Third Division South matches. Divisional champions Fulham won 3-0 in the first match of the season played at St James' Park, whilst Crystal Palace were 1-0 winners in the last league match of the season at the Park.

| CITY PLAYING SQUAD 1932-33 Apps Gls | | | | |
|---|---|---|---|---|
| Name | Pos | Signed from | Apps | Gls |
| John Angus | HB | Scunthorpe & Lindsey U C/S 1930 | 11 | 1 |
| Stanley Barber | HB | Bristol City C/S 1930 | 36 | 4 |
| Arthur Childs | HB | Hull City C/S 1931 | 30 | 3 |
| Reg Clarke | HB | Friernhay 1927 | 42 | 2 |
| Michael Connaboy | F | Wolverhampton Wanderers C/S 1932 | 4 | 1 |
| Arthur Davies | G | Everton C/S 1930 | 42 | |
| James Gray | FB | Liverpool Jan 1930 | 36 | |
| James GumM | W | St James' C/S 1930 | 2 | |
| Andrew Higgins | F | Millwall C/S 1932 | 22 | 9 |
| Harold Houghton | F | Everton Jun 1928 | 42 | 13 |
| Richard Hughes | FB | Bristol City C/S 1932 | 13 | |
| Stanley Hurst | W | Tipton St John Oct 1932 | 8 | |
| John Kennedy | F | Tranmere Rovers C/S 1932 | 15 | 3 |
| Charles Miller | FB | Plymouth Argyle C/S 1926 | 35 | |
| Henry Poulter | F | Sunderland C/S 1932 | 11 | 5 |
| Charles Robinson | HB | Blackpool C/S 1931 | 6 | |
| John Scott | W | Northampton Town C/S 1932 | 37 | 7 |
| Harold Webb | W | Fulham Mar 1933 | 5 | 1 |
| Arthur Welsby | W | Sunderland C/S 1932 | 27 | 5 |
| Fred Whitlow | F | Charlton Athletic C/S 1931 | 32 | 33 |
| Frank Wrightson | F | Fulham Mar 1933 | 6 | 1 |

| City's league results | | |
|---|---|---|
| | Home | Away |
| Aldershot | 0-0 | 1-4 |
| Bournemouth & B.A. | 2-3 | 1-1 |
| Brentford | 1-2 | 2-0 |
| Brighton & H.A. | 4-1 | 1-2 |
| Bristol City | 2-0 | 1-0 |
| Bristol Rovers | 1-0 | 0-1 |
| Cardiff City | 1-0 | 3-1 |
| Clapton Orient | 3-0 | 2-2 |
| Coventry City | 5-0 | 0-4 |
| Crystal Palace | 1-1 | 2-2 |
| Gillingham | 2-1 | 2-1 |
| Luton Town | 2-0 | 0-4 |
| Newport County | 4-0 | 1-1 |
| Northampton Town | 3-1 | 3-5 |
| Norwich City | 2-1 | 0-0 |
| Queens Park Rangers | 2-0 | 3-1 |
| Reading | 4-1 | 2-2 |
| Southend United | 3-0 | 2-1 |
| Swindon Town | 5-0 | 2-2 |
| Torquay United | 5-0 | 3-1 |
| Watford | 5-2 | 0-0 |

| F.A. Cup | | | |
|---|---|---|---|
| Southend United | A | R1 | 1-1 |
| Southend United | H | R1R | 0-1 |

| CITY MANAGER 1932-33 |
|---|
| Billy McDevitt - Appointed April 1929 |

* It was reported that there had been 'tremendous alterations' at Somerton Park since their last visit, when Exeter City travelled to Newport County in October 1932. The ground was under control of a greyhound racing syndicate and they had started work on both grandstands. A special train excursion had brought City supporters for the game.

* When Exeter City travelled to Bournemouth and Boscombe Athletic in February 1933, their journey was described thus:- 'The Exeter City team travelled by motor coach amid Christmas card scenes, the snow lying thick in the higher parts of East Devon and West Dorset, but although the weather was cold and raw, the pitch at Bournemouth was, however, sodden with rain.'

* Two players were signed on the same day from Fulham in March 1933 to assist with the club's drive for promotion. It was reported that the signing of Harold Webb and Frank Wrightson would 'dispel all doubts as to the club's attitude in regard to promotion, as they were acquired at a transfer fee which easily forms a record payment in the history of the Grecians.',

* When second placed Exeter City entertained top of the table, Norwich City, at St James' Park on 1st April 1933, the match referee was Mr. W. Harper, who had taken charge of the previous seasons FA Cup Final, a match in which there was controversy over an incident proceeding one of the Newcastle United goals. No controversy at St James' Park, Exeter though, as City won 2-1 before an attendance of 15,000.

FOOTBALL LEAGUE - DIVISION THREE SOUTH

| | P | W | D | L | F | A | Pts |
|---|---|---|---|---|---|---|---|
| Brentford | 42 | 26 | 10 | 4 | 90 | 49 | 62 |
| Exeter City | 42 | 24 | 10 | 8 | 88 | 48 | 58 |
| Norwich City | 42 | 22 | 13 | 7 | 88 | 55 | 57 |
| Reading | 42 | 19 | 13 | 10 | 103 | 71 | 51 |
| Crystal Palace | 42 | 19 | 8 | 15 | 78 | 64 | 46 |
| Coventry City | 42 | 19 | 6 | 17 | 106 | 77 | 44 |
| Gillingham | 42 | 18 | 8 | 16 | 72 | 61 | 44 |
| Northampton Town | 42 | 18 | 8 | 16 | 76 | 66 | 44 |
| Bristol Rovers | 42 | 15 | 14 | 13 | 61 | 56 | 44 |
| Torquay United | 42 | 16 | 12 | 14 | 72 | 67 | 44 |
| Watford | 42 | 16 | 12 | 14 | 66 | 63 | 44 |
| Brighton & H.A. | 42 | 17 | 8 | 17 | 66 | 65 | 42 |
| Southend United | 42 | 15 | 11 | 16 | 65 | 82 | 41 |
| Luton Town | 42 | 13 | 13 | 16 | 78 | 78 | 39 |
| Bristol City | 42 | 12 | 13 | 17 | 83 | 90 | 37 |
| Queens Park Rangers | 42 | 13 | 11 | 18 | 72 | 87 | 37 |
| Aldershot | 42 | 13 | 10 | 19 | 61 | 72 | 36 |
| Bournemouth & B.A. | 42 | 12 | 12 | 18 | 60 | 81 | 36 |
| Cardiff City | 42 | 12 | 7 | 23 | 69 | 99 | 31 |
| Clapton Orient | 42 | 8 | 13 | 21 | 59 | 93 | 29 |
| Newport County | 42 | 11 | 7 | 24 | 61 | 105 | 29 |
| Swindon Town | 42 | 9 | 11 | 22 | 60 | 105 | 29 |

* The popular bank terrace was completely roofed over during the summer months, to 'provide cover for the shilling supporters.' With one whole side of the ground now under cover, St James' Park was described as 'the cosiest as well as the most compact and convenient arena in the Third Division.'

* Prior to the season commencing the Express and Echo reviewed the forthcoming season and stated: 'Men of fine physique and considerable experience and skill are now engaged to take the vacant positions at Exeter City and the impression is that the Grecians have strengthened their first eleven.'

* On seeing the playing surface at Queen's Park Rangers White City Stadium, Exeter City goalkeeper Arthur Davies said: "It would be a pleasure to beat any team on a ground like this." City did just that, winning 3-1. Although the huge ground looked empty with only 2,500 spectators present.

* With a 5-0 home win over Torquay United, Exeter City went to the top of the Third Division South table on 28th January 1933, with 36 points from the 25 matches played.

* Losing 4-0 at Luton Town on 11th February, this was Exeter City's first defeat for over two months, as their fine form had elevated them into real promotion contenders.

* The City players had to change on the train for their match at Reading, their journey being greatly delayed by 'a mishap on the line.' At Reading West station the officials and players took taxi's to Elm Park to just make the kick off time. Despite the unsatisfactory build-up to the game, City drew 2 -2.

* It was reported in April 1933, that former Exeter City favourite, Percy Varco, would not play football again following an injury whilst appearing for Brighton and Hove Albion. Varco returned to his home town of Fowey in Cornwall, where he later became Mayor.

* The Grecians made their first ever visit to Aldershot on 22nd April 1933. The Shots had previously played in the London Combination. Their ground was stated to have had flower beds behind both goals, giving a picturesque appearance.

* A benefit game for full-back Charlie Miller was played against Plymouth Argyle on 1st May 1933. City won 3-2 before an attendance of 3,000, which it was reported, raised £100.

* Requiring one point to secure the runners-up spot in the Third Division South, City travelled to Southend United for their last match of the season, and duly won 2-1.

* Exeter City had enjoyed their best ever season since joining The Football League in 1920. It was only the third occasion that they had finished in the top half of the table.


* The Express and Echo reported: 'League eminence was rarely gained by the Grecians in former years. Exeter City were a rough team and everyone knew it.'

* Fred Whitlow's scoring feats were phenomenal, especially as he didn't play regularly until October. His tally of 33 goals in 32 starts included hat tricks against Watford, Reading, Southend United, Swindon Town and Newport County.

* The highest attendance of the season at St James' Park was 15,000 for the visit of Norwich City. The best 'on the road' was 16,000 when City visited Brentford.

* It was a good season all round for Exeter City as the reserves won the Championship of the Western League and were also runners-up to Bath City in the Southern League.

Exeter City 1933-34
Back row: Reg Clarke, Dick Hughes, Arthur Davies, Reg Loram
(Trainer), Charlie Miller, Jack Angus
Front row: Jack Scott, Stan Risdon, Stan Hurst, Frank Wrightson,
Jack Barnes, Harry Webb

### CITY PLAYING SQUAD 1933-34

| Name | Pos | Signed from | Apps | Gls |
|---|---|---|---|---|
| John Angus | HB | Scunthorpe & Lindsey U C/S 1930 | 25 | |
| Stanley Barber | HB | Bristol City C/S 1930 | 5 | 1 |
| James Barnes | W | Watford C/S 1933 | 18 | 1 |
| Ronald Boundy | F | Wallasey Oct 1933 | 2 | |
| Arthur Chesters | G | Manchester United C/S 1933 | 9 | |
| Arthur Childs | HB | Hull City C/S 1931 | 4 | |
| Reg Clarke | HB | Friernhay 1927 | 41 | 2 |
| Arthur Davies | G | Everton C/S 1930 | 33 | |
| James Gray | FB | Liverpool Jan 1930 | 41 | |
| James Gumm | W | St James' C/S 1930 | 1 | |
| Alexander Hardie | HB | Plymouth Argyle Oct 1933 | 18 | 1 |
| Harold Houghton | F | Everton Jun 1928 | 29 | 8 |
| Richard Hughes | FB | Bristol City C/S 1932 | 13 | |
| Stanley Hurst | W | Tipton St John Oct 1932 | 34 | 14 |
| Frederick Jasper | W | Budleigh Salterton C/S 1933 | 1 | |
| John Kennedy | F | Tranmere Rovers C/S 1932 | 1 | |
| Charles Miller | FB | Plymouth Argyle C/S 1926 | 28 | |
| Henry Poulter | F | Sunderland C/S 1932 | 11 | 9 |
| Stanley Risdon | HB | Tipton St John C/S 1932 | 8 | 1 |
| John Scott | W | Northampton Town C/S 1932 | 28 | 3 |
| William Smith | FB | Norwich City C/S 1933 | 3 | |
| Thomas Walters | F | Crystal Palace C/S 1933 | 6 | 4 |
| Harold Webb | | Fulham Mar 1933 | 35 | |
| Arthur Welsby | W | Sunderland C/S 1932 | 12 | 3 |
| Fred Whitlow | F | Charlton Athletic C/S 1931 | 28 | 13 |
| Frank Wrightson | F | Fulham Mar 1933 | 28 | 8 |

\* All was not well on the player front just a week prior to the new
season. Forward Harold Houghton was due a benefit and would
not re-sign for the club until he was guaranteed a set amount.
The mater was not resolved until after the season had started.
And a week before the first game, long serving full-back and
captain Charlie Miller had his transfer request granted.

### City's league results

| | Home | Away |
|---|---|---|
| Aldershot | 0-0 | 2-0 |
| Boumemouth & B.A. | 4-0 | 3-1 |
| Brighton & H.A. | 3-0 | 0-2 |
| Bristol City | 2-0 | 1-1 |
| Bristol Rovers | 0-0 | 1-1 |
| Cardiff City | 4-0 | 1-2 |
| Charlton Athletic | 2-0 | 1-4 |
| Clapton Orient | 0-3 | 0-4 |
| Coventry City | 1-0 | 3-1 |
| Crystal Palace | 1-2 | 0-0 |
| Gillingham | 2-0 | 1-1 |
| Luton Town | 4-2 | 2-3 |
| Newport County | 1-1 | 0-1 |
| Northampton Town | 0-2 | 3-5 |
| Norwich City | 3-4 | 1-1 |
| Queens Park Rangers | 1-1 | 0-2 |
| Reading | 4-1 | 1-3 |
| Southend United | 2-0 | 1-3 |
| Swindon Town | 2-2 | 1-1 |
| Torquay United | 4-0 | 2-0 |
| Watford | 3-1 | 0-2 |

### F.A. Cup

| | | | |
|---|---|---|---|
| Northampton Town | A | R1 | 1-2 |

### Third Division South Cup

| | | | |
|---|---|---|---|
| Crystal Palace | H | R1 | 11-6 |
| Watford | H | R2 | 4-2 |
| Coventry City | H | R3 | 1-1 |
| Coventry City | A | R3R | 1-0 |
| Brighton & H.A. | A* | SF | 1-1 |
| Brighton & H.A. | H | SFR | 1-1 |
| Brighton & H.A. | A | SF2R | 4-3 |
| Torquay United | A+ | F | 1-0 |

\* Played at Craven Cottage, Fulham
+ Played at Home Park, Plymouth Argyle

### CITY MANAGER 1933-34
Billy McDevitt - Appointed April 1929

### FOOTBALL LEAGUE - DIVISION THREE SOUTH

| | P | W | D | L | F | A | Pts |
|---|---|---|---|---|---|---|---|
| Norwich City | 42 | 25 | 11 | 6 | 88 | 49 | 61 |
| Coventry City | 42 | 21 | 12 | 9 | 100 | 54 | 54 |
| Reading | 42 | 21 | 12 | 9 | 82 | 50 | 54 |
| Queen's Park Rangers | 42 | 24 | 6 | 12 | 70 | 51 | 54 |
| Charlton Athletic | 42 | 22 | 8 | 12 | 83 | 56 | 52 |
| Luton Town | 42 | 21 | 10 | 11 | 83 | 61 | 52 |
| Bristol Rovers | 42 | 20 | 11 | 11 | 77 | 47 | 51 |
| Swindon Town | 42 | 17 | 11 | 14 | 64 | 68 | 45 |
| Exeter City | 42 | 16 | 11 | 15 | 68 | 57 | 43 |
| Brighton & H.A. | 42 | 15 | 13 | 14 | 68 | 60 | 43 |
| Clapton Orient | 42 | 16 | 10 | 16 | 75 | 69 | 42 |
| Crystal Palace | 42 | 16 | 9 | 17 | 71 | 67 | 41 |
| Northampton Town | 42 | 14 | 12 | 16 | 71 | 78 | 40 |
| Aldershot | 42 | 13 | 12 | 17 | 52 | 71 | 38 |
| Watford | 42 | 15 | 7 | 20 | 71 | 63 | 37 |
| Southaned United | 42 | 12 | 10 | 20 | 51 | 74 | 34 |
| Gillingham | 42 | 11 | 11 | 20 | 75 | 96 | 33 |
| Newport County | 42 | 8 | 17 | 17 | 49 | 70 | 33 |
| Bristol City | 42 | 10 | 13 | 19 | 58 | 85 | 33 |
| Torquay United | 42 | 13 | 7 | 22 | 53 | 93 | 33 |
| Bournemouth & B.A. | 42 | 9 | 9 | 24 | 60 | 102 | 27 |
| Cardiff City | 42 | 9 | 6 | 27 | 57 | 105 | 24 |

* One City player who did have a benefit match was half-back Reg Clarke, Exeter City entertained First Division Leicester City and won 3-2 before an attendance of 6,000.

* Exeter City were top of the Third Division South prior to their visit to Cardiff City on 23rd September 1933, a game they lost 2-1.

* Stanley Rous, later to become Sir Stanley Rous, was the referee for the City versus Queens Park Rangers match on 30th September 1930. The former St Luke's College, Exeter student, was a sports master in a school in Watford and also the Secretary of the Isthmian League.

* Two Exeter City players, John Kennedy and Thomas Walters, made the move to Torquay United on the same day in November 1933.

* The famous amateur club, Corinthians, visited St James' Park to play a friendly against Exeter City on 13th January 1934. The Grecians proved too strong for them though as they ran out 6-1 winners before an attendance of 5,000.

* There was an amazing game at St James' Park in the first round of the Third Division South Cup between Exeter City and Crystal Palace, which produced 17 goals! City won 11-6 with Fred Whitlow scoring six times. City led 4-1 at half-time.

* Goalkeeper Arthur Davies missed his first league match for three years when he was replaced by Arthur Chesters for the visit to Bournemouth & Boscombe Athletic on 27th January 1934.

* Harold Houghton was transferred by Exeter City to Norwich City in March 1934, and then made his debut for his new club at home against the Grecians in a 1-1 draw. Part of the transfer deal involved William Smith moving to Exeter from Norwich.

* John 'Jock' Ditchburn enjoyed a benefit match at St James' Park when Exeter City drew 5-5 with Notts County on 30th April 1934.

* Exeter City became the first ever winners of the Third Division South Cup when a goal from Stan Hurst gave them a 1-0 victory over Torquay United. The Final was played at Home Park, Plymouth before an attendance of 6,198. The cup was presented to captain, Reg Clarke, by the Chairman of Crystal Palace Football Club, Louis Bellattie.

* Three days after the Third Division South Cup Final, Exeter and Torquay met again in the final league match of the season at Plainmoor. Hurst scored two more goals as the Grecians won 2-0 before an attendance of 4,000,

* After his prolific goalscoring feat of the previous season, Fred Whitlow managed 13 in 28 games this time around. He suffered a thigh injury towards the end of the season and as a result missed a number of matches.

* Whitlow was the only City player to register a hat-trick in a league match during the season in the 3-0 home win over Brighton and Hove Albion.

* Highest attendance of the season at St. James' Park was 10,000 who saw a goalless encounter between Exeter City and Bristol Rovers.

* There was disappointment with the final league position after the City had ended the previous season as runners-up. The Grecians' form tailed off badly from February onwards with only two wins in the final fifteen matches.

Back row: Joseph. McClure, M. Lock, Dudley Lewis, F.P. Nichols (Director), Arthur Chesters, Billy McDevitt (Manager), Charlie Miller, Sidney Thomas (Secretary), Edward Keefe, Reg Clarke.
Middle row: J. Lake (Director), E.Edwards (Trainer), Fred Wrightson, Harry Poulter, Jack Angus. Harold Webb, Arthur Davies, William Smith, John Dryden, Fred Jasper, E. Head (Director), Reg Loram (Asst. Trainer), Captain Hunter (Director).
Front row: H. Greenaway (Groundsman), Stan Risdon, Jimmy Gray, Stan Hurst, M.J. McGahey (Chairman), Edward McArthur, Cornelius Tierney, Samuel Dudley, 'Jazzo' (Club Mascot).

## CITY'S LEAGUE RESULTS

|  | Home | Away |
|---|---|---|
| Aldershot | 8-1 | 0-0 |
| Bournemouth & B.A. | 4-1 | 2-3 |
| Brighton & Hove Albion | 3-1 | 0-6 |
| Bristol City | 3-0 | 0-2 |
| Bristol Rovers | 2-2 | 5-5 |
| Cardiff City | 2-1 | 0-5 |
| Charlton Athletic | 3-1 | 0-1 |
| Clapton Orient | 1-1 | 3-0 |
| Coventry City | 2-0 | 1-1 |
| Crystal Palace | 0-6 | 1-0 |
| Gillingham | 2-0 | 1-2 |
| Luton Town | 1-2 | 0-4 |
| Millwall | 0-1 | 0-1 |
| Newport County | 0-1 | 3-1 |
| Northampton Town | 3-0 | 1-2 |
| Queens Park Rangers | 3-0 | 1-1 |
| Reading | 2-3 | 0-2 |
| Southend United | 4-3 | 2-1 |
| Swindon Town | 3-3 | 1-6 |
| Torquay United | 1-1 | 0-3 |
| Watford | 1-1 | 1-0 |

### F.A. Cup

| Charlton Athletic | A | R1 | 2-2 |
|---|---|---|---|
| Charlton Athletic | H | R1R | 5-2 |
| Yeovil & Petters United | A | R2 | 1-4 |

### Third Division South Cup

| Aldershot | H | R1 | 4-0 |
|---|---|---|---|
| Millwall | H | R2 | 5-0 |
| Bristol Rovers | A | SF | 1-3 |

CITY MANAGER 1934-35
Billy McDevitt - Appointed February 1929

## CITY PLAYING SQUAD

| Name | Pos | Signed From | Apps | Gls |
|---|---|---|---|---|
| Jack Angus | HB | Scunthorpe & Lindsey United C/s 1930 | 40 | |
| Hiley Bamsey | HB | Woodbury Apr 1935 | 1 | |
| Arthur Chesters | G | Manchester United C/S 1933 | 31 | |
| Reg Clarke | HB | Southern Railway, Exeter C/S 1927 | 25 | |
| Arthur Davies | G | Everton C/S 1930 | 11 | |
| John Dryden | W | Newcastle United C/S 1934 | 20 | 5 |
| Samuel Dudley | F | Chelsea C/S 1934 | 8 | 1 |
| Jimmy Gray | FB | Liverpool Jan 1930 | 41 | |
| Stan Hurst | W | Tipton St John Apr 1932 | 31 | 8 |
| Edward Keefe | HB | Exminster C/S 1931 | 2 | |
| Dudley Lewis | HB | Bristol Rovers C/S 1934 | 16 | 2 |
| Edward McArthur | F | Middlesbrough C/S 1934 | 15 | 5 |
| Joseph McClure | HB | Brentford C/S 1934 | 5 | |
| Charlie Miller | FB | Plymouth Argyle C/S 1926 | 30 | |
| Henry Poulter | F | Sunderland C/S 1932 | 26 | 16 |
| Stan Risdon | HB | Tipton St John C/S 1932 | 14 | |
| John Scott | W | Northampton Town C/S 1932 | 41 | 7 |
| Thomas Scott | F | Norwich City C/S 1934 | 11 | 3 |
| William Smith | FB | Norwich City C/S 1934 | 10 | |
| Cornelius Tierney | F | Guildford City C/S 1934 | 18 | 1 |
| Harold Webb | HB | Fulham C/S 1933 | 29 | 4 |
| Frank Wrightson | F | Fulham C/S 1933 | 37 | 16 |
| own Goals | | | | 2 |

## THIRD DIVISION SOUTH 1934-35

|  | P | W | D | L | F | A | Pts |
|---|---|---|---|---|---|---|---|
| Charlton Athletic | 42 | 27 | 7 | 8 | 103 | 52 | 61 |
| Reading | 42 | 21 | 11 | 10 | 89 | 65 | 53 |
| Coventry City | 42 | 21 | 9 | 12 | 86 | 50 | 51 |
| Luton Town | 42 | 19 | 12 | 11 | 92 | 60 | 50 |
| Crystal Palace | 42 | 19 | 9 | 14 | 76 | 49 | 47 |
| Watford | 42 | 19 | 9 | 14 | 76 | 49 | 47 |
| Northampton Town | 42 | 19 | 8 | 15 | 65 | 67 | 46 |
| Bristol Rovers | 42 | 17 | 10 | 15 | 73 | 77 | 44 |
| Brighton & Hove Albion | 42 | 17 | 9 | 16 | 69 | 62 | 43 |
| Torquay United | 42 | 18 | 6 | 18 | 81 | 75 | 42 |
| EXETER CITY | 42 | 16 | 9 | 17 | 70 | 75 | 41 |
| Millwall | 42 | 17 | 7 | 18 | 57 | 62 | 41 |
| Queens Park Rangers | 42 | 16 | 9 | 17 | 63 | 72 | 41 |
| Clapton Orient | 42 | 15 | 10 | 17 | 65 | 65 | 40 |
| Bristol City | 42 | 15 | 9 | 18 | 52 | 68 | 39 |
| Swindon Town | 42 | 13 | 12 | 17 | 67 | 78 | 38 |
| Bournemouth & B.A. | 42 | 15 | 7 | 20 | 54 | 71 | 37 |
| Aldershot | 42 | 13 | 10 | 19 | 50 | 75 | 36 |
| Cardiff City | 42 | 13 | 9 | 20 | 62 | 82 | 35 |
| Gillingham | 42 | 11 | 13 | 18 | 55 | 75 | 35 |
| Southend United | 42 | 11 | 9 | 22 | 65 | 78 | 31 |
| Newport County | 42 | 10 | 5 | 27 | 54 | 112 | 25 |

* Having finished the previous season in 9th place, as well as winning the Third Division South Cup, Exeter City entered the 1934-35 campaign full of optimism, but had to make do with a mid-table finish once more, although they did reach the semi-final stage of the Third Division Cup.

* They ended the season in style with a club record league victory, 8-1, at home to Aldershot, with goals from Harry Poulter (3), John Scott, John Dryden, Edward McArthur, Frank Wrightson and a Summerbee own goal. Poulter had also netted a hat-trick in the 3-0 win at Clapton Orient earlier in the season.

* There were also three heavy defeats during the course of the season losing 6-0 at Brighton and Hove Albion, 6-0 at home to Crystal Palace and 6-1 at Swindon Town to show what an inconsistent season it was for the Grecians. They had a run of 8 matches without a win, followed by just two defeats in the next 12!

* The highest attendance of the season at St James' Park for a league match was 9,000 for the visit of Watford. The highest away league attendance was 15,000 who were at Crystal Palace.

* At the start of the season, it was stated in the Express and Echo newspaper: 'Professional football is more commercialised than it used to be before the war, yet the sporting aspects remain, and will no doubt continue to do so.'

* City half-back Edward Keefe rescued a woman from drowning in the Exeter Canal in October 1934, and as a result was awarded the Royal Humane Society's certificate in recognition of his brave action. Keefe had been on his way to St James' Park for training, when he dived in and brought the woman to safety.

* The Grecians lost 2-0 at Plymouth Argyle in April 1935, the match being staged as a benefit for Plymouth Albion Rugby Union Club. The attendance was 3, 000.

* A further benefit match was played for City full-back Jimmy Gray on 1st May 1935. This was against Gray's former club, Liverpool who ran out 3-1 winners, before an attendance of 5,000.

* Music from the B.B.C. was played to spectators for the first time at St James' Park on the visit of Reading in October 1934. This brought a mixed reaction as many said they missed the military bandsmen under the musical leadership of George Newman, who had provided pre-match entertainment for so many years.

* The 5-5 draw at Bristol Rovers in a Third Division South fixture in November 1934 was described as being one of the most amazing and sensational matches ever seen at Eastville.

* The evening prior to Exeter's F.A. Cup first round tie at Charlton Athletic, saw the City directors and players attend a show at the Holborn Empire in London. On the day of the match, which ended 2-2, sirens could be heard from steamers and other craft on the nearby River Thames indicating that thick fog meant tricky conditions for all concerned.

* Trainer Ernie Head took charge of the City first team for the match at Clapton Orient, which ended in a 3-0 win for the Grecians. Manager Billy McDevitt travelled with the City players on the train to Paddington, but then left them there to go off on a scouting mission.

* The final of the Devon Senior Cup, first won by Tavistock in 1890, was staged at St James' Park for the first time in April 1935. Appropriately, Exeter-based Friernhay won the Cup, as they defeated Bideford 1-0.

Back row: Doug Livingstone (Trainer), Tom Dixon, Jack Angus, Henry Poulter, Thomas Scott, Clifford Kirk, Robert Robinson, Arthur Chesters, Wilf Lowton, Charles Miller, Reg Loram (Assistant Trainer), James Dunn

Front row: John Scott, James Gray, Stan Hurst, Keith Richards, Billy McDevitt (Manager), Peter McArdle, C. Cannan, John Fantham, Stan Risdon, Tom McLean.

Sitting on ground: Edward McArthur, Reg Clarke

\* A crowd of around 4,000 attended a special 'Exhibition Match' between Exeter City and Plymouth Argyle played on the ground of Barnstaple Town on 29th April 1936. It was the first time that the two professional teams had met in North Devon., arranged in aid of funds for the Devon County Football Association. Argyle won 4-2, with Dick Ebdon and Tom Scott netting for City.

## CITY'S LEAGUE RESULTS

| | Home | Away |
|---|---|---|
| Aldershot 5-1 | 5-1 | 0-3 |
| Bournemouth & B.A. | 1-3 | 1-1 |
| Brighton & Hove Albion | 3-3 | 1-3 |
| Bristol City | 0-1 | 1-2 |
| Bristol Rovers | 3-1 | 1-6 |
| Cardiff City | 2-0 | 2-5 |
| Clapton Orient | 2-3 | 2-1 |
| Coventry City | 1-3 | 0-3 |
| Crystal Palace | 1-0 | 2-2 |
| Gillingham | 2-5 | 2-2 |
| Luton Town | 1-2 | 1-3 |
| Millwall | 4-3 | 2-2 |
| Newport County | 3-3 | 1-2 |
| Northampton Town | 3-1 | 1-1 |
| Notts County | 0-0 | 1-3 |
| Queens Park Rangers | 0-0 | 1-3 |
| Reading | 4-5 | 0-2 |
| Southend United | 1-0 | 0-4 |
| Swindon Town | 0-3 | 1-1 |
| Torquay United | 1-1 | 1-2 |
| Watford | 1-3 | 0-1 |

### F.A. Cup

| | | Home | Away |
|---|---|---|---|
| Gillingham | H R1 | | 0-4 |

### Third Division South Cup

| | | | Home | Away |
|---|---|---|---|---|
| Gillingham | A R1 | | | 0-0 |
| Gillingham | H R1R | | 4-2 | |
| Crystal Palace | A R2 | | | 2-4 |

CITY MANAGER 1935-36
Billy McDevitt - Appointed February 1929
Jack English - Appointed October 1935

## CITY PLAYING SQUAD

| Name | Pos | Signed from | Apps | Gls |
|---|---|---|---|---|
| Jack Angus HB | HB | Scunthorpe & Lindsey United C/s 1930 | 39 | |
| Hiley Bamsey HB | HB | Woodbury Apr 1935 | 8 | |
| John Beby | G | Darlington Mar 1936 | 10 | |
| Arthur Chesters G | G | Manchester United C/S 1933 | 29 | |
| Reg Clarke HB | HB | Southern Railway, Exeter C/S 1927 | 35 | 6 |
| Wynne Crompton | FB | Crystal Palace C/S 1935 | 7 | |
| James Dunn | F | Everton C/S 1935 | 22 | 4 |
| Richard Ebdon | F | Ottery St Mary C/S 1935 | 24 | 9 |
| John Fantham | HB | Rotherham United C/S 1935 | 6 | 1 |
| Jimmy Gray FB | FB | Liverpool Jan 1930 | 33 | |
| Victor Hoyle | W | Local C/S 1935 | 6 | 1 |
| Stan Hurst W | W | Tipton St John Apr 1932 | 34 | 3 |
| Clifford Kirk | G | Liverpool C/S 1935 | 3 | |
| Wilfred Lowton | FB | Wolverhampton Wanderers C/S 1935 | 18 | |
| Peter McArdle | W | Stoke City C/S 1935 | 9 | 1 |
| Edward McArthur F | F | Middlesbrough C/S 1934 | 8 | 2 |
| James McCambridge | F | Bristol Rovers Sep 1935 | 23 | 14 |
| Thomas McLean | F | Blackburn Rovers C/S 1935 | 21 | 1 |
| Alexander Merrie | F | Aldershot Feb 1936 | 4 | 2 |
| Charlie Miller FB | FB | Plymouth Argyle C/S 1926 | 23 | |
| Henry Poulter F | F | Sunderland C/S 1932 | 2 | 3 |
| Stan Risdon | HB | Tipton St John C/S 1932 | 13 | |
| Reginald Robinson | HB | Huddersfield Town C/S 1935 | 30 | 1 |
| John Scott W | W | Northampton Town C/S 1932 | 27 | 3 |
| Thomas Scott F | F | Norwich City C/S 1934 | 28 | 8 |

## THIRD DIVISION SOUTH 1935-36

| | P | W | D | L | F | A | Pts |
|---|---|---|---|---|---|---|---|
| Coventry City | 42 | 24 | 9 | 9 | 102 | 46 | 57 |
| Luton Town | 42 | 22 | 12 | 8 | 81 | 45 | 56 |
| Reading | 42 | 26 | 2 | 14 | 87 | 62 | 54 |
| Queens Park Rangers | 42 | 22 | 9 | 11 | 84 | 53 | 53 |
| Watford | 42 | 20 | 9 | 13 | 80 | 54 | 49 |
| Crystal Palace | 42 | 22 | 5 | 15 | 96 | 74 | 49 |
| Brighton & H.A. | 42 | 18 | 8 | 16 | 70 | 63 | 44 |
| Bournemouth & B.A. | 42 | 16 | 11 | 15 | 60 | 56 | 43 |
| Notts County | 42 | 15 | 12 | 15 | 60 | 57 | 42 |
| Torquay United | 42 | 16 | 9 | 17 | 62 | 62 | 41 |
| Aldershot | 42 | 14 | 12 | 16 | 53 | 61 | 40 |
| Millwall | 42 | 14 | 12 | 16 | 58 | 71 | 40 |
| Bristol City | 42 | 15 | 10 | 17 | 48 | 59 | 40 |
| Clapton Orient | 42 | 16 | 6 | 20 | 55 | 61 | 40 |
| Northampton Town | 42 | 15 | 8 | 19 | 62 | 90 | 38 |
| Gillingham | 42 | 14 | 9 | 19 | 62 | 90 | 37 |
| Bristol Rovers | 42 | 14 | 9 | 19 | 69 | 95 | 37 |
| Southend United | 42 | 13 | 10 | 19 | 61 | 62 | 36 |
| Swindon Town | 42 | 14 | 8 | 20 | 64 | 73 | 36 |
| Cardiff City | 42 | 13 | 10 | 19 | 60 | 73 | 36 |
| Newport County | 42 | 11 | 9 | 22 | 60 | 111 | 31 |
| Exeter City | 42 | 8 | 11 | 23 | 59 | 93 | 27 |

* Not for the first time the directors of Exeter City made a public appeal for funds in the summer of 1935. They said: "Have confidence. Lend us your financial aid and we will do our best to deliver the goods." Unfortunately, the Grecians were to finish rock bottom of the Third Division South!

* No fewer than nine new directors were elected to the board for the start of the 1935-36 season, as the club increased its share capital.

* Henry Poulter scored a hat-trick in the opening day of the season, 5-1 home win, over Aldershot. However, he was then absent through illness and only made one more league outing.

* When Exeter lost 1-0 at Watford on Wednesday 11th September 1935, the hosts netted in 84th minute when it was reported ... 'The light was so bad that it was impossible to follow the game.'

* The match report for Exeter City's 1-0 home defeat at the hands of Bristol City on 16th September 1935 was not very complimentary! It read .... 'Exeter City are drifting from bad to worse. Their display was crude football of a most unintelligent type. All departments blundered. There was scarcely one redeeming feature about City's inept performance.'

* On 27th September 1935, Exeter City issued the following statement .... 'Arrangements have been made between Exeter City F.C and their manager Mr. McDevitt, that his engagement with the club as their manager should come to an end.'

* The train on which the match referee was travelling for the Exeter City versus Bristol Rovers game was seriously delayed by fog. As a result he didn't make the kick off. A linesman took over as referee and unusually City forward Jimmy McCambridge ran one of the lines! The referee eventually made it to St James' Park after 20 minutes and took over in the middle.

* Two minutes silence was observed by both teams and supporters prior to the kick off between Exeter City and Newport County at St James' Park on 25th January 1936. This was a tribute to King George V who had died earlier in the week. The National Anthem was also played by the Exeter City Military Band.

* Alex Merrie made a sensational debut for Exeter City when he netted in the first minute in a 2-2 draw at Gillingham on 1st February 1936. He also scored the second City goal as well to cap a fine debut.

* After the home defeat against Clapton Orient (2-3), the report stated ....'A second half display bordering on the hopeless brought about another home failure. The chances of escaping either of the two bottom positions are negligible. The blunt truth is that the team is not good enough for the Third Division.'

* Sadly at the City versus Clapton Orient game, former Exeter manager Arthur Chadwick collapsed and died whilst sat in the grandstand. Chadwick had been the Grecians first ever manager in 1908.

* This really had been a season to forget for Exeter City, and was regarded by many as the worst in terms of playing standards and results since the club had joined the professional ranks in 1908.

* Apart from a mid-season revival when the Grecians won six out of seven matches, there was not a lot of cheer for the supporters. Indeed the team also went on a run of 15 league games without a win, including seven straight defeats.

* The highest attendance of the season was 10,000 for the visit of Aldershot on the opening day. The lowest was just 2,000 when Northampton Town were at the Park on 4th April 1936 - a game that City won 3-1.

Exeter City 1936-37
Back row: Reg Clarke, William Barr (Trainer), Ernest Hobbs, Arthur Chesters, George Stimpson, Jack English (Manager), John Shadwell
Front row: Aldred Thompson, John Scott, Rod Williams, Patrick McGill, Fred Urmson, William Brown

* Prior to the start of the season it was reported:- 'Everyone connected with a Football League club learns in the hard school of experience. Exeter City's management have had driven home to then a number of truths in the twelve months past. Some of those truths are the direct outcome of that best forgotten season which drew to a merciful close last May, What for example would be more obvious than that the playing staff was in dire need of a drastic overhaul.

**CITY'S LEAGUE RESULTS**

| | Home | Away |
|---|---|---|
| Aldershot | 1-2 | 1-1 |
| Bournemouth & B.A. | 1-1 | 0-0 |
| Brighton & Hove Albion | 0-4 | 0-1 |
| Bristol City | 3-0 | 1-2 |
| Bristol Rovers | 3-2 | 2-4 |
| Cardiff City | 3-1 | 1-3 |
| Clapton Orient | 0-2 | 0-1 |
| Crystal Palace | 3-2 | 0-8 |
| Gillingham | 1-1 | 2-2 |
| Luton Town | 2-4 | 2-2 |
| Millwall | 1-1 | 3-3 |
| Newport County | 3-1 | 0-2 |
| Northampton Town | 2-5 | 1-2 |
| Notts County | 1-3 | 1-3 |
| Queens Park Rangers | 0-3 | 0-4 |
| Reading | 2-0 | 0-1 |
| Southend United | 2-2 | 4-4 |
| Swindon Town | 1-1 | 1-3 |
| Torquay United | 2-1 | 1-0 |
| Walsall | 3-0 | 2-4 |
| Watford | 2-1 | 1-1 |

**F.A. Cup**

| | | | |
|---|---|---|---|
| Folkestone | H | R1 | 3-0 |
| Walthamstow Avenue | A | R2 | 1-1* |
| Walthamstow Avenue | A | R2 | 3-2 |
| Oldham Athletic | H | R3 | 3-0 |
| Leicester City | H | R4 | 3-1 |
| Preston North End | A | R5 | 3-5 |
| * Abandoned due to fog | | | |

**Third Division South Cup**

| | | | |
|---|---|---|---|
| Cardiff City | H | R1 | 1-0 |
| Torquay United | A | R2 | 1-2 |

CITY MANAGER 1936-37
Jack English - Appointed October 1935

**CITY PLAYING SQUAD**

| Name | Pos | Signed from | Apps | Gls |
|---|---|---|---|---|
| Jack Angus | HB | Scunthorpe & Lindsey United C/S 1930 | 28 | |
| Hiley Bamsey | HB | Woodbury Apr 1935 | 5 | |
| Michael Boyle | FB | Reading C/S 1936 | 23 | |
| William Brown | FB | Watford C/S 1936 | 32 | |
| Walter Bussey | F | Swindon Town Dec 1936 | 20 | 5 |
| Arthur Chesters | G | Manchester United C/S 1933 | 26 | |
| Reg Clarke | HB | Southern Railway, Exeter C/S 1927 | 31 | 2 |
| Richard Ebdon | F | Ottery St Mary C/S 1936 | 3 | |
| Ernest Hobbs | HB | Northampton Town C/S 1936 | 11 | |
| Henry Johnson | F | Southend United C/S 1936 | 11 | 1 |
| John Keane | W | Kilmarnock C/S 1936 | 13 | 1 |
| Patrick McGill | F | Heart of Midlothian C/S 1936 | 25 | 1 |
| William Owen | W | Reading Dec 1936 | 24 | 6 |
| Henry Pollard | HB | Sheffield Wednesday C/S 1936 | 3 | |
| Stanley Pope | F | Tiverton Town C/S 1936 | 13 | 4 |
| Thomas Scott | F | Norwich City C/S 1934 | 17 | 5 |
| John Shadwell | HB | Bury C/S 1936 | 30 | 1 |
| Charles Smith | W | Local C/S 1936 | 4 | |
| Frederick Smith | W | Darlington C/S 1936 | 24 | 4 |
| George Stimpson | FB | Rhyl C/S 1936 | 29 | |
| Aldred Thompson | W | Hartlepools C/S 1936 | 4 | |
| Patrick Tierney | G | Vale of Clyde C/S 1936 | 16 | |
| Frederick Urmson | W | Tranmere Rovers C/S 1936 | 10 | |
| Roderick Williams | F | Norwich City C/S 1936 | 41 | 29 |
| Archibald Young | HB | Bristol Rovers C/S 1936 | 19 | |

**THIRD DIVISION SOUTH 1936-37**

| | P | W | D | L | F | A | Pts |
|---|---|---|---|---|---|---|---|
| Luton Town | 42 | 27 | 4 | 11 | 103 | 53 | 58 |
| Notts County | 42 | 23 | 10 | 9 | 74 | 52 | 56 |
| Brighton & H.A. | 42 | 24 | 5 | 13 | 74 | 43 | 53 |
| Watford | 42 | 19 | 11 | 12 | 85 | 60 | 49 |
| Reading | 42 | 19 | 11 | 12 | 76 | 60 | 49 |
| Bournemouth & B.A. | 42 | 20 | 9 | 13 | 65 | 59 | 49 |
| Northampton Town | 42 | 20 | 6 | 16 | 85 | 68 | 46 |
| Millwall | 42 | 18 | 10 | 14 | 64 | 54 | 46 |
| Queens Park Rangers | 42 | 18 | 9 | 15 | 73 | 52 | 45 |
| Southend United | 42 | 17 | 11 | 14 | 78 | 67 | 45 |
| Gillingham | 42 | 18 | 8 | 16 | 52 | 66 | 44 |
| Clapton Orient | 42 | 14 | 15 | 13 | 52 | 52 | 43 |
| Swindon Town | 42 | 14 | 11 | 17 | 75 | 73 | 39 |
| Crystal Palace | 42 | 13 | 12 | 17 | 62 | 61 | 38 |
| Bristol Rovers | 42 | 16 | 4 | 22 | 71 | 80 | 36 |
| Bristol City | 42 | 15 | 6 | 21 | 58 | 70 | 36 |
| Walsall | 42 | 13 | 10 | 19 | 62 | 84 | 36 |
| Cardiff City | 42 | 14 | 7 | 21 | 54 | 87 | 35 |
| Newport County | 42 | 12 | 10 | 20 | 67 | 98 | 34 |
| Torquay United | 42 | 11 | 10 | 21 | 57 | 80 | 32 |
| Exeter City | 42 | 10 | 12 | 20 | 59 | 88 | 32 |
| Aldershot | 42 | 7 | 9 | 26 | 50 | 89 | 23 |

* After what proved to be disastrous season in 1935-36, manager Jack English 'cleared the decks' and brought in no fewer than sixteen new players prior to the start of the 1936-37 season.

* Sidney H Thomas, who had been secretary if Exeter City since its inception in 1908, stepped down during the summer of 1936. He was one of the founder members of the club in 1904, and combined his roll at Exeter with that of being the managing clerk at local company, Dunn and Baker.

* A new trainer was also appointed in the summer of 1936 as Billy Barr took over from Doug Livingstone. Barr had also been trainer at Walsall, Luton Town, Bristol Rovers and Swindon Town. Livingstone left the Grecians to take up a position at Sheffield United.

* A record attendance for Walthamstow Avenue of 11,131 were present for their round two F.A. Cup tie against Exeter City. Unfortunately with the fog growing ever thicker, the referee consulted both his linesmen and abandoned the tie after 65 minutes with the score at 1-1. The game was eventually played the following Thursday.

* The Exeter City players had lunch at the Royal Clarence Hotel in Exeter prior to their FA Cup fourth round home tie against Leicester City. The visitors had stayed overnight in Taunton. Such was the interest in the game that large queues formed at the Well Street turnstiles prior to them opening. The attendance was 13,731 producing receipts of £1,139. City won 3-1.

* A week after their cup success against Leicester, Exeter suffered their then record defeat when they lost 8-0 at Crystal Palace. This was also Palace's record league victory.

* Prior to their FA Cup fifth round tie at Preston North End, the Exeter City team stopped at the same hotel as the Arsenal players, who were due to play at Burnley. Former Grecian Cliff Bastin was with the Arsenal team and he wished his old team the best of luck. A group of Exeter City supporters walked from the station to the ground with a stuffed seagull (the famous lucky bird, Dido) attached to a long post.

* St James' Park staged its first ever senior representative match on 24th February 1937 when an F.A. Amateur XI lost 1-4 against Combined Universities. The drizzly conditions put a dampener on the attendance as well as less than 1,000 were present.

* Exeter City played First Division Blackburn Rovers at St James' Park on 19th April 1937, as a benefit match for defender, Jack Angus. City lost 4-2 before an attendance of 4,000.

* Apart from the excellent run in the F.A. Cup, this proved to be another very disappointing season as City ended in 21st position in the Third Division South. Had it not been for the goalscoring prowess of Rod Williams, it could have been even worse. Williams ended the season by scoring 8 goals in a run of six matches to take his tally for the season to an impressive 29 goals in 41 outings.

* Exeter City had to apply for re-election to the Football League for the second season in succession, and once again they were successful, although there were fears that should the Grecians find themselves in a similar position then they would be relegated to the Southern League.

* Between 3rd October 1936 and 9th January 1937, the Grecians went 13 league matches without a win.

* The highest crowd of the season for a league match at St James' Park was 11,000 for the Boxing Day visit of Notts County. The lowest was 2,000 when Northampton Town were the visitors in January 1937.

\* After a couple of very poor seasons, a preview of Exeter City's 1937-38 read:-

*'Exeter City's troubles last season lay not so much in the fact that the players were not good enough, as in the way the personnel was ruthlessly changed. There were a lot of many quick change acts in the first half of the season, and it was then that the damage was done. It is when alterations are needlessly made that the effect is the reverse of beneficial.*
*Assuming for example, that the team shows signs of settling down into a useful combination, there is no justification in swapping the men about. But until the true form of the newcomers is correctly assessed there may have to be revisions here and there. This would constitute reasonable team selection,. With 13 newcomers, Exeter's immediate problems may be that of discovering the right blend.*
*There is always that difficulty which has to be faced by a club seeking to emerge from a period of depression. Clubs which are more happily placed do not find the way so hard. They are able to start the new season more or less where they left off last.'*

\* According to local press reports, dated 17th November 1937, Exeter City would be playing Plymouth Argyle in an 'Exhibition Match' at Launceston on 1st December. It was felt it was possible that His Majesty The King, who was due to visit the town on the same day, would watch the game between the reserve teams of the respective clubs. The City and Argyle first teams met on the same day at Home Park in a Devon Professional Championship match. Alas, the King didn't go to the reserve team game, which Argyle won 3-1.

## CITY'S LEAGUE RESULTS

|  | Home | Away |
|---|---|---|
| Aldershot | 0-1 | 1-0 |
| Bournemouth & B.A. | 3-1 | 2-2 |
| Brighton & Hove Albion | 4-0 | 0-6 |
| Bristol City | 3-2 | 1-4 |
| Bristol Rovers | 0-0 | 1-1 |
| Cardiff City | 2-1 | 1-1 |
| Clapton Orient | 2-0 | 1-2 |
| Crystal Palace | 2-2 | 2-2 |
| Gillingham | 3-5 | 1-2 |
| Mansfield Town | 4-0 | 3-2 |
| Millwall | 1-5 | 1-2 |
| Newport County | 2-0 | 2-2 |
| Northampton Town | 4-1 | 0-1 |
| Notts County | 0-3 | 0-0 |
| Queens Park Rangers | 0-4 | 0-4 |
| Reading | 0-2 | 0-1 |
| Southend United | 1-1 | 1-1 |
| Swindon Town | 0-0 | 0-3 |
| Torquay United | 2-0 | 1-2 |
| Walsall | 3-2 | 2-0 |
| Watford | 1-2 | 0-0 |

| F.A. Cup | | | |
|---|---|---|---|
| Folkestone | H | R1 | 1-0 |
| Hull City | H | R2 | 1-2 |

| Third Division South Cup | | | |
|---|---|---|---|
| Southend United | A | R1 | 2-1 |
| Swindon Town | A | R2 | 0-2 |

## CITY MANAGER 1937-38
Jack English - Appointed October 1935

## CITY PLAYING SQUAD

| Name | Pos | Signed from | Apps | Gls |
|---|---|---|---|---|
| Jack Angus | HB | Scunthorpe & Lindsey United C/S 1930 | 36 | |
| Hiley Bamsey | HB | Woodbury Apr 1935 | 28 | |
| Henry Bowl | F | Blackpool C/S 1937 | 34 | 18 |
| William Brown | FB | Watford C/S 1936 | 26 | |
| Walter Bussey | F | Swindon Town Dec 1936 | 36 | 6 |
| Henry Church | G | Oldham Athletic C/S 1937 | 28 | |
| Benjamin Clarke | FB | Sheffield United C/S 1937 | 22 | 1 |
| William Clarke | W | Leicester City C/S 1937 | 12 | 1 |
| Arthur Coles | D | Copplestone C/S 1937 | 2 | |
| Walter Coulston | W | Crystal Palace C/S 1937 | 32 | 2 |
| Thomas Davies | HB | Watford C/S 1937 | 14 | |
| Richard Ebdon | F | Ottery St Mary C/S 1935 | 22 | 6 |
| Vincent Farrell | F | Clapton Orient C/S 1937 | 6 | 4 |
| Terence Kavanagh | HB | Notts County C/S 1937 | 6 | |
| James Liddle | W | Coventry City C/S 1937 | 28 | 8 |
| Patrick McGill | F | Heart of Midlothian C/S 1936 | 9 | |
| Idris Miles | W | Clapton Orient C/S 1937 | 10 | |
| James Miller | G | Kilmarnock Sep 1937 | 1 | |
| Henry Pollard | HB | Sheffield Wednesday C/S 1936 | 1 | |
| Stanley Pope | F | Tiverton Town C/S 1936 | 13 | 6 |
| John Shadwell | HB | Bury C/S 1936 | 40 | 1 |
| William Storey | F | Swindon Town C/S 1937 | 5 | 2 |
| Patrick Tierney | G | Vale of Clyde C/S 1936 | 13 | |
| Henry Topping | FB | Manchester City C/S 1937 | 1 | |
| Robert Wallace | FB | Plymouth Argyle C/S 1937 | 37 | |
| Own Goals | | | | 2 |

## THIRD DIVISION SOUTH 1937-38

|  | P | W | D | L | F | A | Pts |
|---|---|---|---|---|---|---|---|
| Millwall | 42 | 23 | 10 | 9 | 83 | 37 | 56 |
| Bristol City | 42 | 21 | 13 | 8 | 68 | 40 | 55 |
| Queens Park Rangers | 42 | 22 | 9 | 11 | 80 | 47 | 53 |
| Watford | 42 | 21 | 11 | 10 | 73 | 43 | 53 |
| Brighton & H.A. | 42 | 21 | 9 | 12 | 64 | 44 | 51 |
| Reading | 42 | 20 | 11 | 11 | 71 | 63 | 51 |
| Crystal Palace | 42 | 18 | 12 | 12 | 67 | 47 | 48 |
| Swindon Town | 42 | 17 | 10 | 15 | 49 | 49 | 44 |
| Northampton Town | 42 | 17 | 9 | 16 | 51 | 57 | 43 |
| Cardiff City | 42 | 15 | 12 | 15 | 67 | 54 | 42 |
| Notts County | 42 | 16 | 9 | 17 | 50 | 50 | 41 |
| Southend United | 42 | 15 | 10 | 17 | 70 | 68 | 40 |
| Bournemouth & B.A. | 42 | 14 | 12 | 16 | 56 | 57 | 40 |
| Mansfield Town | 42 | 15 | 9 | 18 | 62 | 67 | 39 |
| Bristol Rovers | 42 | 13 | 13 | 16 | 46 | 61 | 39 |
| Newport County | 42 | 11 | 16 | 15 | 43 | 52 | 38 |
| Exeter City | 42 | 13 | 12 | 17 | 57 | 70 | 38 |
| Aldershot | 42 | 15 | 5 | 22 | 39 | 59 | 35 |
| Clapton Orient | 42 | 13 | 7 | 22 | 42 | 61 | 33 |
| Torquay United | 42 | 9 | 12 | 21 | 38 | 73 | 30 |
| Walsall | 42 | 11 | 7 | 24 | 52 | 88 | 29 |
| Gillingham | 42 | 10 | 6 | 26 | 36 | 77 | 26 |

* Prior to the start of the 1937-38 season, the Express and Echo warned .... 'Having had to seek re-election two years running, Exeter City cannot afford to be in the same plight at the end of this season. A third application is bound to be fatal to the club's continuance in The Football League.'

* Former goalkeeper Dick Pym, was appointed assistant trainer during the summer of 1937. He had left City as a player in 1921 to continue this illustrious career with Bolton Wanderers.

* Vince Farrell made a superb debut for Exeter on the opening day of the season, when he scored both goals in City's 2-2 draw at Newport County. He was to only play a further five league matches for the Grecians that season, adding two more goals.

* Henry 'Harry' Bowl also netted twice on his league debut for the Grecians during s 3-2 win over Bristol City at St James' Park in September 1937.

* The 'alarm bells' started to ring as early as October, as City had won just one of their opening ten league matches and were once again bottom of the Third Division South table.

* This was followed by two successive home matches where City defeated, Mansfield Town (4-0) and Northampton Town (4-1), to at least give some hope of an improvement in the teams' fortunes.

* Hull City made their first ever visit to St James' Park for an FA Cup second round tie on 11th December 1937. The visitors had travelled to Exeter the day before and stayed overnight at the Rougemont Hotel. Hull included former Grecian, Charlie Robinson, in their side and won 2-1 before an attendance of 10,297.

* Exeter City's first ever visit to Clapton Orient's new ground at Brisbane Road ended in a 2-1 defeat. Only 4,309 spectators were present.

* The Grecians had a wasted trip to Crystal Palace's Selhurst Park on Christmas Day for a Third Division South fixture. Ten minutes before kick off the referee called the match off as a thick blanket of fog enveloped the ground.

* The contract of William Storey was cancelled by Exeter City in March 1938, so that he could sign for Third Division North outfit, Gateshead. Storey had only moved to Exeter from Swindon Town the previous summer.

* By winning 5-1 in the last game of the season at Exeter City, visitors Millwall, clinched promotion to the Second Division. Supporters of Millwall swarmed onto the St James' Park pitch at the final whistle, one with a large stuffed lion, as they carried their players off towards the dressing room. The attendance was 9,436 that produced match receipts of £570.

* Summing up the season, the Express and Echo reported .... 'There are few regrets at the passing of another season, which, from Exeter City's standpoint, has contained a minimum of pleasing noteworthy features. There is a feeling of relief that the City's existence in The Football League is assured for another term.'

*The average attendance for league matches at St James' Park was equivalent to one in ten of the entire population of the City attending matches. However, it was pointed out that City's average was some 25 per cent below the average for the entire Third Division South.

* Walt Bussey was the only City player to score a hat-trick in a league game during the season, that being against Walsall in the 3-2 home win. Two of Bussey's goals came form the penalty spot.

* City's season had ended almost as badly as it had started, with only one victory (2-0 at home to Clapton Orient) in the final eight matches played.

* There was the usual pre-season optimism that Exeter City would have a good season and this was expressed in the annual preview printed in the local press which read:-

*'From the Arsenal to Rochdale, from the Villa to the smallest club, this is the time of high expectation. For in every board room the view is confidently expressed that this season will be better than the last. Whoever invented the worn phrase about hope springing eternal should have been a football director.*

*How do Exeter City stand? Will the coming season be better and more successful than its immediate predecessors? In endeavouring to analyse the position one helpful point must be that the club has retained all save one of the players who bore the brunt of the Football League campaign last term.*

*This tells us that strictly on the basis of past happenings Exeter City's nucleus of old players should guarantee against an appeal for re-election without being strong enough to be in the front rank of their class.'*

* Before the start of the Football League season, Plymouth Argyle entertained Exeter City at Home Park in a match for the Football League Jubilee (1888-1938). An attendance of 6,807 witnessed a goal feast as Argyle ran out 6-3 winners. Henry Bowl scored two for the Grecians, with their other goal coming from Walt Bussey.

* On the same afternoon, back at St James' Park, there were also nine goals scored, as Exeter City reserves defeated Plymouth Argyle reserves by 8-1. An attendance of 2,000 produced match receipts of £40.

* A few weeks later in a Southern League fixture, City reserves came up against a strong Arsenal side, the game being played at Enfield, as the Grecians were crushed 9-0.

## CITY'S LEAGUE RESULTS

| Home Away | Home | Away |
|---|---|---|
| Aldershot | 3-3 | 0-2 |
| Bournemouth & B.A. | 0-0 | 0-2 |
| Brighton & H.A. | 2-2 | 1-6 |
| Bristol City | 1-1 | 1-4 |
| Bristol Rovers | 2-1 | 1-4 |
| Cardiff City | 1-1 | 2-1 |
| Clapton Orient | 2-1 | 3-3 |
| Crystal Palace | 4-4 | 2-3 |
| Ipswich Town | 3-0 | 2-2 |
| Mansfield Town | 2-0 | 2-4 |
| Newport County | 3-1 | 0-0 |
| Northampton Town | 3-2 | 0-0 |
| Notts County | 1-0 | 1-3 |
| Port Vale | 1-3 | 2-3 |
| Queens Park Rangers | | |
| Reading | 3-2 | 1-1 |
| Southend United | 3-3 | 1-0 |
| Swindon Town | 0-0 | 1-2 |
| Torquay United | 1-2 | 1-0 |
| Walsall | 3-2 | 2-1 |
| Watford | 1-3 | 2-4 |

| F.A. Cup | | |
|---|---|---|
| Torquay United | A R1 | 1-3 |

| Third Division South Cup | | |
|---|---|---|
| Swindon Town | H R1 | 1-1 |
| Swindon Town | A R1R | 3-2 |
| Bournemouth & B.A. | H R2 | 1-2 |

CITY MANAGER 1938-39
Jack English - Appointed October 1935

## CITY PLAYING SQUAD

| Name | Pos | Signed from | Apps | Gls |
|---|---|---|---|---|
| Jack Angus | HB | Scunthorpe & Lindsey United C/S 1930 | 38 | |
| Vincent Blore | G | Crystal Palace C/S 1938 | 4 | |
| Henry Bowl | F | Blackpool C/S 1937 | 42 | 24 |
| William Brown | FB | Watford C/S 1936 | 28 | |
| Walter Bussey | F | Swindon Town Dec 1936 | 18 | 5 |
| Henry Church | G | Oldham Athletic Nov 1937 | 38 | |
| Benjamin Clarke | FB | Sheffield United C/S 1937 | 18 | |
| Richard Ebdon | F | Ottery St Mary C/S 1935 | 42 | 12 |
| William Fellowes | HB | Luton Town C/S 1938 | 42 | 1 |
| Thomas Halliday | FB | Norwich City Feb 1939 | 14 | |
| James Liddle | W | Coventry City C/S 1937 | 15 | 1 |
| John Little | FB | Northampton Town C/S 1938 | 25 | |
| John Millar | W | Benburb C/S 1938 | 9 | 3 |
| Leonard Rich | W | Plymouth Argyle C/S 1938 | 32 | 4 |
| Harold Riley | F | Northampton Town C/S 1938 | 26 | 9 |
| John Shadwell | HB | Bury C/S 1936 | 15 | |
| Roy Southcombe | W | Bideford Apr 1939 | 2 | |
| Charles Sutherley | W | Chudleigh C/S 1938 | 9 | 1 |
| Alexander Turnbull | F | Droylsden C/S 1938 | 14 | 1 |
| Steve Walker | HB | Sheffield United C/S 1938 | 30 | |
| Robert Wallace | FB | Plymouth Argyle C/S 1937 | 1 | |
| Own Goals | | | | 4 |

## THIRD DIVISION SOUTH 1938-39

| | P | W | D | L | F | A | Pts |
|---|---|---|---|---|---|---|---|
| Newport County | 42 | 22 | 11 | 9 | 58 | 45 | 55 |
| Crystal Palace | 42 | 20 | 12 | 10 | 71 | 52 | 52 |
| Brighton & H.A. | 42 | 19 | 11 | 12 | 68 | 49 | 49 |
| Watford | 42 | 17 | 12 | 13 | 62 | 51 | 46 |
| Reading | 42 | 16 | 14 | 12 | 69 | 59 | 46 |
| Queens Park Rangers | 42 | 15 | 14 | 13 | 68 | 49 | 44 |
| Ipswich Town | 42 | 16 | 12 | 14 | 62 | 52 | 44 |
| Bristol City | 42 | 16 | 12 | 14 | 61 | 63 | 44 |
| Swindon Town | 42 | 18 | 6 | 16 | 72 | 77 | 44 |
| Aldershot | 42 | 16 | 12 | 14 | 53 | 66 | 44 |
| Notts County | 42 | 17 | 9 | 16 | 59 | 54 | 43 |
| Southend United | 42 | 16 | 9 | 17 | 61 | 64 | 41 |
| Cardiff City | 42 | 15 | 11 | 16 | 61 | 65 | 41 |
| Exeter City | 42 | 13 | 14 | 15 | 65 | 82 | 40 |
| Bournemouth & B.A. | 42 | 13 | 13 | 16 | 52 | 58 | 39 |
| Mansfield Town | 42 | 12 | 15 | 15 | 44 | 62 | 39 |
| Northampton Town | 42 | 15 | 8 | 19 | 51 | 58 | 38 |
| Port Vale | 42 | 14 | 9 | 19 | 52 | 58 | 37 |
| Torquay United | 42 | 14 | 9 | 19 | 54 | 70 | 37 |
| Clapton Orient | 42 | 11 | 13 | 18 | 53 | 55 | 35 |
| Walsall | 42 | 11 | 11 | 20 | 68 | 69 | 33 |
| Bristol Rovers | 42 | 10 | 13 | 19 | 55 | 61 | 33 |

* The 1938-39 season was overshadowed, from a club point of view, by the tragic death on 12th September of Exeter City full-back, Robert Wallace. He had played in the opening match, was taken ill, but then entered hospital for an operation from which he never recovered.

* For the opening game of the season at Cardiff City, the first ever 'Civic flight' took place when the Mayor of Exeter, the Sheriff, the Town Clerk and invited passengers, flew from Exeter Airport to Cardiff. The Grecians won 2-1, the team having travelled to South Wales by train.

* The club flag was flown at half mast at the Third Division South Cup match against Swindon Town at St James' Park on 14th September, as a mark of respect following the death of Robert Wallace. A collection was also taken to augment a fund which had been opened to help the players' widow.

* Prior to the kick off between Exeter City and Bournemouth & Boscombe Athletic, the players of both sides lined up on the halfway line and the National Anthem played. A report stated ....' This coupled with music of a patriotic nature was a reminder of the Country's deliverance from the threatened catastrophe of a war with Germany.'

* After a good start to the season, City found themselves in 4th place in the Third Division South table on 17th September. However, by 3rd December they had slipped to fourth from bottom.

* Exeter City made their first ever visit to Ipswich Town on 31st December 1938. The Portman Road ground was described as ... 'small, compact, but better than most seen in the Third Division.' .... The game ended 2-2, with snow being piled up along the touchlines, having been cleared from the pitch.

* The local fire brigade pumped gallons of water from the rain-sodden pitch at Bristol Rovers, on the morning of their game with Exeter City on 21st January 1939. It was worthwhile from Rovers' point of view, who won 4-1.

* Exeter City chairman, Captain Hunter, said that the club's financial position was such that if it did not improve then they would have to "put up the shutters."

* City supporters were incensed with the referee at the game against Brighton and Hove Albion at St James' Park, when he sent off Grecians' full back John Little. The player had been badly fouled and then retaliated. The fans felt that the Brighton player should have been sent off, not Little.

* With events in Europe seemingly taking a turn for the worse ,this was reflected in the appeal made prior to kick off in the match at St James' Park against Notts County on 8th April 1939. Exeter City director, and chairman of the local Air Raid Precaution. committee, Mr Fred Cottey. made a speech to the crowd asking for those present to volunteer for National Service.

* The highest attendance of the season at St James' Park was for the very first match. 9,800 were present for the visit of Ipswich Town. The lowest attendance at the Park was 2,228 when City hosted Walsall on 15th February 1939.

*The season ended in great uncertainty as to the future of football with a possible war with Germany on the horizon. It was hoped that matters would be resolved and that the 1939-40 season would lift everyone's spirits.

* By the end of the season the Bob Wallace Memorial Fund totalled £129 16s 3d, including a donation of ten guineas from Plymouth Argyle Football Club.

CITY'S LEAGUE RESULTS

| Home Away | | Home | Away |
|---|---|---|---|
| Northampton Town | | - | 2-1 |
| Port Vale | | - | 1-0 |
| Torquay United | | 2-2 | - |

CITY MANAGER 1939-40
Jack English - Appointed October 1935

## CITY PLAYING SQUAD

| Name | Pos | Signed from | Apps | Gls |
|---|---|---|---|---|
| Jack Angus | HB | Scunthorpe & Lindsey United C/S 1930 | 3 | |
| Jack Blood | FB | Notts County C/S 1939 | 3 | |
| Vincent Blore | G | Crystal Palace C/S 1938 | | |
| Henry Bowl | F | Blackpool C/S 1937 | 3 | 1 |
| Cyril Crawshaw | F | Queen of the South C/S 1939 | | |
| Stanley Cutting | HB | Southampton C/S 1939 | | |
| Richard Ebdon | F | Ottery St Mary C/S 1935 | 3 | 2 |
| William Fellowes | HB | Luton Town C/S 1938 | 3 | |
| Ray Freeman | F | Manchester City C/S 1939 | 1 | |
| James Gallagher | HB | Notts County C/S 1939 | | |
| James Gray | F | Hebburn C/S 1939 | | |
| Thomas Halliday | FB | Norwich City Feb 1939 | | |
| Charles Harthill | W | Wigan Athletic C/S 1939 | | |
| John Little | FB | Northampton Town C/S 1938 | 1 | |
| Harold Riley | F | Northampton Town C/S 1938 | 2 | 2 |
| John Shadwell | HB | Bury C/S 1936 | | |
| Robert Smith | FB | Brentford C/S 1939 | | |
| Frederick Speed | FB | Mansfield Town C/S 1939 | 2 | |
| Charles Sutherley | W | Chudleigh C/S 1938 | 3 | |
| James Thomson | G | Brighton & H.A. C/S 1939 | 3 | |
| Steve Walker | HB | Sheffield United C/S 1938 | 3 | |
| George Wardle | W | Middlesbrough C/S 1939 | 3 | |
| Charles Windle | W | Bury C/S 1939 | | |

THIRD DIVISION SOUTH 1939-40
(As at 2nd Sept 1939 when the Football League Third Division South
was suspended for the duration of the Second World War)

| | P | W | D | L | F | A | Pts |
|---|---|---|---|---|---|---|---|
| Reading | 3 | 2 | 1 | 0 | 8 | 2 | 5 |
| Exeter City | 3 | 2 | 1 | 0 | 4 | 2 | 5 |
| Notts County | 2 | 2 | 0 | 0 | 6 | 3 | 4 |
| Ipswich Town | 3 | 1 | 2 | 0 | 5 | 3 | 4 |
| Brighton & H.A. | 3 | 1 | 2 | 0 | 5 | 4 | 4 |
| Cardiff City | 3 | 2 | 0 | 1 | 5 | 5 | 4 |
| Crystal Palace | 3 | 2 | 0 | 1 | 8 | 9 | 4 |
| Bournemouth & B.A. | 3 | 1 | 1 | 1 | 13 | 4 | 3 |
| Bristol City | 3 | 1 | 1 | 1 | 5 | 5 | 3 |
| Clapton Orient | 3 | 0 | 3 | 0 | 3 | 3 | 3 |
| Mansfield Town | 3 | 1 | 1 | 1 | 8 | 8 | 3 |
| Norwich City | 3 | 1 | 1 | 1 | 4 | 4 | 3 |
| Southend United | 3 | 1 | 1 | 1 | 3 | 3 | 3 |
| Torquay United | 3 | 0 | 3 | 0 | 4 | 4 | 3 |
| Walsall | 3 | 1 | 1 | 1 | 3 | 3 | 3 |
| Queens Park Rangers | 3 | 0 | 2 | 1 | 4 | 5 | 2 |
| Watford | 3 | 0 | 2 | 1 | 4 | 5 | 2 |
| Northampton Town | 3 | 1 | 0 | 2 | 2 | 12 | 2 |
| Aldershot | 3 | 0 | 1 | 2 | 3 | 5 | 1 |
| Swindon Town | 3 | 0 | 1 | 2 | 3 | 5 | 1 |
| Bristol Rovers | 3 | 0 | 1 | 2 | 2 | 7 | 1 |
| Port Vale | 2 | 0 | 1 | 1 | 0 | 1 | 1 |

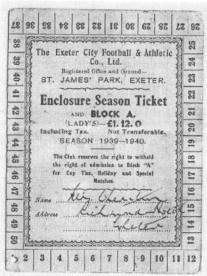

* The numbering of players in Football League matches was used for the first time and this was reported on by the Express and Echo which stated ... 'This is long overdue in the opinion of most people. It is bound to make matches easier for the spectators to follow.'

* Two sets of goal posts were presented to the football club by the Exeter City Supporters' Club prior to the start of the season.

* The signing of Ray Freeman form Manchester City, where he was transfer listed for £400, had a proviso in that he could only play if he could get his release from training as a 'Militia man' from the nearby Topsham Barracks. Still registered with Manchester City, Freeman was therefore on loan to Exeter whilst he was stationed in Devon.

* Exeter City played Plymouth Argyle at St James' Park on 19th August 1939 in a Football Association Jubilee Fund match. The game attracted 6,000 spectators and was won by Argyle, 2-1.

* The Grecians were to play just three Third Division South matches as follows before the competition was abandoned:-
Saturday 26th August 1939 Torquay United H 2-2
Monday 28th August 1939 Northampton Town A 2-1
Saturday 2nd September 1939 Port Vale A 1-0

* The season was ushered in on a note of gravity which was without parallel since 1914 and the onset of the First World War.

* A friendly fixture was played at St James' Park on Wednesday 30th August 1939 between an Exeter City Past XI and a Plymouth Argyle Past XI. City won 7-1. The game had been arranged by the Exeter City Supporters Club.

* A joint statement issued by the Football Association and the Football League on Wednesday 30th August 1939 stated that as they had no information to the contrary, the fixtures would be played as arranged.

* When Exeter City travelled to Port Vale on Saturday 2nd September 1939 they expected that it would be the last Football League fixture they would play with suspension of matches being imminent. So it proved to be.

* The very last match to be played at St James' Park in the 1939-40 season was also on Saturday 2nd September 1939, when the City Reserves and Hereford United drew 0-0 in a Southern League fixture before less than 1,000 spectators.

Exeter City played the following matches:-

| | |
|---|---|
| 20th Jan 1945 | Exeter City 2 Plymouth Argyle 2 Att: 2,720 |
| 10th Feb 1945 | Yeovil Town 2 Exeter City 6 Att: Not known |
| 17th Feb 1945 | Exeter City 4 Royal Marines 1 Att: 2,000 |
| 10th Mar 1945 | Plymouth Argyle 5 Exeter City 1 Att: 2,000 |
| 17th Mar 1945 | Exeter City 2 Yeovil Town 2 Att 1,800 |
| 2nd Apr 1945 | Exeter City 5 Plymouth Argyle 1 Att: 3,500 |
| 21st Apr 1945 | Devonshire Regiment 1 Exeter City 5 Att: 3,000 |

PLAYERS WHO REPRESENTED EXETER CITY 1944-45

| Name | Pos | Signed From |
|---|---|---|
| ??? Allen | F | Royal Marines - Guest |
| Stanley Barnes | HB | ??? - Guest |
| ??? Barry | HB | ??? - Guest |
| ??? Bex | F | ??? - Guest |
| ??? Brenton | HB | ??? - Guest |
| ??? Brown | FB | Motherwell - Guest |
| ??? Clarkson | F | ??? - Guest |
| Frederick Corbett | FB | Manchester City - Guest |
| ??? Crossley | FB | Cliftonville - Guest |
| ??? Dashwood | HB | Fulham - Guest |
| ??? Deacon | HB | Royal Navy Armament Depot - Guest |
| ??? Dixon | HB | Liverpool - Guest |
| Frank Donoghue | FB | Portsmouth - Guest |
| ??? Doyle | W | Leicester City - Guest |
| Richard Ebdon | F | Ottery St Mary C/S 1935 |
| ??? Evans | FB | Royal Marines - Guest |
| William Fellowes | HB | Luton Town C/S 1938 |
| ??? Fowler | HB | Torquay United - Guest |
| Ken Halliday | G | Lyme Regis & R.A.F - Guest |
| ??? Helliar | HB | Torquay United - Guest |
| ??? Higgs | HB | Halifax Town - Guest |
| John Hodge | W | Plymouth Argyle - Guest |
| George Hurst | W | Oldham Athletic - Guest |
| ??? Jackson | FB | ??? Guest |
| Alfred Jeffries | W | Sheffield United - Guest |
| Ronald Jewell | F | Plymouth Argyle - Guest |
| ??? Kimberley | G | ??? - Guest |
| ??? Lucas | FB | Royal Marines - Guest |
| ??? McCartney | F | St Anthony's, Glasgow - Guest |
| ??? Mason | G | Blackpool - Guest |
| Frederick Mitcheson | F | Plymouth Argyle - Guest |
| James Murray | FB | Shawfield Juniors - Guest |
| ??? Neat | F | Third Lanark - Guest |
| ??? Prior | W | ??? - Guest |
| Leonard Rich | FB | Stockport County - Guest |
| Thomas Ryan | HB | Swindon Town - Guest |
| ??? Taylor | G | Grimsby Town - Guest |
| ??? Tuckett | W | Royal Marines - Guest |
| ??? Urquhart | W | Heart Of Midlothian - Guest |
| Steve Walker | HB | Sheffield United C/S 1938 |
| ??? Wheatley | FB | ??? - Guest |
| ??? Williams | G | Lovells Athletic - Guest |

*Exeter City started to appear in a few friendly matches again, the first time the club had played since the shut down in September 1939 due to the Second World War.

*Teams, as can be seen in the list of players, consisted of mainly guest players, several of whom were stationed with the various Forces in the local area.

*St James' Park had a neglected look about it, having been used as base by American troops for the previous years, with even vehicles having been parked and tents erected on the hallowed playing surface!

* With no manager, club secretary Norman Foot took charge of arranging matches and contacting players to complete the teams to represent Exeter City.

* City half-back Steve Walker had guested for Dunfermline Athletic, Doncaster Rovers and Southampton. He had also been wounded in a running fight when the Scharnhorst and Gneisenau made their escape up the English Channel

* City winger George Wardle, stationed in London and guesting for Chelsea, was selected to play for the full Army representative side against the Royal Navy at Ipswich Town's Portman Road ground in February 1945.

* The match receipts from the Exeter City versus Royal Marines match played in February 1945, were donated to the Royal Marines Prisoner of War Fund.

* The Exeter City directors said they required £5,000 to get the club up and running again if they were to compete at Football League level. The closing down of season 1939-40 and that coupled with the summer wage bill, had cost the club at least £2,000.

* The club's balance sheet at June 30th 1944 (issued in April 1945) showed that there was a mortgage loan of £8,000 against St James' Park. Directors' loans amounted to £1,268 and the bank overdraft stood at £1,839.

* During the War, Capt., Hunter, the Exeter City chairman, had died as a result of injuries in the blitz. Mr. M.J. McGahey and Mr. A. Chamberlain, both directors, had also died, so therefore it was decided that all seats on the Exeter City FC board of directors be declared vacant.

* A new board of directors were elected in May 1945, which resulted in one of the club's founders, Mr, Sidney Thomas, becoming chairman. It was also announced that the club's deficit stood at £19,750, and that the better course may have been to gone into liquidation. However, creditors and shareholders would have lost heavily and it was therefore felt that the honest way was to carry on and try to put matters right.

* On 11th May 1945, Exeter City told the Football League that they wanted to be involved again as from the following season.

* Goalkeeper Ken Halliday, an Air Cadet, was killed during training with the Royal Air Force. He had guested for City in one of the early games in the season, on the recommendation of Exeter City player, Reg Clarke.

Exeter City 1945-46
Back row: Edwards, Murray, Goodfellow, Latham, Jordan, Brown, Lee (Groundsman)
Front row: Challis, Wardle, Ebdon, Kernick, Elliot

PLAYERS WHO REPRESENTED EXETER CITY 1945-46
(Only League appearances and goalscorers statistics are shown, as a number only appeared in the Cup matches, but the players are included in the list below)

| Name | Pos | Signed from | Apps | Gls |
|---|---|---|---|---|
| Jack Angus | HB | Scunthorpe & Lindsey United C/S 1930 | 2 | |
| ??? Attwood | F | ??? | | |
| ??? Baxter | W | Bradford Park Avenue - Guest | 1 | |
| Jack Blood | FB | Notts County C/S 1939 | 17 | 1 |
| Ray Bowden | F | ??? | 4 | |
| Harry Boye-Karlsen | F | Norwegian Air Force - Aug 1945 | 1 | |
| ??? Brown | FB | Motherwell - Guest | 7 | |
| ??? Casey | W | Royal Navy - Guest | 2 | 2 |
| Stanley Challis | W | Royal Marines Jul 1945 | 16 | 8 |
| Arthur Coles | HB | Copplestone Jun 1937 | | |
| Cyril Crawshaw | F | Stalybridge Celtic Jul 1939 | | |
| ??? Dalgleish | W | ??? | 1 | |
| Arthur Davison | FB | Stockport County - Guest | | |
| ??? Eastham | HB | ??? | | |
| Richard Ebdon | F | Ottery St Mary C/S 1935 | 16 | 7 |
| ??? Elliott | W | ??? | 1 | |
| Franklin | F | Middlesbrough - Guest | 1 | |
| ??? Gadsby | FB | ??? | | |
| James Gallagher | HB | Notts County C/S 1939 | 2 | |
| Derrick Goodfellow | G | Sheffield Wednesday - Guest | 12 | |
| William Haddington | F | Bradford Park Avenue - Guest | 2 | 1 |
| Harry Haddock | HB | Renfrew Juniors - Guest | 4 | |
| ??? Harris | W | ??? | | |
| Arthur Hydes | F | Newport County Feb 1946 | | |
| ??? Jones | W | ??? | | |
| ??? Jordan | HB | Army Physical Training Corps Jul 1945 | 18 | |
| Philip Joslin | G | Torquay United - Guest | 1 | |
| Dudley Kernick | F | Torquay United - Guest | 8 | 5 |
| William Lambton | G | Nottingham Forest Apr 1946 | | |
| ??? Langford | W | ??? | | |
| Leslie Latham | HB | Aston Villa - Guest | 2 | |
| ??? Lewis | W | Royal Marines Aug 1945 | 6 | |
| John Long | FB | Chester Apr 1946 | | |
| Frederick Mitcheson | F | Ipswich Town - Guest | 9 | 2 |
| James Murray | FB | Shawfield Juniors - Guest | 18 | |
| ??? Perkins | W | ??? | | |
| George Petherbridge | W | Bristol Rovers - Guest | | |
| Batholomew Purvis | FB | North Shields - Guest | 1 | |
| Doug Regan | W | Royal Navy Mar 1945 | | |
| Leonard Rich | FB | Stockport County - Guest | 2 | |
| George Roughton | FB | Manchester United Oct 1945 | 10 | |
| Bernard Singleton | G | Wolverhampton Wanderers Jan 1946 | | |
| ??? Staveley | G | ??? | 1 | |
| Charles Sutherley | W | Chudleigh C/S 1938 | 2 | |
| ??? Thomson | G | ??? | 6 | |
| Roy Tickell | W | Tranmere Rovers Dec 1945 | 4 | |
| ??? Topham | FB | ??? | 2 | |
| Steve Walker | HB | Sheffield United C/S 1938 | 19 | 3 |
| George Wardle | W | Middlesbrough C/S 1939 | 14 | 2 |
| Charles Warren | F | R.A.F. Jul 1945 | 2 | 1 |
| Raymond Wright | F | Wolverhampton Wanderers Mar 1946 | | |

CITY'S LEAGUE RESULTS

| | Home | Away |
|---|---|---|
| Aldershot | 1-4 | 5-3 |
| Bournemouth & B.A. | 0-3 | 1-3 |
| Brighton & H.A. | 3-2 | 2-3 |
| Bristol City | 1-0 | 1-5 |
| Bristol Rovers | 2-2 | 1-2 |
| Cardiff City | 3-2 | 0-0 |
| Crystal Palace | 0-1 | 1-2 |
| Reading | 5-1 | 1-1 |
| Swindon Town | 1-1 | 4-1 |
| Torquay United | 0-2 | 1-3 |

Division Three South Cup (Southern Section)
8th our of 9

| | Home | Away |
|---|---|---|
| Aldershot | 1-0 | 3-5 |
| Bournemouth & B.A. | 3-1 | 1-1 |
| Brighton & H.A. | 0-0 | 2-2 |
| Bristol City | 3-0 | 0-3 |
| Bristol Rovers | 0-1 | 1-2 |
| Cardiff City | 2-1 | 1-5 |
| Crystal Palace | 2-3 | 0-3 |
| Torquay United | 1-1 | 2-0 |

F.A. Cup

| | | | |
|---|---|---|---|
| Trowbridge Town | A | R1 | 3-1 |
| Trowbridge Town | H | R1 | 7-2 |
| Newport County | A | R2 | 1-5 |
| Newport County | H | R2 | 1-3 |

CITY MANAGER 1945-46
George Roughton - Appointed October 1945

\* Prior to the season commencing an appeal was launched for funds to help Exeter City get ready for competitive football once more. By early July 1945, a total of £800 had been raised, although the club had set a goal of £5,000.

\* The Grecians Association was formed with former director Norman Kendall as President. Kendall was on the board in 1908 when the club entered the Southern League. The Association held a number of fund raising events, including a fete at St James' Park.

* Exeter City were members of the Division Three South (South of the Thames) League for season 1945-46. They also played in a cup competition, which was again organised on a league basis.

* At a meeting of the club's board of directors it was stated that they felt that there would be problems during the 1945-46 season, particularly with regards to obtaining players and also the long journeys that would be entailed.

* Prior to the start of the season there was much remedial work carried out to St James' Park. The pitch had to be re-seeded; the Big Bank terracing was overgrown; Buildings erected for military use on the popular terrace had to be removed.

* Before a manager, George Roughton, was appointed in October 1945, all matters concerning the team and signing of players fell upon club secretary Norman Foot, who had carried out a similar task in 1944-45.

* The European Services Baseball Championship Final was played at St. James' Park in August 1945 before an attendance of 1,500. The American Army from France beat the U.S. Navy, Exeter.

* It was reported that over 1,700 supporters attending the game between Exeter City and Swindon Town had travelled by car. 6,300 people gained admission. 429 cars and a taxi were officially counted in the area around the ground. Estimated number of occupants per car was four. Therefore a quarter of the fans had travelled by car.

* Only one hat-trick was recorded by a City player in the 1945-46 season, when Richard 'Digger' Ebdon netted three times in 3-1 home win over Bournemouth and Boscombe Athletic in a Third Division South Cup (Southern Section) fixture.

* The highest attendance recorded at St James' Park during the season was 10,259 for the visit of Crystal Palace in October 1945.

* The club issued the following statement on 20th August 1945:-

*'Owing to the difficulties in reorganising the club and the fact that there are only ten league matches involved, the directors hope that shareholders will agree with the decision that the board have made, namely, not to issue shareholders with tickets for the coming season.*

*When the game returns to normality at the end of the 1945-46 season, a scheme will be put before the shareholders entitled to tickets.*

*With changing money values it is clear that the club cannot hope successfully to weather the necessary reconstruction with a load of many hundreds of shareholders gaining admission to matches without paying.*

*It is felt that shareholders will appreciate the position and will willingly help the City directors to revive the club.*

*With regard to those who bought season tickets for the 1939-40 season, they will be able to use such tickets for league matches for the 1945-46 season.'*

* Exeter City signed their first ever Norwegian player when Harry Boye-Karlsen joined in August 1945. He was a member of the Norwegian Air Force stationed locally. He had caught City's attention when he netted six goals for the Norwegian Air Force whilst playing for them at St James' Park against The Royal Marines.

The popular local cartoonist 'Stil' submitted a number of caricatures of Exeter City players to the Express and Echo for many years after the Second World War. He also drew various local sportsmen and club officials connected with various other sporting organisations.

# The Players

### JOHN ANGUS

A member of City's brilliant Cup side in 1930-1 and has been with the Club long enough to earn a second benefit. Made a memorable first team debut in a Cup-tie at Bury, and was one of the man of the match. Angus has probably made more appearances for the City than any other player, and is still going strong.

### ARTHUR HYDES

Brought out by Ardsley United, a junior club in the Barnsley district. Had a trial with Barnsley, scored three goals and was offered terms, but refused. Went to Leeds and stayed until being transferred to Newport County, whom he helped to win promotion in 1938-9. A shrewd inside forward.

### BERNARD SINGLETON

Another City signing from the Wolves. Young goalkeeper, he has a safe pair of hands. Had barely left school when Major Frank Buckley snapped him up. Served in the Royal Navy during the greater part of the war, and was afterwards transferred to the coal mines.

### BERT HOYLE

While Stan Cullis was serving in Italy, he noted a giant goalkeeper, Bert Hoyle, and recommended him to the Wolves. Hoyle was accordingly signed, but his opportunities were restricted because Scott and Williams, the two international 'keepers, were first and second choice. So Wolves allowed him so come to Exeter.

### BILLY FELLOWES

Born at Tavistock, had a spell with Plymouth Argyle and was allowed to leave on a " free." His ability was appreciated at its true worth by Clapton Orient who made a big profit out of his subsequent transfer to Luton. Fellowes helped Luton to win promotion before joining Exeter. Constructive half-back, and ideal clubman.

### BILLY MUSTARD

Product of the prolific North-Eastern Nursery. Played for Bath City last season and had one outing with Exeter, scoring one of the goals by which the City defeated Plymouth Argyle in a Professional Championship match. His display impressed Mr. Roughton, who promptly booked him on a form during the summer.

### DOUGLAS REGAN

From Devon Minor League football, Regan has made the Football League grade remarkably quickly. Was serving with the Fleet Air Arm when the City spotted him last season. Following a series of good displays with the second team, he was promoted to the first eleven and has not looked back since.

### GEORGE THOMPSON

Irish through and through, and full of his country's traditional good humour. Had experience in the homeland, and then went to Huddersfield, whose Central League side he captained from the right back position last season. Determined defender, he's a difficult man to beat with the ball.

80

### DICK EBDON

'Digger' to every City supporter, and one of the toughest men in the game. Joined the City from his native Ottery St. Mary, and developed into animated forward of the four-figured class just before the war, when Luton and Millwall both made offers. Now scores plenty of goals from the centre-forward position.

### DICK SMART

Good judges predict a bright future for this lad who scored 76 League and Cup goals for Stanley United last term—a tally which, incidentally, broke the Northern Amateur League record. Not big as centre-forwards go, he makes up for this handicap by good positional play and accurate shooting.

### GEORGE WARDLE

On the threshold of big honours, he gained a place in an international trial last season. Hit the headlines as a member of Chelsea's League South Cup winning team in 1945. Fast on the ball clever individualist, George is equally at home at inside or outside right. Previous club Middlesbrough.

### GLYN VAUGHAN

Another of Jack Blood's discoveries. A natural footballer, and an inside-left who is able to make the ball do the work. Son of a former Welsh international.

### STAN CHALLIS

Wing forward with a deadly shot in either foot. Give Challis a reasonable chance, and it's an even bet that he hits the target. Hails from Lympstone. Served with the Royal Marines and made occasional appearances for Crystal Palace during the war. Can play on either flank.

### STEVE WALKER

Came to Exeter from Sheffield United on the recommendation of "Duggie" Livingstone. City's one-time trainer who holds a similar position at Bramall Lane. Versatile and a tireless worker, Steve has filled every position in the half-back line, and three inside-forward positions as well.

### STAN CUTTING

Quick tackling wing half-back and good in distribution as well. City got him from Southampton in 1939. Was previously with Norwich City, the club of his hometown. Saw extensive service overseas with the R.A.F. and took part in many inter-services games out East.

## HARRY HANFORD

Member of Swansea's all-conquering schoolboy side, Hanford was capped as a boy by Wales. He afterwards gained full international honours, and played against England, Scotland & Ireland between 1934 and 1938. Previous clubs: Swansea Town and Sheffield Wednesday. A centre-half who has built his game on the modern defensive style.

## ARTHUR COLES

One of the City's contingent of Devon-born players. He joined the Club as an amateur from Copplestone, becoming a professional in due course. Went to Coleraine in the Irish League in 1938. Served in the R.A.F. throughout the war and played in a number of Service internationals in the Middle and Far East.

## JACK BLOOD

An all-round sportsman. Plays cricket and football equally well. Joined the City from Notts County in 1939, as a left-back. Served with the R.A.F. during the war, and developed into a good centre-half, assisting Liverpool, Southport and other League clubs as a guest player.

## JIMMY MURRAY

Worked as a compositor before the war, and also played football for Shawfield Juniors, Glasgow. Joined the Royal Marines, was posted to Devon, and quickly made a mark in Services League football. Signed by the City last season and made numerous first team appearances at right-back, and one at outside-right.

## JACK LONG

Though he's a full-back now, Jack Long formerly played as a forward, and won schoolboy honours in this department. He gained a captain's rank in the Hampshire Regiment, and was signed by the City last season on the strength of an impressive display with the Southern Command representative side.

## RAY WRIGHT

Joined the City in the second half of last season from the Wolves, and at once showed classtouches as an inside-forward. Port Vale and others wanted him, but he preferred Exeter. One of the team of coaches chosen by the Football Association, Ray toured Norway during the summer.

82

# Exeter City Officials

**Mr. S. H. THOMAS** *(Chairman).*

Player, secretary, director and now chairman of the City club. Mr. S. H. Thomas was in at the birth of Exeter City. No club had a more knowledgable secretary than he proved for nearly 30 years. He has now aspired to the chairmanship, and Exeter City could have no abler man to guide the club's destinies. Sound judgment and a sense of humour are his outstanding qualities.

**NORMAN KENDALL**

**SHUN!**

**JIMMY GALLAGHER**
*(Trainer).*

Though it is correct to say that Jimmy Gallagher is an ex-Guardsman, it would be wrong to suggest that he drills the City lads like a Sergeant Major on parade. Jimmy gets the best out of his charges by instilling into them some of his own abundant enthusiasm and is the life and soul of the party. Biographical note is that he joined Exeter City as a centre-half from Notts County.

**GEORGE ROUGHTON** *(Manager).*

Appointment of George Roughton as the City's manager midway through last season was a wise choice, for he is a good judge of a player, a man of tact and discernment, and patient and understanding of the footballer's problems. In the course of a distinguished playing career, George started in Manchester schoolboy football and later applied for a trial with Manchester United. George was told to "come back when you are a bit bigger" and he subsequently went to Huddersfield, where he remained to develop into one of the best full-backs in the game and earned many honours. The inside touch is that Manchester United were eventually forced to pay thousands of pounds to secure the transfer of a defender whom they could have had for nothing.

**DICK PYM.** **BILLY CRANSHAW** **HAROLD BLACKMORE**

Back row: Dick Ebdon, John Long, Arthur Hydes, Ray Wright, Steve Walker, Harry Hanford
Middle row: Norman Foot (Secretary), George Thompson, Stan Challis, Bill Fellowes, Arthur Coles, Bert Hoyle, Albert Hammond, Glyn Vaughan, James Murray, Jimmy Gallagher (Trainer)
Front row: George Wardle, Bill Mustard, Stan Cutting, George Roughton (Manager), Richard Smart, Bert Bowden, Doug Regan

City's league Results

| | Home | Away |
|---|---|---|
| Aldershot | 4-1 | 0-2 |
| Bournemouth & B.A. | 4-1 | 1-4 |
| Brighton & H.A. | 2-1 | 6-1 |
| Bristol City | 1-3 | 2-2 |
| Bristol Rovers | 3-2 | 0-1 |
| Cardiff City | 0-2 | 0-5 |
| Crystal Palace | 2-1 | 0-1 |
| Ipswich Town | 0-0 | 1-2 |
| Leyton Orient | 3-1 | 1-3 |
| Mansfield Town | 1-0 | 0-1 |
| Northampton Town | 1-0 | 2-1 |
| Norwich City | 3-0 | 3-1 |
| Notts County | 2-2 | 0-0 |
| Port Vale | 1-1 | 2-1 |
| Queens Park Rangers | 3-0 | 0-2 |
| Reading | 1-3 | 0-4 |
| Southend United | 1-5 | 2-2 |
| Swindon Town | 1-1 | 0-2 |
| Torquay United | 1-1 | 1-2 |
| Walsall | 2-2 | 1-2 |
| Watford | 1-0 | 1-3 |

F.A. Cup
Bournemouth & B.A.    A   R1    2-4

CITY MANAGER 1946-47
George Roughton        Appointed Oct 1945

CITY PLAYING SQUAD 1946-47

| Name | Pos | Signed From | Apps | Goals |
|---|---|---|---|---|
| Jack Blood | FB | Notts County May 1939 | 36 | 1 |
| Stan Challis | W | Lympstone Sep 1945 | 4 | 1 |
| Arthur Coles | HB | Coleraine Aug 1946 | 13 | |
| Stan Cutting | HB | Southampton July 1939 | 35 | 2 |
| Dick Ebdon | FB | Ottery St Mary Dec 1935 | 29 | 16 |
| Nbilly Fellowes | HB | Luton Town June 1936 | 14 | |
| Trevor Granville | W | Newport County Oct 1946 | 13 | |
| Harry Haddock | FB | Renfrew Juniors May 1946 | 1 | |
| Albert Hammond | F | Brentford June 1946 | 2 | |
| Harry Hanford | HB | Sheffield Wednesday May 1946 | 36 | |
| Harry Holman | F | Budleigh Salterton Dec 1946 | 4 | 2 |
| Bert Hoyle | G | Wolves Aug 1946 | 19 | |
| Denis Hutchings | W | Axminster Apr 1947 | 5 | |
| Arthur Hydes | F | Newport County Feb 1946 | 4 | |
| John Long | FB | Chester Apr 1946 | 1 | |
| James Murray | F | Shawfield Juniors | 1 | |
| Bill Mustard | W | Bath City May 1946 | 14 | |
| Billy Owen | HB | Newport County Oct 1946 | 20 | 9 |
| Doug Regan | W | Local March 1945 | 37 | 8 |
| Barney Singleton | G | Wolves Jan 1946 | 23 | |
| Richard Smart | F | Stanley United Aug 1946 | 1 | |
| Harry Sutherland | F | Leeds United May 1947 | 1 | |
| Groehe Thompson | FB | Huddersfield Town June 1946 | 38 | |
| Glyn Vaughan | F | Oldham Athletic May 1946 | 4 | |
| Steve Walker | HB | Sheffield United May 1938 | 31 | 2 |
| George Wardle | HB | Middlesbrough June 1939 | 38 | 6 |
| Ray Wright | F | Wolves March 1946 | 38 | 11 |
| Own Goals | | | | 2 |

THIRD DIVISION SOUTH 1946-47

| | P | W | D | L | F | A | Pts |
|---|---|---|---|---|---|---|---|
| Cardiff City | 42 | 30 | 6 | 6 | 93 | 30 | 66 |
| Queens Park Rangers | 42 | 23 | 11 | 8 | 74 | 40 | 57 |
| Bristol City | 42 | 20 | 11 | 11 | 94 | 56 | 51 |
| Swindon Town | 42 | 19 | 11 | 12 | 84 | 73 | 49 |
| Walsall | 42 | 17 | 12 | 13 | 74 | 59 | 46 |
| Ipswich Town | 42 | 16 | 14 | 12 | 61 | 53 | 46 |
| Bournemouth & B.A. | 42 | 18 | 8 | 16 | 72 | 54 | 44 |
| Southend United | 42 | 17 | 10 | 15 | 71 | 60 | 44 |
| Reading | 42 | 16 | 11 | 15 | 83 | 74 | 43 |
| Port Vale | 42 | 17 | 9 | 16 | 68 | 63 | 43 |
| Torquay United | 42 | 15 | 12 | 15 | 52 | 61 | 42 |
| Notts County | 42 | 15 | 10 | 17 | 63 | 63 | 40 |
| Northampton Town | 42 | 15 | 10 | 17 | 72 | 75 | 40 |
| Bristol Rovers | 42 | 16 | 8 | 18 | 59 | 69 | 40 |
| EXETER CITY | 42 | 15 | 9 | 18 | 60 | 69 | 39 |
| Watford | 42 | 17 | 5 | 20 | 61 | 76 | 39 |
| Brighton & H.A. | 42 | 13 | 12 | 17 | 54 | 72 | 38 |
| Crystal Palace | 42 | 13 | 11 | 18 | 49 | 62 | 37 |
| Leyton Orient | 42 | 12 | 8 | 22 | 54 | 75 | 32 |
| Aldershot | 42 | 10 | 12 | 20 | 48 | 78 | 32 |
| Norwich City | 42 | 10 | 8 | 24 | 64 | 100 | 28 |
| Mansfield Town | 42 | 9 | 10 | 23 | 48 | 96 | 28 |

* For many clubs, such as Exeter City, the 1946-47 season was one where they were just glad to be back playing competitive league football. After the shut down during the Second World War, City had played a few friendlies in 1944-45, and 12 months later took part in a special league competition for clubs, based south of the River Thames.

* Not surprisingly supporters were also eager to attend sport once more, and going along to St James' Park was no exception, where the average crowd for the season for league matches was 8,888. The highest crowd at the Park was 13,100 for the visit of Bristol City in September 1946.

* Prior to the start of the season a meeting was arranged by the Grecians Association at the Guildhall, Exeter, attended by the board of directors and supporters. Chairman Mr S.H. Thomas said: "Exeter City are out to build a team to win promotion." He went on to say that only two years previous things had looked desperate as Army huts covered large sections of the terracing and the drainage of the pitch had been ruined.

* With many new signings made by manager George Roughton, and only a handful of players returning to the club who were on the books pre-war, City had a reasonable season, ending in 15th place in the Third Division South.

* The best result was a 6-1 win at Brighton and Hove Albion on Christmas Day. Strangely, both teams travelled back to Exeter on the same train immediately after the game, for the return meeting at St James' Park the following day. City also won that one, but Brighton put up a better showing and only lost 2-1.

* Two players managed to score a hat-trick, one coming in the 6-1 win at Brighton from William Owen, and the other netted by Dick Ebdon in the 4-1 home win over Bournemouth and Boscombe Athletic.

* City had a fairly settled starting line up when you consider no fewer than eight players featured in 30 or more matches for the club. None, however, managed to play in every league match.

* The FA Cup proved to be a disappointment as the Grecians travelled to Bournemouth & Boscombe Athletic for a first round tie and lost 2-4.

* In order to ease congestion at the turnstiles for the visit of Torquay United to St James' Park, the directors decided to install 'change boxes' outside the Well Street and St James' Road entrances. Supporters would therefore be able to get the correct money before passing through the turnstiles and entering the ground.

* Every City match in which he played early on in the season, was an away one for centre-half Harry Hanford. Unable to find a house in Exeter, he had to travel from his Swansea home. For actual away fixtures he often caught the train on his own from Swansea, only to meet up with his team mates at wherever City were playing.

* Arc lights were used for the first time at St James' Park on 31st October 1946, when on a floodlit pitch training took place for part time professionals and the amateurs on the staff. The lights were given to the club by the Grecians Association. They were deemed to be a big success.

* Plans were drawn up in November 1946 for the terracing of the small bank behind the St James' Road goal. It was felt the work could be carried out in sections.

* In February 1947 it was reported that Stan Cutting and George Thompson were sidelined with heavy colds, and this was due to the emergency fuel cuts imposed by the Government of the day, that the City players had all gone without baths after and during their training sessions.

Back row: Dick Ebdon, Harry Bartholomew, Barney Singleton, Cyril Johnstone, William Fallon, Fred Davey, Archie Dymond, Bernard Grant.
Middle row: Harry Sutherland, Reg Gibson, Steve Walker, Ray Wright, Bert Hoyle, Arthur Coles, Jack Blood, Derek Warren.
Front row: Charlie Miller (Asst. Trainer), Dennis Hutchings, Glyn Vaughan, Trevor Granville, Stan Cutting, George Roughton (Manager), Henry Evans, George Thompson, Richard Smart, Doug Regan, Jimmy Gallagher (Trainer).

### City's league results

|  | HOME | AWAY |
|---|---|---|
| Aldershot | 4-0 | 0-0 |
| Bournemouth & B.A. | 1-1 | 1-2 |
| Brighton & H.A. | 1-0 | 1-0 |
| Bristol City | 3-1 | 1-1 |
| Bristol Rovers | 4-0 | 2-2 |
| Crystal Palace | 2-0 | 2-1 |
| Ipswich Town | 1-0 | 0-2 |
| Leyton Orient | 1-1 | 4-2 |
| Newport County | 4-4 | 0-3 |
| Northampton Town | 1-1 | 1-3 |
| Norwich City | 2-0 | 0-3 |
| Notts County | 0-1 | 1-1 |
| Port Vale | 0-0 | 1-1 |
| Queens Park Rangers | 1-2 | 1-3 |
| Reading | 1-0 | 1-2 |
| Southend United | 0-0 | 0-2 |
| Swansea Town | 3-1 | 0-2 |
| Swindon Town | 2-1 | 2-3 |
| Torquay United | 0-2 | 2-1 |
| Walsall | 0-6 | 0-4 |
| Watford | 3-1 | 1-3 |

### F.A. Cup

| Northampton Town | H | R1 | 1-1 |
|---|---|---|---|
| Northampton Town | A | R1R | 0-2 |

CITY MANAGER 1947-48
George Roughton - Appointed October 1945

| CITY PLAYING SQUAD 1947-48 | | | App | G |
|---|---|---|---|---|
| Name | Pos | Signed From | | |
| Jack Angus | HB | Scunthorpe & Lindsey, May 1930 | 3 | |
| Harry Bartholomew | HB | Motherwell May 1947 | 32 | 2 |
| Jack Blood | FB | Notts County May 1939 | 3 | |
| Stan Cutting | HB | Southampton Jul 1939 | 3 | |
| Fred Davey | HB | Crediton Aug 1947 | 10 | |
| Bill Dymond | W | Bristol City Jun 1947 | 17 | 3 |
| Richard Ebdon | F | Ottery St Mary Dec 1935 | 18 | 7 |
| Harry Evans | F | Southampton Apr 1947 | 30 | |
| Peter Fallon | HB | R.A.F Jun 1947 | 2 | |
| William Fallon | W | Notts County Jun 1947 | 8 | 2 |
| Reg Gibson | HB | Plymouth Argyle Jun 1947 | 30 | |
| Trevor Granville | W | Newport County Oct 1946 | 7 | 1 |
| Bert Hoyle | G | Wolverhampton Wanderers Aug 1946 | 9 | |
| Denis Hutchings | W | Axminster Apr 1947 | 26 | 5 |
| Bob Jeffrey | HB | Montrose Oct 1947 | 7 | |
| Cyril Johnstone | FB | Hamilton Academical Jul 1947 | 40 | |
| Angus Mackay | F | Ipswich Town Sep 1947 | 33 | 5 |
| Doug Regan | W | Trialist Mar 1945 | 36 | 11 |
| Stan Rowe | FB | Trialist Oct 1947 | 16 | |
| Barney Singleton | G | Wolverhampton Wanderers Jan 1946 | 33 | |
| Richard Smart | F | Stanley United Aug 1946 | 8 | 2 |
| Harry Sutherland | F | Leeds United May 1947 | 13 | 3 |
| George Thompson | FB | Huddersfield Town Jun 1946 | 25 | 4 |
| Glyn Vaughan | F | Oldham Athletic May 1946 | 2 | |
| Steve Walker | HB | Sheffield United May 1938 | 33 | |
| Ray Wright | F | Wolverhampton Wanderers Mar 1946 | 18 | |
| Own Goals | | | | 4 |

### THIRD DIVISION SOUTH - 1947-48

| | P | W | D | L | F | A | Pt |
|---|---|---|---|---|---|---|---|
| Queens Park Rangers | 42 | 26 | 9 | 7 | 74 | 37 | 61 |
| Bournemouth & B.A. | 42 | 24 | 9 | 9 | 76 | 35 | 57 |
| Walsall | 42 | 21 | 9 | 12 | 70 | 40 | 51 |
| Ipswich Town | 42 | 23 | 3 | 16 | 67 | 61 | 49 |
| Swansea Town | 42 | 18 | 12 | 12 | 70 | 52 | 48 |
| Notts County | 42 | 19 | 8 | 15 | 68 | 59 | 46 |
| Bristol City | 42 | 18 | 7 | 17 | 77 | 65 | 43 |
| Port Vale | 42 | 16 | 11 | 15 | 63 | 54 | 43 |
| Southend United | 42 | 15 | 13 | 14 | 51 | 58 | 43 |
| Reading | 42 | 15 | 11 | 16 | 56 | 58 | 41 |
| EXETER CITY | 42 | 15 | 11 | 16 | 55 | 63 | 41 |
| Newport County | 42 | 14 | 13 | 15 | 61 | 73 | 41 |
| Crystal Palace | 42 | 13 | 13 | 16 | 49 | 49 | 39 |
| Northampton Town | 42 | 14 | 11 | 17 | 58 | 72 | 39 |
| Watford | 42 | 14 | 10 | 18 | 57 | 79 | 38 |
| Swindon Town | 42 | 10 | 16 | 16 | 41 | 46 | 36 |
| Leyton Orient | 42 | 13 | 10 | 19 | 51 | 73 | 36 |
| Torquay United | 42 | 11 | 13 | 18 | 63 | 62 | 35 |
| Aldershot | 42 | 10 | 15 | 17 | 45 | 67 | 35 |
| Bristol Rovers | 42 | 13 | 8 | 21 | 71 | 75 | 34 |
| Norwich City | 42 | 13 | 8 | 21 | 61 | 76 | 34 |
| Brighton & H.A. | 42 | 11 | 12 | 19 | 43 | 73 | 34 |

* Exeter City manager George Roughton rang the changes throughout the course of the 1947-48 season using no fewer than 26 different players in league matches. The home record, apart from a disastrous 0-6 defeat at the hands of Walsall was very good, but not for the first time, the points haul on City's away travels left a little to be desired and as a result the team finished the season in 11th place in the Third Division South.

* Goals were shared throughout the team, with winger Doug Regan being the top scorer with 11. Only two players managed to score more than one goal in any league match, namely Charlie Sutherland against Leyton Orient in a 4-2 victory and Bill Dymond in the 4-0 home win over Aldershot.

* City went out at the first round stage of the FA Cup. After drawing 1-1 at St James' Park against Northampton Town, they lost 2-0 in the replay at The County Ground.

* Highest attendance for a league game at St James' Park was 16,942 for the visit of Notts County, the visitors winning 1-0.

* Biggest win of the season was 4-0 against Bristol Rovers in March 1948. Dymond hit two goals, whilst there was one each for Regan and Evans.

* City started the season poorly recording just three wins in their opening 11 league matches, however, they were to also go on an unbeaten run which stretched for 12 games and included seven victories.

* To meet the convenience of the Reading team and to help supporters to get back from Haldon races, the kick off time for the midweek game was altered from 6pm to 6.15pm.

* Exeter City announced that they had made a profit of £2,149 on the year ended 30th June 1947. Gate receipts were the highest in the club's history totalling £19,845. Repairs and renewals and the upkeep of St James' Park was £4,924, however, the War Department paid £3,821 towards the costs.

* "Trying to get a full-back is harder than getting Dollars from America," said Exeter City manager George Roughton. He had tried to sign a player to fill that position, but after five days of making enquiries, he was unsuccessful.

* Travelling to matches was still proving to be difficult in some cases, and for their game at Aldershot, City had to leave Exeter by early morning train to London, and then onwards by coach. After the game they had to make a hurried exit by coach to Basingstoke, where they caught the train back to Exeter.

* Back from a northern scouting mission in October 1947, City boss George Roughton said that the standard of football up North was pretty grim. One player who had cost his club £800 was described by Roughton as being worth nearer 800 pennies.

* Jack Angus and Dick Ebdon enjoyed a joint benefit match in March 1948, when Exeter City played Plymouth Argyle at St James' Park. The game ended 1-1 and was watched by an attendance of 7,527 producing total match receipts of £648 19s 9d.

* The first ever match to be played at St James' Park on a Good Friday took place on 26th March 1948. The visitors were Bournemouth. The kick off time had to be brought forward to enable the City team to catch the train after the game so that they could fulfil a fixture at Norwich the following day.

* City's 0-6 home defeat against Walsall was described:- 'To have coupled Exeter City's name with the Third Division would have done injustice to the competition. Walsall were made to appear a First Division side as the Grecians cantered around the field aimlessly, with absolutely no determination whatsoever.'

* Exeter City got off to flying start winning their first league match, 5-0 at home to Northampton Town. The performance was described as:- 'Not for years has a City attack possessed such pace, penetration and power as centre-forward Ron Johnson and his henchmen had. The Exeter forwards pulverised the Cobblers defence.',

* After a 6-0 defeat at Swansea Town in October 1948, the alarm bells started to ring, especially so soon after the 9-0 thrashing by Notts County. The Express and Echo reported:- 'The writing is on the wall. Exeter City are on a dangerous slide. It must be halted. Though the opening game of the season indicated that City were a side above average in the Southern section, more recent games have proved the reverse is the case. Time passes on and the City directors cannot afford to waste it. Urgent steps should be taken to strengthen existing resources.'

* Spare a thought for 41 City supporters who travelled by coach to the postponed FA Cup tie at Barnet. They had left Exeter on Friday at midnight, arriving in Victoria coach station at 7am. They went for a walk around the West End, before returning to the coach for the journey to Barnet. With the match off due the London's infamous pea-soup fog, the coach driver waited for conditions to improve before setting off back to Exeter, eventually arriving there on Sunday afternoon!

City's league results

| | Home | Away |
|---|---|---|
| Aldershot | 3-3 | 2-1 |
| Bournemouth & B.A. | 2-3 | 0-1 |
| Brighton & H.A. | 1-1 | 0-2 |
| Bristol City | 1-1 | 0-1 |
| Bristol Rovers | 2-1 | 0-3 |
| Crystal Palace | 3-1 | 1-1 |
| Ipswich Town | 1-3 | 2-2 |
| Leyton Orient | 3-1 | 2-5 |
| Millwall | 3-0 | 1-2 |
| Newport County | 1-2 | 2-0 |
| Northampton Town | 5-1 | 0-4 |
| Norwich City | 4-1 | 0-3 |
| Notts County | 3-1 | 0-9 |
| Port Vale | 2-1 | 1-1 |
| Reading | 1-2 | 0-2 |
| Southend United | 0-0 | 0-0 |
| Swansea Town | 1-1 | 0-6 |
| Swindon Town | 3-1 | 1-1 |
| Torquay United | 2-0 | 1-2 |
| Walsall | 2-1 | 3-4 |
| Watford | 2-1 | 1-0 |

| F.A. Cup | | | |
|---|---|---|---|
| Barnet | A | R1 | 6-2 |
| Hereford United | H | R2 | 2-1 |
| Grimsby Town | A | R3 | 1-2 |

CITY MANAGER 1948-49
George Roughton - Appointed October 1945

CITY PLAYING SQUAD 1948-49

| Name | Pos | Signed from | Apps | Gls |
|---|---|---|---|---|
| Harry Bartholomew | HB | Motherwell May 1947 | 34 | 4 |
| James Clark | FB | Aberdeen Aug 1948 | 26 | 2 |
| Arthur Coles | HB | Coleraine Aug 1946 | 1 | |
| Fred Davey | HB | Crediton Aug 1947 | 7 | |
| Frederick Durrant | F | Queens Park Rangers Feb 1949 | 13 | 4 |
| Bill Dymond | W | Bristol City Jun 1947 | 24 | 5 |
| Harry Evans | F | Southampton Apr 1947 | 11 | |
| Peter FalloN | HB | R.A.F Jun 1947 | 16 | 1 |
| James Gallagher | HB | Notts County Jun 1939 | 1 | |
| Reg Gibson | HB | Plymouth Argyle Jun 1947 | 10 | |
| Bernard Grant | F | Third Lanark Jul 1947 | 2 | |
| William Harrower | HB | Torquay United Jul 1948 | 21 | 4 |
| Bert Hoyle | G | Wolverhampton Wanderers Aug 1946 | 40 | |
| Denis Hutchings | W | Axminster Apr 1947 | 19 | 4 |
| Ronald Johnston | F | Rochdale Jun 1948 | 10 | 2 |
| Cyril Johnstone | FB | Hamilton Academical Jul 1947 | 37 | |
| Angus Mackay | F | Ipswich Town Sep 1947 | 9 | |
| Kenneth Powell | HB | Cardiff City Jun 1948 | 9 | 1 |
| Doug Regan | W | Trialist Mar 1945 | 38 | 14 |
| Roy Rew | F | Sea Mills Feb 1949 | 1 | 1 |
| Stan Rowe | FB | Trialist Oct 1947 | 2 | |
| Barney Singleton | G | Wolverhampton Wanderers Jan 1946 | 5 | |
| Richard Smart | F | Stanley United Aug 1946 | 20 | 5 |
| Archibald Smith | F | Hamilton Academical May 1948 | 20 | 7 |
| Steve Walker | HB | Sheffield United May 1938 | 39 | |
| Derek Warren | FB | Amateur C/S 1948 | 4 | |

THIRD DIVISION SOUTH - 1948-49

| | P | W | D | L | F | A | PTS |
|---|---|---|---|---|---|---|---|
| Swansea Town | 42 | 27 | 8 | 7 | 87 | 34 | 62 |
| Reading | 42 | 25 | 5 | 12 | 77 | 50 | 55 |
| Bournemouth & B.A. | 42 | 22 | 8 | 12 | 69 | 48 | 52 |
| Swindon Town | 42 | 18 | 15 | 9 | 64 | 56 | 51 |
| Bristol Rovers | 42 | 19 | 10 | 13 | 61 | 51 | 48 |
| Brighton & H.A. | 42 | 15 | 18 | 9 | 55 | 55 | 48 |
| Ipswich Town | 42 | 18 | 9 | 15 | 78 | 77 | 45 |
| Millwall | 42 | 17 | 11 | 14 | 63 | 64 | 45 |
| Torquay United | 42 | 17 | 11 | 14 | 65 | 70 | 45 |
| Norwich City | 42 | 16 | 12 | 14 | 67 | 49 | 44 |
| Notts County | 42 | 19 | 5 | 18 | 102 | 68 | 43 |
| Exeter City | 42 | 15 | 10 | 17 | 63 | 76 | 40 |
| Port Vale | 42 | 14 | 11 | 17 | 51 | 54 | 39 |
| Walsall | 42 | 15 | 8 | 19 | 56 | 64 | 38 |
| Newport County | 42 | 14 | 9 | 19 | 68 | 92 | 37 |
| Bristol City | 42 | 11 | 14 | 17 | 44 | 62 | 36 |
| Watford | 42 | 10 | 15 | 17 | 41 | 54 | 35 |
| Southend United | 42 | 9 | 16 | 17 | 41 | 46 | 34 |
| Leyton Orient | 42 | 11 | 12 | 19 | 58 | 80 | 34 |
| Northampton Town | 42 | 12 | 9 | 21 | 51 | 62 | 33 |
| Aldershot | 42 | 11 | 11 | 20 | 48 | 59 | 33 |
| Crystal Palace | 42 | 8 | 11 | 23 | 38 | 76 | 27 |

* In June 1948, Exeter City chairman, Sid Thomas, revealed that the revenue from home matches the previous season had averaged £750, although this was not enough to balance the books. He estimated that the wage bill for the coming year would total £13,000.

* For the first time in the club's history, an assistant manager was appointed in July 1948, this being former player Bill Fellowes, who had originally been signed from Luton Town in 1938.

* Most of the City players took summer jobs. Arthur Coles, Fred Davey and Bert Hoyle worked at local farms. Ray Wright worked at a smallholding in the village of Longdown. Cyril Johnstone, Harry Bartholomew and Doug Regan were employed in the building trade and Stan Rowe was with an engineering company.

* A record attendance of 13,676 was set at Torquay United's Plainmoor ground when Exeter City visited for a Third Division South fixture on 4th September 1948. Torquay won 2-1.

* Having been in existence for just six months, the Exmouth branch of the Grecians' Association reported that membership had grown to 90 by September 1948, but it was estimated that around 500 fans made the trip to home matches.

* An Exeter City player, not named, consulted a doctor on September 1948 with a nervous complaint. The diagnosis was that the trouble was solely due to the barracking that the player had been subjected to in previous matches!

* The Grecians were humiliated at Notts County on 16th October 1948, when they crashed to a record 9-0 defeat. The legendary Tommy Lawton stole the show with four goals, and he was carried from the pitch by jubilant supporters after the final whistle.

* The F.A. Cup first round tie on 27th November 1948 between Barnet and Exeter City was called off fifteen minutes before kick off due to the ever thickening fog. It was estimated that 400 City supporters had made the wasted journey to the game. The teams' travelling and hotel costs had been £170.

* When the F.A. Cup tie between Barnet and Exeter City was rearranged a week later, the Grecians scored their first goal, in a 6-2 win, after just ten seconds, with Harry Bartholomew being on target. Richard Smart netted four of the City goals.

* For the first time since they became a professional club, Exeter City had a home fixture on Christmas Day, with Brighton and Hove Albion being the visitors. A crowd of 7,000 saw a 1-1 draw.

* Trainer Jimmy Gallagher, at the age of 38, was called out of retirement to take his place in the City team that eventually lost 3-0 at Norwich City on New Years Day. The party had travelled the day before, but several players reported unwell on the morning of the match with suspected food poisoning.

* Stan Cutting scored hat-trick of penalties in the City Reserves 4-3 home win over Worcester City in a Southern League fixture in January 1949.

* Notts County forward, Tommy Lawton, who had scored four goals in his sides' 9-0 home win over Exeter earlier in the season, guested for the Grecians in a benefit match for Steve Walker, played against Southampton on 4th April 1949. A crow d of 11,260 saw the game end 1-1.

* The highest attendance of the season that Exeter City played in front of was 29,000 at Swansea Town in October 1948. The Swans won 6-0.

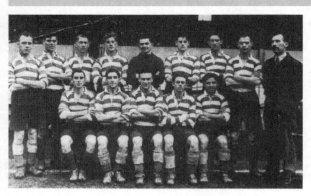

Back row: Cyril Johnstone, Fred Davey, Ray Goddard, Ken Powell, Barney Singleton, Bill Harrower, Jim Clark, Steve Walker, Jimmy Gallagher (Trainer).
Front row: Peter Fallon, Dick Smart, Archie Smith, John Greenwood, Doug Regan.

* By the end of the 1949-50 season, Sid Thomas, chairman of Exeter City revealed that wages and other items had involved an expenditure of £30,000. Attendances for the first team matches at St James' Park had averaged over 10,000, whilst away gates were around 14,000. He added he would like to see that gap narrowing.    Thomas also revealed that in order for the club to have signed Ray Goddard, a director, who wished to remain anonymous loaned the club the transfer fee of £5,000, otherwise they could not have afforded to sign the player.

City's league results

|  | HOME | AWAY |
|---|---|---|
| Aldershot | 1-0 | 2-1 |
| Bournemouth & B.A. | 1-2 | 0-2 |
| Brighton & H.A. | 2-3 | 0-1 |
| Bristol City | 0-0 | 0-1 |
| Bristol Rovers | 2-0 | 0-1 |
| Crystal Palace | 2-1 | 3-5 |
| Ipswich Town | 1-1 | 0-1 |
| Leyton Orient | 1-1 | 1-4 |
| Millwall | 2-1 | 1-3 |
| Newport County | 3-3 | 2-1 |
| Northampton Town | 1-3 | 3-3 |
| Norwich City | 3-1 | 2-1 |
| Notts County | -2 | 0-3 |
| Nottingham Forest | 0-0 | 0-5 |
| Port Vale | 3-1 | 0-1 |
| Reading | 3-4 | 2-3 |
| Southend United | 1- | 0-1 |
| Swindon Town | 3-0 | 1-7 |
| Torquay United | 1-1 | 4-1 |
| Walsall | | |
| Watford | 3-1 | 2-1 |

F.A. Cup

| Millwall | A | R1 | 5-3 |
|---|---|---|---|
| Chester | H | R2 | 2-0 |
| Nuneaton Borough | H | R3 | 3-0 |
| Liverpool | A | R4 | 1-3 |

CITY MANAGER 1949-50
George Roughton - Appointed October 1945

CITY PLAYING SQUAD 1949-50

| Name | Pos | Signed from | App | Gls |
|---|---|---|---|---|
| James Clark | FB | Aberdeen Aug 1948 | 25 | 3 |
| Fred Davey | HB | Crediton Aug 1947 | 32 | |
| Leslie Doyle | HB | Everton Aug 1949 | 10 | |
| Frederick Durrant | F | Queens Park Rangers Feb 1949 | 4 | 1 |
| Peter Fallon | FB | R.A.F Jun 1947 | 25 | 1 |
| Ray Goddard | HB | Plymouth Argyle Dec 1949 | 22 | |
| John Greenwood | HB | Manchester City Jun 1949 | 31 | 1 |
| William Harrower | HB | Torquay United Jul 1948 | 20 | 4 |
| Bert Hoyle | G | Wolverhampton Wanderers Aug 1946 | 14 | |
| Denis Hutchings | W | Axminster Apr 1947 | 4 | |
| Cyril Johnstone | FB | Hamilton Academical Jul 1947 | 41 | |
| Charlie McClelland | W | Blackburn Rovers C/S 1949 | 33 | 8 |
| Angus Mackay | F | Ipswich Town Sep 1947 | 26 | 5 |
| Ronald Mitchell | W | Celtic Aug 1949 | 2 | |
| William Murphy | W | Stirling Albion Nov 1949 | 2 | |
| Kenneth Powell | HB | Cardiff City Jun 1948 | 13 | |
| Doug Regan | W | Trialist Mar 1945 | 27 | 11 |
| Roy Rew | F | Sea Mills Feb 1949 | 3 | 1 |
| Stan Rowe | FB | Trialist Oct 1947 | 19 | |
| Andrew Roy | F | Dunfermline Athletic Aug 1949 | 2 | |
| Barney Singleton | G | Wolverhampton Wanderers Jan 1946 | 28 | |
| Richard Smart | F | Stanley United Aug 1946 | 25 | 14 |
| Archibald Smith | F | Hamilton Academical May 1948 | 31 | 9 |
| Robert Squires | HB | Doncaster Rovers Jun 1949 | 1 | |
| Steve Walker | HB | Sheffield United May 1938 | 8 | 1 |

THIRD DIVISION SOUTH - 1949-50

| | P | W | D | L | F | A | |
|---|---|---|---|---|---|---|---|
| Notts County | 42 | 25 | 8 | 9 | 95 | 50 | |
| Northampton Town | 42 | 20 | 11 | 11 | 72 | 50 | |
| Southend United | 42 | 19 | 13 | 10 | 66 | 48 | |
| Nottingham Forest | 42 | 20 | 9 | 13 | 67 | 39 | |
| Torquay United | 42 | 19 | 10 | 13 | 66 | 63 | |
| Watford | 42 | 16 | 13 | 13 | 45 | 35 | |
| Crystal Palace | 42 | 15 | 14 | 13 | 55 | 54 | |
| Brighton & H.A. | 42 | 16 | 12 | 14 | 57 | 69 | |
| Bristol Rovers | 42 | 19 | 5 | 18 | 51 | 51 | |
| Reading | 42 | 17 | 8 | 17 | 70 | 64 | |
| Norwich City | 42 | 16 | 10 | 16 | 65 | 63 | |
| Bournemouth & B.A. | 42 | 16 | 10 | 16 | 57 | 56 | |
| Port Vale | 42 | 15 | 11 | 16 | 47 | 42 | |
| Swindon Town | 42 | 15 | 11 | 16 | 59 | 62 | |
| Bristol City | 42 | 15 | 10 | 17 | 60 | 61 | |
| Exeter City | 42 | 14 | 11 | 17 | 63 | 75 | |
| Ipswich Town | 42 | 12 | 11 | 19 | 57 | 86 | |
| Leyton Orient | 42 | 12 | 11 | 19 | 53 | 85 | |
| Walsall | 42 | 9 | 16 | 17 | 61 | 62 | |
| Aldershot | 42 | 13 | 8 | 21 | 48 | 60 | |
| Newport County | 42 | 13 | 8 | 21 | 67 | 98 | |
| Millwall | 42 | 14 | 4 | 24 | 55 | 63 | |

* Prior to the start of pre-season training, Exeter City's trainer, ex Sgt. Major of the Grenadier Guards, Jimmy Gallagher, and assistant trainer, former Warrant Officer Stan Cutting of the Royal Air Force, stated they aimed to make City the fittest team in England.

* There was a break in at St. James' Park in August 1949. 27 bottles of lemonade and ginger beer were missing from the refreshment hut, and the intruders then went into the boardroom and drank the remains of Ports, Sherries and Whisky! They also broke into the cupboards containing playing kit, and decided not to take anything, but simply threw shirts and shorts all over the floor.

* Exeter City assistant manager Bill Fellowes resigned in September 1949, 'due to outside business interests.'

* In October 1949 at the weekly meeting of the club's shareholders, it was revealed that the receipts during the last financial year had totalled £30,321. The cost of running Exeter City Football Club amounted to £530 per week. A profit of £2,187 was made on the year.

* A then record fee of £5,000 for Exeter City was paid to Plymouth Argyle for the signature of half-back Ray Goddard in December 1949.

* The Football League fined Millwall £100 and closed their ground for seven days following missiles being thrown at match officials at the end of their first round F.A. Cup tie against Exeter City.

* City conceded 15 goals in three consecutive away matches in December, losing 3-0 at Walsall, 7-1 at Swindon Town, 5-3 at Crystal Palace

* The Nuneaton Borough side arrived in Exmouth on the Thursday before their F.A. Cup third round FA Cup tie at Exeter City. They stayed at the Cranford Hotel and trained on the ground of Exmouth Town. The team also attended a children's pantomime at the Exmouth Church Hall.

* The Grecians received an allocation of 1,600 five-shilling tickets from then First Division leaders, Liverpool, for their F.A. Cup fourth round tie at Anfield in January 1950. The City team stayed in New Brighton and trained at the ground of the Third Division North club on the Thursday and Friday prior to the match.

* The Grecians played before what was then the highest crowd in the club's history when 45,209 were present at Anfield to see Liverpool beat Exeter City 3-1 in the F.A. Cup fourth round on 28th January 1950.

* Unlimited borrowing powers were given to the Exeter City directors when an emergency general meeting of shareholders was held in March 1950. Previously there was a limit of £20,000. At the same meeting it was revealed that the club had bought three houses for use of players and their families at a cost of £10,000

* By winning their last two league matches, Exeter City moved clear of the Third Division South re-election places. The second half of the season had been much better for City with only two defeats in 19 matches.

* Leicester City provided the opposition for a joint benefit match for Jimmy Gallagher and Stan Cutting when they visited St James' Park on 1st May 1950. An attendance of 8,000 saw City win 1-0.

* The highest attendance of the season at St James' Park for a Third Division South fixture was 14,833 for the visit of Torquay United on 11th February 1950.

* City lost two players with cartilage injuries during the season. Half-back Reg Gibson was forced to retire from playing, whilst Fred Durrant had two cartilage's removed from his left knee and played no part in the team after November 1949. He was given a free transfer at the end of the season.

A rare photograph of the Exeter City team during their end of season tour of Holland at Haarlem. The City players are in red shirts and white shorts, whilst the Dutch team are in the striped shirts.

\* A superb goal was scored by Archie Smith in the 1-0 home win against Bristol City in August 1950. It was described as:- 'No finer goal has been seen at St James' Park since the War than the one that gave Exeter City victory. 20 minutes had gone when a pass down the middle by Harrower was collected by Smith, who beat the Bristol City centre-half, and shot with his left foot from 20-yards. The ball was in the top of the net before the goalkeeper could move.

\* Exeter City reserves home game against Chingford in the Southern League in November 1951 was cancelled when the club received the following telegram ... "Very sorry we shall be unable to visit you on Saturday.' .... Chingford FC, due to continuing financial losses, decided they could not continue any longer.

### City's league results

| | HOME | AWAY |
|---|---|---|
| Aldershot | 3-0 | 2-4 |
| Bournemouth & B.A. | 2-1 | 1-1 |
| Brighton & H.A. | 4-2 | 1-4 |
| Bristol City | 1-0 | 1-3 |
| Bristol Rovers | 0-2 | 1-3 |
| Colchester United | 5-0 | 1-0 |
| Crystal Palace | 1-2 | 1-0 |
| Gillingham | 1-2 | 4-9 |
| Ipswich Town | 2-0 | 0-1 |
| Leyton Orient | 0-0 | 3-1 |
| Millwall | 0-1 | 0-5 |
| Newport County | 2-2 | 3-0 |
| Northampton Town | 1-0 | 1-4 |
| Nottingham Forest | 0-5 | 2-2 |
| Norwich City | 1-2 | 0-3 |
| Plymouth Argyle | 3-2 | 1-0 |
| Port Vale | 0-3 | 0-2 |
| Reading | 1-3 | 2-4 |
| Southend United | 1-0 | 1-5 |
| Swindon Town | 1-0 | 0-1 |
| Torquay United | 0-0 | 0-2 |
| Walsall | 1-0 | 2-0 |
| Watford | 3-3 | 2-1 |

### F.A. Cup

| Glastonbury | A | R1 | 2-1 |
|---|---|---|---|
| Swindon Town | H | R2 | 3-0 |
| Grimsby Town | A | R3 | 3-3 |
| Grimsby Town | H | R3R | 4-2 |
| Chelsea | H | R4 | 1-1 |
| Chelsea | A | R4R | 0-2 |

CITY MANAGER 1950-51
George Roughton - Appointed October 1945

### CITY PLAYING SQUAD 1950-51

| Name | Pos | Signed from | Apps | Gls |
|---|---|---|---|---|
| Stan Carter | HB | Amateur Nov 1949 | 1 | |
| Jim Clark | FB | Aberdeen Aug 1948 | 26 | |
| Reg Dare | F | Southampton Aug 1950 | 6 | |
| Fred Davey | HB | Crediton Aug 1947 | 43 | 1 |
| Leslie Doyle HB | HB | Everton Aug 1949 | 22 | |
| William Dunlop | F | Dunfermline Athletic Jun 1950 | 4 | |
| Peter Fallon | HB | R.A.F. Jun 1947 | 37 | 3 |
| Ray Goddard | HB | Plymouth Argyle Dec 1949 | 25 | |
| Arthur Greenaway | F | Plymouth Argyle May 1950 | 1 | |
| Bill Harrower | HB | Torquay United Jul 1948 | 32 | 2 |
| Dennis Hutchings | W | Amateur Jan 1947 | 8 | 1 |
| Cyril Johnstone | FB | Hamilton Academical Jul 1947 | 16 | |
| Graham Lear | G | Exmouth Town Jun 1950 | 3 | |
| Joe Lynn | F | Huddersfield Town Jun 1950 | 29 | 2 |
| Charlie McClelland | W | Blackburn Rovers Jul 1949 | 36 | |
| Angus Mackay | F | Ipswich Town Sep 1947 | 31 | 8 |
| Doug Regan | W | Trialist Mar 1945 | 26 | 7 |
| Stan Rowe | FB | Amateur Sep 1947 | 34 | |
| Ken Salter | G | Cullompton Nov 1950 | 1 | |
| Alan Short | W | Tamerton Aug 1950 | 5 | 1 |
| Barney Singleton | G | Wolverhampton Wanderers Jan 1946 | 42 | 1 |
| Richard Smart | F | Stanley United Aug 1946 | 17 | 4 |
| Archie Smith | F | Hamilton Academical May 1948 | 41 | 21 |
| Peter Smyth | F | Albion Rovers Jun 1950 | 5 | |
| Derek Warren | FB | Axminster Jan 1948 | 14 | |
| Harold Wilkinson | W | Chelsea May 1950 | 1 | |
| Own Goals | | | | 3 |

### THIRD DIVISION SOUTH - 1950-51

| | P | W | D | L | F | A | Pts |
|---|---|---|---|---|---|---|---|
| Nottingham Forest | 46 | 30 | 10 | 6 | 110 | 40 | 70 |
| Norwich City | 46 | 25 | 14 | 7 | 82 | 45 | 64 |
| Reading | 46 | 21 | 15 | 10 | 88 | 53 | 57 |
| Plymouth Argyle | 46 | 24 | 9 | 13 | 85 | 55 | 57 |
| Millwall | 46 | 23 | 10 | 13 | 80 | 57 | 56 |
| Bristol Rovers | 46 | 20 | 15 | 11 | 64 | 42 | 55 |
| Southend United | 46 | 21 | 10 | 15 | 92 | 69 | 52 |
| Ipswich Town | 46 | 23 | 6 | 17 | 69 | 58 | 52 |
| Bournemouth & B.A. | 46 | 22 | 7 | 17 | 65 | 57 | 51 |
| Bristol City | 46 | 20 | 11 | 15 | 64 | 59 | 51 |
| Newport County | 46 | 19 | 9 | 18 | 77 | 70 | 47 |
| Port Vale | 46 | 16 | 13 | 17 | 60 | 65 | 45 |
| Brighton & H.A. | 46 | 13 | 17 | 16 | 71 | 79 | 43 |
| EXETER CITY | 46 | 18 | 6 | 22 | 62 | 85 | 42 |
| Walsall | 46 | 15 | 10 | 21 | 52 | 62 | 40 |
| Colchester United | 46 | 14 | 12 | 20 | 63 | 76 | 40 |
| Swindon Town | 46 | 18 | 4 | 24 | 55 | 67 | 40 |
| Aldershot | 46 | 15 | 10 | 21 | 56 | 88 | 40 |
| Leyton Orient | 46 | 15 | 8 | 23 | 53 | 75 | 38 |
| Torquay United | 46 | 14 | 9 | 23 | 64 | 81 | 37 |
| Northampton Town | 46 | 10 | 16 | 20 | 55 | 67 | 36 |
| Gillingham | 46 | 13 | 9 | 24 | 69 | 101 | 35 |
| Watford | 46 | 9 | 11 | 26 | 54 | 88 | 29 |
| Crystal Palace | 46 | 8 | 11 | 27 | 33 | 84 | 27 |

* The end of the season proved to be little short of disastrous for City as they played four away matches on the trot, lost them all, scored once and conceded fourteen. This was preceded by a 5-1 home defeat at the hands of Third Division South champions, Nottingham Forest.

* It's true to day that the first half of the season was a lot more productive in terms of points than the second. At one stage the Grecians lost just two matches in 10, winning eight of them.

* A run in the FA Cup saw City reach round four and a chance to lock horns with Chelsea at St James' Park. After beating Glastonbury, Swindon Town and Grimsby Town, City then drew 1-1 with Chelsea, losing the replay 0-2.

* After their exit from the FA Cup, City's form slumped alarmingly, and they only registered a further five wins in the remaining 20 league fixtures.

* Highest attendance of the season at St James' Park for a league fixture was a full house of 20,000 for the visit of arch rivals Plymouth Argyle. City won 3-2 with goals from Angus Mackay, Archie Smith and Charlie McClelland.

* Angus Mackay was the only City player to register a league hat-trick during the season, which came in the 4-2 home win over Brighton and Hove Albion. Charlie McClelland got the other goal.

* City used three different goalkeepers during the course of the season. Mainstay was Barney Singleton, but amateur Graham Lear and Ken Salter also got their chance.

* In September 1950, City FC director, Leslie Seward said that the club were not getting the support they deserved and to run it on an economic basis. He added that attendances of 12,000 to 14,000 were needed for home matches. The directors were trying to give people a good team and the Grecians Association were raising money for ground improvements, but their joint efforts were not appreciated as they should have been.

* A new entrance to St James' Park was opened at the Old Tiverton Road end of the ground. The cost of constructing this - £613 - was paid for by the Grecians' Association.

* Because of the similarity in colours, both Exeter City and Swindon Town wore a new look strip for the FA Cup second round tie. The two teams normally played in red and white and under the rules of the competition, both sides had to change. City decided to play in gold shirts with black sleeves and collar. Swindon wore all blue.

* A benefit game was staged at St James' Park for Barney Singleton and Doug Regan in April 1951, when Portsmouth provided the opposition. Before a disappointing attendance of 2,000, Pompey won 2-0.

* Determined to get a ticket for City's FA Cup tie against Chelsea, over 100 supporters were in a queue outside St James' Park long before they went on sale. One 14-year-old was at the head of the queue and had waited for nine hours to ensure he would get one. The club had to face many angry fans who were unlucky and didn't get a ticket, who complained that the sale of them was very badly organised.

* At the end of the season, City went on a short tour of Holland where they played DOS Utrecht (won 3-0), Haarlem Eftal (won 5-3), Hertogenbosch (lost 2-4) and finally a Combined Hague XI (won 2-0).

* The following appeal from Exeter City FC chairman, Sidney Thomas appeared in the Exeter City match programme for the game against Gillingham in August 1951:-

*'The football season, 1951-52, is our 43rd as a professional club, and is likely to be of the greatest importance to use and all smaller clubs. We are living in an age of change and unrest in the soccer world and t is essential that Exeter City should hold a good position at the end of the season, Our supporters can help tremendously towards this end.*

*A little encouragement from the crowd can often turn possible defeat into victory. This particularly applies to our little ground, where almost every whisper can be heard on the field of play, and I am certain that if our supporters will give the necessary encouragement and backing, good results will follow.*

*The club has a good a set of players as we have ever had and it would not require a lot to take the team to the top of the League table. So off we go to season 1951-52 with hopes raised high.'* .... Note that Exeter City ended the season in next to bottom position!!

* The Grecians were losing 1-0 at half-time in their home fixture against Leyton Orient, but the second half was a complete reversal in fortunes. City scored six without reply, with goals from Charlie McClelland (3), Dick Walton (2) and Ivan Armes.

City' s league results

|  | HOME | AWAY |
|---|---|---|
| Aldershot | 0-4 | 1-4 |
| Bournemouth & B.A. | 2-2 | 4-0 |
| Brighton & H.A. | 2-0 | 1-2 |
| Bristol City | 0-0 | 1-1 |
| Bristol Rovers | 0-1 | 2-2 |
| Colchester United | 0-0 | 0-1 |
| Crystal Palace | 0-1 | 1-2 |
| Gillingham | 4-2 | 1-2 |
| Ipswich Town | 2-1 | 4-2 |
| Leyton Orient | 6-1 | 0-3 |
| Millwall | 0-3 | 0-4 |
| Newport County | 3-4 | 0-4 |
| Northampton Town | 0-3 | 1-3 |
| Norwich City | 2-4 | 1-1 |
| Plymouth Argyle | 1-0 | 1-2 |
| Port Vale | 2-0 | 0-3 |
| Reading | 1-4 | 1-2 |
| Shrewsbury Town | 4-2 | 1-2 |
| Southend United | 2-2 | 0-0 |
| Swindon Town | 1-2 | 1-3 |
| Torquay United | 4-0 | 1-5 |
| Walsall | 1-0 | 2-1 |
| Watford | 3-0 | 1-1 |

| F.A. Cup | | | |
|---|---|---|---|
| King's Lynn | A | R1 | 3-1 |
| Ipswich Town | A | R2 | 0-4 |

CITY MANAGER 1951-52
George Roughton - Appointed October 1945
Norman Kirkman - Appointed March 1952

CITY PLAYING SQUAD 1951-52

| Name | Pos | Signed from | Apps | Gls |
|---|---|---|---|---|
| Ivan Armes | HB | Norwich City Dec 1951 | 13 | 2 |
| Samuel Booth | HB | Derry City Aug 1951 | 6 | |
| William Brown | F | Reading Aug 1951 | 7 | |
| Stan Carter | HB | Amateur Nov 1949 | 1 | |
| Jim Clark | FB | Aberdeen Aug 1948 | 17 | |
| William Coley | HB | Northampton Town Jul 1951 | 8 | |
| Fred Davey | HB | Crediton Aug 1947 45 | 45 | |
| Derek Digby | W | Dawlish Town Apr 1949 | 20 | 2 |
| Leslie Doyle | HB | Everton Aug 1949 | 17 | |
| Peter Fallon | HB | R.A.F. Jun 1947 | 17 | 3 |
| Ray Goddard | HB | Plymouth Argyle Dec 1949 | 28 | |
| Bill Harrower | HB | Torquay United Jul 1948 | 12 | |
| Ray Howells | W | Crystal Palace Jul 1951 | 12 | 3 |
| Dennis Hutchings | W | Amateur Jan 1947 | 6 | |
| Norman Kirkman | HB | Southampton Mar 1952 | 8 | |
| Graham Lear | G | Exmouth Town Jun 1950 | 17 | |
| Charlie McClelland | W | Blackburn Rovers Jul 1949 | 35 | 11 |
| Angus Mackay | F | Ipswich Town Sep 1947 | 43 | 21 |
| Robert Mitchell | F | Third Lanark C/S 1951 | 3 | |
| Doug Regan | W | Trialist Mar 1945 | 25 | 5 |
| Stan Rowe | FB | Amateur Sep 1947 | 21 | |
| Barney Singleton | G | Wolverhampton Wanderers Jan 1946 | 29 | |
| Richard Smart | F | Stanley United Aug 1946 | 32 | 8 |
| Archie Smith | F | Hamilton Academical May 1948 | 23 | 5 |
| Richard Walton | FB | Leyton Orient C/S 1951 | 21 | 4 |
| Derek Warren | FB | Axminster Jan 1948 | 37 | |
| Kenneth Wilkins | F | Southampton Oct 1951 | 3 | |
| Own Goals | | | | 1 |

THIRD DIVISION SOUTH - 1951-52

| | P | W | D | L | F | A | Pts |
|---|---|---|---|---|---|---|---|
| Plymouth Argyle | 46 | 29 | 8 | 9 | 107 | 53 | 66 |
| Reading | 46 | 29 | 3 | 14 | 112 | 60 | 61 |
| Norwich City | 46 | 26 | 9 | 11 | 89 | 50 | 61 |
| Millwall | 46 | 23 | 12 | 11 | 74 | 53 | 58 |
| Brighton & H.A. | 46 | 24 | 10 | 12 | 87 | 63 | 58 |
| Newport County | 46 | 21 | 12 | 13 | 77 | 76 | 54 |
| Bristol Rovers | 46 | 20 | 12 | 14 | 89 | 53 | 52 |
| Northampton Town | 46 | 22 | 5 | 19 | 93 | 74 | 49 |
| Southend United | 46 | 19 | 10 | 17 | 75 | 66 | 48 |
| Colchester United | 46 | 17 | 12 | 17 | 56 | 77 | 46 |
| Torquay United | 46 | 17 | 10 | 19 | 86 | 98 | 44 |
| Aldershot | 46 | 18 | 8 | 20 | 78 | 89 | 44 |
| Port Vale | 46 | 14 | 15 | 17 | 50 | 66 | 43 |
| Bournemouth & B.A. | 46 | 16 | 10 | 20 | 69 | 75 | 42 |
| Bristol City | 46 | 15 | 12 | 19 | 58 | 69 | 42 |
| Swindon Town | 46 | 14 | 14 | 18 | 51 | 68 | 42 |
| Ipswich Town | 46 | 16 | 9 | 21 | 53 | 74 | 41 |
| Leyton Orient | 46 | 16 | 9 | 21 | 55 | 68 | 41 |
| Crystal Palace | 46 | 15 | 9 | 22 | 61 | 80 | 39 |
| Shrewsbury Town | 46 | 13 | 10 | 23 | 62 | 86 | 36 |
| Watford | 46 | 13 | 10 | 23 | 57 | 81 | 36 |
| Gillingham | 46 | 11 | 13 | 22 | 71 | 81 | 35 |
| Exeter City | 46 | 13 | 9 | 24 | 65 | 86 | 35 |
| Walsall | 46 | 13 | 5 | 28 | 55 | 94 | 31 |

* There was a dispute amongst the players over terms offered by the club prior to the start of the season. Three threatened to take jobs outside of football. However, no fewer than eight of the players signed on again on the eve of the first pre-season practice match, leaving just one, Peter Fallon, to hold out for better terms, and he signed a few days later.

* Exeter were ready to pay their club record fee to Grimsby Town for Frank Squires in September 1951. However, such were the wage demands of the player that the deal was called off.

* The team missed their 6.30pm train home from Paddington to Exeter after playing their fixture at Watford on 29th September 1951. This was due to the fact they had to wait for the injured Archie Smith to return from the local hospital for stitches to a cut lip. The team had to wait until 11pm for the next train to Exeter, arriving back in Devon at 4am.

* In October 1951, the club announced that they had made a record profit on the previous season of £3,604 5s 11d. Wages, salaries and bonuses accounted for £15,121 5s 6d.

* A ground attendance record of 12,500 watched the King's Lynn versus Exeter City F.A. Cup first round tie.

* The Grecians Association presented the club with a cheque of £313 in December 1951, as the final instalment on the cost of the new Norman Kendall entrance at St James' Park. The total cost of the project had been £613.

* City's amateur goalkeeper, Graham Lear, left the club in December 1951, having obtained work as an architect in London. He had also signed to play for Leytonstone. He remained on Football League forms with the Grecians.

* Signed the previous day from Norwich City, Ivan Armes made his debut for Exeter City in the 4-0 home win over Torquay United on Christmas Day and scored. Twenty-four hours later in the return fixture at Torquay, City lost 1-5! And three days after that City defeated Leyton Orient 6-1 back at St James' Park, such was their inconsistent form.

* Exeter City were the only Football League side that season without an away win until they won 2-0 at Walsall on 5th January 1952.

* Manager George Roughton, in charge since 1945, left the club in March 1952 to take over as boss of Southampton. In his place and arriving in the opposite direction was half-back Norman Kirkham who became the Grecians player-manager.

* Southampton provided the opposition at St James' Park on 2nd April 1952 for the Dick Smart benefit match. City won 3-2 despite being bottom of the Third Division South table at the time.

* Newly appointed player-manager Norman Kirkham had to wait until his seventh match in charge before he saw the Grecians win. A real upset it was too, as rock bottom City beat top of the table Plymouth Argyle, 1-0.

* Exeter City and Walsall had to apply for re-election to the Football League. It was felt that both clubs would be successful despite strong bids from Merthyr Tydfil and Worcester City. And that proved to be the case.

* A combination of poor results and lower attendances had greatly affected the finances at St James' Park, and it was welcome news in May 1952 when the Grecians Association announced they would present a cheque for £400 to alleviate any problems that may have occurred.

* Despite the poor season, Angus Mackay had top scored with an impressive 21 league goals, which proved to be his best tally with the club.

* An Exeter City XI travelled to Bideford in October 1952 to play a match to mark the opening of the North Devon club's new ground, The King George V Playing Field. Before a very good attendance, City won 3-1 with goals from McClelland, Fallon and Murphy.

* There was a surprise when the City reserve team was announced for their game against Gravesend and Northfleet. Left-back Jim Clark, who had been released at the end of the previous season, had been re-signed, following a shortage of players in that position. Sid Thomas, chairman of Exeter City explained that it had been imperative that the club took action quickly to sign another back and Clark had been re-signed for the rest of the season. Since leaving the Grecians he had spent one month on trial with Bradford Park Avenue.

* At the club's Shareholders A.G.M. in November 1952, player-manager Norman Kirkman promised that if early season attendances were maintained, that the directors would not hesitate to spend money on new players. Some of the players who had been bought at the start of the present season had been obtained only by the willingness of the directors to act as guarantors for the fees involved.

* Former Exeter City manager, Jack English, died at his home in Northampton in January 1953. He was 66-years-old. He had played left-back for Sheffield United when they won the F.A. Cup in 1914-15 and appeared for a Football League XI the same season.

City's league results

| | HOME | AWAY |
|---|---|---|
| Aldershot | 2-2 | 1-1 |
| Bournemouth & B.A. | 5-1 | 1-2 |
| Brighton & H.A. | 1-5 | 2-4 |
| Bristol City | 1-1 | 1-4 |
| Bristol Rovers | 0-0 | 0-0 |
| Colchester United | 2-0 | 1-3 |
| Coventry City | 1-0 | 0-1 |
| Crystal Palace | 2-0 | 0-2 |
| Gillingham | 0-0 | 0-1 |
| Ipswich Town | 1-1 | 1-0 |
| Leyton Orient | 0-1 | 0-2 |
| Millwall | 1-0 | 0-0 |
| Newport County | 3-2 | 0-1 |
| Northampton Town | 2-0 | 1-3 |
| Norwich City | 1-0 | 0-2 |
| Queens Park Rangers | 2-2 | 1-1 |
| Reading | 2-0 | 1-3 |
| Shrewsbury Town | 2-2 | 3-1 |
| Southend United | 0-2 | 1-1 |
| Swindon Town | 1-2 | 2-5 |
| Torquay United | 4-1 | 2-5 |
| Walsall | 6-1 | 2-2 |
| Watford | 1-1 | 1-3 |

F.A. Cup
Port Vale          A R1      1-2

CITY MANAGER 1952-53
Norman Kirkman - Appointed March 1952
Tim Ward - Appointed March 1953
Norman Dodgin - Appointed March 1953

THIRD DIVISION SOUTH - 1952-53

| | P | W | D | L | F | A | Pts |
|---|---|---|---|---|---|---|---|
| Bristol Rovers | 46 | 26 | 12 | 8 | 92 | 46 | 64 |
| Millwall | 46 | 24 | 14 | 8 | 82 | 44 | 62 |
| Northampton Town | 46 | 26 | 10 | 10 | 109 | 70 | 62 |
| Norwich City | 46 | 25 | 10 | 11 | 99 | 55 | 60 |
| Bristol City | 46 | 22 | 15 | 9 | 95 | 61 | 59 |
| Coventry City | 46 | 19 | 12 | 16 | 77 | 62 | 50 |
| Brighton & H.A. | 46 | 19 | 12 | 15 | 81 | 75 | 50 |
| Southend United | 46 | 18 | 13 | 15 | 69 | 74 | 49 |
| Bournemouth & B.A. | 46 | 19 | 9 | 18 | 74 | 69 | 47 |
| Watford | 46 | 15 | 17 | 14 | 62 | 63 | 47 |
| Reading | 46 | 19 | 8 | 19 | 69 | 64 | 46 |
| Torquay United | 46 | 18 | 9 | 19 | 87 | 88 | 45 |
| Crystal Palace | 46 | 15 | 13 | 18 | 66 | 82 | 43 |
| Leyton Orient | 46 | 16 | 10 | 20 | 68 | 73 | 42 |
| Newport County | 46 | 16 | 10 | 20 | 70 | 82 | 42 |
| Ipswich Town | 46 | 13 | 15 | 18 | 60 | 69 | 41 |
| Exeter City | 46 | 13 | 14 | 19 | 61 | 71 | 40 |
| Swindon Town | 46 | 14 | 12 | 20 | 64 | 79 | 40 |
| Aldershot | 46 | 12 | 15 | 19 | 61 | 77 | 39 |
| Queens Park Rangers | 46 | 12 | 15 | 19 | 61 | 82 | 39 |
| Gillingham | 46 | 12 | 15 | 19 | 55 | 74 | 39 |
| Colchester United | 46 | 12 | 14 | 20 | 59 | 76 | 38 |
| Shrewsbury Town | 46 | 12 | 12 | 22 | 68 | 91 | 36 |
| Walsall | 46 | 7 | 10 | 29 | 56 | 118 | 24 |

CITY PLAYING SQUAD 1952-53

| Name | Pos | Signed from | Apps | Gls |
|---|---|---|---|---|
| Alexander Anderson | FB | Southampton Jun 1952 | 6 | |
| Ivan Armes | HB | Norwich City Dec 1951 | 1 | |
| Neville Black | F | Newcastle United Jan 1953 | 4 | |
| Samuel Booth | HB | Derry City Aug 1951 | 33 | |
| Jim Clark | FB | Aberdeen Aug 1948 | 1 | |
| James Dailey | F | Birmingham City Aug 1952 | 36 | 12 |
| Fred Davey | HB | Crediton Aug 1947 | 39 | 1 |
| Derek Digby | W | Dawlish Town Apr 1949 | 11 | |
| Leslie Doyle | HB | Everton Aug 1949 | 18 | |
| Peter Fallon | HB | R.A.F. Jun 1947 | 13 | |
| Ray Goddard | HB | Plymouth Argyle Dec 1949 | 37 | |
| Keith Harvey | HB | Crediton Aug 1952 | 6 | |
| Ray Howells | W | Crystal Palace Jul 1951 | 3 | |
| Hugh Kelly | G | Southampton Jun 1952 | 37 | |
| Norman Kirkman | HB | Southampton Mar 1952 | 3 | 1 |
| John Knight | F | Chesterfield Aug 1952 | 36 | 4 |
| Charlie McClelland | W | Blackburn Rovers Jul 1949 | 13 | 5 |
| Angus Mackay | F | Ipswich Town Sep 1947 | 23 | 10 |
| Arnold Mitchell | W | Notts County Jul 1952 | 38 | 10 |
| Edward Murphy | F | Barnsley Jun 1952 | 38 | 7 |
| Doug Regan | W | Trialist Mar 1945 | 17 | 6 |
| Kenneth Rose | F | Chesterfield Jun 1952 | 11 | 3 |
| Stan Rowe | FB | Amateur Sep 1947 | 25 | |
| Barney Singleton | G | Wolverhampton Wanderers Jan 1946 | 9 | |
| Richard Walton | FB | Leyton Orient C/S 1951 | 40 | 1 |
| Francis Wood | HB | Bury Jan 1953 | 8 | |
| Own Goals | | | | 1 |

* Exeter City paid their record transfer fee in August 1952 when they parted with £5,000 for 24-year-old forward, Jim Dailey, from Birmingham City. It was reported that ..... "the directors had to scrape the barrel for the cash to pay the fee."

* The Grecians' game at Coventry City on Monday 29th September 1952 was reported to have finished in almost complete darkness, the hosts winning 1-0, scoring their goal in the 89th minute. The attendance of 8,588 was the lowest at Highfield Road for 20-years.

* Full-back Cyril Johnstone who had to retire from playing through injury, had a benefit match in October 1952 when an attendance of 3,745 saw a Cyril Johnstone XI beat Exeter City 5-1.

* The club reported a loss of £2,927 14s 6d on the year ended 30th June 1952. In their annual report the directors stated that it was not surprising when from the playing point of view the team had one of its worst seasons being compelled to apply for re-election to the Football League. Receipts from matches totalled £25,718 16s 10d.

* In November 1952 it was announced that the club's directors were looking into the possibility of installing floodlights at St James' Park. They said that if and when floodlit football took off then the Grecians wanted to be amongst those clubs who could stage such matches.

* Player-Manager Norman Kirkman left the club in February 1953 to take charge of Bradford Park Avenue. On 6th March 1953, City announced that Barnsley half-back Tim Ward had been appointed player-manager and he watched City win 1-0 at Ipswich Town 24-hours later. Then farce took over! Ward headed back to Barnsley on 12th March after just seven days in charge and was appointed manager of that club instead.

* The first ever floodlit match at St James' Park, a 'switch-on' friendly against Plymouth Argyle on 3rd March 1953 was postponed due to fog! The floodlight system comprised of seven lights on each side of the ground focussed directly on the touchlines, and a further 26 lights for the playing area. The game eventually took place in 9th March 1953 when an attendance of 8,130 were present to see Plymouth Argyle win 3-0.

* A joint benefit match for Fred Davey and Angus Mackay was staged at St James' Park between Exeter City and Cardiff City on 17th March 1953. An attendance of 9,000 saw Cardiff win 3-0 under the new floodlights. They also had a second benefit match on 13th April when Exeter City drew 2-2 with a 'Select XI.'

* A second successive application for re-election to the Football League was avoided when Exeter defeated Coventry City 1-0 at St James' Park on 22nd April 1953, a result that moved them into a position of safety in the league table.

* Exeter's third manager of the season, Norman Dodgin, was appointed on 23rd April 1953. He joined from Northampton Town, having also played for Newcastle United and Reading. His brother, Bill, was the manager of Fulham.

* Peter Fallon enjoyed a benefit match on 27th April 1953, when Exeter City met an 'All Star XI' which included England and Wolverhampton Wanderers player, Wilf Mannion. The visitors won 2-1 before 4,000 spectators.

* Jim Dailey was the only City player to register a hat-trick during the Third Division South season, when he netted three goals in the 6-1 home win over Walsall in September 1952.

* The highest attendance of the season for a league fixture at St James' Park was 15,720 when Norwich City were the visitors on 10th September 1952.

Exeter City 1953-54.

* Derek Digby was transferred from Exeter City to Southampton in September 1953. He therefore linked up once more with his former Grecians' manager George Roughton, who was in charge of the Saints. A day later City used the fee they had received for Digby to sign centre-forward Andy Donaldson from Peterborough United. Donaldson made a sensational debut for City 24-hours later when he scored twice in a 3-0 win at Newport County.

* Two City players asked for a transfer on the same day in October 1953, due to the fact that their families could not settle in Exeter, despite both living in houses owned by the club. Les Samuels family had moved out and returned to Burnley to live, whilst Jim Dailey's wife wanted to move nearer to her family home in Sheffield. Samuels eventually signed for Wrexham, whilst Dailey moved to Workington.

City's League results

| | HOME | AWAY |
|---|---|---|
| Aldershot | 1-3 | 2-1 |
| Bournemouth & B.A. | 1-0 | 1-4 |
| Brighton & Hove Albion | 0-1 | 1-2 |
| Bristol City | 0-1 | 1-5 |
| Colchester United | 1-2 | 1-0 |
| Coventry City | 4-0 | 0-2 |
| Crystal Palace | 7-0 | 0-0 |
| Gillingham | 1-2 | 1-0 |
| Ipswich Town | 1-2 | 1-1 |
| Leyton Orient | 2-1 | 1-3 |
| Millwall | 4-1 | 1-2 |
| Newport County | 1-0 | 3-0 |
| Northampton Town | 1-0 | 2-2 |
| Norwich City | 0-2 | 2-1 |
| Queens Park Rangers | 0-0 | 0-0 |
| Reading | 2-0 | 1-4 |
| Shrewsbury Town | 0-1 | 1-1 |
| Southampton | 4-0 | 0-2 |
| Southend United | 1-1 | 1-0 |
| Swindon Town | 3-1 | 4-2 |
| Torquay United | 1-2 | 2-3 |
| Walsall | 2-1 | 1-1 |
| Watford | 2-1 | 2-0 |

F.A. Cup

| | | | |
|---|---|---|---|
| Hereford United | H | R1 | 1-1 |
| Hereford United | A | R!R | 0-2 |

CITY MANAGER 1953-54
Norman Dodgin - Appointed April 1953

| CITY PLAYING SQUAD 1953-54 | | | League | |
|---|---|---|---|---|
| Name | Pos | Signed From | Apps | Goals |
| Sam Booth | HB | Derry City Aug 1951 | 23 | |
| Jimmy Dailey | F | Birmingham City Aug 1952 | 9 | 1 |
| Fred Davey | HB | Crediton Aug 1947 | 36 | |
| Norman Dodgin | HB | Northampton Town Apr 1953 | 30 | 1 |
| Andy Donaldson | F | Peterborough United Sep 1953 | 33 | 16 |
| Norman Douglass | FB | Chelsea June 53 | 22 | |
| Les Doyle | HB | Everton Aug 1949 | 12 | |
| Bill Ellaway | F | Barnstaple Town Nov 1953 | 8 | 2 |
| Ray Goddard | HB | Plymouth Argyle Dec 1949 | 18 | 2 |
| Keith Harvey | HB | Crediton Aug 1952 | 2 | |
| Hugh Kelly | G | Southampton Jun 1952 | 35 | |
| Jackie Knight | F | Chesterfield Aug 1952 | 20 | 2 |
| Charlie McClelland | W | Blackburn Rovers Jul 1949 | 36 | 19 |
| Angus Mackay | F | Ipswich Town Sep 1947 | 30 | 13 |
| Peter McLean | HB | Reading Aug 1953 | 15 | |
| Arnold Mitchell | HB | Notts County Jul 1952 | 27 | 3 |
| Eddie Murphy | F | Barnsley Jun 1952 | 12 | 1 |
| John Owens | HB | Pontypridd Oct 1953 | 5 | |
| Bill Parker | F | Swindon Town Jul 1953 | 18 | 2 |
| Gerry Priestley | W | Nottingham Forest Jun 1953 | 33 | 5 |
| Stan Rowe | FB | Local Oct 1947 | 7 | |
| Les Samuels | F | Burnley Jul 1953 | 12 | 1 |
| Maurice Setters | HB | Juniors Jan 1954 | | |
| Barney Singleton | G | Wolverhampton Wanderers Jan 1946 | 11 | |
| Jim Storey | FB | Newcastle United Jun 1953 | 9 | |
| Dick Walton | FB | Leyton Orient Dec 1951 | 42 | |

| THIRD DIVISION SOUTH - 1953-54 | | | | | | | |
|---|---|---|---|---|---|---|---|
| | P | W | D | L | F | A | Pts |
| Ipswich Town | 46 | 27 | 10 | 9 | 82 | 51 | 6. |
| Brighton & H.A. | 46 | 26 | 9 | 11 | 86 | 61 | 6. |
| Bristol City | 46 | 25 | 6 | 15 | 88 | 68 | 5. |
| Watford | 46 | 21 | 10 | 15 | 85 | 69 | 5. |
| Northampton Town | 46 | 20 | 11 | 15 | 82 | 55 | 5 |
| Southampton | 46 | 22 | 7 | 17 | 76 | 63 | 5 |
| Norwich City | 46 | 20 | 11 | 15 | 73 | 66 | 5. |
| Reading | 46 | 20 | 9 | 17 | 86 | 73 | 4. |
| EXETER CITY | 46 | 20 | 8 | 18 | 68 | 58 | 4. |
| Gillingham | 46 | 19 | 10 | 17 | 61 | 66 | 4. |
| Leyton Orient | 46 | 18 | 11 | 17 | 79 | 73 | 4. |
| Millwall | 46 | 19 | 9 | 18 | 74 | 77 | 4 |
| Torquay United | 46 | 17 | 12 | 17 | 81 | 88 | 4. |
| Coventry City | 46 | 18 | 9 | 19 | 61 | 56 | 4. |
| Newport County | 46 | 19 | 6 | 21 | 61 | 81 | 4. |
| Southend United | 46 | 18 | 7 | 21 | 69 | 71 | 4. |
| Aldershot | 46 | 17 | 9 | 20 | 74 | 86 | 4. |
| Queens Park Rangers | 46 | 16 | 10 | 20 | 60 | 68 | 4. |
| Bournemouth & BA | 46 | 16 | 8 | 22 | 67 | 70 | 4. |
| Swindon Town | 46 | 15 | 10 | 21 | 67 | 70 | 4. |
| Shrewsbury Town | 46 | 14 | 12 | 20 | 65 | 76 | 4. |
| Crystal Palace | 46 | 14 | 12 | 20 | 60 | 86 | 4. |
| Colchester United | 46 | 10 | 10 | 26 | 50 | 78 | 3. |
| Walsall | 46 | 9 | 8 | 29 | 40 | 87 | 2. |

* This proved to be one of Exeter City's better seasons, finishing in 9th place in the Third Division South, the highest finish since season 1933-34, when a 9th place was also attained. The F.A. Cup proved to be a disappointment though, as the Grecians were beaten by Southern League side, Hereford United, in a first round replay at Edgar Street.

* Winger Charlie McClelland was top scorer in league matches with 19 goals. He had been signed from Blackburn Rovers in July 1949 and went on to make a total of 183 league appearances for City, scoring 60 goals. He left the club at the end of the 1954-55 season and signed for Portland United.

* The highest attendance of the season for a league match at St James' Park was 15,518 for the visit of Torquay United in January 1954. Sadly City lost 2-1!

* The lowest attendance that City played in front of in the 1953-54 Third Division South season was 4,425 when they travelled to Aldershot on Christmas Day. Goals from Arnold Mitchell and Charlie McClelland gave Exeter a 2-1 win.

* Andy Donaldson was the only City player to register a hat-trick in a league match during the season. This he achieved in the 7-0 thrashing of Crystal Palace at St James' Park in January 1954. City's other goals came from Angus Mackay (2), Gerry Priestley and Charlie McClelland.

* Three young Welshmen were signed by Exeter City on the same day in October 1953, two of whom were to go on and play first team football. John Owens, a half-back, was given a professional contract, whilst Norman Packer and Tony Parker were signed on amateur forms. Owens was an upholsterer, whilst Packer, a school teacher, was in the midst of his National Service.

* Exeter City announced that they had made a loss of £573 17s 9d for the year ending 30th June 1953. £6,000 had been spent on transfer fees, whilst sales brought in £2,332. The total wage bill for the year was £14,942. Season ticket sales showed an increase, raising £6,380 4s.

* City full-back Stan Rowe was granted a benefit match which was played against Bristol Rovers in March 1954. An attendance of 2,738 were at St James' Park to see Rovers win 1-0.

* City centre-half Ray Goddard was released from his contract by Exeter City in April 1954, so that he could take over as player-manager at Bideford. He became the third former City player to be managing clubs in North Devon, with Harry Bartholomew at Ilfracombe Town and Arthur Coles at Barnstaple Town.

* The Grecians won the Devon Professional Final (equivalent to today's St Luke's Challenge Bowl) when they defeated Ilfracombe Town 3-0 in the final in North Devon, with goals from Charlie McClelland, Arnold Mitchell and Bill Parker.

* Another benefit game to be played at St James' Park, was staged for Angus Mackay and Fred Davey. City lost 3-1 at St James' Park, to Cardiff City, all three of the Ninian Park club's goals being netted by Welsh International, Trevor Ford.

* City retained 20 players on their staff at the end of the 1953-54 season, namely, Douglass, L. Doyle, Harvey, Priestley, Donaldson, Mackay, McClelland, Mitchell, Setters, Kelly, Walton, Marsh, Rowe, Owens, Davey, Dodgin, Murphy, Ellaway, B. Doyle and Sword

A regular feature of the pre-season preparations for many years was the annual club outing. In August 1954 a party of officials and players, as guests of the directors, enjoyed lunch at Dartmeet. The next halt was Paignton where some of the players enjoyed 6-a-side on the sands. In the evening at the Belgrave Hotel, Torquay, owned by City director, George Gillin, they all enjoyed a dinner, before heading back to Exeter.

* Prior to the season starting player-manager Norman Dodgin said that the previous season was the best the club had enjoyed for 20 years. He expected even better things in 1954-55. He added that he did not look on the club as being called Exeter City, but Dodgin City, for if the team did well, he was a success in his own job.

* By the end of August though City had come in for criticism from the local press, especially following a 2-2 home draw with Colchester United. One article stated: 'This form is not good enough City. It was sub standard because there were too many misdirected passes. Inaccuracy was a bad fault. Exeter were a crude, and ragged side.'

City's League results

| HOME AWAY | HOME | AWAY |
|---|---|---|
| Aldershot | 0-1 | 2-4 |
| Bournemouth & B.A. | 1-1 | 0-2 |
| Brentford | 3-2 | 0-1 |
| Brighton & Hove Albion | 3-1 | 3-5 |
| Bristol City | 0-1 | 0-2 |
| Colchester United | 2-2 | 2-1 |
| Coventry City | 0-0 | 1-1 |
| Crystal Palace | 2-0 | 1-1 |
| Gillingham | 1-1 | 1-1 |
| Leyton Orient | 1-7 | 0-5 |
| Millwall | 1-4 | 2-2 |
| Newport County | 1-1 | 1-2 |
| Northampton Town | 3-1 | 0-2 |
| Norwich City | 0-1 | 0-1 |
| Queens Park Rangers | 2-1 | 2-1 |
| Reading | 3-1 | 0-0 |
| Shrewsbury Town | 1-0 | 1-1 |
| Southampton | 0-1 | 0-3 |
| Southend United | 2-1 | 0-0 |
| Swindon Town | 2-1 | 0-2 |
| Torquay United | 1-2 | 0-1 |
| Walsall | 1-1 | 0-1 |
| Watford | 0-0 | 0-1 |

F.A. Cup
Millwall          A R1      2-3

CITY MANAGER 1954-55
Norman Dodgin - Appointed April 1953

CITY PLAYING SQUAD 1954-55

| Name | Pos | Signed From | Apps | Gls |
|---|---|---|---|---|
| John Anderson | W | Northampton Town Jul 1954 | 7 | |
| Alec Bell | G | Partick Thistle Aug 1954 | 16 | |
| Dennis Callan | HB | Cardiff City May 1954 | 10 | 1 |
| Fred Davey | HB | Crediton Aug 1947 | 33 | 1 |
| Norman Dodgin | HB | Northampton Town Apr 1953 | 3 | |
| Andy Donaldson | F | Peterborough United Sep 1953 | 6 | |
| Norman Douglass | FB | Chelsea Jun 1953 | 41 | |
| Brian Doyle | FB | Stoke City Apr 1954 | 39 | |
| Les Doyle | HB | Everton Aug 1949 | 3 | |
| Thomas Dunne | HB | Leicester City Jul 1954 | 25 | 1 |
| Bill Ellaway | F | Barnstaple Town Nov 1953 | 19 | 6 |
| Keith Harvey | HB | Crediton Aug 1952 | 22 | |
| Frank Houghton | F | Newcastle United C/S 1953 | 18 | 6 |
| Ray John | HB | Barnsley Jul 1954 | 26 | 4 |
| Gordon Kaile | W | Preston North End Aug 1954 | 6 | 1 |
| Hugh Kelly | G | Southampton Jun 1952 | 24 | |
| Charlie McClelland | W | Blackburn Rovers Jul 1949 | 30 | 9 |
| Angus Mackay | F | Ipswich Town Sep 1947 | 31 | 8 |
| Arnold Mitchell | HB | Notts County Jul 1952 | 45 | 1 |
| Geoffrey Morton | G | Southend United Sep 1954 | 6 | |
| Eddie Murphy | F | Barnsley Jun 1952 | 25 | 2 |
| John Owens | HB | Pontypridd Oct 1953 | 9 | |
| Gerry Priestley | W | Nottingham Forest Jun 1953 | 9 | 1 |
| Graham Rees | F | Pontypridd Youth Sept 1954 | 5 | 1 |
| Maurice Setters | HB | Juniors Jan 1954 | 9 | |
| Peter Thomas | F | Cardiff City Dec 1954 | 24 | 4 |
| Dick Walton | FB | Leyton Orient Dec 1951 | 14 | 1 |
| Evan Williams | FB | Cardiff City May 1954 | 1 | |

THIRD DIVISION SOUTH - 1954-55

| | P | W | D | L | F | A | Pts |
|---|---|---|---|---|---|---|---|
| Bristol City | 46 | 30 | 10 | 6 | 101 | 47 | 70 |
| Leyton Orient | 46 | 26 | 9 | 11 | 89 | 47 | 61 |
| Southampton | 46 | 24 | 11 | 11 | 75 | 51 | 59 |
| Gillingham | 46 | 20 | 15 | 11 | 77 | 66 | 55 |
| Millwall | 46 | 20 | 11 | 15 | 72 | 68 | 51 |
| Brighton & H.A. | 46 | 20 | 10 | 16 | 76 | 63 | 50 |
| Watford | 46 | 18 | 14 | 14 | 71 | 62 | 50 |
| Torquay United | 46 | 18 | 12 | 16 | 82 | 82 | 48 |
| Coventry City | 46 | 18 | 11 | 17 | 67 | 59 | 47 |
| Southend United | 46 | 17 | 12 | 17 | 83 | 80 | 46 |
| Brentford | 46 | 16 | 14 | 16 | 82 | 82 | 46 |
| Norwich City | 46 | 18 | 10 | 18 | 60 | 60 | 46 |
| Northampton Town | 46 | 19 | 8 | 19 | 73 | 81 | 46 |
| Aldershot | 46 | 16 | 13 | 17 | 75 | 71 | 45 |
| Queens Park Rangers | 46 | 15 | 14 | 17 | 69 | 75 | 44 |
| Shrewsbury Town | 46 | 16 | 10 | 20 | 70 | 78 | 42 |
| Bournemouth & B.A. | 46 | 12 | 18 | 16 | 57 | 65 | 42 |
| Reading | 46 | 13 | 15 | 18 | 65 | 73 | 41 |
| Newport County | 46 | 11 | 16 | 19 | 60 | 73 | 38 |
| Crystal Palace | 46 | 11 | 16 | 19 | 52 | 80 | 38 |
| Swindon Town | 46 | 11 | 15 | 20 | 46 | 64 | 37 |
| Exeter City | 46 | 11 | 15 | 20 | 47 | 73 | 37 |
| Walsall | 46 | 10 | 14 | 22 | 75 | 86 | 34 |
| Colchester United | 46 | 9 | 13 | 24 | 53 | 91 | 31 |

* With the St James' Park playing surface having been re-seeded, the Exeter City players undertook their pre-season training at Heavitree United's Wingfield Park ground and also used a council pitch at Marsh Barton in the city.

* Wing-half Maurice Setters, regarded by many as a real prospect for the future, played in a youth trial for the England team in a match staged on the ground of Notts County in October 1954. He had joined City originally as an outside right.

* Angus Mackay scored from the penalty spot in three successive league matches at St James' Park, against Queens Park Rangers, Southend United and Brentford respectively.

* The Board of Directors were keen to arrange midweek floodlit friendly matches and in October 1954, they said they had so far approached Arsenal, Chelsea, Manchester United, Newcastle United, Portsmouth and Wolverhampton Wanderers without success. French club Racing De Paris had also declined an invitation.

* After a 2-0 defeat at Bristol City on 30th October 1954, the Express and Echo reported: 'These unpalatable facts must be faced. Exeter City's goalscoring record is as bad as any in the Football League. The continuous drift towards the bottom of the table goes on.' In the very next game at St. James' Park, City were thumped 7-1 by Leyton Orient.

* A fall in attendances and increased expenses were a major factor in that Exeter City posted a loss in November 1954, of £2,260 9s 2d for the year ending 30th June 1954. Expenditure totalled £40,656 16s 9d. Match receipts totalled £25,974 19s 5d.

* Maurice Setters was transferred to West Bromwich Albion for a fee of £3,000 in January 1955. The City directors said it was a financial necessity. It was common knowledge that the current attendances of 7,000 were nothing like sufficient to keep a Third Division club going. City chairman Sidney Thomas added that they needed an average 0f 11,000.

* Norman Packer, an amateur with Exeter City, was selected to play for the British Army XI against Essex in February 1955. He was to enter the teaching profession on completion of his National Service and become a part-time professional with the Grecians,

* Exeter City played Austrian side, F.C. Colombia, in a friendly on Monday 21st February 1955. Played on a snow covered St James' Park pitch, the Grecians won 4-2 with goals from Peter Thomas, Angus Mackay, Charlie McClelland and Andy Donaldson.

* Famous trumpeter, Eddie Calvert, became an Exeter City shareholder in April 1955, when he bought £100 worth. Calvert was the cousin of Exeter forward Frank Houghton.

* Full-back Brian Doyle asked the club for a transfer in April 1955 as he felt that the St James' Park crowd were barracking him. City manager Norman Dodgin felt that the barrackers were not giving Doyle a chance, as he was a "grand player and always puts the team first."

* Thanks to Leyton Orient defeating Walsall 4-1, Exeter City were saved from having to apply for re-election to the Football League again. The result meant that both Walsall and Colchester United were the re-election candidates, leaving Exeter safe with one game still to play.

* Long serving match reporter for the Express and Echo, Lionel Wotton, died at the age of 52 in May 1955. He had covered City's matches for the newspaper under the name of 'Nomad' since 1933, having joined the paper as a 16-year-old.

* The Grecians Association presented Exeter City with a cheque for £1,000 at their annual dinner of the Executive Committee held at the Royal Clarence Hotel, Exeter. Since their formation in 1945-46, the Grecians Association had raised around £12,000 for the parent club.

* An attempt by the Inland Revenue to make Exeter City pay more rates because a 'good samaritan' repainted the roof of the main grandstand failed when the club appealed against the increase.   They had proposed that an increase of rateable assessing from £234 to £247 be applied. The original assessment had been agreed in 1935 and had remained unchanged since then. The proposal for the increase was because of an advertisement on the roof of the grandstand. The increase was rejected by the valuation panel for Exeter, East and North Devon.

In 1952 the roof of the grandstand had been in a bad state and club could not afford to lay out £300 to have it repainted. Fortunately a supporter of the club came to the rescue, and being connected with an oil company, it was agreed that he would repaint the roof in return for an advertisement.

* The Grecians Association announced they would be having a membership drive in July 1955. They were aiming for 2,000 members, by the end of the season. It had dropped to just 400.

* A new attractive programme cover, featuring an image of Exeter Cathedral, was introduced for the season. The aim of it, brought in at the instigation of the Exeter Information Bureau was to publicise the City of Exeter.

### City's League results

| | Home | Away |
|---|---|---|
| Aldershot | 2-1 | 0-1 |
| Bournemouth & B.A. | 2-0 | 0-0 |
| Brentford | 2-3 | 0-2 |
| Brighton & Hove Albion | 0-5 | 0-1 |
| Colchester United | 0-0 | 1-5 |
| Coventry City | 2-3 | 2-2 |
| Crystal Palace | 6-1 | 1-0 |
| Gillingham | 2-1 | 1-2 |
| Ipswich Town | 2-2 | 2-2 |
| Leyton Orient | 1-1 | 1-1 |
| Millwall | 3-1 | 0-2 |
| Newport County | 2-0 | 2-1 |
| Northampton Town | 3-1 | 0-3 |
| Norwich City | 1-1 | 1-2 |
| Queens Park Rangers | 2-0 | 0-1 |
| Reading | 0-2 | 2-1 |
| Shrewsbury Town | 3-0 | 0-2 |
| Southampton | 3-2 | 0-5 |
| Southend United | 0-1 | 0-6 |
| Swindon Town | 1-2 | 1-0 |
| Torquay United | 0-0 | 1-3 |
| Walsall | 1-1 | 1-3 |
| Watford | 1-2 | 3-2 |

### F.A. Cup

| | | | |
|---|---|---|---|
| Coventry City | A | R1 | 1-0 |
| Hendon | H | R2 | 6-2 |
| Stoke City | H | R3 | 0-0 |
| Stoke City | A | R3R | 0-3 |

### CITY MANAGER 1955-56
Norman Dodgin - Appointed April 1953

### CITY PLAYING SQUAD 1955-56

| Name | Pos | Signed From | Apps | Gls |
|---|---|---|---|---|
| Ted Buckle | F | Everton Jul 1955 | 28 | 5 |
| Ronnie Burke | F | Rotherham United Jun 1955 | 30 | 10 |
| Fred Davey | HB | Crediton Aug 1947 | 31 | |
| Brian Doyle | FB | Stoke City Apr 1954 | 33 | |
| Thomas Dunne | HB | Leicester City Jul 1954 | 12 | |
| Bill Ellaway | F | Barnstaple Town Nov 1953 | 4 | 1 |
| Theo Foley | FB | Home Farm Feb 1955 | 4 | |
| Ian Grinney | W | Crediton Sep 1954 | 2 | |
| Keith Harvey | HB | Crediton Aug 1952 | 41 | |
| Frank Houghton | F | Newcastle United C/S 1953 | 4 | 1 |
| George Hunter | G | Derby County Aug 1955 | 43 | |
| Ray Iggledon | F | Leeds United Jul 1955 | 27 | 8 |
| Ray John | HB | Barnsley Jul 1954 | 40 | 8 |
| Hugh Kelly | G | Southampton Jun 1952 | 3 | |
| Arnold Mitchell | HB | Notts County Jul 1952 | 45 | 4 |
| Eddie Murphy | F | Barnsley Jun 1952 | 19 | 3 |
| Norman Packer | HB | Pontypridd Jul 1955 | 1 | |
| Stephen Parr | FB | Liverpool May 1955 | 5 | |
| John Porteous | HB | Plymouth Argyle Mar 1955 | 13 | |
| Graham Rees | F | Pontypridd Youth Sept 1954 | 20 | 4 |
| Dennis Simpson | W | Reading May 1955 | 27 | 4 |
| Alan Sword | F | Newcastle United Sept 1953 | 9 | 4 |
| Keith Thomas | W | Plymouth Argyle Mar 1956 | 10 | 1 |
| Peter Thomas | F | Cardiff City Dec 1954 | 5 | |
| Dick Walton | FB | Leyton Orient Dec 1951 | 18 | |
| William Whiteside | W | Portadown Nov 1955 | 3 | 1 |
| George Willis | F | Plymouth Argyle Mar 1956 | 13 | 2 |
| Fred Worthington | F | Leicester City Jul 1955 | 16 | 1 |
| Own Goals | | | | 1 |

THIRD DIVISION SOUTH - 1955-56

| | P | W | D | L | F | A | Pts |
|---|---|---|---|---|---|---|---|
| Leyton Orient | 46 | 29 | 8 | 9 | 106 | 49 | 66 |
| Brighton & H.A. | 46 | 29 | 7 | 10 | 112 | 50 | 65 |
| Ipswich Town | 46 | 25 | 14 | 7 | 106 | 60 | 64 |
| Southend United | 46 | 21 | 11 | 14 | 88 | 80 | 53 |
| Torquay United | 46 | 20 | 12 | 14 | 86 | 63 | 52 |
| Brentford | 46 | 19 | 14 | 13 | 69 | 66 | 52 |
| Norwich City | 46 | 19 | 13 | 14 | 86 | 82 | 51 |
| Coventry City | 46 | 20 | 9 | 17 | 73 | 60 | 49 |
| Bournemouth & B.A. | 46 | 19 | 10 | 17 | 63 | 51 | 48 |
| Gillingham | 46 | 19 | 10 | 17 | 69 | 71 | 48 |
| Northampton Town | 46 | 20 | 7 | 19 | 67 | 71 | 47 |
| Colchester United | 46 | 18 | 11 | 17 | 76 | 81 | 47 |
| Shrewsbury Town | 46 | 17 | 12 | 17 | 69 | 66 | 46 |
| Southampton | 46 | 18 | 8 | 20 | 91 | 81 | 44 |
| Aldershot | 46 | 12 | 16 | 18 | 70 | 90 | 40 |
| Exeter City | 46 | 15 | 10 | 21 | 58 | 77 | 40 |
| Reading | 46 | 15 | 9 | 22 | 70 | 79 | 39 |
| Queens Park Rangers | 46 | 14 | 11 | 21 | 64 | 86 | 39 |
| Newport County | 46 | 15 | 9 | 22 | 58 | 79 | 39 |
| Walsall | 46 | 15 | 8 | 23 | 68 | 84 | 38 |
| Watford | 46 | 13 | 11 | 22 | 52 | 85 | 37 |
| Millwall | 46 | 15 | 6 | 25 | 83 | 100 | 36 |
| Crystal Palace | 46 | 12 | 10 | 24 | 54 | 83 | 34 |
| Swindon Town | 46 | 8 | 14 | 24 | 34 | 78 | 30 |

* Exeter City appointed a new groundsman, Sonny Clarke in the summer of 1955, and he was to serve the club for very many years, which eventually earned him a testimonial match against Derby County.

* The club made a profit of £272 on the year ending 30th June 1955, but the overall deficit stood at £18,605. Income for the year was £36,561, whilst wages, bonuses and pension schemes accounted for £17,906. travel, hotel and removal expenses totalled £3,961.

* The Grecians made a dreadful start to the season, winning just one of their opening 12 Third Division South fixtures. The one success was 3-1 at home to Millwall, when two goals from Ray John and one from Arnold Mitchell earned the points.

* In October 1955, Arnold Mitchell and Eddie Murphy both played for the Southern League XI against the previous season's League Champions, Yeovil Town, the game taking place at Huish.

* Trouble flared at the final whistle after Exeter City had beaten Aldershot 2-1. The home fans were incensed at the 'rough' tactics employed by the visitors which led to one City supporter striking Aldershot centre-half Charlie Billington as he walked toward the dressing room, and other supporters had to be restrained. A few weeks later the club were instructed to post warning notices by the Football Association that this would not be tolerated in the future.

* Following a meeting of the club's shareholders, Exeter City increased its share capital to £25,000 in November 1955 by the creation of 8,000 ordinary £1 shares.

* In November 1955, Chairman Mr. S.H. Thomas said that the club needed to find £700 per week to cover their running costs and without the support of the Grecians Association and Exmouth (Exeter City) Supporters Club it was doubtful if Exeter City could survive. It was also announced that two directors had unexpectedly resigned, Fred Cottey and Les Seward.

* The Exmouth (Exeter City) Supporters Club presented a new playing strip to the Grecians. With City's FA Cup third round opponents, Stoke City, playing in red and white stripes, Exeter played in blue and white shirts and shorts.

* The FA Cup tie between Exeter City and Stoke City was filmed for the first time ever. A cine camera had been given to the club along with a projector by Exeter director, Albert Line, with the idea that matches could be filmed and played back to show up any tactical errors.

* Exeter City played a friendly match against an International XI at St James' Park on 16th January 1956. The visitors included the likes of George Swindin, Wally Barnes, George Hardwick, Frank Broome and Charlie Mitten. City won 3-2 before an attendance of 7,322.

* Slipping ever nearer to the Football League re-election places, City manager Norman Dodgin recruited two players from Plymouth Argyle on 1st March 1956 in an effort to reverse the teams fortune. George Willis was signed for a fee of £250, whilst John Porteous cost £300. Both players made their debuts in a 3-1 win over Northampton Town, the first win for over two months, with Willis scoring one of the goals.

* There was controversy when City dropped the in form forward, Ted Buckle, from their side against Shrewsbury Town at Gay Meadow in April 1956. The reason was, had he played, then the Grecians, as part of the original transfer deal, would have had to pay Everton a further £500. Buckle was reinstated the following game and the transfer concluded with Everton.

* The highest attendance of the season for a league game at St James' Park was 13,991 for the visit of Torquay United on 3rd September 1955.

Back row: John Porteous, Keith Harvey, Steve Parr, Frank Houghton, John Lobbett, George Hunter, John Ferrier, Alan Marsh, Norman Packer.
Middle row: Graham Bowkett, Alan Sword, John Currie, Keith Thomas, Colin Beer, Eric Phoenix, Dennis Simpson, Ray John
Front row: Graham Rees, Brian Doyle, David Robinson, Ronnie Burke, Arnold Mitchell, Theo Foley, John Divers, George Willis, Ted Buckle

City's League results

| | HOME | AWAY |
|---|---|---|
| Aldershot | 1-1 | 4-1 |
| Bournemouth & B.A. | 1-2 | 1-3 |
| Brentford | 1-1 | 0-3 |
| Brighton & Hove Albion | 1-3 | 0-3 |
| Colchester United | 0-2 | 0-4 |
| Coventry City | 4-2 | 0-1 |
| Crystal Palace | 2-1 | 0-0 |
| Gillingham | 4-0 | 1-2 |
| Ipswich Town | 1-2 | 0-3 |
| Millwall | 1-1 | 3-1 |
| Newport County | 2-0 | 1-1 |
| Northampton Town | 0-0 | 1-1 |
| Norwich City | 0-0 | 0-1 |
| Plymouth Argyle | 2-1 | 0-5 |
| Queens Park Rangers | 0-0 | 3-5 |
| Reading | 1-1 | 0-4 |
| Shrewsbury Town | 5-1 | 2-1 |
| Southampton | 0-4 | 2-2 |
| Southend United | 6-1 | 0-2 |
| Swindon Town | 3-2 | 5-3 |
| Torquay United | 1-1 | 0-1 |
| Walsall | 0-1 | 0-2 |
| Watford | 1-2 | 1-1 |

F.A. Cup
| | | |
|---|---|---|
| Plymouth Argyle | A R1 | 0-2 |

CITY MANAGER 1956-57
Norman Dodgin - Appointed April 1953

CITY PLAYING SQUAD 1956-57

| Name | Pos | Signed From | Apps | Gls |
|---|---|---|---|---|
| Colin Beer | W | Exbourne C/S 1955 | 4 | 2 |
| Alec Bell | G | Partick Thistle Aug 1954 | 6 | |
| Ted Buckle | F | Everton Jul 1955 | 37 | 7 |
| Ronnie Burke | F | Rotherham United Jun 1955 | 12 | 4 |
| Dennis Churms | F | Coventry City Mar 1957 | 10 | |
| James Currie | F | Falkirk Jun 1956 | 45 | 17 |
| John Divers | W | Clyde May 1956 | 12 | 1 |
| Brian Doyle | FB | Stoke City Apr 1954 | 28 | |
| John Ferrier | FB | Clyde May 1956 | 31 | |
| Keith Harvey | HB | Credition Aug 1952 | 43 | 6 |
| Frank Houghton | F | Newcastle United C/S 1953 | 5 | 3 |
| George Hunter | G | Derby County Aug 1955 | 40 | |
| Ray John | HB | Barnsley Jul 1954 | 46 | 5 |
| George Lackenby | HB | Newcastle United Dec 1956 | 24 | 4 |
| Arnold Mitchell | HB | Notts County ul 1952 | 33 | 3 |
| Norman Packer | HB | Pontypridd Jul 1955 | 7 | |
| Stephen Parr | FB | Liverpool May 1955 | 3 | |
| Eric Phoenix | F | Gillingham Jun 1956 | 5 | |
| John Porteous | HB | Plymouth Argyle Mar 1955 | 27 | |
| Graham Rees | F | Pontypridd Youth Sept 1954 | 23 | 2 |
| Dennis Simpson | W | Reading May 1955 | 3 | |
| Noel Simpson | HB | Coventry City Feb 1957 | 16 | |
| Keith Thomas | W | Plymouth Argyle Mar 1956 | 33 | 5 |
| George Willis | F | Plymouth Argyle Mar 1956 | 13 | 1 |
| Own Goals | | | | 1 |

THIRD DIVISION SOUTH - 1956-57

| | P | W | D | L | F | A | Pts |
|---|---|---|---|---|---|---|---|
| Ipswich Town | 46 | 25 | 9 | 12 | 101 | 54 | 59 |
| Torquay United | 46 | 24 | 11 | 11 | 89 | 64 | 59 |
| Colchester United | 46 | 22 | 14 | 10 | 84 | 56 | 58 |
| Southampton | 46 | 22 | 10 | 14 | 76 | 52 | 54 |
| Bournemouth & B.A. | 46 | 19 | 14 | 13 | 88 | 62 | 52 |
| Brighton & H.A. | 46 | 19 | 14 | 13 | 86 | 65 | 52 |
| Southend United | 46 | 18 | 12 | 16 | 73 | 65 | 48 |
| Brentford | 46 | 16 | 16 | 14 | 78 | 76 | 48 |
| Shrewsbury Town | 46 | 15 | 18 | 13 | 72 | 79 | 48 |
| Queens Park Rangers | 46 | 18 | 11 | 17 | 61 | 60 | 47 |
| Watford | 46 | 18 | 10 | 16 | 72 | 75 | 46 |
| Newport County | 46 | 16 | 13 | 17 | 65 | 62 | 45 |
| Reading | 46 | 18 | 9 | 19 | 80 | 81 | 45 |
| Northampton Town | 46 | 18 | 9 | 19 | 66 | 73 | 45 |
| Walsall | 46 | 16 | 12 | 18 | 80 | 74 | 44 |
| Coventry City | 46 | 16 | 12 | 18 | 74 | 84 | 44 |
| Millwall | 46 | 16 | 12 | 18 | 64 | 84 | 44 |
| Plymouth Argyle | 46 | 16 | 11 | 19 | 68 | 73 | 43 |
| Aldershot | 46 | 15 | 12 | 19 | 79 | 92 | 42 |
| Crystal Palace | 46 | 11 | 18 | 17 | 62 | 75 | 40 |
| Exeter City | 46 | 12 | 13 | 21 | 61 | 79 | 37 |
| Gillingham | 46 | 12 | 13 | 21 | 54 | 85 | 37 |
| Swindon Town | 46 | 15 | 6 | 25 | 66 | 96 | 36 |
| Norwich City | 46 | 8 | 15 | 23 | 61 | 94 | 31 |

* Thirty sheep were 'signed on' by Exeter City in July 1956, joining the groundstaff in preparing the St James' Park pitch. They got on so well that their original three-day stay was extended to a week, by which time they had cropped the grass really short.

*In July 1956, the Directors decided to play recorded music over the tannoy at St James' Park, rather than the previous live performances from the Exeter British Railways Southern Region Band. They also announced that the cost of the match programme would increase from threepence to fourpence. Reserve team issues would remain the same price at one penny.

* The Grecians failed to score in their opening four Third Division South matches, a club record. Game number five resulted in them drawing 1-1 at home to Torquay United.

* Groundsman Sonny Clarke took delivery of a bulldozer in September 1956, to be used to level the orchard behind the Big Bank terracing, in readiness for a practice area for the club and would be ideal for five-a-side games.

* 19-year-old Colin Beer made a dream debut for Exeter City on 15th September 1956, when he scored twice in his team's 6-1 home win over Southend United.

* In the year ending 30th June 1956, Exeter City lost £3,977 to take the total deficit to £24,126. The loss was almost entirely brought about by the club spending money in the transfer market, which cost £6,241. Match receipts totalled £27,171, and season tickets brought in £4,984. Wages, bonuses and pension costs was a club record £18,250, whilst travel and hotel expenses totalled £4,476.

* A letter expressing a vote of no confidence in the policy of the Exeter City directors towards the Exmouth (Exeter City) Supporters Club was received in November 1956. It stated that football was on the 'down grade and that the directors were to blame. if it goes on much longer, it will be closed doors for Exeter City.'

* The Exeter City versus Plymouth Argyle FA Cup first round tie was made all ticket. Prices were as follows:- Grandstand 6s; Enclosure 3s 6d; Ground 2s 6d; Boys 1s.

* Floodlights were used for the first time for a Saturday afternoon Football League fixture at St James' Park for the visit of Watford 10th November 1956.

* Frank Houghton sustained a double fracture of the leg in the 5-0 beating at Plymouth Argyle in January 1957 which ended his playing career.

* A joint statement issued by the Grecians Association and the Exeter City board of directors on 2nd March 1957, read as follows:- 'Owing to the serious financial situation of the club, the directors have requested the Grecian Association to agree to the transfer to the clubs account the amount of £1,100 reserved for ground improvements. As a result in the marked decline in attendances at St James' Park this money is required to meet immediate working expenses.'

* Manager Norman Dodgin left the club on 1st April 1957, following a decision by the board of directors. The players were unhappy and they called a meeting to discuss the situation, and as a result gave their support for Dodgin.

* Albert Line was appointed chairman of Exeter City in April 1957 and immediately called the players to a meeting to explain the club's predicament, with attendances falling sharply. Line said this would be the start of a new era for the club as he set about putting his aims into practice, including a reconstruction of the board of directors.

* A joint benefit match for Arnold Mitchell and Keith Harvey was played against a Manager's All Star XI in April I1957. City won 2-1 before an attendance of 3,322.

Back row: David Butterworth, not known, Ted Calland, Peter Rapley,
Dennis Churms, Norman Packer, Alec Bell, George Hunter, Dilwyn Hill,
Tom Wilson, Keith Harvey, Jim Currie, Arnold Mitchell
Middle row: Harry Hanford (Trainer), Sonny Clarke (Groundsman), Derek
Waterman, Trevor Atkins, not known, Graham Rees, Dave Robinson,
Les MacDonald, Noel Simpson, Mike Cleverley, Tom Skuse, Ray John,
Theo Foley, Frank Houghton (Assistant Trainer)
Front row: Jimmy Rigby (Director), William Crawshaw (Director), Albert
Line (Chairman), Sidney Thomas (President), Albert Ford (Director),
John Watts (Director), George Gilbert (Secretary)

City's League results

| | HOME | AWAY |
|---|---|---|
| Aldershot | 3-0 | 2-2 |
| Bournemouth & B.A. | 1-2 | 1-2 |
| Brentford | 3-5 | 0-1 |
| Brighton & Hove Albion | 2-0 | 2-2 |
| Colchester United | 4-3 | 0-3 |
| Coventry City | 1-0 | 1-6 |
| Crystal Palace | 0-1 | 0-2 |
| Gillingham | 1-3 | 1-1 |
| Millwall | 2-0 | 0-3 |
| Newport County | 0-2 | 2-2 |
| Northampton Town | 0-1 | 0-9 |
| Norwich City | 2-2 | 2-3 |
| Plymouth Argyle | 4-2 | 0-1 |
| Port Vale | 1-0 | 2-3 |
| Queens Park Rangers | 0-0 | 1-1 |
| Reading | 1-1 | 0-2 |
| Shrewsbury Town | 2-1 | 0-1 |
| Southampton | 2-2 | 0-6 |
| Southend United | 0-5 | 0-2 |
| Swindon Town | 0-1 | 1-5 |
| Torquay United | 5-1 | 3-1 |
| Walsall | 2-1 | 0-3 |
| Watford | 1-2 | 4-5 |

F.A. Cup
Bath City    A R1    1-2

CITY PLAYING SQUAD 1957-58

| Name | Pos | Signed From | Apps | Gls |
|---|---|---|---|---|
| Trevor Atkins | F | Local C/S 1956 | 1 | 1 |
| Ian Atkinson | F | Carlisle United Jul 1957 | 8 | 2 |
| Colin Beer | W | Exbourne c/s 1955 | 1 | |
| Alec Bell | G | Partick Thistle Aug 1954 | 18 | |
| David Butterworth | F | Guildford City May 1957 | 17 | |
| Ted Calland | F | Torquay United Jul 1957 | 34 | 15 |
| Dennis Churms | F | Coventry City Mar 1957 | 34 | 8 |
| James Currie | F | Falkirk Jun 1956 | 9 | 2 |
| Gordon Dale | W | Portsmouth Oct 1957 | 31 | |
| Theo Foley | FB | Home Farm Feb 1955 | 34 | 1 |
| Keith Harvey | HB | crediton Aug 1952 | 37 | 2 |
| Dilwyn Hill | F | Pontypridd Jun 1955 | 10 | 2 |
| George Hunter | G | Derby County Aug 1955 | 28 | |
| Ray John | HB | Barnsley Jul 1954 | 26 | 1 |
| Brian Lightly | HB | Portsmouth Jun 1957 | 4 | |
| Les MacDonald | FB | Portsmouth Jun 1957 | 31 | |
| Arnold Mitchell | HB | Notts County Jul 1952 | 43 | 4 |
| John Nicholls | F | Cardiff City Nov 1957 | 16 | 8 |
| Ken Oliver | HB | Derby County Jan 1958 | 16 | |
| Norman Packer | HB | Pontypridd Jul 1955 | 7 | |
| Peter Rapley | W | Portsmouth Jun 1957 | 9 | 4 |
| Graham Rees | F | Pontypridd Youth Sept 1954 | 25 | 1 |
| David Robinson | W | Whipton Dec 1954 | 15 | 4 |
| Noel Simpson | HB | Coventry City Feb 1957 | 17 | |
| Nelson Stiffle | W | Bournemouth & B.A. Mar 1958 | 9 | |
| Derek Waterman | HB | Guildford City Jun 1957 | 4 | |
| Thomas Wilson | W | Reading Jul 1957 | 22 | 2 |

CITY MANAGER 1957-58
Bill Thompson - Appointed May 1957
Frank Broome - Appointed January 1958

THIRD DIVISION SOUTH - 1957-58

| | P | W | D | L | F | A | Pts |
|---|---|---|---|---|---|---|---|
| Brighton & H.A. | 46 | 24 | 12 | 10 | 88 | 64 | 60 |
| Brentford | 46 | 24 | 10 | 12 | 82 | 56 | 58 |
| Plymouth Argyle | 46 | 25 | 8 | 13 | 67 | 48 | 58 |
| Swindon Town | 46 | 21 | 15 | 10 | 79 | 50 | 57 |
| Reading | 46 | 21 | 13 | 12 | 79 | 51 | 55 |
| Southampton | 46 | 22 | 10 | 14 | 112 | 72 | 54 |
| Southend United | 46 | 21 | 12 | 13 | 90 | 58 | 54 |
| Norwich City | 46 | 19 | 15 | 12 | 75 | 70 | 53 |
| Bournemouth & B.A. | 46 | 21 | 9 | 16 | 81 | 74 | 51 |
| Queens Park Rangers | 46 | 18 | 14 | 14 | 64 | 65 | 50 |
| Newport County | 46 | 17 | 14 | 15 | 73 | 67 | 48 |
| Colchester United | 46 | 17 | 13 | 16 | 77 | 79 | 47 |
| Northampton Town | 46 | 19 | 6 | 21 | 87 | 79 | 44 |
| Crystal Palace | 46 | 15 | 13 | 18 | 70 | 72 | 43 |
| Port Vale | 46 | 16 | 10 | 20 | 67 | 58 | 42 |
| Watford | 46 | 13 | 16 | 17 | 59 | 77 | 42 |
| Shrewsbury Town | 46 | 15 | 10 | 21 | 49 | 71 | 40 |
| Aldershot | 46 | 12 | 16 | 18 | 59 | 89 | 40 |
| Coventry City | 46 | 13 | 13 | 20 | 61 | 81 | 39 |
| Walsall | 46 | 14 | 9 | 23 | 61 | 75 | 37 |
| Torquay United | 46 | 11 | 13 | 22 | 49 | 74 | 35 |
| Gillingham | 46 | 13 | 9 | 24 | 52 | 81 | 35 |
| Millwall | 46 | 11 | 9 | 26 | 63 | 91 | 31 |
| Exeter City | 46 | 11 | 9 | 26 | 57 | 99 | 31 |

* Exeter City named their new manager as Bill Thompson in May 1957, who had been in charge at Guildford City. He said he would work seven days per week and believed that Exeter would have their best season for a long time.

* The club sustained two heavy defeats in the first two home matches of the season. Chairman Albert Line said in his programme notes for the visit of Southend United to St James' Park that it was a start of a new era for the club, however, the Grecians lost 0-5. In the next home match they lost 3-5 to Brentford.

* In September 1957, City manager Bill Thompson, who preferred to sit in the Directors Box watching matches, said: "I believe the team manager has no place and no right to be on the touchline." Two months later he was quoted as saying: "Players do not need to be told what to do. They should know what to do for themselves."

* Keith Harvey was selected to play for the Third Division South XI against the Third Division North at Crystal Palace on 30th October 1957.

* Exeter City were not renowned for paying big transfer fees, but in October 1957 they did so to sign winger Gordon Dale from Portsmouth. Interestingly most record books state that City paid £7,000, but the club minute books clearly state £5,000.

* The club reported a loss of £1,198 for the year ending 30th June 1957. Wages, salaries and bonuses totalled £17,505, whilst travel, hotel and removal expenses accounted for £3,794. Match receipts brought in £21,109, whilst the Grecians Association made donations of £6,950.

* The Grecians made an embarrassing FA Cup first round exit at Southern League, Bath City, losing 2-1, in a performance described as 'showing as much fight as a cream puff.'

* Following a meeting in December 1957, between the club chairman and the players, (they were seen both collectively and individually), a week later it was the turn of manager Bill Thompson, to discuss the disappointing league position of the club.

* Following the 5-1 defeat at Swindon Town, six days later, on 10th January 1958, it was announced that the manager, Bill Thompson, had his contract terminated.

* The day after Thompson's departure, City were crushed 6-0 at Southampton, however, this did not put off former England international, Frank Broome, who watched the game and was duly appointed manager after a meeting with the chairman and some of the directors.

* Although there was a slight improvement under Frank Broome, the team hit a new low when they were thrashed 9-0 at Northampton Town on 12th April 1958, equalling the club's biggest Football League defeat.

* The disastrous season ended with Exeter 'sitting' at the bottom of the Third Division South, and thus having to apply for re-election to The Football League'. The bottom 12 clubs of the Southern and Northern section were to form the new Fourth Division. Fortunately the Grecians received a lot of support from fellow league clubs and were duly re-elected.

* Despite the poor season, one player did hit a league hat-trick, when Johnny Nicholls, along with a goal from Arnold Mitchell, gave the Grecians a very satisfying 4-2 victory over rivals, Plymouth Argyle. The game also attracted the highest attendance of the season at St. James' Park, 13, 598.

* City had a run of six straight defeats in November and December 1957, scoring five goals and conceding seventeen. They then followed that by winning three games in succession, including achieving the 'double' over Torquay United, during the Christmas period,

Exeter City playing squad and club directors, season 1958-59.

Playing in the newly formed Fourth Division, Exeter City were to face some lengthy journeys to fulfil fixtures. Their first away match was at Darlington on Saturday 30th August and from there they would go to Barrow on the Monday evening.

Travelling by rail their itinerary was as follows:- Exeter depart 10.30am Friday. Arrive Darlington 8.23pm. Depart Darlington Sunday 2.35pm. Arrive Barrow 10.30pm. Depart Barrow Tuesday 9am. Arrive Exeter 7.50pm. It was stated that it would cost £6 1s 6d per man in rail fares.

It was reported that the share that City would get from the Darlington gate may reach £100, and from the Barrow game around £50. Yet the rail fares cost over £80 and for hotels for fours nights at least £70.   On top of that they had to add the cost of meals for five days for manager Frank Broome, trainer Eddie Nash and 12 players at least, and maybe one director.

City's first expedition to the North could therefore cost them £100 from their own pockets. This left practically nothing from the reserve game gate to pay a wage bill bordering on the £300 mark.

### City's league results

| | Home | Away |
|---|---|---|
| Aldershot | 2-0 | 0-1 |
| Barrow | 4-0 | 0-1 |
| Bradford Park Avenue | 4-0 | 3-0 |
| Carlisle United | 2-1 | 2-1 |
| Chester | 1-1 | 2-4 |
| Coventry City | 2-1 | 0-2 |
| Crewe Alexandra | 3-0 | 0-0 |
| Crystal Palace | 3-1 | 1-1 |
| Darlington | 2-2 | 1-1 |
| Gateshead | 1-1 | 2-1 |
| Gillingham | 3-0 | 2-0 |
| Hartlepools United | 3-0 | 3-3 |
| Millwall | 3-1 | 1-1 |
| Northampton Town | 3-4 | 1-1 |
| Oldham Athletic | 3-2 | 1-2 |
| Port Vale | 3-4 | 3-5 |
| Shrewsbury Town | 1-0 | 0-3 |
| Southport | 3-2 | 1-0 |
| Torquay United | 2-2 | 4-3 |
| Walsall | 3-0 | 0-3 |
| Watford | 3-0 | 1-2 |
| Workington | 1-0 | |
| York City | 0-2 | 2-0 |

### F.A. Cup

| | | | |
|---|---|---|---|
| Brentford | A | R1 | 2-3 |

CITY MANAGER 1958-59
Frank Broome Appointed February 1958

### CITY PLAYING SQUAD 1958-59

| Name | Position | Signed From | Apps | Gls |
|---|---|---|---|---|
| Brian Birch | F | Barrow Sept 1958 | 7 | 1 |
| David Butterworth | HB | Guildford City Dec 1957 | 8 | |
| Ted Calland | F | Torquay United Jul 1957 | 44 | 27 |
| Gordon Dale | W | Portsmouth Oct 1957 | 41 | 2 |
| Theo Foley | FB | Home Farm Mar 1955 | 46 | |
| Keith Harvey | HB | Crediton Aug 1952 | 13 | 3 |
| Dilwyn Hill | F | Pontypridd Jun 1955 | 2 | 1 |
| George Hunter | G | Derby County Aug 1955 | 36 | |
| Ray John | HB | Barnsley Jul 1954 | 6 | |
| John Lobbett | G | Barnstaple Town Mar 1956 | 10 | |
| Les MacDonald | FB | Portsmouth Jun 1957 | 39 | |
| Arnold Mitchell | HB | Notts County Jul 1952 | 46 | 7 |
| Johnny Nicholls | F | Cardiff City Nov 1957 | 39 | 15 |
| Ken Oliver | HB | Derby County Jan 1958 | 46 | |
| Norman Packer | HB | Army Jul 1955 | 2 | |
| Graham Rees | F | Pontypridd YC Sep 1954 | 43 | 22 |
| David Robinson | HB | Whipton Dec 1954 | 1 | |
| Nelson Stiffle | W | Bournemouth & B.A. Mar 1958 | 44 | 8 |
| Jimmy Thompson | HB | Oldham Athletic Dec 1958 | 26 | 1 |
| Brian Whitnall | FB | Scunthorpe United Jul 1958 | 7 | |

### FOURTH DIVISION - 1958-59

| | P | W | D | L | F | A | Pts |
|---|---|---|---|---|---|---|---|
| Port Vale | 46 | 26 | 12 | 8 | 110 | 58 | 64 |
| Coventry City | 46 | 24 | 12 | 10 | 84 | 47 | 60 |
| York City | 46 | 21 | 18 | 7 | 73 | 52 | 60 |
| Shrewsbury Town | 46 | 24 | 10 | 12 | 101 | 63 | 58 |
| EXETER CITY | 46 | 23 | 11 | 12 | 87 | 61 | 57 |
| Walsall | 46 | 21 | 10 | 15 | 95 | 64 | 52 |
| Crystal Palace | 46 | 20 | 12 | 14 | 90 | 71 | 52 |
| Northampton Town | 46 | 21 | 9 | 16 | 85 | 78 | 51 |
| Millwall | 46 | 20 | 10 | 16 | 76 | 69 | 50 |
| Carlisle United | 46 | 19 | 12 | 15 | 62 | 65 | 50 |
| Gillingham | 46 | 20 | 9 | 17 | 82 | 77 | 49 |
| Torquay United | 46 | 16 | 12 | 18 | 78 | 77 | 44 |
| Chester | 46 | 16 | 12 | 18 | 72 | 84 | 44 |
| Bradford Park Avenue | 46 | 18 | 7 | 21 | 75 | 77 | 43 |
| Watford | 46 | 16 | 10 | 20 | 81 | 79 | 42 |
| Darlington | 46 | 13 | 16 | 17 | 66 | 68 | 42 |
| Workington | 46 | 12 | 17 | 17 | 63 | 78 | 41 |
| Crewe Alexandra | 46 | 15 | 10 | 21 | 74 | 88 | 40 |
| Hartlepools United | 46 | 15 | 10 | 21 | 74 | 88 | 40 |
| Gateshead | 46 | 16 | 8 | 22 | 56 | 85 | 40 |
| Oldham Athletic | 46 | 16 | 4 | 26 | 59 | 84 | 36 |
| Aldershot | 46 | 14 | 7 | 25 | 63 | 97 | 35 |
| Barrow | 46 | 9 | 10 | 27 | 51 | 104 | 28 |
| Southport | 46 | 7 | 12 | 27 | 41 | 86 | 26 |

* Had the Grecians' form not fallen away in the last third of the season, then there is little doubt that Exeter City would have attained promotion for the first time in their history. As it was they missed out by one point, having to beat Shrewsbury Town in the last game of the season, only to lose 0-3 and the Shrews were promoted instead.

* Goalscoring was never a problem for City with no fewer than three players reaching double figures and Ted Calland in particular hitting a magnificent 27 league goals.

* City won just five of their final 18 league matches and it cost them dearly. Unfortunately they had to do without goalkeeper George Hunter for a few of those games as he sustained a broken leg in the game at home to Port Vale, his place being taken by John Lobbett.

* Such was the settled side that City were able to field, no fewer than three players were ever present for the 46 game campaign, whilst four others played 40 or more.

* In what was the first season of the newly formed Fourth Division, City played a number of teams from the North of England that they hadn't done so before. It wasn't unusual to stay away over a weekend to play matches, such as at York City and Gateshead, or Crewe Alexandra and Workington in order to cut down on both travelling and costs.

* The City chairman right at the start of the season felt that the Southern teams would dominate the newly formed division, and that he was not happy with the fact that they had to now travel a lot more to fulfil the fixtures at added expense.

* Highest league attendance of the season at St James' Park was 13,102 for the visit of Torquay United.

* Despite all the goals that City scored, only one player netted a hat-trick - Graham Rees - but amazingly he still finished on the losing side as Exeter lost 5-3 at Port Vale.

* Exeter City had a new look for their FA Cup first round tie at Brentford. They wore tangerine shirts, with black edgings white shorts and socks. Both teams had to change their colours as both normally played in red and white so City bought a new strip. City lost the tie 3-2.

* Although City had put themselves in debt by spending £13,000 on players and were still relegated to the Fourth Division for 1958-59, the benefits were now being felt said City chairman Albert Line at the club's annual meeting. He went on to say that he thought Second Division football was nearer than many people believed.

* The City board of directors paid the cost of sending the players off for a mid-season break to Bournemouth in February 1959. It was originally intended for the players to stay at the chairman's hotel in Falmouth, but due to building alterations that was not possible, so they went to Bournemouth for a few days instead.

* Manager Frank Broome said: "The Fourth Division is no good. The biggest trouble is the travelling. Twice the team has had to go on trips which have kept them away from Exeter for five days. That means away from training as well. We are not making any money from the games either. Midweek trips are simply terrible."

* Having missed out on promotion by one point, City chairman, Albert Line said he was optimistic for the future. He was confident that the stepping stones of success had been laid. Plans for next season would be drawn up and the board of directors resolved to bring to Exeter football of the highest quality as soon as possible.

Back row: Jimmy Thompson, Keith Harvey, Barry Pulman, Mike Cleverly, Trevor Atkins, Bob Rackley, Alan Jones, Les MacDonald, Andy Micklewright, David Butterworth, Dilwyn Hill, Norman Packer, Peter Rapley.

Middle row: Eddie Nash (Trainer), Ken Oliver, Arnold Mitchell, Nelson Stiffle, Brian Whitnall, Brian Birch, John Lobbett, Ray Cragg, Graham Rees, Theo Foley, Ted Calland, Gordon Dale, David Pryde (Asst. Trainer).

Front row: Frank Broome (Manager), Les Kerslake (Director), Jack Watts (Director), Billy Crawshaw (Director), George Gillin (Chairman), Jack Cowley (Director), Jack Warne (Director), H.B. White (Director), George Gilbert (Secretary).

\* Following a meeting of the Exeter City board of directors in June 1959, it was confirmed that they had adjusted the sliding incentive wage scale for the players contracts for the 1959-60 season. They had improved upon the proposed £5 drop from the first team to the reserves, which most of the first team players had rejected as being not acceptable. The board stated that the wage scale compared with most good clubs and were far better than some.

City's league results

| | HOME | AWAY |
|---|---|---|
| Aldershot | 3-1 | 0-1 |
| Barrow | 2-2 | 3-3 |
| Bradford Park Avenue | 3-1 | 0-1 |
| Carlisle United | 1-3 | 4-0 |
| Chester | 2-0 | 0-1 |
| Crewe Alexandra | 2-4 | 1-1 |
| Crystal Palace | 2-2 | 0-1 |
| Darlington | 0-0 | 1-0 |
| Doncaster Rovers | 4-2 | 1-0 |
| Gateshead | 2-1 | 0-1 |
| Gillingham | 2-0 | 1-2 |
| Hartlepools United | 5-0 | 3-4 |
| Millwall | 2-2 | 3-2 |
| Northampton Town | 1-1 | 1-1 |
| Notts County | 3-3 | 0-3 |
| Oldham Athletic | 4-3 | 2-1 |
| Rochdale | 4-1 | 0-3 |
| Southport | 1-1 | 2-3 |
| Stockport County | 2-1 | 0-1 |
| Torquay United | 1-0 | 3-2 |
| Walsall | 1-2 | 2-2 |
| Watford | 2-0 | 2-5 |
| Workington | 1-0 | 1-2 |

F.A. Cup

| | | | |
|---|---|---|---|
| Barnstaple Town | H | R1 | 4-0 |
| Brentford | H | R2 | 3-1 |
| Luton Town | H | R3 | 1-2 |

CITY MANAGER 1959-60
Frank Broome Appointed February 1958

CITY PLAYING SQUAD 1959-60

| Name | Pos | Signed From | Apps | Gls |
|---|---|---|---|---|
| Trevor Atkins | F | Local C/S 1956 | 2 | 2 |
| Peter Bennett | F | Plymstock Aug 1959 | 5 | 5 |
| Brian Birch | F | Barrow Sept 1958 | 12 | |
| David Butterworth | HB | Guildford City Dec 1957 | 1 | |
| Ted Calland | F | Torquay United Jul 1957 | 27 | 7 |
| Gordon Dale | W | Portsmouth Oct 1957 | 26 | 5 |
| Theo Foley | FB | Home Farm Mar 1955 | 45 | |
| Keith Harvey | HB | Crediton Aug 1952 | 23 | |
| Dilwyn Hill | F | Pontypridd Jun 1955 | 2 | |
| Alan Jones | G | Cardiff City Jul 1959 | 32 | |
| John Lobbett | G | Barnstaple Town Mar 1956 | 14 | |
| Les MacDonald | FB | Portsmouth Jun 1957 | 40 | |
| Andy Micklewright | F | Swindon Town Jul 1959 | 38 | 11 |
| Arnold Mitchell | HB | Notts County Jul 1952 | 42 | |
| Ken Oliver | HB | Derby County Jan 1958 | 30 | |
| Peter Rapley | W | Portsmouth Jun 1957 | 1 | |
| Graham Rees | F | Pontypridd YC Sep 1954 | 42 | 17 |
| Nelson Stiffle | W | Bournemouth & B.A. Mar 1958 | 41 | 9 |
| Jimmy Thompson | HB | Oldham Athletic Dec 1958 | 44 | 6 |
| Eric Welsh | W | Distillery Sept 1959 | 4 | |
| Brian Whitnall | FB | Scunthorpe United Jul 1958 | 6 | |
| Jack Wilkinson | F | Poole Town Oct 1959 | 29 | 16 |
| Own Goals | | | | 2 |

FOURTH DIVISION - 1959-60

| | P | W | D | L | F | A | Pts |
|---|---|---|---|---|---|---|---|
| Walsall | 46 | 28 | 9 | 9 | 102 | 60 | 65 |
| Notts County | 46 | 26 | 8 | 12 | 107 | 69 | 60 |
| Torquay United | 46 | 26 | 8 | 12 | 84 | 58 | 60 |
| Watford | 46 | 24 | 9 | 13 | 92 | 67 | 57 |
| Millwall | 46 | 18 | 17 | 11 | 84 | 61 | 53 |
| Northampton Town | 46 | 22 | 9 | 15 | 85 | 63 | 53 |
| Gillingham | 46 | 21 | 10 | 15 | 74 | 69 | 52 |
| Crystal Palace | 46 | 19 | 12 | 15 | 84 | 64 | 50 |
| Exeter City | 46 | 19 | 11 | 16 | 80 | 70 | 49 |
| Stockport County | 46 | 19 | 11 | 16 | 58 | 54 | 49 |
| Bradford Park Avenue | 46 | 17 | 15 | 14 | 70 | 68 | 49 |
| Rochdale | 46 | 18 | 10 | 18 | 65 | 60 | 46 |
| Aldershot | 46 | 18 | 9 | 19 | 77 | 74 | 45 |
| Crewe Alexandra | 46 | 18 | 9 | 19 | 79 | 88 | 45 |
| Darlington | 46 | 17 | 9 | 20 | 63 | 73 | 43 |
| Workington | 46 | 14 | 14 | 18 | 68 | 60 | 42 |
| Doncaster Rovers | 46 | 16 | 10 | 20 | 69 | 76 | 42 |
| Barrow | 46 | 15 | 11 | 20 | 77 | 87 | 41 |
| Carlisle United | 46 | 15 | 11 | 20 | 51 | 66 | 41 |
| Chester | 46 | 14 | 12 | 20 | 59 | 7 | 40 |
| Southport | 46 | 10 | 14 | 22 | 48 | 92 | 34 |
| Gateshead | 46 | 12 | 9 | 25 | 58 | 86 | 33 |
| Oldham Athletic | 46 | 8 | 12 | 26 | 41 | 83 | 28 |
| Hartlepools United | 46 | 10 | 7 | 29 | 59 | 109 | 27 |

* Chairman Albert Line resigned on 2nd June 1959, due to 'health reasons' although he had made a statement to the Press regarding the club's financial position a couple of days earlier, which the rest of the board felt were inaccurate. George Gillin, a Torquay hotelier was appointed chairman in Line's place.

* A number of ground improvements were undertaken in the summer of 1960 including re-seating part of the enclosure in front of the grandstand, re-roofing of the Cowshed terrace where necessary, and replacing 300 railway sleepers on the covered terrace.

* The first half of the season was dominated by off the field events, for in October 1959, Albert Line stated that the board should be reconstituted with younger members taking over. He was not going to attend any more meetings as there was an unhappy atmosphere.

* Exeter City made a small profit of £224 on the year ended 30th June 1959. Salaries, wages and bonuses cost £24,484, whilst gate receipts totalled £25,691.

* Manager Frank Broome offered to resign in October 1959, but the directors rejected this. It was thought that Broome was unhappy at the club, with his contract running out in August 1961. At the same time it was agreed that the players should on a sliding scale of wages to reach the maximum of £20 per week by March 1960 if the team were in the top four of the table.

* During the half-time interval of the Exeter City versus Crewe fixture, spectators cheered when someone leapt the fence and paraded in front of the main stand with a banner stating that they wanted Frank Broome to stay. After the game a crowd of 200 gathered outside the ground with shouts of 'Go home Gillin.'

* The directors issued statement in October 1959 which explained their decision for removing Albert Line as vice chairman. 'Part of it read:- 'Under Mr Line's chairmanship Exeter City has spent nearly £20,000 on players in two seasons. This has caused serious financial problems that the club now finds itself troubled with. The policy of the present board is to strive to a more solvent position.' At the AGM of the shareholders a few days later, Line did not seek re-election due to continuing ill health.

* In early December 1959 there were strong rumours that the club would be cutting their playing staff to just 16 for the following season and that the reserves would switch from the Southern League to the Western League. The 'A' team in the South Western League would be abandoned altogether. This was confirmed at a board meeting later in the month as a cost cutting measure.

* The third round F.A. Cup tie against Luton Town at St James' Park was all ticket, with prices being set at - Grandstand 7s 6d; Ground 2s 6d. The tie, won by Luton, drew a crowd of 20,193.

* City were the victims of an astonishing refereeing decision at Workington in April 1960. Jimmy Thompson 'scored' with a 30-yard shot in the 83rd minute, the ball rebounding back into play off the net stanchion, but the referee signalled to play on, much to the amazement of both teams, as he thought the ball had hit a post.

* Manager Frank Broome was offered a similar job at Carlisle United in April 1960, but he turned it down preferring to stay in the south of England. The following month, Broome was appointed manager of Southend United.

* Exeter City retained just 12 players at the end of the season, with 17 others being transfer-listed or freed. It was hoped with reduced expenditure the club would be able to buy five or six players for the following season.

* The club received 40 applications for the post of player-manager and they appointed Glen Wilson, the long serving Brighton and Hove Albion, half-back.

* Speaking at a dinner for the players and officials of Exeter City F.C. in his Torquay hotel, chairman George Gillin said that he was confident that with a united effort City may go one step further than just being near the top as in the two previous seasons. Earlier in the day the players and officials had been on their annual outing, which took them to the Manor Hotel, Moretonhampstead where they played games of Squash, Badminton, Tennis and Golf before enjoying lunch.

* At the Annual General meeting of Exeter City shareholders in August 1960, chairman George Gillin stated that by cutting the playing staff and entering a team in the Western League instead of having sides in the Southern League and the South Western League, Exeter City would save about £5,000. The average gate receipts at St James' Park for a Southern League fixture was between £25 and £40 and that had to cover two weeks expenses which was £500 or more.

* When Exeter City centre-half Keith Harvey returned to his home in Crediton, after playing in a 2-0 defeat at Southport, he found the ground floor under a foot of water due to flooding. He was allowed to miss training for a couple of days whilst he continued with the clean up.

City's league results

| | HOME | AWAY |
|---|---|---|
| Accrington Stanley | 2-4 | 1-0 |
| Aldershot | 1-0 | 1-3 |
| Barrow | 2-2 | 1-1 |
| Bradford Park Avenue | 4-2 | 2-5 |
| Carlisle United | 0-0 | 2-2 |
| Chester | 4-1 | 4-4 |
| Crewe Alexandra | 0-1 | 0-2 |
| Crystal Palace | 2-3 | 0-0 |
| Darlington | 1-3 | 0-3 |
| Doncaster Rovers | 2-0 | 1-2 |
| Gillingham | 2-0 | 2-4 |
| Hartlepools United | 2-1 | 0-0 |
| Mansfield Town | 0-2 | 3-2 |
| Millwall | 2-3 | 2-2 |
| Northampton Town | 1-3 | 1-3 |
| Oldham Athletic | 3-0 | 2-5 |
| Peterborough United | 3-4 | 1-7 |
| Rochdale | 1-0 | 1-3 |
| Southport | 2-1 | 0-2 |
| Stockport County | 2-1 | 0-0 |
| Workington | 0-0 | 1-3 |
| Wrexham | 1-0 | 1-3 |
| York City | 2-1 | 1-6 |

F.A. Cup

| Bournemouth & B.A. | H R1 | 1-1 |
|---|---|---|
| Bournemouth & B.A. | A R1R | 1-3 |

Football League Cup

| Manchester United | H R1 | 1-1 |
|---|---|---|
| Manchester United | A R1R | 1-4 |

CITY MANAGER 1960-61
Glen Wilson Appointed May 1960

| CITY PLAYING SQUAD 1960-61 | | | | |
|---|---|---|---|---|
| Name | Pos | Signed From | Apps | Gls |
| Peter Bennett | F | Plymstock Aug 1959 | 1 | |
| Graham Bond | F | Torquay United Oct 1960 | 10 | 4 |
| Ray Carter | F | Torquay United Oct 1960 | 25 | 13 |
| Gordon Dale | W | Portsmouth Oct 1957 | 26 | 1 |
| Fred Donaldson | F | Port Vale Aug 1960 | 36 | 6 |
| Theo Foley | FB | Home Farm Mar 1955 | 26 | |
| Peter Gordon | F | Watford Jun 1960 | 24 | 3 |
| Alan Grant | HB | Brighton & H.A. Jun 1960 | 4 | |
| Bernard Harrison | W | Southampton Jul 1960 | 18 | 4 |
| Keith Harvey | HB | Crediton Aug 1952 | 36 | |
| Reg Jenkins | F | Plymouth Argyle Dec 1960 | 20 | 6 |
| Alan Jones | G | Cardiff City Jul 1959 | 26 | |
| John Lobbett | G | Barnstaple Town Mar 1956 | 20 | |
| Les MacDonald | FB | Portsmouth Jun 1957 | 46 | |
| Arnold Mitchell | HB | Notts County Jul 1952 | 20 | |
| Norman Packer | HB | Pontypridd Jul 1955 | 1 | |
| Graham Rees | F | Pontypridd YC Sep 1954 | 42 | 14 |
| Jimmy Thompson | HB | Oldham Athletic Dec 1958 | 35 | 3 |
| Eric Welsh | W | Distillery Sept 1959 | 7 | |
| Brian Whitnall | FB | Scunthorpe United Jul 1958 | 19 | |
| Jack Wilkinson | F | Poole Town Oct 1959 | 19 | 10 |
| Alvan Williams | HB | Bradford Park Avenue Aug 1960 | 19 | 1 |
| Peter Williams | HB | Plymouth Argyle Apr 1960 | 1 | |
| Glen Wilson | HB | Brighton & H.A. May 1960 | 25 | 1 |

FOURTH DIVISION - 1960-61

| | P | W | D | L | F | A | Pts |
|---|---|---|---|---|---|---|---|
| Peterborough United | 46 | 28 | 10 | 8 | 134 | 65 | 66 |
| Crystal Palace | 46 | 29 | 6 | 11 | 110 | 69 | 64 |
| Northampton Town | 46 | 25 | 10 | 11 | 90 | 62 | 60 |
| Bradford Park Avenue | 46 | 26 | 8 | 12 | 84 | 74 | 60 |
| York City | 46 | 21 | 9 | 16 | 80 | 60 | 51 |
| Millwall | 46 | 21 | 8 | 17 | 97 | 86 | 50 |
| Darlington | 46 | 18 | 13 | 15 | 78 | 70 | 49 |
| Workington | 46 | 21 | 7 | 18 | 74 | 76 | 49 |
| Crewe Alexandra | 46 | 20 | 9 | 17 | 61 | 67 | 49 |
| Aldershot | 46 | 18 | 9 | 19 | 79 | 69 | 45 |
| Doncaster Rovers | 46 | 19 | 7 | 20 | 76 | 78 | 45 |
| Oldham Athletic | 46 | 19 | 7 | 20 | 79 | 88 | 45 |
| Stockport County | 46 | 18 | 9 | 19 | 57 | 66 | 45 |
| Southport | 46 | 19 | 6 | 21 | 69 | 67 | 44 |
| Gillingham | 46 | 15 | 13 | 18 | 64 | 66 | 43 |
| Wrexham | 46 | 17 | 8 | 21 | 62 | 56 | 42 |
| Rochdale | 46 | 17 | 8 | 21 | 60 | 66 | 42 |
| Accrington Stanley | 46 | 16 | 8 | 22 | 74 | 88 | 40 |
| Carlisle United | 46 | 13 | 13 | 20 | 61 | 79 | 39 |
| Mansfield Town | 46 | 16 | 6 | 24 | 71 | 78 | 38 |
| Exeter City | 46 | 14 | 10 | 22 | 66 | 94 | 38 |
| Barrow | 46 | 13 | 11 | 22 | 52 | 79 | 37 |
| Hartlepools United | 46 | 12 | 8 | 26 | 71 | 103 | 32 |
| Chester | 46 | 11 | 9 | 26 | 61 | 104 | 31 |

* Exeter City's first team players would earn £18 per week, however, if the team was in the top four, then they would get a £2 per week bonus.

* Admission prices for the 1960-61 season were fixed at:- Ground 2s 6d; Standing Enclosure 3s; Enclosure Seats 4s; Grandstand Seats 6s; Season Tickets £7.

* Exeter City lost £2,513 on the year ended 30th June 1960. £3,000 was spent on ground improvements, whilst the Grecians Association handed over £12,800. Match receipts totalled £27,769. Wages accounted for £24,852 and travel and hotel expenses came to £5,442.

* Arnold Mitchell played his 320th league match for City when he lined up against Carlisle United on the opening day of the season. A club record, previously held by Reg Clarke.

* in his programme notes for the above game against Carlisle, Player-Manager Glen Wilson, wrote:- 'Two seasons in the Fourth Division is way too long. We must increase our efforts to get back into the Third Division as quickly as possible.'

* The Grecians were drawn at home to Manchester United in the first round of the new Football League Cup competition. The match was made all-ticket. An attendance of 14,494 saw the Grecians hold their famous visitors to a 1-1 draw. A week later City lost the replay at Old Trafford 4-1, before a crowd of 15,662.

* The club appointed a new secretary in October 1960, Jimmy Cook, who had previously been secretary of Montrose F.C for five years. However, he quit the job at St James' Park after just three weeks for 'personal reasons.'

* Following City's 2-2 home draw with Barrow on 3rd December 1960, the club slumped to the bottom of the Fourth Division, having gone nine games without a win, and conceding thirteen goals in the last three matches.

* Chairman George Gillin announced on 9th January 1961 that the club were in acute financial trouble and it was difficult to say where the wages were coming from week by week. Eight days later, following a board meeting, it was revealed that the club had offered St James' Park to Exeter City Council for the sum of £60,000, and then rent it back from them. At a Council meeting in March, the proposal was turned down with only two councillors voting in favour.

* The following month the Board stated that they would run a team of 15 or 16 professionals the following season and scrap the reserves, which would save £7,000 alone. Admission prices would also have to rise by sixpence for the ground and one shilling and sixpence for the grandstand. They said that if the club was to function, then supporters must be expected to pay a realistic price.

* In March 1961, Player-Manager Glen Wilson told five of his players that they would be available on free transfers as part of the cutbacks in readiness for the following season.

* The Fourth Division fixture between Exeter City and Crewe Alexandra on Wednesday 15th March was postponed due to fog. However, Crewe stayed over another 24 hours and the match went ahead the following evening, with the visitors winning 1-0.

* Despite winning their final match of the season, a 2-0 home win over Gillingham, Exeter City still found themselves in the bottom four of the Fourth Division and therefore had to apply for re-election to The Football League.

* On 5th May 1961, it was announced that only ten players would be retained, thus the club would be seeking to make five or six signings for the following season.

* Player-Manager Glen Wilson turned down the chance to become manager of his former club, Brighton and Hove Albion in May 1961, preferring to stay with Exeter City.

*To encourage supporters to buy their season tickets early and to help the club's cash flow position during the summer months, it was announced that the cost of some season tickets for the 1961-62 season would be reduced.

"The board have decided that all seasons for the grandstand purchased by 24th June shall be issued for £6 instead of £7," said chairman Reg Rose. "In addition season tickets will be available for the popular bank at £3."

Summer wages would cost the club £4,000 and during that time the only source of income was from season ticket sales and money raised by the Grecians Association.

* City player-manager Glen Wilson contacted his Plymouth Argyle counterpart, Neil Dougall, with a view to signing transfer listed forward George Kirby. Wilson said: "I was very interested until hearing the fee that Argyle wanted - £20,000 - That is a ridiculous price as far as we are concerned. We haven't got anything like that kind of money. If we had I would rather spend it on a new stand for the supporters."

* Following the Grecians defeat at non-league Dartford in the FA Cup, the players were ordered to attend extra training, two sessions per day. Trainer Eddie Nash said: "What we are lacking at the moment is effort and the extra training sessions will enable the players to be built up to extra effort just by habit."

Player-manager Glen Wilson added: "I have not been satisfied with the teams performances over the last few games. There ought to be more fight for the club and if I don't get it for 90 minutes on a Saturday, then I will make sure I get it midweek during training. We are in an uncomfortable position in the league and I don't want the team sliding any lower."

City's league results

|  | HOME | AWAY |
|---|---|---|
| Accrington Stanley | 3-0 | * |
| Aldershot | 2-1 | 1-1 |
| Barrow | 3-0 | 0-3 |
| Bradford City | 1-2 | 1-5 |
| Carlisle United | 4-0 | 1-2 |
| Chester | 5-0 | 1-1 |
| Chesterfield | 4-1 | 0-2 |
| Colchester United | 0-2 | 0-2 |
| Crewe Alexandra | 2-1 | 1-3 |
| Darlington | 0-1 | 0-1 |
| Doncaster Rovers | 1-5 | 1-3 |
| Gillingham | 1-3 | 2-2 |
| Hartlepools United | 1-1 | 0-0 |
| Mansfield Town | 2-1 | 1-3 |
| Millwall | 1-1 | 0-2 |
| Oldham Athletic | 3-3 | 1-1 |
| Rochdale | 1-3 | 0-3 |
| Southport | 1-1 | 1-1 |
| Stockport County | 4-3 | 0-1 |
| Tranmere Rovers | 1-0 | 4-3 |
| Workington | 3-1 | 1-3 |
| Wrexham | 1-1 | 2-1 |
| York City | 2-1 | 1-2 |

*Accrington Stanley resigned

| F.A. Cup | | | |
|---|---|---|---|
| Dartford | H | R1 | 3-3 |
| Dartford | A | R1R | 1-2 |

| Football League Cup | | | |
|---|---|---|---|
| Mansfield Town | A | R1 | 2-5 |

CITY MANAGER 1961-62
Glen Wilson Appointed May 1960

CITY PLAYING SQUAD 1961-62

| Name | Pos | Signed From | Apps | Gls |
|---|---|---|---|---|
| Archie Blue | F | Hearts Jul 1961 | 34 | 6 |
| Alan Brown | F | Brighton & H.A. Jan 1962 | 11 | 3 |
| Ray Carter | F | Torquay United Oct 1960 | 40 | 18 |
| Peter Gordon | F | Watford Jun 1960 | 43 | 9 |
| Keith Harvey | HB | Crediton Aug 1952 | 44 | 2 |
| Geoff Hudson | FB | Halifax Town Jul 1962 | 41 | |
| Mike Hughes | HB | Cardiff City Jul 1961 | 17 | |
| Reg Jenkins | F | Plymouth Argyle Dec 1960 | 39 | 8 |
| Alan Jones | G | Cardiff City Jul 1959 | 32 | |
| Les MacDonald | FB | Portsmouth Jun 1957 | 43 | |
| John McMillan | W | Cardiff City Oct 1961 | 8 | 1 |
| Arnold Mitchell | HB | Notts County Jul 1952 | 16 | |
| Graham Rees | F | Pontypridd YC Sep 1954 | 25 | |
| Derrick Sullivan | HB | Cardiff City Jun 1961 | 44 | |
| Colin Tinsley | G | Darlington Jul 1961 | 12 | |
| Eric Welsh | W | Distillery Sept 1959 | 20 | 6 |
| Brian Whitnall | FB | Scunthorpe United Jul 1958 | 4 | |
| Glen Wilson | HB | Brighton & H.A. May 1960 | 11 | 1 |
| Own Goals | | | | 2 |

FOURTH DIVISION - 1961-62

| | P | W | D | L | F | A | Pts |
|---|---|---|---|---|---|---|---|
| Millwall | 44 | 23 | 10 | 11 | 87 | 62 | 56 |
| Colchester United | 44 | 23 | 9 | 12 | 104 | 71 | 55 |
| Wrexham | 44 | 22 | 9 | 13 | 96 | 56 | 53 |
| Carlisle United | 44 | 22 | 8 | 14 | 64 | 63 | 52 |
| Bradford City | 44 | 21 | 9 | 14 | 94 | 86 | 51 |
| York City | 44 | 20 | 10 | 14 | 84 | 53 | 50 |
| Aldershot | 44 | 22 | 5 | 17 | 81 | 60 | 49 |
| Workington | 44 | 19 | 11 | 14 | 69 | 70 | 49 |
| Barrow | 44 | 17 | 14 | 13 | 74 | 58 | 48 |
| Crewe Alexandra | 44 | 20 | 6 | 18 | 79 | 70 | 46 |
| Oldham Athletic | 44 | 17 | 12 | 15 | 77 | 70 | 46 |
| Rochdale | 44 | 19 | 7 | 18 | 71 | 71 | 45 |
| Darlington | 44 | 18 | 9 | 17 | 61 | 73 | 45 |
| Mansfield Town | 44 | 19 | 6 | 19 | 77 | 66 | 44 |
| Tranmere Rovers | 44 | 20 | 4 | 20 | 70 | 81 | 44 |
| Stockport County | 44 | 17 | 9 | 18 | 70 | 69 | 43 |
| Southport | 44 | 17 | 9 | 18 | 61 | 71 | 43 |
| Exeter City | 44 | 13 | 11 | 20 | 62 | 77 | 37 |
| Chesterfield | 44 | 14 | 9 | 21 | 70 | 87 | 37 |
| Gillingham | 44 | 13 | 11 | 20 | 73 | 94 | 37 |
| Doncaster Rovers | 44 | 11 | 7 | 26 | 60 | 85 | 29 |
| Hartlepools United | 44 | 8 | 11 | 25 | 52 | 101 | 27 |
| Chester | 44 | 7 | 12 | 25 | 54 | 96 | 26 |

*Accrington Stanley resigned from League and their record was expunged

* Prior to the start of the season Exeter City announced a record loss of £7,160 on the year ending June 1961. Match and ground receipts totalled £22,660, and the club's overall deficit now stood at £39,445.

* The terracing alongside the grandstand, between there and Big Bank and known as 'The Transport Mens Enclosure' would not be used for the 1961-62, as it was in need of repair and the club felt that it was better to close the area instead.

* In August 1961, club chairman Reg Rose considered calling a public meeting to discuss Exeter City's financial position. He said that it had been left to two men to put in thousands of pounds and though they had publicly appealed for help, they never received any replies. Had it not been for director George Gillin, who carried the club financially for three years, then there would be no Exeter City.

* Bolivian team, C.A.R. La Paz played a friendly at St James' Park on 20th October 1961, with City winning 3-1 before an attendance of 5,004. It also marked the first team debut of 15-year-old apprentice, Peter Rutley, who played for the final 15 minutes of the game.

* A planning application to build a £150,000 20-lane bowling alley at the back of the Big Bank terracing was turned down by the city council.

* The Grecians lost to Southern League Dartford in the first round of the FA Cup. After being held to a replay at St James' Park, they lost the replay in Kent.

* Another prestige friendly took place at St. James' Park on 22nd November 1961 when Exeter City entertained O.F.K. Belgrade, the visitors winning 4-2 in front of 3,548 spectators.

* Player-manager Glen Wilson was one of the favourites to take over as manager of Tranmere Rovers in December 1961, a job that carried a salary of £2,000 per year. City chairman Reg Rose said the club would not stand in the way if Wilson wanted to go to Tranmere. However, Wilson turned the job down saying that Exeter City could become a very good club.

* In January 1962 Exeter City chairman Reg Rose made a public appeal, mainly to traders and businessmen of the city, to raise money for the club through the issue of £5 loan receipts. He said that the club could not go on much longer steadily losing money without reaching the same stage as Accrington Stanley who were thinking of resigning from The Football League. The financial situation at Exeter City was described as being grave.

* Club chairman Reg Rose bought the £17,000 mortgage on St. James' Park and hoped to stabilise expenditure during the season. Including the mortgage the club had total debts of around £40,000 and without substantial help of the Red and White pool and the Supporters Club, City would still lose around £250 per week.

* Four days before City were due to travel to play at Accrington Stanley, the Lancashire club went into liquidation with debts of £60,000. City secretary Keith Honey said that the postponement of the fixture would save the club £160 in hotel and travelling expenses.

* Player-manager Glen Wilson was dismissed by the club on 30th April 1962. The following day he was replaced by Cyril Spiers, who had previously managed Cardiff City and Crystal Palace. Spiers said that the future accent at Exeter City would be on youth and that he never could resist a challenge.

* Ray Carter was the only City player to score a hat-trick in what was otherwise another poor playing season. He hit three goals in the 3-3 home draw with Oldham Athletic and eventually top scored for the season with 18 league goals.

A hard hitting article appeared in the local press in November 1962 which was quite critical of the club, which read as follows:-

*'On and off the field Exeter City are in deep trouble. The club may not be facing a financial crisis, but no amount of whitewash will cover the fact that from the playing point of view they have progressed not one step since 1959, and that internal relationships are equally poor.*

*The playing performances are entirely devoid of any sense of pattern or plan which might be shown in the club's administration. The internal relations are devoid of any team work which the players might show on the pitch.*

*Three seasons ago, even when the team were losing, you could be sure of seeing a consistent performance. They always tried to play the same style of football. This season the side clicks one game and fails the next. It is all too haphazard.*

*Three seasons ago the club had little or no money to spend, but everyone else was anxious to try and raise more and no one was more willing than the Grecians Association. Today the directors are willing to dip their hands in their pockets to buy players that are desperately needed, but the Supporters Club will not.*

*Exeter City chairman Reg Rose has not helped matters by declaring in the press ...*"My feelings are that the Grecians Association dispute with the club is purely a domestic matter and that it has done the club no good at all to have the matter aired in the press. We have recently lost out on signing three players because of the bad press that Exeter City are receiving.'

The Grecians Association have gone so far as to pass a vote of no confidence in the direction or management of the club and are withholding

## City's league results

| | HOME | AWAY |
|---|---|---|
| Aldershot | 4-2 | 1-1 |
| Barrow | 0-2 | 2-0 |
| Bradford City | 0-2 | 3-2 |
| Brentford | 2-2 | 1-3 |
| Chester | 2-1 | 1-3 |
| Chesterfield | 2-2 | 1-1 |
| Crewe Alexandra | 1-1 | 0-1 |
| Darlington | 1-3 | 1-0 |
| Doncaster Rovers | 0-1 | 1-1 |
| Gillingham | 0-0 | 0-4 |
| Hartlepools United | 3-1 | 2-0 |
| Lincoln City | 1-1 | 1-4 |
| Mansfield Town | 0-3 | 0-1 |
| Newport County | 1-0 | 0-4 |
| Oldham Athletic | 2-1 | 2-1 |
| Oxford United | 1-1 | 1-3 |
| Rochdale | 0-2 | 0-3 |
| Southport | 2-1 | 3-1 |
| Stockport County | 0-1 | 3-4 |
| Torquay United | 0-3 | 0-3 |
| Tranmere Rovers | 2-1 | 1-2 |
| Workington | 1-0 | 1-3 |
| York City | 2-1 | 3-3 |

**F.A. Cup**

| | | | |
|---|---|---|---|
| Gravesend & Northfleet | A | R1 | 2-3 |

**Football League Cup**

| | | | |
|---|---|---|---|
| Aldershot | A | R1 | 0-2 |

CITY MANAGER 1962-63
Cyril Spiers Appointed May 1962

## CITY PLAYING SQUAD 1962-63

| Name | Pos | Signed From | Apps | Gls |
|---|---|---|---|---|
| Des Anderson | HB | Glenavon Aug 1962 | 44 | |
| James Boag | G | Bath City Oct 1962 | 2 | |
| Ray Carter | F | Torquay United Oct 1960 | 40 | 19 |
| Derek Grace | F | Queens Park Rangers May 1962 | 1 | |
| Brian Green | F | Altrincham Aug 1962 | 9 | 1 |
| Keith Harvey | HB | Crediton Aug 1952 | 22 | 2 |
| John Henderson | F | Charlton Athletic Nov 1962 | 24 | 8 |
| Mike Hughes | HB | Cardiff City Jul 1961 | 19 | |
| Brian Jenkins | W | Cardiff City Jun 1961 | 34 | 3 |
| David Johnston | FB | Leicester City May 1962 | 10 | |
| Les MacDonald | FB | Portsmouth Jun 1957 | 28 | |
| John McMillan | W | Cardiff City Oct 1961 | 12 | |
| Arnold Mitchell | HB | Notts County Jul 1952 | 40 | 5 |
| Roy Patrick | FB | Southampton Mar 1963 | 18 | |
| Barry Pierce | F | York City Jul 1962 | 28 | 4 |
| Graham Rees | F | Pontypridd YC Sep 1954 | 29 | 4 |
| Peter Rutley | HB | Apprentice Jul 1961 | 8 | |
| James Sanders | HB | Cheltenham Town Aug 1962 | 20 | 1 |
| Charlie Sells | F | Queens Park Rangers Aug 1962 | 14 | 3 |
| Cecil Smyth | FB | Distillery Aug 1962 | 39 | |
| Colin Tinsley | G | Darlington Jul 1961 | 44 | 1 |
| Eric Welsh | W | Distillery Sept 1959 | 21 | 4 |
| Own Goals | | | | 2 |

## FOURTH DIVISION - 1962-63

| | P | W | D | L | F | A | Pts |
|---|---|---|---|---|---|---|---|
| Brentford | 46 | 27 | 8 | 11 | 98 | 64 | 62 |
| Oldham Athletic | 46 | 24 | 11 | 11 | 95 | 60 | 59 |
| Crewe Alexandra | 46 | 24 | 11 | 11 | 86 | 58 | 59 |
| Mansfield Town | 46 | 24 | 9 | 13 | 108 | 69 | 57 |
| Gillingham | 46 | 22 | 13 | 11 | 71 | 49 | 57 |
| Torquay United | 46 | 20 | 16 | 10 | 75 | 56 | 56 |
| Rochdale | 46 | 20 | 11 | 15 | 67 | 59 | 51 |
| Tranmere Rovers | 46 | 20 | 10 | 16 | 81 | 67 | 50 |
| Barrow | 46 | 19 | 12 | 15 | 82 | 80 | 50 |
| Workington | 46 | 17 | 13 | 16 | 76 | 68 | 47 |
| Aldershot | 46 | 15 | 17 | 14 | 73 | 69 | 47 |
| Darlington | 46 | 19 | 6 | 21 | 72 | 87 | 44 |
| Southport | 46 | 15 | 14 | 17 | 72 | 106 | 44 |
| York City | 46 | 16 | 11 | 19 | 67 | 62 | 43 |
| Chesterfield | 46 | 13 | 16 | 17 | 70 | 64 | 42 |
| Doncaster Rovers | 46 | 14 | 14 | 18 | 64 | 77 | 42 |
| Exeter City | 46 | 16 | 10 | 20 | 57 | 77 | 42 |
| Oxford United | 46 | 13 | 15 | 18 | 70 | 71 | 41 |
| Stockport County | 46 | 15 | 11 | 20 | 56 | 70 | 41 |
| Newport County | 46 | 14 | 11 | 21 | 76 | 90 | 39 |
| Chester | 46 | 15 | 9 | 22 | 51 | 66 | 39 |
| Lincoln City | 46 | 13 | 9 | 24 | 68 | 89 | 35 |
| Bradford City | 46 | 11 | 10 | 25 | 64 | 93 | 32 |
| Hartlepools United | 46 | 7 | 11 | 28 | 56 | 104 | 25 |

* A season that will be remembered for the 'Big Freeze' when the UK was covered by snow and ice for weeks. Exeter City only played once between 29th December and 2nd March. The season was extended, with City playing their last game on 22nd May at Crewe Alexandra.

* Exeter City entered the F.A. Youth Cup for the very first time, with manager Cyril Spiers accent very much on young players, he felt this would benefit the club.

* The club made a loss of £3,190 on the year ending 30th June 1962. There was a total deficiency of £42,635. Gate receipts had dropped by £2,500. The Grecians' Association had donated £8,750.

* City made a terrible start to the season and didn't win until their ninth league game, that being a 2-1 home win over York City.

* With the team struggling, in October 1962, chairman Reg Rose said that the board were not just sitting back and watching the team spend another season at the bottom of the Fourth Division. The board realised that they had to do something about the forward line and outlined plans to bring three good class forwards to the club.

* Brighton and Hove Albion reported Exeter City to the Football League in October 1962 for non-payment of the final instalment of the transfer fee for Glen Wilson. Exeter owed Brighton £1,400.

* Exeter City crashed out of the F.A. Cup first round to Southern League Gravesend and Northfleet, losing 3-2. City complained about the floodlights which were not switched on, and also had keeper Colin Tinsley carried off injured in the 65th minute. Not a good day for the Grecians!

* The Exeter City players had a nightmare journey home from Stockport County after losing 4-3 there on Boxing Day. They left Manchester by the midnight train and did not arrive in Exeter until 9am the following day. The train had been held up by snow drifts and battled through blizzards.

* Such was the severity of the winter that in February there was 8 inches of snow on the St James' Park pitch, and at least 3 inches of hard packed ice underneath.

* On 7th February 1963 it was announced that the contract of City manager Cyril Spiers had been terminated. Trainer Jack Edwards would take charge of the team on a caretaker basis. Edwards transformed the team's fortunes and they climbed away from the bottom of the Fourth Division.

* After playing, and winning 2-0 at Barrow on 2nd March 1965, the City team then made the short trip across town to watch Barrow play Workington in the Rugby League Cup.

* Wing-half Jimmy Sanders had his contract cancelled by mutual consent. The player said that his wife and three children were living in a rented house in Bristol, and he was in digs in Exeter. He simply could not make ends meet. He had hoped that the City would have found him a club house to live in, but that was not possible.

* With just one game remaining, it was announced that Jack Edwards had been appointed manager. The board of directors felt that he had achieved a certain amount of success since he took over as caretaker following the departure of Cyril Spiers and commanded a great deal of popularity and respect.

* The highest attendance of the season for a league match at St James' Park was for the opening game against Torquay United when 9,676 were present.

* The lowest attendance that City played in front of in a Fourth Division fixture was 1,403 at Rochdale on 11th May 1963. City lost 0-3.

* In September 1963 Exeter City announced that they were to stop travelling to away matches by train as it was too expensive. Instead they were to have a coach fitted out with swivel seats and tables so that the players could travel in comfort.

City club secretary, Keith Honey, said: "As far as we are concerned British Railways have priced themselves out of business. Most of our fellow Fourth Division teams are in the North, so we face a great deal of travelling. From bitter experience we have found we cannot trust the railway timetables.

"This means we can never afford to leave ourselves just 30 minutes in the timetable for changing trains. We have to get there on time or face a heavy fine from the Football League for being late. There is no reduction in the dining cars for parties, but now we are going by coach we book meals in hotels on the way at about half the cost."

* A new incentive scheme was introduced that may have helped bring players to St James' Park. There was a crowd bonus paid to players whereby they would receive extra in wages should the attendance at home matches attract more than 5,000 through the turnstiles. Part-timer Graham Rees was one of two players nominated to put the bonus scheme to the City board of directors. Rees said: "We have made £7 to £8 out of it so far. This may not sound too much, but when it comes in £1 or £2 extra payments in your pay packet each week, it is quite useful. The payers have been quite pleased with the new scheme."

* There was feeling that Exeter City were becoming disenchanted with their reserve team. Despite costing a good deal of money to run, it was stated that in a competition of the Western League's standard the team should be near the top. Instead they found themselves near the bottom.

## CITY PLAYING SQUAD 1963-64

| Name | Pos | Signed From | Apps | Gls |
|------|-----|-------------|------|-----|
| Des Anderson | HB | Glenavon Aug 1962 | 46 | |
| Alan Banks | F | Cambridge City Oct 63 | 28 | 18 |
| Alan Barnett | G | Grimsby Town Jul 1963 | 45 | |
| John Cochrane | W | Brighton & H.A. Aug 1963 | 2 | |
| Dermot Curtis | F | Ipswich Town Aug 1963 | 32 | 9 |
| John Edgar | F | Hartlepools United Jul 1963 | 6 | |
| Derek Grace | F | Queens Park Rangers May 1962 | 32 | 4 |
| Dave Hancock | HB | Torquay United Mar 1964 | 9 | |
| Keith Harvey | HB | Crediton Aug 1952 | 46 | 5 |
| John Henderson | F | Charlton Athletic Nov 1962 | 22 | 6 |
| George Ley | W | Hitchin Town Sep 1963 | 14 | 1 |
| Les MacDonald | FB | Portsmouth Jun 1957 | 42 | |
| Arnold Mitchell | HB | Notts County Jul 1952 | 38 | 3 |
| George Northcott | F | Cheltenham Town Aug 1963 | 1 | |
| Jimmy Parkhill | G | Cliftonville Sep 1963 | 1 | |
| Roy Patrick | FB | Southampton Mar 1963 | 7 | |
| Peter Phoenix | W | Rochdale Oct 1963 | 15 | 1 |
| Graham Rees | F | Pontypridd YC Sep 1954 | 45 | 6 |
| Peter Rutley | HB | Apprentice Jul 1961 | 2 | |
| Cecil Smyth | FB | Distillery Aug 1962 | 44 | 1 |
| George Spiers | F | Crusaders Aug 1963 | 5 | |
| Adrian Thorne | F | Plymouth Argyle Dec 1963 | 24 | 6 |
| Own Goals | | | | 2 |

### City's league results

| | HOME | AWAY |
|------|------|------|
| Aldershot | 0-0 | 1-0 |
| Barrow | 0-0 | 1-1 |
| Bradford Park Ave. | 2-3 | 2-3 |
| Bradford City | 4-1 | 2-1 |
| Brighton & H.A. | 0-0 | 2-1 |
| Carlisle United | 1-0 | 0-3 |
| Chester | 3-0 | 0-2 |
| Chesterfield | 6-1 | 1-0 |
| Darlington | 1-1 | 1-1 |
| Doncaster Rovers | 3-1 | 0-1 |
| Gillingham | 0-0 | 0-0 |
| Halifax Town | 0-0 | 0-2 |
| Hartlepools United | 2-1 | 1-1 |
| Lincoln City | 0-0 | 1-1 |
| Newport County | 3-1 | 1-0 |
| Oxford United | 3-2 | 2-0 |
| Rochdale | 0-1 | 3-1 |
| Southport | 1-1 | 1-1 |
| Stockport County | 2-0 | 0-0 |
| Torquay United | 0-0 | 1-1 |
| Tranmere Rovers | 5-0 | 1-2 |
| Workington | 2-1 | 0-0 |
| York City | 1-0 | 2-1 |

### F.A. Cup

| | | | |
|------|---|----|-----|
| Shrewsbury Town | H | R1 | 2-1 |
| Bristol City | H | R2 | 0-2 |

### Football League Cup

| | | | |
|------|---|----|-----|
| Oxford United | A | R1 | 1-0 |
| Hull City | A | R2 | 0-1 |

### CITY MANAGER 1962-63
Jack Edwards - Appointed May 1963

### FOURTH DIVISION - 1963-64

| | P | W | D | L | F | A | Pts |
|------|----|----|----|----|----|----|----|
| Gillingham | 46 | 23 | 14 | 9 | 59 | 30 | 60 |
| Carlisle United | 46 | 25 | 10 | 11 | 113 | 58 | 60 |
| Workington | 46 | 24 | 11 | 11 | 76 | 52 | 59 |
| Exeter City | 46 | 20 | 18 | 8 | 62 | 37 | 58 |
| Bradford City | 46 | 25 | 6 | 15 | 76 | 62 | 56 |
| Torquay United | 46 | 20 | 11 | 15 | 80 | 54 | 51 |
| Tranmere Rovers | 46 | 20 | 11 | 15 | 85 | 73 | 51 |
| Brighton & H.A. | 46 | 19 | 12 | 15 | 71 | 52 | 50 |
| Aldershot | 46 | 19 | 10 | 17 | 83 | 78 | 48 |
| Halifax Town | 46 | 17 | 14 | 15 | 77 | 77 | 48 |
| Lincoln City | 46 | 19 | 9 | 18 | 67 | 75 | 47 |
| Chester | 46 | 19 | 8 | 19 | 65 | 60 | 46 |
| Bradford P.A. | 46 | 18 | 9 | 18 | 75 | 81 | 45 |
| Doncaster Rovers | 46 | 15 | 12 | 19 | 70 | 75 | 42 |
| Newport County | 46 | 17 | 8 | 21 | 64 | 73 | 42 |
| Chesterfield | 46 | 15 | 12 | 19 | 57 | 71 | 42 |
| Stockport County | 46 | 15 | 12 | 19 | 50 | 58 | 42 |
| Oxford United | 46 | 14 | 13 | 19 | 59 | 63 | 41 |
| Darlington | 46 | 14 | 12 | 20 | 66 | 93 | 40 |
| Rochdale | 46 | 12 | 15 | 19 | 56 | 59 | 39 |
| Southport | 46 | 15 | 9 | 22 | 63 | 88 | 39 |
| York City | 46 | 14 | 7 | 25 | 52 | 66 | 35 |
| Hartlepools United | 46 | 12 | 9 | 25 | 54 | 93 | 33 |
| Barrow | 46 | 6 | 18 | 22 | 51 | 93 | 30 |

* The season was to end as being the best thus far in the club's Football League history as they secured promotion for the first time to the Third Division.

* Prior to the season commencing a major job was undertaken of re-roofing the Old Grandstand. Put off for several years, it became urgent after a 6' section of guttering fell onto the pitch surrounds.

* The club made only their second profit since the Second World War on the year ending June 1963. The profit of £7,569 was partly due to the increase contributions of the Grecians Association and the development fund lottery. Wages cost increased to £28,070, whilst travelling expenses were £4,482.

* For the first time in the club's history an Exeter City player - Dermot Curtis - had been picked to play for his country in a full international. Curtis appeared for Eire against Austria in Vienna on 25th September 1963.

* The Grecians paid a fee, eventually totalling £5,200 for inside-forward Alan Banks, from Southern League Cambridge City. £3,200 went to Cambridge, whilst a further £2,000 went to Liverpool who still held his Football League registration.

* In November 1963, the club announced that they were looking to replace the older players' houses with newer builds. This they felt would attract quality players to Exeter City if accommodation could be offered as well.

* The Board of Directors were seeking to replace the floodlights, which had been installed in 1953, following complaints from visiting sides and the City players. It was expected that a new system would cost £8,000.

* In February 1964 the club were actively seeking to purchase a 15 acre site close to the city centre to develop for practice pitches and training facilities. They were advertising for land that could be used for that purpose.

* An attendance of 16,141 for the visit of Torquay United to St James' Park on Good Friday 1964 was the highest for many a season between the two clubs. The game, which was all ticket, ended goalless.

* City's 1-0 victory at Chesterfield on 13th April took them to the top of the Fourth Division, with three games remaining. Eight days later they then defeated the Spirerites in the return game at St. James' Park by 6-1 in front of an attendance of 9,449.

* Exeter needed at least a point in their final game of the season at fellow promotion chasing, Workington, to be assured of promotion. A special train fare of 70/- return was offered for the many City fans who made the long trek north and they were rewarded with a goalless draw, thus City were indeed promoted for the first time in their history.

* At the final whistle all 22 players, of Exeter and Workington, appeared in the directors' box to acknowledge the crowd who had swarmed onto the pitch at Borough Park, The City players the went back to their dressing room to celebrate with champagne.

* City chairman, Reg Rose said that now the club had won promotion, he didn't want to stop, and would be hoping that this was the beginning, not the end of success to come the club's way.

* Within days it was announced that adult admission prices for Third Division football at St James' Park the following season would be set at 4/- for the ground, an increase of 6d. Season tickets would be increased from £7 to £8.

* A new contract was offered and signed by manager Jack Edwards, the directors stating that he had been very fair in his approach to them, and so they were willing to agree to his terms.

*Financial backing from the traders of the city of Exeter, and a new family atmosphere for supporters were two of the things needed at St James' Park, City fundraising organiser Fred Easton told supporters at an open meeting at the ground in July 1964. He said it was about time the trades people of Exeter supported the cub. As far as the regular supporter was concerned, he added that a social club was needed where the older people could get together in the afternoons and evenings with a Ladies section as well. He outlined plans which the City F.C. directors had drawn up for the social centre on the club's property.

* Exeter City's vice chairman, George Gillin, admitted that he had been approached by Plymouth Argyle directors to join their board in July 1964. Gillin, 72, said: "I have been offered the position of chairman with Argyle and the offer requires much consideration."

Stockport-born Gillin, had recently stated that promotion with Exeter City was the happiest day in his 35 years with football. He made his first west country connections with Plymouth Argyle when he was a shareholder with two seats in the directors box.

The Torquay hotelier then joined the board of Torquay United and was chairman for four of his six years there. In 1964 he moved to St James' Park and apart from a short break, he served as director, chairman and vice-chairman ever since then.

* Exeter City's goalscoring forward Alan Banks found himself with a problem prior to the Football League Cup tie at home to Gillingham - no boots!

When it was discovered that one of the ground staff boys had forgotten to collect the boots from the repairers and there was no one at the shop, things looked decidedly bad for the popular player.

Luckily programme editor, Maurice Golesworthy volunteered to collect the keys to the shop and pick up the boot. He managed to get back to the ground just four minutes before kick off! It proved to be worthwhile as Banks scored his first goal of the season in the 2-0 win over Gillingham.

### CITY PLAYING SQUAD 1964-65

| Name | Pos | Signed From | Apps | Gls |
|------|-----|-------------|------|-----|
| Des Anderson | HB | Glenavon Aug 1962 | 43 | 1 |
| Alan Banks | F | Cambridge City Oct 1963 | 19 | 8 |
| Alan Barnett | G | Grimsby Town Jul 1963 | 5 | |
| Wilf Carter | F | Plymouth Argyle May 1964 | 26 | 4 |
| Dermot Curtis | F | Ipswich Town Aug 1963 | 42 | 9 |
| Bryce Fulton | FB | Plymouth Argyle Jul 1964 | 15 | |
| Derek Grace | F | Queens Park Rangers May 1962 | 7 | |
| Dave Hancock | HB | Torquay United Mar 1964 | 31 | 3 |
| Keith Harvey | HB | Crediton United Aug 1952 | 42 | 5 |
| George Ley | W | Hitchin Town Sep 1963 | 15 | 1 |
| Les MacDonald | FB | Portsmouth Jun 1957 | 15 | |
| Arnold Mitchell | HB | Notts County Jul 1952 | 43 | 3 |
| Roy Patrick | FB | Southampton Mar 1963 | 25 | |
| Barry Redwood | F | Newton Abbot Spurs May 1962 | 1 | 1 |
| Graham Rees | F | Pontypridd YC Sep 1954 | 33 | 7 |
| Peter Rutley | HB | Apprentice Jul 1961 | 6 | |
| Peter Shearing | G | Portsmouth Jun 1964 | 41 | |
| Cecil Smyth | FB | Distillery Aug 1962 | 40 | |
| Adrian Thorne | F | Plymouth Argyle Dec 1963 | 17 | 2 |
| Eric Welsh | W | Distillery Sep 1959 | 40 | 7 |
| Own Goals | | | | 1 |

City's league results

| | HOME | AWAY |
|---|------|------|
| Barnsley | 3-0 | 0-0 |
| Bournemouth & B.A. | 1-3 | 2-2 |
| Brentford | 0-0 | 1-2 |
| Bristol City | 0-1 | 1-1 |
| Bristol Rover | 0-1 | 1-1 |
| Carlisle United | 0-0 | 1-2 |
| Colchester United | 2-0 | 1-1 |
| Gillingham | 1-1 | 1-0 |
| Grimsby Town | 4-1 | 1-2 |
| Hull City | 0-2 | 1-3 |
| Luton Town | 5-1 | 2-1 |
| Mansfield Town | 2-3 | 1-2 |
| Oldham Athletic | 2-1 | 0-2 |
| Peterborough United | 4-2 | 0-0 |
| Port Vale | 2-1 | 1-0 |
| Queens Park Rangers | 2-2 | 0-0 |
| Reading | 2-2 | 2-2 |
| Scunthorpe United | 1-3 | 0-0 |
| Shrewsbury Town | 0-1 | 0-1 |
| Southend United | 1-1 | 0-0 |
| Walsall | 0-1 | 1-2 |
| Watford | 1-0 | 0-1 |
| Workington | 0-0 | 1-0 |

F.A. Cup

| | | | |
|---|---|---|---|
| Hayes | H | R1 | 1-0 |
| Shrewsbury Town | H | R2 | 1-2 |

Football League Cup

| | | | |
|---|---|---|---|
| Gillingham | H | R1 | 2-0 |
| Bradford City | H | R2 | 3-5 |

CITY MANAGER 1962-63
Jack Edwards - Appointed May 1963
Ellis Stuttard - Appointed January 1965

THIRD DIVISION - 1964-5

| | P | W | D | L | F | A | Pts |
|---|---|---|---|---|---|---|-----|
| Carlisle United | 46 | 25 | 10 | 11 | 76 | 53 | 60 |
| Bristol City | 46 | 24 | 11 | 11 | 92 | 55 | 59 |
| Mansfield Town | 46 | 24 | 11 | 11 | 95 | 61 | 59 |
| Hull City | 46 | 23 | 12 | 11 | 91 | 57 | 58 |
| Brentford | 46 | 24 | 9 | 13 | 83 | 55 | 57 |
| Bristol Rovers | 46 | 20 | 15 | 11 | 82 | 58 | 55 |
| Gillingham | 46 | 23 | 9 | 14 | 70 | 50 | 55 |
| Peterborough United | 46 | 22 | 7 | 17 | 85 | 74 | 51 |
| Watford | 46 | 17 | 16 | 13 | 71 | 64 | 50 |
| Grimsby Town | 46 | 16 | 17 | 13 | 68 | 67 | 49 |
| Bournemouth & B.A. | 46 | 18 | 11 | 17 | 72 | 63 | 47 |
| Southend United | 46 | 19 | 8 | 19 | 78 | 71 | 46 |
| Reading | 46 | 16 | 14 | 16 | 70 | 70 | 46 |
| Queens Park Rangers | 46 | 17 | 12 | 17 | 72 | 80 | 46 |
| Workington | 46 | 17 | 12 | 17 | 58 | 69 | 46 |
| Shrewsbury Town | 46 | 15 | 12 | 19 | 76 | 84 | 42 |
| Exeter City | 46 | 12 | 17 | 17 | 51 | 52 | 41 |
| Scunthorpe United | 46 | 14 | 12 | 20 | 65 | 72 | 40 |
| Walsall | 46 | 15 | 7 | 24 | 55 | 80 | 37 |
| Oldham Athletic | 46 | 13 | 10 | 23 | 61 | 83 | 36 |
| Luton Town | 46 | 11 | 11 | 24 | 51 | 94 | 33 |
| Port Vale | 46 | 9 | 14 | 23 | 41 | 76 | 32 |
| Colchester United | 46 | 10 | 10 | 26 | 50 | 89 | 30 |
| Barnsley | 46 | 9 | 11 | 26 | 54 | 90 | 29 |

* Despite winning promotion Exeter City reported a loss of £10,986 on the year ended 30th June 1964. They spent £13,000 on players' transfer fees. Travelling and hotel expenses totalled £4,595, whilst wages and bonuses came to £30,972. The club now had a total deficiency of £45,052.

* The Grecians started life in the Third Division with a visit from Peterborough United on 22nd August 1964, the game attracting a bumper crowd of 10,281. City won 4-2 with goals from Arnold Mitchell, Keith Harvey, Dermot Curtis and Graham Rees.

* The Football League banned Exeter City from staging any more games under the St James' Park floodlights in October 1964, stating that the lights were not up to standard. City appealed against the decision explaining that a new £8,000 system was being installed. The League relented to allow the Grecians to play Brentford, but then days later enforced the ban again.

* Ironically there was a major power cut prior to the kick off against Brentford and the game was delayed for 45 minutes. The fault was traced to a cable near the ground.

* The club appointed their first ever female company secretary in October 1964. Patricia Smith, who lived in Exeter had held a similar post elsewhere, but had no previous experience before with a football club. However, she had left the Grecians by the following January to be replaced by Dick Miller, son of former Exeter player Charlie Miller.

* In November 1964, the board of directors announced that they were to contest an 1883 covenant prohibiting them from building on part of their land at Old Tiverton Road. They were hoping to build a clubhouse, but it had raised strong objections from a resident in Old Tiverton Road itself.

* Exeter City's new floodlights were officially used for the first time when a friendly was played against the Arsenal first team on 2nd December 1964. The visitors won 4-1 before an attendance of 11,507.

* Following City's 5-1 home win over Luton Town in January 1965, came the shock news that manager Jack Edwards had resigned. He was unhappy with the fact that the club had appointed Ellis Stuttard as chief scout without him knowing anything about it, Internal squabbles and nothing else had forced him to resign and he felt that the players and himself could have been treated better following their promotion season.

* Within 24-hours of Jack Edwards resigning as manager, Ellis Stuttard was appointed caretaker-manager. Meanwhile the City directors issued a statement denying any dissention within the club, as Edwards had suggested, nor amongst the players. Within days Stuttard was officially appointed manager.

* Tragedy struck the cub and in particular leading scorer Alan Banks, as the City striker broke his right leg in the game against Port Vale at St. James' Park on 6th February 1965. Banks had scored twice prior to the injury as City won 2-1.

* City player, Barry Redwood, 18, was told to retire from playing in March 1965, following a head injury in a reserve team game at Bridport The blow affected his eyesight and there was a chance if he got another knock he would do permanent damage. A testimonial game against Swindon Town was played the following month, City winning 3-0 before a crowd of 1,882, which raised £401 for Redwood.

* Arnold Mitchell was announced as being the first ever winner of the Supporters' Club Player Of The Year in April 1965.

* At the end of the season, City chairman, Reg Rose, said: "Another year has passed with it's full quota of troubles, trials and tribulations. What has been achieved? Our finances are better, our assets more substantial. Quite conceivably we could be knocking at the door of a higher division next season."

The Exeter City squad return for pre-season training prior to the 1965-66 season.
Back row: George McLean, Des Anderson, Bruce Fulton, Alan Barnett.
Middle row (the two players looking at camera: Cecil Smyth, George Ley.
Front row seated: Jeff Tolchard, Mike Balson, Arnold Mitchell, Peter Shearing, Dermot Curtis, Alan Banks, Keith Harvey, Alan Riding, Unknown, Dennis Peapell.

City's league results

| | HOME | AWAY |
|---|---|---|
| Bournemouth & B.A. | 1-0 | 1-0 |
| Brentford | 5-0 | 2-1 |
| Brighton & H.A. | 2-0 | 1-2 |
| Bristol Rovers | 1-0 | 0-2 |
| Gillingham | 3-1 | 1-1 |
| Grimsby Town | 2-0 | 1-1 |
| Hull City | 1-4 | 1-6 |
| Mansfield Town | 2-2 | 0-0 |
| Millwall | 1-2 | 0-3 |
| Oldham Athletic | 4-0 | 1-3 |
| Oxford United | 1-2 | 1-0 |
| Peterborough United | 2-5 | 0-2 |
| Queens Park Rangers | 0-0 | 0-1 |
| Reading | 1-2 | 1-4 |
| Scunthorpe United | 4-0 | 1-2 |
| Shrewsbury Town | 0-0 | 0-4 |
| Southend United | 1-1 | 2-4 |
| Swansea Town | 1-1 | 0-1 |
| Swindon Town | 1-1 | 2-2 |
| Walsall | 0-2 | 1-1 |
| Watford | 1-2 | 0-3 |
| Workington | 2-1 | 1-6 |
| York City | 0-2 | 0-2 |

F.A. Cup

| | | | |
|---|---|---|---|
| Bedford Town | H | R1 | 1-2 |

Football League Cup

| | | | |
|---|---|---|---|
| Colchester United | A | R1 | 1-2 |

CITY MANAGER 1965-66
Ellis Stuttard - Appointed February 1965

## CITY PLAYING SQUAD 1965-66

| Name | Pos | Signed from | Apps | Gls |
|---|---|---|---|---|
| Des Anderson | HB | Glenavon Aug 1962 | 9+2 | |
| Alan Banks | F | Cambridge City Oct 1965 | 38 | 17 |
| Alan Barnett | G | Grimsby Town Jul 1963 | 7 | |
| Jimmy Blain | FB | Carlisle United Oct 1965 | 24+1 | 1 |
| Colin Buckingham | HB | Plymouth Argyle Sep 1965 | 28 | |
| Wilf Carter | F | Plymouth Argyle May 1964 | 22 | 2 |
| Dermot Curtis | F | Ipswich Town Aug 1963 | 17 | 5 |
| Ray Elliott | F | Charlton Athletic Mar 1966 | 4 | |
| John Evans | F | Carlisle United Mar 1966 | 7+1 | |
| Bryce Fulton | FB | Plymouth Argyle Jul 1964 | 22 | |
| Ray Harford | HB | Charlton Athletic Jan 1966 | 17 | |
| Keith Harvey | HB | Crediton Aug 1952 | 40 | 3 |
| Ray Keeley | F | Charlton Athletic Mar 1966 | 7 | 1 |
| Jack Kennedy | F | Charlton Athletic Nov 1965 | 22+1 | 4 |
| George Ley | FB | Hitchin Town Sep 1963 | 31 | 3 |
| Les MacDonald | FB | Portsmouth Jun 1957 | 10 | |
| George McLean | F | Grimsby Town Jun 1965 | 34 | 11 |
| Arnold Mitchell | HB | Notts County Jul 1952 | 19 | 1 |
| Dennis Peapell | HB | Swindon Town Jul 1965 | 23+1 | 1 |
| Graham Rees | W | Pontypridd YC Sep 1954 | 13 | 1 |
| Alan Riding | F | Colchester United Jul 1964 | 1 | |
| Peter Shearing | G | Portsmouth Jun 1964 | 39 | |
| Cecil Smyth | FB | Distillery Aug 1962 | 44 | |
| Bruce Stuckey | W | Apprentice Feb 1965 | 14 | 1 |
| Jeff Tolchard | W | Torquay United Jul 1965 | 1 | |
| Eric Welsh | W | Distillery Sep 1959 | 13 | 2 |

## THIRD DIVISION - 1965-66

| | P | W | D | L | F | A | Pts |
|---|---|---|---|---|---|---|---|
| Hull City | 46 | 31 | 7 | 8 | 109 | 62 | 69 |
| Millwall | 46 | 27 | 11 | 8 | 76 | 43 | 65 |
| Queens Park Rangers | 46 | 24 | 9 | 13 | 95 | 65 | 57 |
| Scunthorpe United | 46 | 21 | 11 | 14 | 80 | 67 | 53 |
| Workington | 46 | 19 | 14 | 13 | 67 | 57 | 52 |
| Gillingham | 46 | 22 | 8 | 16 | 62 | 54 | 52 |
| Swindon Town | 46 | 19 | 13 | 14 | 74 | 48 | 51 |
| Reading | 46 | 19 | 13 | 14 | 70 | 63 | 51 |
| Walsall | 46 | 20 | 10 | 16 | 77 | 64 | 50 |
| Shrewsbury Town | 46 | 19 | 11 | 16 | 73 | 64 | 49 |
| Grimsby Town | 46 | 17 | 13 | 16 | 68 | 62 | 47 |
| Watford | 46 | 17 | 13 | 16 | 55 | 51 | 47 |
| Peterborough United | 46 | 17 | 12 | 17 | 80 | 66 | 46 |
| Oxford United | 46 | 19 | 8 | 19 | 70 | 74 | 46 |
| Brighton & H.A. | 46 | 16 | 11 | 19 | 67 | 65 | 43 |
| Bristol Rovers | 46 | 14 | 14 | 18 | 64 | 64 | 42 |
| Swansea Town | 46 | 15 | 11 | 20 | 81 | 96 | 41 |
| Bournemouth & B.A. | 46 | 13 | 12 | 21 | 38 | 56 | 38 |
| Mansfield Town | 46 | 15 | 8 | 23 | 59 | 89 | 38 |
| Oldham Athletic | 46 | 12 | 13 | 21 | 55 | 81 | 37 |
| Southend United | 46 | 16 | 4 | 26 | 54 | 83 | 36 |
| EXETER CITY | 46 | 12 | 11 | 23 | 53 | 79 | 35 |
| Brentford | 46 | 10 | 12 | 24 | 48 | 69 | 32 |
| York City | 46 | 9 | 9 | 28 | 53 | 106 | 27 |

* Season 1965-66 proved to be a hugely disappointing one for Exeter City as they ended being relegated back to the Fourth Division after just two seasons at the higher level. A terrible second half of the season condemned them to the drop.

* There was unrest behind the scenes as well which resulted in manager Ellis Stuttard taking more of a backroom role and allowing Jock Basford then City coach taking charge of the team (he was to later become manager after Stuttard was dismissed), and the former Charlton Athletic youth manager/scout quickly used his contacts to bring in the likes of Jack Kennedy, Ray Harford, Ray Keeley and Ray Elliott, all from Charlton, however, the move was to be too late and City only won four of their last 24 league matches.

* The way the Grecians started the season, two consecutive 4-0 home wins over Oldham Athletic and Scunthorpe United respectively, there could have been no thought of a possible struggle, or even relegation.

* The FA Cup and Football League Cup didn't bring any success either. City lost to Southern League Bedford Town at St James' Park, going down 1-2, in the first round. It was at the same stage that the Grecians made their exit from the Football League Cup, as they lost 2-1 at Colchester United.

* Alan Banks did exceptionally well to top the scoring charts with 17 league goals in what was a struggling team. having fully recovered from the broken leg he had sustained in the previous season.

* Highest league attendance at St James' Park was 9,132 for the visit of Swansea Town on 27th December 1965. The game ended all square at 1-1, with Banks netting for City.

* Heaviest defeat of the season was the 6-1 thrashing at far flung Workington. City only had a George Ley goal to celebrate after their longest trip of the season.

* Exeter City's two supporters' clubs, The Grecians' Association and the Supporters Club amalgamated in August 1965. The Grecians Association had been formed in 1944, whilst the Supporters Club were formed in 1964. The new body had a reported combined membership of 7,500.

* City entered a team in the Exeter and District Basketball League, with ten players having stated they would play, namely, Cecil Smyth, Alan Barnett, Mike Balson, Peter Arbury, Wilf Carter, Des Anderson, Les MacDonald, Phil Richardson, Bobby House and Chris Taylor.

* Winger Eric Welsh was sold to Carlisle United in October 1965, and making the move in the opposite direction was Jimmy Blain, who went on to be a great servant to the Grecians.

* City played a friendly against Czech side, Slovan Bratislava at the Park, which drew an attendance of 5,000. City won 4-1 with goals from Bruce Stuckey, George McLean, Jimmy Blain and an own goal from Hrivnak.

* A telephone call from the Football League to Exeter City saved the club's first team making a lengthy, unnecessary journey. The call was to say that the Grecians' fixture at Peterborough had been called off due to snow. City secretary Dick Miller was able to stop the coach at Ilchester by getting a cafe proprietor to put a noticeboard on the side of the road so that the players on the coach could see it as they passed through.

* In March 1966 City chairman Reg Rose was so incensed with the team after five successive defeats that he talked of immediate action to stop the slump and their displays had been a disgrace. The board would not sit back and accept the sort of performances that had been taking place.

* Exeter City transferred two players to Plymouth Argyle as soon as the previous season had ended. Top scorer Alan Banks and goalkeeper Peter Shearing joined Argyle for a combined fee of £8,000. Argyle had also made a bid for City centre-half Ray Harford.

* The team would also be without the long serving Arnold Mitchell, who had been given a free transfer. The 37-year-old had made 495 league appearances for the Grecians, and fully intended to keep playing by joining a local non-league club. Fifteen of Arnold's nineteen years in football were spent with Exeter City.

* Exeter City manager Jock Basford asked the supporters to bear with the team in it's early days of the 1966-67 season. Most of the players were youngsters and needed encouragement and time to settle down. No one imagined that City would go shooting back up into the Third Division right away, but supporters did want to see evidence of "method, effort and enthusiasm."

* By September 1966, Basford said he had been pleased with the way things had gone for his team. He said that as always, supporters were impatient for results, but when one was team building from scratch after relegation, it takes time, especially as City had parted company with 16 players.

### CITY PLAYING SQUAD 1966-67

| Name | Pos | Signed from | Apps | Gls |
|---|---|---|---|---|
| Mike Balson | HB | Bridport May 1965 | 2 | |
| Jimmy Blain | FB | Carlisle United Oct 1965 | 37(2) | 3 |
| Colin Buckingham | HB | Plymouth Argyle Sep 1965 | 1 | |
| Ray Elliott | F | Charlton Athletic Mar 1966 | 24 | 3 |
| Ben Embury | FB | Tottenham Hotspur Jun 1966 | 25(2) | |
| John Evans | F | Carlisle United Mar 1966 | 4 | 2 |
| Peter Godfrey | W | Chesterfield Jun 1966 | 42 | 4 |
| Ray Harford | HB | Charlton Athletic Jan 1966 | 38 | 1 |
| Keith Harvey | HB | Crediton Aug 1952 | 7 | |
| Ken Jones | G | Charlton Athletic Jun 1966 | 17 | |
| Ray Keeley | F | Charlton Athletic Mar 1966 | 38(1) | 9 |
| Jack Kennedy | F | Charlton Athletic Nov 1965 | 18 | 2 |
| George Ley | FB | Hitchin Town Sep 1963 | 33 | 2 |
| George McLean | F | Grimsby Town Jun 1965 | 13 | 1 |
| Richard McNeil | F | Leicester City Jun 1966 | 31 | 11 |
| Bobby Nash | FB | Queens Park Rangers Jun 1966 | 1 | |
| Jim Ryan | F | Hastings United Jan 1967 | 20 | 5 |
| Roger Smith | W | Tottenham Hotspur Jun 1966 | 6 | 3 |
| John Smout | G | Crystal Palace Jun 1966 | 29 | |
| Cecil Smyth | FB | Distillery Aug 1962 | 25(2) | |
| Bruce Stuckey | W | Apprentice Feb 1965 | 11(2) | 2 |
| Ken Thompson | HB | Ipswich Town Jun 1966 | 38(1) | 1 |
| Ernie Wilkinson | HB | Arsenal Jun 1966 | 46 | |
| Own Goals | | | | 1 |

### City's league results

| | HOME | AWAY |
|---|---|---|
| Aldershot | 1-1 | 0-1 |
| Barnsley | 0-3 | 1-2 |
| Barrow | 1-2 | 0-5 |
| Bradford City | 2-2 | 1-1 |
| Bradford Park Avenue | 4-1 | 2-2 |
| Brentford | 1-0 | 1-3 |
| Chester | 2-0 | 2-0 |
| Chesterfield | 1-1 | 0-1 |
| Crewe Alexandra | 2-0 | 2-2 |
| Halifax Town | 3-2 | 0-0 |
| Hartlepools united | 1-1 | 1-3 |
| Lincoln City | 1-0 | 1-1 |
| Luton Town | 2-1 | 0-4 |
| Newport County | 0-0 | 2-3 |
| Notts County | 1-0 | 1-0 |
| Port Vale | 0-1 | 0-2 |
| Rochdale | 0-0 | 0-1 |
| Southend United | 0-1 | 0-0 |
| Southport | 0-0 | 1-1 |
| Stockport County | 0-3 | 0-1 |
| Tranmere Rovers | 1-4 | 1-1 |
| Wrexham | 4-1 | 0-0 |
| York City | 3-1 | 4-2 |

| F.A. Cup | | | |
|---|---|---|---|
| Luton Town | H | R1 | 1-1 |
| Luton Town | A | R1R | 0-2 |

| Football League Cup | | | |
|---|---|---|---|
| Torquay United | H | R1 | 2-2 |
| Torquay United | A | R1R | 2-1 |
| Cardiff City | A | R2 | 1-0 |
| Walsall | H | R3 | 1-2 |

### CITY MANAGER 1966-67
Walter 'Jock' Basford - Appointed June 1966

### FOURTH DIVISION - 1966-67

| | P | W | D | L | F | A | Pts |
|---|---|---|---|---|---|---|---|
| Stockport County | 46 | 26 | 12 | 8 | 69 | 42 | 64 |
| Southport | 46 | 23 | 13 | 10 | 69 | 42 | 59 |
| Barrow | 46 | 24 | 11 | 11 | 76 | 54 | 59 |
| Tranmere Rovers | 46 | 22 | 14 | 10 | 66 | 43 | 58 |
| Crewe Alexandra | 46 | 21 | 12 | 13 | 70 | 55 | 54 |
| Southend United | 46 | 22 | 9 | 15 | 70 | 49 | 53 |
| Wrexham | 46 | 16 | 20 | 10 | 76 | 62 | 52 |
| Hartlepools United | 46 | 22 | 7 | 17 | 66 | 64 | 51 |
| Brentford | 46 | 18 | 13 | 15 | 58 | 56 | 49 |
| Aldershot | 46 | 18 | 12 | 16 | 72 | 57 | 48 |
| Bradford City | 46 | 19 | 10 | 17 | 74 | 62 | 48 |
| Halifax Town | 46 | 15 | 14 | 17 | 59 | 68 | 44 |
| Port Vale | 46 | 14 | 15 | 17 | 55 | 58 | 43 |
| Exeter City | 46 | 14 | 15 | 17 | 50 | 60 | 43 |
| Chesterfield | 46 | 17 | 8 | 21 | 60 | 63 | 42 |
| Barnsley | 46 | 13 | 15 | 18 | 60 | 64 | 41 |
| Luton Town | 46 | 16 | 9 | 21 | 59 | 73 | 41 |
| Newport County | 46 | 12 | 16 | 18 | 56 | 63 | 40 |
| Chester | 46 | 15 | 10 | 21 | 54 | 78 | 40 |
| Notts County | 46 | 13 | 11 | 22 | 53 | 72 | 37 |
| Rochdale | 46 | 13 | 11 | 22 | 53 | 75 | 37 |
| York City | 46 | 12 | 11 | 23 | 65 | 79 | 35 |
| Bradford Park Avenue | 46 | 11 | 13 | 22 | 52 | 79 | 35 |
| Lincoln City | 46 | 9 | 13 | 24 | 58 | 82 | 31 |

* Ellis Stuttard resigned as manager of Exeter City in June 1966, with Jock Basford taking over. For all intents and purposes, Basford had been in charge for the last seven matches of the previous season, while Stuttard had a General Manager's role.

* Basford was keen to promote younger players and as a result a number were signed during the summer of 1966, from the likes of Ipswich Town, Arsenal, Tottenham Hotspur and Leicester City etc.

* The club introduced a concession priced season ticket (£2 10s) for old age pensioners to gain admittance to league matches.

* Long serving Keith Harvey, and Player Of The Year for 1965-66, was appointed trainer in July 1966, although he was still registered as a player. He was recalled to play for the first team in the FA Cup first round tie against Luton Town the following November.

* City, perhaps controversially, changed the colour of their shirts and shorts for the 1966-67 season. It was to be all white with red trimmings.

* The Grecians lost £4,006 on the year ending 30th June 1966. Revenue from home gates decreased to £19,849. Wages accounted for £40,800, whilst travelling and hotel expenses accounted for £6,379. The profit and loss account showed an overall deficiency of £43,680.

* Former Plymouth Argyle chairman, Ron Blindell was approached by the club to join the board or even take the club over in November 1966. It was then revealed that the deal was off, despite several hours of talks, with the City board having an apparent change of mind, when they were asked to sign everything over at a meeting before Blindell left the ground, which they could not agree too.

* City manager Jock Basford was against the possible idea of clubs loaning out players to teams such as Exeter. He said: "The idea is a bit of a dream and there could be many snags."

* In January 1967 it was announced that Exeter City would scrap their reserve team for the following season and cut their professional playing staff to a maximum of 16, all with first team potential. With attendances down, and as a consequence, revenue, the board of directors appealed to all supporters in Exeter to help the club.

* A month later the decision (see above) to scrap the reserves was rescinded, as the City directors decided to keep a team in the Western League, but scrap the Colts team and withdraw from the Exeter and District League.

* City's newly appointed chairman, Les Kerslake, appealed to supporters to get along to the game against Barrow in February 1967, as the previous Saturday match with Luton Town produced the lowest crowd, 3,744, in the entire Football League that day. Just 3,550 were present for the visit of Barrow!

* The directors made another u-turn in April 1967, when they stated that the club would after all only operate with one team for the next season and a playing staff of around 16 full professionals. The club were in talks with St Luke's College who might use St James' Park for their Western League fixtures.

* After several days of speculation on whether City manager Jock Basford was resigning, on 10th April 1967 City chairman Les Kerslake said that Basford was not under contract to Exeter City and had been relieved of his duties as team manager. Approaches would be made to former Grecians' manager, Frank Broome, who was working in Australia. He accepted the offer and was back in Exeter to take charge on 8th May.

*Portsmouth signed Exeter City full-back George Ley for a fee of £8,000 on 31st April 1967. He had been on the transfer list since the previous January.

* Jimmy Blain became the Exeter City Player Of The Year for the 1966-67 season.

The following article appeared in the local press prior to the start of the 1967-68 season:-

'During the course of the 1967-68 season, Exeter City players will travel something like 10,000 miles in the Fourth Division, allowing of course a few hundred miles one way or another. In addition there are possible cup ties and perhaps one or two other games.

Supporters are hoping that history will repeat itself, for the last time Exeter City went to Bradford City on the opening day of the season was in August 1963, and the Grecians went on to win promotion.

Manager Frank Broome had the following message for supporters:-

"I sincerely hope that supporters will give the lads time to settle down before they jump to any conclusions. I can assure you that the players will be giving 100 per cent effort which we can expect from them.

"We have no real worries except for the unfortunate operations and injuries which do not often accumulate in such proportions. We wish the supporters, happy watching and hope we can provide the sort of football and entertainment they want to see."

Club chairman Les Kerslake added: "This is the start of my first season as chairman and as a life long supporter of the club, the early promise I can make is that every effort will be made to provide a successful team at St James' Park.

"During my previous experience as a director, I have only known success in the club and I sincerely hope this will be repeated this season. Every effort will be made by the board of directors to provide entertaining football which will give value for money."

City's league results

|  | HOME | AWAY |
|---|---|---|
| Aldershot | 3-0 | 0-0 |
| Barnsley | 2-0 | 1-2 |
| Bradford City | 4-1 | 1-2 |
| Bradford Park Avenue | 0-0 | 1-0 |
| Brentford | 0-3 | 1-5 |
| Chester | 1-0 | 1-3 |
| Chesterfield | 1-1 | 1-1 |
| Crewe Alexandra | 1-4 | 0-2 |
| Darlington | 0-0 | 1-0 |
| Doncaster Rovers | 0-1 | 1-3 |
| Halifax Town | 0-0 | 1-1 |
| Hartlepools united | 0-0 | 1-3 |
| Lincoln City | 0-0 | 1-1 |
| Luton Town | 0-5 | 0-0 |
| Newport County | 2-1 | 1-1 |
| Notts County | 3-3 | 0-1 |
| Port Vale | 3-1 | 0-1 |
| Rochdale | 3-1 | 2-2 |
| Southend United | 0-2 | 0-1 |
| Swansea Town | 1-3 | 1-1 |
| Workington | 1-0 | 0-1 |
| Wrexham | 2-2 | 0-0 |
| York City | 3-1 | 0-4 |

F.A. Cup

| Nuneaton Borough | A | R1 | 0-0 |
|---|---|---|---|
| Nuneaton Borough | H | R1R | 0-0 |
| Nuneaton Borough | N* | R12R | 1-0 |
| Walsall | H | R2 | 1-3 |

* Played at Ashton Gate, Bristol City.

Football League Cup

| Torquay United | A | R1 | 0-0 |
|---|---|---|---|
| Torquay United | H | R1R | 0-3 |

CITY MANAGER 1967-68
Frank Broome - Appointed May 1967

CITY PLAYING SQUAD 1967-68

| Name | Pos | Signed from | Apps | Gls |
|---|---|---|---|---|
| Mike Balson | HB | Bridport May 1965 | 37(1) | |
| Alan Banks | F | Plymouth Argyle Nov 1967 | 27 | 6 |
| Jimmy Blain | FB | Carlisle United Oct 1965 | 44 | 5 |
| John Corr | W | Arsenal Jul 1967 | 17(1) | 7 |
| Dennis Coughlin | F | Swansea Town Mar 1968 | 13 | 2 |
| Campbell Crawford | FB | West Bromwich Albion Jul 1967 | 36(1) | 1 |
| Dermot Curtis | F | Torquay United Jun 1967 | 35 | 6 |
| Ben Embury | FB | Tottenham Hotspur Jun 1966 | 11(1) | |
| Micky Fudge | W | West Bromwich Albion Jun 1967 | 32(1) | 6 |
| Ian Hamilton | F | Bristol Rovers Jun 1967 | 4 | 1 |
| Stuart Hart | W | Corinthians (Australia) Aug 1967 | 20(2) | 1 |
| Keith Harvey | HB | Crediton Aug 1952 | 34 | |
| Cliff Huxford | HB | Southampton Jun 1967 | 40(1) | 1 |
| John Newman | HB | Plymouth Argyle Nov 1967 | 30 | 1 |
| Alan Pinkney | F | St Luke's College Feb 1968 | 5 | 1 |
| John Smout | G | Crystal Palace Jun 1966 | 46 | |
| Cecil Smyth | FB | Distillery Aug 1962 | 40 | |
| Bruce Stuckey | W | Apprentice Feb 1965 | 12 | 3 |
| Keith Whatling | W | Ipswich Town Jul 1967 | 10 | 2 |
| Ernie Wilkinson | HB | Arsenal Jun 1966 | 13(1) | |
| Own Goals | | | | 2 |

FOURTH DIVISION - 1967-68

| | P | W | D | L | F | A | Pts |
|---|---|---|---|---|---|---|---|
| Luton Town | 46 | 27 | 12 | 7 | 87 | 44 | 66 |
| Barnsley | 46 | 24 | 13 | 9 | 68 | 46 | 61 |
| Hartlepools United | 46 | 25 | 10 | 11 | 60 | 46 | 60 |
| Crewe Alexandra | 46 | 20 | 18 | 8 | 74 | 49 | 58 |
| Bradford City | 46 | 23 | 11 | 12 | 72 | 51 | 57 |
| Southend United | 46 | 20 | 14 | 12 | 77 | 58 | 54 |
| Chesterfield | 46 | 21 | 11 | 14 | 71 | 50 | 53 |
| Wrexham | 46 | 20 | 13 | 13 | 72 | 53 | 53 |
| Aldershot | 46 | 18 | 17 | 11 | 70 | 55 | 53 |
| Doncaster Rovers | 46 | 18 | 15 | 13 | 66 | 56 | 51 |
| Halifax Town | 46 | 15 | 16 | 16 | 52 | 49 | 46 |
| Newport County | 46 | 16 | 13 | 17 | 58 | 63 | 45 |
| Lincoln City | 46 | 17 | 9 | 20 | 71 | 68 | 43 |
| Brentford | 46 | 18 | 7 | 21 | 61 | 64 | 43 |
| Swansea Town | 46 | 16 | 10 | 20 | 63 | 77 | 42 |
| Darlington | 46 | 12 | 17 | 17 | 47 | 53 | 41 |
| Notts County | 46 | 15 | 11 | 20 | 53 | 79 | 41 |
| Port Vale | 46 | 12 | 15 | 19 | 61 | 72 | 39 |
| Rochdale | 46 | 12 | 14 | 20 | 51 | 72 | 38 |
| Exeter City | 46 | 11 | 16 | 19 | 45 | 65 | 38 |
| York City | 46 | 11 | 14 | 21 | 65 | 68 | 36 |
| Chester | 46 | 9 | 14 | 23 | 57 | 78 | 32 |
| Workington | 46 | 10 | 11 | 25 | 54 | 87 | 31 |
| Bradford Park Avenue | 46 | 4 | 15 | 27 | 30 | 82 | 23 |

* At the A.G.M. of the Exeter City Supporters Club in July 1967, Exeter City FC chairman Les Kerslake said that the return of Frank Broome as manager made him think that the club were getting back some of the spirit that used to be there.

* Exeter City did not have enough fit players for their first pre-season friendly match against Swansea Town, so therefore accepted the offer of using visiting winger Brian Grey to make up the numbers. City lost 5-2.

* The injury crisis continued and the Football League allowed the Grecians to play new signing, Brian Hart, against Torquay United in the League Cup, despite not having been signed 14-days before as the rules of the competition stated. Hart was to sustain a broken leg later in the season, in match at home to Aldershot in December 1967.

* It was announced that Exeter City had made a loss of £3,983 on the year ending 31st May 1967. Their overall deficit now stood at £47,414. Home gate receipts totalled £20,582, whist fund-raising brought in £14.435.

* After losing 1-0 at Workington in October 1967, City manager Frank Broome described his teams' display as "disgraceful for a professional team to have played as badly as that."

* The Bishop of Exeter stood on the Big Bank at St James' Park along with other City supporters, as he watched the Grecians draw 2-2 with Wrexham in October 1967.

* Exeter City played a Select XI at St James' Park in October 1967, in a benefit match for full-back Cecil Smyth. City lost 1-3, with former Grecian Alan Banks netting twice for the Select team.

* Winger Bruce Stuckey was sold to First Division, Sunderland in October 1967 for a fee of £15,000. A few days later City signed John Newman and Alan Banks from Plymouth Argyle.

* City found themselves bottom of the Fourth Division after their 4-0 defeat at York City on 25th November 1967.

* Having been signed from Arsenal in the summer, John Corr was immediately sidelined with a fractured kneecap. His debut therefore did not come until 16th December 1967, when he scored twice in a 4-2 home win over Bradford City.

* Exeter signed St Luke's College student, Alan Pinkney in February 1968. He was a regular player for the College side in the Western League and had guested in the Cecil Smyth Benefit match.

* In March 1968 the Board of Directors said that the club would continue with the policy of just having one side for the following season. and employing around 16 professionals.

* Following a 1-0 home defeat against Lincoln City in April 1968, the Express and Echo reported:- 'Now even a fairy Godmother with a wand capable of producing almost any miracle could be struggling to turn this team into one which could avoid having to apply for re-election.'

* Despite only drawing 0-0 at home to Darlington in the final match of the season, results elsewhere went in Exeter City's favour, and they just managed to avoid the Fourth Division re-election places.

* Prior to the season commencing the City Board of Directors had hoped for an increase in average attendances for matches at St James' Park, but that was never going to be the case as the team struggled. The highest crowd of the season at the Park was 5,046 for the visit of Aldershot, whilst the lowest was 3,323 when Doncaster Rovers were the opposition.

* Only one player, goalkeeper John Smout, was ever present throughout City's league matches. He had only missed two matches since having made his debut in November 1966.

Exeter City 1968-69
Back row: Alan Pinkney, Campbell Crawford, Cecil Smyth, Jimmy Blain
Middle row: John Corr, Dermot Curtis, Mike Balson, Peter Shearing, Brian Sharples, John Kirkman, Keith Harvey, Bert Edwards (Trainer).
Front row: Keith Whatling, John Mitten, Frank Broome (Manager), John Newman, David Pleat.

| City's league results | Home | Away |
|---|---|---|
| Aldershot | 0-0 | 0-2 |
| Bradford Park Avenue | 4-2 | 1-2 |
| Bradford City | 2-3 | 0-1 |
| Brentford | 2-2 | 1-0 |
| Chester | 2-2 | 1-0 |
| Chesterfield | 3-0 | 0-2 |
| Colchester United | 1-1 | 0-1 |
| Darlington | 2-0 | 2-1 |
| Doncaster Rovers | 0-0 | 1-3 |
| Grimsby Town | 2-2 | 2-1 |
| Halifax Town | 2-1 | 1-2 |
| Lincoln City | 3-0 | 2-3 |
| Newport County | 2-0 | 1-2 |
| Notts County | 0-0 | 1-3 |
| Peterborough United | 0-1 | 1-1 |
| Port Vale | 3-1 | 0-1 |
| Rochdale | 2-2 | 1-1 |
| Scunthorpe United | 3-1 | 1-2 |
| Southend United | 1-2 | 1-6 |
| Swansea Town | 0-1 | 0-2 |
| Workington | 1-0 | 0-3 |
| Wrexham | 5-3 | 2-2 |
| York City | 5-0 | 2-0 |

| F.A. Cup | | | |
|---|---|---|---|
| Newport County | H | R1 | 0-0 |
| Newport County | A | R1R | 3-1 |
| Colchester United | A | R2 | 1-0 |
| Manchester United | H | R3 | 1-3 |

| Football League Cup | | | |
|---|---|---|---|
| Plymouth Argyle | A | R1 | 0-0 |
| Plymouth Argyle | H | R1R | 0-0 |
| Plymouth Argyle | N* | R1R | 1-0 |
| Sheffield Wednesday | H | R2 | 3-1 |
| Tottenham Hotspur | A | R3 | 3-6 |

*Second replay at Plainmoor, Torquay United

CITY MANAGER 1968-69
Frank Broome - Appointed May 1967
John Newman - Appointed April 1969

CITY PLAYING SQUAD 1968-69

| Name | Pos | Signed from | Apps | Gls |
|---|---|---|---|---|
| Mike Balson | HB | Bridport Aug 1965 | 37 | 2 |
| Alan Banks | F | Plymouth Argyle Nov 1967 | 22 | 13 |
| Fred Binney | F | Torquay United Feb 1969 | 17 | 11 |
| Jimmy Blain | FB | Carlisle United Oct 1965 | 42 | 2 |
| Peter Bullock | F | Colchester United Jul 1968 | 14 | 2 |
| John Corr | W | Arsenal Jul 1967 | 25+1 | 5 |
| Campbell Crawford | FB | West Bromwich Albion Jul 1967 | 13+4 | 1 |
| Dermot Curtis | F | Ipswich Town Aug 1963 | 29+2 | 4 |
| Keith Harvey | HB | Crediton Aug 1952 | 25+1 | |
| John Kirkham | M | Peterborough United Jul 1968 | 31+1 | 6 |
| John Mitten | W | Plymouth Argyle Jul 1968 | 35+2 | 7 |
| John Newman | HB | Plymouth Argyle Nov 1967 | 39+1 | |
| Graham Parker | M | Lincoln City Mar 1969 | 11 | |
| Alan Pinkney | F | St Luke's College Feb 1968 | 2 | |
| David Pleat | W | Shrewsbury Town Jul 1968 | 43 | 8 |
| John Rowlands | F | Torquay United Jan 1969 | 1 | |
| Brian Sharples | HB | Birmingham City Dec 1968 | 11 | 1 |
| Peter Shearing | G | Portsmouth Jun 1964 | 46 | |
| Cecil Smyth | FB | Distillery Aug 1962 | 38+1 | |
| Keith Whatling | W | Ipswich Town Jul 1967 | 9+3 | 1 |
| John Wingate | | Dawlish Town Feb 1969 | 16 | 3 |

FOURTH DIVISION - 1968-69

| | P | W | D | L | F | A | Pts |
|---|---|---|---|---|---|---|---|
| Doncaster Rovers | 46 | 21 | 17 | 8 | 65 | 38 | 59 |
| Halifax Town | 46 | 20 | 17 | 9 | 53 | 37 | 57 |
| Rochdale | 46 | 18 | 20 | 8 | 68 | 35 | 56 |
| Bradford City | 46 | 18 | 20 | 8 | 65 | 46 | 56 |
| Darlington | 46 | 17 | 18 | 11 | 62 | 45 | 52 |
| Colchester United | 46 | 20 | 12 | 14 | 57 | 53 | 52 |
| Southend United | 46 | 19 | 13 | 14 | 78 | 61 | 51 |
| Lincoln City | 46 | 17 | 17 | 12 | 54 | 52 | 51 |
| Wrexham | 46 | 18 | 14 | 14 | 61 | 52 | 50 |
| Swansea Town | 46 | 19 | 11 | 16 | 58 | 54 | 49 |
| Brentford | 46 | 18 | 12 | 16 | 64 | 65 | 48 |
| Workington | 46 | 15 | 17 | 14 | 40 | 43 | 47 |
| Port Vale | 46 | 16 | 14 | 16 | 46 | 46 | 46 |
| Chester City | 46 | 16 | 13 | 17 | 76 | 66 | 45 |
| Aldershot | 46 | 19 | 7 | 20 | 66 | 66 | 45 |
| Scunthorpe United | 46 | 18 | 8 | 20 | 61 | 60 | 44 |
| EXETER CITY | 46 | 16 | 11 | 19 | 66 | 65 | 43 |
| Peterborough United | 46 | 13 | 16 | 17 | 60 | 57 | 42 |
| Notts County | 46 | 12 | 18 | 16 | 48 | 57 | 42 |
| Chesterfield | 46 | 13 | 15 | 18 | 43 | 50 | 41 |
| York City | 46 | 14 | 11 | 21 | 53 | 75 | 39 |
| Newport County | 46 | 11 | 14 | 21 | 49 | 74 | 36 |
| Grimsby Town | 46 | 9 | 15 | 22 | 47 | 69 | 33 |
| Bradford Park Avenue | 46 | 5 | 10 | 31 | 32 | 106 | 20 |

* In the FA Cup, City defeated Newport County after a replay at Somerton Park, then Colchester United away, to earn a huge game against Manchester United in round three. A sell-out crowd saw United win 3-1, but not before the Grecians had given them a real fright.

* City also reached round three in the Football League Cup. It took three games to dispose of rivals Plymouth Argyle in the first round, before City upset all the odds by beating Sheffield Wednesday 3-1 at St James' Park. They then faced a daunting task at Tottenham Hotspur in round three, but what a fight they put up, eventually going down 6-3, the only team that season to score three goals at White Hart Lane.

* The league form was pretty patchy. The loss of Alan Banks through injury was a big blow, but the signing of Fred Binney on loan from Torquay United proved to be a good move as he scored 11 goals in just 17 appearances.

* It was only when Binney was in the side in the last quarter of the season that City began to consistently string a run of results together and indeed in their final 15 matches, only lost three times, which was promotion form.

* One of the most stunning league performances as far as entertaining supporters was concerned, was the 5-3 home win over Wrexham. David Pleat gave what many regard as his best performance in a Grecians shirt, scoring one of the goals. Binney netted twice and there were goals for Dermot Curtis and Brian Sharples.

* The highest attendance of the season for a league fixture at St James' Park was 12,714 for the visit of Southend United, three weeks prior to the Cup tie against Manchester United. Anyone attending the Southend game were given a voucher guaranteeing them a ticket for United. The previous home game had attracted just 3,851!

* Admission charges were raised substantially for the visit of Manchester United. Grandstand tickets were priced at 12s 6d as opposed to 6s, whilst it cost 6s to stand on the terracing against the usual price of 3s. Club chairman Les Kerslake said Exeter's share of the gate would be roughly £1,200. The board felt that the regular 4,000 supporters would not begrudge the club the opportunity of obtaining the increased admission charges from the 'wandering thousands.'

* Centre-forward John Rowlands was signed on loan from Torquay United, played one game and then, within hours, was off to sign for Cape Town City in South Africa.

* There was trouble all the way round for City when they played against Chester. Even before the game kicked off, Goalkeeper Peter Shearing's car broke down on the way to the ground at Ide. Manager Frank Broome went to fetch him, but found the Police were there and rushed them back to St James' Park in time for the kick off. Then it was discovered that John Newman was held up in holiday traffic. The A.A. came to his rescue escorting him through the traffic, but he still arrived 25 minutes late. Dermot Curtis picked originally as substitute had to play. When Newman arrived, he took over as sub, but went on the 53rd minute when Keith Harvey was injured.

* Just days before the final match of the season, it was announced that John Newman had taken over as player-manager, replacing Frank Broome who had left three months earlier.

Back row: Jimmy Blain, Graham Parker, Mike Blason, John Giles, Cecil Smyth
Middle row: Keith Harvey (Trainer), David Pleat, John Wingate, Peter Shearing, Brian Sharples, Steve Morris, John Mitten
Front row: John Corr, Alan Banks, John Newman (Player-Manager), Campbell Crawford, Bruce Walker

\* Exeter City created an unwanted record at the start of the 1969-70 season as for the first time since they became a professional club in 1908, they failed to get a single point from their first four games of the season. One supporter commented: "When you recall some the dismal campaigns this club has had during a history of long up hill struggle, it is difficult to believe that they have never before got off to such a poor start."

\* Shortly before the end of City's game against Port Vale at St. James' Park, the referee stopped the game after a cushion had been thrown onto the pitch following an unpopular offside decision. The referee held the match up for a few minutes whilst an announcement was made to the crowd that action would be taken if there was any more trouble.

## City's League Results

| | Home | Away |
|---|---|---|
| Aldershot | 2-1 | 0-1 |
| Bradford Park Avenue | 3-0 | 1-2 |
| Brentford | 2-2 | 0-2 |
| Chester | 1-0 | 0-2 |
| Chesterfield | 1-1 | 1-2 |
| Colchester United | 2-1 | 1-2 |
| Crewe Alexandra | 3-0 | 1-1 |
| Darlington | 1-2 | 0-4 |
| Grimsby Town | 0-1 | 0-2 |
| Hartlepool | 6-0 | 0-2 |
| Lincoln City | 1-2 | 0-1 |
| Newport County | 1-1 | 0-2 |
| Northampton Town | 1-0 | 0-2 |
| Notts County | 1-1 | 0-4 |
| Oldham Athletic | 0-2 | 1-1 |
| Peterborough United | 1-1 | 1-1 |
| Port Vale | 1-2 | 0-2 |
| Scunthorpe United | 4-1 | 0-0 |
| Southend United | 3-0 | 1-1 |
| Swansea Town | 6-0 | 0-0 |
| Workington | 5-1 | 2-1 |
| Wrexham | 1-0 | 0-3 |
| York City | 2-1 | 0-1 |

## Football League Cup

| | | | |
|---|---|---|---|
| Bristol City | H | R1 | 1-1 |
| Bristol City | A | R1R | 2-3 |

## F.A. Cup

| | | | |
|---|---|---|---|
| Fulham | H | R1 | 2-0 |
| Northampton Town | A | R2 | 1-1 |
| Northampton Town | H | R1R | 0-0 |
| Northampton Town | N | R12R | 1-2* |

\* Played at County Ground, Swindon Town

CITY MANAGER 1969-70
John Newman - Appointed April 1969

## CITY PLAYING SQUAD 1969-70

| | | | League | |
|---|---|---|---|---|
| Name | Pos | Signed From | Apps | Goals |
| Mike Balson | HB | Juniors Aug 1965 | 41 | 1 |
| Alan Banks | F | Plymouth Argyle, Nov 1967 | 34+2 | 10 |
| Fred Binney | F | Torquay United, Mar 1970 | 7 | 1 |
| Jimmy Blain | FB | Carlisle United Oct 1965 | 41 | 2 |
| John Corr | W | Arsenal Jul 1967 | 16+1 | 4 |
| Campbell Crawford | FB | West Bromwich Albion, July 1967 | 37+1 | 1 |
| Joe Gadston | F | Bristol Rovers Nov 1969 | 26 | 9 |
| John Giles | M | Bristol City May 1969 | 28+1 | 1 |
| John Mitten | W | Plymouth Argyle Jul 1969 | 43 | 9 |
| Steve Morris | FB | Bristol City Jun 1969 | 28+5 | 1 |
| John Newman | HB | Plymouth Argyle Nov 1967 | 4 | |
| Graham Parker | M | Lincoln City Mar 1969 | 39 | |
| David Pleat | W | Shrewsbury Town Jul 1968 | 23+2 | 5 |
| Brian Sharples | HB | Birmingham City Dec 1968 | 41 | 2 |
| Peter Shearing | G | Plymouth Argyle Jul 1968 | 27 | |
| Bruce Walker | W | Bradford City Jun 1969 | 21+3 | 2 |
| Bob Wilson | G | Cardiff City Jan 1970 | 19 | |
| John Wingate | M | Dawlish Town Feb 1969 | 31+6 | 8 |
| Own Goals | | | | 1 |

## FOURTH DIVISION 1969-70

| | P | W | D | L | F | A | Pts |
|---|---|---|---|---|---|---|---|
| Chesterfield | 46 | 27 | 10 | 9 | 77 | 32 | 64 |
| Wrexham | 46 | 26 | 9 | 11 | 84 | 49 | 61 |
| Swansea Town | 46 | 21 | 18 | 7 | 66 | 45 | 60 |
| Port Vale | 46 | 20 | 19 | 7 | 61 | 33 | 59 |
| Brentford | 46 | 20 | 16 | 10 | 58 | 39 | 56 |
| Aldershot | 46 | 20 | 13 | 13 | 78 | 65 | 53 |
| Notts County | 46 | 22 | 8 | 16 | 73 | 62 | 52 |
| Lincoln City | 46 | 17 | 16 | 13 | 66 | 52 | 50 |
| Peterborough United | 46 | 17 | 14 | 15 | 77 | 69 | 48 |
| Colchester United | 46 | 17 | 14 | 15 | 64 | 63 | 48 |
| Chester | 46 | 21 | 6 | 19 | 58 | 66 | 48 |
| Scunthorpe United | 46 | 18 | 10 | 18 | 67 | 65 | 46 |
| York City | 46 | 16 | 14 | 16 | 55 | 62 | 46 |
| Northampton Town | 46 | 16 | 12 | 18 | 64 | 55 | 44 |
| Crewe Alexandra | 46 | 16 | 12 | 18 | 51 | 51 | 44 |
| Grimsby Town | 46 | 14 | 15 | 17 | 54 | 58 | 43 |
| Southend United | 46 | 15 | 10 | 21 | 59 | 85 | 40 |
| EXETER CITY | 46 | 14 | 11 | 21 | 57 | 59 | 39 |
| Oldham Athletic | 46 | 13 | 13 | 20 | 60 | 65 | 39 |
| Workington | 46 | 12 | 14 | 20 | 46 | 64 | 38 |
| Darlington | 46 | 13 | 10 | 23 | 53 | 73 | 36 |
| Hartlepool | 46 | 10 | 10 | 26 | 42 | 82 | 30 |
| Bradford Park Avenue | 46 | 6 | 11 | 29 | 41 | 96 | 23 |

* One of the strangest results of the season was when Exeter City defeated, later to be promoted, Swansea Town 6-0 at St James' Park, the Welsh club's heaviest defeat of the campaign. Jimmy Blain and John Corr both netted doubles, whilst there was also a goal each for John Wingate and John Mitten.

* City's away record was nothing short of shocking,. They had to wait until 13th December before they won on the road, 2-1 at Workington. This proved to be the only away victory of the entire season.

* There was quite a battle in round two of the FA Cup, as it took three games to decide a winner. City drew 1-1 at Northampton Town, drew 0-0 back at St James' Park, and then lost the second replay, 1-2, played on the neutral ground of Swindon Town.

* Joe Gadston was signed from Bristol Rovers for a fee of £1,000 in November 1969, and by the end of the season he had repaid that fee by netting nine league goals.

* Only one player scored a hat-trick for City during the season, that being Alan Banks, whose treble helped the Grecians to a 6-0 home win over Hartlepool United.

* The highest attendance of the season for a league match at St James' Park was 6,700 for the visit of Newport County on Boxing Day. The lowest league crowd City played in front of was 1,342 at Workington.

* Exeter City were granted permission to sell beer on the terraces at three home matches, when Exeter Magistrates decided that the experiment could go ahead from 30th August 1969, after local Police had raised no objection.

* In September 1969 the club announced that they had made a profit on the previous season of £8,897. This reduced the club's overall deficit to £42,348. Gate receipts had increased to total £42,033, but wages and player signing on fees had also increased for the season to £35,407.

* On New Years Day 1970, Exeter City Supporters' Club launched a 1970s Appeal Fund, to raise cash to be used by team manager John Newman in the transfer market. Twelve days later the fund totalled a miserly £9! And on 15th January it was decided to close the Appeal Fund and refund those who had donated.

* After goalkeeper Peter Shearing broke his arm in the 2-0 defeat at Port Vale, City had to move quickly to sign a replacement, namely Bob Wilson, on loan from Cardiff City.

* Graham Parker was voted Exeter City Player of the Year and had proved to be one of the Grecians' most consistent players since being signed from Lincoln City the previous season.

* Around 130 City fans took part in a sponsored walk in March 1970, which raised over £500. Some of that was used to buy tracksuits for the players.

* In April 1970, City announced that admission prices would be increased for the following season. Terrace price would be six shillings, children three shillings. Stand tickets were to cost ten shillings. Stand season tickets were to be priced at £9 10s, whilst those for the terraces would be £6. City Chairman Les Kerslake said that the club regretted the increases, but the cost of everything was rising and most clubs in the Football League would have to raise prices as a result.

* City did win one trophy, the Tiverton Hospital Cup, as a strong side beat Tiverton Town 7-2 at Ladysmead. John Mitten and Dave Pleat scored two each and there were goals for Joe Gadston, Alan Banks and Graham Parker.

Back row: Joe Gadson, Brian Sharples, Graham Parker, John Mitten, Alan Banks
Middle row: John Corr, Campbell Crawford, Peter Shearing, Mike Balson, Bob Wilson, John Wingate, John Newman (Player-Manager)
Front row: Steve Morris, Jimmy Blain, Barry Rowan, Fred Binney, John Giles

* There were stories of a possible takeover at Exeter City F.C. just before the season commenced. Former chairman Reg Rose confirmed that approaches had been made to him about a possible bid to take control. Rose, who retired as chairman in 1967 due to ill health said he would be prepared to go back to St James' Park and form a new board of directors.

The current chairman, Les Kerslake said he knew nothing about the moves, but said he would be prepared to meet Rose and discuss anything. Rose still retained shares in the club, but when he left the board he had stated that it would be very unlikely he would return even after a prolonged convalescence leave. The hurly burly nature of a football club directorship was incompatible with his heart condition.

| City's League Results | HOME | AWAY |
| --- | --- | --- |
| Aldershot | 4-1 | 2-2 |
| Barrow | 4-2 | 1-1 |
| Bournemouth | 0-0 | 1-4 |
| Brentford | 1-0 | 0-5 |
| Cambridge United | 1-0 | 0-2 |
| Chester | 3-1 | 1-3 |
| Colchester United | 2-2 | 1-1 |
| Crewe Alexandra | 6-2 | 1-4 |
| Darlington | 2-1 | 2-3 |
| Grimsby Town | 4-0 | 2-1 |
| Hartlepool United | 1-1 | 0-3 |
| Lincoln City | 0-0 | 1-4 |
| Newport County | 1-1 | 1-0 |
| Northampton Town | 1-1 | 2-2 |
| Notts County | 0-1 | 1-1 |
| Oldham Athletic | 0-2 | 1-2 |
| Peterborough United | 3-2 | 3-1 |
| Scunthorpe United | 1-1 | 0-3 |
| Southend United | 2-0 | 0-0 |
| Southport | 2-1 | 2-0 |
| Stockport County | 2-1 | 3-0 |
| Workington | 0-1 | 0-1 |
| York City | 0-2 | 2-2 |

| Football League Cup | | | |
| --- | --- | --- | --- |
| Swansea City | H | R1 | 0-0 |
| Swansea City | A | R1R | 2-4* |
| * after extra time | | | |

| F.A. Cup | | | |
| --- | --- | --- | --- |
| Swansea City | A | R1 | 1-4 |

CITY MANAGER 1970-71
John Newman - Appointed April 1969

| CITY PLAYING SQUAD 1970-71 | | | | |
| --- | --- | --- | --- | --- |
| Name | Pos | Signed From | Apps | Gls |
| Mike Balson | HB | Juniors Aug 1965 | 44+1 | |
| Alan Banks | F | Plymouth Argyle Nov 1967 | 40+1 | 21 |
| Fred Binney | F | Torquay United Mar 1970 | 30 | 8 |
| Jimmy Blain | FB | Carlisle United Oct 1965 | 38 | |
| John Corr | W | Arsenal Jul 1967 | 17+3 | 3 |
| Campbell Crawford | FB | West Bromwich Albion Jul 1967 | 46 | |
| Joe Gadston | F | Bristol Rovers Nov 1969 | 39 | 18 |
| Jimmy Giles | HB | Aldershot Mar 1971 | 11 | 2 |
| John Giles | M | Bristol City May 1969 | 17+1 | 1 |
| John Mitten | W | Plymouth Argyle Jul 1969 | 18+2 | 1 |
| Fred Molyneux | Hb | Plymouth Argyle Feb 1971 | 2 | |
| Steve Morris | Fb | Bristol City Jun 1969 | 22+1 | |
| John Newman | HB | Plymouth Argyle Nov 1967 | 14 | |
| Graham Parker | M | Lincoln City Mar 1969 | 35 | 2 |
| Barry Rowan | W | Plymouth Argyle Jul 1970 | 38+2 | 7 |
| Brian Sharples | HB | Birmingham City Dec 1968 | 16 | 1 |
| Peter Shearing | G | Plymouth Argyle Jul 1968 | 6 | |
| Bob Wilson | G | Cardiff City Jan 1970 | 40 | |
| John Wingate | M | Dawlish Town Feb 1969 | 33+2 | 3 |

| FOURTH DIVISION 1970-71 | P | W | D | L | F | A | Pts |
| --- | --- | --- | --- | --- | --- | --- | --- |
| Notts County | 46 | 24 | 12 | 10 | 81 | 46 | 60 |
| Bournemouth & B.A. | 46 | 24 | 12 | 10 | 81 | 46 | 60 |
| Oldham Athletic | 46 | 24 | 11 | 11 | 88 | 63 | 59 |
| York City | 46 | 23 | 10 | 13 | 78 | 54 | 56 |
| Chester City | 46 | 24 | 7 | 15 | 69 | 55 | 55 |
| Colchester United | 46 | 21 | 12 | 13 | 70 | 54 | 54 |
| Northampton Town | 46 | 19 | 13 | 14 | 63 | 59 | 51 |
| Southport | 46 | 21 | 6 | 19 | 63 | 57 | 57 |
| EXETER CITY | 46 | 17 | 14 | 15 | 67 | 68 | 48 |
| Workington | 46 | 18 | 12 | 16 | 48 | 49 | 48 |
| Stockport County | 46 | 16 | 14 | 16 | 49 | 65 | 46 |
| Darlington | 46 | 17 | 11 | 18 | 58 | 57 | 45 |
| Aldershot | 46 | 14 | 17 | 15 | 66 | 71 | 45 |
| Brentford | 46 | 18 | 8 | 20 | 66 | 62 | 44 |
| Crewe Alexandra | 46 | 18 | 8 | 20 | 75 | 76 | 44 |
| Peterborough United | 46 | 18 | 7 | 21 | 70 | 71 | 43 |
| Scunthorpe United | 46 | 15 | 13 | 18 | 56 | 61 | 43 |
| Southend United | 46 | 14 | 15 | 17 | 53 | 66 | 43 |
| Grimsby Town | 46 | 18 | 7 | 21 | 57 | 71 | 43 |
| Cambridge United | 46 | 15 | 13 | 18 | 51 | 66 | 43 |
| Lincoln City | 46 | 13 | 13 | 20 | 70 | 71 | 39 |
| Newport County | 46 | 10 | 8 | 28 | 55 | 85 | 28 |
| Hartlepool United | 46 | 8 | 12 | 26 | 34 | 74 | 28 |
| Barrow | 46 | 7 | 8 | 31 | 51 | 90 | 22 |

* Exeter City enjoyed their best final placing in the Fourth Division since they were promoted in 1963-64. Player-manager John Newman guided his team to 9th place, with two players reaching double figures in terms of goals. Alan Banks led the way with 21 league goals, closely followed by Joe Gadston with 18.

* Banks hit the only hat-trick of City's league season when the Grecians beat Grimsby Town 4-1 at St James' Park, the other goal being netted by Fred Binney.

* The best result of the season was the 6-2 hiding of Crewe Alexandra at the Park, before 4,769 spectators. Banks and Gadston scored two each, whilst John Giles and Corr got one apiece.

* An early first round exit was made in the FA Cup as City lost 4-1 at Swansea City. They also went out at the same stage in the Football League Cup against the same opponents. After a goalless draw at the Park, City went down 4-2 after extra-time in the replay.

* The highest attendance of the season for a Fourth Division fixture at the Park was 7,918 for the visit of Bournemouth & Boscombe Athletic, whilst the lowest was 3,437 for the game against Southport. A notable 18,002 turned up for City's final game at Notts County, the hosts celebrating that they had won the Fourth Division championship, but they didn't get things their own way as a Gadston goal gave City a point.

* John Hillier was appointed as Exeter City's first ever Commercial Manager in September 1970 and his target was to raise £15,000 in his first year. He had previously been working for Devon County Council.

* The club launched a new look match programme, although there was much discussion as to why Maurice Golesworthy's notes had been dispensed with. He had been a familiar face on match days at the Park for the previous 22 years and was the envy of most Football League clubs for the wealth of information he had at his fingertips.

* The Grecians reported a net loss of £8,164 on the year. There was a big drop in revenue from home gates and transfer fees paid increased. The club's total deficit stood at £50,515. Wages costs rose to £35,407 for the year, however, travelling and hotel costs showed a slight decrease at £4,792.

* Defender Fred Molyneux, signed on loan from Plymouth Argyle, played two matches, stayed one week, and then signed for Tranmere Rovers! He always said that he wanted to return to Lancashire if the opportunity arose, but was happy to join City as he was out of the team at Argyle and transfer listed.

* Outline planning permission was granted by Exeter City Council for the construction of a clubhouse at the top of the Big Bank terracing at St James" Park.

* Alan Banks was presented with an engraved silver salver for breaking the club's goalscoring record, previously held by Graham Rees with 89 goals. He was presented with the salver by the Mayor of Exeter, himself a former City player, Percy Hilton, before the game against Brentford in February 1971.

* Exeter City made a transfer deadline day signing in March 1971, when they paid £3,000 for Aldershot's 24-year-old centre-half Jimmy Giles. When Exeter had visited Aldershot a couple of weeks earlier, Giles had come on as substitute for the Shots and headed the home side into the lead. City drew the game 2-2.

* At the end of the season, City winger Barry Rowan, was loaned to Dallas Tornado for three months in the American Professional League. Four years earlier he had played in the same league for Oakland Clippers and then Detroit Cougars.

* An Exeter City Supporters Association was formed in July 1971. It was stated that the purpose of the new association was to raise funds for Exeter City Football Club by adopting a professional approach to fund raising as nearly all the other League clubs had found necessary in recent years.

City director, Wally Rice, said that the income of the club had been far too low in the past to achieve anything more than meagre success. The club aimed at promotion to Division Three and if this was to be achieved and the team was to remain there, new players and additional reserve strength was essential.

Exeter City FC would have control over the association finances and the secretary, Eric Budd, the official organiser of social events, would be responsible to the club. Russell Thomas, Exeter City's secretary was the association treasurer.

Membership of the association would cost 15p and this would entitle members to advantages including the O.A.P. scheme giving reduced admission to matches at St James' Park. Coaches would be organised to away matches and activities included twice weekly bingo sessions, a Golden Goal competition and a 200 Club.

* During the summer of 1971 the popular side stand was re-roofed. A new players entrance was constructed at the old Grecians Entrance and a new facade had been placed over the turnstiles to improve the appearance of the main stand.

In addition the refreshment huts had all been painted and the guest room under the main stand had been totally redecorated to ensure it was more suitable to entertain visiting directors and their guests.

City's League Results

|  | HOME | AWAY |
|---|---|---|
| Aldershot | 1-0 | 0-0 |
| Barrow | 7-1 | 0-0 |
| Brentford | 0-1 | 0-1 |
| Bury | 3-2 | 3-4 |
| Cambridge United | 3-4 | 1-0 |
| Chester | 1-1 | 2-1 |
| Colchester United | 3-3 | 0-3 |
| Crewe Alexandra | 3-1 | 1-0 |
| Darlington | 3-0 | 1-2 |
| Doncaster Rovers | 1-0 | 1-2 |
| Gillingham | 1-1 | 2-0 |
| Grimsby Town | 3-4 | 0-3 |
| Hartlepool United | 1-0 | 0-1 |
| Lincoln City | 1-2 | 1-4 |
| Newport County | 1-0 | 0-0 |
| Northampton Town | 1-3 | 1-1 |
| Peterborough United | 3-2 | 3-3 |
| Reading | 0-0 | 0-3 |
| Scunthorpe United | 1-0 | 0-3 |
| Southend United | 0-0 | 0-3 |
| Southport | 1-3 | 0-4 |
| Stockport County | 2-0 | 4-0 |
| Workington | 0-2 | 0-0 |

F.A. Cup

| Crawley Town | A | R1 | 0-0 |
| Crawley Town | H | R1R | 2-0 |
| Swansea City | A | R2 | 0-0 |
| Swansea City | H | R2R | 0-1 |

Football League Cup

| Bristol Rovers | H | R1 | 0-3 |

CITY MANAGER 1971-72
John Newman - Appointed April 1969

### CITY PLAYING SQUAD 1971-72

| Name | Pos | Signed From | Apps | Gls |
|---|---|---|---|---|
| Mike Balson | HB | Juniors Aug 1965 | 46 | 1 |
| Alan Banks | FB | Plymouth Argyle Nov 1967 | 31(5) | 7 |
| Fred Binney | FB | Torquay United Mar 1970 | 39 | 17 |
| Jimmy Blain | FB | Carlisle United Oct 1965 | 40(2) | 1 |
| Campbell Crawford | FB | West Bromwich Albion Jul 1967 | 30(2) | |
| Joe Gadston | FB | Bristol Rovers Nov 1969 | 20 | 3 |
| Dave Gibson | M | Aston Villa Jan 1972 | 23 | 1 |
| Jimmy Giles | HB | Aldershot Mar 1971 | 42 | 1 |
| John Giles | M | Bristol City May 1969 | 10(3) | |
| Tony Morrin | M | Barrow Jul 1971 | 31 | 5 |
| Steve Morris | FB | Bristol City Jun 1969 | 11(5) | 1 |
| John Neale | W | Barnstaple Town Mar 1972 | 2(2) | |
| John Newman | HB | Plymouth Argyle Nov 1967 | 4 | |
| Graham Parker | M | Lincoln City Mar 1969 | 33(1) | 4 |
| Barry Rowan | W | Plymouth Argyle Jul 1970 | 33(1) | 8 |
| Steve Stacey | FB | Bristol City Sep 1971 | 30 | |
| Bob Wilson | G | Cardiff City Jan 1970 | 46 | |
| John Wingate | M | Dawlish Town Feb 1969 | 35(1) | 9 |

FOURTH DIVISION 1971-72

| | P | W | D | L | F | A | Pts |
|---|---|---|---|---|---|---|---|
| Grimsby Town | 46 | 28 | 7 | 11 | 88 | 56 | 63 |
| Southend United | 46 | 24 | 12 | 10 | 81 | 55 | 60 |
| Brentford | 46 | 24 | 11 | 11 | 76 | 44 | 59 |
| Scunthorpe United | 46 | 22 | 13 | 11 | 56 | 37 | 57 |
| Lincoln City | 46 | 21 | 14 | 11 | 77 | 59 | 56 |
| Workington | 46 | 16 | 19 | 11 | 50 | 34 | 51 |
| Southport | 46 | 18 | 14 | 14 | 66 | 46 | 50 |
| Peterborough United | 46 | 17 | 16 | 13 | 82 | 64 | 50 |
| Bury | 46 | 19 | 12 | 15 | 73 | 59 | 50 |
| Cambridge United | 46 | 17 | 14 | 15 | 62 | 60 | 48 |
| Colchester United | 46 | 19 | 10 | 17 | 70 | 69 | 48 |
| Doncaster Rovers | 46 | 16 | 14 | 16 | 56 | 63 | 46 |
| Gillingham | 46 | 16 | 13 | 17 | 61 | 67 | 45 |
| Newport County | 46 | 18 | 8 | 20 | 60 | 72 | 44 |
| Exeter City | 46 | 16 | 11 | 19 | 61 | 68 | 43 |
| Reading | 46 | 17 | 8 | 21 | 56 | 76 | 42 |
| Aldershot | 46 | 9 | 22 | 15 | 48 | 54 | 40 |
| Hartlepool United | 46 | 17 | 6 | 23 | 58 | 69 | 40 |
| Darlington | 46 | 14 | 11 | 21 | 64 | 82 | 39 |
| Chester | 46 | 10 | 18 | 18 | 47 | 56 | 38 |
| Northampton Town | 46 | 12 | 13 | 21 | 66 | 79 | 37 |
| Barrow | 46 | 13 | 11 | 22 | 40 | 71 | 37 |
| Stockport County | 46 | 9 | 14 | 23 | 55 | 87 | 32 |
| Crewe Alexandra | 46 | 10 | 9 | 27 | 43 | 69 | 29 |

* Exeter City made a net loss of £1,888 on the year ending 31st May 1971. The club's deficit stood at £52,400. Fundraising brought in £11,311, but revenue from gate receipts dropped to £27,901. The Directors estimated that the value of the land and buildings at St James' Park to be well in excess of £30,000.

* The club offered the 16 professional players the biggest incentives ever, with a scheme based on crowd figures and scoring goals, which would boost each individual players' bank balance considerably should they be successful.

* City started the season with a 4-0 loss at Southport, their heaviest opening day defeat for 14 years. It was not a good weekend for manager John Newman who also had his hotel room broken into and the contents of a bag stolen including a cheque book and cash.

* It was announced, in September 1971, that the club hoped to have a reserve team again for the following season, to play in the Exeter and District League. However, four months later there had been a change of heart as the Grecians applied to join the Western League.

* Comedian and Luton Town Director, Eric Morecambe, visited the Exeter City dressing rooms prior to the game against Southport in October 1971. Morecambe, and Ernie Wise were appearing at the ABC Cinema in Exeter and came along to watch the game. City lost 3-1. Wise preferred to spend the day in Sidmouth.

* Manager John Newman handed in his resignation immediately after the defeat against Southport . Four days later a letter was written on behalf of all the players to Newman urging him to change his mind, and that persuaded him to do so.

* Exmouth hotelier, Frank Betts, offered Exeter City's players a £14,000 bonus, but to earn it, they had to win the FA Cup! Security was lodged with the Bank to cover the amount. The odds on City winning the trophy were 10,000 to 1.

*Exeter City launched their new club song - 'The Exeter City March' - at the game against Brentford in December 1971. Director Walter Rice, whose idea it was, wanted the  ... "Skinheads in the Cowshed to lead the crowd in song."

* City manager John Newman had been frustrated in attempts to sign players and said: "Exeter have never been a good home to players because it is not a very stable club. That is one of the reasons. The other is they do not want to be so far away from the football areas and the west country is I am afraid.'

* The club launched a 'Buy A Player' appeal in March 1972, with the aim of raising £5,000 by 1st June, Commercial manager John Hillier was the driving force behind the fundraising initiative. Twenty-four hours after the launch the fund stood at 50p!

* Exeter's game at Grimsby Town on 18th March 1972 was abandoned after just 18 minutes when fog got ever thicker off the North Sea. The referee waited for 10 minutes to see if it would clear, but then called a halt to the game.

* The club introduced a 'Golden Gate' for the match against Colchester United at St James' Park on 15th April,. Admission through that entrance cost 50p instead of the usual 30p. The extra cash would go to the 'Buy A Player' appeal.

* The Grecians went goal crazy in their final home match of the season against Barrow as they won 7-1. Alan Banks headed home his 100th league goal for the club. This proved to be Barrow's last game in the Football League as they failed to gain re-election for the following season.

* Work commenced in June 1972 on the construction of a clubhouse at St James' Park which would cost £8,500. Of the cost £6,500 was provided at a low rate of interest by a local firm and £2,000 was made available by the four man board of directors of Exeter City.

The building, which was to be located on top of the Big Bank terracing, was 64 foot long and 24 foot wide, containing a long bar and a skittle alley.

City director and P.R.O. Wally Rice said: "The club's directors have been most anxious to have the building in the past year, but I am sure supporters do not know what difficulties have been involved.

"First there was the question of the cost and the dislocation of accommodation. Secondly there was the problem of negotiating the final sponsorship for a large part of the construction and furnishing of the new clubhouse.

"The directors are keen to have the building opened, both to bring in additional income and to provide a home for the Supporters Association where they can meet together with the players. officials and directors."

* With attendances in decline everywhere, manager John Newman made a rallying call for them to return in December 1972. Despite the team sitting at the top end of the Fourth Division, Newman said: "We cannot survive on the gates of 4,000 that we have been getting, even though we are doing better than most in the Fourth Division.

"Attendances are down everywhere this season, but surely we can now expect 5,000 as we are in the top four of the division? There is a long way to go if we are to win promotion and everyone wants to keep the form going, encouraged by higher attendances,"

### City's League Results

| | HOME | AWAY |
|---|---|---|
| Aldershot | 1-0 | 0-0 |
| Barnsley | 2-1 | 1-1 |
| Bradford City | 5-1 | 0-4 |
| Bury | 1-1 | 1-2 |
| Cambridge United | 3-1 | 3-1 |
| Chester | 0-0 | 1-0 |
| Colchester United | 1-0 | 2-1 |
| Crewe Alexandra | 0-0 | 0-1 |
| Darlington | 1-1 | 0-0 |
| Doncaster Rovers | 0-1 | 1-5 |
| Gillingham | 3-2 | 0-1 |
| Hartlepool United | 1-1 | 0-0 |
| Hereford United | 1-0 | 0-1 |
| Lincoln City | 2-0 | 2-2 |
| Mansfield Town | 4-2 | 0-3 |
| Newport County | 0-0 | 0-2 |
| Northampton Town | 4-1 | 2-1 |
| Peterborough United | 1-1 | 1-1 |
| Reading | 0-0 | 0-2 |
| Southport | 0-1 | 0-1 |
| Stockport County | 3-0 | 0-1 |
| Torquay United | 3-2 | 2-0 |
| Workington | 4-2 | 1-3 |

| F.A. Cup | | | |
|---|---|---|---|
| Walton & Hersham | A | R1 | 1-2 |

| Football League Cup | | | |
|---|---|---|---|
| Brighton & H.A. | A | R1 | 1-2 |

CITY MANAGER 1972-73
John Newman - Appointed April 1969

### CITY PLAYING SQUAD 1972-73

| Name | Pos | Signed From | Apps | Gls |
|---|---|---|---|---|
| Mike Balson | HB | Juniors Aug 1965 | 42 | 4 |
| Alan Banks | F | Plymouth Argyle Nov 1967 | 6(5) | 1 |
| John Benson | FB | AFC Bournemouth Mar 1973 | 4 | |
| Fred Binney | F | Plymouth Argyle Nov 1967 | 46 | 28 |
| Jimmy Blain | FB | Carlisle United Oct 1965 | 29(3) | |
| Keith Clapham | HB | AFC Bournemouth Jul 1972 | 21(5) | |
| Allen Clarke | G | Charlton Athletic Feb 1973 | 8 | |
| Campbell Crawford | FB | West Bromwich Albion Jul 1967 | 29(2) | |
| Dave Gibson | M | Aston Villa Jan 1972 | 30(1) | 2 |
| Jimmy Giles | HB | West Bromwich Albion Jul 1967 | 44 | 1 |
| Tony Morrin | M | Barrow Jul 1971 | 39(1) | 2 |
| John Neale | W | Barnstaple Town Mar 1972 | 12 | |
| Graham Parker | M | Lincoln City Mar 1969 | 30 | 3 |
| Dick Plumb | F | Charlton Athletic Aug 1972 | 38 | 11 |
| Barry Rowan | W | Plymouth Argyle Jul 1970 | 5(2) | |
| Tony Scott | W | AFC Bournemouth Jun 1972 | 30 | |
| Steve Stacey | FB | Bristol City Sep 1971 | 27(2) | |
| Bob Wilson | G | Cardiff City Jan 1970 | 38 | |
| John Wingate | M | Dawlish Town Feb 1969 | 28(7) | 4 |
| Own Goals | | | | 1 |

### FOURTH DIVISION 1972-73

| | P | W | D | L | F | A | Pts |
|---|---|---|---|---|---|---|---|
| Southport | 46 | 26 | 10 | 10 | 71 | 48 | 62 |
| Hereford United | 46 | 23 | 12 | 11 | 66 | 38 | 58 |
| Cambridge United | 46 | 20 | 17 | 9 | 67 | 57 | 57 |
| Aldershot | 46 | 22 | 12 | 12 | 60 | 38 | 56 |
| Newport County | 46 | 22 | 12 | 12 | 64 | 44 | 56 |
| Mansfield Town | 46 | 20 | 14 | 12 | 78 | 51 | 54 |
| Reading | 46 | 17 | 18 | 11 | 51 | 38 | 52 |
| Exeter City | 46 | 18 | 14 | 14 | 57 | 51 | 50 |
| Gillingham | 46 | 19 | 11 | 16 | 63 | 58 | 49 |
| Lincoln City | 46 | 16 | 16 | 14 | 64 | 57 | 48 |
| Stockport County | 46 | 18 | 12 | 16 | 53 | 53 | 48 |
| Bury | 46 | 14 | 14 | 18 | 58 | 51 | 46 |
| Workington | 46 | 17 | 12 | 17 | 59 | 61 | 46 |
| Barnsley | 46 | 14 | 16 | 16 | 58 | 60 | 44 |
| Chester | 46 | 14 | 15 | 17 | 61 | 52 | 43 |
| Bradford City | 46 | 16 | 11 | 19 | 61 | 65 | 43 |
| Doncaster Rovers | 46 | 15 | 12 | 19 | 49 | 58 | 42 |
| Torquay United | 46 | 12 | 17 | 17 | 44 | 47 | 41 |
| Peterborough United | 46 | 14 | 13 | 19 | 71 | 76 | 41 |
| Hartlepool United | 46 | 12 | 17 | 17 | 34 | 49 | 41 |
| Crewe Alexandra | 46 | 9 | 18 | 19 | 38 | 61 | 36 |
| Colchester United | 46 | 10 | 11 | 25 | 48 | 76 | 31 |
| Northampton Town | 46 | 10 | 11 | 25 | 40 | 73 | 31 |
| Darlington | 46 | 7 | 15 | 24 | 42 | 85 | 29 |

*Admission charges for the 1972-73 season for Football League matches at St James' Park were as follows:- Grandstand 60p; Ground 40p, O.A.P's and Juveniles all at half price for all first team League matches. For reserve team matches in the Western League, only the grandstand would be open - 20p for adults; half price for O.A.P's and Juveniles.

* Exeter City paid a fee of £5,000 for former Yeovil Town forward Dick Plumb, who arrived from Charlton Athletic a day before the season commenced.

* The City players went into the recording studio to make a record, the 'A' side being called 'Swing Along With City' and the 'B' side featuring forward Fred Binney solo, singing 'Football Fan.' The record was released in September 1972.

* John Wingate was measured to have the hardest shot of any of the City players when a computerised speed and timing machine was used at St James' Park in September 1972. Wingate was timed at 59.20mph. Barry Rowan came in at 57.40mph and Mike Balson at 54.80mph.

* Exeter City's 3-0 home win over Stockport County at St James' Park was overshadowed by the sudden death of match referee Jim Finn. He collapsed on the field in the 60th minute and stretchered off before being taken to hospital. Efforts to revive him in the dressing room failed.

* The City Board of Directors were concerned at the slump in the average attendance at St James' Park as early as September 1972. Director Walter Rice said it was a matter of grave concern and that receipts from home games were barely enough to pay half the wage bill. The average at the time was 3,757.

* The club announced that they had made a loss of £1,113 on the year ending 31st May 1972. Gate receipts had dropped to £27,542. A further £13,800 came in fundraising. Wages costs totalled £42,809. Travelling and hotel expenses accounted for £5,075.

* Exeter City staged a testimonial match for former player, Brian Sharples, who had been forced to retire through injury. The opposition were Aston Villa on 24th October 1972 and a crowd of 4,921 saw the teams draw 2-2. Sharples estimated he would make £1,750 from the game.

* The name of the football club was changed at the AGM of shareholders in November 1972. Instead of 'The Exeter City Football and Athletic Company Limited' it would now be 'Exeter City Association Football Club Limited.'

* Exeter City suffered a humiliating 2-1 defeat in the FA Cup first round when they lost at Isthmian League side, Walton and Hersham.

* Robert Rowden quit as secretary of Exeter City in December 1972, after just five months in the job, saying: "I feel that the facilities in which I am expected to work at St James' Park are inadequate."

* Keith Harvey quit as trainer of Exeter City in January 1973 to take up employment with the Post office. This ended a 20-year association with the club, that he joined as a player.

* Exeter City ran an excursion train to their away fixture at Gillingham in February 1973, the first time that they had done so since the promotion season of 1963-64.

* The club increased admission charges in March 1973 after the introduction of Value Added Tax. Stand tickets were increased from 60p to 65p, and ground admission prices increased from 40p to 45p.

* The club also hired the special Leagueliner train from the Football League to take the team and supporters to the fixture at Peterborough United in April 1973. Commercial manager John Hillier said that it had cost £1,000 to hire, but they had made a profit of £300 on the venture.

Back row: John Neale, Keith Clapham, Brian Joy, Graham Parker
Middle row: John Newman (Manager), Dick Plumb, Bob Wilson, Mike
Balson, Allen Clarke, Dave Gibson, John Wingate, Jack Edwards
(Trainer)
Front Row: Jimmy Giles, Tony Morrin, Fred Binney, Fred Dart
(Chairman), Jimmy Blain, Tony Scott, Campbell Crawford

### City's League Results

| HOME AWAY | HOME | AWAY |
|---|---|---|
| Barnsley | 6-2 | 0-3 |
| Bradford City | 0-0 | 0-1 |
| Brentford | 2-1 | 1-0 |
| Bury | 0-3 | 0-0 |
| Chester City | 2-1 | 1-0 |
| Colchester United | 1-0 | 0-1 |
| Crewe Alexandra | 2-0 | 5-2 |
| Darlington | 3-0 | 0-1 |
| Doncaster Rovers | 1-2 | 0-1 |
| Gillingham | 2-1 | 1-2 |
| Hartlepool United | 2-0 | 3-1 |
| Lincoln City | 0-1 | 1-2 |
| Mansfield Town | 1-1 | 3-3 |
| Newport County | 0-1 | 1-2 |
| Northampton Town | 1-1 | 2-1 |
| Peterborough United | 1-2 | 0-2 |
| Reading | 0-1 | 1-4 |
| Rotherham United | 0-0 | 0-4 |
| Scunthorpe United | 4-0 | |
| Stockport County | 2-1 | 1-0 |
| Swansea City | 2-0 | 0-2 |
| Torquay United | 4-2 | 0-0 |
| Workington | 1-1 | 1-3 |

### Football League Cup

| | | |
|---|---|---|
| Swansea City | A R1 | 1-1 |
| Swansea City | H R1R | 2-1 aet |
| Rotherham United | A R2 | 4-1 |
| West Bromwich Albion | A R3 | 3-1 |
| Wolves | A R4 | 1-3 |

### F.A. Cup

| | | |
|---|---|---|
| Alvechurch | H R1 | 0-1 |

CITY MANAGER 1973-74
John Newman - Appointed April 1969

## CITY PLAYING SQUAD 1973-74

| Name | Pos | Signed From | Apps | Gls |
|---|---|---|---|---|
| Mike Balson | D | Bridport Aug 1965 | 24+1 | 1 |
| Fred Binney | F | Torquay United Mar 1970 | 38 | 25 |
| Jimmy Blain | D | Carlisle United Oct 1965 | 15+2 | |
| Keith Bowker | F | Birmingham City Dec 1973 | 25 | 7 |
| Keith Clapham | GD | AFC Bournemouth Sep 1972 | 32+2 | |
| Allen Clarke | G | Charlton Athletic Feb 1973 | 8 | |
| Campbell Crawford | D | West Bromwich Albion Jul 1967 | 33 | |
| Alan Devlin | F | Dundee United Nov 1973 | 1 | |
| Dave Gibson | M | Aston Villa Jan 1972 | 16+1 | |
| Jimmy Giles | D | Aldershot Mar 1971 | 43 | 2 |
| Peter Hatch | D | Oxford United Dec 1973 | 24 | |
| Brian Joy | D | Doncaster Rovers Jul 1973 | 29+1 | |
| Tony Morrin | M | Barrow Jul 1971 | 28+1 | 3 |
| John Neale | W | Barnstaple Town Mar 1972 | 16+6 | 1 |
| Graham Parker | M | Lincoln City Mar 1969 | 32 | 3 |
| Dick Plumb | F | Charlton Athletic Aug 1972 | 21 | 6 |
| Tony Scott | W | Bournemouth Jun 1972 | 21 | 4 |
| Ken Wallace | W | Hereford United Sep 1973 | 8+2 | 1 |
| Bob Wilson | G | Cardiff City Jan 1970 | 37 | |
| John Wingate | M | Dawlish Town Feb 1969 | 44 | 5 |
| Own Goals | | | | 2 |

### FOURTH DIVISION - 1973-74

| | P | W | D | L | F | A | Pts |
|---|---|---|---|---|---|---|---|
| Peterborough United | 46 | 27 | 11 | 8 | 75 | 38 | 65 |
| Gillingham | 46 | 25 | 12 | 9 | 90 | 49 | 62 |
| Colchester United | 46 | 24 | 12 | 10 | 73 | 36 | 60 |
| Bury | 46 | 24 | 11 | 11 | 81 | 49 | 59 |
| Northampton Town | 46 | 20 | 13 | 13 | 63 | 48 | 53 |
| Reading | 46 | 16 | 19 | 11 | 58 | 37 | 51 |
| Chester City | 46 | 17 | 15 | 14 | 54 | 55 | 49 |
| Bradford City | 46 | 17 | 14 | 15 | 58 | 52 | 48 |
| Newport County | 46 | 16 | 14 | 16 | 56 | 65 | 45 |
| EXETER CITY | 45 | 18 | 8 | 19 | 58 | 55 | 44 |
| Hartlepool United | 46 | 16 | 12 | 18 | 48 | 47 | 44 |
| Lincoln City | 46 | 16 | 12 | 18 | 63 | 67 | 44 |
| Barnsley | 46 | 17 | 10 | 19 | 58 | 64 | 44 |
| Swansea City | 46 | 16 | 11 | 19 | 45 | 46 | 43 |
| Rotherham United | 46 | 15 | 13 | 18 | 56 | 58 | 43 |
| Torquay United | 46 | 13 | 17 | 16 | 52 | 57 | 43 |
| Mansfield Town | 46 | 13 | 17 | 16 | 62 | 69 | 43 |
| Scunthorpe United | 45 | 14 | 12 | 19 | 47 | 64 | 42 |
| Brentford | 46 | 12 | 16 | 18 | 48 | 50 | 40 |
| Darlington | 46 | 13 | 13 | 20 | 40 | 62 | 39 |
| Crewe Alexandra | 46 | 14 | 10 | 22 | 43 | 71 | 38 |
| Doncaster Rovers | 46 | 12 | 11 | 23 | 47 | 80 | 35 |
| Workington | 46 | 11 | 13 | 22 | 43 | 74 | 35 |
| Stockport County | 46 | 7 | 20 | 19 | 44 | 69 | 34 |

* This proved to be an eventful season to say the least, no more so than the saga of the game that never was at Scunthorpe United. With several players sidelined through injury or illness and backed by doctor's certificates, City requested a postponement of the game. The Football League decided they knew more about medical matters than the club doctor and refused, ordering City to travel, even though they only had nine fit players. City didn't go, and as a result the Football League fined them and ordered them to pay Scunthorpe costs in what was regarded as one of the most unjust cases for many a year.

* It was also the season when a power workers dispute meant that floodlights couldn't be used for certain games. So this led to earlier kick offs or even playing on a Sunday afternoon to avoid any planned power cuts.

* The Grecians reached the fourth round of the Football League Cup to be knocked out by Wolverhampton Wanders in a tie that was staged on a Tuesday afternoon at Molineux. City lost 5-1. To reach that stage they had beaten Swansea City, Rotherham United and West Bromwich Albion.

* City travelled to Rotherham United twice in the same week with very different results. On the Wednesday night they defeated their hosts 4-1 in the Football League Cup, but the following Saturday went back to Millmoor, only to lose 0-4 in a Fourth Division fixture!

* Fred Binney led the way in the goalscoring charts with 25 league goals, which not surprisingly attracted the attention of many clubs. He left City at the end of the season to join Brighton and Hove Albion for a fee of £25,000, with Lammie Robertson and John Templeman moving in the opposite direction as part of the deal.

* The FA Cup was a complete disaster as City suffered one of their all too frequent humiliating defeats at the hands of non-league opposition. They lost 1-0 to Alvechurch at St James' Park in the first round.

* The highest attendance of the season for a league match at St James' Park was 6,822 when Reading won 1-0.

* In complete contrast, there were a miserable 693 (and that included at least two City fans, yours truly being one of them!) at Borough Park, Workington, where City lost 3-1, Graham Parker scoring the Grecians' goal.

* Fred Binney netted two hat-tricks in league matches during the course of the season. The first came in a remarkable 5-2 win at Crewe Alexandra, when Tony Morrin and Keith Bowker got the other City goals. His second hat-trick of the season followed in a 4-0 home win over Scunthorpe United, Bowker again being the score sheet.

* Despite scoring on his debut for Dundee United against Morton in January 1970, Alan Devlin only made a handful of first team outings for the Tannadice club. He then played in Hong Kong and despite getting an offer to sign for Motherwell, linked up with Exeter City in July 1973, initially on trial. He made his debut for the Grecians in an FA Cup first round tie at St James' Park against Alvechurch, which the non-leaguers won. His only appearance in a league match for Exeter also ended in defeat against Peterborough United, again played at the Park, in March 1974. He was released at the end of the season.

* Just under 6,000 were inside St James' Park for the local derby against Torquay United in March 1974. There were plenty of goals as City ran out 4-2 winners, with Fred Binney (2), Tony Morrin and an own goal making up the Grecians' tally.

Back row: Peter Hatch, Michael Horne, Tony Ridley, Bob Wilson, Hedley Steele
Middle row: Jack Edwards (Trainer), John Neale, John Templeman, John Rutter, Keith Bowker, Bobby Hodge, John Newman (Manager).
Front row: Graham Weeks, Nicky Jennings, Lammie Robertson, Keith Clapham, Brian Joy, Tony Morrin, Alan Hooker.

City's league results

|  | Home | Away |
|---|---|---|
| Barnsley | 4-2 | 0-1 |
| Bradford City | 1-0 | 1-0 |
| Brentford | 1-0 | 0-2 |
| Cambridge United | 1-4 | 1-1 |
| Chester | 1-0 | 1-1 |
| Crewe Alexandra | 2-0 | 1-2 |
| Darlington | 4-1 | 0-2 |
| Doncaster Rovers | 2-1 | 3-3 |
| Hartlepool United | 1-0 | 3-0 |
| Lincoln City | 1-2 | 0-5 |
| Mansfield Town | 0-1 | 2-3 |
| Newport County | 3-1 | 2-1 |
| Northampton Town | 2-2 | 1-1 |
| Reading | 0-2 | 0-3 |
| Rochdale | 2-1 | 1-1 |
| Rotherham United | 0-4 | 1-1 |
| Scunthorpe United | 0-0 | 1-2 |
| Shrewsbury Town | 1-0 | 2-2 |
| Southport | 1-0 | 0-3 |
| Stockport County | 4-1 | 2-3 |
| Swansea City | 1-2 | 2-0 |
| Torquay United | 0-0 | 2-2 |
| Workington | 1-0 | 1-0 |

F.A. Cup

| Newport County | H | R1 | 1-2 |
|---|---|---|---|

Football League Cup

| Swansea City | H | R1 | 3-1 |
|---|---|---|---|
| Hereford United | H | R2 | 0-1 |

CITY MANAGER 1974-75
John Newman - Appointed April 1969

CITY PLAYING SQUAD 1974-75

| Name | Position | Signed From | | |
|---|---|---|---|---|
| Alan Beer | F | Weymouth Nov 1974 | 27 | 9 |
| Len Bond | G | Bristol City Nov 1974 | 30 | |
| Keith Bowker | F | Birmingham City Dec 73 | 43 | 18 |
| Keith Clapham | D | AFC Bournemouth Sept 1972 | 19+2 | |
| Jimmy Giles | D | Aldershot Mar 1971 | 43 | 2 |
| Peter Hatch | D | Oxford United Dec 1973 | 41 | 1 |
| Bobby Hodge | W | Apprentice Jul 1974 | 27+5 | 4 |
| Alan Hooker | D | Apprentice Jul 1974 | 7+2 | |
| Nicky Jennings | W | Portsmouth May 1974 | 19 | 4 |
| Brian Joy | D | Doncaster Rovers Jul 1973 | 45 | 2 |
| Tony Morrin | M | Barrow Jul 1971 | 39 | 3 |
| David Munks | D | Swindon Town Dec 1974 | 11 | |
| John Neale | W | Barnstaple Town Mar 72 | 21+6 | 3 |
| Lammie Robertson | M | Brighton & H.A. Jun 1974 | 42 | 10 |
| John Rutter | D | AFC Bournemouth Jul 1974 | 31 | 1 |
| Hedley Steele | D | Tiverton Town Jul 1974 | 6+1 | 1 |
| John Templeman | D | Brighton & H.A. Jun 1974 | 39 | 2 |
| Bob Wilson | G | Cardiff City Jan 1970 | 16 | |

FOURTH DIVISION - 1974-75

| | P | W | D | L | F | A | Pts |
|---|---|---|---|---|---|---|---|
| Mansfield Town | 46 | 28 | 12 | 6 | 90 | 40 | 68 |
| Shrewsbury Town | 46 | 26 | 10 | 10 | 80 | 43 | 62 |
| Rotherham United | 46 | 22 | 15 | 9 | 71 | 41 | 59 |
| Chester City | 46 | 23 | 11 | 12 | 64 | 38 | 57 |
| Lincoln City | 46 | 21 | 15 | 10 | 79 | 48 | 57 |
| Cambridge United | 46 | 20 | 14 | 12 | 62 | 44 | 54 |
| Reading | 46 | 21 | 10 | 15 | 63 | 47 | 52 |
| Brentford | 46 | 18 | 13 | 15 | 63 | 47 | 52 |
| EXETER CITY | 46 | 19 | 11 | 16 | 60 | 63 | 49 |
| Bradford City | 46 | 17 | 13 | 16 | 56 | 51 | 47 |
| Newport County | 46 | 19 | 9 | 18 | 68 | 75 | 47 |
| Hartlepool United | 46 | 16 | 11 | 19 | 52 | 62 | 43 |
| Torquay United | 46 | 14 | 14 | 18 | 46 | 61 | 42 |
| Barnsley | 46 | 15 | 11 | 20 | 62 | 65 | 41 |
| Northampton Town | 46 | 15 | 11 | 20 | 67 | 73 | 41 |
| Doncaster Rovers | 46 | 14 | 12 | 20 | 65 | 79 | 40 |
| Crewe Alexandra | 46 | 11 | 18 | 17 | 34 | 47 | 40 |
| Rochdale | 46 | 13 | 13 | 20 | 59 | 75 | 39 |
| Stockport County | 46 | 12 | 14 | 20 | 59 | 75 | 38 |
| Darlington | 46 | 13 | 10 | 23 | 54 | 67 | 36 |
| Swansea City | 46 | 15 | 6 | 25 | 46 | 73 | 36 |
| Workington | 46 | 10 | 11 | 25 | 36 | 66 | 31 |
| Scunthorpe United | 46 | 7 | 15 | 24 | 41 | 78 | 29 |

* Exeter City finished the season just above mid-table with manager John Newman having once again achieved much with a relatively small playing squad. In his first full season with the Grecians, Keith Bowker led the way with 18 league goals.

* No player recorded a hat-trick in a league match, however, Bowker, (five times), Lammie Robertson, John Neale, Tony Morrin and Alan Beer all netted twice in a league game.

* Most successful signing during the season was striker Alan Beer, who arrived in a £5,000 deal from Weymouth. He went on to net 9 goals in 27 league starts and proved to be a bargain buy.

* Admission prices to St James' Park for the 1974-75 season were:- Grandstand 90p; Ground 45p; Ground senior citizens and juniors 25p. Entry to City reserve team matches (Grandstand only) was 20p, with senior citizens and juniors 10p.

* For the third season running, City were knocked out of the FA Cup at the first round stage, this time by Newport County, who won 2-1 at St. James' Park.

* The Grecians reached round two of The Football League Cup. After beating Swansea City at the Park, 3-1, they then faced Hereford United, also at home, but the men from Edgar Street netted the only goal of the game.

* In November 1974 City chairman Gerald Vallance revealed that the club were losing £300 per week and that could not go on. He added: "I am confident we will see out this season, but as for next, that is another matter." Exeter had to average between 4,500 and 5,000 to break even, but with the average gate at the time just 3,209 they were some way short. The club's weekly wages bill was £850.

* Manager John Newman was critical of the City fans following a match in March 1975. He said: "I will always accept criticism provided it is backed by good reasoning and judgement, but I cannot accept the barracking and abuse levelled at players after only ten minutes."

* City reserves were left without a goalkeeper in October 1974, so they borrowed Allan Trump who was playing for Budleigh Salterton. Trump, who had appeared for City before, was also later to become the club's Chief Executive a few years later.

* Norman Ngwanya arrived at the club in April 1975, having paid all his own expenses from his home in Bulawayo (then Rhodesia, now Zimbabwe). He had been playing for South African First Division side, Moroka Swallows. The 24-year-old right winger was to stay with City for a month in the hope of earning a contract with the club. His ambition had always been to play in England.

* Highest attendance of the season for a League match at St James' Park was 7,271 for the visit of Torquay United on Boxing Day 1974. The game ended goalless. The lowest attendance was 2,565 when City defeated Crewe Alexandra with goals from Lammie Robertson (penalty) and Keith Bowker.

* For the third time in four seasons, Jimmy Giles was the Exeter City Player of the Year. His trophy was presented to him by Plymouth Argyle strikers, Billy Rafferty and Paul Mariner, during an awards night held at Zhivago's in Exeter. Doug Tootell was Amateur Player of the Year, whilst Supporter of the Year was Graham Sparks from Branscombe. Bill Dimond picked up the Commercial Manager's award.

* Leicester City provided the opposition for the Alan Banks testimonial match played at the Park in May 1975. On a rainy night, 3,546 fans turned out to see the teams draw 1-1. Graham Parker scored for City and Frank Worthington for Leicester.

* Exeter City players were given a glimpse into the future in August 1975 when clairvoyant Madame Rosina, complete with 300-year-old crystal ball, dropped into St James' Park to give her predictions for the coming season.

One of her customers happened to be an Exeter City fan who wanted to know how his team would fare in the Fourth Division. Rosina explained that she would only be able to give a prediction if she went to the club. To her surprise this was arranged and she was greeted with some scepticism by the City players.

Rosina's prediction was: "They have a lot of potential, but at the moment I do not think they have been knitted into a team, although this will no doubt come as the season progresses.

"Exeter will have a good season and finish well in the top half. I can see a good cup run for them as well. Large gates and a lot of travelling involved."

* The Grecians experimented with a 3.15pm kick off for their early season Saturday afternoon fixtures. But by October 1975, they decided to revert to the traditional 3pm kick off. Exeter City secretary, Pat Wakeham, said: "It was an experiment we felt was worth trying, but it has not been the success we hoped for."

* Manager John Newman was not encouraged by the pre-match interest for the visit of table-topping Lincoln City in January 1976. He said:-

"Lincoln City should be the top attraction of the season as Fourth Division leaders, but at the moment it does not loo k that way. The pre-match ticket sales are not very encouraging at the moment.

"There still appears to be a little bit of apathy towards the club in the city. After all we have only lost four games out of the last 20." (The attendance for the game was 3,858).

City's league results

| | HOME | AWAY |
|---|---|---|
| AFC Bournemouth | 1-0 | 0-1 |
| Barnsley | 2-0 | 0-0 |
| Bradford City | 0-0 | 0-0 |
| Brentford | 0-0 | 1-5 |
| Cambridge United | 1-2 | 1-0 |
| Crewe Alexandra | 2-2 | 0-0 |
| Darlington | 1-1 | 0-0 |
| Doncaster Rovers | 1-0 | 0-0 |
| Hartlepool United | 3-1 | 1-2 |
| Huddersfield Town | 4-1 | 1-0 |
| Lincoln City | 0-0 | 1-4 |
| Newport County | 3-0 | 3-3 |
| Northampton Town | 0-0 | 1-3 |
| Reading | 4-1 | 3-4 |
| Rochdale | 1-0 | 1-0 |
| Scunthorpe United | 5-4 | 1-0 |
| Southport | 2-0 | 0-1 |
| Stockport County | 2-0 | 1-2 |
| Swansea City | 3-0 | 3-0 |
| Torquay United | 0-0 | 0-1 |
| Tranmere Rovers | 0-2 | 1-1 |
| Watford | 1-3 | 0-2 |
| Workington | 1-0 | 0-1 |

F.A. Cup

| Cardiff City | A R1 | 2-6 |
|---|---|---|

Football League Cup

| Newport County | A R1 | 1-1 |
|---|---|---|
| Newport County | H R1R | 2-0 |
| Torquay United | A R2 | 1-1 |
| Torquay United | H R2R | 1-2 |

CITY MANAGER 1975-76
John Newman - Appointed April 1969

CITY PLAYING SQUAD 1975-76

| Name | Po | Signed From | Apps | Gls |
|---|---|---|---|---|
| Alan Beer | F | Weymouth Nov 1974 | 46 | 20 |
| Keith Bowker | F | AFC Bournemouth Sept 1972 | 42 | 13 |
| Keith Clapham | D | AFC Bournemouth Sept 1972 | 0(1) | |
| Peter Hatch | D | Oxford United Dec 1973 | 43 | 1 |
| Bobby Hodge | W | Apprentice Jul 1974 | 23(2) | 3 |
| Alan Hooker | D | Apprentice Jul 1974 | 26(2) | |
| John Hore | D | Plymouth Argyle Mar 1976 | 11 | |
| Nicky Jennings | W | Portsmouth May 1974 | 34 | 2 |
| Mike Jordan | F | Clyst Valley Jul 1975 | 10(1) | 3 |
| Brian Joy | D | Doncaster Rovers Jul 1973 | 15 | |
| Richard Key | G | Coventry City Jul 1975 | 37 | |
| Tony Morrin | M | Barrow Jul 1971 | 28 | 2 |
| Graham Moxham | W | Bideford Jul 1975 | 4(2) | |
| David Munks | D | Swindon Town Dec 1974 | 9 | |
| Lammie Robertson | M | Brighton & H.A. Jun 1974 | 44 | 4 |
| John Rutter | D | AFC Bournemouth Aug 1974 | 0(1) | |
| Bobby Saxton | D | Plymouth Argyle Sep 1975 | 39 | 1 |
| John Templeman | D | Brighton & H.A. Jun 1974 | 42(1) | 3 |
| Bob Wilson | G | ardiff City Jan 1970 | 9 | |
| John Wingate | F | AFC Bournemouth Jul 1975 | 44(1) | 2 |

FOURTH DIVISION - 1975-76

| | P | W | D | L | F | A | Pts |
|---|---|---|---|---|---|---|---|
| Lincoln City | 46 | 32 | 10 | 4 | 111 | 39 | 74 |
| Northampton Town | 46 | 29 | 10 | 7 | 87 | 40 | 68 |
| Reading | 46 | 24 | 12 | 10 | 70 | 51 | 60 |
| Tranmere Rovers | 46 | 24 | 10 | 12 | 89 | 55 | 58 |
| Huddersfield Town | 46 | 21 | 14 | 11 | 56 | 41 | 56 |
| AFC Bournemouth | 46 | 20 | 12 | 14 | 57 | 48 | 52 |
| Exeter City | 46 | 18 | 14 | 14 | 56 | 47 | 50 |
| Watford | 46 | 22 | 6 | 18 | 62 | 62 | 50 |
| Torquay United | 46 | 18 | 14 | 14 | 55 | 63 | 50 |
| Doncaster Rovers | 46 | 19 | 11 | 16 | 75 | 69 | 49 |
| Swansea City | 46 | 16 | 15 | 15 | 66 | 57 | 47 |
| Barnsley | 46 | 14 | 16 | 16 | 52 | 48 | 44 |
| Cambridge United | 46 | 14 | 15 | 17 | 58 | 62 | 43 |
| Hartlepool United | 46 | 16 | 10 | 20 | 62 | 78 | 42 |
| Rochdale | 46 | 12 | 18 | 16 | 40 | 54 | 42 |
| Crewe Alexandra | 46 | 13 | 15 | 18 | 58 | 57 | 41 |
| Bradford City | 46 | 12 | 17 | 17 | 63 | 65 | 41 |
| Brentford | 46 | 14 | 13 | 19 | 56 | 60 | 41 |
| Scunthorpe United | 46 | 14 | 10 | 22 | 50 | 59 | 38 |
| Darlington | 46 | 14 | 10 | 22 | 48 | 57 | 38 |
| Stockport County | 46 | 13 | 12 | 21 | 43 | 76 | 38 |
| Newport County | 46 | 13 | 9 | 24 | 57 | 90 | 35 |
| Southport | 46 | 8 | 10 | 28 | 41 | 77 | 26 |
| Workington | 46 | 7 | 7 | 32 | 30 | 87 | 21 |

* Prior to the season starting, manager John Newman said: "The club has had an extremely sticky time to get through the Summer period. We have jumped through a little crisis and it will depend on the season ahead whether we are able to keep the present situation going."

* The financial alarm bells rang loudly after the opening home match of the season against Southport drew just 2,844 through the St James' Park turnstiles. Chairman Gerald Vallance said that the club needed to average 4,000, otherwise it would not survive. Attendances continued to fall and the club struggled financially throughout the season.

* Exeter City played Coventry City in a testimonial for their former long serving player and trainer, Keith Harvey. The game took place at St James' Park on 2nd September 1975 and ended 2-2, with a disappointing 2,098 in attendance.

* There was a feisty meeting between Exeter City and Cambridge United in September 1975, which saw a player form each side sent off and three others booked. Lammie Robertson was red carded along with Eades of Cambridge for fighting one another.

* Experienced defender, Bobby Saxton, was signed for a fee of £4,000 from Plymouth Argyle in September 1975. He was later to become player-manager of the Grecians.

* In November 1975, Welsh team manager Alan Smith, confirmed that he was following the progress of Exeter City striker Alan Beer and that he could be called up into the Under-21 squad.

* Australian international Adrian Alston scored a hat-trick for Cardiff City as they crushed Exeter City 6-2 at Ninian Park in the first round of the FA Cup,

* In almost farcical conditions,, City defeated Bournemouth 1-0 at St James' Park in January 1976. Winds, gusting up to 70mph made it impossible to keep the ball on the ground. Thirteen floodlight bulbs also fused during the game.

* Former President of F.I.F.A., Sir Stanley Rous, attended Exeter City's match against Lincoln City in January 1976. He was joined by the chairman of the Football Association, Sir Andrew Stephen.

* Alan Beer, who topped the goalscoring for City in 1975-76, scored hat-trick against Scunthorpe United in the final match, a nine-goal thriller, with Exeter winning 5-4. Sadly it was watched by the lowest gate of the season, just 1,863.

* Exeter City announced that they had made a record loss of £30,909 on the 1974-75 season. Gate receipts had slumped to just £19,591. Wages and signing on fees went up by more than £10,000 on the previous season. Chairman Gerald Vallance said: "It is certain that the next six months are going to be extremely difficult financially speaking."

* Commercial Manager Ray Ellis introduced match sponsorship for the first time when Dunns Motors of Sidwell Street, Exeter were sponsors for the visit of Torquay United. Renwick Travel also sponsored a game for a record fee of £300.

* With Exeter City having just missed out on promotion, ending the season in 7th place, the club announced that they would not be increasing admission charges for the following season - 1976-77. Grandstand season tickets would be priced at £23; Ground season tickets £13. Matchday admission priced would be £1.20p for the Grandstand and 65p to the Ground.

* Chairman Gerald Vallance resigned from the board of directors at the end of the season stating that his plan to strengthen the board with the appointment of two more directors was not agreed. A few days later Clifford Hill took over as chairman of the club stating: "I have every faith in Exeter City as a viable soccer club."

City's league results

| | Home | Away |
|---|---|---|
| AFC Bournemouth | 1-1 | 0-2 |
| Aldershot | 3-0 | 2-2 |
| Barnsley | 1-0 | 4-3 |
| Bradford City | 0-0 | 1-1 |
| Brentford | 3-2 | 0-1 |
| Cambridge United | 1-1 | 1-1 |
| Colchester United | 1-0 | 1-3 |
| Crewe Alexandra | 3-0 | 0-2 |
| Darlington | 1-0 | 1-2 |
| Doncaster Rovers | 0-2 | 3-0 |
| Halifax Town | 1-0 | 2-1 |
| Hartlepool United | 3-1 | 2-2 |
| Huddersfield Town | 2-0 | 1-0 |
| Newport County | 1-0 | 3-0 |
| Rochdale | 2-1 | 2-1 |
| Scunthorpe United | 2-0 | 1-4 |
| Southend United | 3-1 | 0-2 |
| Southport | 3-1 | 1-1 |
| Stockport County | 2-1 | 0-0 |
| Swansea City | 2-0 | 0-0 |
| Torquay United | 3-0 | 1-0 |
| Watford | 2-2 | 1-4 |
| Workington | 0-0 | 3-1 |

Back row: Harry Holman, Tony Morrin, Mike Jordan, Nicky Jennings, Tony Kellow
Middle row: John Hore, John Templeman, Mike Green, Phil Howe, Richard Key, Graham Weeks, Keith Clapham, Alan Hooker
Front row: Lammie Robertson, Alan Beer, Bobby Saxton (Player-Manager), Bobby Hodge, Peter Hatch

F.A. Cup

| | | | |
|---|---|---|---|
| Southend United | H | R1 | 1-1 |
| Southend United | A | R1R | 1-2* |
| *After extra time | | | |

* According to bookmakers, Ladbrokes, Exeter City would be a good bet for promotion at the end of 1976-77. Before the season started they made City second favourites to win the Fourth Division championship at odds of 8-1, behind Huddersfield Town. Exeter were also 2-1 to win promotion to the Third Division.

Football League Cup

| | | | |
|---|---|---|---|
| Plymouth Argyle | A | R1 | 1-0 |
| Plymouth Argyle | H | R1 | 1-0 |
| Norwich City | H | R2 | 1-3 |

CITY PLAYING SQUAD 1976-77

| Name | Position | Signed From | App | Gls |
|---|---|---|---|---|
| John Baugh | G | St Luke's College Feb 1977 | 15 | |
| Alan Beer | F | Weymouth Nov 1974 | 38 | 21 |
| Keith Clapham | D | AFC Bournemouth Sept 1972 | 7+2 | |
| Peter Darke | D | Plymouth Argyle Oct 1976 | 5 | |
| Geoff Gay | M | Bolton Wanderers Mar 1977 | 5+1 | |
| Mike Green | D | Apprentice Nov 1975 | 0+1 | |
| Peter Hatch | D | Oxford United Dec 1973 | 43 | 2 |
| Bobby Hodge | W | Apprentice Jul 1974 | 35 | 7 |
| Harry Holman | F | Chelsea Jul 1976 | 7 | |
| John Hore | D | Plymouth Argyle Mar 1976 | 46 | |
| Alan Hooker | D | Apprentice Jul 1974 | 13 | |
| Nicky Jennings | W | Portsmouth May 1974 | 43 | 7 |
| Mike Jordan | F | Apprentice Jul 1975 | 5+2 | |
| Tony Kellow | F | Falmouth Town Jul 1976 | 44 | 19 |
| Richard Key | G | Coventry City Jul 1975 | 31 | |
| Tony Morrin | M | Barrow Jul 1971 | 15 | |
| Forbes Phillipson-Masters | D | Southampton Sep 1976 | 6 | |
| Lee Roberts | D | Shrewsbury Town Mar 1977 | 5+2 | |
| Lammie Robertson | M | Brighton & H.A. Jun 1974 | 43 | 9 |
| Bobby Saxton | D | Plymouth Argyle Sep 1975 | 28 | 2 |
| John Templeman | D | Brighton & H.A. Jun 1974 | 35 | 1 |
| Graham Weeks | M | Apprentice Mar 1976 | 37+3 | 1 |
| Own Goals | | | | 1 |

CITY MANAGER 1976-77
John Newman - Appointed April 1969
Bobby Saxton - Appointed January 1977

FOURTH DIVISION - 1974-75

| | P | W | D | L | F | A | Pts |
|---|---|---|---|---|---|---|---|
| Cambridge United | 46 | 26 | 13 | 7 | 87 | 40 | 65 |
| EXETER CITY | 46 | 25 | 12 | 9 | 70 | 46 | 62 |
| Colchester United | 46 | 25 | 9 | 12 | 77 | 43 | 59 |
| Bradford City | 46 | 23 | 13 | 10 | 78 | 51 | 59 |
| Swansea City | 46 | 23 | 9 | 14 | 62 | 39 | 55 |
| Barnsley | 46 | 23 | 9 | 14 | 62 | 39 | 55 |
| Watford | 46 | 18 | 15 | 13 | 67 | 50 | 51 |
| Doncaster Rovers | 46 | 21 | 9 | 16 | 71 | 65 | 51 |
| Huddersfield Town | 46 | 19 | 12 | 15 | 60 | 49 | 50 |
| Southend United | 46 | 15 | 19 | 12 | 52 | 45 | 49 |
| Darlington | 46 | 18 | 13 | 15 | 59 | 64 | 49 |
| Crewe Alexandra | 46 | 19 | 11 | 16 | 47 | 60 | 49 |
| AFC Bournemouth | 46 | 15 | 18 | 13 | 54 | 44 | 48 |
| Stockport County | 46 | 13 | 19 | 14 | 53 | 57 | 45 |
| Brentford | 46 | 18 | 7 | 21 | 77 | 76 | 43 |
| Torquay United | 46 | 17 | 9 | 20 | 59 | 67 | 43 |
| Aldershot | 46 | 16 | 11 | 19 | 49 | 59 | 43 |
| Rochdale | 46 | 13 | 12 | 21 | 50 | 59 | 38 |
| Newport County | 46 | 14 | 10 | 22 | 42 | 58 | 38 |
| Scunthorpe United | 46 | 13 | 11 | 22 | 49 | 73 | 37 |
| Halifax Town | 46 | 11 | 14 | 21 | 47 | 58 | 36 |
| Hartlepool United | 46 | 10 | 12 | 24 | 47 | 73 | 32 |
| Southport | 46 | 3 | 19 | 24 | 33 | 77 | 25 |
| Workington | 46 | 4 | 11 | 31 | 41 | 102 | 19 |

* For only the second time in the history of Exeter City, the Grecians won promotion, by finishing as runners-up in the Fourth Division. They started the season with long serving John Newman as manager, but when he left to take over at Grimsby Town, Bobby Saxton was appointed as player-manager.

* City had an amazing end to the season to clinch promotion when they won 11 of their last 14 matches, losing just once at Brentford.

* In one of the games, they were trailing 3-0 at half-time at Barnsley, however, the Grecians turned on a stunning performance and hit back to win 4-3! This all but clinched promotion. However, that was finally confirmed in the very next match at Doncaster Rovers, where Exeter won 3-0 before hundreds of travelling fans.

* Not surprisingly the highest attendance of the season at St James' Park for a league fixture was the very last game when 10,751 saw City defeat Aldershot 3-0. This was in complete contrast to the opening home fixture of the season when 3,606 were present to see a 1-1 draw with Cambridge United.

* The 40 goal partnership of Alan Beer and Tony Kellow did much to ensure that City were promoted and proved once again that if you have two consistent goalscorers in the side, then success will be more than a possibility.

* City went out of the FA Cup at the first round stage. After being held to a 1-1 draw at the Park by Southend United, they then lost the replay 2-1 after extra-time.

* There was a local derby in the first round of the Football League Cup, played over two legs. City won both ties 1-0, to advance to round two where they lost at home to Norwich City, 1-3.

* In December 1976, City chairman Gerald Vallance reported that the club had lost £22,451 on the previous year. He added: "I do not think the club could stand another loss like that. It would be the end. Even so, I am confident that Exeter City will see out this season. In fact, things are looking a little brighter."

* When Bobby Saxton took over as player-manager in January 1977, he said: "It has always been my ambition to go into management. I am sure we have a chance of promotion and I am sure I can keep it going."

* City's promotion hopes were dealt a severe blow in the game against Crewe at Gresty Road, when goalkeeper Richard Key sustained a broken ankle. On loan midfielder Geoff Gay, from Bolton Wanderers, made his City debut by taking over between the posts. For the remainder of the season, St Luke's College student, John Baugh replaced Key and was part of what proved to be a very successful couple of months.

* Exeter City Commercial Manager, Ray Ellis, 31, was elected as treasurer of the Football League Commercial Manager's Association in March 1977, being elected unanimously at the Association's annual general meeting held in Leicester. This was the first time a representative from a Fourth Division club had been on the management committee. Ellis had joined City as Commercial Manager three years earlier.

* Player-manager Saxton also made one other signing before the March transfer deadline as he signed Lee Roberts from Shrewsbury Town. The player was later to sign a longer term deal with the club.

* Exeter City captain, John Hore said: "This is my second promotion season, having gone up with Plymouth Argyle. That was marvellous, but I rate the Exeter success as an even greater achievement considering the small squad we have. It is a fantastic achievement.

Exeter City 1977-78
Back row: Keith Ford, Keith Bowker, Harry Holman, Bobby Saxton
(Player-Manager)
Middle row: Lammie Robertson, John Templeman, John Baugh, Richard
Key, Phil Howe, Bobby Hodge, Peter Hatch
Front row: Jack Edwards (Trainer), Nicky Jennings, Graham Weeks,
John Hore, Tony Kellow, Alan Beer, Tony Long (Physio)
On ground: Paul Smythe, Roy Ireland

* Admission prices for matches at St James' Park were:- Grandstand £1.50p; Ground 80p; Senior Citizens and Juveniles 50p;
For reserve team, Western League fixtures, the Grandstand
admission price was 25p, with Senior Citizens and Juveniles 15p.

City's league results

|  | Home | Away |
|---|---|---|
| Bradford City | 1-0 | 2-1 |
| Bury | 2-2 | 0-5 |
| Cambridge United | 2-4 | 1-2 |
| Carlisle United | 0-1 | 0-2 |
| Chester City | 1-1 | 1-2 |
| Chesterfield | 0-0 | 0-0 |
| Colchester United | 0-0 | 1-3 |
| Gillingham | 2-1 | 0-1 |
| Hereford United | 1-0 | 0-4 |
| Lincoln City | 3-0 | 2-1 |
| Oxford United | 2-1 | 0-0 |
| Peterborough United | 1-0 | 1-1 |
| Plymouth Argyle | 0-0 | 2-2 |
| Portsmouth | 0-1 | 1-1 |
| Port Vale | 4-1 | 0-4 |
| Preston North End | 2-0 | 0-0 |
| Rotherham United | 1-0 | 0-1 |
| Sheffield Wednesday | 2-1 | 1-2 |
| Shrewsbury Town | 1-1 | 2-0 |
| Swindon Town | 0-0 | 0-4 |
| Tranmere Rovers | 4-2 | 1-2 |
| Walsall | 1-1 | 3-1 |
| Wrexham | 0-1 | 1-2 |

F.A. Cup

| Newport County | A | R1 | 1-1 |
|---|---|---|---|
| Newport County | H | R1R | 4-2 |
| Minehead | A | R2 | 3-0 |
| Wolverhampton Wanderers | H | R3 | 2-2 |
| Wolverhampton Wanderers | A | R3R | 1-3 |

Football League Cup

| Plymouth Argyle | A | R1 | 2-2 |
|---|---|---|---|
| Plymouth Argyle | H | R1 | 0-0 |
| Plymouth Argyle | A | R1R | 1-0 |
| Aston Villa | H | R2 | 1-3 |

CITY MANAGER 1977-78
Bobby Saxton - Appointed January 1977

| CITY PLAYING SQUAD 1977-78 | | | | |
|---|---|---|---|---|
| Name | Position | Signed From | | |
| John Baugh | G | St Luke's College Feb 1977 | 5 | |
| Alan Beer | F | Weymouth Nov 1974 | 3 | 2 |
| Keith Bowker | F | Cambridge United Aug 1977 | 46 | 9 |
| John Delve | M | Plymouth Argyle Mar 1978 | 11 | 1 |
| Dick Forbes | M | St Luke's College Apr 1978 | 2 | |
| Jimmy Giles | D | Charlton Athletic Dec 1977 | 23 | |
| Peter Hatch | D | Oxford United Dec 1973 | 38+1 | |
| Gary Heale | F | Luton Town Dec 1977 | 3+1 | |
| Bobby Hodge | W | Apprentice Jul 1974 | 31+1 | 4 |
| Harry Holman | F | Chelsea Jul 1976 | 36+1 | 8 |
| John Hore | D | Plymouth Argyle Mar 1976 | 46 | |
| Fred Ingham | F | Falmouth Town Sep 1977 | 4+2 | 1 |
| Nicky Jennings | W | Portsmouth May 1974 | 23+5 | 2 |
| Tony Kellow | F | Falmouth Town Jul 1976 | 46 | 14 |
| Richard Key | G | Coventry City Jul 1975 | 41 | |
| Colin Randell | M | Plymouth Argyle Sep 1977 | 40 | 1 |
| Lee Roberts | D | Shrewsbury Town Sep 1977 | 24+2 | 2 |
| Lammie Robertson | M | Brighton & H.A. Jun 1974 | 3+1 | 2 |
| Bobby Saxton | D | Plymouth Argyle Sep 1975 | 25 | |
| John Templeman | D | Brighton & H.A. Jun 1974 | 44 | |
| Graham Weeks | M | Apprentice Mar 1976 | 12+1 | |
| Own Goals | | | | 2 |

THIRD DIVISION - 1977-78

|  | P | W | D | L | F | A | Pts |
|---|---|---|---|---|---|---|---|
| Wrexham | 46 | 23 | 15 | 8 | 78 | 45 | 61 |
| Cambridge United | 46 | 23 | 12 | 11 | 72 | 51 | 58 |
| Preston North End | 46 | 20 | 16 | 10 | 63 | 38 | 56 |
| Peterborough United | 46 | 20 | 16 | 10 | 47 | 33 | 56 |
| Chester City | 46 | 16 | 22 | 8 | 59 | 56 | 54 |
| Walsall | 46 | 18 | 17 | 11 | 61 | 50 | 53 |
| Gillingham | 46 | 15 | 20 | 11 | 67 | 60 | 50 |
| Colchester United | 46 | 15 | 18 | 13 | 55 | 44 | 48 |
| Chesterfield | 46 | 17 | 14 | 15 | 58 | 49 | 48 |
| Swindon Town | 46 | 16 | 16 | 14 | 67 | 60 | 48 |
| Shrewsbury Town | 46 | 16 | 15 | 15 | 63 | 57 | 47 |
| Tranmere Rovers | 46 | 16 | 15 | 15 | 57 | 52 | 47 |
| Carlisle United | 46 | 14 | 19 | 13 | 59 | 59 | 47 |
| Sheffield Wednesday | 46 | 15 | 16 | 15 | 50 | 52 | 46 |
| Bury | 46 | 13 | 19 | 14 | 62 | 56 | 45 |
| Lincoln City | 46 | 15 | 15 | 16 | 53 | 61 | 45 |
| EXETER CITY | 46 | 15 | 14 | 17 | 49 | 50 | 44 |
| Oxford United | 46 | 13 | 14 | 19 | 64 | 67 | 40 |
| Plymouth Argyle | 46 | 11 | 17 | 18 | 61 | 68 | 39 |
| Rotherham United | 46 | 13 | 13 | 20 | 51 | 68 | 39 |
| Port Vale | 46 | 8 | 20 | 18 | 46 | 67 | 36 |
| Bradford City | 46 | 12 | 10 | 24 | 56 | 86 | 34 |
| Hereford United | 46 | 9 | 14 | 23 | 34 | 60 | 32 |
| Portsmouth | 46 | 7 | 17 | 22 | 41 | 75 | 31 |

* The Grecians found life in the Third Division hard going after the previous season's promotion. However, they suffered a huge blow right at the start of the campaign when Alan Beer sustained a serious knee injury in only the third match, having already scored twice. The injury proved to be career threatening and he never played again.

* City also sold talented midfield schemer Lammie Robertson to Leicester City and then signed Colin Randell from Plymouth Argyle as a replacement.

* In view of the on the field setbacks, a 17th place finish was not so bad, and had they turned a few more draws into victories, then City would have finished a lot higher. But they did struggle for goals once Beer had been sidelined.

* The team had a good run in the FA Cup reaching the third round after they had disposed of Newport County after a replay, and Minehead. They were then drawn at home to First Division Wolverhampton Wanderers and drew 2-2. City lost the replay 3-1.

* Adverse publicity was generated over the decision by the club's board of directors to increase ticket prices by 100 per cent for the third round FA Cup tie against Wolverhampton Wanderers. Grandstand tickets rose from £1.50p to £3, whilst it cost £1.50p for a place in the Cowshed and £1.20p for the rest of the ground.

* In the Football League Cup, it took three matches to overcome the first round challenge of Plymouth Argyle, City eventually winning 1-0. However, in round two they lost 3-1 to Aston Villa at St James' Park

* For the first time ever in a season, two players managed to score twice from the penalty spot in a game. Robertson did so in the 4-1 home win over Port Vale, and Tony Kellow did likewise in a 2-4 home defeat at the hands of Cambridge United.

* One notable and popular signing during the season, was the return of centre-half Jimmy Giles from Charlton Athletic. He took over in the team from player-manager Bobby Saxton, and was to prove an excellent acquisition over the next few seasons.

* Lee Roberts also returned to the club, the Shrewsbury Town defender having joined for a fee of £8,000. Player-manager Saxton had made enquiries for Roberts since the player had enjoyed a successful loan spell at Exeter the previous season.

* Exeter City and Plymouth Argyle received the red carpet treatment when they ran out onto St James' Park for their Football League Cup tie. They ran along a red carpet laid courtesy of the match sponsors, John Holt Carpets of Exeter. A familiar face was present, that of former City player Jimmy Blain, who worked for the sponsors.

* During the summer of 1977 extensive alterations took place under the grandstand at St James' Park. The old boardroom and tea room were made into one large Vice Presidents Lounge. The idea was to encourage supporters to become Vice Presidents, paying £50 per season. City quickly signed up 20 Vice Presidents and it was hoped many more would join as the season progressed.

* It was announced in November 1977 that Exeter City had made a profit of £4,411 in the previous season. Gate receipts had increased to £49,813, whilst commercial activities had brought in £40,857. The directors were of the opinion that the value of the land and buildings at St James' Park exceeded the book value of £40,674. The clubs total debt stood at £118,934.

* Millwall had made an offer to sign Tony Kellow during the course of the season. However, they were told that he was not for sale and that the rumour of an offer of £100,000 for the player being made were not true.

* Singer Elton John, then chairman of Watford Football Club, was given the best possible tonic as he battled against a mystery illness at an exclusive Harley Street clinic.

Thanks to the Exeter-based Express and Echo newspaper he was able to listen to the Football League Cup fourth round tie between Exeter City and Watford via a personal phone line by his bedside.

The offer had been gratefully accepted and arrangements were made to ring Echo reporter Martin Dean at regular intervals during the match. Elton must have been cheered to learn that Watford won 2-0.

* On signing for Blackpool in November 1978, Exeter City's leading goalscorer, Tony Kellow said: "I am a little bit sad that I am leaving because Exeter City has been a good club for me. They gave me a big break, but I think I am bettering myself in a lot of respects.

"Blackpool are a bigger club. I would like to move to a higher grade of football, but manager Bob Stokoe sold me Blackpool. I never dreamed of this sort of thing happening when I was playing for Falmouth Town."

* A dispute between Exeter City manager Bobby Saxton and young striker Harry Holman came to ahead when it was revealed that the player had walked out on the club in November 1978. He had failed to report on Saturday after being selected for a reserve team game at Saltash United. It was believed that Holman, who was on the transfer list, felt that he should have been in the first team and that he would need to move to another club for League football.

* Although the departure of manager Bobby Saxton and the remainder of the Exeter City coaching staff for Plymouth Argyle in January 1979 may have left a sour taste for some City supporters, no animosity was shown by City chairman Gerald Vallance.

"I feel that these men are leaving to better themselves," said Vallance. "We can only wish them well in their new jobs at Home Park."

* At the end of the season groundsman Sonny Clarke and electrician Pat Green were busy at work installing 13 new mercury halide floodlights on the grandstand side of the ground. Green had erected the club's original lights in 1953. The old lights had become obsolete due to the acute shortage of bulbs and their output was less than the new ones.

City's league results

| | Home | Away |
|---|---|---|
| Blackpool | 3-0 | 1-1 |
| Brentford | 2-2 | 0-0 |
| Bury | 2-1 | 2-4 |
| Carlisle United | 3-2 | 1-1 |
| Chester | 0-1 | 0-1 |
| Chesterfield | 3-1 | 1-0 |
| Colchester United | 2-1 | 2-2 |
| Gillingham | 0-0 | 0-2 |
| Hull City | 3-1 | 0-1 |
| Lincoln City | 3-2 | 1-0 |
| Mansfield Town | 0-0 | 1-1 |
| Oxford United | 2-0 | 2-3 |
| Peterborough United | 1-0 | 1-1 |
| Plymouth Argyle | 1-0 | 2-4 |
| Rotherham United | 2-0 | 1-2 |
| Sheffield Wednesday | 2-2 | 1-2 |
| Shrewsbury Town | 0-1 | 1-4 |
| Southend United | 0-0 | 1-1 |
| Swansea City | 2-1 | 0-1 |
| Swindon Town | 1-2 | 1-1 |
| Tranmere Rovers | 3-0 | 2-2 |
| Walsall | 3-1 | 2-2 |
| Watford | 0-0 | 0-1 |

| F.A. Cup | | |
|---|---|---|
| Brentford | H 1-0 | R1 |
| Maidstone United | A 0-1 | R2 |

| Football League Cup | | |
|---|---|---|
| A.F.C. Bournemouth | A 1-0 | R1 |
| A.F.C. Bournemouth | H 1-1 | R1 |
| Blackburn Rovers | H 2-1 | R2 |
| Bolton Wanderers | H 2-1 | R3 |
| Watford | H 0-2 | R4 |

CITY PLAYING SQUAD 1978-79

| Name | Pos | Signed From | Apps | Gls |
|---|---|---|---|---|
| Keith Bowker | F | Northampton Town Aug 1977 | 26+3 | 11 |
| John Delve | M | Plymouth Argyle Mar 1978 | 42 | 6 |
| Dick Forbes | M | St Luke's College Apr 1978 | 7+1 | |
| Jimmy Giles | D | Charlton Athletic Dec 1977 | 43 | 1 |
| Peter Hatch | D | Oxford United Dec 1973 | 45 | 2 |
| Bobby Hodge | W | Apprentice Jul 1974 | 4 | |
| Harry Holman | F | Chelsea Jul 1976 | 4+4 | 1 |
| John Hore | D | Plymouth Argyle Mar 1976 | 44 | |
| Fred Ingham | F | Falmouth Town Sep 1977 | 0+2 | |
| Roy Ireland | M | Apprentice Feb 1979 | 0+1 | |
| Tony Kellow | F | Falmouth Town Jul 1976 | 17 | 7 |
| Ian Main | G | St. Luke's College Sep 1978 | 13 | |
| Tony Mitchell | D | St. Luke's College Jul 1977 | 10 | |
| Steve Neville | F | Southampton Sep 1978 | 36 | 9 |
| Vince O'Keefe | G | A.P. Leamington Jun 1978 | 33 | |
| Ian Pearson | F | Millwall Nov 1978 | 18 | 3 |
| Colin Randell | M | Plymouth Argyle Sep 1977 | 38 | 3 |
| Lee Roberts | D | Shrewsbury Town Sep 1977 | 41 | 3 |
| Phil Roberts | D | Hereford United Feb 1979 | 2 | |
| Peter Rogers | | Bath City Feb 1979 | 11 | 3 |
| John Sims | F | Notts County Dec 1978 | 25 | 11 |
| John Templeman | D | Brighton & H.A. Jun 1974 | 45 | 1 |
| Osher Williams | W | Southampton Aug 1978 | 2+1 | |

CITY MANAGER 1978-79
Bobby Saxton - Appointed January 1977
Brian Godfrey - Appointed January 1979

THIRD DIVISION - 1978-79

| | P | W | D | L | F | A | Pts |
|---|---|---|---|---|---|---|---|
| Shrewsbury Town | 46 | 21 | 19 | 6 | 61 | 41 | 61 |
| Watford | 46 | 24 | 12 | 10 | 83 | 52 | 60 |
| Swansea City | 46 | 24 | 12 | 10 | 83 | 61 | 60 |
| Gillingham | 46 | 21 | 17 | 8 | 65 | 42 | 59 |
| Swindon Town | 46 | 25 | 7 | 14 | 74 | 52 | 57 |
| Carlisle United | 46 | 15 | 22 | 9 | 53 | 42 | 52 |
| Colchester United | 46 | 17 | 17 | 12 | 60 | 55 | 51 |
| Hull City | 46 | 19 | 11 | 16 | 66 | 61 | 49 |
| EXETER CITY | 46 | 17 | 15 | 14 | 61 | 56 | 49 |
| Brentford | 46 | 19 | 9 | 18 | 53 | 49 | 47 |
| Oxford United | 46 | 14 | 18 | 14 | 44 | 50 | 46 |
| Blackpool | 46 | 18 | 9 | 19 | 61 | 59 | 45 |
| Southend United | 46 | 15 | 15 | 16 | 51 | 49 | 45 |
| Sheffield Wednesday | 46 | 13 | 19 | 14 | 53 | 53 | 45 |
| Plymouth Argyle | 46 | 15 | 14 | 17 | 67 | 68 | 44 |
| Chester City | 46 | 14 | 16 | 16 | 57 | 61 | 44 |
| Rotherham United | 46 | 17 | 10 | 19 | 49 | 55 | 44 |
| Mansfield Town | 46 | 12 | 19 | 15 | 51 | 52 | 43 |
| Bury | 46 | 11 | 20 | 15 | 59 | 65 | 42 |
| Chesterfield | 46 | 13 | 14 | 19 | 51 | 65 | 40 |
| Peterborough United | 46 | 11 | 14 | 21 | 44 | 63 | 36 |
| Walsall | 46 | 10 | 12 | 24 | 56 | 71 | 32 |
| Tranmere Rovers | 46 | 6 | 16 | 24 | 45 | 78 | 28 |
| Lincoln City | 46 | 7 | 11 | 28 | 41 | 88 | 25 |

* Had it not been four consecutive defeats at the end of the season, Exeter City would have improved even more on their very good 9th place finish in the Third Division, especially as the club had a change of manager halfway through the season.

* The Grecians also had a good run in the Football League Cup. After defeating Bournemouth, Blackburn Rovers and Bolton Wanderers, City, in round four, lost to Watford (0-2) at St. James' Park.

* In the FA Cup, after beating Brentford 1-0 at St James' Park, City travelled to Maidstone United and lost 1-0.

* There were several changes made to the squad during the season, not least of which saw leading scorer Tony Kellow join Blackpool for a fee of £125,000. Kellow had attracted various bids from clubs, but Blackpool won the day for the former Falmouth Town man. Later on, arrivals would include Ian Pearson from Millwall for £25,000, Steve Neville from Southampton and John Sims from Notts County.

* Winger Bobby Hodge was another departure as he signed for Colchester United for a fee of £15,000. He had played a part in the City team that won promotion in 1976-77.

* Winger Osher Williams was signed on loan from Southampton in September 1978. He only made three league appearances however, before returning to the Saints. He later played for Stockport County.

* Former City players, Dick Pym and Harold Blackmore were invited back to the Park to see two of their old teams in action as Exeter City defeated Bolton Wanderers 2-1. Both players had been transferred to Bolton from the Grecians in late 1920s and appeared in the FA Cup Final.

* City had a run of nine unbeaten league matches, of which six were won. This coincided with the arrival of John Sims and Ian Pearson in the side.

* The club staged a testimonial match for Alan Beer, who had to retire from playing due to a knee injury. City played West Bromwich Albion, with the game ending 2-2 before an attendance of 4,474.

* Manager Bobby Saxton left the club in January 1979, to take over as Plymouth Argyle manager. Jack Edwards, who had guided the team to promotion in 1963-64 was appointed caretaker manager. However, within days, Bath City boss Brian Godfrey had been appointed manager of Exeter City and Edwards reverted to his previous role.

* Nicky Jennings was another player to be granted a testimonial and he was lucky in that visitors Nottingham Forest had just signed the game's first ever £1m player, Trevor Francis, who made his debut for them. City lost 0-5 to Forest before an attendance of 9,479, with receipts totalling £12,000.

* When Exeter City visited Blackpool for a Third Division fixture in April 1979, the hosts, who included Tony Kellow in their side (and he scored!) had their then lowest ever attendance for a Football League match when 3,136 saw a 1-1 draw,.

* Just 984 paying spectators were present at Prenton Park for Tranmere Rovers game against Exeter City in March 1979. The game ended 2-2 with City's goals being scored by John Sims and Lee Roberts.

* Midfielder Colin Randell was voted to be City's Player of the Year. Randell who had been signed by City from Plymouth Argyle in September 1977 for a fee of £10,000, was later to follow ex-City boss Saxton back to Plymouth.

* Amateur Player of the Year was St Luke's College student, Dick Forbes, whilst Roy Ireland became the Youth Player of the Year.

* It was announced in October 1979 that the Exeter City board of directors were to carry out improvements to St. James' Park. The Express and Echo reported:-

'Although the Park is by no means the worst ground in the Football League, it is hardly the suitable setting for the degree of Third Division success at which the club is aimed. A run down image is no good to an ambitious club. Take for example the player who comes west to look the club over before deciding whether or not to sign for the City. If first impressions are anything to go on, one could understand players taking one look and going home.

'One could say improvements are not before time, but whereas successive boards have come and gone, leaving the ground to slip into decay, the current board have called a halt. No one can point an accusing finger in their direction when it comes to ambition on and off the field.'

* Following the fourth round Football League Cup defeat at Anfield, speaking about Exeter City, Liverpool manager Bob Paisley said: "All credit to Exeter. I thought they did extremely well. I always expected it to be hard. I thought the Exeter goalkeeper, Vince O'Keefe, was magnificent. Someone said beforehand that he could not play, but he was as good as any goalkeeper who has been here this season."

City manager Brian Godfrey added: "We were playing against the Football League champions and there are plenty of clubs who go to Anfield and do not do as well as we did. I just hope we can carry the spirit we showed into our League games. We won't be playing Liverpool every week."

City's league results

| | Home | Away |
|---|---|---|
| Barnsley | 2-1 | 2-2 |
| Blackburn Rovers | 2-0 | 1-1 |
| Blackpool | 1-0 | 0-1 |
| Brentford | 0-0 | 2-0 |
| Bury | 1-0 | 0-3 |
| Carlisle United | 1-2 | 1-4 |
| Chester | 1-0 | 3-1 |
| Chesterfield | 1-2 | 0-3 |
| Colchester United | 3-1 | 0-0 |
| Gillingham | 3-1 | 0-1 |
| Grimsby Town | 1-2 | 1-5 |
| Hull City | 2-2 | 2-2 |
| Mansfield Town | 2-1 | 1-0 |
| Millwall | 2-1 | 1-5 |
| Oxford United | 0-0 | 0-2 |
| Plymouth Argyle | 2-2 | 0-2 |
| Reading | 1-0 | 1-2 |
| Rotherham United | 1-1 | 0-2 |
| Sheffield United | 3-1 | 1-3 |
| Sheffield Wednesday | 1-0 | 1-0 |
| Southend United | 4-2 | 0-4 |
| Swindon Town | 4-1 | 3-2 |
| Wimbledon | 0-2 | 2-2 |

F.A.Cup
| Aldershot | A 1-4 | R1 |
|---|---|---|

Football League Cup
| Hereford United | A 3-1 | R1 |
|---|---|---|
| Hereford United | H 2-1 | R1 |
| Doncaster Rovers | a 1-3 | R2 |
| Doncaster Rovers | H 5-1* | R2 |
| Birmingham City | A 2-1 | R3 |
| Liverpool | A 0-2 | R4 |

* After extra-time.

CITY PLAYING SQUAD 1979-80

| Name | Pos | Signed From | Apps | Gls |
|---|---|---|---|---|
| Andy Bell | | Taunton Town Jul 1979 | 2+1 | |
| Keith Bowker | F | Northampton Town Aug 1977 | 21+6 | 8 |
| John Delve | M | Plymouth Argyle Mar 1978 | 42 | 1 |
| Dick Forbes | M | St Luke's College Apr 1978 | 16+1 | 3 |
| Jimmy Giles | D | Charlton Athletic Dec 1977 | 42 | 2 |
| Peter Hatch | D | Oxford United Dec 1973 | 44 | 6 |
| John Hore | D | Plymouth Argyle Mar 1976 | 46 | |
| Roy Ireland | M | Apprentice Feb 1979 | 3+1 | |
| Tony Kellow | F | Blackpool Mar 1980 | 10 | 5 |
| Ian Main | G | St. Luke's College Sep 1978 | 26 | |
| Tony Mitchell | D | St. Luke's College Jul 1977 | 34 | |
| Steve Neville | F | Southampton Sep 1978 | 40+3 | 8 |
| Vince O'Keefe | G | A.P. Leamington Jun 1978 | 20 | |
| Ian Pearson | F | Millwall Nov 1978 | 9+1 | 3 |
| Ray Pratt | F | Merthyr Tydfil Mar 1980 | 5+2 | 2 |
| Dave Pullar | W | Portsmouth Jul 1979 | 43 | 10 |
| Lee Roberts | D | Shrewsbury Town Sep 1977 | 14+3 | 3 |
| Phil Roberts | D | Hereford United Feb 1979 | 31+1 | |
| Martyn Rogers | D | Bath City Jul 1979 | 11 | |
| Peter Rogers | F | Bath City Feb 1979 | 39+4 | 5 |
| John Sims | F | Notts County Dec 1978 | 8+1 | |
| Own Goals | | | | 4 |

CITY MANAGER 1979-80
Brian Godfrey - Appointed January 1979

Third Division 1979-80

| | P | W | D | L | F | A | Pts |
|---|---|---|---|---|---|---|---|
| Grimsby Town | 46 | 26 | 10 | 10 | 73 | 42 | 62 |
| Blackburn Rovers | 46 | 25 | 9 | 12 | 58 | 36 | 59 |
| Sheffield Wednesday | 46 | 21 | 16 | 9 | 81 | 47 | 58 |
| Chesterfield | 46 | 23 | 11 | 12 | 71 | 46 | 57 |
| Colchester United | 46 | 20 | 12 | 14 | 64 | 56 | 52 |
| Carlisle United | 46 | 18 | 12 | 16 | 66 | 56 | 48 |
| Reading | 46 | 16 | 16 | 14 | 66 | 65 | 48 |
| EXETER CITY | 46 | 19 | 10 | 17 | 60 | 68 | 48 |
| Chester City | 46 | 17 | 13 | 16 | 49 | 57 | 47 |
| Swindon Town | 46 | 19 | 8 | 19 | 71 | 63 | 46 |
| Barnsley | 46 | 16 | 14 | 16 | 53 | 56 | 46 |
| Sheffield United | 46 | 18 | 10 | 18 | 59 | 66 | 46 |
| Rotherham United | 46 | 18 | 10 | 18 | 58 | 66 | 46 |
| Millwall | 46 | 16 | 13 | 17 | 65 | 59 | 45 |
| Plymouth Argyle | 46 | 16 | 12 | 18 | 59 | 55 | 44 |
| Gillingham | 46 | 14 | 14 | 18 | 49 | 51 | 42 |
| Oxford United | 46 | 14 | 13 | 19 | 57 | 62 | 41 |
| Blackpool | 46 | 15 | 11 | 20 | 62 | 74 | 41 |
| Brentford | 46 | 15 | 11 | 20 | 59 | 73 | 41 |
| Hull City | 46 | 12 | 16 | 18 | 51 | 69 | 40 |
| Bury | 46 | 16 | 7 | 23 | 45 | 59 | 39 |
| Southend United | 46 | 14 | 10 | 22 | 47 | 57 | 38 |
| Mansfield Town | 46 | 10 | 16 | 20 | 47 | 58 | 36 |
| Wimbledon | 46 | 10 | 14 | 22 | 52 | 81 | 34 |

* The 1979-80 season proved to be a very good one for Exeter City, as not only did they finish a creditable 8th in the Third Division, they also enjoyed a run in the Football League Cup that ultimately ended in the fourth round. The only real downside of the season was the first round FA Cup defeat at Aldershot.

* The League Cup started with a two-leg first round tie against Hereford United. City travelled to Edgar Street for the first leg and a Keith Bowker hat-trick helped them to a 3-1 win.

* The first round second leg against Hereford resulted in a 2-1 win for City before an attendance of 4,312, with goals from Dave Pullar and Ian Pearson.

* On to round two and again it was played over two legs. It must have seemed a huge hill to climb for the Grecians after they lost 3-1 at Doncaster Rovers' Belle Vue ground, with only a Pullar goal to show for their efforts.

* One of the great St James' Park nights of League Cup football occurred in the second leg, for after extra-time in a fascinating tie, City won 5-1. Bowker netted twice and there were goals from Peter Hatch, Steve Neville (penalty) and John Sims.

* There was a real shock result in round three as Exeter travelled to Birmingham City and won 2-1. Neville hit both the goals before an attendance of 13,669.

* So onto round four and City had earned themselves a trip to Anfield and the chance to take on Liverpool. It wasn't until the second half that the hosts managed to find a way through the resolute City defence and they went on to win 2-0 before 21,000. City's team that night was:- O'Keefe, Mitchell, Hore, Giles, Delve, Hatch, Forbes, Pullar, Neville, Bowker, Pearson.

* The highest league attendance of the season at St James' Park was for the match against Plymouth Argyle, when 10,489 made their way through the turnstiles.

* The lowest league attendance of the season at St James' Park was 2,648 when Colchester United visited in December 1979 and were beaten 3-1

* One of the highlights of the season was the return of goalscoring legend, Tony Kellow, who had been re-signed from Blackpool for a fee of £65,000. He wasted no time in getting back into the goalscoring groove and in the 10 matches that he played after returning, he had netted five goals.

* Signed on the same day as Kellow, to beat the annual transfer deadline, was striker Ray Pratt from Merthyr Tydfil. He was to go on and net 46 goals during his stay at City.

* Admission prices at St James' Park for the 1979-80 season were:- Grandstand £2 10p; Ground £1.15p; Transfer from ground to the enclosure 65p. For reserve team games in the Western League, adults paid 30p, senior citizens and children 20p.

* In October 1979 Exeter City announced club record profits of £101,861. However, much of the money came from a single transaction, the transfer of Tony Kellow to Blackpool. The profit enabled the club to wipe out virtually all of their debts and start on a series of ground improvements.

* Only John Hore played in every league match for City. The former Plymouth Argyle defender went on to make a total of 193 league appearances for the Grecians.

* It was reported that a group of local businessmen had formed a consortium to make a bid to take over the club. This was dismissed by the club's board of directors and nothing further was heard on the matter.

# 1980/81  Football League Division 3  8th from 24

## CITY PLAYING SQUAD 1980-81

| Name | Pos | Signed From | Apps | Gls |
|------|-----|-------------|------|-----|
| Len Bond | G | St. Louis (USA) Oct 1980 | 17 | |
| John Delve | M | Plymouth Argyle Mar 1978 | 36 | 4 |
| Phil Fisher | W | Bridgend Town Feb 1981 | 3 | |
| Dick Forbes | M | St Luke's College Apr 1978 | 30(2) | 2 |
| Jimmy Giles | D | Charlton Athletic Dec 1977 | 22 | 2 |
| Peter Hatch | D | Oxford United Dec 1973 | 45 | 2 |
| Roy Ireland | M | Apprentice Feb 1979 | 14(2) | |
| Tony Kellow | F | Blackpool Mar 1980 | 46 | 25 |
| Ian Main | G | St. Luke's College Sep 1978 | 24 | |
| Tony Mitchell | D | St. Luke's College Jul 1977 | 3 | |
| Steve Neville | F | Southampton Sep 1978 | 14 | 5 |
| Steve Nute | G | Apprentice Apr 1980 | 5 | |
| Ian Pearson | F | Millwall Nov 1978 | 40(1) | 4 |
| Ray Pratt | F | Merthyr Tydfil Mar 1980 | 8(9) | 4 |
| Frank Prince | M | Bristol Rovers Jul 1980 | 21 | 1 |
| Dave Pullar | W | Portsmouth Jul 1979 | 24(1) | 5 |
| Lee Roberts | D | Shrewsbury Town Sep 1977 | 24 | 2 |
| Phil Roberts | D | Hereford United Feb 1979 | 44 | |
| Martyn Rogers | D | Bath City Jul 1979 | 37 | |
| Peter Rogers | F | Bath City Feb 1979 | 34(6) | 6 |
| John Sparrow | D | Chelsea Jan 1981 | 15 | 1 |
| Own Goals | | | | 1 |

### City's league results

| | Home | Away |
|------|------|------|
| Barnsley | 0-1 | 0-1 |
| Blackpool | 0-0 | 0-0 |
| Brentford | 0-0 | 1-0 |
| Burnley | 0-0 | 0-1 |
| Carlisle United | 2-0 | 1-1 |
| Charlton Athletic | 4-3 | 0-1 |
| Chester | 2-2 | 0-1 |
| Chesterfield | 2-2 | 0-1 |
| Colchester United | 4-0 | 2-1 |
| Fulham | 1-0 | 1-0 |
| Gillingham | 2-1 | 5-1 |
| Huddersfield Town | 1-4 | 0-5 |
| Hull City | 1-3 | 3-3 |
| Millwall | 2-0 | 0-1 |
| Newport County | 2-2 | 1-2 |
| Oxford United | 1-1 | 2-1 |
| Plymouth Argyle | 1-1 | 2-0 |
| Portsmouth | 2-0 | 0-5 |
| Reading | 3-1 | 1-2 |
| Rotherham United | 2-1 | 1-3 |
| Sheffield United | 1-1 | 1-3 |
| Swindon Town | 3-4 | 2-2 |
| Walsall | 0-3 | 3-1 |

### Third Division 1980-81

| | P | W | D | L | F | A | Pts |
|------|---|---|---|---|---|---|-----|
| Rotherham United | 46 | 24 | 13 | 9 | 62 | 32 | 61 |
| Barnsley | 46 | 21 | 17 | 8 | 72 | 45 | 59 |
| Charlton Athletic | 46 | 25 | 9 | 12 | 63 | 44 | 59 |
| Huddersfield Town | 46 | 21 | 14 | 11 | 71 | 40 | 56 |
| Chesterfield | 46 | 23 | 10 | 13 | 72 | 48 | 56 |
| Portsmouth | 46 | 22 | 9 | 15 | 55 | 47 | 53 |
| Plymouth Argyle | 46 | 19 | 14 | 13 | 56 | 44 | 52 |
| Burnley | 46 | 18 | 14 | 14 | 60 | 48 | 50 |
| Brentford | 46 | 14 | 19 | 13 | 52 | 49 | 47 |
| Reading | 46 | 18 | 10 | 18 | 62 | 62 | 46 |
| Exeter City | 46 | 16 | 13 | 17 | 62 | 66 | 45 |
| Newport County | 46 | 15 | 13 | 18 | 64 | 61 | 43 |
| Fulham | 46 | 15 | 13 | 18 | 57 | 64 | 43 |
| Oxford United | 46 | 13 | 17 | 16 | 39 | 47 | 43 |
| Gillingham | 46 | 12 | 18 | 16 | 48 | 58 | 42 |
| Millwall | 46 | 14 | 14 | 18 | 43 | 60 | 42 |
| Swindon Town | 46 | 13 | 15 | 18 | 51 | 56 | 41 |
| Chester | 46 | 15 | 11 | 20 | 41 | 48 | 41 |
| Carlisle United | 46 | 14 | 13 | 19 | 57 | 70 | 41 |
| Walsall | 46 | 13 | 15 | 18 | 59 | 74 | 41 |
| Sheffield United | 46 | 14 | 13 | 19 | 65 | 62 | 40 |
| Colchester United | 46 | 14 | 11 | 21 | 45 | 65 | 39 |
| Blackpool | 46 | 9 | 14 | 23 | 45 | 75 | 32 |
| Hull City | 46 | 8 | 16 | 22 | 40 | 71 | 32 |

### F.A.Cup

| | | | |
|------|------|------|------|
| Leatherhead | H | 5-0 | R1 |
| Millwall | A | 1-0 | R2 |
| Maidstone United | A | 4-2 | R3 |
| Leicester City | A | 1-1 | R4 |
| Leicester City | H | 3-1 | R4R |
| Newcastle United | A | 1-1 | R5 |
| Newcastle United | H | 4-0 | R5R |
| Tottenham Hotspur | A | 0-2 | R6 |

### Football League Cup

| | | |
|------|------|------|
| Bristol Rovers | H | 1-1 |
| Bristol Rovers | A | 1-1 |

*After extra-time.
Bristol Rovers won 7-6 on penalties.

CITY MANAGER 1980-81
Brian Godfrey - Appointed January 1979

* Even though he had got his playing squad sorted for the coming season, which was just five weeks away, manager Brian Godfrey liked nothing better than to drive the tractor and roller around the Cat and Fiddle training ground. In July 1980 he said: "There is no time for taking things easy." Godfrey added that he had a good tutor in farmer Danny Yeo who kept an eye on the ground. You cannot imagine many managers today helping out with the preparation of their respective training grounds!

* The season will always be remembered for the run in the F.A. Cup which took Exeter City to the quarter-final stage for the second time in their history. The previous occasion being in 1931.

* Groundsman Sonny Clarke completed 25 years in the job on 9th August 1980. The Board of Directors decided to mark this achievement by arranging a testimonial game for him at St. James' Park against Derby County on 13th October. City won 3-2 before a disappointingly low attendance of 1,504.

* Exeter City player, Ian Pearson, along with his wife, Jackie, commenced a milk delivery business in the Redhills area of the city, saying: "It is for when I finish playing football."

* Goalkeeper Len Bond had a torrid time of things on his debut for City, when lining up at St James' Park against Swindon Town. Although Exeter scored three, they also conceded four.

* The Grecians celebrated Christmas in style as they defeated arch rivals, Plymouth Argyle 2-0 at Home Park on Boxing Day, before an attendance of 14,792. Tony Kellow and Dave Pullar got the City goals.

* Exeter M.P., John Hannam, sent Exeter City a good luck telegram prior to their FA Cup tie at Leicester City.

* The large travelling support of Exeter City fans (approx. 2,000) who saw the Grecians draw 1-1 at Leicester City in the fourth round of the F.A. Cup, included one, Mike Gallon, who journeyed all the way from Western Australia. Gallon had emigrated their 15 years earlier, but his mother still lived in Exeter.

*City sensationally dumped First Division Leicester City out of the FA Cup when they won the fourth round replay 3-1, which included a hat-trick netted by Tony Kellow. The tie was watched by an attendance of 15,268.

* Exeter restaurateur Gino Vece, later to become a director at Exeter City, offered the players a bonus of £100 per man if they won or drew at Newcastle United in the fifth round of the FA Cup.

* The Grecians caused a sensation when drawing 1-1 at Newcastle United, with a late equaliser from Lee Roberts. But there was an even bigger sensation as the televised replay back at the 'real' St James' Park ended in a 4-0 win for Exeter City before an attendance of 17,668. City's scorers on a memorable night were Peter Hatch, Ian Pearson, Peter Rogers and Martyn Rogers.

*Police were called to quell angry Exeter City fans who had queued for hours, only to find that by the time they reached the front of the queue, the 3,500 ticket allocation for the quarter-final FA Cup tie at Tottenham Hotspur had run out. City Commercial Manager, Ray Ellis, said: "I have had enough. I have been threatened and abused. I called in the Police as a precaution."

* An impassioned plea was made to City manager Brian Godfrey to ask him to get a ticket for the Spurs cup tie as he was unable to pick one up in person, fell on deaf ears when it was discovered that the Exeter fan was detained by Her Majesty's Pleasure in Exeter Prison! He was due to be released 24 hours before the big game.

* It was no surprise when leading goalscorer Tony Kellow was voted Exeter City Player of the Year at the end of the 1980-81 season. Kellow had netted 32 league and cup goals, including two hat-tricks.

* Young professional Roy Ireland netted a hat-trick in a reserve team game against Swansea City , and was told on the same day that he was to be released on a free transfer!

CITY PLAYING SQUAD 1981-82

| Name | Pos | Signed From | Apps | Gls |
|---|---|---|---|---|
| Len Bond | G | St. Louis (USA) Oct 1980 | 31 | |
| Joe Cooke | D | Oxford United Jun 1981 | 17 | 3 |
| Steve Davey | M | Portsmouth Aug 1981 | 15 | |
| John Delve | M | Plymouth Argyle Mar 1978 | 40 | 3 |
| Phil Fisher | W | Bridgend Town Feb 1981 | 6(2) | 1 |
| George Foster | D | Plymouth Argyle Dec 1981 | 28 | |
| Paul Giles | M | Cardiff City Mar 1982 | 9 | 1 |
| Peter Hatch | D | Oxford United Dec 1973 | 20(2) | 3 |
| Frank Howarth | M | Apprentice Aug 1982 | 1(1) | |
| Tony Kellow | F | Blackpool Mar 1980 | 46 | 21 |
| Graeme Kirkup | D | Apprentice May 1981 | 8 | |
| Mike Lester | M | Barnsley Aug 1981 | 18(1) | 6 |
| Ian Main | G | St. Luke's College Sep 1978 | 15 | |
| Nicky Marker | D | Apprentice May 1981 | 11(3) | 1 |
| Tony Mitchell | D | St. Luke's College Jul 1977 | 13 | |
| Ray Pratt | F | Merthyr Tydfil Mar 1980 | 23(7) | 9 |
| Frank Prince | M | Bristol Rovers Jul 1980 | 6(4) | 1 |
| Dave Pullar | W | Portsmouth Jul 1979 | 27(3) | 2 |
| Lee Roberts | D | Shrewsbury Town Sep 1977 | 23(2) | 4 |
| Phil Roberts | D | Hereford United Feb 1979 | 26(1) | |
| Stuart Robertson | M | Burnley Mar 1982 | 5(1) | |
| Martyn Rogers | D | Bath City Jul 1979 | 35(1) | 4 |
| Peter Rogers | F | Bath City Feb 1979 | 42 | 10 |
| Peter Shaw | D | Charlton Athletic Nov 1981 | 3 | |
| John Sparrow | D | Chelsea Jan 1981 | 38 | 1 |
| Own Goals | | | | 1 |

City's league results

| | Home | Away |
|---|---|---|
| Brentford | 3-1 | 0-2 |
| Bristol City | 4-0 | 2-3 |
| Bristol Rovers | 1-3 | 2-3 |
| Burnley | 2-1 | 3-3 |
| Carlisle United | 2-1 | 2-3 |
| Chester | 3-0 | 2-0 |
| Chesterfield | 0-3 | 1-2 |
| Doncaster Rovers | 2-1 | 0-3 |
| Fulham | 1-0 | 1-4 |
| Gillingham | 1-1 | 3-2 |
| Huddersfield Town | 1-0 | 1-1 |
| Lincoln City | 1-2 | 0-2 |
| Millwall | 5-4 | 1-5 |
| Newport County | 1-0 | 1-1 |
| Oxford United | 1-2 | 0-0 |
| Plymouth Argyle | 1-1 | 1-2 |
| Portsmouth | 3-3 | 0-2 |
| Preston North End | 4-3 | 0-1 |
| Reading | 4-3 | 0-4 |
| Southend United | 1-1 | 1-2 |
| Swindon Town | 1-2 | 2-3 |
| Walsall | 2-0 | 1-2 |
| Wimbledon | 2-1 | 1-1 |

F.A.Cup
| Brentford | A 0-2 | R1 |
|---|---|---|

Football League Cup
| Cardiff City | A 1-2 | R1 |
|---|---|---|
| Cardiff City | H 3-1 | R1 |
| Liverpool | A 0-5 | R2 |
| Liverpool | H 0-6 | R2 |

Third Division 1981-82

| | P | W | D | L | F | A | Pts |
|---|---|---|---|---|---|---|---|
| Burnley | 46 | 21 | 17 | 8 | 66 | 49 | 80 |
| Carlisle United | 46 | 23 | 11 | 12 | 65 | 50 | 80 |
| Fulham | 46 | 21 | 15 | 10 | 77 | 51 | 78 |
| Lincoln City | 46 | 21 | 14 | 11 | 66 | 40 | 77 |
| Oxford United | 46 | 19 | 14 | 13 | 63 | 49 | 71 |
| Gillingham | 46 | 20 | 11 | 15 | 64 | 56 | 71 |
| Southend United | 46 | 18 | 15 | 13 | 63 | 51 | 69 |
| Brentford | 46 | 19 | 11 | 16 | 56 | 47 | 68 |
| Millwall | 46 | 18 | 13 | 15 | 62 | 62 | 67 |
| Plymouth Argyle | 46 | 18 | 11 | 17 | 64 | 56 | 65 |
| Chesterfield | 46 | 18 | 10 | 18 | 67 | 58 | 64 |
| Reading | 46 | 17 | 11 | 18 | 67 | 75 | 62 |
| Portsmouth | 46 | 14 | 19 | 13 | 56 | 51 | 61 |
| Preston North End | 46 | 16 | 13 | 17 | 50 | 56 | 61 |
| Bristol Rovers | 46 | 18 | 9 | 19 | 58 | 65 | 61* |
| Newport County | 46 | 14 | 16 | 16 | 54 | 54 | 58 |
| Huddersfield Town | 46 | 15 | 12 | 19 | 64 | 59 | 57 |
| Exeter City | 46 | 16 | 9 | 21 | 71 | 84 | 57 |
| Doncaster Rovers | 46 | 13 | 17 | 16 | 55 | 68 | 56 |
| Walsall | 46 | 13 | 14 | 19 | 51 | 55 | 53 |
| Wimbledon | 46 | 14 | 11 | 21 | 61 | 75 | 53 |
| Swindon Town | 46 | 13 | 13 | 20 | 55 | 71 | 52 |
| Bristol City | 46 | 11 | 13 | 22 | 40 | 65 | 46 |
| Chester | 46 | 7 | 11 | 28 | 36 | 78 | 32 |

* Two points deducted by Football League

CITY MANAGER 1981-82
Brian Godfrey - Appointed January 1979

* Prior to the season starting, manager Brian Godfrey signed a new three-year contract. This was announced after several weeks of negotiations, the new deal keeping him at St James' Park until July 1984. members of the City coaching staff also accepted improved terms.

City chairman Gerald Vallance revealed: "The negotiations have been very difficult. Obviously we are delighted with what Brian has done for us, but I think all clubs are in a difficult financial situation at the moment."

* The pre-season friendly against Chelsea at St James' Park, which the visitors won 1-0, produced unsavoury scenes in the city centre after the final whistle. Various fights broke out and number of arrests were made, with up to 200 people involved in one incident.

* Cup fever gripped St James' Park when the Grecians were drawn against Liverpool in the second round of the Football League Cup. Everyone wanted to see the League Cup holders, however, the first leg was to be played At Anfield, and hundreds made their way from Devon

* Liverpool proved to be far too strong for Exeter City, as they won the first leg 5-0 and then thrashed the Grecians 6-0 back at St James' Park. The aggregate score of 11-0 was a record for the competition.

* Midfielder Steve Davey took over in goal during City's 3-1 defeat at Brentford, after Len Bond had to leave the field with concussion after 15 minutes. Davey, who had played as an emergency keeper when at Hereford United, said: "Nobody else was putting their hand up to take over in goal, so I suppose it had to be me."

* Tony Kellow netted the 100th League goal of his career when he was on target in the 4-3 home win against Preston North End in October 1981. City's fourth goal was Kellow's 100th, having also scored earlier in the match as well.

* City gave a trial to Holland Under-21 international Frans Koenan who had played 12 league matches for Newcastle United the previous season. He played just the one game, a match to mark the official opening on a new social club at Cullompton Rangers, when Exeter City played Bridgwater Town.

* Exeter City were presented with a cheque for £1,000 before the home game with Reading by the Pepsi Cola's South West Area Manager. The money was for topping the Pepsi Golden Goals table for Division Three for the month of October. Half the cash was to go to a charity nominated by the club.

* In February 1982, the club stated that all profits that they had made over previous seasons had been used to keep the afloat. The Financial Director, Ian Webb, gave assurances, however, that the club would not be allowed to slip back into the financial nightmares of the 1960s and 70s.

* Later in the month Webb added that average Third Division player earned £10,000 per year and that the present playing staff was more than Exeter City could afford. It cost £20,000 per month to run the club, however, gate receipts were not meeting that figure. The club did announce a profit of £32,785 on the year ending 30th June 1981, thanks to the run in the FA Cup and the sale of Steve Neville to Sheffield United.

* Alarm bells again rang in May 1982 when Exeter City Chairman, Gerald Vallance admitted the club's present financial position was disappointing. There had been a fall in income in every respect. The club's share of away gates had dropped, and average attendances at St James; Park were down by 400 per match. It was expected that the loss on the year would be over £100,000. It was hoped that fundraising would help offset the £70,000 in savings that the club were seeking to make.

*As a result of the cutbacks, only eight players were retained at the end of the season. It was expected that manager Brian Godfrey would have to operate with a squad of 16 players the following season. The reserve team would play in the Devon and Exeter Premier League, rather than the far too costly London Midweek League as it had been doing.

CITY PLAYING SQUAD 1982-83

| Name | Pos | Signed From | Apps | Gls |
|------|-----|-------------|------|-----|
| Len Bond | G | St. Louis (USA) Oct 1980 | 45 | |
| John Burke | W | Sheffield United Mar 1983 | 3 | |
| David Crown | W | Portsmouth Mar 1983 | 6(1) | 3 |
| Grant Davies | D | Newport County Feb 1983 | 7 | |
| John Delve | M | Plymouth Argyle Mar 1978 | 44 | 5 |
| Aidan Gibson | W | Derby County Jul 1982 | 17(1) | 1 |
| David Harle | M | Doncaster Rovers Jul 1982 | 36(1) | 6 |
| Steve Hatter | D | Fulham Sep 1982 | 11 | 1 |
| Frank Howarth | M | Apprentice Aug 1982 | 3(2) | |
| Tony Kellow | F | Blackpool Mar 1980 | 31(2) | 10 |
| Graeme Kirkup | D | Apprentice May 1981 | 15(2) | |
| Martin Ling | W | Apprentice Jul 1982 | 0(1) | |
| Stan McEwan | D | Blackpool Jul 1982 | 37 | 6 |
| Nicky Marker | D | Apprentice May 1981 | 18 | 1 |
| Steve Neville | F | Sheffield United Oct 1982 | 33 | 17 |
| Leighton Phillips | D | Charlton Athletic Mar 1983 | 10 | |
| Ray Pratt | F | Merthyr Tydfil Mar 1980 | 17(14)9 | |
| Dave Pullar | W | Portsmouth Jul 1979 | 30(2) | 5 |
| Lee Roberts | D | Shrewsbury Town Sep 1977 | 9 | |
| Martyn Rogers | D | Bath City Jul 1979 | 37(1) | 1 |
| Peter Rogers | F | Bath City Feb 1979 | 43 | 10 |
| Peter Shepherd | G | Plymouth Argyle Aug 1982 | 1 | |
| John Sparrow | D | Chelsea Jan 1981 | 9(1) | 1 |
| Patrick Thomas | M | Apprentice Jun 1982 | 0(1) | |
| Keith Viney | D | Portsmouth Aug 1982 | 44 | 4 |
| Own Goals | | | | 1 |

Third Division 1982-83

| | P | W | D | L | F | A | Pts |
|------|---|---|---|---|---|---|-----|
| Portsmouth | 46 | 27 | 10 | 9 | 74 | 41 | 91 |
| Cardiff City | 46 | 25 | 11 | 10 | 76 | 50 | 86 |
| Huddersfield Town | 46 | 23 | 13 | 10 | 84 | 49 | 82 |
| Newport County | 46 | 23 | 9 | 14 | 76 | 54 | 78 |
| Oxford United | 46 | 22 | 12 | 12 | 71 | 53 | 78 |
| Lincoln City | 46 | 23 | 7 | 16 | 77 | 51 | 76 |
| Bristol Rovers | 46 | 22 | 9 | 15 | 84 | 58 | 75 |
| Plymouth Argyle | 46 | 19 | 8 | 19 | 61 | 66 | 65 |
| Brentford | 46 | 18 | 10 | 18 | 88 | 77 | 64 |
| Walsall | 46 | 17 | 13 | 16 | 64 | 63 | 64 |
| Sheffield United | 46 | 19 | 7 | 20 | 62 | 64 | 64 |
| Bradford City | 46 | 16 | 13 | 17 | 68 | 69 | 61 |
| Gillingham | 46 | 16 | 13 | 17 | 58 | 59 | 61 |
| AFC Bournemouth | 46 | 16 | 13 | 17 | 59 | 68 | 61 |
| Southend United | 46 | 15 | 14 | 17 | 66 | 65 | 59 |
| Preston North End | 46 | 15 | 13 | 18 | 60 | 69 | 58 |
| Millwall | 46 | 14 | 13 | 19 | 64 | 77 | 55 |
| Wigan Athletic | 46 | 15 | 9 | 22 | 60 | 72 | 54 |
| Exeter City | 46 | 14 | 12 | 20 | 81 | 104 | 54 |
| Orient | 46 | 15 | 9 | 22 | 64 | 88 | 54 |
| Reading | 46 | 12 | 17 | 17 | 64 | 79 | 53 |
| Wrexham | 46 | 12 | 15 | 19 | 56 | 76 | 51 |
| Doncaster Rovers | 46 | 9 | 11 | 26 | 57 | 97 | 38 |
| Chesterfield | 46 | 8 | 13 | 25 | 43 | 68 | 37 |

City's league results

| | Home | Away |
|------|------|------|
| AFC Bournemouth | 4-2 | 0-2 |
| Bradford City | 2-1 | 3-3 |
| Brentford | 1-7 | 1-4 |
| Bristol Rovers | 0-1 | 4-4 |
| Cardiff City | 0-2 | 0-2 |
| Chesterfield | 2-3 | 3-1 |
| Doncaster Rovers | 3-0 | 1-6 |
| Gillingham | 2-2 | 4-4 |
| Huddersfield Town | 3-4 | 1-1 |
| Lincoln City | 3-1 | 1-4 |
| Millwall | 2-1 | 2-5 |
| Newport County | 0-1 | 1-1 |
| Orient | 2-0 | 1-5 |
| Oxford United | 3-1 | 1-1 |
| Plymouth Argyle | 1-0 | 0-1 |
| Portsmouth | 1-1 | 2-3 |
| Preston North End | 5-1 | 2-2 |
| Reading | 2-2 | 1-3 |
| Sheffield United | 0-3 | 0-3 |
| Southend United | 4-3 | 1-1 |
| Walsall | 4-3 | 2-3 |
| Wigan Athletic | 2-1 | 0-1 |
| Wrexham | 3-3 | 2-1 |

F.A. Cup

| | | |
|------|------|------|
| Plymouth Argyle | A 0-2 | R1 |

Football League Cup

| | | |
|------|------|------|
| Newport County | H 1-2 | R1 |
| Newport County | A 0-6 | R1 |

Football League Trophy

| | | |
|------|------|------|
| Bristol City | H 2-1 | G |
| Newport County | A 1-5 | G |
| Torquay United | A 2-3 | G |

CITY MANAGER 1982-83
Brian Godfrey - Appointed January 1979

* Admission prices to St James' Park for the 1982-83 season were:- Ground - Adult £1.80p; Ground - Senior Citizens and Juveniles £1; Transfer from Ground to the Enclosure £1.20p; Reserves and youth matches, Adults - 50p; Senior Citizens and Juveniles 30p.

* In September 1982, Club chairman Clifford Hill told a meeting of the Exeter Chamber of Commerce that City would be keen to bring in a big name player if local business would sponsor the deal and the players' wages. In return n the company or group of companies would be free to use the player for publicity and public relations work.

Hill said: "We have to market the club in the city, so lets see what the tycoons in Exeter can do?"

* Exeter City were the team to watch if you wanted to see goals. They ended the season scoring more goals (81) than most of the other clubs in the Division, but at the same time conceded more than any other (104)!

* Pre-season preparations didn't start very well as Exeter lost over two legs to Weymouth in the Western Counties Floodlight League Cup Final, a match that had been held over from the previous season. The Grecians were humiliated in the second leg at Weymouth, losing 6-1!

*The Grecians has a disastrous week early September. They lost 6-1 at Doncaster Rovers on 10th September and four days later travelled to Newport County in The Football League Cup and lost 6-0!

* In the same month Exeter City sacked three of their coaching staff and it was reported that the youth development scheme may have to be scrapped in a desperate bid, not for the first time, for financial survival.

* Vice chairman Clifford Hill said: "We have no panic. Just a realisation of facts. We have had a crisis which we think we have averted by prompt action. The message to all is to rally around and we within the club will do our utmost to provide Exeter with a football club to be proud of."

* A week later the club secretary, Pat Wakeham, who had been in the post for 10 years, was made redundant, as another cost cutting measure.

*It was rumoured that the club were heading for a loss of £250,000 and it was within a hair's breath of closing down. It was only directors agreeing to unsecured loans (described by vice chairman Clifford Hill as not being acceptable) that kept the club afloat.

* Despite the club's financial woes, they somehow managed to find £10,000 to re-sign Steve Neville from Sheffield United, following a one month loan deal. This proved to be an excellent signing as Neville went on to become City's leading scorer.

* Exeter City took part in the inaugural Football League Trophy competition for Third and Fourth Division clubs, but never got beyond the early group stages, with Newport County again inflicting a heavy defeat upon them winning 5-1 at Somerton Park.

* Steve Neville was on the mark in the 1-0 home win over neighbours Plymouth Argyle on 27th December to give City fans a late Christmas present. The game also attracted the highest attendance of the season, 9,168

* Apprentice Martin Ling made his debut as a substitute in the 3-0 defeat at Sheffield United in March 1983. Much was expected of Ling, who went on to captain the England Youth side in one match against an England Public Schools XI.

* City suffered their heaviest home defeat for quite some time when going down 1-7 to Brentford in April 1983. A week later they then lost 5-1 at Orient, thus conceding their 100th league goal of the season during the course of that game.

* The following game after the defeat at Orient saw City edge home in a 4-3 thriller at St James' Park against Southend United, with Steve Neville netting a hat-trick. The other goal was scored by the on-loan David Crown.

* The lowest attendance of the season for any of Exeter City's Third Division matches was 1,788, who saw Chesterfield lose 3-1 at home to the Grecians in April 1983. The lowest attendance at St James' Park for a league match was 2,272 when Reading were the visitors in December 1982.

* Goalkeeper Len Bond made the most league appearances for City, missing just one match when his place went to Peter Shepherd for the game against Bradford City at St James' Park, which proved to be the only match that he played in.

EXETER CITY 1983-84
Back row: Martyn Rogers, Ray Pratt, Nicky Marker, Graeme Kirkup, Frank Howarth, Tony Kellow.
Middle row: Martin Ling, Darren Clifford, Symon Burgher, Len Bond, Leon Smith, Michael Lane, Adrain Robson, Malcolm Musgrove (Coach).
Front row: Dick Forbes, Tony Dennis, David Harle, Gerry Francis (Player-Manager), Keith Viney, Peter Rogers, Steve Neville

THIRD DIVISION - 1983-84

| | P | W | D | L | F | A | Pts |
|---|---|---|---|---|---|---|---|
| Oxford United | 46 | 28 | 11 | 7 | 91 | 50 | 95 |
| Wimbledon | 46 | 26 | 9 | 11 | 97 | 76 | 87 |
| Sheffield United | 46 | 24 | 11 | 11 | 86 | 53 | 83 |
| Hull City | 46 | 23 | 14 | 9 | 71 | 38 | 83 |
| Bristol Rovers | 46 | 22 | 13 | 11 | 68 | 54 | 79 |
| Walsall | 46 | 22 | 9 | 15 | 68 | 61 | 75 |
| Bradford City | 46 | 20 | 11 | 15 | 73 | 65 | 71 |
| Gillingham | 46 | 20 | 10 | 16 | 74 | 69 | 70 |
| Millwall | 46 | 18 | 13 | 15 | 71 | 65 | 67 |
| Bolton Wanderers | 46 | 18 | 10 | 18 | 56 | 60 | 64 |
| Orient | 46 | 18 | 9 | 19 | 71 | 81 | 63 |
| Burnley | 46 | 16 | 14 | 16 | 76 | 61 | 62 |
| Newport County | 46 | 16 | 14 | 16 | 76 | 61 | 62 |
| Lincoln City | 46 | 17 | 10 | 19 | 59 | 62 | 61 |
| Wigan Athletic | 46 | 16 | 13 | 17 | 46 | 56 | 61 |
| Preston North End | 46 | 15 | 11 | 20 | 66 | 66 | 56 |
| AFC Bournemouth | 46 | 16 | 7 | 23 | 63 | 73 | 55 |
| Rotherham United | 46 | 15 | 9 | 22 | 57 | 64 | 54 |
| Plymouth Argyle | 46 | 13 | 12 | 21 | 56 | 62 | 51 |
| Brentford | 46 | 11 | 16 | 19 | 69 | 79 | 49 |
| Scunthorpe United | 46 | 9 | 19 | 18 | 54 | 73 | 46 |
| Southend United | 46 | 10 | 14 | 22 | 55 | 76 | 44 |
| Port vale | 46 | 11 | 10 | 25 | 51 | 83 | 43 |
| EXETER CITY | 46 | 6 | 15 | 25 | 50 | 84 | 33 |

City's league results

| | Home | Away |
|---|---|---|
| AFC Bournemouth | 0-2 | 1-3 |
| Bolton Wanderers | 2-2 | 0-1 |
| Bradford City | 0-2 | 3-1 |
| Brentford | 1-2 | 0-3 |
| Bristol Rovers | 1-2 | 0-2 |
| Burnley | 1-1 | 0-4 |
| Gillingham | 0-0 | 1-3 |
| Hull City | 2-1 | 0-1 |
| Lincoln City | 0-3 | 1-1 |
| Millwall | 3-2 | 0-3 |
| Newport County | 1-2 | 0-1 |
| Orient | 3-4 | 2-2 |
| Oxford United | 3-1 | 1-1 |
| Plymouth Argyle | 1-1 | 2-2 |
| Port Vale | 1-1 | 2-2 |
| Preston North End | 2-1 | 1-2 |
| Rotherham United | 0-1 | 0-1 |
| Scunthorpe United | 1-1 | 1-3 |
| Sheffield United | 1-2 | 2-2 |
| Southend United | 3-3 | 3-0 |
| Walsall | 0-1 | 1-4 |
| Wigan Athletic | 1-1 | 1-1 |
| Wimbledon | 0-3 | 1-2 |

F.A. Cup

| | | |
|---|---|---|
| Maidstone United | H 1-1 | R1 |
| Maidstone United | A 1-2 | R1R |

Football League Cup

| | | |
|---|---|---|
| Cardiff City | H 2-3 | R1 |
| Cardiff City | A 1-2 | R1 |

CITY MANAGER 1983-84
Gerry Francis - Appointed July 1983

CITY PLAYING SQUAD 1983-84

| Name | Pos | Signed From | Apps | Gls |
|---|---|---|---|---|
| Hugh Atkinson | M | Wolverhampton Wanderers Oct 1983 | 28 | 1 |
| Joe Auguste | F | Hounslow Town Sept 1983 | 7+3 | |
| Len Bond | G | St. Louis (USA) Oct 1980 | 45 | |
| Richard Crabtree | G | Dawlish Town Jul 1983 | 1 | |
| Tony Dennis | W | Plymouth Argyle Aug 1983 | 3+1 | |
| Ian Evans | D | Barnsley Aug 1983 | 4 | |
| Gerry Francis | M | Coventry City Jul 1983 | 28 | 3 |
| David Harle | M | Doncaster Rovers Jul 1982 | 6 | |
| Steve Harrower | M | Dawlish Town Jan 1984 | 10+3 | 1 |
| Jim Hicks | D | Warwick University Sep 1983 | 3 | |
| Frank Howarth | D | Apprentice Nov 1982 | 6+5 | |
| Tony Kellow | F | Blackpool Mar 1980 | 7+1 | |
| Graeme Kirkup | D | Apprentice May 1983 | 36 | 1 |
| Michael Lane | FB | Apprentice Jul 1983 | 1 | |
| Martin Ling | M | Apprentice Jan 1984 | 23+6 | |
| Roy McDonough | F | Southend United Jan 1984 | 15+1 | |
| Stan McEwan | D | Blackpool Jul 1982 | 28 | 9 |
| Nicky Marker | D | Apprentice May 1983 | 28+3 | |
| Russell Musker | M | Bristol City Oct 1983 | 6 | |
| Steve Neville | F | Sheffield United Oct 1982 | 40+3 | 9 |
| Mark O'Connor | M | Queens Park Rangers Oct 1983 | 38 | 1 |
| Ray Pratt | F | Merthyr Tydfil Mar 1980 | 30+6 | 16 |
| Peter Rogers | F | Bath City Feb 1979 | 25 | 5 |
| John Sims | F | Torquay United Feb 1984 | 12+2 | 3 |
| Peter Taylor | W | Maidstone United Oct 1983 | 8 | |
| Keith Viney | D | Portsmouth Aug 1982 | 42 | |
| Simon Webster | D | Tottenham Hotspur Nov 1983 | 26 | |
| Own Goals | | | | 1 |

* The season started with great optimism as Exeter City made headline news with the appointment of former England international Gerry Francis as player-manager. That optimism continued as City arranged a meet the manager evening at both Tiverton Town F.C. and Exmouth Town F.C..

* It soon became evident that whilst the City directors had done well to get such a high profile appointment to manage the club, they then failed to back him in the transfer market, and as a result Francis was left to sign free transfers, non-contract players and loanees.

* It proved to be one of the most disastrous seasons in the club's history, as the Grecians finished rock bottom of the Third Division and were relegated, and Francis left his job as player-manager before it ended.

* It took until December before City registered a home victory when they defeated Hull City 2-1 with goals from Hugh Atkinson and Ray Pratt.

* Amongst the high profile signings on short contacts, thanks to the various contacts that Francis had, were Welsh International centre-half Ian Evans, who featured in the opening four games and then former England man, Peter Taylor, who managed 8 appearances before returning to the club he was signed from, Maidstone United.

* Needless to say attendances dipped alarmingly, and this was so in contrast with the hopes at the opening game when 4,742 were present to see Walsall win 1-0. Things got so bad that by the time Southend United visited the Park in March 1984, only 1,782 bothered to make their way through the St James' Park turnstiles.

* City were knocked out at the first round stage in both the F.A. Cup and the Football League Cup, losing to Maidstone United and Cardiff City respectively.

* Two players were brought in on a long term loan, namely Tottenham Hotspur, defender Simon Webster and midfielder Mark O'Connor from Queen's Park Rangers, and both were regulars in the struggling City team.

* Considering what a poor time City had, Ray Pratt did remarkably well to top score with 16 goals. Almost a third of the number of the goals scored by the entire team.

* Stan McEwan scored nine goals in 28 matches, but wanted a transfer, and so he was a big loss to City as he moved on to Hull City for a fee of £5,000 in February 1984.

* There was much discontent off the field as well, as City director Dan McCauley wanted to give the manager more money to work with, which included the issue of a further £60,000 of shares, but the other board members did not. As a result of McCauley's public differences with the board, he was removed as a director.

* In December 1983 the club announced that they had made a loss of £92,983 for year ending May 1983. They were in total deficit of £299,291. Wages costs for the season accounted for £287,815, whilst in the plus side the commercial department raised £93,250 and increase of £11,000.

* Exeter City appointed their first ever official Club Chaplain, Richard Chewter. Aged 29, he had moved to Exeter two years earlier and become a City supporter. He said: "I do not pray for goals. I pray for souls."

* Exeter City's associate schoolboy goalkeeper, Howard Whitehouse made his full debut for England Schools against Switzerland in May 1984. He had already played 45 minutes for the side in West Germany the previous month. Despite the impressive start to his career, Whitehouse never became a full time professional with City.

Exeter City 1984-85
Back row: Martyn Rogers, Graeme Kirkup, Jim McNichol, Roy McDonough, John Sims, Jim Iley (Manager), Nicky Marker, Ray Pratt, Danny O'Shea, Symon Burgher, Phil King
Middle row: Malcolm Musgrove (Chief Coach), Steve Neville, Martin Ling, Keith Viney, Steve Harrower, Frank Howarth, Mike Radford (Youth Development Officer).
Sat on ground: Neville Crocker, Michael Lane, Andy Phillips, Darren Clifford

City's league results

| | Home | Away |
|---|---|---|
| Aldershot | 3-0 | 1-1 |
| Blackpool | 1-1 | 0-3 |
| Bury | 0-2 | 2-2 |
| Chester City | 1-1 | 3-1 |
| Chesterfield | 0-1 | 1-5 |
| Colchester United | 1-5 | 4-3 |
| Crewe Alexandra | 0-2 | 0-0 |
| Darlington | 1-1 | 1-2 |
| Hartlepool United | 3-2 | 1-1 |
| Halifax Town | 1-0 | 3-2 |
| Hereford United | 0-0 | 2-1 |
| Mansfield Town | 0-0 | 2-2 |
| Northampton Town | 5-0 | 2-5 |
| Peterborough United | 0-1 | 0-0 |
| Port Vale | 2-1 | 1-5 |
| Rochdale | 1-1 | 0-2 |
| Scunthorpe United | 2-1 | 1-7 |
| Southend United | 2-1 | 0-1 |
| Stockport County | 0-2 | 0-1 |
| Swindon Town | 1-1 | 0-2 |
| Torquay Unied | 4-3 | 1-1 |
| Tranmere Rovers | 0-1 | 2-3 |
| Wrexham | 2-0 | 0-2 |

F.A. Cup
| | | |
|---|---|---|
| Enfield | H 2-2 | R1 |
| Enfield | A 0-3 | R1R |

Football League Cup
| | | |
|---|---|---|
| Cardiff City | H 1-0 | R1 |
| Cardiff City | A 0-2 | R1 |

Freight Rover Trophy
| | | |
|---|---|---|
| Newport County | A 0-3 | R1 |
| Newport County | H 1-1 | R1 |

CITY MANAGER 1984-85
Jim Iley - Appointed June 1984

CITY PLAYING SQUAD 1984-85

| Name | Pos | Signed From | Apps | Gls |
|---|---|---|---|---|
| Leigh Barnard | M | Swindon Town Feb 1985 | 6 | 2 |
| Symon Burgher | M | Apprentice Feb 1985 | 11(3) | |
| Darren Clifford | M | Apprentice Nov 1984 | 0(1) | |
| Phil Coleman | D | Chelmsford City Dec 1984 | 6 | |
| Ian Davies | D | Carlisle United Dec 1984 | 5 | |
| Steve Harrower | M | Dawlish Town Jan 1984 | 25(6) | 1 |
| Frank Howarth | D | Apprentice Nov 1982 | 11(8) | 1 |
| Phil King | D | Apprentice Jan 1985 | 15(1) | |
| Graeme Kirkup | D | Apprentice May 1983 | 35(3) | |
| Martin Ling | M | Apprentice Jan 1984 | 42(1) | 6 |
| Doug McClure | D | Queens Park Rangers Nov 1984 | 0(1) | |
| Roy McDonough | F | Southend United Jan 1984 | 5 | 1 |
| Jim McNichol | D | Brentford Jul 1984 | 42 | 5 |
| Nicky Marker | D | Apprentice May 1983 | 45 | |
| Trevor Morgan | F | Bristol City Nov 1984 | 27 | 9 |
| Steve Neville | F | Sheffield United Oct 1982 | 16 | 1 |
| Danny O'Shea | M | Arsenal Aug 1984 | 45 | 2 |
| Forbes Phillipson-Masters | D | Bristol City Mar 1985 | 5(2) | 1 |
| Ray Pratt | F | Merthyr Tydfil Mar 1980 | 33 | 19 |
| Martyn Rogers | D | Bath City Jul 1979 | 8(1) | |
| John Sims | F | Torquay United Feb 1984 | 11 | 3 |
| Lee Smelt | G | Cardiff City Mar 1985 | 13 | |
| Kevin Smith | F | Cambridge United Oct 1984 | 21(4) | 2 |
| Nigel Smith | M | Bristol City Nov 1984 | 1 | |
| Keith Viney | D | Portsmouth Aug 1982 | 45 | 1 |
| Jeff Wood | G | Happy Valley (Hong Kong) Aug 1984 | 33 | |
| Own Goals | | | | 3 |

Fourth Division 1984-85

| | P | W | D | L | F | A | Pts |
|---|---|---|---|---|---|---|---|
| Chesterfield | 46 | 26 | 13 | 7 | 64 | 35 | 91 |
| Blackpool | 46 | 24 | 14 | 8 | 73 | 39 | 86 |
| Darlington | 46 | 24 | 13 | 9 | 66 | 49 | 85 |
| Bury | 46 | 24 | 12 | 10 | 76 | 50 | 84 |
| Hereford United | 46 | 22 | 11 | 13 | 65 | 47 | 77 |
| Tranmere Rovers | 46 | 24 | 3 | 19 | 83 | 66 | 75 |
| Colchester United | 46 | 20 | 14 | 12 | 87 | 65 | 74 |
| Swindon Town | 46 | 21 | 9 | 16 | 62 | 58 | 72 |
| Scunthorpe United | 46 | 19 | 14 | 13 | 83 | 62 | 71 |
| Crewe Alexandra | 46 | 18 | 12 | 16 | 65 | 69 | 66 |
| Peterborough United | 46 | 16 | 14 | 16 | 54 | 53 | 62 |
| Port Vale | 46 | 14 | 18 | 14 | 61 | 59 | 60 |
| Aldershot | 46 | 17 | 8 | 21 | 56 | 63 | 59 |
| Mansfield Town | 46 | 13 | 18 | 15 | 41 | 38 | 57 |
| Wrexham | 46 | 15 | 9 | 22 | 67 | 70 | 54 |
| Chester City | 46 | 15 | 9 | 22 | 60 | 72 | 54 |
| Rochdale | 46 | 13 | 14 | 19 | 55 | 69 | 53 |
| Exeter City | 46 | 13 | 14 | 19 | 57 | 79 | 53 |
| Hartlepool United | 46 | 14 | 10 | 22 | 54 | 67 | 52 |
| Southend United | 46 | 13 | 11 | 22 | 58 | 83 | 50 |
| Halifax Town | 46 | 15 | 5 | 26 | 42 | 69 | 50 |
| Stockport County | 46 | 13 | 8 | 25 | 58 | 79 | 47 |
| Northampton Town | 46 | 14 | 5 | 27 | 53 | 74 | 47 |
| Torquay United | 46 | 9 | 14 | 23 | 38 | 63 | 41 |

* After a disastrous previous season which ended in relegation, not surprisingly many changes were made to the playing staff as well as the appointment of a new manager, Jim Iley.

* It was a season when a handful of young apprentices made their debuts or established themselves in the first team, notably, Symon Burgher, Darren Clifford, Phil King, Graeme Kirkup, Nicky Marker and Martin Ling.

* Once again it proved to be a less than satisfactory season which saw City struggling in the Fourth Division and bringing in a number of players during the course of it, both loan and non-contact players.

* It wasn't until just before the first match of the season that City had a senior goalkeeper on their books. Even the pre-season photo shoot of the squad did not have a keeper in the picture! Jeff Wood eventually signed, having returned from playing for Happy Valley in Hong Kong.

* In January 1985 it was reported that City chairman Byron Snell said: "in Jim Iley we have got a first class manager who is prepared to stick to his task. He has got the full support of the Board." - Just over three months later Iley was sacked!

* Iley took the unusual step of calling a public meeting to put his side of the story and relate various events that had taken place during his spell at in charge at St James' Park, much to the embarrassment and anger of the Board of Directors. The packed meeting took place in the Sidwell Street Methodist Church Hall.

* Iley later took Exeter City to the County Court to press for damages for wrongful dismissal. After an initial appearance, and approaching the club to settle out of court, the long running dispute finally came to a conclusion when Iley announced in February 1986 that an amicable settlement had indeed been reached between himself and Exeter City.

* John Hore, who was caretaker manager after the departure of Iley was not happy when he claimed he had been promised the manager's job by the Exeter City chairman, but was overlooked in favour of Colin Appleton. Hore said: "I have been led up the garden path. I cannot accept the way on which the chairman and the Board of Directors have conducted themselves in this matter."

* Exeter City had four days to forget in March 1985. They travelled to Scunthorpe United on the 19th and were thrashed 7-1, with Trevor Morgan getting the Grecians' goal. Four days later they were on the road again, this time to Colchester United, and once again City were soundly beaten, losing 5-1, with Morgan again getting his name on the score sheet.

* Worryingly from the financial point of view, average attendances for league matches at St James' Park were down by 1,000 per game to 2,352. The lowest attendance of the season was just 1,825 for the visit of Colchester United. Only 1,859 bothered to attend the last home match of the season against Tranmere Rovers.

* Considering it was another poor season of football, striker Ray Pratt did remarkably well, top scoring with 9 goals. He would probably have got more had he not missed the last 12 matches through injury.

* Pratt was also the only City player that season to score a hat-trick in league fixture, coming against Torquay United at St James' Park on Boxing Day, in a thrilling 4-3 victory.

* Steve Neville was transferred to Bristol City in November 1984 for a fee of £12,000, plus Trevor Morgan making a move in the opposite direction as part of the deal.

EXETER CITY 1985-86

Back Row: Club Apprentices

Middle Row: Mike Radford (Youth Development Officer), ??? , Darren Gale, Jim McNichol, Aiden McCaffery, John Shaw, Nicky Marker, Keith Viney, Graeme Kirkup, Phil King, Colin Appleton (Manager).

Front Row: Martin Ling, Ray Pratt, Tony Kellow, Trevor Morgan, Gary Jackson, Steve Harrower, Alan Crawford

City's league results

|  | Home | Away |
|---|---|---|
| Aldershot | 2-0 | 0-4 |
| Burnley | 0-2 | 1-3 |
| Cambridge United | 0-0 | 1-1 |
| Chester City | 1-3 | 1-2 |
| Colchester United | 2-2 | 1-1 |
| Crewe Alexandra | 1-2 | 1-0 |
| Hartlepool United | 1-2 | 0-0 |
| Halifax Town | 1-0 | 0-1 |
| Hereford United | 3-2 | 1-4 |
| Mansfield Town | 0-1 | 1-2 |
| Northampton Town | 1-2 | 2-2 |
| Orient | 1-1 | 2-2 |
| Peterborough United | 1-0 | 1-1 |
| Port Vale | 1-0 | 0-0 |
| Preston North End | 3-0 | 2-2 |
| Rochdale | 2-0 | 1-1 |
| Scunthorpe United | 2-0 | 0-1 |
| Southend United | 0-2 | 0-2 |
| Stockport County | 1-0 | 1-1 |
| Swindon Town | 0-3 | 1-2 |
| Torquay Unied | 2-2 | 2-1 |
| Tranmere Rovers | 1-0 | 1-0 |
| Wrexham | 0-1 | 1-1 |

F.A. Cup

| Cardiff City | H 2-1 | R1 |
|---|---|---|
| Bristol City | A 2-1 | R2 |
| Everton | A 0-1 | R3 |

Football League Cup

| Plymouth Argyle | A 1-2 | R1 |
|---|---|---|
| Plymouth Argyle | H 2-0 | R1 |
| Aston Villa | H 1-4 | R2 |
| Aston Villa | A 1-8 | R2 |

Freight Rover Trophy

| Wolverhampton Wanderers | H | 1-1 |
|---|---|---|
| Torquay United | A | 0-1 |

CITY MANAGER 1985-86
Colin Appleton - Appointed June 1985

## CITY PLAYING SQUAD 1985-86

| Name | Pos | Signed From | Apps | Gls |
|---|---|---|---|---|
| Alan Crawford | W | Bristol City Jul 1985 | 33 | 3 |
| Darren Gale | F | Swansea City Sep 1985 | 17(1) | 5 |
| Mel Gwinnett | G | Bradford City Aug 1985 | 2 | |
| Steve Harrower | M | Dawlish Town Jan 1984 | 32(2) | 6 |
| John Impey | D | Torquay United Aug 1985 | 26 | |
| Garry Jackson | M | Manchester City Sep 1985 | 31(1) | 2 |
| Peter Johnson | D | Whitby Town Mar 1986 | 5 | |
| Tony Kellow | F | Newport County Jul 1985 | 24(9) | 9 |
| Danny Keough | M | Manchester United Oct 1985 | 31(1) | |
| Alan Kimble | D | Charlton Athletic Aug 1985 | 1 | |
| Gary Kimble | W | Charlton Athletic Aug 1985 | 1 | |
| Phil King | D | Apprentice Jan 1985 | 9(2) | |
| Graeme Kirkup | D | Apprentice May 1983 | 8 | |
| Martin Ling | M | Apprentice Jan 1984 | 45 | 8 |
| Aiden McCaffrey | D | Bristol Rovers Jul 1985 | 31(2) | |
| Jim McNichol | D | Brentford Jul 1984 | 45 | 5 |
| Nicky Marker | D | Apprentice May 1983 | 40 | |
| Richard Massey | D | Apprentice Jul 1984 | 2 | |
| Trevor Morgan | F | Bristol City Nov 1984 | 4 | |
| Ray Pratt | F | Merthyr Tydfil Mar 1980 | 10(8) | 2 |
| John Shaw | G | Bristol City Jul 1985 | 44 | |
| Keith Viney | D | Portsmouth Aug 1982 | 45 | 2 |
| Mark Walsh | M | Auckland (New Zealand) Aug 1985 | 0(1) | |
| Warren Ward | F | Lincoln City Feb 1986 | 14 | 3 |
| Andrew Webber | F | Swansea City Sep 1985 | 1 | |
| Paul Williams | F | Saltash United Aug 1985 | 1(1) | |
| Own Goals | | | | 2 |

Fourth Division 1985-86

| | P | W | D | L | F | A | Pts |
|---|---|---|---|---|---|---|---|
| Swindon Town | 46 | 32 | 6 | 8 | 82 | 43 | 102 |
| Chester City | 46 | 23 | 15 | 8 | 83 | 50 | 84 |
| Mansfield Town | 46 | 23 | 12 | 11 | 74 | 47 | 81 |
| Port Vale | 46 | 21 | 16 | 9 | 67 | 37 | 79 |
| Orient | 46 | 20 | 12 | 14 | 79 | 64 | 72 |
| Colchester United | 46 | 19 | 13 | 14 | 88 | 63 | 70 |
| Hartlepool United | 46 | 20 | 10 | 16 | 68 | 67 | 70 |
| Northampton Town | 46 | 18 | 10 | 18 | 79 | 58 | 64 |
| Southend United | 46 | 18 | 10 | 18 | 69 | 67 | 64 |
| Hereford United | 46 | 18 | 10 | 18 | 74 | 73 | 64 |
| Stockport County | 46 | 17 | 13 | 16 | 63 | 71 | 64 |
| Crewe Alexandra | 46 | 18 | 9 | 19 | 54 | 61 | 63 |
| Wrexham | 46 | 17 | 9 | 20 | 68 | 80 | 60 |
| Burnley | 46 | 16 | 11 | 19 | 60 | 65 | 59 |
| Scunthorpe United | 46 | 15 | 14 | 17 | 50 | 55 | 59 |
| Aldershot | 46 | 17 | 7 | 22 | 66 | 74 | 58 |
| Peterborough United | 46 | 13 | 17 | 16 | 52 | 64 | 56 |
| Rochdale | 46 | 14 | 13 | 19 | 57 | 77 | 55 |
| Tranmere Rovers | 46 | 15 | 9 | 22 | 65 | 80 | 54 |
| Halifax Town | 46 | 14 | 12 | 20 | 60 | 71 | 54 |
| Exeter City | 46 | 13 | 15 | 18 | 47 | 59 | 54 |
| Cambridge United | 46 | 15 | 9 | 22 | 65 | 80 | 54 |
| Preston North End | 46 | 11 | 10 | 25 | 54 | 89 | 43 |
| Torquay United | 46 | 9 | 10 | 27 | 43 | 88 | 37 |

* Newly appointed manager Colin Appleton faced a monumental task having a small playing budget and attempting to improve the fortunes of the club of the previous two seasons. Unfortunately, City ended the season in 21st place, and played some of their home fixtures in front of less than 2,000 fans at St James' Park.

* Two notable signings right at the start of the season, were the Kimble twins, Alan and Gary, who moved to Exeter City on loan from Charlton Athletic. This was the first time that twins had played for the City first team, although their stay was a brief one and they only featured in one league match, a 2-0 home defeat against Southend United.

* With a small playing budget, Appleton used the loan market and also signed non-contract players. On loan, in addition to the Kimble's came Warren Ward from Lincoln City. Non-contract players were Peter Johnson (Whitby Town), Mark Walsh (who had been playing in New Zealand), Andrew Webber (Swansea City) and Paul Williams (Saltash United).

* Goalscoring proved to be a problem for the team, and at one stage there was a run of six consecutive league matches without City finding the back of the opposition net.

* Leading goalscorer with 9 league goals, was the 'evergreen' Tony Kellow, who had been signed from Newport County, for a third spell with the club. Winger and youth product Martin Ling, netted 8 league goals, his best season since making a first team breakthrough, missing just one league game.

* Alarm bells started to ring as regards the club's financial position, with average attendances for league matches at St James' Park having slumped to just 1,972, in comparison to 2,352 the previous season.

* The highest attendance of the season in a Fourth Division match at St James' Park was 2,868 for the opening day of the season fixture against Port Vale. The lowest of the season was just 1,369 when City played out a goalless draw with Cambridge United.

* Richard Massey became the latest product of the Exeter City youth scheme to make his first team debut when lining up against Northampton Town in April 1986. He joined fellow squad members, Graeme Kirkup, Phil King, Nicky Marker and Martin Ling, to play league football for the Grecians that season.

* In the FA Cup, Exeter put up a tremendous fight at Goodison Park in the third round of the FA Cup, and it a late goal to ensure that their hosts went through to the next stage before an attendance of just under 23,000.

* The Grecians had reached the second round stage of The Football League Cup, which was played on a home and away basis. After going down 1-4 at home to Aston Villa, they faced a huge task in the second leg, and suffered their record League Cup defeat as they lost 8-1. Alan Crawford netted for City.

* Tony Kellow scored in three successive league matches from the penalty spot, and they proved to be the only goals scored in each of the games. His first came against Halifax Town at the Park (1-0 on 23rd October) and that was followed by one against Hartlepool United (also at home, 1-2) and then one at Peterborough United (1-1).

* One of Colin Appleton's most successful signings was midfielder Danny Keough, who had previously played for Manchester United. He was signed in October 1985 and was virtually an ever present after making his debut against Hartlepool United at St. James' Park.

*Despite the disappointing season, City had a run of three successive league wins on two occasions. They defeated Preston North End, Crewe Alexandra and Aldershot, and later in the season won against Hereford United, Torquay United and Rochdale.

EXETER CITY 1986-87
Back row: Chris Small, Richard Hancox, Clive Nelson, Warren Hadley, Richard Smeath, Richard Massey, Jamie Harris, Scott Hiley, Mark Robson.
Middle row: Steve Pugh, Mel Gwinnett, Sean Priddle, Nicky Marker, Andy Watson, Keith Viney, Aiden McCaffrey, John Shaw, Darren Gale, Colin Appleton (Manager).
Front row: Paul Batty, Steve Harrower, Brendan O'Connell, Tony Kellow, Dean Roberts, Danny Keough, Gary Jackson

### City's league results

| | Home | Away |
|---|---|---|
| Aldershot | 4-0 | 1-2 |
| Burnley | 3-0 | 0-0 |
| Cambridge United | 1-1 | 2-2 |
| Cardiff City | 0-0 | 0-0 |
| Colchester United | 2-0 | 1-1 |
| Crewe Alexandra | 1-0 | 2-2 |
| Hartlepool United | 2-0 | 0-1 |
| Halifax Town | 2-2 | 0-2 |
| Hereford United | 1-0 | 1-1 |
| Lincoln City | 2-0 | 1-1 |
| Northampton Town | 1-1 | 0-4 |
| Orient | 1-0 | 0-2 |
| Peterborough United | 1-1 | 2-2 |
| Preston North End | 1-2 | 1-2 |
| Rochdale | 1-1 | 0-0 |
| Scunthorpe United | 0-0 | 1-3 |
| Southend United | 0-0 | 1-2 |
| Stockport County | 4-0 | 0-0 |
| Swansea City | 2-2 | 0-1 |
| Torquay United | 2-2 | 1-1 |
| Tranmere Rovers | 1-0 | 0-1 |
| Wolverhampton Wanderers | 1-3 | 2-2 |
| Wrexham | 4-2 | 0-0 |

### F.A. Cup
| | | | |
|---|---|---|---|
| Cambridge United | H | 1-1 | R1 |
| Cambridge United | A | 0-2 | R1R |

### Football League Cup
| | | | |
|---|---|---|---|
| Newport County | H | 0-0 | R1 |
| Newport County | A | 0-1 | R1 |

### Freight Rover Trophy
| | | | |
|---|---|---|---|
| Bristol City | H | 1-1 | R1 |
| Bristol Rovers | A | 1-1 | R1 |
| Port Vale | H | 0-1 | R1 |

### CITY MANAGER 1986-87
Colin Appleton - Appointed June 1985

### Fourth Division 1986-87

| | P | W | D | L | F | A | Pts |
|---|---|---|---|---|---|---|---|
| Northampton Town | 46 | 30 | 9 | 7 | 103 | 53 | 99 |
| Preston North End | 46 | 26 | 12 | 8 | 72 | 47 | 90 |
| Southend United | 46 | 25 | 5 | 16 | 68 | 55 | 80 |
| Wolverhampton Wanderers | 46 | 24 | 7 | 15 | 69 | 50 | 79 |
| Colchester United | 46 | 21 | 7 | 18 | 64 | 56 | 70 |
| Aldershot | 46 | 20 | 10 | 16 | 64 | 57 | 70 |
| Orient | 46 | 20 | 9 | 17 | 64 | 61 | 69 |
| Scunthorpe United | 46 | 18 | 12 | 16 | 73 | 57 | 66 |
| Wrexham | 46 | 15 | 29 | 11 | 70 | 51 | 65 |
| Peterborough United | 46 | 17 | 14 | 15 | 57 | 50 | 65 |
| Cambridge United | 46 | 17 | 11 | 18 | 60 | 62 | 62 |
| Swansea City | 46 | 17 | 11 | 18 | 56 | 61 | 62 |
| Cardiff City | 46 | 15 | 16 | 15 | 48 | 50 | 61 |
| Exeter City | 46 | 11 | 23 | 12 | 53 | 49 | 56 |
| Halifax Town | 46 | 15 | 10 | 21 | 59 | 74 | 55 |
| Hereford United | 46 | 14 | 11 | 21 | 60 | 61 | 53 |
| Crewe Alexandra | 46 | 13 | 14 | 19 | 70 | 72 | 53 |
| Hartlepool United | 46 | 11 | 18 | 17 | 44 | 65 | 51 |
| Stockport County | 46 | 13 | 12 | 21 | 40 | 69 | 51 |
| Tranmere Rovers | 46 | 11 | 17 | 18 | 54 | 72 | 50 |
| Rochdale | 46 | 11 | 17 | 18 | 54 | 73 | 50 |
| Burnley | 46 | 12 | 13 | 21 | 53 | 74 | 49 |
| Torquay United | 46 | 10 | 18 | 18 | 56 | 72 | 48 |
| Lincoln City | 46 | 12 | 12 | 22 | 45 | 65 | 48 |

### CITY PLAYING SQUAD 1986-87

| Name | Pos | Signed From | Apps | Gls |
|---|---|---|---|---|
| Paul Batty | M | Chesterfield Jul 1986 | 30(3) | 2 |
| Steve Biggins | F | Trelleborg FF (Sweden) Oct 1986 | 14 | 2 |
| Martin Butler | F | York City Feb 1967 | 4 | 1 |
| Dean Edwards | F | Wolverhampton Wanderers Mar 1987 | 11 | 5 |
| Peter Foley | F | Witney Town Mar 1987 | 1 | |
| Darren Gale | F | Swansea City Sep 1985 | 2 | |
| Mel Gwinnett | G | Bradford City Aug 1985 | 3 | |
| Steve Harrower | M | Dawlish Town Jan 1984 | 30(4) | |
| Garry Jackson | M | Manchester City Sep 1985 | 3 | |
| Sean Joyce | M | Doncaster Rovers Nov 1986 | 1 | |
| Tony Kellow | F | Newport County Jul 1985 | 22(11) | 15 |
| Danny Keough | M | Manchester United Oct 1985 | 40 | |
| Aiden McCaffrey | D | Bristol Rovers Jul 1985 | 24(1) | |
| Nicky Marker | D | Apprentice May 1983 | 43 | 1 |
| Richard Massey | D | Apprentice Jul 1984 | 3 | |
| Brendan O'Connell | F | Portsmouth Jul 1986 | 34(8) | 8 |
| Paul Olsson | M | Hull City Mar 1987 | 8 | |
| Sean Priddle | M | Wimbledon Jul 1986 | 18 | 1 |
| Stephen Pugh | D | Torquay United Aug 1986 | 23(1) | 1 |
| Dean Roberts | F | Bolton Wanderers Jul 1986 | 23(2) | 7 |
| Mark Robson | W | Apprentice Dec 1986 | 26 | 7 |
| John Shaw | G | Bristol City Jul 1985 | 43 | |
| Shaun Taylor | D | Bideford Dec 1986 | 23 | |
| Keith Viney | D | Portsmouth Aug 1982 | 45 | 1 |
| Andy Watson | D | Huddersfield Town Jul 1986 | 29 | 1 |
| Paul Williams | F | Saltash United Aug 1985 | 3(7) | |
| Own Goals | | | | 1 |

* At last there were signs of an improvement in Exeter City's fortunes, as they finished in 14th place in the Fourth Division. The improved form was also reflected in an increase in average attendances (2,628) at St James' Park in comparison to the 1,972 the previous season.

* Once again Tony Kellow was the main goalscorer, however new signing Brendan O'Connell and Dean Roberts also made useful contributions, as did Dean Edwards who only featured in the final 11 matches of the season, having been signed from Wolverhampton Wanderers.

* Exeter City obtained international clearance to sign 32-year-old Steve Biggins from Swedish club, Trelleborg FF in October 1986. Biggins had previously played for Hednesford Town, Shrewsbury Town, Oxford United, Derby Wolverhampton Wanderers and Port Vale. After a promising start at City, Biggins' form fell away and he left to join Telford United.

* There were no joy in the Cups, as the Grecians made disappointing first round exits in the FA Cup, the Football League Cup and the Freight Rover Trophy.

* Highest attendance of the season at St James' Park for a league fixture was 4,915 for the very last home fixture of the season, when Wolverhampton Wanderers were the visitors, and they brought a large travelling support.

* The lowest attendance of the season at St. James' Park for a league fixture was 1,525 when Scunthorpe United were the visitors in April 1987.

* Kellow netted six times from the penalty spot, and only two of those games ended in defeat. He scored from the spot in two successive games at Lincoln City (1-1) and Rochdale (1-1) at St James' Park.

* Non-contract player Peter Foley, better known for his time at Oxford United, where he scored 71 goals in 277 league matches, was signed from Witney Town in March 1987. However, he only played in one match for the Grecians, a 2-2 draw at Peterborough United.

* One of manager Colin Appleton's best signings during his stay at the club, was that of central defender Shaun Taylor from Bideford in December 1986. He went on to play 23 league matches that season, but by the time he left the club in a £200,000 transfer to Swindon Town in July 1991, he had played in City's Fourth Division championship winning team of 1990 and featured in 200 league games, scoring 26 goals.

* Two players were signed on loan during the season, Martin Butler and Sean Joyce. Butler arrived from York City in February 1987 and his only goal scored in the four games that he played for the Grecians came on his debut in a 4-2 home win against Wrexham. Joyce played just one match for Exeter, against Northampton Town, after being signed from Doncaster Rovers in November 1986.

* Apprentice winger, Mark Robson, was signed on a full contract in December 1986, but not before he had already featured in a handful of first team matches, the first of which was against Lincoln City two months earlier, as he scored in the 2-0 home win. He was to score seven league goals in a very promising first season.

* Results 'on the road' were pretty disappointing to say the least. Not a single win was recorded in league fixtures, although City did draw in 13 of the 23 away matches played, the most of any team in the Fourth Division. Their paltry tally of 16 goals scored was the worst in the division.

* City drew no fewer than 23 of the 46 league matches played, the most in the entire Fourth Division. They were everyone's favourites on the pools coupon! Losing just twice at St James' Park, City also had the best home defensive record in the division, conceding just 17 goals at St. James' Park.

CITY PLAYING SQUAD 1987-88

| Name | Pos | Signed From | Apps | Gls |
|------|-----|-------------|------|-----|
| Paul Batty | M | Chesterfield Jul 1986 | 29(3) | 6 |
| Roy Carter | M | Newport County Jul 1987 | 37(4) | 2 |
| Eamonn Collins | M | Portsmouth Nov 1987 | 8(1) | |
| Richard Cooper | M | Lincoln City Jul 1987 | 30(3) | 1 |
| John Delve | M | Gloucester City Oct 1987 | 12(1) | 1 |
| Dean Edwards | F | Wolverhampton Wanderers Mar 1987 | 40(3) | 12 |
| Mel Gwinnett | G | Bradford City Aug 1985 | 24 | |
| Jamie Harris | F | Apprentice Aug 1986 | 5(4) | 1 |
| Steve Harrower | M | Dawlish Town Jan 1984 | 43(3) | 2 |
| Scott Hiley | D | Apprentice Aug 1986 | 12(3) | 1 |
| Tony Kellow | F | Newport County Jul 1985 | 5(11) | 4 |
| Nicky Marker | D | Apprentice May 1983 | 11 | |
| Richard Massey | D | Apprentice Jul 1984 | 17(6) | 1 |
| Simon Milton | M | Ipswich Town Nov 1987 | 2 | 3 |
| Gordon Nisbet | D | Plymouth Argyle Jun 1987 | 12 | |
| Brendan O'Connell | F | Portsmouth Jul 1986 | 39 | 11 |
| Paul Olsson | M | Hull City Mar 1987 | 30(5) | 2 |
| Stephen Phillips | F | Peterborough United Sept 1987 | 5(1) | 1 |
| Darren Rowbotham | F | Plymouth Argyle Oct 1987 | 20(3) | 2 |
| John Shaw | G | Bristol City Jul 1985 | 22 | |
| Shaun Taylor | D | Bideford Dec 1986 | 41 | 1 |
| Keith Viney | D | Portsmouth Aug 1982 | 46 | |
| Andy Watson | D | Huddersfield Town Jul 1986 | 12(1) | |
| Paul Williams | F | Saltash United Aug 1985 | 4(2) | 1 |
| Own Goals | | | | 1 |

City's league results

| | Home | Away |
|---|------|------|
| Bolton Wanderers | 1-1 | 0-1 |
| Burnley | 1-2 | 0-3 |
| Cambridge United | 3-0 | 1-2 |
| Cardiff City | 0-2 | 2-3 |
| Carlisle United | 1-1 | 0-0 |
| Colchester United | 0-2 | 2-0 |
| Crewe Alexandra | 3-1 | 0-0 |
| Darlington | 4-1 | 1-4 |
| Hartlepool United | 1-0 | 1-3 |
| Halifax Town | 1-2 | 0-2 |
| Hereford United | 2-2 | 1-1 |
| Leyton Orient | 2-3 | 3-2 |
| Newport County | 3-0 | 1-1 |
| Peterborough United | 0-1 | 1-1 |
| Rochdale | 1-1 | 0-0 |
| Scarborough | 1-0 | 1-3 |
| Scunthorpe United | 1-1 | 1-1 |
| Stockport County | 2-1 | 1-2 |
| Swansea City | 3-1 | 2-0 |
| Torquay United | 0-1 | 1-1 |
| Tranmere Rovers | 0-1 | 1-2 |
| Wolverhampton Wanderers | 2-4 | 0-3 |
| Wrexham | 1-1 | 0-3 |

F.A. Cup

| | | |
|---|---|---|
| Leyton Orient | A 0-2 | R1 |

Football League Cup

| | | |
|---|---|---|
| AFC Bournemouth | A 1-1 | R1 |
| AFC Bournemouth | H 1-3 | R1 |

Sherpa Van Trophy

| | | |
|---|---|---|
| Port Vale | A 0-2 | R1 |
| Newport County | H 0-1 | R1 |

CITY MANAGER 1987-88
Colin Appleton - Appointed June 1985
John Delve (Caretaker Manager)
- Appointed December 1987

The 1987-88 campaign was to be last season that supporters were able to see the legendary Tony Kellow wear the red an white of Exeter City. In his final season with the club he netted four goals in sixteen outings. By then he had firmly etched his name in the record books, becoming the Grecians all-time leading goalscorer with a tally of 129 goals in his three spells with the club. Having signed for Exeter from Falmouth Town, Kellow also played for Blackpool, Plymouth Argyle, Swansea City and Newport County. His name lives on in 2012 as a show on local radio, Radio Exe, is named in his honour - 'Kellow's Bootlaces.'

Fourth Division 1987-88

| | P | W | D | L | F | A | Pts |
|---|---|---|---|---|---|---|-----|
| Wolverhampton Wanderers | 46 | 27 | 9 | 10 | 82 | 43 | 90 |
| Cardiff City | 46 | 24 | 13 | 9 | 66 | 41 | 85 |
| Bolton Wanderers | 46 | 22 | 12 | 12 | 66 | 42 | 78 |
| Scunthorpe United | 46 | 20 | 17 | 9 | 76 | 51 | 77 |
| Torquay United | 46 | 21 | 14 | 11 | 66 | 41 | 77 |
| Swansea City | 46 | 20 | 10 | 16 | 62 | 56 | 70 |
| Peterborough United | 46 | 20 | 10 | 16 | 52 | 53 | 70 |
| Leyton Orient | 46 | 19 | 12 | 15 | 85 | 63 | 69 |
| Colchester United | 46 | 19 | 10 | 17 | 47 | 51 | 67 |
| Burnley | 46 | 20 | 7 | 19 | 57 | 62 | 67 |
| Wrexham | 46 | 20 | 6 | 20 | 69 | 58 | 66 |
| Scarborough | 46 | 17 | 14 | 15 | 56 | 48 | 65 |
| Darlington | 46 | 18 | 11 | 17 | 71 | 69 | 65 |
| Tranmere Rovers | 46 | 19 | 9 | 18 | 61 | 53 | 64* |
| Cambridge United | 46 | 16 | 13 | 17 | 50 | 52 | 61 |
| Hartlepool United | 46 | 15 | 14 | 17 | 50 | 57 | 59 |
| Crewe Alexandra | 46 | 13 | 19 | 14 | 57 | 53 | 58 |
| Halifax Town | 46 | 14 | 14 | 18 | 54 | 59 | 55** |
| Hereford United | 46 | 14 | 12 | 20 | 41 | 59 | 54 |
| Stockport County | 46 | 12 | 15 | 19 | 44 | 58 | 51 |
| Rochdale | 46 | 11 | 15 | 20 | 47 | 76 | 48 |
| Exeter City | 46 | 11 | 13 | 22 | 53 | 68 | 46 |
| Carlisle United | 46 | 12 | 8 | 26 | 57 | 86 | 44 |
| Newport County | 46 | 6 | 7 | 33 | 35 | 105 | 25 |

* Tranmere had 2 points deducted.
** Halifax Town had 1 point deducted.

*After improving their league position the previous season, City slipped back towards the bottom of the Fourth Division, and were knocked out of both the FA Cup, the Football League Cup and the Sherpa Van Trophy at the first round stage.

* Manager Colin Appleton left the club in December 1987, resigning due to personal reasons. Midfielder John Delve, took over as caretaker manager until the end of the season, having returned to the club, having played for Gloucester City, and working on the Grecians' lottery scheme.

* Delve was unhappy at the end of the season when he was overlooked for the manager's job on a permanent basis, with Terry Cooper being appointed instead. He then left the club. Whilst Delve felt he was hard done by, the appointment of Cooper coincided with some very good times for Exeter City.

* One significant transfer that did take place was a player exchange deal involving Nicky Marker moving to Plymouth Argyle, with Darren Rowbotham arriving at St. James' Park. Both moves proved to be beneficial for the players concerned.

* Simon Milton was brought in on loan from Ipswich Town and although he only played twice, he scored three goals. He netted twice on his debut in a 2-1 home win against Stockport County, and then scored in the following match, a 4-1 defeat at Darlington.

* Highest attendance of the season for a league match at St James' Park was 6,281 for the visit of Torquay United, 3rd October 1987. The lowest league attendance at the Park was just 1,515 when Darlington were the visitors, 30th April 1988.

* The average attendance for league matches at St James' Park was 2,463, down from 2,628 of the previous season. Needless to say there was very little money available for manager Colin Appleton, or caretaker John Delve to attract players to Exeter.

* Legendary goalscorer, Tony Kellow, was to play his final season at the club, used in a handful of matches and mainly a substitute. He had made a total of 332 league appearances for Exeter City in three spells with the club, and scored 129 goals.

* For the fourth consecutive season, Exeter City opened their league campaign with a win, this time 3-0 against Cambridge United, with new signing Roy Carter scoring twice, and the other goal coming from Brendan O'Connell. The attendance of only 2,650 for that first game of the season, must have been a little worrying.

* Exeter had a terrible second half of the season, for they recorded just four wins in 23 matches, against Swansea City (home 3-1), Hartlepool United (home 1-0), Scarborough (home 1-0) and Darlington (home 4-1).

* They also went 19 games without winning an away match in the league and had to wait until the following season before they were successful again, stretching the winless run to 23 matches.

* Despite the less than impressive season, one player did score a hat-trick. Dean Edwards achieved the feat in the 4-1 home win over Darlington. He was top scorer in league games with 12 goals.

* Two youth players made the first team break through. Scott Hiley made his debut against Burnley in October 1987, whilst Jamie Harris lined up for his first start against Peterborough United the following March.

* Exeter attracted their then lowest attendance for a Football League Trophy match (known as the Sherpa Van Trophy for 1987-88) when only 1,006 took the trouble to go along to St James' Park for the visit of Newport County. The Grecians lost 1-0 to a side that eventually finished rock bottom of the Fourth Division.

Back Row: Terry Cooper (Manager), Chris Banks, Tommy Langley, Graham Withey, Mel Gwinnett, Shaun Taylor, Richard Smeath, Keith Viney, Jamie Harris, Lee Rogers, Mike Radford (Youth Development Officer).
Middle row: Steve Neville, Richard Cooper, Scott Hiley, Paul Batty, Chris Small , Darren Rowbotham, Steve Harrower.
Front Row: Jonathan Hawkins , Chris Vinnicombe, Stuart Smith, Martin Parker, Alan Roberts, Jimmy Dugdale, Paul Gadson, Robert Dodds, Darren Jarman

| City's league results | Home | Away |
|---|---|---|
| Bolton Wanderers | | |
| Burnley | 3-0 | 0-3 |
| Cambridge United | 0-3 | 0-2 |
| Carlisle United | 3-0 | 0-1 |
| Colchester United | 4-2 | 0-4 |
| Crewe Alexandra | 1-2 | 1-2 |
| Darlington | 2-1 | 2-2 |
| Doncaster Rovers | 3-0 | 1-2 |
| Grimsby Town | 2-1 | 1-2 |
| Halifax Town | 4-1 | 3-0 |
| Hartlepool United | 2-1 | 2-2 |
| Hereford United | 3-1 | 0-1 |
| Leyton Orient | 1-1 | 0-4 |
| Lincoln City | 0-1 | 0-2 |
| Peterborough United | 3-1 | 1-0 |
| Rochdale | 5-1 | 1-2 |
| Rotherham United | 0-0 | 1-0 |
| Scarborough | 1-0 | 1-2 |
| Scunthorpe United | 2-2 | 0-2 |
| Stockport County | 2-2 | 0-4 |
| Torquay United | 3-0 | 4-0 |
| Tranmere Rovers | 0-1 | 0-2 |
| Wrexham | 0-2 | 0-3 |
| York City | 2-0 | 1-3 |

| F.A. Cup | | | |
|---|---|---|---|
| Bognor Regis Town | A | 1-2 | R1 |

| Football League Cup | | | |
|---|---|---|---|
| Bristol City | A | 0-1 | R1 |
| Bristol City | H | 0-1 | R1 |

| Sherpa Van Trophy | | | |
|---|---|---|---|
| Bristol City | A | 0-2 | PR |
| Bristol Rovers | H | 1-1 | PR |

CITY MANAGER 1988-89
Terry Cooper - Appointed May 1988

Fourth Division 1988-89

| | P | W | D | L | F | A | Pts |
|---|---|---|---|---|---|---|---|
| Rotherham United | 46 | 22 | 16 | 8 | 76 | 35 | 82 |
| Tranmere Rovers | 46 | 21 | 17 | 8 | 62 | 43 | 80 |
| Crewe Alexandra | 46 | 21 | 15 | 10 | 67 | 48 | 78 |
| Scunthorpe United | 46 | 21 | 14 | 11 | 77 | 57 | 77 |
| Scarborough | 46 | 21 | 14 | 11 | 67 | 52 | 77 |
| Leyton Orient | 46 | 21 | 12 | 13 | 86 | 50 | 75 |
| Wrexham | 46 | 19 | 14 | 13 | 77 | 63 | 71 |
| Cambridge United | 46 | 18 | 14 | 14 | 71 | 62 | 68 |
| Grimsby Town | 46 | 17 | 15 | 14 | 65 | 59 | 66 |
| Lincoln City | 46 | 18 | 10 | 18 | 64 | 60 | 64 |
| York City | 46 | 17 | 13 | 16 | 62 | 63 | 64 |
| Carlisle United | 46 | 15 | 15 | 16 | 53 | 52 | 60 |
| Exeter City | 46 | 18 | 6 | 22 | 65 | 68 | 60 |
| Torquay United | 46 | 17 | 8 | 21 | 45 | 60 | 59 |
| Hereford United | 46 | 14 | 16 | 16 | 66 | 72 | 58 |
| Burnley | 46 | 14 | 13 | 19 | 52 | 61 | 55 |
| Peterborough United | 46 | 14 | 12 | 20 | 52 | 74 | 54 |
| Rochdale | 46 | 13 | 14 | 19 | 56 | 82 | 53 |
| Hartlepool United | 46 | 14 | 10 | 22 | 50 | 78 | 52 |
| Stockport County | 46 | 10 | 21 | 15 | 54 | 52 | 51 |
| Halifax Town | 46 | 13 | 11 | 22 | 69 | 75 | 50 |
| Colchester United | 46 | 12 | 14 | 20 | 60 | 70 | 50 |
| Doncaster Rovers | 46 | 13 | 10 | 23 | 49 | 78 | 49 |
| Darlington | 46 | 8 | 18 | 20 | 53 | 76 | 42 |

CITY PLAYING SQUAD 1988-89

| Name | Pos | Signed From | Apps | Gls |
|---|---|---|---|---|
| Chris Banks | D | Port Vale May 1988 | 43(2) | 1 |
| Paul Batty | M | Chesterfield Jul 1986 | 15 | 1 |
| Ian Benjamin | F | Chester City Feb 1989 | 20 | 3 |
| Richard Cooper | M | Lincoln City Jul 1987 | 25(4) | 1 |
| Richard Dryden | D | Bristol Rovers Mar 1989 | 21 | |
| Mel Gwinnett | G | Bradford City Aug 1985 | 17 | |
| Carl Harris | W | Rochdale Dec 1988 | 11(5) | 1 |
| Jamie Harris | F | Apprentice Aug 1986 | 1(4) | |
| Steve Harrower | M | Dawlish Town Jan 1984 | 18 | |
| Herbie Heath | D | Darlaston Feb 1989 | 3(2) | |
| Scott Hiley | D | Apprentice Aug 1986 | 36(1) | 5 |
| Mark Jones | D | Walsall Nov 1988 | 5 | |
| Tommy Langley | F | Aldershot Jul 1988 | 14(7) | 2 |
| Brian McDermott | W | Cardiff City Feb 1989 | 19 | 1 |
| Kevin Miller | G | Newquay Mar 1989 | 3 | |
| Steve Neville | W | Bristol City Jul 1988 | 38 | 14 |
| Martin Parker | M | Trainee Jul 1986 | 0(1) | |
| Paul Roberts | D | Tampa Bay Rowdies Dec 1988 | 3 | |
| Lee Rogers | D | Bristol City Jun 1988 | 45 | |
| Darren Rowbotham | F | Plymouth Argyle Oct 1987 | 45 | 20 |
| Keith Smith | F | Alfreton Town Jan 1989 | 2(13) | 2 |
| Shaun Taylor | D | Bideford Dec 1986 | 46 | 6 |
| Steve Tupling | M | Cardiff City Jan 1989 | 8(1) | 1 |
| Keith Viney | D | Portsmouth Aug 1982 | 3 | |
| Chris Vinnicombe | D | Trainee Jul 1986 | 21(4) | |
| Dave Walter | G | Bideford Nov 1988 | 26 | |
| Graham Withey | F | Cheltenham Town Jul 1988 | 5(2) | 2 |
| Richard Young | F | Southend United Mar 1989 | 13(1) | 4 |
| Own Goals | | | | 1 |

* The appointment of Terry Cooper in May 1988 was like a breath of fresh air, with a completely new approach taken by the Yorkshireman on and off the field. His dry sense of humour being a particular feature in the way he handled players and supporters.

* The 1988-89 season was a transitional one for Cooper as he reshaped his playing squad, but at the same time guiding the team to a mid-table position.

*Darren Rowbotham hit 20 league goals, the first City player to do so since Tony Kellow scored 21 in 1981-82. Rowbotham formed a striking partnership with Steve Neville who had returned to the club for a third spell, scoring 14 league goals.

* The one down side of the season was the defeat at non-league Bognor Regis Town in the first round of the F.A. Cup. This prompted Cooper to say: "We were like a soggy pasty."

* Striker Jamie Harris was taken ill on the coach on the way to the game at Leyton Orient, suffering from partial paralysis of one side of his face, dizziness and loss of balance. It was feared that he had meningitis, but tests proved otherwise and he was able to travel back with the team. City lost 4-0 which led to Cooper describing his players as a "team of pansies."

* Having settled into the club as manager, in October 1988, Terry Cooper said: "I am quite confident I can build a good team here. We are three players short of a good team. But the club is in debt and the bank are on our backs. I might just have to wait until the end of the season to get the players I want." A month later Cooper signed a two-year deal with the Grecians, having previously worked without one.

* Midfielder Paul Batty underwent his third knee operation in the space of ten months in January 1989, keeping him out of action for the rest of the season.

* Despite the improvement on the field, attendances at St James' Park still remained low. Only 1,725 turned up for the 4-1 home win over Halifax Town. It was felt that the low crowds was due to the fact that City had gone seven years without any hint of success. The average attendance for a league match at St James' Park was 2,680.

* It was not a good day when City travelled to play at Scunthorpe United in February 1989. Not only did they lose 2-0, but on the way home the team coach broke down on the M5 between Tewkesbury and Cheltenham, and they were left waiting for three hours until they were able to continue their journey back to Exeter.

* As from March 1989, it was announced that City would allow up to six supporters to travel on the team coach to away fixtures at a cost of £85 each. This would include the cost of travel, hotel accommodation and meals. It would help offset the heavy costs of away travel which was averaging £700 per away game.

* Newquay goalkeeper, Kevin Miller, was handed his Football League debut by Exeter City against Rotherham United, after regular number one, Dave Walter was suspended, and second year apprentice keeper, Richard Smeath, was sidelined through injury. Miller kept a clean sheet and at the end of the season was signed on professional terms by the Grecians, the start of a very successful career.

* In May 1989, Financial Director, Murray Couch, was reported as saying that Exeter City were still in debt to the tune of around £500,000. However the club were appreciative of the support they were getting and as a result admission prices would be frozen for the following season at £5 for the Grandstand and £3 for the rest of the ground.

## CITY PLAYING SQUAD 1989-90

| Name | Pos | Signed From | Apps | Gls |
|------|-----|-------------|------|-----|
| Danny Bailey | M | Wealdstone Aug 1989 | 46 | 1 |
| Paul Batty | M | Chesterfield Jul 1986 | 15+5 | 2 |
| Ian Benjamin | F | Chester City Feb 1989 | 10+2 | 1 |
| Mark Cooper | M | Bristol City Oct 1989 | 1+3 | |
| Tony Coyle | W | Northwich Victoria Nov 1989 | 1 | |
| Richard Dryden | D | Bristol Rovers Sep 1988 | 30 | 7 |
| Gary Elkins | D | Fulham Dec 1989 | 5 | |
| Paul Eshelby | W | Endcliffe United Dec 1989 | 1 | |
| Tony Frankland | M | Trainee Jul 1990 | 3+1 | |
| Karl Goddard | D | Bradford City Dec 1989 | 0+1 | |
| Steve Harrower | M | Dawlish Town Jan 1984 | 3+4 | |
| Scott Hiley | D | Apprentice Aug 1986 | 45+1 | |
| Tom Kelly | D | York City Mar 1990 | 11+1 | 2 |
| Brian McDermott | W | Cardiff City Feb 1989 | 38+3 | 3 |
| Jim McNichol | D | Torquay United Aug 1989 | 33 | 8 |
| Angus McPherson | D | Rangers Mar 1990 | 11 | 1 |
| Kevin Miller | G | Newquay Mar 1989 | 28 | |
| Steve Neville | W | Bristol City Jul 1988 | 42 | 14 |
| Lee Rogers | D | Bristol City Jun 1988 | 13+3 | |
| Darren Rowbotham | F | Plymouth Argyle Oct 1987 | 31+1 | 20 |
| Ben Rowe | F | Bristol City Sep 1989 | 4+6 | 2 |
| Clive Stafford | D | Colchester United Feb 1990 | 2 | |
| Kevin Summerfield | M | Plymouth Argyle Mar 1990 | 4 | |
| Shaun Taylor | D | Bideford Dec 1986 | 45+1 | 6 |
| Chris Vinnicombe | D | Trainee Jul 1989 | 14 | 1 |
| Dave Walter | G | Bideford Nov 1988 | 18 | |
| Clive Whitehead | M | Portsmouth Jul 1989 | 36+2 | 5 |
| Richard Young | F | Southend United Mar 1989 | 16+12 | 6 |
| Own Goals | | | | 4 |

## FOURTH DIVISION - SEASON 1989-90

| | P | W | D | L | F | A | Pts |
|------|---|---|---|---|---|---|-----|
| EXETER CITY | 46 | 28 | 5 | 13 | 83 | 48 | 89 |
| Grimsby Town | 46 | 22 | 13 | 11 | 70 | 47 | 79 |
| Southend United | 46 | 22 | 9 | 15 | 61 | 48 | 75 |
| Stockport County | 46 | 21 | 11 | 14 | 68 | 62 | 73 |
| Maidstone United | 46 | 22 | 7 | 17 | 77 | 61 | 73 |
| Cambridge United | 46 | 21 | 10 | 15 | 76 | 66 | 73 |
| Chesterfield | 46 | 19 | 14 | 13 | 63 | 50 | 71 |
| Carlisle United | 46 | 21 | 8 | 17 | 61 | 60 | 71 |
| Peterborough United | 46 | 17 | 17 | 12 | 59 | 46 | 68 |
| Lincoln City | 46 | 18 | 14 | 14 | 48 | 49 | 68 |
| Scunthorpe United | 46 | 17 | 15 | 14 | 69 | 54 | 66 |
| Rochdale | 46 | 20 | 6 | 20 | 52 | 55 | 66 |
| York City | 46 | 16 | 16 | 14 | 55 | 53 | 64 |
| Gillingham | 46 | 17 | 11 | 18 | 46 | 48 | 62 |
| Torquay United | 46 | 15 | 12 | 19 | 53 | 66 | 57 |
| Burnley | 46 | 14 | 14 | 18 | 45 | 55 | 56 |
| Hereford United | 46 | 15 | 10 | 21 | 56 | 62 | 55 |
| Scarborough | 46 | 15 | 10 | 21 | 60 | 73 | 55 |
| Hartlepool United | 46 | 15 | 10 | 21 | 66 | 88 | 55 |
| Doncaster Rovers | 46 | 14 | 9 | 23 | 53 | 60 | 51 |
| Wrexham | 46 | 13 | 12 | 21 | 51 | 67 | 51 |
| Aldershot | 46 | 12 | 14 | 20 | 49 | 69 | 50 |
| Halifax Town | 46 | 12 | 13 | 21 | 57 | 65 | 49 |
| Colchester United | 46 | 11 | 10 | 25 | 48 | 75 | 43 |

### City's league results

| | Home | Away |
|------|------|------|
| Aldershot | 2-0 | 1-0 |
| Burnley | 2-1 | 0-1 |
| Cambridge United | 3-2 | 2-3 |
| Carlisle United | 0-0 | 0-1 |
| Chesterfield | 2-1 | 1-2 |
| Colchester United | 2-1 | 1-0 |
| Doncaster Rovers | 1-0 | 1-2 |
| Gillingham | 3-1 | 1-1 |
| Grimsby Town | 2-1 | 0-1 |
| Halifax Town | 2-0 | 2-1 |
| Hartlepool United | 3-1 | 3-0 |
| Hereford United | 2-0 | 1-2 |
| Lincoln City | 3-0 | 5-1 |
| Maidstone United | 2-0 | 0-1 |
| Peterborough United | 2-0 | 3-4 |
| Rochdale | 5-0 | 0-1 |
| Scarborough | 3-2 | 2-1 |
| Scunthorpe United | 1-0 | 4-5 |
| Southend United | 2-1 | 2-1 |
| Stockport County | 1-1 | 1-2 |
| Torquay United | 3-0 | 2-0 |
| Wrexham | 1-1 | 1-1 |
| York City | 3-1 | 0-3 |

### F.A. Cup

| | | | |
|------|------|-----|-----|
| Dartford | A | 1-1 | R1 |
| Dartford | H | 4-1 | R1R |
| Maidstone United | A | 1-1 | R2 |
| Maidstone United | H | 3-2 | R2R |
| Norwich City | H | 1-1 | R3 |
| Norwich City | A | 0-2 | R3R |

### Football League Cup

| | | | |
|------|------|-----|-----|
| Swansea City | H | 3-0 | R1 |
| Swansea City | A | 1-1 | R1 |
| Blackburn Rovers | H | 3-0 | R2 |
| Blackburn Rovers | A | 1-2 | R2 |
| Blackpool | H | 3-0 | R3 |
| Sunderland | H | 2-2 | R4 |
| Sunderland | A | 2-5 | R4R |

### Leyland Daf Cup

| | | | |
|------|------|-----|-----|
| Torquay United | H | 2-0 | PR |
| Bristol Rovers | A | 0-3 | PR |
| Shrewsbury Town | A | 1-0 | R1 |
| Maidstone United | A | 0-2 | R2 |

### CITY MANAGER 1989-90
Terry Cooper - Appointed May 1988

Terry Cooper became the first Exeter City manager to guide a team to a Football League divisional championship. The former Leeds United and England international had been at the club for just two seasons, but transformed the fortunes of the Grecians with a number of astute signings.

Unbeaten in the league at St James' Park, the team stormed to the Fourth Division championship, being ten points in front of runners up, Grimsby Town.

They also made progress in all three of the cup competitions, which included reaching the third round stage of the FA Cup and the fourth round of the Football League Cup.

* The season ended in triumph for Exeter City as they lifted the Fourth Division Championship trophy, thus being promoted for only the third time in the club's history. It was the first major trophy the Grecians had won since their success in the Third Division South Cup in 1934.

* The Express and Echo reported: 'Exeter City are back in the Third Division. They clinched promotion with a tremendous win over Southend United and now need two points from their last three games for their first ever Championship. The champagne flowed freely after City had guaranteed a top three place in front of a near capacity crowd.'

* At the start of the season, Ladbrokes, the bookmakers, had offered odds of 20-1 on Exeter City winning the Fourth Division Championship.

* Despite missing the last 14 games due to a serious knee injury, Darran Rowbotham still top scored in league games with an impressive 20 goals. Would he have reached 30 had he remained fit?

* Only midfielder Danny Bailey was an ever-present in the City league season, featuring in all 46 matches. However, Karl Goddard, only made one substitute appearance, the former Leeds United player being signed on non-contract forms.

* The highest attendance of the season at St James' Park was for the match against Southend United, when 8,271 made their way through the turnstiles.

* The lowest attendance of the season at St James' Park was 2,754 when Cambridge United visited in September 1989 and were beaten 3-2.

* Exeter City's average home crowd was 4,859, an increase of 81.4 per cent on their previous season. Only Burnley and Grimsby Town had better averages in the Division.

* Defender Jim McNichol was the only player to score a hat-trick for City in the league, including a goal from the penalty spot, in the 5-0 home win over Rochdale in March 1990.

* Manager Terry Cooper was cleaning windows, when he thought, that's it, and promptly set off to sign winger Tony Coyle from Northwich Victoria, who was to play only one game for the Grecians.

* After winning promotion, Terry Cooper was quoted as saying: "I don't want to stay in football for the rest of my life, but I won't leave Exeter City for any other club."

* City reached the third round of the FA Cup, beating Dartford and Maidstone United after replays. They were then drawn at home to Norwich City, the tie ending all square at 1-1. In the replay at Carrow Road, Norwich won 2-0.

* Exeter had a good run in the Football League Cup. They beat Swansea City, Blackburn Rovers and Blackpool to earn themselves a fourth round home tie against Sunderland. After drawing 2-2, City then lost the replay at Roker Park, going down 2-5.

* In November 1989, City sold Chris Vinnicombe to Glasgow Rangers. the club received £200,000 as an initial down payment, and would then receive £100,000 when the player made 20, 30 and 40 appearances. Rangers also agreed to pay a further £100,000 if Vinnicombe won an England cap.

* The City Board of Directors decided to increase admission prices to St James' Park by £1 all round for the Football League Cup ties against Sunderland and the FA Cup tie with Norwich City. Admission to the stand would increase to £6, and to the terraces to £4. Most supporters praised the club for not exploiting their success starved faithful and considered fair weather fans deserved to pay that little bit extra.

| | Home | Away |
|---|---|---|
| AFC Bournemouth | 2-0 | 1-2 |
| Birmingham City | 0-2 | 1-1 |
| Bolton Wanderers | 2-1 | 0-1 |
| Bradford City | 2-2 | 0-3 |
| Brentford | 1-1 | 0-1 |
| Bury | 2-0 | 1-3 |
| Cambridge United | 0-1 | 0-1 |
| Chester City | 1-1 | 2-1 |
| Crewe Alexandra | 3-0 | 1-1 |
| Fulham | 0-1 | 2-3 |
| Grimsby Town | 0-0 | 1-2 |
| Huddersfield Town | 2-2 | 0-1 |
| Leyton Orient | 2-0 | 0-1 |
| Mansfield Town | 2-0 | 2-0 |
| Preston North End | 4-0 | 0-1 |
| Reading | 1-3 | 0-1 |
| Rotherham United | 2-0 | 4-2 |
| Shrewsbury Town | 3-0 | 2-2 |
| Southend United | 1-2 | 1-2 |
| Stoke City | 2-0 | 1-2 |
| Swansea City | 2-0 | 3-0 |
| Tranmere Rovers | 0-0 | 0-1 |
| Wigan Athletic | 1-0 | 1-4 |

| F.A. Cup | | | |
|---|---|---|---|
| Cambridge United | H | 1-2 | R1 |

| Football League. Cup | | | |
|---|---|---|---|
| Notts County | H | 1-1 | R1 |
| Notts County | A | 0-1 | 1R |

| Leyland Daf Cup | | | |
|---|---|---|---|
| Cardiff City | A | 1-0 | PR |
| Hereford United | H | 2-2 | PR |
| Aldershot | H | 1-0 | R1 |
| Cambridge United | H | 1-2 | R2 |

EXETER CITY 1990-91

Back row: Terry Cooper (Manager), ??? , Nick Tanner, Richard Dryden, Kevin Miller, Richard Young, Steve Berryman, Jim McNichol, Paul Eshelby, Jon Brown, Steve Harrower, Mike Radford (Youth Development Officer), Mike Davenport (Physio).

Middle row: Brian McDermott, Scott Hiley, Tom Kelly, Danny Bailey, Shaun Taylor, Mark Cooper, Gordon Hobson, Steve Neville, Clive Whitehead.

Front Row: Paul Batty, Ben Rowe, Tony Frankland, Graham Waters, Jamie Day, Lee Annunziata, ??? , Andrew Tibbenham, Toby Redwood.

CITY MANAGER 1990-91
Terry Cooper - Appointed May 1988

| CITY PLAYING SQUAD 1990-91 | | | | |
|---|---|---|---|---|
| Name | Pos | Signed From | Apps | Gls |
| Danny Bailey | M | Wealdstone Aug 1989 | 17(1) | 1 |
| Paul Batty | M | Chesterfield Jul 1986 | 9(2) | |
| Darren Boughey | W | Stoke City March 1991 | 8 | 1 |
| Jon Brown | D | Denaby United Jun 1990 | 26(3) | |
| Peter Cawley | D | Southend United Nov 1990 | 7 | |
| Mark Cooper | M | Bristol City Oct 1989 | 42 | 11 |
| Richard Dryden | D | Bristol Rovers Sep 1988 | 41 | 6 |
| Paul Eshelby | W | Endcliffe United Dec 1989 | 9(9) | 1 |
| Tony Frankland | M | Trainee Jul 1990 | 0(3) | |
| Scott Hiley | D | Apprentice Aug 1986 | 46 | 2 |
| Gordon Hobson | W | Lincoln City Aug 1990 | 37 | 7 |
| Murray Jones | F | Bristol City Jan 1991 | 16(4) | 3 |
| Tom Kelly | D | York City Mar 1990 | 13(9) | 1 |
| Brian McDermott | W | Cardiff City Feb 1989 | 8 | |
| Jim McNichol | D | Torquay United Aug 1989 | 9 | |
| Gary Marshall | W | Scunthorpe United Oct 1990 | 31(1) | 3 |
| Kevin Miller | G | Newquay Mar 1989 | 46 | |
| Trevor Morgan | F | Happy Valley (Hong Kong) Nov 1990 | 14(3) | 3 |
| Steve Neville | W | Bristol City Jul 1988 | 35(5) | 11 |
| Pat O'Toole | M | Leicester City Dec 1990 | 6 | |
| Gordon Owen | W | Blackpool Dec 1990 | 4 | |
| Lee Rogers | D | Bristol City Jun 1988 | 6(1) | |
| Darren Rowbotham | F | Plymouth Argyle Oct 1987 | 9(4) | 3 |
| Ben Rowe | F | Bristol City Sep 1989 | 1(1) | |
| Shaun Taylor | D | Bideford Dec 1986 45 | 4 | |
| Clive Whitehead | M | Portsmouth Jul 1989 | 8 | |
| Richard Young | F | Southend United Mar 1989 | 3(4) | |
| Own Goals | | | | 1 |

THIRD DIVISION - SEASON 1990-91

| | P | W | D | L | F | A | Pts |
|---|---|---|---|---|---|---|---|
| Cambridge United | 46 | 25 | 11 | 10 | 75 | 45 | 86 |
| Southend United | 46 | 26 | 7 | 13 | 67 | 51 | 85 |
| Grimsby Town | 46 | 24 | 11 | 11 | 66 | 34 | 83 |
| Bolton Wanderers | 46 | 24 | 11 | 11 | 64 | 50 | 83 |
| Tranmere Rovers | 46 | 23 | 9 | 14 | 64 | 46 | 78 |
| Brentford | 46 | 21 | 13 | 12 | 59 | 47 | 76 |
| Bury | 46 | 20 | 13 | 13 | 67 | 56 | 73 |
| Bradford City | 46 | 20 | 10 | 16 | 62 | 54 | 70 |
| AFC Bournemouth | 46 | 19 | 13 | 14 | 58 | 58 | 70 |
| Wigan Athletic | 46 | 20 | 9 | 17 | 71 | 54 | 69 |
| Huddersfield Town | 46 | 18 | 13 | 13 | 57 | 51 | 67 |
| Birmingham City | 46 | 16 | 17 | 13 | 45 | 49 | 65 |
| Leyton Orient | 46 | 18 | 10 | 18 | 55 | 58 | 64 |
| Stoke City | 46 | 16 | 12 | 18 | 55 | 59 | 60 |
| Reading | 46 | 17 | 8 | 21 | 53 | 66 | 59 |
| Exeter City | 46 | 16 | 9 | 21 | 58 | 52 | 57 |
| Preston North End | 46 | 15 | 11 | 20 | 54 | 67 | 56 |
| Shrewsbury Town | 46 | 14 | 10 | 22 | 61 | 68 | 52 |
| Chester City | 46 | 14 | 9 | 23 | 46 | 58 | 51 |
| Swansea City | 46 | 13 | 9 | 24 | 49 | 72 | 46 |
| Fulham | 46 | 10 | 16 | 20 | 41 | 56 | 46 |
| Crewe Alexandra | 46 | 11 | 11 | 24 | 62 | 80 | 44 |
| Rotherham United | 46 | 10 | 12 | 24 | 50 | 87 | 42 |
| Mansfield Town | 46 | 8 | 14 | 24 | 42 | 63 | 38 |

*Following the success of the previous season, Exeter City found it a little tougher going in the Third Division and surrendered their long term unbeaten record at St James' Park in the very first match when they lost to Reading. However, by the end of the season they did enough to establish themselves at the higher level.

* Manager Terry Cooper continued to wheel and deal in the transfer market, and among a number of signings he paid fees for were Gordon Hobson (£20,000), Gary Marshall (£25.000) and Murray Jones (£30,000).

* Disappointingly average attendances for league matches at St. James' Park was 4,285, which was a drop of 600 on the previous season.

* Long term injury victim and leading goalscorer Darren Rowbotham was kept on the sidelines until the end of March, when he showed a glimpse of what the team had been missing scoring four goals in nine full starts and four substitute appearances.

* City expanded their commercial activities by taking on a lease on 'Pennies' a bric-a-brac shop in St James' Road outside the ground which had closed down. The Commercial team were to use it as their headquarters as well as running a club shop, called The Near Post.

* Exeter City midfielder Clive Whitehead left the club in October 1990 to become player-manager of Yeovil Town. He quickly signed Steve Harrower from the Grecians for a fee of £5,000 and he was followed to Yeovil by Brian McDermott for £10,000. However, Whitehead was sacked as manager of Yeovil in April 1991.

* Following a Football Association hearing into serious allegations made by a former Exeter City chairman, of a £27,000 overpayment in grant aid by the Football Grounds Improvement Trust for safety work at St James' Park, they announced their verdict in December 1990. Three directors and one former board member were found guilty of misconduct giving them bans from football ranging from 3 months to 12 months and fines ranging from £2,000 to £5,000.

* Popular midfielder Danny Bailey was sold to Reading for £50,000 two days before Christmas. He had originally joined the club on a free transfer from Wealdstone.

* The club had a court action taken against them for non payment of Police charges in January 1991. Devon County Council obtained a High Court judgement as City owed £22,000 for Police charges at St. James' Park. The matter was eventually resolved without a court appearance.

* In March 1991 it was announced that Exeter had sacked striker Richard Young for a breach of contract, who had not been seen at St James' Park for some time, nor had he contacted manager Terry Cooper.

* Former Exeter City defender Chris Vinnicombe captained the England under-21 side against the Republic of Ireland in March 1991. A meteoric rise for the player who had been sold by the Grecians to Glasgow Rangers in November 1989.

* Grecians' supporter Norman Shiel staged an exhibition of Exeter City memorabilia at the local Royal Albert Museum in Exeter in March 1991. It was officially opened by deposed City chairman, Ivor Doble and was to run for four weeks.

* Exeter's home match against Shrewsbury Town on 6th April 1991 was abandoned at half-time after a monsoon-like storm swamped the playing surface in minutes leaving parts of the pitch like a lake. City had led 1-0 at the time.

* It was reported that the club announced they had a commitment to create an all-seater stadium by the end of the century. Secretary Stuart Brailey said that until, or unless, the situation changed, City would continue to plan to seat all spectators.

*An increase in admission prices for the following season, 1991-92, was announced in April 1991. Grandstand seats at St James' Park would go up by £1 to £7. A full price season ticket for the stand would cost £161.

**EXETER CITY 1991-92**
Back row: Jon Brown, Kevin Maloy, David Cole, Kevin Miller, Scott Daniels.
Third row: Mike Davenport (Physio), Gordon Hobson, Gary Marshall, Steve O'Shaughnessy, Dave Cooper, Chris O'Donnell, Tony Frankland, Graham Waters, Mike Radford (Youth Development Officer).
Second row: Scott Hiley, Steve Moran, Mark Cooper, Alan Ball (Manager), Steve Williams (Assistant Player-Manager), Darren Rowbotham, Tom Kelly.
Front row: Glen Sprod, Mark Brown, Neil Fairchild, Zac Locke, Craig Taylor, Toby Redwood.

### CITY PLAYING SQUAD 1991-92

| Name | Pos | Signed From | App | Gls |
|------|-----|-------------|-----|-----|
| Jon Brown | D | Denaby United Jun 1990 | 33(2) | |
| Gary Chapman | F | Notts County Sep 1991 | 17(3) | 4 |
| David Cole | D | Rochdale Aug 1991 | 0(2) | |
| Andy Cook | D | Southampton Sep 1991 | 38 | |
| David Cooper | D | Luton Town Aug 1991 | 9(4) | |
| Mark Cooper | M | Bristol City Oct 1989 | 3 | 1 |
| Mark Damerell | W | Plymouth Argyle Dec 1991 | 1 | |
| Scott Daniels | D | Colchester United Aug 1991 | 43 | 3 |
| Eamonn Dolan | F | Birmingham City Sep 1991 | 5(2) | |
| Dean Edwards | F | Unattached Dec 1991 | 4 | |
| Andy Harris | M | Birmingham City Nov 1991 | 5(1) | |
| Vince Hilaire | W | Stoke City Sep 1991 | 24(9) | 4 |
| Scott Hiley | D | Apprentice Aug 1986 | 33 | 1 |
| Gordon Hobson | W | Lincoln City Aug 1990 | 0(1) | |
| John Hodge | W | Falmouth Town Sep 1991 | 16(7) | 1 |
| John Humphrey | F | Millwall Dec 1991 | 2 | |
| Tom Kelly | D | York City Mar 1990 | 32 | 5 |
| Kevin Maloy | G | Taunton Town Jul 1991 | 4 | |
| Gary Marshall | W | Scunthorpe United Oct 1990 | 17(11) | 3 |
| Paul Masefield | D | Cheltenham Town Feb 1992 | 1 | |
| Kevin Miller | G | Newquay Mar 1989 | 42 | |
| Steve Moran | F | Reading Aug 1991 | 31(3) | 19 |
| Andy Morris | F | Chesterfield Mar 1992 | 4(3) | 2 |
| Ken O'Doherty | D | Huddersfield Town Aug 1991 | 2 | |
| Chris O'Donnell | D | Leeds United Aug 1991 | 2 | |
| Steve O'Shaughnessy | D | Rochdale Jul 1991 | 1(2) | |
| Toby Redwood | D | School Nov 1988 | 1 | |
| Mark Robson | W | Tottenham Hotspur Jan 1992 | 7(1) | 1 |
| Darren Rowbotham | F | Plymouth Argyle Oct 1987 | 5 | 1 |
| Ian Thompstone | F | Oldham Athletic Jan 1992 | 14 | 3 |
| Alan Tonge | M | Horwich R.M.I. Dec 1991 | 3 | |
| Graham Waters | W | Oxford United Jul 1991 | 1(1) | |
| Peter Whiston | D | Torquay United Sep 1991 | 36 | 3 |
| Steve Williams | M | Luton Town Aug 1991 | 36 | |
| Paul Wimbleton | M | Maidstone United Sep 1991 | 35(1) | 4 |
| Own Goals | | | | 2 |

### City's league results

| | Home | Away |
|------|------|------|
| AFC Bournemouth | 0-3 | 0-1 |
| Birmingham City | 2-1 | 0-1 |
| Bolton Wanderers | 2-2 | 2-1 |
| Bradford City | 1-0 | 1-1 |
| Brentford | 1-2 | 0-3 |
| Bury | 5-2 | 1-3 |
| Chester City | 0-0 | 2-5 |
| Darlington | 4-1 | 2-5 |
| Fulham | 1-1 | 0-0 |
| Hartlepool United | 1-1 | 1-3 |
| Huddersfield Town | 0-1 | 0-0 |
| Hull City | 0-3 | 2-1 |
| Leyton Orient | 2-0 | 0-1 |
| Peterborough United | 2-2 | 1-1 |
| Preston North End | 4-1 | 3-1 |
| Reading | 2-1 | 0-1 |
| Shrewsbury Town | 1-0 | 1-6 |
| Stockport County | 2-1 | 1-4 |
| Stoke City | 0-0 | 2-5 |
| Swansea City | 2-1 | 0-1 |
| Torquay United | 1-0 | 0-1 |
| West Bromwich Albion | 1-1 | 3-6 |
| Wigan Athletic | 0-1 | 1-4 |

### F.A. Cup

| | | | |
|------|------|------|------|
| Colchester United | A | 0-0 | R1 |
| Colchester United | H | 0-0* | R1R |
| Swansea City | H | 0-0 | R2 |
| Swansea City | A | 2-1 | R2R |
| Portsmouth | H | 1-2 | R3 |

### Football League. Cup

| | | | |
|------|------|------|------|
| Birmingham City | H | 0-1 | R1 |
| Birmingham City | A | 0-4 | R1 |

### Autoglass Trophy

| | | | |
|------|------|------|------|
| Torquay United | H | 2-1 | PR |
| Hereford United | A | 1-2 | PR |
| West Bromwich Albion | A | 1-0 | R1 |
| Peterborough United | A | 0-1 | R2 |

### CITY MANAGER 1991-92
Alan Ball - Appointed Aug 1991

### THIRD DIVISION - SEASON 1991-92

| | P | W | D | L | F | A | Pts |
|------|---|---|---|---|---|---|-----|
| Brentford | 46 | 25 | 7 | 14 | 81 | 55 | 82 |
| Birmingham City | 46 | 23 | 12 | 11 | 69 | 52 | 81 |
| Huddersfield Town | 46 | 22 | 12 | 12 | 59 | 38 | 78 |
| Stoke City | 46 | 21 | 14 | 11 | 69 | 49 | 77 |
| Stockport County | 46 | 22 | 10 | 14 | 75 | 49 | 76 |
| Peterborough United | 46 | 20 | 14 | 12 | 65 | 58 | 74 |
| West Bromwich Albion | 46 | 19 | 14 | 13 | 64 | 49 | 71 |
| AFC Bournemouth | 46 | 20 | 11 | 15 | 52 | 48 | 71 |
| Fulham | 46 | 19 | 13 | 14 | 57 | 53 | 70 |
| Leyton Orient | 46 | 18 | 11 | 17 | 62 | 52 | 65 |
| Hartlepool United | 46 | 18 | 11 | 17 | 57 | 57 | 65 |
| Reading | 46 | 16 | 13 | 17 | 59 | 62 | 61 |
| Bolton Wanderers | 46 | 14 | 17 | 15 | 57 | 56 | 59 |
| Hull City | 46 | 16 | 11 | 19 | 54 | 54 | 59 |
| Wigan Athletic | 46 | 15 | 14 | 17 | 58 | 64 | 59 |
| Bradford City | 46 | 13 | 19 | 14 | 62 | 61 | 58 |
| Preston North End | 46 | 15 | 12 | 19 | 61 | 72 | 57 |
| Chester City | 46 | 14 | 14 | 18 | 56 | 59 | 56 |
| Swansea City | 46 | 14 | 14 | 18 | 55 | 65 | 56 |
| Exeter City | 46 | 14 | 11 | 21 | 57 | 80 | 53 |
| Bury | 46 | 13 | 12 | 21 | 55 | 74 | 51 |
| Shrewsbury Town | 46 | 12 | 11 | 23 | 53 | 68 | 47 |
| Torquay United | 46 | 13 | 8 | 25 | 42 | 68 | 47 |
| Darlington | 46 | 10 | 7 | 29 | 56 | 90 | 37 |

* This was a season of transition, with a new manager appointed, England World Cup winner, Alan Ball, and a whole host of players coming and going as he tried to mould his own squad. Previous manager Terry Cooper decided to take up an appointment with Birmingham City.

* Prior to the start of the season there was unrest between the supporters and the board of directors. A group of City fans invaded the directors box during one of the pre-season matches as their way of showing that they were far from happy with ongoing events.

* Ball quickly realised what a mountain he had to climb, as City conceded 14 goals in their opening three matches. He quickly reshaped the playing squad which included striker Darren Rowbotham going to local rivals Torquay United in exchange for defender Peter Whiston.

* One of Ball's former Southampton team mates, Steve Moran, topped City's scoring charts, and the manager also introduced home grown starlet Martin Phillips into his side.

* Moran scored all four of City's goals in the 4-1 home win against Darlington in October 1991.

* It was also a season where Exeter City avoided relegation by the narrowest of margins, even though they could have dropped into Division Four right up to the last day of the season. Although losing 5-2 at Darlington, there were scenes of celebration when it was realised that despite the defeat, results had gone for them and City would remain in the Third Division.

* The Grecians had ended the season in poor form with only one win in eleven league matches. Their only success was a 2-1 home win against Birmingham City. They then went eight matches without a victory, losing seven and drawing one.

* The average attendance for league matches at St. James' Park was 3,627, a considerable drop on the previous season when it was 4,285.

* In October 1991 it was announced that Exeter City were to carry out improvements to the floodlighting system at a reported cost of £60,000. The Football League had insisted that clubs should have a system of at least 250 lux. City's lights were only between 180 and 200 lux. The improvements and cabling would bring the lights up to 500 lux.

* A minutes silence was held prior to kick off at Exeter City's FA Cup second round tie against Swansea City, as a mark of respect for former Grecians, Arsenal and England winger, Cliff Bastin, who had died earlier that week.

* in April 1992 Exeter City sacked eight gatemen after an undercover swoop on alleged turnstile fiddling. Club officials said they were forced to act after it was discovered that spectators were getting into St. James' Park for nothing on matchdays. It was reported that City were alerted by an off duty policeman attending a game.

* The Exeter City Supporters' Club held talks with the board of directors over the lack of facilities in the Cowshed terracing and offered financial assistance to make improvements. This included the building of toilets at the St. James' Road end of the terracing.

* There was a testimonial match for defender Jim McNichol at the end of the season on 4th May 1992, when Exeter City entertained West Ham United. The Hammers won 2-1 before an attendance of 2,380.

* Asked about his thoughts when arriving at Exeter City as manager at the start of the season, Alan Ball said: "I joined without a clue about the problems on the board of directors, or behind the scenes, or with the playing staff. It had been a really traumatic time for me on more ways than one.":

* Just before the season started, Exeter City Commercial Manager Mike Lewis left the club and described what it was like behind the scenes at St James' Park.

"In the last 20 months that I have been at Exeter City, we have had more trauma and drama than you get in five years of Coronation Street," he said.

"We had been through a hell of a lot. I felt I was in need of a break and you just don't get them in football, so I felt the time was right to resign."

Lewis was replaced with the appointment of Steve Birley, who said: "Commercially, I am going to set the place on fire. I am thrilled to bits to get the job and am relishing the challenge."

* Kick off times of Exeter City's pre-season friendlies had to be changed as the floodlight improvements had not been completed. The games against Charlton Athletic, West Ham United and Luton Town were to have 7pm starts instead of 7.30pm.

* In August 1992, The Football Association Disciplinary Committee fined Exeter City £6,000, suspended for 12 months, after the club had to face them due their poor record the previous season.

Board spokesman Allen Trump said: "We have got off quite lightly so far. We expect a dramatic improvement from the players. Fortunately we put forward a good enough case at the commission to get the fine suspended."

## CITY PLAYING SQUAD 1992-93

| Name | Pos | Signed From | Apps | Gls |
|------|-----|-------------|------|-----|
| Danny Bailey | M | Fulham Dec 1992 | 27 | |
| Kevin Bond | D | AFC Bournemouth Aug 1992 | 17(1) | |
| Jon Brown | D | Denaby United Jun 1990 | 40 | 1 |
| Gary Chapman | F | Notts County Sep 1991 | 3(1) | 1 |
| Eamonn Collins | M | Colchester United Jul 1992 | 8(3) | |
| Andy Cook | D | Southampton Sep 1991 | 32 | 1 |
| David Cooper | D | Luton Town Aug 1991 | 16(4) | |
| Scott Daniels | D | Colchester United Aug 1991 | 26 | 2 |
| Eamonn Dolan | F | Birmingham City Sep 1991 | 10(9) | 4 |
| Richard Evans | W | Bristol Rovers Oct 1992 | 5 | 2 |
| Joe Gallen | F | Watford Dec 1992 | 6 | |
| Andy Harris | M | Birmingham City Nov 1991 | 23(5) | 1 |
| Scott Hiley | D | Apprentice Aug 1986 | 33 | 3 |
| John Hodge | W | Falmouth Town Sep 1991 | 41(1) | 9 |
| Ronnie Jepson | F | Preston North End Jul 1992 | 35(3) | 8 |
| Tom Kelly | D | York City Mar 1990 | 20(2) | 1 |
| Mark Loram | F | Torquay United Sep 1992 | 2(1) | |
| Jim McIntyre | F | Bristol City Feb 1993 | 12(3) | 3 |
| Kevin Miller | G | Newquay Mar 1989 | 44 | |
| Jason Minett | D | Norwich City Mar 1993 | 11(1) | |
| Steve Moran | F | Reading Aug 1991 | 19(4) | 8 |
| Vince O'Keefe | G | Retired Aug 1992 | 2 | |
| Martin Phillips | W | School Jul 1992 | 0(6) | |
| Toby Redwood | D | School Nov 1988 | 3(3) | |
| Stuart Storer | W | Bolton Wanderers Mar 1993 | 10 | 4 |
| Craig Taylor | D | Trainee Jul 1990 | 2(3) | |
| Alan Tonge | M | Horwich R.M.I. Dec 1991 | 13(2) | 1 |
| Peter Whiston | D | Torquay United Sep 1991 | 27 | 3 |
| Chris White | D | Peterborough United Mar 1993 | 11 | |
| Steve Williams | M | Luton Town Aug 1991 | 8(4) | |
| Own Goals | | | | 2 |

### City's league results

| | Home | Away |
|---|------|------|
| AFC Bournemouth | 1-1 | 3-1 |
| Blackpool | 0-1 | 0-2 |
| Bolton Wanderers | 1-3 | 1-4 |
| Bradford City | 0-1 | 1-3 |
| Brighton & Hove Albion | 2-3 | 0-3 |
| Burnley | 2-2 | 1-3 |
| Chester City | 2-0 | 3-0 |
| Fulham | 1-2 | 1-1 |
| Hartlepool United | 3-1 | 3-1 |
| Huddersfield Town | 1-2 | 0-0 |
| Hull City | 1-1 | 0-4 |
| Leyton Orient | 1-0 | 0-5 |
| Mansfield Town | 2-0 | 0-0 |
| Plymouth Argyle | 2-0 | 3-0 |
| Port Vale | 1-1 | 2-2 |
| Preston North End | 0-1 | 2-2 |
| Reading | 0-0 | 3-2 |
| Rotherham United | 0-2 | 1-1 |
| Stockport County | 2-2 | 2-2 |
| Stoke City | 2-2 | 1-1 |
| Swansea City | 0-2 | 0-0 |
| West Bromwich Albion | 2-3 | 0-2 |
| Wigan Athletic | 0-0 | 1-0 |

### F.A. Cup

| | | |
|---|---|---|
| Kidderminster Harriers | H 1-0 | R1 |
| Swansea City | H 2-5 | R2 |

### Football League. Cup

| | | |
|---|---|---|
| Birmingham City | H 0-0 | R1 |
| Birmingham City | A 4-1 | R1 |
| Oldham Athletic | H 0-1 | R2 |
| Oldham Athletic | A 0-0 | R2 |

### Autoglass Trophy

| | | |
|---|---|---|
| Torquay United | H 5-0 | R1 |
| Plymouth Argyle | A 1-1 | R1 |
| Reading | H 2-2* | R2 |
| Brighton & Hove Albion | A 1-0 | R3 |
| Swansea City | A 3-2 | R4 |
| Port Vale | A 1-2 | Area Final |
| Port Vale | H 1-1 | Area Final |

* Exeter won 4-2 on penalties.

### CITY MANAGER 1992-93
Alan Ball - Appointed Aug 1991

### DIVISION TWO - SEASON 1992-93

| | P | W | D | L | F | A | Pts |
|---|---|---|---|---|---|---|-----|
| Stoke City | 46 | 27 | 12 | 7 | 73 | 34 | 93 |
| Bolton Wanderers | 46 | 27 | 9 | 10 | 80 | 41 | 90 |
| Port Vale | 46 | 26 | 11 | 9 | 79 | 44 | 89 |
| West Bromwich Albion | 46 | 25 | 10 | 11 | 88 | 54 | 85 |
| Swansea City | 46 | 20 | 13 | 13 | 65 | 47 | 73 |
| Stockport County | 46 | 19 | 15 | 12 | 81 | 57 | 72 |
| Leyton Orient | 46 | 21 | 9 | 16 | 69 | 53 | 72 |
| Reading | 46 | 18 | 15 | 13 | 66 | 51 | 69 |
| Brighton & Hove Albion | 46 | 20 | 9 | 17 | 63 | 59 | 69 |
| Bradford City | 46 | 18 | 14 | 14 | 69 | 67 | 68 |
| Rotherham United | 46 | 17 | 14 | 15 | 60 | 60 | 65 |
| Fulham | 46 | 16 | 17 | 13 | 57 | 55 | 65 |
| Burnley | 46 | 15 | 16 | 15 | 57 | 59 | 61 |
| Plymouth Argyle | 46 | 16 | 12 | 18 | 59 | 64 | 60 |
| Huddersfield Town | 46 | 17 | 9 | 20 | 54 | 61 | 60 |
| Hartlepool United | 46 | 14 | 12 | 20 | 42 | 60 | 54 |
| AFC Bournemouth | 46 | 12 | 17 | 17 | 45 | 52 | 53 |
| Blackpool | 46 | 12 | 15 | 19 | 63 | 75 | 51 |
| Exeter City | 46 | 11 | 17 | 18 | 54 | 69 | 50 |
| Hull City | 46 | 13 | 11 | 22 | 46 | 69 | 50 |
| Preston North End | 46 | 13 | 8 | 25 | 65 | 94 | 47 |
| Mansfield Town | 46 | 11 | 11 | 24 | 52 | 80 | 44 |
| Wigan Athletic | 46 | 10 | 11 | 25 | 43 | 72 | 41 |
| Chester City | 46 | 8 | 5 | 33 | 49 | 102 | 29 |

* With the F.A. Premier League being formed, this resulted in the lower divisions in the Football League being renamed, so Exeter City found themselves in Division Two, which was formerly Division Three!

* Once again there was quite a turnover of players as manager Alan Ball continued to 'reshape' his playing squad. Exeter also paid transfer fees for Ronnie Jepson (£60,000) and Stuart Storer (£25,000).

* To overcome an early goalkeeping crisis, former Grecian Vince O'Keefe was persuaded to come out of retirement to line up for the Club again in the opening match of the season. He was working for the Professional Footballers Association at the time. He was to make one further outing later in the season.

* Alan Ball utilised the loan transfer market during the season bringing in Jim McIntyre, who formed a good partnership with Jepson during his stay at St. James' Park.

* The Grecians were just one step away from a first ever appearance at Wembley when they reached the Southern Area Final (played over two legs) in the Autoglass Trophy against Port Vale. Sadly it was not to be as City lost 3-2 on aggregate.

* The most rewarding victory, as far as City fans were concerned, was the comprehensive display and 3-0 win at old rivals Plymouth Argyle. A league double was therefore completed against the Argyle, with Exeter having won 2-0 at St. James' Park.

* As part of the previous seasons transfer of Exeter City full-back, Chris Vinnicombe, to Glasgow Rangers, a friendly was staged at St James' Park in September 1992. However, there was bitter disappointment that Rangers sent a reserve team, including Vinnicombe, as they drew 1-1 before an attendance of just 2,300.

* A month later Exeter City secretary, Mike Holladay declared himself unhappy with the size of the crowds at St. James' Park, which were averaging around 3,300 instead of the target figure of 4,000.

* In November 1992 the Football League imposed a transfer embargo upon the club - the second that season - as the Grecians had not settled a payment due to striker Gary Chapman, his signing on fee. Two days later Commercial manager Steve Birley described the club's current position as "turbulent."

* Exeter's FA Cup second round tie at St. James' Park against Swansea City was abandoned due to a floodlight failure, with the visitors leading 2-1. A few days later in the rearranged tie, Swansea won 5-2.

* Exeter City's financial worries had reached a stage in January 1993 where the Club faced a winding up order. Chairman Gerald Vallance said the Inland Revenue had not been paid for a month and went on to say: "Slumping gates, indifferent home form, have cut income. The directors have had to dip into their own pockets to help pay the wages and as many other bills as they can. The monthly wage bill is £40,000 per month."

* A month later it was revealed that the Devon and Cornwall Police were owed £50,000 by the Grecians. They were insisting that the bill be paid, certainly by the start of the following season.

* Striker Eamonn Dolan was diagnosed with testicular cancer immediately after the Autoglass Trophy tie against Port Vale. This would ultimately end his playing career.

* The Club appointed their first ever Chief Executive, when Allen Trump, who was company secretary and director, took on the role, which would start from 1st July 1993.

* In May 1993 the Club faced a new financial embarrassment when their accounts were not submitted to Companies House on time. Exeter, it was reported, failed to reply to a written demand for an explanation from Companies House and therefore faced further penalties.

Back Row: Gary Rice, Adam Shearer , Matthew Hare, Matthew Harris , Jon Richardson

First Row: Scott Daniels, Toby Redwood, Stuart Storer, Peter Fox, Chris White, Jason Minett, Andy Harris

Second Row: Peter Whiston , Ronnie Robinson, Gary Worthington, Russell Coughlin, Jon Brown, Mark Brown, Craig Taylor, David Cooper

Third Row (Seated): Danny Bailey, Ronnie Jepson, Mike Chapman (Physio), Alan Ball (Manager), Mike Radford (Youth Development Officer), George Kent (Scout), Alan Tonge, Jason Percival

Front Row (Sitting on Ground): Richard Pears, Phil Lafferty , Kevin Darch, Mark Hutchings , Anthony Thirlby, Jimmy Ball, Barry McConnell, Martin Phillips, Andrew Rollason

CITY PLAYING SQUAD 1993-94

| Name | Pos | Signed From | Apps | Gls |
|------|-----|-------------|------|-----|
| David Adekola | F | Bury Feb 94 | 1(2) | 1 |
| Danny Bailey | M | Fulham Dec 1992 | 29(5) | |
| Kevin Bond | D | AFC Bournemouth Aug 1992 | 1 | |
| Jon Brown | D | Denaby United Jun 1990 | 18(5) | |
| Mike Cecere | F | Walsall Jan 1994 | 2 | |
| David Cooper | D | Luton Town Aug 1994 | 0(1) | |
| Mark Cooper | M | Wycombe Wanderers Feb 1994 | 21 | 8 |
| Russell Coughlin | M | Swansea City Jul 1993 | 35 | |
| Scott Daniels | M | Colchester United Aug 1991 | 39(2) | 2 |
| Simon Davies | M | Manchester United Dec 1993 | 5(1) | 1 |
| Peter Fox | G | Stoke City Jul 1993 | 25(1) | |
| Mark Gavin | W | Bristol City Feb 1994 | 12 | |
| Andy Gosney | G | Birmingham City Oct 1993 | 1 | |
| Andy Harris | M | Birmingham City Nov 1991 | 4 | |
| Ronnie Jepson | F | Preston North End Jul 1992 | 16 | 13 |
| Andy Llewellyn | D | Bristol City Mar 1994 | 15 | |
| Allen McKnight | G | South China FC Mar 1994 | 9(1) | |
| David Mehew | M | Bristol Rovers Mar 1994 | 5(2) | |
| Jason Minett | D | Norwich City Mar 1993 | 34(4) | 1 |
| Nicky Morgan | F | Bristol City Feb 1994 | 12 | 4 |
| Richard Pears | M | Trainee Jul 1992 | 6(5) | 1 |
| Jason Percival | F | Stoke City Jul 1993 | 0(4) | |
| Martin Phillips | W | School Jul 1992 | 7(2) | |
| Toby Redwood | D | School Nov 1988 | 11(2) | |
| Jon Richardson | D | Trainee Aug 1991 | 4(3) | |
| Ronnie Robinson | D | Peterborough United Jul 1993 | 21(1) | 1 |
| Mickey Ross | F | Portsmouth Aug 1993 | 26(1) | 9 |
| Stuart Storer | W | Bolton Wanderers Mar 1993 | 44 | 2 |
| Anthony Thirlby | M | Trainee Jul 1992 | 7(3) | |
| Alan Tonge | M | Horwich R.M.I. Dec 1991 | 0(1) | |
| Robbie Turner | F | Notts County Feb 1994 | 22 | 3 |
| Kenny Veysey | G | Reading Oct 1993 | 11(1) | |
| Peter Whiston | D | Torquay United Sep 1991 | 22 | 1 |
| Chris White | D | Peterborough United Mar 1993 | 7(1) | |
| Steve Wigley | W | Portsmouth Aug 1993 | 22(1) | 1 |
| Gavin Worboys | F | Notts County Dec 1993 | 4 | 1 |
| Gary Worthington | F | Wigan Athletic Jul 1993 | 8(7) | 1 |
| Own Goals | | | | 2 |

City's league results

| | Home | Away |
|---|---|---|
| AFC Bournemouth | 0-2 | 1-1 |
| Barnet | 0-0 | 1-2 |
| Blackpool | 1-0 | 0-1 |
| Bradford City | 0-0 | 0-6 |
| Brentford | 2-2 | 1-2 |
| Brighton & Hove Albion | 1-1 | 0-0 |
| Bristol Rovers | 1-0 | 1-1 |
| Burnley | 4-1 | 2-3 |
| Cambridge United | 0-5 | 0-3 |
| Cardiff City | 2-2 | 0-2 |
| Fulham | 6-4 | 0-3 |
| Hartlepool United | 2-1 | 2-1 |
| Huddersfield Town | 2-3 | 1-0 |
| Hull City | 0-1 | 1-5 |
| Leyton Orient | 1-0 | 1-1 |
| Plymouth Argyle | 2-3 | 0-1 |
| Port Vale | 1-1 | 0-3 |
| Reading | 4-6 | 0-1 |
| Rotherham United | 1-1 | 0-3 |
| Stockport County | 1-2 | 0-4 |
| Swansea City | 1-0 | 0-2 |
| Wrexham | 5-0 | 1-1 |
| York City | 1-2 | 0-3 |

F.A. Cup

| | | | |
|---|---|---|---|
| Farnborough Town | A | 3-1 | R1 |
| Leyton Orient | A | 1-1 | R2 |
| Leyton Orient | H | 2-2 | R2* |
| Aston Villa | H | 0-1 | R3 |

*Exeter City won on penalties.

Football League. Cup

| | | | |
|---|---|---|---|
| Walsall | A | 0-0 | R1 |
| Walsall | H | 2-1 | R1 |
| Derby County | H | 1-3 | R2 |
| Derby County | A | 0-2 | R2 |

Autoglass Trophy

| | | | |
|---|---|---|---|
| Swansea City | A | 0-2 | R1 |
| Plymouth Argyle | H | 1-0 | |

CITY MANAGER 1993-94
Alan Ball - Appointed Aug 1991
Terry Cooper - Appointed January 1994

DIVISION TWO - SEASON 1993-94

| | P | W | D | L | F | A | Pts |
|---|---|---|---|---|---|---|---|
| Reading | 46 | 26 | 11 | 9 | 81 | 44 | 89 |
| Port Vale | 46 | 26 | 10 | 10 | 79 | 46 | 88 |
| Plymouth Argyle | 46 | 25 | 10 | 11 | 88 | 56 | 85 |
| Stockport County | 46 | 24 | 13 | 9 | 74 | 44 | 85 |
| York City | 46 | 21 | 12 | 13 | 64 | 40 | 75 |
| Burnley | 46 | 21 | 10 | 15 | 79 | 58 | 73 |
| Bradford City | 46 | 19 | 13 | 14 | 61 | 53 | 70 |
| Bristol Rovers | 46 | 20 | 10 | 16 | 60 | 59 | 70 |
| Hull City | 46 | 18 | 14 | 14 | 62 | 54 | 68 |
| Cambridge United | 46 | 19 | 9 | 18 | 79 | 73 | 66 |
| Huddersfield Town | 46 | 17 | 14 | 15 | 58 | 61 | 65 |
| Wrexham | 46 | 17 | 11 | 18 | 66 | 77 | 62 |
| Swansea City | 46 | 16 | 12 | 18 | 56 | 58 | 60 |
| Brighton & Hove Albion | 46 | 15 | 14 | 17 | 60 | 67 | 59 |
| Rotherham United | 46 | 15 | 13 | 18 | 63 | 66 | 58 |
| Brentford | 46 | 13 | 19 | 14 | 57 | 55 | 58 |
| AFC Bournemouth | 46 | 14 | 15 | 17 | 51 | 59 | 57 |
| Leyton Orient | 46 | 14 | 14 | 18 | 57 | 71 | 56 |
| Cardiff City | 46 | 13 | 15 | 18 | 66 | 79 | 54 |
| Blackpool | 46 | 16 | 5 | 25 | 63 | 75 | 53 |
| Fulham | 46 | 14 | 10 | 22 | 50 | 63 | 52 |
| Exeter City | 46 | 11 | 12 | 23 | 52 | 83 | 45 |
| Hartlepool United | 46 | 9 | 9 | 28 | 41 | 87 | 36 |
| Barnet | 46 | 5 | 13 | 28 | 41 | 86 | 28 |

* This proved to be an eventful season both on and off the field. It was also a season that resulted in Exeter City being relegated. Manager Alan Ball left the club immediately after the FA Cup tie against Aston Villa to take over at Southampton and was replaced by Terry Cooper for his second spell at the club. It was hoped he could rekindle the promotion glory days of 1990, but it was not to be.

* Problems really mounted off the field with the financial alarm bells ringing and staff unrest, although it was to be the following season that it all came to a head with almost disastrous results.

* Between November 1993 and March 1994, the Grecians won just two matches as they slid down the table into the relegation places.

* Manager Terry Cooper introduced a number of players to the squad as well as promoting trainees, Anthony Thirlby, Richard Pears and Jon Richardson into the team.

*Although striker Ronnie Jepson was sold to Huddersfield Town for £60,000 in November 1993, his 13 league goals up to that point still made him the club top scorer at the end of the season!

* City also spent money in the transfer market, notably, Ronnie Robinson (£25,000) and Mark Gavin (£10,000).

* No fewer than four goalkeepers played for City during the season, although one of them, Andy Gosney, didn't even complete a full 90 minutes being carried off injured in the crazy 4-6 home defeat against Reading.

* City also won a home game 6-4, four weeks after the Reading defeat, as Fulham were beaten, Mickey Ross netted a hat-trick.

* Comedian Freddie Starr made an offer to buy Exeter City in September 1993, however, the club issued a statement which read: "The board does not consider the approach by Mr. Starr to be in the best interests of Exeter City Football Club." Starr made a second offer of £200,000 to buy out majority shareholder Clifford Hill and even took his place on the St James' Park terracing as the Grecians defeated Wrexham 5-0. His second bid was also rejected.

* There was complete unrest at St James' Park in September 1993 as back room staff and manager Alan Ball visited the home of Club president and majority shareholder Clifford Hill. They demanded the immediate resignation of the club's Chief Executive, Allen Trump, whom they were unhappy with. Ball said he could no longer work with him. Trump did resign but remained on the board of directors for a couple of months. Trump said that the club had an estimated deficit of £200,000 and sooner or later someone had to inject some money.

* In December 1993 it was revealed that Exeter City had made a loss of almost £350,000 on the previous financial year. By the end of June 1992 the club were in debt to £900,000. The club's wage bill, including £270,000 spent on transfers topped the £1m mark for the first time in the club's history.

* Despite their financial woes, plans were revealed in January 1994 to eventually turn the Big Bank terracing into an all-seater stand, with a pub and leisure facilities underneath. It was expected to cost around £1m, with various grants being sought to help offset the cost.

* Not surprisingly there was a big clear out of players at the end of what was a traumatic season. Nine players were released with manager Terry Cooper saying: "I have really got to clear the decks and my hands are tied really. I have 21 players signed for next season and if I am going to strengthen in the areas I want to, then I have to make room on the wage bill."

EXETER CITY 1994-95
Back row: Mark Gavin, Mark Cooper, Dave Cooper, Tony Thirlby, Gary Rice, Martin Phillips, Danny Bailey, Micky Ross, Jason Minett
Centre row: Russell Coughlin, Ronnie Robinson, Peter Whiston, Mark Came, Peter Fox, Robbie Turner, Andy Woodman, Stuart Storer, Scott Daniels, Jon Richardson, Richard Pears
Front row: Mike Cecere, Mike Chapman (Physio), Trevor Morgan (Assistant Manager), Terry Cooper (manager), George Kent (Scout), Mike Radford (Youth Development Officer), Colin Anderson.

### City's league results

|                     | Home | Away |
|---------------------|------|------|
| Barnet              | 1-2  | 1-1  |
| Bury                | 0-4  | 0-0  |
| Carlisle United     | 1-1  | 0-1  |
| Chesterfield        | 1-2  | 0-2  |
| Colchester United   | 1-0  | 1-3  |
| Darlington          | 0-2  | 0-2  |
| Doncaster Rovers    | 1-5  | 0-3  |
| Fulham              | 0-1  | 0-4  |
| Gillingham          | 3-0  | 0-3  |
| Hartlepool United   | 2-1  | 2-2  |
| Hereford United     | 1-1  | 0-3  |
| Lincoln City        | 1-0  | 0-2  |
| Mansfield Town      | 2-3  | 1-1  |
| Northampton Town    | 0-0  | 1-2  |
| Preston North End   | 0-1  | 1-0  |
| Rochdale            | 0-0  | 1-0  |
| Scarborough         | 5-2  | 0-0  |
| Scunthorpe United   | 2-2  | 0-3  |
| Torquay United      | 1-2  | 0-0  |
| Walsall             | 1-3  | 0-1  |
| Wigan Athletic      | 2-4  | 1-3  |

### F.A. Cup

|               |   |     |    |
|---------------|---|-----|----|
| Crawley Town  | H | 1-0 | R1 |
| Colchester United | H | 1-2 | R2 |

### Football League. Cup

|              |   |     |    |
|--------------|---|-----|----|
| Swansea City | H | 2-2 | R1 |
| Swansea City | A | 0-2 | R1 |

### Auto Windscreens Shield

|                 |   |     |    |
|-----------------|---|-----|----|
| Plymouth Argyle | A | 3-1 | R1 |
| Cardiff City    | H | 1-1 | R1 |
| Cardiff City    | H | 1-0 | R2 |
| Shrewsbury Town | A | 1-3 | R3 |

### CITY MANAGER 1994-95
Terry Cooper - Appointed January 1994

### CITY PLAYING SQUAD 1994-95

| Name | Pos | Signed From | Apps | Gls |
|------|-----|-------------|------|-----|
| Colin Anderson | D | Hereford United Jul 1994 | 21 | 1 |
| Danny Bailey | M | Fulham Dec 1992 | 14 | 1 |
| Mike Barrett | G | Liskeard Athletic Dec 1994 | 4 | |
| Ross Bellotti | G | Trainee Jul 1994 | 1(1) | |
| Jon Brown | D | Denaby United Jun 1990 | 32(5) | 2 |
| Mark Came | D | Chester City Jul 1994 | 32 | 1 |
| Mike Cecere | F | Walsall Jan 1994 | 27(1) | 10 |
| David Cooper | D | Luton Town Aug 1994 | 14 | |
| Mark Cooper | M | Wycombe Wanderers Feb 1994 | 31(9) | 6 |
| Russell Coughlin | M | Swansea City Jul 1993 | 23(2) | |
| Scott Daniels | D | Colchester United Aug 1991 | 6(1) | |
| Peter Fox | G | Stoke City Jul 1993 | 31 | |
| Mark Gavin | W | Bristol City Feb 1994 | 37 | 2 |
| Jason Minett | D | Norwich City Mar 1993 | 38 | 2 |
| Trevor Morgan | F | Birmingham City Sep 1994 | 4(5) | 1 |
| Richard Pears | F | Trainee Jul 1992 | 12(7) | 1 |
| Martin Phillips | W | School Jul 1992 | 18(6) | 2 |
| Gary Rice | D | Trainee Jul 1994 | 5(5) | |
| Jon Richardson | D | Trainee Aug 1991 | 38 | 1 |
| Ronnie Robinson | D | Peterborough United Jul 1993 | 16(1) | |
| Mickey Ross | F | Portsmouth Aug 1993 | 1 | |
| Stuart Storer | W | Bolton Wanderers Mar 1993 | 21(2) | 2 |
| Anthony Thirlby | M | Trainee Jul 1992 | 20(7) | 2 |
| Robbie Turner | F | Notts County Feb 1994 | 10(1) | 1 |
| Andy Woodman | G | Crystal Palace Jul 1994 | 6 | |
| Own Goals | | | | 1 |

### DIVISION THREE - SEASON 1994-95

|                   | P  | W  | D  | L  | F  | A  | Pts |
|-------------------|----|----|----|----|----|----|-----|
| Carlisle United   | 42 | 27 | 10 | 5  | 67 | 31 | 91  |
| Walsall           | 42 | 24 | 11 | 7  | 75 | 40 | 83  |
| Chesterfield      | 42 | 23 | 12 | 7  | 62 | 37 | 81  |
| Bury              | 42 | 23 | 11 | 8  | 73 | 36 | 80  |
| Preston North End | 42 | 19 | 10 | 13 | 58 | 41 | 67  |
| Mansfield Town    | 42 | 18 | 11 | 13 | 84 | 59 | 65  |
| Scunthorpe United | 42 | 18 | 8  | 16 | 68 | 63 | 62  |
| Fulham            | 42 | 16 | 14 | 12 | 60 | 54 | 62  |
| Doncaster Rovers  | 42 | 17 | 10 | 15 | 58 | 43 | 61  |
| Colchester United | 42 | 16 | 10 | 16 | 56 | 64 | 58  |
| Barnet            | 42 | 15 | 11 | 16 | 56 | 63 | 56  |
| Lincoln City      | 42 | 15 | 11 | 16 | 54 | 55 | 56  |
| Torquay United    | 42 | 14 | 13 | 15 | 54 | 57 | 55  |
| Wigan Athletic    | 42 | 14 | 10 | 18 | 53 | 60 | 52  |
| Rochdale          | 42 | 12 | 14 | 16 | 44 | 67 | 50  |
| Hereford United   | 42 | 12 | 13 | 17 | 45 | 62 | 49  |
| Northampton Town  | 42 | 10 | 14 | 18 | 45 | 67 | 44  |
| Hartlepool United | 42 | 11 | 10 | 21 | 43 | 69 | 43  |
| Gillingham        | 42 | 10 | 11 | 21 | 46 | 64 | 41  |
| Darlington        | 42 | 11 | 8  | 23 | 43 | 57 | 41  |
| Scarborough       | 42 | 8  | 10 | 24 | 49 | 70 | 34  |
| Exeter City       | 42 | 8  | 10 | 24 | 36 | 70 | 34  |

* By April 1995, the Club were in serious trouble, and the last home match of the season against Fulham, saw a black edged programme produced, as it could have been, in theory, the very last game played by Exeter City.

* if the previous season was a bad one for Exeter City, then was even worse. Bottom of the entire Football League and only saved from being relegated to the Conference due to Macclesfield Town's ground not meeting the ground grading standards required for promotion. But worse then that, the club almost folded altogether.

* The final game of the season was at Northampton Town, and although City lost, the result was the least of the worries for the huge travelling support, for at the end of the match there were emotional scenes as fans did not know at that point whether they would ever be able to watch Exeter City play again.

* Manager Terry Cooper resigned due to ill health before the season ended and Peter Fox took over in a caretaker capacity, before eventually being given the job in June 1995.

* The Club were in a terrible financial mess and not for the first time in their history the overall position looked very bleak, although on this occasion it was even worse than that if it was at all possible!

* In what many regarded as a rash move, St James' Park was sold to Beazer Homes, thus raising cash to pay off debts. But the house builders announced plans to eventually build on the site and City fans were both horrified and very concerned for the future. It was reported that the club prior to the sale of the ground, had debts of £1.2m.

* An application to move to a new stadium at an out of town site at Matford was turned down by the planners.

*Things became very desperate and the board of directors only had one option left open for them, to allow the Club to slide into administration.

* The purse strings were therefore controlled not by the directors, but by the administrators whose first move was to announce cutbacks in the staff.

* A couple of offers were made to buy the Club, one from two people based in the West Midlands. Nothing came of the discussions though and as the days ticked by it became ever more likely that the Club would simply fold, as the administrator warned that there was not enough money to continue past a certain date.

* The off the field events overshadowed completely what had been a dismal playing season as well. Just minutes away from not being able to guarantee a £390,000 financial package with The Football League for the 1995-96 season, agreement was reached thanks to some generous sponsors and friends of the Club, much to the relief of those waiting outside the Club solicitors for an announcement.

*Exeter City Council, worried, like everyone else, that the city were about to lose what was, after all, a valuable community asset, that of a football club, negotiated a deal to buy back St James' Park from Beazer Homes, and then in turn leased it back to the football club.

* The Council were keen to develop the community side of the Club, but for the supporters, they were just simply relieved once more that something positive had occurred.

*Eventually the Grecians were able to come out of administration and run their own affairs once more, safe in the knowledge that at least the ground they played on would not be suddenly sold off for housing.

* The financial situation was also eased as winger Martin Phillips was sold to Manchester City - then managed by former Exeter City boss Alan Ball - for a club record fee of £500,000. The fee received enabled the Grecians to come out of administration.

Back row: Mark Cooper, Mark Gavin, Russell Coughlin, Anthony Thirlby, Jamie Morgan, Barry McConnell, Neil Parsley, Richard Neno

Middle row: Eamonn Dolan, Robbie Turner, Mark Came, Mike Cecere, Ross Belotti, Jon Richardson, Matthew Hare, Colin Anderson, Gary Rice

Front row: Richard Pears, Danny Bailey, Mike Chapman (Physio), George Kent (Scout), Peter Fox (manager), Noel Blake (Player Asst-Manager), Mike Radford (Youth Development Officer), Martin Phillips, Nicky Medlin

City's league results

| | Home | Away |
|---|---|---|
| Barnet | 1-0 | 2-3 |
| Bury | 1-1 | 0-2 |
| Cardiff City | 2-0 | 1-0 |
| Carlisle United | 1-0 | 1-1 |
| Chester City | 1-2 | 2-2 |
| Colchester United | 2-2 | 1-1 |
| Darlington | 0-1 | 0-1 |
| Doncaster Rovers | 1-0 | 0-2 |
| Fulham | 2-1 | 1-2 |
| Gillingham | 0-0 | 0-1 |
| Hartlepool United | 1-0 | 0-0 |
| Hereford United | 0-2 | 2-2 |
| Leyton Orient | 2-2 | 3-0 |
| Lincoln City | 1-1 | 1-0 |
| Mansfield Town | 2-2 | 1-1 |
| Northampton Town | 1-2 | 0-0 |
| Plymouth Argyle | 1-1 | 2-2 |
| Preston North End | 1-1 | 0-2 |
| Rochdale | 2-0 | 2-4 |
| Scarborough | 2-0 | 0-0 |
| Scunthorpe United | 1-0 | 0-4 |
| Torquay United | 0-0 | 2-0 |
| Wigan Athletic | 0-4 | 0-1 |

F.A. Cup

| | | |
|---|---|---|
| Peterborough United | H 0-1 | R1 |

Football League. Cup

| | | |
|---|---|---|
| Torquay United | A 0-0 | R1 |
| Torquay United | H 1-1 | R1 |

\* Torquay won on away goals

Auto Windscreens Shield

| | | |
|---|---|---|
| Brentford | A 1-1 | R1 |
| AFC Bournemouth | H 0-2 | R2 |

CITY MANAGER 1995-96
Peter Fox - Appointed June 1995

CITY PLAYING SQUAD 1995-96

| Name | Pos | Signed From | Apps | Gls |
|---|---|---|---|---|
| Colin Anderson | D | Hereford United Jul 1994 | 5(8) | |
| Danny Bailey | M | Fulham Dec 1992 | 41(1) | 1 |
| Noel Blake | D | Stoke City Aug 1995 | 44 | 2 |
| Lee Bradbury | F | Portsmouth Dec 1995 | 14 | 5 |
| Leon Braithwaite | W | Bishop's Stortford Nov 1995 | 14(9) | 3 |
| Paul Buckle | M | Torquay United Oct 1995 | 22 | 2 |
| Mark Came | D | Chester City Jul 1994 | 38 | 4 |
| Mike Cecere | F | Walsall Jan 1994 | 5(8) | 1 |
| Mark Chamberlain | W | Brighton & Hove Albion Aug 1995 | 29(4) | 1 |
| Mark Cooper | M | Wycombe Wanderers Feb 1994 | 26(1) | 6 |
| Russell Coughlin | M | Swansea City Jul 1993 | 6(2) | |
| Adrian Foster | F | Gillingham Mar 1996 | 4(3) | |
| Peter Fox | G | Stoke City Jul 1993 | 46 | |
| Mark Gavin | W | Bristol City Feb 1994 | 24(4) | 2 |
| Matthew Hare | D | Trainee Jul 1995 | 10(3) | |
| Darren Hughes | D | Northampton Town Nov 1995 | 25(1) | |
| Barry McConnell | F | Trainee Aug 1995 | 1(7) | |
| Nicky Medlin | M | Trainee Aug 1995 | 2(4) | |
| Jamie Morgan | M | Plymouth Argyle Aug 1995 | 2(4) | |
| Chris Myers | M | Scarborough Mar 1996 | 7(1) | |
| Neil Parsley | D | West Bromwich Albion Aug 1995 | 29(3) | |
| Richard Pears | F | Trainee Jul 1992 | 19(3) | 5 |
| Martin Phillips | W | School Jul 1992 | 11(2) | 3 |
| Gary Rice | D | Trainee Jul 1994 | 17(2) | |
| Jon Richardson | D | Trainee Aug 1991 | 43 | 1 |
| Mickey Ross | F | Plymouth Argyle Nov 1995 | 7 | |
| John Sharpe | W | Manchester City Feb 1996 | 9(5) | 1 |
| Anthony Thirlby | M | Trainee Jul 1992 | 0(2) | |
| Robbie Turner | F | Notts County Feb 1994 | 6(6) | 3 |
| Own Goals | | | | 4 |

DIVISION THREE - SEASON 1995-96

| | P | W | D | L | F | A | Pts |
|---|---|---|---|---|---|---|---|
| Preston North End | 46 | 23 | 17 | 6 | 78 | 38 | 86 |
| Gillingham | 46 | 22 | 17 | 7 | 49 | 20 | 83 |
| Bury | 46 | 22 | 13 | 11 | 66 | 48 | 79 |
| Plymouth Argyle | 46 | 22 | 12 | 12 | 68 | 49 | 78 |
| Darlington | 46 | 20 | 18 | 8 | 60 | 42 | 78 |
| Hereford United | 46 | 20 | 14 | 12 | 65 | 47 | 74 |
| Colchester United | 46 | 18 | 18 | 10 | 61 | 51 | 72 |
| Chester City | 46 | 18 | 16 | 12 | 72 | 53 | 70 |
| Barnet | 46 | 18 | 16 | 12 | 65 | 45 | 70 |
| Wigan Athletic | 46 | 20 | 10 | 16 | 62 | 56 | 70 |
| Northampton Town | 46 | 18 | 13 | 15 | 51 | 44 | 67 |
| Scunthorpe United | 46 | 15 | 15 | 16 | 67 | 61 | 60 |
| Doncaster Rovers | 46 | 16 | 11 | 19 | 49 | 60 | 59 |
| Exeter City | 46 | 13 | 18 | 15 | 46 | 53 | 57 |
| Rochdale | 46 | 14 | 13 | 19 | 57 | 61 | 55 |
| Cambridge United | 46 | 14 | 12 | 20 | 61 | 71 | 54 |
| Fulham | 46 | 12 | 17 | 17 | 57 | 63 | 53 |
| Lincoln City | 46 | 13 | 14 | 19 | 57 | 73 | 53 |
| Mansfield Town | 46 | 11 | 20 | 15 | 54 | 64 | 53 |
| Hartlepool United | 46 | 12 | 13 | 21 | 47 | 67 | 49 |
| Leyton Orient | 46 | 12 | 11 | 23 | 44 | 63 | 47 |
| Cardiff City | 46 | 11 | 12 | 23 | 41 | 64 | 45 |
| Scarborough | 46 | 8 | 16 | 22 | 39 | 69 | 40 |
| Torquay United | 46 | 5 | 14 | 27 | 30 | 84 | 29 |

* Considering the utter turmoil and uncertainty surrounding the Club in the summer of 1995, newly appointed player-manager Peter Fox did a remarkable job in guiding the team to a mid-table finish in 1995-96.

* His squad was a mixture of experience and youngsters who had progressed via the Club's youth scheme. Experience included the likes of assistant player-manager Noel Blake, who had been a team mate of Fox at Stoke City. Former England international winger, Mark Chamberlain, was another player well known to City's management duo and he signed for the Grecians as well.

* Needless to say Fox and Blake had little money in the budget to make signings, so had to use their contacts in order to bring in players, on free transfers, and with a few loan signings.

* The one downside of the squad in 1995-96 was the lack of goals, which were really hard to come by, so much so Mark Cooper topped the scoring charts with only six league goals to his credit, welcome as they were!

* It was also a little worrying and disappointing that less than 3,000 were present at St James' Park for the opening game of the season, a 1-0 defeat against Darlington.

* The Grecians reached the giddy heights of fourth in the league table following their 2-1 home win against Fulham in September 1995, but the team then went 12 matches without a win and consequently by then had dipped to 14th place.

* Striker Mickey Ross returned to the club for a second spell in November 1995 in an effort to score goals. This time he was signed on loan from Plymouth Argyle, but he failed to hit the back of the net during his stay at St James' Park.

* A player-exchange deal in October 1995, involved two midfield players, with City's Russell Coughlin going to Torquay United, whilst Paul Buckle came in the opposite direction.

* The Grecians signed winger Leon Braithwaite from Hemel Hempstead in November 1995 and he became a favourite of the St James' Park faithful, being noted for his speed, if not his shooting!

* Another notable arrival was John Sharpe from Manchester City. He was the brother of England and Manchester United winger, Lee Sharpe.

*Striker Lee Bradbury was signed on loan from Portsmouth and his 5 goals in 14 league outings was the kick start of a career that eventually saw him leave Pompey for Manchester City a fee of £3m! Had City had the financial resources available to them, there were reports that they may well have attempted to have kept him, instead of the player returning to Portsmouth.

* Average attendances for league matches at St. James ' Park was 3,442, a big improvement on the previous season when it was 2,484. Apart from Wigan Athletic, the crowds at Exeter showed the biggest increase of any club in Division Three.

* Not for the first time, Exeter City's final league match of the season coincided with their hosts Preston North End celebrating winning the Divisional Championship. As a result a bumper 18,700 were at Deepdale to see North End defeat the Grecians 2-0. Unfortunately some City supporters who had travelled to the game were unable to gain admittance to the ground when it was full, despite reportedly having match tickets to do so.

* One notable award the Club won was being judged as having the best match programme in the entire Football League. The programme won a string of awards every season between 1993-94 and 2010-11, such was the high consistency of the publication.

Back row: Marcus Dailly, Leon Braintwaite, Sufyan Ghazghazi, Darren Hughes, Mark Chamberlain

Middle row: George Kent (Scout), Mike Chapman (Physio), Eamonn Dolan, Jon Richardson, Ashley Bayes, Richard Pears, Matthew Hare, Mike Radford (Youth Development Officer), Noel Blake (Player Asst-Manager)

Front row: Nicky Medlin, Danny Bailey, Tim Steele, Peter Fox (Manager), Barry McConnell, Chris Myers, Gary Rice.

### City's league results

| | Home | Away |
|---|---|---|
| Barnet | 1-1 | 0-3 |
| Brighton & H.A. | 2-1 | 0-1 |
| Cambridge United | 0-1 | 2-3 |
| Cardiff City | 2-0 | 1-2 |
| Carlisle United | 2-1 | 0-2 |
| Chester City | 1-5 | 1-2 |
| Colchester United | 0-3 | 0-1 |
| Darlington | 3-2 | 1-0 |
| Doncaster Rovers | 1-1 | 2-1 |
| Fulham | 0-1 | 1-1 |
| Hartlepool United | 2-0 | 1-1 |
| Hereford United | 1- | 2-1 |
| Hull City | 0-0 | 0-2 |
| Leyton Orient | 3-2 | 1-1 |
| Lincoln City | 3-3 | 3-2 |
| Mansfield Town | 0-0 | 1-0 |
| Northampton Town | 0-1 | 1-4 |
| Rochdale | 0-0 | 0-2 |
| Scarborough | 2-2 | 4-3 |
| Scunthorpe United | 0-1 | 1-4 |
| Swansea City | 1-2 | 1-3 |
| Torquay United | 1-1 | 0-2 |
| Wigan Athletic | 0-1 | 0-2 |

### F.A. Cup

| | | | |
|---|---|---|---|
| Bristol Rovers | A | 2-1 | R1 |
| Plymouth Argyle | A | 1-4 | R2 |

### Football League. Cup

| | | | |
|---|---|---|---|
| Barnet | H | 0-4 | R1 |
| Barnet | A | 0-2 | R1 |

### Auto Windscreens Shield

| | | | |
|---|---|---|---|
| Cardiff City | A | 1-1 | R2 |
| Peterborough United | H | 0-1 | R2 |

\* - Note: Exeter were given a bye in round one.

### CITY MANAGER 1996-97
Peter Fox - Appointed June 1995

### CITY PLAYING SQUAD 1996-97

| Name | Pos | Signed From | Apps | Gls |
|---|---|---|---|---|
| Lee Baddeley | D | Cardiff City Feb 1997 | 8(3) | |
| Danny Bailey | M | Fulham Dec 1992 | 32(3) | 2 |
| Ashley Bayes | G | Torquay United Jul 1996 | 41 | |
| Paul Birch | M | Doncaster Rovers Mar 1997 | 2 | |
| Noel Blake | D | Stoke City Aug 1995 | 46 | 6 |
| Leon Braithwaite | W | Bishop's Stortford Nov 1995 | 26(12) | 5 |
| Mark Chamberlain | W | Brighton & Hove Albion Aug 1995 | 22(4) | 3 |
| Glenn Crowe | F | Wolverhampton Wanderers Feb 1997 | 10 | 5 |
| Marcus Dailly | M | Dundee Aug 1996 | 8(9) | |
| Steve Flack | F | Cardiff City Sep 1996 | 20(7) | 4 |
| Peter Fox | G | Stoke City Jul 1993 | 5 | |
| Brian Gayle | D | Sheffield United Aug 1996 | 10 | |
| Sufyan Ghazghazi | F | Trainee Jul 1996 | 1(5) | |
| Matthew Hare | D | Trainee Jul 1995 | 16(9) | 1 |
| Lee Hodges | M | West Ham United Sep 1996 | 16(1) | |
| Darren Hughes | D | Northampton Town Nov 1995 | 33(3) | 1 |
| Barry McConnell | F | Trainee Aug 1995 | 20(14) | |
| Gary McKeown | M | Dundee Dec 1996 | 3 | |
| Nicky Medlin | M | Trainee Aug 1995 | 7(4) | 1 |
| Jason Minett | M | Lincoln City Jan 1997 | 13 | |
| Chris Myers | M | Scarborough Mar 1996 | 31(2) | 2 |
| Richard Pears | F | Trainee Jul 1996 | 6(2) | 1 |
| Jason Rees | M | Portsmouth Jan 1997 | 7 | |
| Gary Rice | D | Trainee Jul 1994 | 9(6) | |
| Jon Richardson | D | Trainee Aug 1991 | 42(1) | 1 |
| Neil Richardson | D | Rotherham United Nov 1996 | 14 | |
| Darren Rowbotham | F | Shrewsbury Town Oct 1996 | 25 | 9 |
| John Sharpe | W | Manchester City Feb 1997 | 19(2) | 1 |
| Tim Steele | W | Hereford United Aug 1996 | 14(14) | 3 |
| Own Goals | | | | 3 |

### DIVISION THREE - SEASON 1996-97

| | P | W | D | L | F | A | Pts |
|---|---|---|---|---|---|---|---|
| Wigan Athletic | 46 | 26 | 9 | 11 | 84 | 51 | 87 |
| Fulham | 46 | 25 | 12 | 9 | 72 | 38 | 87 |
| Carlisle United | 46 | 24 | 12 | 10 | 67 | 44 | 84 |
| Northampton Town | 46 | 20 | 12 | 14 | 67 | 44 | 72 |
| Swansea City | 46 | 21 | 8 | 17 | 62 | 58 | 71 |
| Chester City | 46 | 18 | 16 | 12 | 55 | 43 | 70 |
| Cardiff City | 46 | 20 | 9 | 17 | 56 | 54 | 69 |
| Colchester United | 46 | 17 | 17 | 12 | 62 | 51 | 68 |
| Lincoln City | 46 | 18 | 12 | 16 | 70 | 69 | 66 |
| Cambridge United | 46 | 18 | 11 | 17 | 53 | 59 | 65 |
| Mansfield Town | 46 | 16 | 16 | 14 | 47 | 45 | 64 |
| Scarborough | 46 | 16 | 15 | 15 | 65 | 68 | 63 |
| Scunthorpe United | 46 | 18 | 9 | 19 | 59 | 62 | 63 |
| Rochdale | 46 | 14 | 16 | 16 | 58 | 58 | 58 |
| Barnet | 46 | 14 | 16 | 16 | 46 | 51 | 58 |
| Leyton Orient | 46 | 15 | 12 | 19 | 50 | 58 | 57 |
| Hull City | 46 | 13 | 18 | 15 | 44 | 50 | 57 |
| Darlington | 46 | 14 | 10 | 22 | 64 | 78 | 52 |
| Doncaster Rovers | 46 | 14 | 10 | 22 | 52 | 66 | 52 |
| Hartlepool United | 46 | 14 | 9 | 23 | 53 | 66 | 51 |
| Torquay United | 46 | 13 | 11 | 22 | 46 | 62 | 50 |
| Exeter City | 46 | 12 | 12 | 22 | 48 | 73 | 48 |
| Brighton & H.A. | 46 | 13 | 10 | 23 | 53 | 70 | 47 |
| Hereford United | 46 | 11 | 14 | 21 | 50 | 65 | 47 |

1996-97 proved to be a much harder season for the Grecians than the previous one. They were knocked out of the League Cup at the first round stage, and lost to great rivals Plymouth Argyle in the FA Cup. City eventually finished 22nd in the division, just one point above the relegation place to the Conference.

* Once again goalscoring proved to be a problem, with City netting an average of just over a goal a game. It wasn't until the return of favourite Darren Rowbotham in February that they began to score more regularly and he was to top score with 9.

* Rowbotham wasn't the only Grecian to return to the club for a second spell, He was joined by Jason Minett, signed from Lincoln City.

* Manager Peter Fox did pay his first transfer fee though, £10,000 for striker Steve Flack from Cardiff City. This proved to be a great investment as Flack became a loyal servant over several seasons.

*Assistant player-manager Noel Blake was the only member of the squad to be an ever present. He was used in the latter stages of some games as an attacker in an effort to bolster the goal-shy forwards.

* Lee Hodges arrived on loan from West Ham United and was such a success that he was presented with a commemorative salver by chairman Ivor Doble on his last appearance for the club.

* Glenn Crowe was another player to appear on loan for the Grecians, being signed from Wolverhampton Wanderers. He had a successful stay in Devon, scoring five goals in ten matches. On his return to Wolves, he was later called up into the Republic of Ireland 'B' team.

* In September 1996 Exeter City Football Club signed a 25-year lease with the owners of St James' Park, Exeter City Council, which secured football at the ground until the year 2021 at least. The agreement followed the purchase of the ground by the Council during the summer from Beazer Homes.

* Average attendances for league fixtures at St James' Park fell from 3,442 (1995-96) to 3,014 as finances were once again very stretched, with prudent use of the playing budget a necessity.

* The Exeter City Football Trust, which had been formed in the aftermath of the club going into administration, continued to thrive and fund raise, including sportsman's dinners, golf tournaments, quiz nights, disco's, skittles and bucket collections.

* In October 1996, Exeter City Football Club's Chief Executive, Bernard Frowd, made a special trip to Buckingham Palace, where he was presented with his O.B.E., an honour that was bestowed upon him earlier in the year.

* Discussions were held with the Exeter City Council as regards redeveloping the Big Bank end of St James' Park. The plan was to demolish the outdated terracing and replace it with a covered enclosure. Initially this was to be seated grandstand, although that never came to fruition.

* The first issue of a new club magazine, 'Exeter City News.' appeared in February 1997. It didn't prove to be a success, however, and lasted only until the following season.

* Exeter City fans were asked by Uri Geller to watch his programme on Westcountry TV in February 1997. He felt that all City supporters should think positively and the team would steadily climb the Third Division table. In the final game of the season at the Park against Chester City, Uri placed a 'crystal' behind one of the goals which would enable the Grecians to avoid relegation. They lost 1-5!

* Former Exeter City midfielder, Tom Kelly, had a benefit match staged for him at Torquay United's Plainmoor ground in May 1997, when an Exeter City Select XI provided the opposition.

Back row: Andy Cyrus, Jamie Vittles, ???, Sufyan Ghazghazi, Jimmy Gardner

Middle row: George Kent (Scout), Mike Radford (Youth Development Officer), Peter Fox (Manager), Chris Fry, Steve Flack, Ashley Bayes, Lee Baddeley, Barry McConnell, Noel Blake (Player Asst-Manager), Eamonn Dolan (Community officer), Mike Chapman (Physio)

Front row: Paul Birch, Nicky Medlin, Shaun Gale, Darren Rowbotham, Jon Richardson, Leon Braithwaite, Matthew Hare, Jason Minett

### DIVISION THREE 1997-98

| | P | W | D | L | F | A | Pts |
|---|---|---|---|---|---|---|---|
| Notts County | 46 | 29 | 12 | 5 | 82 | 43 | 99 |
| Macclesfield Town | 46 | 23 | 13 | 10 | 63 | 44 | 82 |
| Lincoln City | 46 | 20 | 15 | 11 | 60 | 51 | 75 |
| Colchester United | 46 | 21 | 11 | 14 | 72 | 60 | 74 |
| Torquay United | 46 | 21 | 11 | 14 | 68 | 59 | 74 |
| Scarborough | 46 | 19 | 15 | 12 | 67 | 58 | 72 |
| Barnet | 46 | 19 | 13 | 14 | 61 | 51 | 70 |
| Scunthorpe United | 46 | 19 | 12 | 15 | 56 | 52 | 69 |
| Rotherham United | 46 | 16 | 19 | 11 | 67 | 61 | 67 |
| Peterborough United | 46 | 18 | 13 | 15 | 63 | 51 | 67 |
| Leyton Orient | 46 | 19 | 12 | 15 | 62 | 47 | 66 |
| Mansfield Town | 46 | 16 | 17 | 13 | 64 | 55 | 65 |
| Shrewsbury Town | 46 | 16 | 13 | 17 | 61 | 62 | 61 |
| Chester City | 46 | 17 | 10 | 19 | 60 | 61 | 61 |
| Exeter City | 46 | 15 | 15 | 16 | 68 | 63 | 60 |
| Cambridge United | 46 | 14 | 18 | 14 | 63 | 57 | 60 |
| Hartlepool United | 46 | 12 | 23 | 11 | 61 | 53 | 59 |
| Rochdale | 46 | 17 | 7 | 22 | 56 | 55 | 58 |
| Darlington | 46 | 14 | 12 | 20 | 56 | 72 | 54 |
| Swansea City | 46 | 13 | 11 | 22 | 49 | 62 | 50 |
| Cardiff City | 46 | 9 | 23 | 14 | 48 | 52 | 50 |
| Hull City | 46 | 11 | 8 | 27 | 56 | 83 | 41 |
| Brighton & H.A. | 46 | 6 | 17 | 23 | 38 | 66 | 35 |
| Doncaster Rovers | 46 | 4 | 8 | 34 | 30 | 113 | 20 |

## CITY PLAYING SQUAD 1997-98

| Name | Pos | Signed From | Apps | Gls |
|---|---|---|---|---|
| Lee Baddeley | D | Cardiff City Feb 1997 | 29(3) | 1 |
| Ashley Bayes | G | Torquay United Jul 1996 | 45 | |
| Paul Birch | M | Doncaster Rovers Mar 1977 | 31(2) | 5 |
| Noel Blake | D | Stoke City Aug 1995 | 36(2) | 1 |
| Leon Braithwaite | W | Bishop's Stortford Nov 1995 | 0(5) | 1 |
| Geoff Breslan | M | Trainee Jul 1996 | 0(1) | |
| Billy Clark | D | Bristol Rovers Oct 1997 | 31 | 3 |
| Chris Curran | D | Plymouth Argyle Jul 1997 | 9 | |
| Andy Cyrus | D | Crystal Palace Jul 1997 | 17(4) | |
| Mark Devlin | M | Stoke City Oct 1997 | 31(2) | 2 |
| James Dungey | G | Plymouth Argyle Dec1997 | 1 | |
| Steve Flack | F | Cardiff City Sep 1996 | 37(4) | 14 |
| Chris Fry | M | Colchester United Jul 1997 | 16(12) | 1 |
| Shaun Gale | D | Barnet Jun 1997 | 42(1) | 4 |
| Jimmy Gardner | W | Cardiff City Jul 1997 | 19(4) | 1 |
| Sufyan Ghazghazi | F | Trainee Jul 1996 | 1(8) | |
| Matthew Hare | D | Trainee Jul 1995 | 5(2) | |
| Peter Holcroft | M | Swindon Town Aug 1997 | 3(3) | |
| Chris Holloway | M | Trainee Jul 1996 | 4(2) | |
| Neil Illman | F | Plymouth Argyle Dec 1997 | 6(2) | 2 |
| Barry McConnell | F | Trainee Aug 1995 | 10(6) | 6 |
| Nicky Medlin | M | Trainee Aug 1995 | 11(9) | |
| Jason Minett | D | Lincoln City Jan 1997 | 6 | |
| Martin Phillips | W | Manchester City Mar 1998 | 7(1) | |
| Jon Richardson | D | Trainee Aug 1991 | 41 | 2 |
| Darren Rowbotham | F | Shrewsbury Town Oct 1996 | 42(1) | 20 |
| Paul Tisdale | M | Bristol City Dec 1997 | 10 | 1 |
| John Wilkinson | W | Trainee Jul 1995 | 0(1) | |
| John Williams | F | Walsall Aug 1997 | 16(20) | 4 |

### City's League Results

| | Home | Away |
|---|---|---|
| Barnet | 0-0 | 2-1 |
| Brighton & H.A. | 2-1 | 3-1 |
| Cambridge United | 1-0 | 1-2 |
| Cardiff City | 1-1 | 1-1 |
| Chester City | 5-0 | 1-1 |
| Colchester United | 0-1 | 2-1 |
| Darlington | 1-0 | 2-3 |
| Doncaster Rovers | 5-1 | 1-0 |
| Hartlepool United | 1-1 | 1-1 |
| Hull City | 3-0 | 2-3 |
| Leyton Orient | 2-2 | 0-1 |
| Lincoln City | 1-2 | 1-2 |
| Macclesfield Town | 1-3 | 2-2 |
| Mansfield Town | 1-0 | 2-3 |
| Notts County | 2-5 | 1-1 |
| Peterborough United | 0-0 | 1-1 |
| Rochdale | 3-0 | 0-3 |
| Rotherham United | 3-1 | 0-1 |
| Scarborough | 1-1 | 1-4 |
| Scunthorpe United | 2-3 | 1-2 |
| Shrewsbury Town | 2-2 | 1-1 |
| Swansea City | 1-0 | 1-2 |
| Torquay United | 1-1 | 2-1 |

**F.A. Cup**

| | | | |
|---|---|---|---|
| Northampton Town | H | 1-1 | R1 |
| Northampton Town | A | 1-2 | R1R |

**Football League Cup**

| | | | |
|---|---|---|---|
| Walsall | H | 0-2 | R1 |
| Walsall | A | 0-1 | R1 |

**Auto Windscreens Shield**

| | | | |
|---|---|---|---|
| Bristol Rovers | H | 1-2 | R2 |

\* Exeter given bye in Round 1

CITY Manager 1997-98          1997-98
Peter Fox - Appointed June 1995

* Exeter City made a terrific start to the season and actually found themselves top of the table for a short while after winning four matches and drawing once in their opening five games. However, although they were still in fourth place in December, the Grecians' form slipped away and the season ended with an eventual 15th place.

* The middle part of the season was very poor in terms of good league results with only three wins in 21 matches and the early season promise was soon forgotten about as the team slipped down the table.

*Darren Rowbotham proved his worth once more as he topped the scoring with 20 league goals, the first City player to score that many since 1989-90 when ... Rowbotham!!! - in his first spell with the club, netted 21.

* Peter Fox started his third season in charge at St James' Park, but still had to work within a tight financial budget. During the summer he signed Chris Curran, Andy Cyrus, Chris Fry, Shaun Gale (for a £10,000 fee), Jimmy Gardner and John Williams.

*As the season progressed further arrivals at the cub included the experienced Billy Clark from Bristol Rovers and Mark Devlin from Stoke City. Fox also went into the loan market, with one player signed being Paul Tisdale, who was later to become manager at Exeter a few years later.

*A popular return to the club was made by locally produced winger, Martin Phillips, who rejoined the Grecians in March 1998 for a loan spell until the end of the season. Having been sold by Exeter for £500,000, Phillips featured in the last eight matches of the season.

* There was no joy in any of the cup competitions, with early exits being made in them all. City fans were starved of success as far as cup ties were concerned, a run in one of them was long overdue.

* The club magazine, 'Exeter City F.C. News' never really took off in terms of sales, however, in September 1997, managing editor, Bill Cooper, was supplied with a sponsored car by J.F.E. Nissan. A sales outlet for the magazine was opened in the Exmouth Indoor Market for a short while. The magazine folded after a couple of seasons.

* Following a number of complaints, the Club made an appeal in the Grecian Gazette match programme with regards to bad language at games at St James' Park. With increasing numbers of families and youngsters attending games, supporters were reminded that the stewards had the power to remove anyone using foul and abusive language.

* City's Chief Executive, Bernard Frowd, stated just how important revenue from commercial ventures was to the club, when a new Commercial Manager, Keith Hartshorn was appointed in December 1997. He said: "The club has to consider carefully what is required of the Commercial Department. The ability of the club to raise income from its own commercial and sponsorship activity is getting increasingly vital and we need to redouble our efforts."

* Highest attendance of the season at St James' Park for a league fixture was against Devon neighbours, Torquay United, when 8,350 saw the teams draw 1-1 on 28th December 1997. This, incidentally, was the first time Exeter had ever played a home league match on a Sunday. They had previously played away on a Sunday to the likes of Newport County and Reading etc.

* Lowest attendance of the season for a league fixture was a pitiful 1,186 at Doncaster Rovers at the end of August. City won the game 1-0.

Back row: Chris Fry, Scott Walker , Chris Holloway, Jon Gittens, Steve Flack, Shaun Gale, Barry McConnell, Jimmy Gardner, Luke Vinnicombe

Middle row: Lee Baddeley, Jon Richardson, Chris Curran, Darren Rowbotham, Danny Potter, Ashley Bayes, John Wilkinson, Gavin Chesterfield, Danny Harris

Front row: Graeme Power, Geoff Brelan, Noel Blake (Asst Manager), George Kent (Scout), Peter Fox (Manager), Mike Radford (Youth Development Officer) Simon Shakeshaft (Physio), Jason Rees, Billy Clark

## CITY PLAYING SQUAD 1998-99

| Name | Pos | Signed From | Apps | Gls |
|------|-----|-------------|------|-----|
| Lee Baddeley | D | Cardiff City Feb 1997 | 23 | |
| Ashley Bayes | G | Torquay United Jul 1996 | 41 | |
| Noel Blake | D | Stoke City Aug 1995 | 4(3) | |
| Geoff Breslan | M | Trainee Jul 1996 | 24(10) | 4 |
| Billy Clark | D | Bristol Rovers Oct 1997 | 8(2) | |
| Glen Crowe | F | Wolverhampton Wanderers Aug 1998 | 3(6) | |
| David Crown | W | Portsmouth Mar 1983 | | |
| Chris Curran | D | Plymouth Argyle Jul 1997 | 30(4) | 4 |
| Steve Flack | F | Cardiff City Sep 1996 | 38(6) | 11 |
| Chris Fry | M | Colchester United Jul 1997 | 27(5) | 2 |
| Shaun Gale | D | Barnet Jun 1997 | 21(6) | |
| Jimmy Gardner | W | Cardiff City Jul 1997 | 23(4) | |
| John Gittens | D | Torquay United Jul 1998 | 44 | 2 |
| Chris Holloway | M | Trainee Jul 1996 | 27(7) | 1 |
| Barry McConnell | F | Trainee aug 1995 | 15(7) | 5 |
| Danny Potter | G | Weymouth Aug 1998 | 5 | |
| Graeme Power | D | Bristol Rovers Aug 1998 | 40 | |
| Brian Quailey | F | West Bromwich Albion Dec 1998 | 8(4) | 2 |
| Jason Rees | M | Cambridge United Jul 1998 | 44 | 1 |
| Jin Richardson | D | Trainee Aug 1991 | 39(1) | 2 |
| Darren Rowbotham | F | Shrewsbury Town Oct 996 | 28(4) | 6 |
| Peter Smith | M | Trainee Jul 1998 | 0(10 | |
| Robert Speakman | F | Trainee Jul 1998 | 0(1) | |
| Paul Tosh | F | Hibernian Feb 1999 | 8(2) | 2 |
| Warren Waugh | F | Trainee Jul 1998 | 0(7) | |
| John Wilkinson | W | Trainee Jl 1995 | 6(12) | 2 |
| Own Goals | | | | 3 |

City's League Results

| | Home | Away |
|------|------|------|
| Barnet | 1-0 | 1-0 |
| Brentford | 0-1 | 0-3 |
| Brighton & H.A. | 1-0 | 1-0 |
| Cambridge United | 0-3 | 1-1 |
| Cardiff City | 0-2 | 0-1 |
| Carlisle United | 2-0 | 3-1 |
| Chester City | 0-1 | 0-0 |
| Darlington | 0-0 | 0-4 |
| Halifax Town | 2-1 | 1-1 |
| Hartlepool United | 2-1 | 3-4 |
| Hull City | 3-0 | 1-2 |
| Leyton Orient | 1-1 | 0-2 |
| Mansfield Town | 2-1 | 1-0 |
| Peterborough United | 2-0 | 1-4 |
| Plymouth Argyle | 1-1 | 0-1 |
| Rochdale | 2-1 | 1-1 |
| Rotherham United | 3-0 | 0-0 |
| Scarborough | 1-0 | 0-1 |
| Scunthorpe United | 2-2 | 0-2 |
| Shrewsbury Town | 0-1 | 1-1 |
| Southend United | 2-1 | 0-0 |
| Swansea City | 4-0 | 0-2 |
| Torquay United | 1-1 | 0-1 |

F.A. Cup

| | | | |
|------|------|------|------|
| Tamworth | A | 2-2 | R1 |
| Tamworth | H | 4-1 | R1R |
| Bristol Rovers | H | 2-2 | R2 |
| Bristol Rovers | A | 0-5 | R2R |

Football League Cup

| | | | |
|------|------|------|------|
| Ipswich Town | H | 1-1 | R1 |
| Ipswich Town | A | 1-5 | R1 |

Auto Windscreens Shield

| | | | |
|------|------|------|------|
| Southend United | H | 3-1 | R2 |
| Cambridge United | A | 1-1+ | R3 |

+ Cambridge won 5-3 on pens
* Exeter given bye in Round 1

CITY MANAGER 1998-99
Peter Fox - Appointed June 1995

DIVISION THREE SEASON 1998-99

| | P | W | D | L | F | A | Pts |
|------|---|---|---|---|---|---|-----|
| Brentford | 46 | 26 | 7 | 13 | 79 | 56 | 85 |
| Cambridge United | 46 | 23 | 12 | 11 | 78 | 48 | 81 |
| Cardiff City | 46 | 22 | 14 | 10 | 60 | 39 | 80 |
| Scunthorpe United | 46 | 22 | 8 | 16 | 69 | 58 | 74 |
| Rotherham United | 46 | 20 | 13 | 13 | 79 | 61 | 73 |
| Leyton Orient | 46 | 19 | 15 | 12 | 68 | 59 | 72 |
| Swansea City | 46 | 19 | 14 | 13 | 56 | 48 | 71 |
| Mansfield Town | 46 | 19 | 10 | 17 | 60 | 58 | 67 |
| Peterborough United | 46 | 18 | 12 | 16 | 72 | 56 | 66 |
| Halifax Town | 46 | 17 | 15 | 14 | 58 | 56 | 66 |
| Darlington | 46 | 18 | 11 | 17 | 69 | 58 | 65 |
| Exeter City | 46 | 17 | 12 | 17 | 47 | 50 | 63 |
| Plymouth Argyle | 46 | 17 | 10 | 19 | 58 | 54 | 61 |
| Chester City | 46 | 13 | 18 | 15 | 57 | 66 | 57 |
| Shrewsbury Town | 46 | 14 | 14 | 18 | 52 | 63 | 56 |
| Barnet | 46 | 14 | 13 | 19 | 54 | 71 | 55 |
| Brighton & H.A. | 46 | 16 | 7 | 23 | 49 | 66 | 55 |
| Southend United | 46 | 14 | 12 | 20 | 52 | 58 | 54 |
| Rochdale | 46 | 13 | 15 | 18 | 42 | 55 | 54 |
| Torquay United | 46 | 12 | 17 | 17 | 47 | 58 | 53 |
| Hull City | 46 | 14 | 11 | 21 | 44 | 62 | 53 |
| Hartlepool United | 46 | 13 | 12 | 21 | 52 | 65 | 51 |
| Carlisle United | 46 | 11 | 16 | 19 | 43 | 53 | 49 |
| Scarborough | 46 | 14 | 6 | 26 | 50 | 77 | 48 |

* This was a season where Exeter City spent most of it in the middle of the league table, never going any higher than 12th, although they did slip down as far as 19th following the 1-0 away defeat against arch rivals, Plymouth Argyle, in December 1998, a game that was watched by the highest attendance of the season for a league match played by City, when 11,936 were present at Home Park.

* Manager Peter Fox and his assistant Noel Blake started their fourth season in charge by once again having to be thrifty in the transfer market due the financial position at St James' Park.

* Two notable and experienced players to be signed prior to the start of the season were Jon Gittens and Jason Rees. However, a number of players who had made their way via the club's youth scheme, ably run by Mike Radford, also got their chance, including Geoff Breslan, Chris Holloway, Barry McConnell, Jon Richardson, Peter Smith, Robert Speakman, Warren Waugh and John Wilkinson.

* Goalscoring proved to be a problem, with an average of one per game, as Steve Flack top scored with 11 league goals. The team went five league matches without scoring at one stage. City's best spell of the season in January and February saw them go six matches unbeaten, which included four wins.

* City also had two separate spells during the season when they went seven matches without a win, which summed up their season, as not being consistent enough to make any impact.

* The Grecians were almost the 'victims' of an all too familiar giant killing in the first round of the FA Cup, as it took an injury time equaliser from Jon Richardson to earn a 2-2 draw at Tamworth. The non-leaguers were soundly beaten 4-1 in the replay back at St James' Park. Playing in the Tamworth side was former Exeter City player, Tim Steele.

* Ipswich Town were the visitors to St James' Park for the first round first leg of the Football League Cup, a team that the Grecians had not played since the days of the Third Division South. They gave a good account of themselves as they held Ipswich to a 1-1 draw before a disappointing attendance of 3,233. but then lost the return leg 5-1 in Suffolk to end any hopes of a run in the competition.

* Average attendance for league matches at St James' Park was 3,154, which was worryingly down on the previous season when it was 3,988.

* The subject of ground redevelopment was high on the agenda and work was expected to start the following season on demolishing the much loved Cowshed terrace to be replaced by a seated stand, which would incorporate executive boxes, thus hopefully increasing the club's revenue.

* Highest attendance of the season at St James' Park was not surprisingly for the visit of Plymouth Argyle when 6,746 were present. The lowest was just 1,929 when City defeated Rotherham United 3-0.

* Once again City used the loan market to bring in Glen Crowe (for his second spell at the club), Brian Quailey and Paul Tosh. All were strikers, and whilst Crowe didn't find the back of the net, the other two did, with a couple of goals each during their stay at the club.

* Scarborough finished rock bottom of the Football League and thus dropped into the Conference. What wasn't known at the time was that the Boro' chairman, John Russell, would later join the Grecians in the ill fated 2002-03 season, which ended on relegation to the Conference!

## CITY PLAYING SQUAD 1999-2000

| Name | Pos | Signed | Apps | Gls |
|------|-----|--------|------|-----|
| Gary Alexander | F | West Ham United Aug 1999 | 37 | 16 |
| Frank Bennett | F | Bristol Rovers Feb 2000 | 8(1) | 1 |
| Noel Blake | D | Stoke City Aug 1995 | 2(5) | 1 |
| Lee Boylan | F | Trelleborg (Sweden) Nov 1999 | 3(3) | 1 |
| Shayne Bradley | F | Southampton Sep 1999 | 6(2) | 1 |
| Geoff Breslan | M | Trainee Jul 1996 | 16(13) | |
| Aaron Brown | M | Bristol City Jan 2000 | 4(1) | 1 |
| Paul Buckle | M | Colchester United Jul 1999 | 27 | 1 |
| John Cornforth | M | Scunthorpe United Feb 2000 | 12 | 2 |
| Chris Curran | D | Plymouth Argyle Jul 1997 | 36(2) | 1 |
| Rob Dewhurst | D | Hull City Aug 1999 | 21(2) | 2 |
| Lee Ellington | F | Hull City Mar 2000 | 0(1) | |
| Steve Flack | F | Cardiff City Sep 1996 | 19(21) | 2 |
| Shaun Gale | D | Barnet Jun 1997 | 18(5) | 1 |
| John Gittens | D | Torquay United Jul 1998 | 18(5) | 1 |
| Chris Holloway | M | Trainee Jul 1996 | 20(4) | 1 |
| Alex Inglethorpe | F | Leyton Orient Feb 2000 | 0(1) | |
| Lee Jarman | D | Merthyr Tdfil Mar 2000 | 7 | |
| David Lee | D | Colchester United Feb 2000 | 3(1) | |
| Steve Lovell | F | Portsmouth Mar 2000 | 4(1) | 1 |
| Barry McConnell | F | Trainee Aug 1995 | 16(9) | 1 |
| Jason Matthews | G | Nuneaton Borough Aug 1999 | 11(1) | |
| Stuart Naylor | G | Walsall Aug 1999 | 31 | |
| Kofi Nyamah | W | Luton Town Jul 1999 | 23(12) | 1 |
| Danny Potter | G | Weymouth Aug 1998 | 4 | |
| Graeme Power | D | Bristol Rovers Aug 1998 | 29(1) | |
| Jason Rees | M | Cambridge United Jul 1998 | 42(1) | 4 |
| Jon Richardson | D | Trainee Aug 1991 | 35 | 1 |
| Jamie Robinson | D | Torquay United Jan 1999 | 11(1) | |
| Darren Rowbotham | F | Shrewsbury Town Oct 1996 | 13(5) | 2 |
| Peter Smith | M | Trainee Jul 1998 | 3(4) | |
| Robert Speakman | F | Trainee Jul 1998 | 4(13) | 3 |
| Jukka Vanninen | M | Roveniemi Rops (Finland) Dec 1999 | 3(2) | |
| Warren Waugh | F | Trainee Jul 1998 | 0(3) | |
| Ben Worrall | M | Scarborough Aug 1999 | 1(3) | |

## DIVISION THREE SEASON 1999-2000

| | P | W | D | L | F | A | Pts |
|---|---|---|---|---|---|---|-----|
| Swansea City | 46 | 24 | 13 | 9 | 51 | 30 | 85 |
| Rotherham United | 46 | 24 | 12 | 10 | 72 | 36 | 84 |
| Northampton Town | 46 | 25 | 7 | 14 | 63 | 45 | 82 |
| Darlington | 46 | 21 | 16 | 9 | 66 | 36 | 79 |
| Peterborough United | 46 | 22 | 12 | 12 | 63 | 54 | 78 |
| Barnet | 46 | 21 | 12 | 13 | 59 | 53 | 75 |
| Hartlepool United | 46 | 21 | 9 | 16 | 60 | 49 | 72 |
| Cheltenham Town | 46 | 20 | 10 | 16 | 50 | 42 | 70 |
| Torquay United | 46 | 19 | 12 | 15 | 62 | 52 | 69 |
| Rochdale | 46 | 18 | 14 | 14 | 57 | 54 | 68 |
| Brighton & H.A. | 46 | 17 | 16 | 13 | 64 | 47 | 67 |
| Plymouth Atgyle | 46 | 16 | 18 | 12 | 55 | 51 | 66 |
| Macclesfield | 46 | 18 | 11 | 17 | 66 | 61 | 65 |
| Hull City | 46 | 15 | 14 | 17 | 43 | 43 | 59 |
| Lincoln City | 46 | 15 | 14 | 17 | 67 | 69 | 59 |
| Southend United | 46 | 15 | 11 | 20 | 53 | 61 | 56 |
| Mansfield Town | 46 | 16 | 8 | 22 | 50 | 65 | 56 |
| Halifax Town | 46 | 12 | 16 | 18 | 44 | 58 | 54 |
| Leyton Orient | 46 | 13 | 13 | 20 | 47 | 52 | 52 |
| York City | 46 | 12 | 16 | 18 | 39 | 53 | 52 |
| Exeter City | 46 | 11 | 11 | 24 | 46 | 72 | 44 |
| Shrewsbury Town | 46 | 9 | 13 | 24 | 40 | 67 | 40 |
| Carlisle United | 46 | 9 | 12 | 25 | 42 | 75 | 39 |
| Chester City | 46 | 10 | 9 | 27 | 44 | 79 | 39 |

## City's League Results

| | Home | Away |
|---|------|------|
| Barnet | 0-0 | 2-2 |
| Brighton & H.A. | 0-0 | 2-4 |
| Carlisle United | 1-1 | 0-0 |
| Cheltenham Town | 1-2 | 1-3 |
| Chester City | 0-2 | 1-1 |
| Darlington | 1-4 | 0-1 |
| Halifax Town | 1-0 | 0-1 |
| Hartlepool United | 1-2 | 1-2 |
| Hull City | 1-0 | 0-4 |
| Leyton Orient | 1-3 | 1-4 |
| Lincoln City | 3-0 | 0-1 |
| Macclesfield Town | 0-3 | 0-1 |
| Mansfield Town | 1-0 | 1-1 |
| Northampton Town | 1-2 | 1-2 |
| Peterborough United | 2-2 | 1-3 |
| Plymouth Argyle | 1-1 | 0-1 |
| Rochdale | 2-0 | 2-0 |
| Rotherham United | 3-1 | 0-5 |
| Shrewsbury Town | 1-2 | 4-1 |
| Southend United | 0-1 | 2-1 |
| Swansea City | 1-1 | 0-3 |
| Torquay United | 3-2 | 0-1 |
| York City | 2-1 | 0-0 |

### F.A. Cup

| | | | |
|---|---|---|---|
| Eastwood Town | H | 2-1 | R1 |
| Aldershot Town | H | 2-0 | R2 |
| Everton | H | 0-0 | R3 |
| Everton | A | 0-1 | R3R |

### Football League Cup

| | | | |
|---|---|---|---|
| Birmingham City | A | 0-3 | R1 |
| Birmingham City | H | 1-2 | R1 |

### Auto Windscreens Shield

| | | | |
|---|---|---|---|
| Swansea City | H | 2-0 | R2 |
| Torquay United | H | 1-0 | R3 |
| Bristol City | A | 0-4 | SF |
| Bristol City | H | 1-1 | SF |

* Exeter were given a bye in Round One

## CITY MANAGER 1999-2000

Peter Fox - Appointed June 1995
Noel Blake - Appointed January 2000

* It proved to be a season of contrasts, for like the previous campaign, Exeter City were top of the Third Division after the first month, but then slid away to finish in 21st place.

* Newcomers to the City squad at the beginning of the season were, Paul Buckle, Rob Dewhurst, Stuart Naylor, Kofi Nyamah and Ben Worrall, but the most significant signing was Gary Alexander, who joined on a season long loan from West Ham United. He went on to become the club's leading goalscorer with 16 league goals.

* City again used the loan market during the course of the season, but no one were as successful as Alexander. Frank Bennett, Shayne Bradley and Steve Lovell - all three being strikers - had a loan spell at St James' Park.

* Exeter also signed their first ever Finnish-born player, Jukka Vanninen, but the midfielder was to feature in just five league matches before being released.

* Towards the end of season, players were signed on short term or non-contract terms including, Lee Ellington, Lee Jarman and David Lee, none of whom were to be retained for the following season.

* On a positive note, no fewer than seven players featured in the first team during the course of the season, who had progressed via the club's youth development scheme.

* The Grecians did reach the third round of the FA Cup though and a bumper St James' Park crowd (6,045—only three sides of three ground were open due to redevelopment work) watched Everton being held to a goalless draw. City lost the replay 1-0 but drew a lot of praise for the way in which they had matched their Premiership opponents over the two games.

* Exeter had lost goalkeeper Stuart Naylor with concussion at half-time in the Cup tie against Everton at the Park, and so debutant Jason Matthews took over for the second half and gave a great performance not being overawed by the situation he suddenly found himself in.

* The team also reached the Southern Area semi-final of the Auto Windscreens Shield. But their dreams of a trip to Wembley were shattered when they lost 4-0 at Bristol City in the first leg. Although the teams drew back at St James' Park, Exeter were beaten before the start.

* Ground redevelopment was well advanced, with the much loved Cowshed terracing demolished and replaced by an all seater stand, and the Big Bank terrace rebuilt and covered. It was argued that the improvements had to take place to meet the minimum standards required by The Football League, but the Doble Stand in particular later proved to be a real millstone around the clubs necks as money was owed to Mowlem who constructed it. And even then it was not finished, with nothing being built underneath the stand, it being just an empty shell.

* The average attendance for league matches fell once again to 3,014. The highest attendance of the season for a league match was 5,263 for the visit of Torquay United in November 1999.

* The lowest attendance at St James' Park was just 964 for the visit of Swansea City in the second round of the Auto Windscreens Shield, a competition that fails to capture the interest of supporters at its early stages.

* Manager Peter Fox resigned in January 2000, frustrated with the way results had gone in the past twelve months. Fox had been a popular manager, but at the end of the day, he like many before him, was unable to achieve the results that everyone so desired. His assistant Noel Blake was appointed in his place, and like Fox, this was also his first managerial appointment.

## CITY PLAYING SQUAD 2000-1

| Name | Pos | Signed from | Apps | Gls |
|---|---|---|---|---|
| Kwame Ampadu | M | Leyton Orient Jul 2000 | 29(7) | |
| Jon Ashton | D | Plymouth Argyle Jul 2000 | 7(6) | |
| Gary Birch | F | Walsall Mar 2001 | 6(3) | 2 |
| Noel Blake | D | Stoke City Aug 1995 | 3(2) | |
| Geoff Breslan | M | Trainee Jul 1996 | 0(2) | |
| Paul Buckle | M | Colchester United Jul 1999 | 39(2) | 3 |
| Mark Burrows | D | Coventry City Ul 2000 | 21(8) | |
| Jamie Campbell | D | Brighton & H.A. Jul 2000 | 42 | 2 |
| John Cornforth | M | Scunthorpe United Feb 2000 | 11(1) | |
| Chris Curran | D | Plymouth Argyle Jul 1997 | 26 | |
| Steve Epesse-Titi | D | Wolverhampton Wanderers Mar 2001 | 5(1) | |
| Steve Flack | F | Cardiff City May 1996 | 33(7) | 13 |
| Kevin Francis | F | Castleton Gabriels Nov 2000 | 3(4) | 1 |
| Stuart Fraser | G | Stoke City Jul 2000 | 5(1) | |
| Gavin Holligan | F | West Ham United Oct 2000 | 3 | |
| Chris Holloway | M | Trainee Jul 1996 | 0(4) | |
| Carl Hutchings | M | Bristol City Nov 2000 | 2 | |
| Alex Inglethorpe | F | Leyton Orient Feb 2000 | 11(7) | 2 |
| Barry McConnell | F | Trainee Aug 1995 | 3(1) | |
| Jamie Mudge | F | Trainee Jul 2000 | 0(3) | |
| Graeme Power | D | Bristol Rovers Aug 1998 | 34(1) | 1 |
| Kevin Rapley | F | Notts County Nov 2000 | 6(1) | |
| Mark Rawlinson | M | AFC Bournemouth Jul 2000 | 18(7) | 2 |
| Paul Read | F | SK Ostersund (Sweden) Nov 2000 | 10(1) | 1 |
| Chrisian Roberts | F | Cardiff City Jul 2000 | 33(9) | 8 |
| Darren Roberts | F | Scarborough Jul 2000 | 3(5) | |
| Andy Roscoe | M | Mansfield Town Jul 2000 | 33(10) | 1 |
| Darren Rowbotham | F | Shrewsbury Town Oct 1996 | 18(7) | |
| Robert Speakman | F | Trainee Jul 1998 | 0(1) | |
| Damian Spencer | F | Bristol City Mar 2001 | 2(4) | |
| Francis Tierney | W | Witton Albion Nov 2000 | 4(3) | 1 |
| Graeme Tomlinson | W | Macclesfield Town Jun 2000 | 13(11) | 1 |
| Arjen Van Heusden | G | Cambridge United Aug 2000 | 41 | |
| Neil Whitworth | D | Hull City Aug 2000 | 34 | 1 |
| John Wilkinson | W | Trainee Jul 1995 | 0(1) | |
| Lee Zabek | M | Bristol Rovers Jul 2000 | 26(5) | |
| Own Goals | | | | 1 |

City's League Results

| Home | Home | Away |
|---|---|---|
| Barnet | 1-0 | 1-1 |
| Blackpool | 2-0 | 0-3 |
| Brighton & H.A. | 1-0 | 0-2 |
| Cardiff City | 1-2 | 1-0 |
| Carlisle United | 1-0 | 1-0 |
| Cheltenham Town | 0-2 | 0-1 |
| Chesterfield | 1-1 | 0-2 |
| Darlington | 1-1 | 1-1 |
| Halifax Town | 0-0 | 1-3 |
| Hartlepool United | 1-1 | 0-2 |
| Hull City | 0-1 | 1-2 |
| Kidderminster Harriers | 2-1 | 0-0 |
| Leyton Orient | 2-3 | 1-2 |
| Lincoln City | 0-0 | 1-3 |
| Macclesfield Town | 0-0 | 2-0 |
| Mansfield Town | 0-0 | 1-1 |
| Plymouth Argyle | 0-2 | 0-1 |
| Rochdale | 0-1 | 0-3 |
| Scunthorpe United | 2-1 | 2-0 |
| Shrewsbury Town | 1-0 | 0-2 |
| Southend United | 2-2 | 1-1 |
| Torquay United | 1-1 | 1-2 |
| York City | 3-1 | 3-0 |

| F.A. Cup | | | |
|---|---|---|---|
| Walsall | A | 0-4 | R1 |

| Football League Cup | | | |
|---|---|---|---|
| Swindon Town | A | 1-1 | R1 |
| Swindon Town | H | 1-2 | R1 |

| LDV Trophy | | | |
|---|---|---|---|
| Wycombe Wanderers | A | 0-1 | R1 |

CITY MANAGER 2000-1
Noel Blake - Appointed January 2000

## DIVISION THREE SEASON 2000-1

| | P | W | D | L | F | A | Pts |
|---|---|---|---|---|---|---|---|
| Brighton & H.A. | 46 | 28 | 8 | 10 | 73 | 35 | 92 |
| Cardiff City | 46 | 23 | 13 | 10 | 95 | 58 | 82 |
| Chesterfield | 46 | 25 | 14 | 7 | 79 | 42 | 80 |
| Hartlepool United | 46 | 21 | 14 | 11 | 71 | 54 | 77 |
| Leyton Orient | 46 | 20 | 15 | 11 | 59 | 51 | 75 |
| Hull City | 46 | 19 | 17 | 10 | 47 | 39 | 74 |
| Blackpool | 46 | 22 | 6 | 18 | 74 | 58 | 72 |
| Rochdale | 46 | 18 | 17 | 11 | 59 | 48 | 71 |
| Cheltenham Town | 46 | 18 | 14 | 14 | 59 | 52 | 68 |
| Scunthorpe United | 46 | 18 | 11 | 17 | 62 | 52 | 65 |
| Southend United | 46 | 15 | 18 | 13 | 55 | 53 | 63 |
| Plymouth Argyle | 46 | 15 | 13 | 18 | 54 | 61 | 58 |
| Mansfield Town | 46 | 15 | 13 | 18 | 64 | 72 | 58 |
| Macclesfield Town | 46 | 14 | 14 | 18 | 51 | 62 | 56 |
| Shrewsbury Town | 46 | 15 | 10 | 21 | 49 | 65 | 55 |
| Kidderminster Harriers | 46 | 13 | 14 | 19 | 47 | 61 | 53 |
| York City | 46 | 13 | 13 | 20 | 42 | 53 | 52 |
| Lincoln City | 46 | 12 | 15 | 19 | 58 | 66 | 51 |
| Exeter City | 46 | 12 | 14 | 20 | 40 | 58 | 50 |
| Darlington | 46 | 12 | 13 | 21 | 44 | 56 | 49 |
| Torquay United | 46 | 12 | 13 | 21 | 52 | 77 | 49 |
| Carlisle United | 46 | 11 | 15 | 20 | 42 | 65 | 48 |
| Halifax Town | 46 | 12 | 11 | 23 | 54 | 68 | 47 |
| Barnet | 46 | 12 | 9 | 25 | 67 | 81 | 45 |

* Noel Blake in his first managerial appointment struggled to make headway and it was difficult to keep tabs just who was on the books, for no fewer than 36 players featured in the first team alone. Consistency is not a word too often associated with Exeter City, and that was certainly the case as far as team selection was concerned.

* Despite the huge turnover of players, City struggled badly at the foot of the Football League, and it was only after the intervention of former Tottenham Hotspur legend, Steve Perryman, who had been brought to the club by Grecians' director Joe Gadston, that possibly prevented Exeter dropping out of the league altogether. Working alongside Blake, he somehow managed to steady the ship and garnish enough points to avoid the drop. Gadston had been at Brentford when Perryman was the manager there, hence the connection, and what a good one it proved to be as the Spurs man later returned to the club to become Director of Football.

* Results in the cup competitions were disappointing, going out at the first round stage in the FA Cup, the Football League Cup and the LDV Vans Trophy.

* Surprisingly the average attendances for league matches at St James' Park showed a healthy increase on the previous season. An average of 3,708 came through the turnstiles an increase of 700 per game.

* The highest attendance of the season at the Park for a league game was 5,150 for the visit of Carlisle United in February 2001.

* The lowest attendance that City played in front of in a league match that season was 1,322 when they travelled to Barnet in September 2000.

* Arriving at the club for the start of the 2000-01 season were a number of players, that included midfielder Kwame Ampadu, who twelve years later was still working for Exeter City in a youth development role.

* Once more City signed a handful of players on loan as the season progressed, namely, Gary Birch, the giant striker Kevin Francis, who had made his name at Stockport County, Gavin Holligan, Carl Hutchings, Kevin Rapley, and Damian Spencer. All were strikers, but none of them really made too much impression.

* Defender Steve Epesse-Titi became the first French-born player to wear the red and white of Exeter City when he was signed from Wolverhampton Wanderers in March 2001, but he only stayed until the end of the season, moving on to join Kidderminster Harriers, and then Clyde.

* Exeter also signed their first ever Dutch-born goalkeeper. In Arjen Van Heusden, arriving from Cambridge United. He proved to be an excellent acquisition, as he went on to feature in 41 league matches in his first season at the club.

* Goalscoring, not for the first time, proved to be a problem in league matches, with only Steve Flack (13) and Christian Roberts (8) netting with any regularity. Roberts had arrived on a free transfer from Cardiff City in July 2000 and was noted for his pace as well as his goalscoring ability.

* The first half of the season was a disaster with only four wins in the league up until January 2001, and two of those came in successive matches against York City and Carlisle United.

* The alarm bells really started to sound following a 6-1 defeat Cardiff City on New Years Day and many felt that relegation to the Conference was inevitable unless there was a dramatic change of form.

*With all three Devon clubs in the same division, it was of great disappointment to City supporters that Exeter failed to beat Torquay United or Plymouth Argyle in the four matches against them.

## CITY PLAYING SQUAD 2001-2

| Name | Pos | Signed From | App | Gls |
|---|---|---|---|---|
| Les Afful | F | Trainee July 2000 | 0(2) | |
| Kwame Ampadu | M | Leyton Orient Jul 2000 | 33(3) | |
| Martin Barlow | M | Plymouth Argyle Jul 2001 | 26(4) | |
| Gary Birch | F | Walsall Aug 2001 | 5(10) | |
| Geoff Breslan | M | Trainee Jul 1996 | 21(12) | 2 |
| Paul Buckle | M | Colchester United Jul 1999 | 19(6) | 1 |
| Mark Burrows | D | Coventry City Jul 2000 | 6(3) | |
| Jamie Campbell | D | Brighton & H.A. Jul 2000 | 20(0) | 1 |
| Glenn Cronin | M | Cherry Orchard Jul 1998 | 24(6) | 1 |
| Chris Curran | D | Plymouth Argyle Jul 1997 | 35(2) | |
| Cherif Diallo | F | Scarborough Sep 2001 | 0(2) | |
| Stuart Elliot | D | Scarborough Jan 2002 | 0(1) | |
| Steve Flack | F | Cardiff City Sep 1996 | 27(9) | 6 |
| Stuart Fraser | G | Stoke Jul 2000 | 10(2) | |
| Shaun Goff | D | Trainee Jul 2000 | 2 | |
| Matthew Gregg | G | Crystal Palace Sep 2001 | 2 | |
| Marcus Gross | D | Trainee Jul 1999 | 1 | |
| Dylan Kerr | D | Hamilton Academical Aug 2001 | 5 | 1 |
| Sean McCarthy | F | Plymouth Argyle Jul 2001 | 18(8) | 6 |
| Barry McConnell | F | Trainee Aug 1995 | 30(2) | |
| Reinier Moor | F | Trainee Jul 1999 | 0(2) | |
| Graeme Power | D | Bristol Rovers Aug 1998 | 36(1) | 1 |
| Paul Read | F | SK Ostersund (Sweden) Nov 2000 | 3(12) | |
| Jay Richardson | M | Chelsea Jul 2001 | 5(13) | |
| Christian Roberts | F | Cardiff City Jul 2000 | 34(3) | 11 |
| Andy Roscoe | M | Mansfield Town Jul 2000 | 35(3) | 7 |
| Graeme Tomlinson | W | Macclesfield Town Jun 2000 | 25(7) | 5 |
| Arjen Van Heusden | G | Cambridge United Aug 2000 | 33 | |
| Andy Walker | G | St. Albans City Aug 2001 | 1 | |
| Alex Watson | D | Torquay United Jul 2001 | 42(1) | 1 |
| Neil Whitworth | D | Hull City Aug 2000 | 12(3) | |
| Lee Zabek | M | Bristol Rovers Jul 2000 | 2 | |
| Own Goals | | | | 2 |

## City's League Results

| | Home | Away |
|---|---|---|
| Bristol Rovers | 1-0 | 0-0 |
| Carlisle United | 1-0 | 0-1 |
| Cheltenham Town | 0-2 | 1-3 |
| Darlington | 0-4 | |
| Halifax Town | 0-0 | 1-1 |
| Hartlepool United | 0-2 | 0-2 |
| Hull City | 1-3 | 0-2 |
| Kidderminster Harriers | 2-1 | 1-3 |
| Leyton Orent | 0-0 | 1-1 |
| Lincoln City | 1-1 | 0-0 |
| Luton Town | 2-2 | 0-3 |
| Macclesfield Town | 0-0 | 2-1 |
| Mansfield Town | 0-1 | 1-0 |
| Oxford United | 3-2 | 2-1 |
| Plymouth | 2-3 | 0-3 |
| Rochdale | 1-1 | 0-2 |
| Rushden & Diamonds | 1-1 | 1-2 |
| Scunthorpe United | 0-4 | 4-3 |
| Shrewsbury Town | 2-2 | 1-0 |
| Southend United | 2-1 | 1-3 |
| Swansea City | 0-3 | 2-4 |
| Torquay United | 0-0 | 2-0 |
| York City | 2-1 | 3-2 |

**F.A. Cup**

| | | | |
|---|---|---|---|
| Cambridge City | H | 3-0 | R1 |
| Dagenham & Redbridge | H | 0-0 | R2 |
| Dagenham & Redbridge | A | 0-3 | R2R |

**Football League Cup**

| | | | |
|---|---|---|---|
| Walsall | H | 0-1 | R1 |

**LDV Trophy**

| | | | |
|---|---|---|---|
| Cambridge United | H | 1-2 | R1 |

CITY MANAGER 2001-2
Noel Blake - Appointed January 2000
John Cornforth - Appointed September 2001

* When the season began, little did anyone know what was to unfold over the next 12 months. It proved, yet again, to be a real struggle both on and off the field. Even a change of manager, with John Cornforth taking over from Noel Blake did little to improve matters, although to be fair with hardly any resources at their disposal it was not surprising that whoever was in charge of the team would have an uphill battle. To the credit of Carnforth he did guide the team to a 16th place finish.

* While manager John Cornforth looked after on the field matters, which included the club having to go to the Professional Footballers Association to pay the players for the month of February, club chairman Ivor Doble was keen to sell his interest. He made no secret of his wish to sell, but with debts believed then to be in the region of £2m, attracting a buyer was never going to be easy. Doble was known to have been talking with a number of consortia including reported fans favourite headed by former director Joe Gadston.

## DIVISION THREE SEASON 2001-02

| | P | W | D | L | F | A |
|---|---|---|---|---|---|---|
| Plymouth Argyle | 46 | 31 | 9 | 6 | 71 | 28 |
| Luton Town | 46 | 30 | 7 | 9 | 96 | 48 |
| Mansfield Town | 46 | 24 | 7 | 15 | 72 | 60 |
| Cheltenham Town | 46 | 21 | 15 | 10 | 66 | 49 |
| Rochdale | 46 | 21 | 15 | 10 | 65 | 52 |
| Rushden & Diamonds | 46 | 20 | 13 | 13 | 69 | 53 |
| Hartlepool United | 46 | 20 | 11 | 15 | 74 | 48 |
| Scunthorpe United | 46 | 19 | 14 | 13 | 74 | 56 |
| Shrewsbury Town | 46 | 20 | 10 | 16 | 64 | 53 |
| Kidderminster Harriers | 46 | 19 | 9 | 18 | 56 | 47 |
| Hull City | 46 | 16 | 13 | 17 | 57 | 51 |
| Southend United | 46 | 15 | 13 | 18 | 51 | 54 |
| Macclesfield Town | 46 | 15 | 13 | 18 | 41 | 52 |
| York City | 46 | 16 | 9 | 21 | 54 | 67 |
| Darlington | 46 | 15 | 11 | 20 | 60 | 71 |
| Exeter City | 46 | 14 | 13 | 19 | 54 | 56 |
| Carlisle United | 46 | 12 | 16 | 18 | 49 | 56 |
| Leyton Orient | 46 | 13 | 13 | 20 | 55 | 71 |
| Torquay United | 46 | 12 | 15 | 19 | 46 | 63 |
| Swansea City | 46 | 13 | 12 | 21 | 53 | 77 |
| Oxford United | 46 | 11 | 14 | 21 | 53 | 62 |
| Lincoln City | 46 | 10 | 16 | 20 | 44 | 62 |
| Bristol Roves | 46 | 11 | 12 | 23 | 40 | 60 |
| Halifax Town | 46 | 8 | 12 | 26 | 39 | 84 |

* It wasn't long into the season before there were signs that it was going to be another struggle, with one win in the opening ten league matches. As a result manager Noel Blake decided he had enough and resigned.

* The club turned to midfielder John Cornforth to take over, who had been assisting Blake with coaching. After a period in temporary charge during which time City reached the lofty heights of 10th place, he was given the job on a permanent basis. Alas, after that results started to fall away again and the Grecians slid down the table to eventually end the season in 16th place.

* The team ended the season as badly as they had started it, with only one win in their final eleven matches, when they defeated York City 2-1 at St. James' Park.

* The goalkeeping position was filled by no fewer than four different players, namely, Stuart Fraser, Matthew Gregg, Arjan Van Heusden and Andy Walker.

*Gary Birch returned to the club from Walsall for a second loan spell at St James' Park, but didn't hit the back of the net in 15 league appearances.

* One notable arrival in September 2001, although he was to feature in just two substitute outings, was Cherif Diallo from Scarborough. He became the first Senegalese player to appear for the Grecians.

* Many supporters never even saw Stuart Elliott play for Exeter City! Signed on a non-contract basis in January 2002 after being released by Scarborough, he was to make a brief substitute appearance at Macclesfield Town, before moving on to sign for Merthyr Tydfil.

* Going out at the first round stage of both the Football League Cup and the LDV Vans Trophy, Exeter did at least get to round two in the F.A. Cup. But they were held to a goalless draw at home to then non-leaguers Dagenham and Redbridge, and then lost the replay, which was televised to make it a horror show for City fans.

* The average attendance for league matches at St James' Park fell to 3,313. The highest gate of the season at the Park was 6,756 for the visit of Plymouth Argyle in September 2001.

* The lowest league attendance that City played in front of was just 1,719 when they won 2-1 at Macclesfield Town in February 2002. The lowest crowd of the season at the Park was 1,047 who watched Cambridge United win 2-1 in the LDV Vans Trophy.

* Leading goalscorer Christian Roberts left the club in March 2002, when Bristol City paid a fee of £10,000 for him, which seemed a bargain at the time. Once he had left City struggled to score goals in their final six matches of the season, netting just three times.

* No fewer than six players who appeared in the first team had been products of the club's youth scheme, with Geoff Breslan and Barry McConnell appearing in over 30 games each. Three of the six made their league debuts, namely, Marcus Gross, Shaun Goff and Reinier Moor.

*Events off the field started to dominate proceedings as club chairman Ivor Doble, the majority shareholder, had publicly stated for some time that he wanted to sell. After what seemed like weeks and weeks of discussions, he eventually handed over to former Scarborough chairman, John Russell and ex-Swansea City owner Mike Lewis. It very quickly proved to be a disastrous move as the following season turned into something of a 'soap opera.'

CITY PLAING SQUAD 2002-03

| Name | Pos | Signed From | Apps | Gls |
|---|---|---|---|---|
| Colin Alcide | F | Gainsborough Trinity Nov 2002 | 1 | |
| Kwame Ampadu | M | Leyton Orient Jul 2000 | 18(5) | |
| Phil Baker | D | Bangor City Apr 2003 | 5(1) | |
| Lee Barnard | F | Tottenham Hotspur Nov 2002 | 3 | |
| Geoff Breslan | M | Trainee Jul 1996 | 0(10) | |
| Lewis Buxton | D | Portsmouth Oct 2002 | 4 | |
| James Coppinger | F | Newcastle United Jul 2002 | 35(8) | 5 |
| Glenn Cronin | M | Cherry Orchard Jul 1998 | 28(11) | |
| Chris Curran | D | Plymouth Argyle Jul 1997 | 10(3) | |
| Sean Devine | F | Wycombe Wanderers Jan 2003 | 21(2) | 8 |
| Steve Flack | F | Cardiff City Sep 1996 | 39(1) | 13 |
| Stuart Fraser | G | Stoke City Jul 2000 | 0(1) | |
| Santos Gaia | D | Corinthians (Brazil) Jul 2002 | 33 | 1 |
| Don Goodman | F | Walsall Aug 2002 | 11(2) | 1 |
| Paul Harries | F | Wollongong Wolves (Australia) Sep 2002 | 0(1) | |
| Scott Hiley | D | Portsmouth Sep 2002 | 37 | |
| Ciaran Kilheeney | F | Mossley Mar 2003 | 0(4) | |
| Matthew Lock | M | Trainee Aug 2002 | 1(2) | |
| Barry McConnell | F | Trainee Aug 1995 | 13(8) | |
| Kevin Miller | G | Barnsley Jul 2002 | 46 | |
| Reinier Moor | F | Trainee Jul 1999 | 2(15) | 3 |
| Scott Partridge | F | Rushden & Diamonds Dec 2002 | 2(2) | 2 |
| Carl Pettefer | M | Portsmouth Oct 2002 | 30(1) | 1 |
| George Pilkington | D | Everton Nov 2002 | 7 | |
| Graeme Power | D | Bristol Rovers Aug 1998 | 27(3) | |
| Andy Roscoe | M | Mansfield Town Jul 2000 | 23(10) | 3 |
| Lee Sharpe | W | Bradford City Aug 2002 | 4 | 1 |
| Gareth Sheldon | W | Scunthorpe United May 2002 | 7(12) | 1 |
| Michael Simpkins | D | Cardiff City Sep 2002 | 4(1) | |
| Cleveland Taylor | W | Bolton Wanderers Aug 2002 | 1(2) | |
| Martin Thomas | M | Oxford United Aug 202 | 22(4) | 3 |
| Chris Todd | D | Drogheda United Jan 2003 | 12 | |
| Adam Virgo | D | Brighton & H.A. Nov 2002 | 8(1) | |
| Justin Walker | M | Lincoln City Aug 2002 | 35(4) | 5 |
| Alex Watson | D | Torquay United Jul 2001 | 3 | |
| Adrian Whitbread | D | Reading Jan 2003 | 7 | |
| Neil Whitworth | D | Hull City Aug 2000 | 7(1) | |
| Own Goals | | | | 3 |

City's league results

| Home | Home | Away |
|---|---|---|
| AFC Bournemouth | 1-3 | 0-2 |
| Boston United | 0-2 | 3-0 |
| Bristol Rovers | 0-0 | 1-1 |
| Bury | 1-2 | 0-1 |
| Cambridge United | 1-2 | 1-2 |
| Carlisle United | 1-0 | 2-0 |
| Darlington | 0-4 | 2-2 |
| Hartlepool United | 1-2 | 1-2 |
| Hull City | 3-1 | 2-2 |
| Kidderminster Harriers | 2-5 | 3-4 |
| Leyton Orient | 1-0 | 1-1 |
| Lincoln City | 2-0 | 0-1 |
| Macclesfield Town | 1-1 | 1-1 |
| Oxford United | 2-2 | 2-2 |
| Rochdale | 1-1 | 3-3 |
| Rushden & Diamonds | 1-1 | 0-1 |
| Scunthorpe United | 1-1 | 1-1 |
| Shrewsbury Town | 1-1 | 0-1 |
| Southend United | 1-0 | 0-1 |
| Swansea City | 1-0 | 1-0 |
| Torquay united | 1-2 | 0-1 |
| Wrexham | 1-0 | 0-4 |
| York City | 0-1 | 2-0 |

F.A. Cup

| | | |
|---|---|---|
| Forest Green Rovers | A | 0-0 | R1 |
| Forest Green Rovers | H | 2-1 | R1R |
| Rushden & Diamonds | H | 3-1 | R2 |
| Charlton Athletic | A | 1-3 | R3 |

Football League Cup

| | | |
|---|---|---|
| Brighton & H.A. | A | 1-2 | R1 |

LDV Trophy

| | | |
|---|---|---|
| Bristol Rovers | H | 1-0 | R1 |
| Cardiff City | H | 0-3 | R2 |

CITY MANAGER 2002-
John Comforth Appointed September 2001
Neil McNab Appointed October 2002
Gary Peters Appointed February 2003

* The spotlight was on what was doing on off the pitch rather than on it throughout the 2002-3 season. Things came to a head in May 2003 when it was reported that Police made two arrests after launching an inquiry into alleged financial irregularities at Exeter City Football Club.

Fraud squad officers from the Devon and Cornwall force executed a warrant at a private address in Swansea in connection with the investigation. Twenty officers, including a team from the Fraud Squad and the high-tech crime unit, executed warrants at private addresses in Exeter, and went to the football club's offices at St James' Park.

Police confirmed that a probe - code named Operation Roe - into the football club's financial position was under way after several days of planning.

Chairman John Russell and vice-chairman Mike Lewis had earlier announced that they had called in accountants to study options open to them after an FA audit described the Grecians' financial position as 'perilous'.

Five former directors had recently quit the club after a boardroom row. And celebrity Uri Geller, who was due to join the club board, also severed his links with Russell and Lewis after a dispute between them.

DIVISION THREE 2002/3

| | P | W | D | L | F | A | Pts |
|---|---|---|---|---|---|---|---|
| Rushden & Diamonds | 46 | 24 | 15 | 7 | 73 | 47 | 87 |
| Hartlepool United | 46 | 24 | 13 | 9 | 71 | 51 | 85 |
| Wrexham | 46 | 23 | 15 | 8 | 84 | 50 | 84 |
| AFC Bournemouth | 46 | 20 | 14 | 12 | 60 | 48 | 74 |
| Scunthorpe United | 46 | 19 | 15 | 12 | 68 | 49 | 72 |
| Lincoln City | 46 | 18 | 16 | 12 | 46 | 37 | 70 |
| Bury | 46 | 18 | 16 | 12 | 57 | 56 | 70 |
| Oxford United | 46 | 19 | 12 | 15 | 57 | 47 | 69 |
| Torquay United | 46 | 16 | 18 | 12 | 71 | 71 | 66 |
| York City | 46 | 17 | 15 | 14 | 52 | 53 | 66 |
| Kidderminster Harriers | 46 | 16 | 15 | 15 | 62 | 63 | 63 |
| Cambridge United | 46 | 16 | 13 | 17 | 67 | 70 | 61 |
| Hull City | 46 | 14 | 17 | 15 | 58 | 53 | 59 |
| Darlington | 46 | 12 | 18 | 16 | 58 | 59 | 54 |
| Boston United | 46 | 15 | 13 | 18 | 55 | 56 | 54* |
| Macclesfield Town | 46 | 14 | 12 | 20 | 57 | 63 | 54 |
| Southend United | 46 | 17 | 3 | 26 | 47 | 59 | 54 |
| Leyton Orient | 46 | 14 | 11 | 21 | 51 | 61 | 53 |
| Rochdale | 46 | 12 | 16 | 18 | 63 | 70 | 52 |
| Bristol Rovers | 46 | 12 | 15 | 19 | 50 | 57 | 51 |
| Swansea City | 46 | 12 | 13 | 21 | 48 | 65 | 49 |
| Carlisle United | 46 | 13 | 10 | 23 | 52 | 78 | 49 |
| Exeter City | 46 | 11 | 15 | 20 | 50 | 64 | 48 |
| Shrewsbury Town | 46 | 9 | 14 | 23 | 62 | 92 | 41 |

* Boston United 4 points deducted for financial issues

* This was a season that could be best described as bizarre, tragic etc. And the ended with the new owners John Russell and Mike Lewis being arrested, and the club eventually saved from going out of business altogether by the hard work of leading members of the Exeter City Supporters' Trust.

* At the start of the season Lewis said: "We are practical, reasonable men. Our target within three years is to get the club back to a position where it is washing its face again - by that I mean not losing money."

* The involvement of celebrity Uri Geller and son Daniel - who were listed as co-chairman and co-vice-chairman - raised the profile of the club. Then there was the bizarre sight of pop megastar Michael Jackson parading around St James' Park in a vintage car. He, along with illusionist David Blaine, had been persuaded to visit Exeter by his friend Uri Geller.

* The Grecians continued to make headlines and after failing to lure Paul Gascoigne out of retirement to play for Exeter City, the signing (against the wishes of manager John Cornforth) of former Manchester United winger Lee Sharpe was announced on a reported £3,000 per game contract. He stayed for a month.

* On 11th September the club reported record £500,000 losses in the year up to June 2002. Russell land Lewis revealed how they planned to cut City's £1.8m debts with a ground redevelopment plan. The only drawback being that St James' Park was owned by Exeter City Council, who showed little enthusiasm for the project.

* It was no surprise when the duo's next move was to sack manager John Cornforth and replace him with Neil McNab, with his assistant being Gary Bennett. McNab had been recommended by former City manager Alan Ball.

* Meanwhile there were reports of employment tribunals, unpaid bills, uneasy creditors and threats of winding up orders. The City Council then publicly demanded to know why charities had received no cash from Jackson's summer appearance - as did firms still waiting for payment for the equipment and services they supplied for the event.

* By early December, nine companies had lodged County Court judgements against the club and the Sheriff of Devon had even taken 'walking possession' of the floodlights at St James' Park.

* Results in league matches were nothing short of disastrous, however, the team did reach the third round of the FA Cup before losing to Charlton Athletic. Some of the money earned from that tie - £75,000 of it - went on a record signing, Sean Devine, from Wycombe Wanderers.

* In February 2003, after just three wins from 20 league games McNab and Bennett were shown the door. Ex-Preston North End manager Gary Peters was appointed in their place 24-hours later.

* A transfer embargo was imposed by the Football League for failing to meet an instalment of Devine's fee, six directors resigned following an FA report into the state of City's finances and the Gellers (who had never registered as directors) left the board on the advice of concerned officials at the Football League.

* Despite the odds stacked against him, Peters somehow managed to guide his beleaguered team to pick up 20 points during the 13 matches he was in charge, but it was not quite enough to prevent Exeter City sliding out of the Football League into the Conference.

* On 12th May, Lewis and Russell arrived at St James' Park to find the locks to their office in the St James' Centre had been changed by landlords OTR, who then agreed to let them use a single room in the building.

* The end came for Russell and Lewis when they, along with Russell's wife, were arrested and interviewed - but not charged - by fraud squad officers investigating alleged financial irregularities at the club.

* Ivor Doble, former chairman, club president and majority shareholder at St James' Park, called on the duo to quit the Grecians. They did indeed quit allowing the Supporters' Trust to complete their takeover at St James's Park. Gary Peters also left the club. And 74 years of Football League history for Exeter City FC were over ... for now!

* For months the supporters had been ever strengthening the hand of the Exeter City Supporters' Trust. What had started off as a very small group was getting more powerful by the day with all sorts of professional expertise being offered to them.

* When the chance to step in and help the club arrived, the Trust were able to be in a very good position to run Exeter City on a day by day basis, albeit, at first on a temporary arrangement.

* Former chairman Ivor Doble asked the Trust to take charge and after long and detailed discussions, he passed his majority shareholding to them.

197

## CITY PLAYING SQUAD 2003-4

| Name | Pos | Signed | Apps | Gls |
|------|-----|--------|------|-----|
| Les Afful | F | Trainee Jul 2000 | 17(13) | 2 |
| Kwame Ampadu | M | Leyton Orient Jul 2000 | 29(10) | |
| James Bittner | G | Chippenham Town Jul 2003 | 37 | |
| Sean Canham | F | Trainee Aug 2001 | 10(11) | 5 |
| Graham Cheeseman | F | Bridgwater Town Aug 2003 | 0(2) | |
| James Coppinger | F | Newcastle United Jul 2002 | 36(3) | 8 |
| Glenn Cronin | M | Cherry Orchard Jul 1998 | 40 | 5 |
| Sean Devine | F | Wycombe Wanderers Jan 2003 | 24(9) | 20 |
| Steve Flack | F | Cardiff City Sep 1996 | 24(13) | 6 |
| Santos Gaia | D | Corinthians (Brazil) Jul 2002 | 39 | 4 |
| Scott Hiley | D | Portsmouth Sep 2002 | 42 | |
| Alex Jeannin | D | Darlington Jul 2003 | 39 | 2 |
| Dwayne Lee | F | Aldershot Town Sep 2003 | 18(3) | 3 |
| Barry McConnell | F | Trainee Aug 1995 | 13(7) | 2 |
| Reinier Moor | F | Trainee Jul 1999 | 7(5) | 2 |
| Dean Moxey | M | Trainee Jul 2002 | 9(8) | 2 |
| Lewis Reed | M | Trainee Jul 2002 | 0(1) | |
| Martin Rice | G | Trainee Dec 2002 | 5(2) | |
| Gareth Sheldon | W | Scunthorpe United May 2002 | 30(4) | 8 |
| Andy Taylor | M | Manchester United Oct 2003 | 0(7) | |
| Martin Thomas | M | Oxford United Aug 2002 | 5(6) | |
| Chris Todd | D | Drogheda United Jan 2003 | 38(1) | 1 |
| Own Goals | | | | 1 |

* Following relegation to the Conference, the club was taken over by the Exeter City Supporters Trust. Later in May 2007 two of the Directors who had been in charge during disastrous season 2002–2003 were convicted of fraudulent trading at the club, John Russell receiving a prison sentence and Mike Lewis a community service sentence.

Several million pounds in debt and with no big investor in sight, the Trust kept the club going through fund-raising activities amongst rank-and-file supporters.

Complex legal arguments with both Inland Revenue and football authorities meant that City's first season of non-league football was plagued by off-the-field uncertainty.

* After just two weeks of feverish work alongside Bishop Fleming, a firm of accountants, the new supporter-run board decided to issue a Company Voluntary Arrangement (CVA) proposal, by which they declared the club insolvent and offered to pay their creditors, owed a hopeless £3m in total, 10p in the pound.

Their major debts were to the builders, Mowlem - owed around £800,000 for building two stands at the ground - £500,000 outstanding in tax and VAT, a £160,000 loan from the Football Foundation, and a mighty £1.1m in loans from former directors including around £700,000 to former club chairman Ivor Doble.

### City's Conference Results

| | Home | Away | |
|------|------|------|---|
| Accrington Stanley | 3-2 | 2-1 | |
| Aldershot Town | 2-1 | 1-2 | |
| Barnet | 1-1 | 3-2 | |
| Burton Albion | 2-0 | 4-3 | |
| Chester City | 2-1 | 2-3 | |
| Dagenham & Redbridge | 1-1 | 2-0 | |
| Farnborough Town | 1-1 | 2-1 | |
| Forest Green Rovers | 2-2 | 5-2 | |
| Gravesend & Northfleet | 0-1 | 2-3 | |
| Halifax Town | 1-1 | 0-2 | |
| Hereford United | 0-1 | 1-1 | |
| Leigh R.M.I. | 3-2 | 1-1 | |
| Margate | 1-1 | 1-0 | |
| Morecambe | 4-0 | 3-0 | |
| Northwich Victoria | 2-0 | 1-1 | |
| Scarborough | 0-0 | 3-2 | |
| Shrewsbury Town | 3-2 | 2-2 | |
| Stevenage Borough | 1-0 | 2-2 | |
| Tamworth | 3-2 | 1-2 | |
| Telford United | 0-3 | 0-2 | |
| Woking | 1-2 | 0-1 | |

| F.A. Cup | | | |
|------|------|------|---|
| Gravesend & Northfleet | H | 0-0 | Q4 |
| Gravesend & Northfleet | A | 3-3 | Q4* |
| Exeter City lost 6-5 on pens | | | |

> 

| LDV Trophy | | | |
|------|------|------|---|
| Hereford United | A | 0-2 | R1 |

| F.A.Trophy | | | |
|------|------|------|---|
| Hereford United | H | 3-2 | R3 |
| King's Lynn | A | 3-0 | R4 |
| Arlesey Town | H | 3-0 | R5 |
| Aldershot Town | A | 1-2 | R6 |

CITY MANAGER
Eamonn Dolan - Appointed August 2003

### Football Conference Season 2003-4

| | P | W | D | L | F | A | Pts |
|------|---|---|---|---|---|---|-----|
| Chester City | 42 | 27 | 11 | 4 | 85 | 34 | 92 |
| Hereford United | 42 | 28 | 7 | 7 | 103 | 44 | 91 |
| Shrewsbury Town | 42 | 20 | 14 | 8 | 67 | 42 | 74 |
| Barnet | 42 | 19 | 14 | 9 | 60 | 46 | 71 |
| Aldershot Town | 42 | 20 | 10 | 12 | 80 | 67 | 70 |
| Exeter City | 42 | 19 | 12 | 11 | 71 | 57 | 69 |
| Morecambe | 42 | 20 | 7 | 15 | 66 | 66 | 67 |
| Stevenage Borough | 42 | 18 | 9 | 15 | 58 | 52 | 63 |
| Woking | 42 | 15 | 16 | 11 | 65 | 52 | 61 |
| Accrington Stanley | 42 | 15 | 13 | 14 | 68 | 61 | 58 |
| Gravesend & Northfleet | 42 | 14 | 15 | 13 | 69 | 66 | 57 |
| Telford United | 42 | 15 | 10 | 17 | 49 | 51 | 55 |
| Dagenham & Redbridge | 42 | 15 | 9 | 18 | 59 | 64 | 54 |
| Burton Albion | 42 | 15 | 7 | 20 | 57 | 59 | 51* |
| Scarborough | 42 | 12 | 15 | 15 | 51 | 54 | 51 |
| Margate | 42 | 14 | 9 | 19 | 56 | 64 | 51 |
| Tamworth | 42 | 13 | 10 | 19 | 49 | 68 | 49 |
| Forest Green Rovers | 42 | 12 | 12 | 18 | 58 | 80 | 48 |
| Halifax Town | 42 | 12 | 8 | 22 | 43 | 65 | 44 |
| Farnborough Town | 42 | 10 | 9 | 23 | 53 | 74 | 39 |
| Leigh RMI | 42 | 7 | 8 | 27 | 46 | 97 | 29 |
| Northwich Victoria | 42 | 4 | 11 | 27 | 30 | 80 | 23 |

* Burton Albion deducted 1 point

* After a calamitous 2002-03 season which saw the club relegated to the Conference, there was still much left to do following the takeover by the Exeter City Supporters' Trust before the start of the club's venture into the world of non-league.

* A substantial sum of money had to be raised just to get through the summer. There was an amazing amount of hard work, both trying to raise finance and from a band of volunteers who beavered away on working on the ground and the stands which had been neglected over the years.

* The club decided to appoint the hugely popular Eamonn Dolan as manager, who accepted the position in June 2003. Dolan had retired from playing at the club after being diagnosed with testicular cancer and then became Exeter City's Community Officer. He had the vast experience of Steve Perryman to call upon once more, who had returned to the City to offer his services and generally work as Dolan's assistant.

* It was a whole new adventure for everyone, members of the Trust now in control of the club, sponsors, management and players, and of course the supporters, as unfamiliar teams such as Leigh R.M.I. and Margate were visiting St James' Park.

* It was still a struggle and the club began to see some light when they successfully negotiated a CVA with its creditors. Unfortunately the Inland Revenue were not impressed and they challenged the ruling in Court.

* City were to use just 22 players during the season, with finance still very much an issue at the club, with much to be sorted out.

* Dolan worked wonders with the players he had, promising youngsters coming through the system and blooding them early into the first team. Amazingly City found themselves in a challenging play-off place for virtually the whole of the season.

* A poor run of results towards the end of the campaign prevented them from making an attempt to win back a Football League place at the first attempt.

* it seemed that every week a new obstacle was placed in the clubs way. Not least of which was the threat of a points deduction by the Conference, then points being docked because of a player being allegedly registered after a transfer embargo was in place. City kept their points total though, the Conference deciding not to go ahead with either claim.

* Trust members, of which there were over 1,400 by the end of the 2003-04 season, were asked to put their hands in their pockets on more than one occasion to stave off further cash flow problems.

* There was a real buzz and positive feeling about the club for the first time in several seasons. This was now a true supporters' club - a supporter owned club and a community club.

* In May 2004 Exeter City Football Club celebrated their centenary with a prestige friendly against a Brazil Masters XI, the Grecians having been the first club to have played the Brazilian international team way back in 1914. It was fitting way to end what had been a real learning curve of a season for the club, but what a contrast to the previous twelve months it had been!

* Exeter City were the third best supported club in the Conference, averaging 3,665 for matches at St. James' Park. The highest attendance was for the final match against Accrington Stanley in April 2004 when an amazing 8,256 were present to witness a 3-2 win. However, the Grecians were to miss out on the play offs by just one point.

* Record signing Sean Devine, who had arrived at the club for £75,000 the previous season, topped the goalscoring charts with an impressive 20 goals in the Conference.

## CITY PLAYING SQUAD 2004-05

| Name | Pos | Signed From | Apps | Gls |
|---|---|---|---|---|
| Les Afful | F | Trainee Jul 2000 | 33(6) | |
| Kwame Ampadu | M | Leyton Orient Jul 2000 | 29(1) | 1 |
| James Bittner | G | Chippenham Town Jul 2003 | 5 | |
| Paul Buckle | M | Weymouth Dec 2004 | 9(2) | 1 |
| Sean Canham | F | Trainee Aug 2001 | 1(1) | |
| Danny Clay | M | Trainee Jul 2003 | 9(4) | |
| Glenn Cronin | M | Cherry Orchard Jul 1998 | 3(1) | |
| Sean Devine | F | Wycombe Wanderers Jan 2003 | 25(12) | 11 |
| Jake Edwards | F | Yeovil Town Jul 2004 | 22(12) | 6 |
| Steve Flack | F | Cardiff City Sep 1996 | 20(16) | 12 |
| Santos Gaia | D | Corinthians (Brazil) Jul 2002 | 33 | 7 |
| Scott Hiley | D | Portsmouth Sep 2002 | 42 | 1 |
| Kezie Ibe | F | Yeovil Town Dec 2004 | 2(2) | 1 |
| Alex Jeannin | D | Darlington Jul 2003 | 33 | 2 |
| Paul Jones | G | Leyton Orient Nov 2004 | 22(1) | |
| Barry McConnell | F | Trainee Aug 1995 | 5(5) | 3 |
| Marcus Martin | M | Plymouth Argyle Aug 2004 | 9(12) | 1 |
| Dean Moxey | M | Trainee Jul 2000 | 22(8) | 3 |
| Lee Phillips | F | Weymouth Feb 2005 | 11(3) | 4 |
| Gary Sawyer | D | Plymouth Argyle Aug 2004 | 27(5) | 2 |
| Gareth Sheldon | W | Scunthorpe United May 2002 | 18(10) | 4 |
| Wayne O'Sullivan | M | Plymouth Argyle Aug 2004 | 1(8) | 1 |
| Martin Rice | G | Trainee Dec 2002 | 15 | |
| Andy Taylor | M | Manchester United Oct 2003 | 39(2) | 5 |
| Chris Todd | D | Drogheda United Jan 2003 | 27 | 1 |
| Steve Tully | D | Weymouth Feb 2005 | 0(2) | |
| Own Goals | | 5 | | |

## Football Conference 2004/5

| | P | W | D | L | F | A | Pts |
|---|---|---|---|---|---|---|---|
| Barnet | 42 | 26 | 8 | 8 | 90 | 44 | 86 |
| Hereford United | 42 | 21 | 11 | 10 | 68 | 41 | 74 |
| Carlisle United | 42 | 20 | 13 | 9 | 74 | 37 | 73 |
| Aldershot Town | 42 | 21 | 10 | 11 | 68 | 52 | 73 |
| Stevenage Borough | 42 | 22 | 6 | 14 | 65 | 52 | 72 |
| Exeter City | 42 | 20 | 11 | 11 | 71 | 50 | 71 |
| Morecambe | 42 | 19 | 14 | 9 | 69 | 50 | 71 |
| Woking | 42 | 18 | 14 | 10 | 58 | 45 | 68 |
| Halifax Town | 42 | 19 | 9 | 14 | 73 | 56 | 66 |
| Accrington Stanley | 42 | 18 | 11 | 13 | 72 | 58 | 65 |
| Dagenham & Redbridge | 42 | 19 | 8 | 15 | 68 | 60 | 65 |
| Crawley Town | 42 | 16 | 9 | 17 | 50 | 50 | 57 |
| Scarborough | 42 | 14 | 14 | 14 | 60 | 46 | 56 |
| Gravesend & Northfleet | 42 | 13 | 11 | 18 | 58 | 64 | 50 |
| Tamworth | 42 | 14 | 11 | 17 | 53 | 63 | 50* |
| Burton Albion | 42 | 13 | 11 | 18 | 50 | 66 | 50 |
| York City | 42 | 11 | 10 | 21 | 39 | 65 | 43 |
| Canvey Island | 42 | 9 | 15 | 18 | 53 | 65 | 42 |
| Northwich Victoria | 42 | 14 | 10 | 18 | | | 41+ |
| Forest Green Rovers | 42 | 6 | 15 | 21 | 41 | 81 | 33 |
| Farnborough Town | 42 | 6 | 11 | 25 | 35 | 89 | 29 |
| Leigh R.M.I. | 42 | 4 | 6 | 32 | 31 | 98 | 18 |

\* Tamworth deducted 3 points for breach of rules

+ Northwich Victoria deducted 10 points for entering administration

### City's Conference Results

| | Home | Away |
|---|---|---|
| Accrington Stanley | 1-2 | 0-0 |
| Aldershot Town | 3-1 | 1-2 |
| Barnet | 0-3 | 0-1 |
| Burton Albion | 3-1 | 0-1 |
| Canvey Island | 0-1 | 2-2 |
| Carlisle United | 0-0 | 2-0 |
| Crawley Town | 3-2 | 1-0 |
| Dagenham & Redbridge | 1-1 | 3-2 |
| Farnborough Town | 2-1 | 1-2 |
| Forest Green Rovers | 2-0 | 3-2 |
| Gravesend & Northfleet | 3-0 | 1-1 |
| Halifax Town | 2-1 | 1-2 |
| Hereford United | 4-0 | 2-1 |
| Leigh R.M.I. | 5-1 | 1-0 |
| Morecambe | 1-1 | 2-2 |
| Northwich Victoria | 2-3 | 2-1 |
| Scarborough | 3-1 | 1-1 |
| Stevenage Borough | 2-0 | 2-3 |
| Tamworth | 2-2 | 2-1 |
| Woking | 0-0 | 3-3 |
| York City | 0-1 | 2-1 |

### F.A. Cup

| | | | |
|---|---|---|---|
| Braintree Town | H | 2-0 | Q4 |
| Grimsby Town | H | 1-0 | R1 |
| Doncaster Rovers | H | 2-1 | R2 |
| Manchester United | A | 0-0 | R3 |
| Manchester United | H | 0-2 | R3R |

### LDV Tropy

| | | | |
|---|---|---|---|
| Oxford United | A | 2-2 | R1* |
| Swindon Town | H | 1-2 | R2 |

\* Exeter won 3-1 on pens

### F.A. Trophy

| | | | |
|---|---|---|---|
| Billericay Town | A | 2-2 | R3 |
| Billericay Town | H | 2-0 | R3R |
| Tamworth | A | 3-0 | R4 |
| Stamford | A | 1-0 | R5 |
| Grays Athletic | A | 1-4 | R6 |

### CITY MANAGER 2004-5

Eamonn Dolan - Appointed June 2003
Alex Inglethorpe - Appointed October 2004

* With the Exeter City Supporters' Trust running the football club, they still had the matter of trying to appease creditors and reduce the huge debt. They were, however, about to have a massive stroke of good fortune thanks to the F.A. Cup!

* The second season in the Conference didn't start off too well and by the end of October the Grecians found themselves in a disappointing 15th place.

* The ever popular Eamonn Dolan left the club as manager to take over running the youth academy at Reading, and City moved quickly to appoint former player, Alex Inglethorpe, as their new boss, who would work alongside the club's Director of Football, Steve Perryman.

* Having beaten Braintree Town, Grimsby Town and Doncaster Rovers in the F.A. Cup, Exeter City were drawn away to Manchester United in round three, guaranteeing a massive pay day, no matter the result.

* All of a sudden Inglethorpe found himself leading the team out at Old Trafford, amid much media attention. Premier League team against one from the Conference? Foregone conclusion wasn't it? A huge travelling support made their way to Manchester and couldn't quite believe the outcome. True United didn't play their full strength side, but what a result! City had held them to a goalless draw.

* Needless to say the media were swarming around the club like bees to honey and the replay back at St James' Park would be shown live on television. This time United boss Sir Alex Ferguson really did play his first choice line up, and although the Grecians once again put up a great show, they lost 0 -2.

* The reward for the two games against United was that the club's finances were once again put on an even keel almost at a stroke. Someone really was looking down on Exeter City in a favourable light!

* Defender Steve Tully returned to the club for a second spell when he signed from Weymouth in February 2005, and he would go on to play a major part in the revival of the club's playing fortunes during the next few seasons.

* After the excitement of the F.A. Cup the season just got better and better. The team reached the sixth round of the F.A. Trophy before losing to Grays Athletic, and in the league the team strung together some good results to lift them into a possible play off position in the Conference.

* Could City bounce back to the Football League? Unfortunately no, despite winning their last three matches of the season against Crawley Town, Gravesend and Northfleet and Carlisle United. They ended the season missing out on the play offs by just one point. A great achievement considering the first three months of the season.

* Average attendances at St James' Park for Conference home matches was 3,389, the second highest in the division. The highest gate for a Conference match at the Park was 4,529 against Scarborough, a game the Grecians won 3-1.

* With the greater number of Supporters Trust members, all contributing their monthly fee, the increase mainly due to the Manchester United game, the club were now in a position to make a real attempt at climbing out of the Conference the following season.
.

## CITY PLAYING SQUAD 2005-06

| Name | Pos | Signed From | Apps | Gls |
|------|-----|-------------|------|-----|
| Les Afful | F | Trainee Jul 2000 | 4(6) | 1 |
| Paul Buckle | M | Tiverton Town Mar 2005 | 24(4) | 3 |
| Matthew Bye | M | Trainee Jul 2005 | 0(1) | |
| Wayne Carlisle | W | Leyton Orient Jan 2006 | 4(2) | 1 |
| Jon Challinor | M | Aldershot Town Jul 2005 | 40(2) | 12 |
| Danny Clay | M | Trainee Jul 2003 | 1(2) | |
| Glenn Cronin | M | Cherry Orchard Jul 1998 | 28(2) | |
| Jake Edwards | F | Yeovil Town Jul 2004 | 8(6) | 1 |
| Craig Farrell | F | Carlisle United Jul 2005 | 26(12) | 8 |
| Steve Flack | F | Cardiff City Sep 1996 | 11(26) | 5 |
| George Friend | D | Trainee Mar 2006 | 1 | |
| Santos Gaia | D | Corinthians (Brazil) Jul 2002 | 14(3) | |
| Matthew Gill | M | Notts County Jan 2006 | 13(3) | 1 |
| Scott Hiley | D | Portsmouth Sep 2002 | 13(1) | |
| Billy Jones | D | Kidderminster Harriers Jul 2005 | 36(1) | 7 |
| Paul Jones | G | Leyton Orient Nov 2004 | 37 | |
| Jamie Mackie | F | Milton Keynes Dons Jul 2005 | 13(11) | 3 |
| Dean Moxey | M | Trainee Jul 2002 | 12(9) | 1 |
| Lee Phillips | F | Weymouth Feb 2005 | 34(3) | 13 |
| Anton Robinson | M | Millwall Dec 2005 | 0(1) | |
| Gary Sawyer | D | Plymouth Argyle Jul 2004 | 26(4) | |
| Tony Scully | W | Notts County Sep 2005 | 10(3) | 3 |
| Danny Seaborne | D | Trainee May 2005 | 4 | 1 |
| Martin Rice | G | Trainee Dec 2002 | 5 | |
| Andy Taylor | M | Manchester United Oct 2003 | 29(6) | |
| Chris Todd | D | Drogheda United Jan 2003 | 41 | 4 |
| Chris Vinnicombe | D | Tiverton Town Aug 2005 | 1(2) | |
| Craig Watkins | W | Sutton United Aug 2005 | 0(5) | 1 |
| Danny Woodards | D | Wycombe Wanderers Oct 2005 | 27 | |

Barry McConnell Testimonial Programme, v Charlton Athletic

### City's Conference results

| | Home | Away |
|---|------|------|
| Accrington Stanley | 1-3 | 2-1 |
| Aldershot Town | 4-0 | 0-1 |
| Altrincham | 3-1 | 1-1 |
| Burton Albion | 1-2 | 0-2 |
| Cambridge United | 4-0 | 1-2 |
| Canvey Island | 0-2 | 1-1 |
| Crawley Town | 4-0 | 2-0 |
| Dagenham & Redbridge | 3-1 | 2-2 |
| Forest Green Rovers | 0-0 | 0-0 |
| Gravesend & Northfleet | 1-0 | 2-0 |
| Grays Athletic | 1-2 | 0-3 |
| Halifax Town | 4-2 | 0-2 |
| Hereford United | 1-2 | 2-0 |
| Kidderminster Harriers | 1-0 | 2-1 |
| Morecambe | 2-0 | 2-2 |
| Scarborough | 1-1 | 1-0 |
| Southport | 5-0 | 3-0 |
| Stevenage Borough | 0-2 | 0-2 |
| Tamworth | 3-0 | 1-1 |
| Woking | 1-1 | 0-1 |
| York City | 1-3 | 2-4 |

**F.A. Cup**

| | | |
|---|---|---|
| Stevenage Borough | H 0-1 | Q4 |

**Football League Trophy**

| | | |
|---|---|---|
| Milton Keynes Dons | A 2-3 | R1 |

**F.A. Trophy**

| | | |
|---|---|---|
| Bishop's Stortford | H 2-1 | R1 |
| Histon | H 3-2 | R2 |
| Cambridge City | H 1-0 | R3 |
| Salisbury City | H 3-1 | R4 |
| Grays Athletic | H 2-1 | SF |
| Grays Athletic | A 0-2 | SF |

### CITY MANAGER 2005-06
Alex Inglethorpe - Appointed October 2004

### Football Conference

| | P | W | D | L | F | A | Pts |
|---|---|---|---|---|---|---|-----|
| Accrington Stanley | 42 | 28 | 7 | 7 | 76 | 45 | 91 |
| Hereford United | 42 | 22 | 14 | 6 | 59 | 33 | 80 |
| Grays Athletic | 42 | 21 | 13 | 8 | 94 | 55 | 76 |
| Halifax Town | 42 | 21 | 12 | 9 | 55 | 40 | 75 |
| Morecambe | 42 | 22 | 8 | 12 | 68 | 41 | 74 |
| Stevenage Borough | 42 | 19 | 12 | 11 | 62 | 44 | 69 |
| Exeter City | 42 | 18 | 9 | 15 | 65 | 48 | 63 |
| York City | 42 | 17 | 12 | 13 | 63 | 48 | 63 |
| Burton Albion | 42 | 16 | 12 | 14 | 50 | 52 | 60 |
| Dagenham & Redbridge | 42 | 16 | 10 | 16 | 63 | 59 | 58 |
| Woking | 42 | 14 | 14 | 14 | 58 | 47 | 56 |
| Cambridge United | 42 | 15 | 10 | 8 | 51 | 57 | 55 |
| Aldershot | 42 | 16 | 6 | 20 | 61 | 74 | 54 |
| Canvey Island | 42 | 13 | 12 | 17 | 47 | 58 | 51 |
| Kidderminster Harriers | 42 | 13 | 11 | 18 | 39 | 55 | 50 |
| Gravesend & Northfleet | 42 | 13 | 10 | 19 | 45 | 57 | 49 |
| Crawley Town | 42 | 12 | 11 | 19 | 48 | 55 | 47 |
| Southport | 42 | 10 | 10 | 22 | 36 | 68 | 40 |
| Forest Green Rovers | 42 | 8 | 14 | 20 | 49 | 62 | 38 |
| Tamworth | 42 | 8 | 14 | 20 | 32 | 63 | 38 |
| Scarborough | 42 | 9 | 10 | 23 | 40 | 66 | 37 |
| Altrincham | 42 | 10 | 11 | 21 | 40 | 71 | 23* |

* Altrincham deducted 18 points for breach of league rules

* Having ended the previous season strongly and just missing out on a play off spot, optimism was high for another good campaign, and that proved to be correct as City won their first four matches (Gravesend away 2-0, Kidderminster home 1-0, Morecambe home 2-0, Accrington away 2-1), to go top of the Conference. Accrington would become Conference champions after this early season setback.

* Newcomers to the City squad included defender Billy Jones, former Exeter player Chris Vinnicombe, midfielder Jon Challinor, strikers Craig Farrell and Jamie Mackie.

* City continued to be around the promotion play off places through until January 2006, and topped the table again in November following a 1-1 draw at Altrincham.

* They also strung together another run of four consecutive wins as they defeated Halifax Town at home 4-2, Crawley away 2-0, Tamworth home 3-1, and Kidderminster away 2-1.

* Form dipped in the second half of season and it was ultimately to cost them any hopes of a return to the Football League, let alone a play off opportunity. Indeed, City won just four of their last seventeen matches in the Conference. Losing 15 Conference matches during the season, was simply too many to make a realistic and consistent challenge at the top of the division.

* Steve Flack scored one of the fastest hat-tricks in club history when he netted all three goals in the opening 14 minutes against Southport at St James' Park in March 2006. City led 4-0 at half-time, but could only add one further goal in the second half.

* Although knocked out of both the F.A. Cup and the Football League Trophy early on, the team did enjoy a fruitful run in the F.A. Trophy and came within a whisker of playing at Wembley in the final, before Grays Athletic beat them 3-2 on aggregate in the semi-final.

* A number of players arrived during the season, some for just a short stay. Winger Wayne Carlisle came from Leyton Orient, Midfielders Matthew Gill from Notts County, and Anton Robinson from Millwall, winger Tony Scully also from Notts County, and another wide player, Craig Watkins who joined from Sutton United.

* Once again it was pleasing to see the home grown players appear in the first team, and the club had high hopes of George Friend, Dean Moxey and Danny Seaborne in particular. All three would be sold for welcome transfer fees in later seasons.

* With City finishing in 7th place and eleven points short of a play off place, it was perhaps a little disappointing, however, bridges continued to be built off the field as the club got more and more involved with the local community.

* Attendances continued to climb at St James' Park with an average of 3,790 for Conference matches, the highest in the division. The highest attendance for a game was 6,682 who were present for the 1-2 defeat against Grays Athletic.

* The lowest attendance Exeter City played in front of was just 641 at Canvey Island in April 2006, the game ended 1-1.

* One notable success that should be mentioned were the regular work parties of volunteers who helped not only on a match day, but also during the week and summer months, as they carried out all manner of tasks from picking up littler immediately after the final whistle, to painting and making repairs where necessary to the ground and the St James' Centre, the latter continuing to be the administrative and social hub of the club.

CITY PLAYING SQUAD 2006-07

| Name | Pos | Signed From | App | Gls |
|------|-----|-------------|-----|-----|
| Patrick Ada | D | St Albans City Jul 2006 | 5(1) | |
| Paul Buckle | M | Tiverton Town Mar 2005 | 26(3) | 3 |
| Wayne Carlisle | W | Leyton Orient Jan 2006 | 21(3) | 5 |
| Jon Challinor | M | Aldershot Town Jul 2005 | 32(10) | 9 |
| Danny Clay | M | Trainee Jul 2003 | 2(3) | |
| Bertie Cozic | M | Aldershot Town Jul 2006 | 15(15) | 1 |
| Rob Edwards | D | Blackpool Aug 2006 | 43 | 1 |
| Lee Elam | W | Weymouth Jan 2007 | 19(1) | 7 |
| George Friend | D | Trainee Mar 2006 | 0(2) | |
| Matthew Gill | M | Notts County Jan 2006 | 46 | 1 |
| Billy Jones | D | Kidderminster Harriers Jul 2005 | 46 | 10 |
| Paul Jones | G | Leyton Orient Nov 2004 | 21 | |
| Richard Logan | F | Weymouth Jan 2007 | 10(7) | 4 |
| Jamie Mackie | F | Milton Keynes Dons Jul 2005 | 22(18) | 5 |
| Dean Moxey | M | Trainee Jul 2002 | 11(12) | 2 |
| Lee Phillips | F | Weymouth Feb 2005 | 21(15) | 4 |
| Martin Rice | G | Trainee Dec 2002 | 25(1) | |
| Jon Richardson | D | Forest Green Rovers Jul 2006 | 13(6) | |
| Danny Seaborne | D | Trainee May 2005 | 3(1) | 1 |
| Adam Stansfield | F | Hereford United Jun 2006 | 26(12) | 9 |
| Andy Taylot | M | Manchester United Oct 2003 | 26(4) | |
| Chris Todd | D | Drogheda United Jan 2003 | 25 | 1 |
| Steve Tully | D | Weymouth Jan 2007 | 17 | |
| Danny Woodards | D | Wycombe Wanderers Oct 2005 | 21(1) | |
| Own Goals | | | | 4 |

City's Conference results

| | Home | Away |
|------|------|------|
| Aldershot Town | 0-0 | 2-3 |
| Altrincham | 2-1 | 2-1 |
| Burton Albion | 3-0 | 0-1 |
| Cambridge United | 2-0 | 3-1 |
| Crawley Town | 1-1 | 3-0 |
| Dagenham & Redbridge | 3-2 | 1-4 |
| Forest Green Rovers | 1-0 | 1-2 |
| Gravesend & Northfleet | 1-3 | 2-2 |
| Grays Athletic | 2-1 | 2-2 |
| Halifax Town | 4-1 | 1-2 |
| Kidderminster Harriers | 1-1 | 2-0 |
| Morecambe | 1-0 | 2-2 |
| Northwich Victoria | 1-1 | 0-1 |
| Oxford United | 2-1 | 0-1 |
| Rushden & Diamonds | 0-0 | 0-3 |
| St. Albans City | 4-2 | 2-1 |
| Southport | 2-1 | 1-0 |
| Stafford Rangers | 1-2 | 1-0 |
| Stevenage Borough | 1-1 | 0-0 |
| Tamworth | 1-0 | 0-1 |
| Weymouth | 4-0 | 1-2 |
| Woking | 1-0 | 2-0 |
| York City | 1-1 | 0-0 |

Play Offs

| | | | |
|------|---|-----|----|
| Oxford United | H | 0-1 | SF |
| Oxford United | A | 2-1* | SF |
| Morecambe | N^ | 1-2 | |

\* Exeter City won 4-3 on penalties.
^ at Wembley

F.A. Cup

| | | | |
|------|---|-----|----|
| AFC Wimbledon | H | 2-1 | Q4 |
| Stockport County | H | 1-2 | R1 |

F.A. Trophy

| | | | |
|------|---|-----|----|
| Heybridge Swifts | H | 3-0 | R1 |
| Kidderminster Harriers | H | 0-1 | R2 |

\* Paul Tisdale was appointed manager of Exeter City in June 2006, and was to become the club's most successful in their history, guiding the Grecians to two consecutive promotions and two Wembley appearances.

He was perhaps a surprise choice at the time, although he had played for City on loan as midfield player some years before, having also appeared for Southampton, Northampton own (loan), Huddersfield Town (loan), Bristol City, Finn Pa, Panionios and Yeovil Town.

An injury forced him to give up playing regularly and he became a coach with university side, Team Bath, in 2000. Helping them win four promotions and enjoying a fine run in the FA Cup in 2002-03, when they lost to Mansfield Town in the first round proper, Tisdale was noted for his studious style of management and coaching.

That prompted Exeter City to offer him a contract at St James' Park and he proved to be an immediate success leading the team to Wembley for the Conference play off final in his first season in charge. But that was to be only the start of a successful period with the Grecians.

CITY MANAGER 2006-07
Paul Tisdale - Appointed June 2006

Football Conference

| | P | W | D | L | F | A | Pts |
|------|---|---|---|---|---|---|-----|
| Dagenham & Redbridge | 46 | 28 | 11 | 7 | 93 | 48 | 95 |
| Oxford United | 46 | 22 | 15 | 9 | 66 | 33 | 81 |
| Morecambe | 46 | 23 | 12 | 11 | 64 | 46 | 81 |
| York City | 46 | 23 | 11 | 12 | 65 | 45 | 80 |
| Exeter City | 46 | 22 | 12 | 12 | 67 | 48 | 78 |
| Burton Albion | 46 | 22 | 9 | 15 | 52 | 47 | 75 |
| Gravesend & Northfleet | 46 | 21 | 11 | 14 | 63 | 56 | 74 |
| Stevenage Borough | 46 | 20 | 10 | 16 | 76 | 66 | 70 |
| Aldershot Town | 46 | 18 | 11 | 17 | 64 | 62 | 65 |
| Kidderminster Harriers | 46 | 17 | 12 | 17 | 43 | 50 | 63 |
| Weymouth | 46 | 18 | 9 | 19 | 56 | 73 | 63 |
| Rushden & Diamonds | 46 | 17 | 11 | 18 | 58 | 54 | 62 |
| Northwich Victoria | 46 | 18 | 4 | 24 | 51 | 69 | 58 |
| Forest Green Rovers | 46 | 13 | 18 | 15 | 59 | 64 | 57 |
| Woking | 46 | 15 | 12 | 19 | 56 | 61 | 57 |
| Halifax Town | 46 | 15 | 10 | 21 | 55 | 62 | 55 |
| Cambridge United | 46 | 15 | 10 | 21 | 57 | 66 | 55 |
| Crawley Town | 46 | 17 | 12 | 17 | 52 | 52 | 53* |
| Grays Athletic | 46 | 13 | 13 | 20 | 56 | 55 | 52 |
| Stafford Rangers | 46 | 14 | 10 | 22 | 49 | 71 | 52 |
| Altrincham | 46 | 13 | 12 | 21 | 53 | 67 | 51 |
| Tamworth | 46 | 13 | 9 | 24 | 43 | 61 | 48 |
| Southport | 46 | 11 | 14 | 21 | 57 | 67 | 47 |
| St Albans City | 46 | 10 | 10 | 26 | 57 | 89 | 40 |

\* Crawley Town deducted 10 points
for entering administration.

* Exeter City commenced their fourth season of Conference football with a new manager at the helm. Former Grecian loanee, Paul Tisdale had made his name as a coach with university side Team Bath, and was perhaps at the time a surprise choice to take over from Alex Inglethorpe who had linked up with Tottenham Hotspur as a youth coach.

* The appointment of Tisdale proved to be a master stroke as he enjoyed success in each of his first three seasons with the club. In his first he brought in some experience to add to his squad in the shape of Rob Edwards. Other new arrivals prior to the first game were Patrick Ada; Bertie Cozic (thus becoming the second Frenchman to play for City); the return of Jon Richardson for his second spell at the club; Adam Stansfield, a former trialist who signed from Hereford United.

* The Grecians got away to a good start with only one defeat in their opening seven Conference matches, and were never out of the top ten places all season. Although they didn't head the table, the highest position they reached was third, following a 3-0 home win against Burton Albion in February 2007.

* Exeter signed three players from Weymouth in the second half of the season, the Dorset club struggling financially and being forced to release players. Steve Tully returned to the club after a previous brief spell, and he was joined by striker Richard Logan and winger Lee Elam.

* Elam made a spectacular debut netting a hat-trick in the 4-0 victory over his former club Weymouth. Oddly he was then dropped for the next game against Dagenham and Redbridge, being named as one of the substitutes.

* It quickly became apparent that manager Tisdale had a very different style to any other who had been in charge at St James' Park. An astute tactical judge, he picked a team which he felt would be best suited to each game, rather than simply keeping an unchanged line up just because they had won the previous match.

* The Grecians ended the season very strongly and won five of their last seven matches, the last of which against Southport, attracted an attendance of 6.670, the best of the season. The 2-1 win confirmed that City would be in the Conference play offs fir the first time.

* There then proved to be an epic struggle in the play off semi-final against Oxford United. City eventually got through to play at Wembley for the first time in their history when they won a penalty shoot out in the second leg.

* So on to Wembley! A crowd of just over 40,000, with easily half of those supporting Exeter City, were to experience heartbreak. Although City took the lead through a Lee Phillips goal, their opponents, Morecambe, hit back to score twice and thus win promotion to the Football League.

* One sour note and one for the record books, was the fact that City midfielder Matthew Gill was sent off in the closing seconds of the final, thus becoming the very first player to be red-carded at the new Wembley.

* The road to Wembley had boosted the numbers of those wanting to join the Exeter City Supporters' Trust which guaranteed them a ticket at any all-ticket match.

* Leading scorer for Exeter was surprisingly not a striker, but defender Billy Jones, who netted ten goals, four of them from the penalty spot.

* The average attendance for Conference matches at St James' Park was 3,627. The lowest attendance that City played in front of was 784 at Northwich Victoria, which the hosts won 1-0.

CITY PLAYING SQUAD 2007-08

| Name | Pos | Signed From | Apps | Gls |
|------|-----|-------------|------|-----|
| Frankie Artus | M | Bristol City Aug 2007 | 8(2) | |
| Steve Basham | F | Oxford United Jul 2007 | 15(17) | 5 |
| Wayne Carlisle | W | Leyton Orient Jan 2006 | 24(8) | 4 |
| Bertie Cozic | M | Aldershot Town Jul 2006 | 10(5) | |
| Rob Edwards | D | Blackpool Aug 2006 | 46 | 1 |
| Lee Elam | W | Weymouth Jan 2007 | 9(14) | 3 |
| George Friend | D | Trainee Mar 2006 | 27(3) | 1 |
| Matthew Gill | M | Notts County Jan 2006 | 43 | 3 |
| Ryan Harley | M | Weston-Super-Mare Dec 2007 | 9(3) | 1 |
| Paul Jones | G | Leyton Orient Nov 2004 | 7 | |
| Richard Logan | F | Weymouth Jan 2007 | 28(13) | 18 |
| Jamie Mackie | F | Milton Keynes Dons Jul 2005 | 21(3) | 11 |
| Andy Marriott | G | Boston United Jul 2007 | 39 | |
| Dean Moxey | M | Trainee Jul 2002 | 43(2) | 9 |
| Jon Richardson | D | Forest Green Rovers Jul 2006 | 15(4) | |
| Danny Seaborne | D | Trainee May 2005 | 24 | 2 |
| Liam Sercombe | M | Trainee Jun 2007 | 4(3) | |
| Adam Stansfield | F | Hereford United Jun 2006 | 36(5) | 11 |
| Andy Taylor | M | Manchester United Oct 2003 | 19(1) | |
| Matt Taylor | D | Team Bath Jul 2007 | 40 | 9 |
| Steve Tully | D | Weymouth Jan 2007 | 38(1) | |
| Ben Watson | F | Grays Athletic Mar 2008 | 1(8) | 1 |
| Own Goals | | | | 4 |

City's Conference results

| | Home | Away |
|------|------|------|
| Aldershot Town | 1-1 | 0-2 |
| Altrincham | 2-1 | 4-1 |
| Burton Albion | 1-4 | 4-4 |
| Cambridge United | 1-1 | 1-0 |
| Crawley Town | 2-0 | 2-2 |
| Droylsden | 1-1 | 3-2 |
| Ebbsfleet United | 1-1 | 1-1 |
| Farsley Celtic | 2-1 | 2-0 |
| Forest Green Rovers | 3-3 | 1-1 |
| Gravesend & Northfleet | | |
| Grays Athletic | 1-0 | 2-0 |
| Halifax Town | 1-0 | 3-0 |
| Histon | 2-1 | 2-2 |
| Kidderminster Harriers | 1-0 | 0-4 |
| Northwich Victoria | 2-1 | 0-0 |
| Oxford United | 2-0 | 2-2 |
| Rushden & Diamonds | 2-2 | 2-0 |
| Salisbury City | 4-2 | 0-2 |
| Stafford Rangers | 4-1 | 5-1 |
| Stevenage Borough | 4-0 | 1-0 |
| Torquay United | 4-3 | 0-1 |
| Weymouth | 0-0 | 1-3 |
| Woking | 2-2 | 1-1 |
| York City | 1-1 | 2-3 |

| Play Offs | | | |
|------|------|------|------|
| Torquay United | H | 1-2 | SF |
| Torquay United | A | 4-1 | SF |
| Cambridge United | N* | 1-0 | |
| * at Wembley | | | |

| F.A. Cup | | | |
|------|------|------|------|
| Ebbsfleet United | A | 3-1 | Q4 |
| Stevenage Borough | H | 4-0 | R1 |
| Bury | A | 0-1 | R2 |

| F.A. Trophy | H | 3-0 | R1 |
|------|------|------|------|
| Salisbury City | A | 0-3 | R2 |
| Rushden & Diamonds | A | 0-3 | R3 |

* After the disappointment of defeat at Wembley in the previous season, Exeter City experienced the opposite feeling in May 2008 as the team triumphed 1-0 against Cambridge United in the Conference Play Off Final.

Asked how it felt at Wembley for a second time, manager Paul Tisdale said: "It was a fantastic day, to see everybody there. The club had vision of what had to be done, and then to actually come real, is unbelievable.

"The victory parade through Exeter was a fantastic day. To get to the Guildhall and lift it up the cup in front of all those people, and get a cheer was fantastic, then to see all the people lining the streets.

"I had the cup sat on my mantelpiece for 5 days, and have a photo of my boy Sam, sat inside the cup. He's not wearing a thing, and wondering what he's doing in it. Well, I hope it's been cleaned. When the lads were drinking out of it, at the ball, I didn't tell them that!"

Asked what his next dream for Exeter City was, Tisdale continued: "In terms of progression for the club, it would be easy to say promotion again. It took 5 years, and now the next step would be to improve in small ways, in every area.

"We might get promoted, we might not. Improve at the same rate, with the support base, and financial side. It's not an easy dream, but every element needs to improve."

CITY MANAGER 2007-08
Paul Tisdale - Appointed June 2006

Football Conference

| | P | W | D | L | F | A | Pts |
|------|---|---|---|---|---|---|-----|
| Aldershot Town | 46 | 31 | 8 | 7 | 82 | 48 | 101 |
| Cambridge United | 46 | 25 | 11 | 10 | 68 | 41 | 86 |
| Torquay United | 46 | 26 | 8 | 12 | 83 | 57 | 86 |
| Exeter City | 46 | 22 | 17 | 7 | 83 | 58 | 83 |
| Burton Albion | 46 | 23 | 12 | 11 | 79 | 56 | 81 |
| Stevenage Borough | 46 | 24 | 7 | 15 | 82 | 55 | 79 |
| Histon | 46 | 20 | 12 | 14 | 76 | 67 | 72 |
| Forest Green Rovers | 46 | 19 | 14 | 13 | 76 | 59 | 71 |
| Oxford United | 46 | 20 | 11 | 15 | 56 | 48 | 71 |
| Grays Athletic | 46 | 19 | 13 | 14 | 58 | 47 | 70 |
| Ebbsfleet United | 46 | 19 | 12 | 15 | 65 | 61 | 69 |
| Salisbury City | 46 | 18 | 14 | 14 | 70 | 60 | 68 |
| Kidderminster Harriers | 46 | 19 | 10 | 17 | 74 | 57 | 67 |
| York City | 46 | 17 | 11 | 18 | 71 | 74 | 62 |
| Crawley Town | 46 | 19 | 9 | 18 | 73 | 67 | 60* |
| Rushden & Diamonds | 46 | 15 | 14 | 17 | 55 | 55 | 59 |
| Woking | 46 | 12 | 17 | 17 | 53 | 61 | 53 |
| Weymouth | 46 | 11 | 13 | 22 | 53 | 73 | 46 |
| Northwich Victoria | 46 | 11 | 11 | 24 | 52 | 78 | 44 |
| Halifax Town | 46 | 12 | 16 | 18 | 61 | 70 | 42+ |
| Altrincham | 46 | 9 | 14 | 23 | 56 | 82 | 41 |
| Farsley Celtic | 46 | 10 | 9 | 27 | 48 | 86 | 39 |
| Stafford Rangers | 46 | 5 | 10 | 31 | 42 | 99 | 25 |
| Droylsden | 46 | 5 | 9 | 32 | 46 | 103 | 24 |

* Crawley Town deducted 6 points
+ Halifax Town deducted 10 points

* Having lost in the Conference Play off Final the previous season, would Exeter City be able to maintain their push for promotion back to the Football League? Although they started off being unbeaten in their opening five matches and were top of the table, they then went five games without a win, thus falling to 10th place.

* A few additions had been made by manager Paul Tisdale to his squad as he brought in Frankie Artus on loan, and signed Steve Basham, Andy Marriott and Matt Taylor. The latter had been signed from Tisdale's former club, Team Bath. A full contract was also given to youth product Liam Sercombe.

* Further arrivals during the course of the season were midfielder Ryan Harley from Weston-Super-Mare and striker Ben Watson from Grays Athletic.

* From the end of September onwards the team never dropped lower than 8th place in the Conference. The team went on a run of just one defeat (losing 1-0 to Torquay United) in fifteen matches in the middle of the season.

* They also finished the season strongly when they secured three wins and two draws in their final matches, ensured that City would once again be in the play-offs.

* To reach Wembley once more they had to overcome neighbours Torquay United. Needless to say there was immense interest in the two-legged semi-finals. The Grecians lost 2-1 in the first leg at St James' Park, but then proceeded to put in a tremendous performance at Plainmoor running out 4-1 winners.

* So it was off to Wembley again for the second year running. This time they were to face Cambridge United. Exeter certainly seemed very relaxed about the prospect having been there 12 months earlier and so knew what to expect on the day.

*Once again the Grecians supporters turned out in their thousands as a crowd of 42,511 saw the only goal of the game netted by Rob Edwards in the 22nd minute. Exeter City were back in the Football League after five seasons in the Conference and they were very much a different club to the one that had suffered relegation and almost financial melt down at the end of 2002-03.

* After the final whistle, Exeter manager Paul Tisdale said his players deserved promotion: "It's absolutely fantastic. I'm very proud to have been part of this football club. It was a terribly long second half - the last 10 minutes were excruciating. The support was wonderful, I'm delighted for them" He said it won't be easy next season, but added: "It's a high quality problem - let's enjoy it."

* As is tradition the team and back room staff went on an open top tour of Exeter city centre where the streets were lined with thousands of well wishers and supporters, before they attended a civic reception at the Guildhall.

* Paul Tisdale had taken the club to two Wembley finals in consecutive seasons, unheard of prior to his appointment. Now he had the task of guiding them in League Two of the Football League.

* The Grecians were now something of a role model for supporters' owned clubs, certainly in the Football League, and as a result were contacted by other clubs who wanted to go down the same road.

* City averaged 3,705 for home matches in the Conference, with a season high of 7,839 coming not surprisingly against Torquay United. The lowest crowd they played in front of in the Conference was just 841 at Crawley Town in March 2008.

## CITY PLAYING SQUAD 2008-09

| Name | Pos | Signed From | App | Gls |
|------|-----|-------------|-----|-----|
| Troy Archibald-Henville | D | Tottenham Hotspur Jan 2008 | 19 | |
| Steve Basham | F | Oxford United Jul 2007 | 12(11) | 2 |
| Bertie Cozic | M | Aldershot Town Jul 2006 | 14(6) | |
| Rob Edwards | D | Blackpool Aug 2006 | 44 | |
| Stuart Fleetwood | F | Charlton Athletic Mar 2009 | 7(2) | 3 |
| George Friend | D | Trainee Mar 2006 | 4 | |
| Matthew Gill | M | Notts County Jan 2006 | 43 | 9 |
| Ryan Harley | M | Weston-Super-Mare Dec 2007 | 25(6) | 4 |
| Paul Jones | G | Leyton Orient Nov 2004 | 46 | |
| Richard Logan | F | Weymouth Jan 2007 | 18(12) | 4 |
| Craig McAllister | F | Oxford United Jul 2008 | 8(22) | 7 |
| Dean Moxey | M | Trainee Jul 2002 | 41(2) | 4 |
| Fred Murray | D | Stevenage Borough Sep 2008 | 3(3) | |
| Jack Obersteller | M | Millwall May 2008 | 3(4) | |
| Manny Panther | M | York City Jul 2008 | 15(7) | 2 |
| Alex Russell | M | Cheltenham Town Feb 2009 | 7 | |
| Neil Saunders | M | Team Bath Jul 2007 | 15(2) | 3 |
| Danny Seaborne | D | Trainee May 2005 | 31(2) | 1 |
| Liam Sercombe | M | Trainee Jun 2007 | 16(13) | 2 |
| Chris Shephard | M | Trainee Jun 2007 | 0(2) | |
| Adam Stansfield | F | Hereford United Jun 2006 | 32(5) | 10 |
| Marcus Stewart | F | Yeovil Town Jul 2008 | 35(1) | 7 |
| Matt Taylor | D | Team Bath Jul 2007 | 29(2) | 2 |
| Steve Tully | D | Weymouth Jan 2007 | 35(1) | |
| Ben Watson | F | Grays Athletic Mar 2008 | 4(8) | 2 |
| Own Goals | | | | 3 |

### City's League Results

| | Home | Away |
|------|------|------|
| Accrington Stanley | 2-1 | 1-2 |
| AFC Bournemouth | 1-3 | 1-0 |
| Aldershot Town | 3-2 | 0-1 |
| Barnet | 2-1 | 1-0 |
| Bradford City | 1-0 | 1-4 |
| Brentford | 0-2 | 1-1 |
| Bury | 0-0 | 1-1 |
| Chester City | 2-0 | 0-0 |
| Chesterfield | 1-6 | 1-2 |
| Dagenham & Redbridge | 2-1 | 2-1 |
| Darlington | 2-0 | 1-1 |
| Gillingham | 3-0 | 0-1 |
| Grimsby Town | 0-0 | 2-2 |
| Lincoln City | 2-1 | 1-0 |
| Luton Town | 0-1 | 2-1 |
| Macclesfield Town | 4-0 | 4-1 |
| Morecambe | 2-2 | 1-1 |
| Notts County | 2-2 | 1-2 |
| Port Vale | 1-0 | 3-1 |
| Rochdale | 4-1 | 2-2 |
| Rotherham United | 1-1 | 1-0 |
| Shrewsbury Town | 0-1 | 1-1 |
| Wycombe Wanderers | 1-0 | 1-1 |

| F.A. Cup | | |
|------|------|------|
| Curzon Ashton | A 2-3 | R1 |

| Football League Cup | | |
|------|------|------|
| Southampton | H 1-3 | R1 |

| Johnstone's Paint Trophy | | |
|------|------|------|
| Shrewsbury Town | H 1-2 | R1 |

Programme for the FA Cup tie at Curzon Ashton—possibly the most humiliating defeat the club have ever suffered

**CITY MANAGER 2007-08**
Paul Tisdale - Appointed June 2006

### League Two

| | P | W | D | L | F | A | Pts |
|------|----|----|----|----|----|----|-----|
| Brentford | 46 | 23 | 16 | 7 | 65 | 36 | 85 |
| Exeter City | 46 | 22 | 13 | 11 | 65 | 50 | 79 |
| Wycombe Wanderers | 46 | 20 | 18 | 8 | 54 | 33 | 78 |
| Bury | 46 | 21 | 15 | 10 | 63 | 43 | 78 |
| Gillingham | 46 | 21 | 12 | 13 | 58 | 55 | 75 |
| Rochdale | 46 | 19 | 13 | 14 | 70 | 59 | 70 |
| Shrewsbury Town | 46 | 17 | 18 | 11 | 61 | 44 | 69 |
| Dagenham & Redbridge | 46 | 19 | 11 | 16 | 77 | 53 | 68 |
| Bradford City | 46 | 18 | 13 | 15 | 66 | 55 | 67 |
| Chesterfield | 46 | 16 | 15 | 15 | 62 | 57 | 63 |
| Morecambe | 46 | 15 | 18 | 13 | 53 | 56 | 63 |
| Darlington | 46 | 20 | 12 | 14 | 61 | 44 | 62* |
| Lincoln City | 46 | 14 | 17 | 15 | 53 | 52 | 59 |
| Rotherham United | 46 | 21 | 12 | 13 | 60 | 46 | 58+ |
| Aldershot Town | 46 | 14 | 12 | 20 | 59 | 80 | 54 |
| Accrington Stanley | 46 | 13 | 11 | 22 | 42 | 59 | 50 |
| Barnet | 46 | 11 | 15 | 20 | 56 | 74 | 48 |
| Port Vale | 46 | 13 | 9 | 24 | 44 | 66 | 48 |
| Notts County | 46 | 11 | 14 | 21 | 49 | 69 | 47 |
| Macclesfield Town | 46 | 13 | 8 | 25 | 45 | 77 | 47 |
| AFC Bournemouth | 46 | 17 | 12 | 17 | 59 | 51 | 46** |
| Grimsby Town | 46 | 9 | 14 | 23 | 51 | 69 | 41 |
| Chester City | 46 | 8 | 13 | 25 | 43 | 81 | 37 |
| Luton Town | 46 | 13 | 17 | 16 | 58 | 65 | 26++ |

\* Darlington deducted 10 points
+ Rotherham United deducted 17 points
** AFC Bournemouth deducted 17 points
++ Luton Town deducted 30 points

*Back in the Football League for the first time since 2003, needless to say the start of the season was eagerly anticipated, but little did anyone know then just how successful it was going to be.

* Manager Paul Tisdale showed great faith with the squad that had won the Conference Play-off Final at Wembley, but did bring in midfielders Jack Obersteller and Manny Panther, striker Craig McAllister and the vastly experienced forward, Marcus Stewart.

* Although the Grecians opened the season with a 1-1 draw at Darlington, it has to be said that they took a while to get used to league football. And by the end of September they found themselves in 11th place.

* The first home match back in the league was against Shrewsbury Town before an attendance of just under 5,000, however, disappointingly City lost 1-0.

* From October onwards, however, City began to hit a rich vein of form and put together a run of seven unbeaten matches which lifted them to third place in the League Two table.

* Not having an auspicious record against non-league opposition in the F.A. Cup, Exeter were drawn away to Curzon Ashton in the first round. Despite a late revival, City lost 3-2.

* They had also gone out of both the Carling Cup (Football League Cup) and the Johnstone's Paint Trophy at the first round stage, and whilst a little disappointing it did enable the squad to concentrate fully on the league.

* With another run of only one defeat in ten league matches, Exeter were right up amongst the automatic and play-off hopefuls and when they went in to the return game against Darlington, which they won 2-0, they were in 5th place.

* Attendances naturally increased as City were seen to be in with a real chance of promotion again and this optimism was only heightened when in March and April they won 6, drew four and only lost twice.

* Striker Stuart Fleetwood was brought to the club on loan from Charlton Athletic in March 2009 to add to the teams attacking options.

* The final home of the season against Morecambe attracted an attendance of 8,544, but the Lancashire side were to keep City fans in suspense as far as automatic promotion was concerned, as they drew 2-2. Everything now rested on the final match.

* That took the Grecians to their final game at Rotherham United, who were playing their matches at the Don Valley Stadium in Sheffield. The Grecians needed a victory to have any chance of automatic promotion , and this was duly achieved thanks to a goal from Richard Logan before a huge travelling support as part of the 6,184 crowd, which included an estimated 2.500 from Exeter.

* To win two successive promotions was an historic moment for the club and the scenes at the end of the match at Rotherham reflected that. City players were mobbed in a running track invasion and it was a full 45 minutes before the last few left the stadium.

* Exeter boss Paul Tisdale admitted it had been "a long hard slog". He said of the win at Rotherham: "The last 20 minutes were torture. We did it the hard way by missing a penalty when we could have made it safe. It's a great achievement for us - back to back promotions - and we are in League One. It's going to be tough next season, but we'll enjoy our promotion first."

* The average attendance at St James' Park for the League Two season was 4,939, a third up on the figure for the previous season. The highest crowd that City played in front of in League Two was 12,683 at Bradford City. The lowest was just 1,169 for the Grecians' visit to Accrington Stanley.

CITY PLAYING SQUAD 2009-10

| Name | Pos | Signed From | App | Gls |
|---|---|---|---|---|
| Troy Archibald-Henville | D | Tottenham Hotspur Jan 2008 | 13(2) | |
| Joe Burnell | M | Oxford United Jul 2009 | 4(4) | |
| Barry Corr | F | Swindon Town Jul 2009 | 17(17) | 3 |
| Bertie Cozic | M | Aldershot Town Jul 2006 | 21(8) | 2 |
| Richard Duffy | D | Millwall Jul 2009 | 41(1) | 1 |
| James Dunne | M | Arsenal Jul 2009 | 18(5) | 3 |
| Rob Edwards | D | Blackpool Aug 2006 | 17(4) | |
| Stuart Fleetwood | F | Charlton Athletic Sep 2009 | 16(11) | 4 |
| George Friend | D | Trainee Mar 2006 | 13 | 1 |
| Scott Golbourne | D | Reading Jul 2009 | 30(4) | |
| Marcus Haber | F | West Bromwich Albion Feb 2010 | 3(2) | |
| Ryan Harley | M | Weston-Super-Mare Dec 2007 | 43(1) | 10 |
| Oscar Jansson | G | Tottenham Hotspur Sep 2009 | 7 | |
| Paul Jones | G | Leyton Orient Nov 2004 | 26 | |
| Richard Logan | F | Weymouth Jan 2007 | 4(30) | 4 |
| Craig McAllister | F | Oxford United Jul 2008 | 0(4) | |
| Andy Marriott | G | Boston United Jul 2007 | 13 | |
| Craig Noone | W | Plymouth Argyle Sep 2009 | 7 | 2 |
| James Norwood | F | Eastbourne Town Jul 2009 | 2(1) | |
| Alex Russell | M | Cheltenham Town Feb 2009 | 27(2) | 1 |
| Neil Saunders | M | Team Bath Jul 2007 | 2(4) | |
| Danny Seaborne | D | Trainee May 2005 | 17(2) | |
| Liam Sercombe | M | Trainee Jun 2007 | 25(3) | 1 |
| Adam Stansfield | F | Hereford United Jun 2006 | 19(8) | 7 |
| Marcus Stewart | F | Yeovil Town Jul 2008 | 36(5) | 2 |
| Matt Taylor | D | Team Bath Jul 2007 | 46 | 5 |
| Ryan Taylor | F | Rotherham United Mar 2010 | 3(4) | |
| Steve Tully | D | Weymouth Jan 2007 | 36(2) | 1 |
| Ben Watson | F | Grays Athletic Mar 2008 | 0(1) | |
| Own Goals | | | | 1 |

City's results

| | Home | Away |
|---|---|---|
| Brentford | 3-0 | 0-0 |
| Brighton & H.A. | 0-1 | 0-2 |
| Bristol Rovers | 1-0 | 0-1 |
| Carlisle United | 2-3 | 1-0 |
| Charlton Athletic | 1-1 | 1-2 |
| Colchester United | 2-0 | 2-2 |
| Gillingham | 1-1 | 0-3 |
| Hartlepool United | 3-1 | 1-1 |
| Huddersfield Town | 2-1 | 0-4 |
| Leeds United | 2-0 | 1-2 |
| Leyton Orient | 0-0 | 1-1 |
| Millwall | 1-1 | 0-1 |
| Milton Keynes Dons | 1-2 | 1-1 |
| Norwich City | 1-1 | 1-3 |
| Oldham Athletic | 1-1 | 0-2 |
| Southampton | 1-1 | 1-3 |
| Southend United | 1-0 | 0-0 |
| Stockport County | 0-1 | 3-1 |
| Swindon Town | 1-1 | 1-1 |
| Tranmere Rovers | 2-1 | 1-3 |
| Walsall | 2-1 | 0-3 |
| Wycombe Wanderers | 1-1 | 2-2 |
| Yeovil Town | 1-1 | 1-2 |

F.A. Cup
| Nuneaton Town | A | 4-0 | R1 |
| Milton Keynes Dons | A | 3-4 | R2 |

Football League Cup
| Queens Park Rangers | H | 0-5 | R1 |

Johnstone's Paint Trophy
| Swindon Town | H | 1-1 | R2 |
Exeter City were given a bye in round one.

CITY MANAGER 2009-10
Paul Tisdale - Appointed June 2006

League One

| | P | W | D | L | F | A | Pts |
|---|---|---|---|---|---|---|---|
| Norwich City | 46 | 29 | 8 | 9 | 89 | 47 | 95 |
| Leeds United | 46 | 25 | 11 | 10 | 77 | 44 | 86 |
| Millwall | 46 | 24 | 13 | 9 | 76 | 44 | 85 |
| Charlton Athletic | 46 | 23 | 15 | 8 | 71 | 48 | 84 |
| Swindon Town | 46 | 22 | 16 | 8 | 73 | 57 | 82 |
| Huddersfield Town | 46 | 23 | 11 | 12 | 82 | 56 | 80 |
| Southampton | 46 | 23 | 14 | 9 | 85 | 47 | 73* |
| Colchester United | 46 | 20 | 12 | 14 | 64 | 52 | 72 |
| Brentford | 46 | 14 | 20 | 12 | 55 | 52 | 62 |
| Walsall | 46 | 16 | 14 | 16 | 60 | 63 | 62 |
| Bristol Rovers | 46 | 19 | 5 | 22 | 59 | 70 | 62 |
| Milton Keynes Dons | 46 | 17 | 9 | 20 | 60 | 68 | 60 |
| Brighton & H.A. | 46 | 15 | 14 | 17 | 56 | 60 | 59 |
| Carlisle United | 46 | 15 | 13 | 18 | 63 | 66 | 58 |
| Yeovil Town | 46 | 13 | 14 | 19 | 55 | 59 | 53 |
| Oldham Athletic | 46 | 13 | 13 | 20 | 39 | 57 | 52 |
| Leyton Orient | 46 | 13 | 12 | 21 | 53 | 63 | 51 |
| Exeter City | 46 | 11 | 18 | 17 | 48 | 60 | 51 |
| Tranmere Rovers | 46 | 14 | 9 | 23 | 45 | 72 | 51 |
| Hartlepool United | 46 | 14 | 11 | 21 | 59 | 67 | 50^ |
| Gillingham | 46 | 12 | 14 | 20 | 48 | 64 | 50 |
| Wycombe Wanderers | 46 | 10 | 15 | 21 | 56 | 76 | 45 |
| Southend United | 46 | 10 | 13 | 23 | 51 | 72 | 43 |
| Stockport County | 46 | 5 | 10 | 31 | 35 | 95 | 25 |

Programme for the Exeter v Derby pre-season game, featuring Dean Moxey, recently sold to Derby for £350,000 plus.

* Southampton 10 points deducted for breaching insolvency regulations.
^Hartlepool United deducted 3 points for fielding ineligible player.

* Just two years after playing at Altrincham before an attendance of 1,318, Exeter City now found themselves travelling to Leeds United for their first match in League One where they came mighty close to earning a point before 27,681. Although they lost 2-1 and had a player sent off, City did enough on that showing to hopefully more than hold their own in the higher division.

* Newcomers to the squad for the start of the season were defenders Richard Duffy and Scott Golbourne, midfielders Joe Burnell and James Dunne, strikers Barry Corr and James Norwood. The latter player had his wages paid for by a group of City supporters who contributed a monthly sum.

* Stuart Fleetwood was signed on loan from Charlton Athletic in September 2009, and another striker, Canadian-born Marcus Haber arrived on loan from West Bromwich Albion in February 2010. He became the first Canadian to play for the Grecians.

* Not surprisingly City didn't find it quite as easy as the previous season and for much of the season were found in the lower reaches of the League One table.

* Only two matches were won in League One in the first two months of the season, those being against Carlisle United and Tranmere Rovers as the team slipped into 20th place in the table.

* It was a season where the Grecians used three goalkeepers, namely Oscar Jansson (on loan from Tottenham Hotspur), Paul Jones, and the vastly experienced Andy Marriott, who was also working at the club's Cat and Fiddle training ground in a secretarial capacity.

* Goals were hard to come by and by the end of the season it was a midfield player who topped the scoring charts, when the talented Ryan Harley hit ten league goals.

* A familiar 'face' returned to Exeter City on loan in March 2010, when defender George Friend was signed on loan from Wolverhampton Wanderers. He had been transferred by the Grecians to Wolves in September 2008 for £350,000.

* One defeat in the final twelve league matches enabled the Grecians to give themselves a chance of another season in League One, but it all rested on the final match, against a team who had beaten them 4-0 earlier in the campaign, Huddersfield Town.

* There was plenty at stake at both ends of the table when Exeter entertained Huddersfield Town in what was the final game of the season. The Grecians had yet to secure their League One status for another year and entered the final day of the season with just goal difference keeping them outside the relegation zone. The Terriers, who had won seven of their last nine, could in theory have still secured automatic promotion, but with the play-offs a more likely option they would be keen to maintain their momentum. City warmed the hearts of Grecians to secure their League One status for another year thanks to a fine 2-1 win in front of a crowd of 8,383

* After the victory over Huddersfield, manager Paul Tisdale said: "It's a wonderful achievement and our supporters have something to celebrate again this summer, There have been ups and downs, but they know how to dig in and the last few months have been terrific, a real team effort. I'm delighted, I'm relieved, I'm excited, but above all I'm very proud to be part of this great football club. We are a club where the supporters own the club and I don't think there's a club in the country that respects their supporters as much as we do, so I'm delighted for them."

* The average attendance at St James' Park for League One matches was 5,832, an increase of just over 18% on the previous season. The lowest league crowd that City played in front of 3,983 at Hartlepool United.

211

## CITY PLAYING SQUAD 2010-11

| Name | Pos | Signed From | App | Gls |
|---|---|---|---|---|
| Troy Archibald-Henville | D | Tottenham Hotspur Jan 2008 | 32(4) | 1 |
| Scot Bennett | D | Trainee Mar 2008 | 0(1) | |
| Bertie Cozic | M | Aldershot Town Jul 2006 | 4(7) | |
| James Cureton | F | Norwich City Jul 2010 | 34(7) | 17 |
| Richard Duffy | D | Millwall Jul 2009 | 41(1) | 2 |
| James Dunne | M | Arsenal Jul 2009 | 36(6) | 1 |
| Rob Edwards | D | Blackpool Aug 2006 | 6(3) | |
| Scott Golbourne | D | Reading Jul 2009 | 42(2) | 2 |
| Ben Hamer | G | Reading Jan 2011 | 18 | |
| Ryan Harley | M | Weston-Super-Mare Dec 2007 | 40(2) | 10 |
| Billy Jones | D | Crewe Alexandra Jun 2008 | 27(2) | |
| Paul Jones | G | Leyton Orient Nov 2004 | 18 | |
| Artur Krysiak | G | Birmingham City May 2010 | 10 | |
| Richard Logan | F | Weymouth Jan 2007 | 22(18) | 11 |
| Daniel Nardiello | F | Blackpool Jul 2010 | 15(15) | 10 |
| Tom Nicholls | F | Trainee Apr 2011 | 0(1) | |
| David Noble | M | Bristol City Jan 2010 | 29(7) | |
| James Norwood | F | Eastbourne Town Jul 2009 | 1 | |
| John O'Flynn | F | Barnet Jul 2010 | 22(9) | 6 |
| Liam Sercombe | M | Trainee Jun 2007 | 38(4) | 3 |
| Marcus Stewart | F | Yeovil Town Jul 2008 | 2(6) | |
| Matt Taylor | D | Team Bath Jul 2007 | 26(2) | 2 |
| Jake Thomson | W | Southampton Jul 2010 | 1(15) | |
| Paul Tisdale | M | Team Bath Jun 2006 | 0(1) | |
| Steve Tully | D | Weymouth Jan 2007 | 42(1) | 1 |

*Exeter City surprised many by not only just missing out on a play-off place in League One by one point, but by finishing the season strongly to end in 8th position.

Immediately after the final match of the season, a 2-1 win at Sheffield Wednesday, Manager Paul Tisdale summed up the season.
"I'm very proud of the team and very proud to be manager of a terrific club. It's been a great year and we've had to overcome numerous issues, most notably the passing of Adam Stansfield and we've come through it."

He added: "We've done things in a very respectful way. I hope we keep this side together. I urge them to stay with it, although I know there are riches elsewhere.

"This club is different," said Tisdale. "It is totally different and part of it is being serious, you don't lose that seriousness, but you have to enjoy every minute you get."

Commenting on his surprise run out in that final game, Tisdale, 38, said: "I belive it's my first Football League game for 13 years since I last played for Exeter away at Scarborough. It was just a wonderful experience to be part of a team winning at Hillsborough - it was a great moment for me."

### City's results

| | Home | Away |
|---|---|---|
| AFC Bournemouth | 2-0 | 0-3 |
| Brentford | 2-4 | 1-1 |
| Brighton & H.A. | 1-2 | 0-3 |
| Bristol Rovers | 2-2 | 2-0 |
| Carlisle United | 2-1 | 2-2 |
| Charlton Athletic | 1-0 | 3-1 |
| Colchester United | 2-2 | 1-5 |
| Dagenham & Redbridge | 2-1 | 1-1 |
| Hartlepool United | 1-2 | 3-2 |
| Huddersfield Town | 1-4 | 1-0 |
| Leyton Orient | 2-1 | 0-3 |
| Milton Keynes Dons | 1-1 | 0-1 |
| Notts County | 3-1 | 2-0 |
| Oldham Athletic | 2-0 | 3-3 |
| Peterborough United | 2-2 | 0-3 |
| Plymouth Argyle | 1-0 | 0-2 |
| Rochdale | 1-0 | 1-0 |
| Sheffield Wednesday | 5-1 | 2-1 |
| Southampton | 1-2 | 0-4 |
| Swindon Town | 1-0 | 0-0 |
| Tranmere Rovers | 1-1 | 0-4 |
| Walsall | 2-1 | 1-2 |
| Yeovil Town | 2-3 | 3-1 |

| F.A. Cup | | |
|---|---|---|
| Bury | A 0-2 | R1 |

| Football League Cup | | |
|---|---|---|
| Ipswich Town | H 2-3 | R1 |

| Johnstone's Paint Trophy | | |
|---|---|---|
| Yeovil Town | A 3-1 | R1 |
| Hereford United | A 3-0 | R2 |
| Plymouth Argyle | A 2-1 | R3 |
| Bristol Rovers | A 2-2* | SF |
| Brentford | A 1-1 | SAF |
| Brentford | H 1-2 | SAF |

* Exeter City won 5-4 on penalties

CITY MANAGER 2010-11
Paul Tisdale - Appointed June 2006

### League One

| | P | W | D | L | F | A | Pts |
|---|---|---|---|---|---|---|---|
| Brighton & H.A. | 46 | 28 | 11 | 7 | 85 | 40 | 95 |
| Southampton | 46 | 28 | 8 | 10 | 86 | 38 | 92 |
| Huddersfield Town | 46 | 25 | 12 | 9 | 77 | 48 | 87 |
| Peterborough United | 46 | 23 | 10 | 13 | 106 | 75 | 79 |
| Milton Keynes Dons | 46 | 23 | 8 | 15 | 67 | 60 | 77 |
| AFC Bournemouth | 46 | 19 | 14 | 13 | 75 | 54 | 71 |
| Leyton Orient | 46 | 19 | 13 | 14 | 71 | 62 | 70 |
| Exeter City | 46 | 20 | 10 | 16 | 66 | 73 | 70 |
| Rochdale | 46 | 18 | 14 | 14 | 63 | 55 | 68 |
| Colchester United | 46 | 16 | 14 | 16 | 57 | 63 | 62 |
| Brentford | 46 | 17 | 10 | 19 | 55 | 62 | 61 |
| Carlisle United | 46 | 16 | 11 | 19 | 60 | 62 | 59 |
| Charlton Athletic | 46 | 15 | 14 | 17 | 62 | 66 | 59 |
| Yeovil Town | 46 | 16 | 11 | 19 | 56 | 65 | 59 |
| Sheffield Wednesday | 46 | 16 | 10 | 20 | 67 | 67 | 58 |
| Hartlepool United | 46 | 15 | 12 | 19 | 47 | 65 | 57 |
| Oldham Athletic | 46 | 13 | 17 | 16 | 53 | 60 | 56 |
| Tranmere Rovers | 46 | 15 | 11 | 20 | 53 | 60 | 56 |
| Notts County | 46 | 14 | 8 | 24 | 46 | 60 | 50 |
| Walsall | 46 | 12 | 12 | 22 | 56 | 75 | 48 |
| Dagenham & Redbridge | 46 | 12 | 11 | 23 | 52 | 70 | 47 |
| Bristol Rovers | 46 | 11 | 12 | 23 | 48 | 82 | 45 |
| Plymouth Argyle | 46 | 15 | 7 | 24 | 51 | 74 | 42* |
| Swindon Town | 46 | 9 | 14 | 23 | 50 | 72 | 41 |

* Plymouth Argyle deducted 10 for entering administration.

* Exeter City were beginning to get a reputation for finishing a season strongly, and 2010-11 proved to be no different with seven wins on their last nine League One matches. This put the team on the brink of a possible play off position for the Championship- - an incredible achievement. Alas, at the end of the day they just missed out.

* Manager Paul Tisdale donned his boots once more in the final game of the season at Sheffield Wednesday. He was introduced as a late substitute, and not even the players knew he had named himself on the bench! It was his first Exeter outing since February 1998 when he was on loan from Bristol City. The Grecians won the game to complete the double over Sheffield Wednesday.

* Signed on a free transfer after being released by Norwich City, Jamie Cureton soon got on the goalscoring trail and ended the season with 17 League goals.

* Other newcomers to the squad at the start of the season were goalkeeper Artur Krysiak (becoming the first Polish born player to play league football for the Grecians), defender Billy Jones (his second spell at the club), winger Jake Thomson and strikers Daniel Nardiello and John O'Flynn.

* Although City had a disappointing time in both the Football League Cup and the FA Cup, they did reach the Southern Area Final of the Johnstone's Paint Trophy. They had to do it the hard way as every round was an away tie, including a memorable victory over great rivals Plymouth Argyle at Home Park.

* The most comprehensive display and victory of the season in League One was the 5-1 home win against Sheffield Wednesday, who were chasing a promotion spot at the time.

* Having stated that he was not going to renew his contract, goalkeeper Paul Jones moved to Peterborough United on loan, the club he eventually signed for. As a result this left City with just Artur Krysiak, so they signed Reading keeper Ben Hamer on loan, and he was to feature in 18 league matches.

* Midfielder Ryan Harley, who had been linked with a possible move to Brighton and Hove Albion, eventually joined Swansea City in January 2011, but was then immediately loaned back to the Grecians for the rest of the season. He was to never play a league game for the Swans though, for in August 2011, he did indeed sign for Brighton for a fee of £250,000.

* Tom Nichols became the latest product of Exeter City's youth scheme to make his first team debut at league level when he was introduced as a substitute in the last game of the season at Sheffield Wednesday.

*Defender Rob Edwards, who had played a major role during City's rise from Conference to League One announced that he was retiring from playing to concentrate on coaching. Edwards had already been in charge of City's reserve team and was to become Paul Tisdale's assistant manager the following season.

* Despite a successful season the average attendance for league matches at St James' Park showed a fall of over 400 per game. The final figure of 5,393 compared with 5,832 for the previous season.

* The highest attendance of the season at St James' Park was not surprisingly against Plymouth Argyle when 7,869 made their way through the turnstiles for what was the penultimate match of the campaign.

* The highest away attendance that the Grecians played in front of was at Charlton Athletic where a massive 24,767 saw Exeter far from being overawed and winning 3-1.

* The lowest attendance that City played in front of in a League One fixture was 2,005 at Dagenham & Redbridge. The game ended all square at 1-1.

*The club were shocked by the death of City striker Adam Stansfield in August 2010. The player had battled against cancer since first being diagnosed early in the year. Stansfield joined the Exeter squad for the first day of pre-season training in July, but his condition deteriorated rapidly and he died on 10 August 2010. The club also announced the shirt number 9 would be retired for nine seasons.

CITY PLAYING SQUAD 2011-12

| Name | Pos | Signed | App | Gls |
|------|-----|--------|-----|-----|
| Troy Archibald-Henville | D | Tottenham Hotspur Jan 2008 | 45 | 2 |
| Pat Baldwin | D | Southend United Mar 2012 | 9 | |
| Guillem Bauza | M | Northampton Town May 2011 | 12(15) | 2 |
| Scot Bennett | D | Trainee Mar 2008 | 13(2) | 3 |
| Nicholas Bignall | F | Reading Aug 2011 | 3 | |
| Danny Coles | D | Bristol Rovers Jun 2011 | 28(3) | 2 |
| James Cureton | F | Leyton Orient Mar 2012 | 5(2) | 1 |
| Lauri Dalla Valle | F | Fulham Mar 2012 | 3(1) | |
| Aaron Dawson | D | Trainee May 2010 | 2 | |
| Richard Duffy | D | Millwall Jul 2009 | 22(6) | |
| James Dunne | M | Arsenal Jul 2009 | 43(1) | 2 |
| Jonathan Fortune | D | Free Agent Mar 2012 | 5 | |
| Elliott Frear | W | Trainee Mar 2009 | 5(5) | |
| Scott Golbourne | D | Reading Jul 2009 | 26 | |
| Alan Gow | M | East Bengal (India) Mar 2012 | 6(1) | 3 |
| Chris Hackett | W | Millwall Dec 2011 | 5 | |
| Billy Jones | D | Crewe Alexandra Jun 2010 | 16(2) | 1 |
| Jimmy Keohane | M | Bristol City Aug 2011 | 0(3) | |
| Artur Krysiak | G | Birmingham City May 2010 | 38 | |
| Richard Logan | F | Weymouth Jan 2007 | 12(17) | 5 |
| Callum McNish | M | Southampton Jul 2011 | 2(3) | |
| Daniel Nardiello | F | Blackpool Jul 2010 | 28(8) | 9 |
| Tom Nicholls | F | Trainee Apr 2011 | 2(5) | 1 |
| David Noble | M | Bristol City Jan 2010 | 42 | 2 |
| Matthew Oakley | M | Leicester City Sep 2011 | 7 | |
| Luke O'Brien | D | Bradford City Jan 2012 | 2(1) | |
| John O'Flynn | F | Barnet Jul 2010 | 8(16) | 2 |
| Lenny Pidgeley | G | Bradford City Jun 2011 | 8(2) | |
| Rohan Ricketts | W | Free Agent Mar 2012 | 0(1) | |
| Liam Sercombe | M | Trainee Jun 2007 | 27(6) | 7 |
| Chris Shephard | W | Trainee Jun 2007 | 6(4) | |
| Jake Taylor | F | Reading Sep 2011 | 25(4) | 3 |
| Steve Tully | D | Weymouth Jan 2007 | 42(2) | |
| Rowan Vine | F | Queens Park Rangers Aug 2011 | 4(1) | |
| Matthew Whichelow | F | Watford Sep 2011 | 2 | |
| Own Goals | | | | 1 |

| City's league results | Home | Away |
|-----------------------|------|------|
| AFC Bournemouth | 0-2 | 0-2 |
| Brentford | 1-2 | 0-2 |
| Bury | 3-2 | 0-2 |
| Carlisle United | 0-0 | 1-4 |
| Charlton Athletic | 0-1 | 0-2 |
| Chesterfield | 2-1 | 2-0 |
| Colchester United | 1-1 | 0-2 |
| Hartlepool United | 0-0 | 0-2 |
| Huddersfield Town | 0-4 | 0-2 |
| Leyton Orient | 3-0 | 0-3 |
| Milton Keynes Dons | 0-2 | 0-3 |
| Notts County | 1-1 | 1-2 |
| Oldham Athletic | 2-0 | 0-0 |
| Preston North End | 1-2 | 0-1 |
| Rochdale | 3-1 | 2-3 |
| Scunthorpe United | 0-0 | 0-1 |
| Sheffield United | 2-2 | 4-4 |
| Sheffield Wednesday | 2-1 | 0-3 |
| Stevenage | 1-1 | 0-0 |
| Tranmere Rovers | 3-0 | 0-3 |
| Walsall | 4-2 | 2-1 |
| Wycombe Wanderers | 1-3 | 1-3 |
| Yeovil Town | 1-1 | 2-2 |

| F.A. Cup | | | |
|----------|---|-----|-----|
| Walsall | H | 1-1 | R1 |
| Walsall | A | 2-3* | R1R |

*After extra time

| Football League Cup | | | |
|---------------------|---|-----|----|
| Yeovil Town | H | 2-0 | R1 |
| Liverpool | H | 1-3 | R2 |

| Johnstone's Paint Trophy | | | |
|--------------------------|---|------|----|
| Plymouth Argyle | H | 1-1* | R1 |
| Swindon Town | H | 1-2 | R2 |

* Exeter won 3-0 on pens.

CITY MANAGER 2011-12
Paul Tisdale - Appointed June 2006

League One

| | P | W | D | L | F | A | Pts |
|---|---|---|---|---|---|---|-----|
| Charlton Athletic | 46 | 30 | 11 | 5 | 82 | 36 | 101 |
| Sheffield Wednesday | 46 | 28 | 9 | 9 | 81 | 48 | 93 |
| Sheffield United | 46 | 27 | 9 | 10 | 92 | 51 | 90 |
| Huddersfield Town | 46 | 21 | 18 | 7 | 79 | 47 | 81 |
| Milton Keynes Dons | 46 | 22 | 14 | 10 | 84 | 47 | 80 |
| Stevenage | 46 | 18 | 19 | 9 | 69 | 44 | 73 |
| Notts County | 46 | 21 | 10 | 15 | 75 | 63 | 73 |
| Carlisle United | 46 | 18 | 15 | 11 | 65 | 66 | 69 |
| Brentford | 46 | 18 | 13 | 15 | 63 | 51 | 67 |
| Colchester United | 46 | 13 | 20 | 13 | 61 | 66 | 59 |
| AFC Bournemouth | 46 | 15 | 13 | 18 | 48 | 52 | 58 |
| Tranmere Rovers | 46 | 14 | 14 | 18 | 49 | 53 | 56 |
| Hartlepool United | 46 | 14 | 14 | 18 | 50 | 55 | 56 |
| Bury | 46 | 15 | 11 | 20 | 60 | 79 | 56 |
| Preston North End | 46 | 13 | 15 | 18 | 54 | 68 | 54 |
| Oldham Athletic | 46 | 14 | 12 | 20 | 50 | 66 | 54 |
| Yeovil Town | 46 | 14 | 12 | 20 | 59 | 80 | 54 |
| Scunthorpe United | 46 | 10 | 22 | 14 | 55 | 59 | 52 |
| Walsall | 46 | 10 | 20 | 16 | 51 | 57 | 50 |
| Leyton Orient | 46 | 13 | 11 | 22 | 48 | 75 | 50 |
| Wycombe Wanderers | 46 | 11 | 10 | 25 | 65 | 88 | 43 |
| Chesterfield | 46 | 10 | 12 | 24 | 56 | 80 | 42 |
| Exeter City | 46 | 10 | 12 | 24 | 46 | 75 | 42 |
| Rochdale | 46 | 8 | 14 | 24 | 47 | 81 | 38 |

* Pre-season optimism was higher than usual due to the fact that the team had narrowly missed out on a play-off place the previous season, however, 2011-12 was to prove to be one that saw the side struggle, never replace the key players that had left, and suffer a string of injuries.

* Without defender Matt Taylor, who signed for Charlton Athletic, Ryan Harley who had returned to Swansea and then on to Brighton, and top scorer Jamie Cureton who had left to sign for Leyton Orient. City manager Paul Tisdale had quite a task in finding replacements for such talented players.

* Newcomers to the squad prior to the big kick off were goalkeeper Lenny Pidgeley, defender Danny Coles, midfielders Guillem Bauza, Jimmy Keohane and Callum McNish. But it was in the goalscoring department that City were sadly lacking.

* In an effort to add some spice to the attack, City entered the loan market at various stages during the season and signed Nicholas Bignall, Lauri Dalla Valle, Chris Hackett, Rowan Vine and Matthew Whichelow.

* With results not going the Grecians' way and attendances falling, alarm bells started to sound as regard budgeted finances, and when manager Paul Tisdale stated that he had nothing left in his playing budget, it was only due to the benevolence of sponsors and anonymous donors that their was a last throw of the dice in an attempt to avoid falling into league Two. A number of newcomers arrived on the scene. Most notably and certainly the most successful signing was midfielder Alan Gow, who became the first City player to be signed from an Indian club.

* Exeter though were hit by a series of injuries to key players and even lost defender Danny Coles in a freak training ground collision, when he sustained broken bones in his back which kept him out for rest of the season.

* Supporters did get the opportunity to see Liverpool at St James' Park, however, as they visited for a second round Football League Cup tie. That was one of the few highlights of the season, City losing 3-1.

* It was in League One matches though that City really struggled to score goals. Statistics reveal all when it is noted that the leading scorer, Danny Nardiello, had just nine goals to his name. The Grecians failed to hit the back of the net in 22 League One games. There was an exception to the scarcity of goals when Exeter amazingly drew 4-4 at Sheffield United.

* Exeter were all but relegated a few weeks prior to when it was actually confirmed, for although it was mathematically possible to avoid the drop, few believed that they would on their form shown. This was summed up when they led 2-0 at fellow strugglers Rochdale, only to lose 3-2.

* With City having slipped back into League Two, it was reported that the playing budget would be cut, partly due to falling attendances, and manager Paul Tisdale had a 'rebuilding job' on his hands.

* Assistant manager Rob Edwards summed the season up when he said: ""We have had injuries and it hasn't been one player, it has been three or four at a time. It has been a tough season for everyone and that includes the players as well. The club wants to be a club that produces good young players that will move on and I think the club will be one that has a strong team one year and will then look to rebuild."

* One positive aspect at the end of the season was that no fewer than six of the Under-18 team were given full professional contracts, and they were likely to be part of a much younger looking squad that would compete in League Two in 2012-13.